INTRODUCTION TO CONTRACTS AND RESTITUTION FOR PARALEGALS

INTRODUCTION TO CONTRACTS AND RESTITUTION FOR PARALEGALS

Martin A. Frey
Professor of Law
The University of Tulsa
College of Law

Terry H. Bitting
Attorney at Law
Tulsa, Oklahoma

West Publishing Company
St. Paul New York Los Angeles San Francisco

Copyediting: Margaret Albrecht
Cover design: John Och
Figures: Alice Thiede, Cartographics

50 W. Kellogg Boulevard
P.O. Box 64526
St. Paul, MN 55164–1003

Printed in the United States of America

Library of Congress Cataloging-in-Publication Data
Frey, Martin A.
An introduction to contracts and restitution for paralegals
Martin A. Frey, Terry H. Bitting.

p. cm.—(West's paralegal series)
Includes index.
ISBN 0–314–64064–9
1. Contracts—United States. 2. Restitution—United States.
I. Bitting, Terry H. II. Title. III. Series.

KF801.F74 1988 346.73′022—dc19

[347.30622] 87–34158
CIP

To
Phyllis and David
and
Larry and Brian

Table of Contents

Table of Cases

Preface

The growth of paralegal and legal assistants' programs over the past few years has been dramatic. Not only do more attorneys rely on paralegals and legal assistants each year, but they ask them to perform more complicated assignments. As the use of paralegals and legal assistants increases, their training becomes more sophisticated and more demanding.

As with all relatively new programs, the development of teaching materials lags behind the use of paralegals and legal assistants. Often paralegals and legal assistants have not had materials specifically designed for their needs. This has been true in the area of contracts law where the materials used have been borrowed from business law or law school programs rather than designed especially for paralegal and legal assistants' programs. This book is intended to fill that void.

This text introduces the law of contracts and its corollary, the law of restitution. It is written with the basic premise that the law of contracts need not be a jumble of unrelated rules. To remove the mystery from the law of contracts, we have developed a "road map" for analyzing breach of contract and restitution liability. This text follows the road map. A thorough knowledge of this analytical structure is essential whether the client's problem requires the negotiation and drafting of a contract or involves a contractual relationship gone awry.

The text is divided into six parts. Each of the first five parts addresses a step in the road-map analysis. The sixth part goes beyond the original two contracting parties and investigates third party interests in the contract.

Part 1. Step One: Scope—Determining the Applicable Law

Part 2. Step Two: Contract Formation

Part 3. Step Three: Contracts That Are Unenforceable

Part 4. Step Four: Performance and Breach of the Contract

Part 5. Step Five: Plaintiff's Remedies for the Defendant's Breach of Contract

Part 6. Third Party Interests

We have written this book for the students. Each point of law is developed with a clear statement of the rule, an example of how the rule applies to a set of facts, and a short problem. The problem provides an opportunity for students to explore the dimensions of the rule. This exercise breathes life into the rule. At times, a case will follow the problem so the students can gain an understanding of how a court might apply the rule to a set of facts. A case is included for illustrative purposes and not for its statement of the rule. Cases also serve to remind us that contracts deal with real people with real problems.

Because the law of those contracts involving the sale of goods has been codified in the Uniform Commercial Code, a number of UCC sections have been included. This presents students with an opportunity to become familiar with statutory as well as case law. To provide a broader base, the Uniform Consumer Credit Code and a few miscellaneous statutes are briefly introduced. Several samplings of statutes will be presented so students understand that not all states share the same rules. The statutory differences also provide students with the opportunity to compare and contrast various rules.

We have provided students with practical as well as theoretical information. The analytical structure and the decision trees that naturally flow from the structure form a practical foundation for the book. This approach extends well beyond the classroom. A chapter on drafting a contract stresses good writing. Specific clauses often found in a written contract, such as choice of law, forum selection, disclaimers, limitation on remedies, attorneys' fees and costs, and liquidated damages are discussed. Diagrams are included to aid the learning process.

We welcome your comments. We hope that you will find the following materials informative and challenging.

M. A. F.
T. H. B.

Tulsa, Oklahoma
January 1988

Acknowledgments

We have been fortunate to have a number of very fine people encourage and assist us in preparing this book. Our research assistant, Teresa Dreiling, The University of Tulsa College of Law, Class of 1987, organized fifteen years of accumulated case clippings and notes, so we could effectively write. Our research assistants at Washington University School of Law (St. Louis), Rosalie M. Crouch, Class of 1988, John M. Naylor, Class of 1987, and Beth J. Solomon, Class of 1988, found cases, contributed examples and problems, and critiqued drafts. Our research assistant, Lisa M. Janoski, The University of Tulsa College of Law, Class of 1989, read copy, galley and page proofs. Special thanks to Phyllis H. Frey for her encouragement throughout this project and her assistance in the editorial process. Each has left his or her mark. Finally, we wish to thank Eleanor Thompson of Washington University School of Law and Sally Totty of The University of Tulsa College of Law for preparing the many drafts of the manuscript. Without their cheerful and efficient efforts with word processing, we would probably still be writing about offer.

Last, but not least, we wish to thank our friends at West Publishing for their commitment to this project and for their efforts in transforming manuscript into book. Their good spirits and suggestions were invaluable. Special thanks to Susan Tubb, our editor, and Peggy Adams, our production editor, and to all those who worked on this book.

INTRODUCTION

Contracts play a role in every phase of daily life. The food, the clothes, and the cars we buy, the shelter we rent or buy, and the jobs at which we work are all transactions of a contractual nature. Contractual relationships are the cornerstone of our society.

Contracts allow people to set priorities and to order their lives. Contracts are consensual. They are entered into by agreement of the parties. Contracts are not imposed upon the parties by government. Contracting parties exercise "freedom of contract." The terms the parties select for their contracts are the terms that govern their relationship. These terms are the "law" between the parties.

This text introduces the law of contracts and its coroiiary, the law of restitution. It is written with the basic premise that the law of contracts need not be a jumble of unrelated rules. To remove the mystery from the law of contracts, the authors have developed an analytical structure that can be used for evaluating all contracts problems. A thorough knowledge of this analytical structure is essential whether the client's problem requires the negotiation and drafting of a contract or involves a contractual relationship gone awry.

Chapter 1 presents a "road map" for analyzing breach of contract and restitution liability. This text follows the road map. Each of the first five parts of the text addresses a step in the road map analysis. The sixth part goes beyond the original two contracting parties and investigates third party interests in the contract.

Part 1. Step One: Scope—Determining the Applicable Law
Part 2. Step Two: Contract Formation
Part 3. Step Three: Contracts That Are Unenforceable
Part 4. Step Four: Performance and Breach of the Contract
Part 5. Step Five: Plaintiff's Remedies for the Defendant's Breach of the Contract
Part 6. Third Party Interests

Restitution as the basis for a cause of action (when a breach of contract action does not exist) will be discussed at each step of the analysis. As you read each part, chapter, and section, refer to the road map for the contracts/restitution analysis (Chapter 1) when evaluating the transactions in question. Use the road map as a guide. If you understand the importance of each step in its proper order and the alternatives available when a contract has not been formed, was not enforceable, or has not been breached, you will have an excellent foundation upon which to analyze contracts questions. In addition, you will have learned the necessary elements for contracting, and this will be a valuable aid in interviewing potential clients and creating drafts of their agreements for your attorney.

The law of contracts comes from two primary sources: the legislature (statutes and codes) and the courts (case law). Within a state, the legislature contributes to the development of the law of contracts by enacting statutes and codes. Traditionally, statutes are created from the wide assortment of bills introduced each year by legislators. The proposed legislation is assigned to legislative committees for study, hearings, and amendments. The legislative goal is to create rules of law in the best interest of the citizens of the state. The legislature does not resolve disputes between litigants.

In recent years, legislatures have had the opportunity to enact more than piecemeal legislation. Through the efforts of the Commission on Uniform State Laws and the American Law Institute, state legislatures have been presented thoroughly researched and carefully drafted codes. One such code is the Uniform Commercial Code (UCC), a uniform code that has been enacted (with state modifications) in forty-nine states and the District of Columbia. The UCC covers a range of topics including sale of goods, commercial paper, letters of credit, documents of title, and secured transactions. Creation of such codes promotes uniformity within a state and among the states at an affordable cost.

The U.S. Congress also contributes statutes that relate to the law of contracts. One example, the Magnuson-Moss Warranty–Federal Trade Commission Improvement Act, establishes minimum standards for written warranties and limitations on disclaimers of implied warranties for consumer products.

The Federal Trade Commission and other administrative agencies also contribute to the law of contracts. The Federal Trade Commission Regulations for Door-to-Door Sales, for example, provides the buyer in a home solicitation sale with a cooling off period.

Case law contributes heavily to the law of contracts. Unlike legislation and administrative regulations, case law develops on a case by case basis. When a statute or regulation is applicable, the court relates the facts in the case before it to that statute or regulation. If no statute or regulation is applicable, the court is free to create rules to resolve the dispute before it. A court must wait for a set of litigants to bring their dispute before it for resolution. The court's responsibility is to resolve disputes between litigants. Generally, the court only addresses the questions of law necessary for resolution of the dispute. As a result, the law develops in a hit or miss fashion. When studying the law of contracts in a particular state, it is common to find areas of contracts law that the courts of that state have yet to interpret. The litigants before that state's courts may not have raised questions involving those particular areas of the law for the courts to consider. When an issue that has not been previously decided by a particular court is first raised, it is called a "case of first impression."

Within a state, a number of courts contribute to the case law of that jurisdiction. Although some states have only a two level judicial system (a trial court and an appellate court), many have a three level system (a trial court, an intermediate appellate court, and a high appellate court). While the trial court is often called the district court, the intermediate appellate court the court of appeals, and the high appellate court the supreme court, some jurisdictions label their courts differently. For example, the trial court in New York is the Supreme Court and the high appellate court is the Court of Appeals. In some states, appeals are taken from the trial court to the intermediate appellate court. In others, appeals are taken from the trial court to the highest appellate court where the case is either retained or delegated to an intermediate appellate court. Some states permit appeals to be taken from the intermediate court to the high appellate court, but other states only allow certiorari to be sought, leaving the decision of whether to hear the case to the higher appellate court. Whether the decision of the intermediate court is final also varies from state to state.

Federal courts also hear contracts cases. Generally, federal courts apply the contracts law of the appropriate state to these cases. Because so many courts are involved in the development of contracts law within each state, the law within that state is not necessarily wholly consistent.

Establishment of a hierarchy of courts within the state results in opinions of some courts taking precedence over opinions of other courts. Because each opinion relative to a point of law is not always reviewed by the highest court in the state, conflicting opinions may exist among the various intermediate appellate courts. Case law, once reported, always appears in its reported form because there is no mechanism for periodic review and updating. Precedent can change only when the court, in an appropriate case, writes an opinion overruling or distinguishing existing precedent.

Individuals and groups constantly attempt to influence the legislative and judicial decision making process. Special interest groups lobby members of the legislature and the various agencies. Organizations, such as the Commission on Uniform State Laws, have been successful in thoroughly researching and drafting codes for legislative consideration. Another organization, the American Law Institute, has had unprecedented success in shaping the law through its Restatement of the Law series. The Restatements have addressed Contracts, Property, Torts, Restitution, Agency, Trusts, Conflict of Laws, Security, Judgments, and Foreign Relations of the United States. Each Restatement, by blending some of "what the law is" with "what the law ought to be," has greatly influenced legal thought in the twentieth century. While the Restatement is not legislation and therefore is not "the law," judges are often influenced by individual sections of a Restatement and incorporate these sections in their judicial opinions. A Restatement section, if incorporated, becomes a part of the case law for that jurisdiction.

The Restatement of Contracts was approved and promulgated by the American Law Institute in May 1932. The legendary Professor Samuel Williston of the Harvard Law School faculty served as Chief Reporter, and Professor Arthur L. Corbin of the Yale University Law School faculty served as a Special Adviser and the Reporter on Remedies. This work greatly influenced the law of contracts. Revision of the Restatement of Contracts began in 1962 and was completed by the Institute in 1979. This revision is entitled Restatement (Second) of Contracts. Excerpts of these Restatements will be used throughout this text.

The American Law Institute and the National Conference of Commissioners on Uniform State Law joined forces to produce the Uniform Commercial Code. Unlike the Restatements, which were not intended for the legislatures as suggested legislation, the Uniform Commercial Code was intended for that purpose. One of its main objectives was to create uniformity throughout U.S. jurisdictions. The first official draft of the UCC was promulgated in 1951 and enacted in Pennsylvania in 1953, effective July 1, 1954. Although a subsequent draft appeared in 1957, it was the 1962 Official Draft of the UCC that was widely accepted by state legislatures. Major revisions of various UCC articles have occurred in 1972 (article 9, secured transactions), 1978 (article 8, investment securities) and 1987 (article 2A, leases).

While the UCC was designed to create uniformity among the various jurisdictions, some care must be exercised when researching a UCC problem. As states have enacted the UCC, they have tailored some of its sections to suit their particular interests. Therefore, some variation does exist among the states and a researcher must check for state variations when comparing judicial decisions discussing various UCC sections.

Finally, one should not forget the legion of law professors, practitioners, judges, and law students who write the treatises and law journal articles that contribute to a wealth of information concerning what the law of contracts is and what the law of contracts ought to be.

Welcome to the world of Cardozo, Corbin, Llewellyn, Traynor, and Williston, to name a few. You join good company.

1

A ROAD MAP FOR ANALYZING THE LAW OF CONTRACTS AND RESTITUTION

Section 1. A ROAD MAP FOR THE LAW OF CONTRACTS

Chapter 1 is the most important chapter in this text. It gives you an overview of the analytical process for evaluating a dispute involving a contract and is a point of reference for all topics discussed in the text. If you use this chapter as intended and review it as you work through each subsequent chapter, you will have firmly in mind an analytical process for evaluating a transaction involving a contract. You also will understand whether another form of relief, a restitution action, may be available if a breach of contract action is unavailable.

There are five steps for analyzing the law of contracts and restitution. Within each step, issues of major importance are identified and discussed. Because each step is the foundation for the next, it is important to understand each step before going on to the next.

STEP ONE: SCOPE—DETERMINING THE APPLICABLE LAW

The threshold step in the contracts analysis addresses scope questions. The scope step determines the set of rules under which the game will be played. Scope questions arise in a number of different settings. In a state with competing federal and state rules, is the transaction governed by federal rather than state law? In a transaction taking place in a number of states or nations, which state's or nation's law governs? In a state where several sets of rules appear to apply to the transaction, which set prevails? The determination of the set of rules under which the game will be played is commonly referred to as choice of law.

A conflict may exist between federal and state law. Federal law, for example, may override state law in some aspects of a consumer transaction.

EXAMPLE

Buyer purchases a VCR for home use from a department store. The Seller of a consumer product, in making a written warranty, must follow the requirements set forth in the federal Magnuson-Moss Warranty Act. This Act establishes federal minimum standards for written warranties, limitations on disclaimers of implied warranties, and remedies, separate and apart from state remedies. Buyer, therefore, acquires rights under federal law that exceed those rights acquired under state law.

If state law applies, geographic considerations raise choice of laws questions. In a transaction spanning several states, which state's law governs must be determined at the outset.

EXAMPLE

The New York owner of a yacht moored in a marina in Maine mails a letter from New York to a potential Buyer in California promising to sell her the yacht and to deliver it to a Florida marina. The California Buyer sends a letter to the New York Seller accepting the Seller's terms. Before this letter is received by the Seller, the Buyer telegraphs the Seller rejecting the Seller's offer. The Seller sells the yacht to a third party at a price lower than she would have received from the original California Buyer. May the Seller successfully sue the original Buyer for the difference between the original contract price and the substitute contract price? If the laws of California, Florida, Maine, and New York are not the same, and if the laws of different states would produce different answers, which state's laws apply is the threshold question.

Once the appropriate state is determined, the investigation considers whether a special body of law within that state applies to the transaction. If the transaction is a sale of goods, for example, the appropriate state's version of the Uniform Commercial Code (UCC) will govern the transaction rather than the state's common law.

EXAMPLE

An Owner takes her car to a garage for repair. The car needs new parts, body work, and painting. The bill is itemized at $300 labor and $300 parts. After three months, the paint blisters. If the transaction is governed by the UCC (sale of goods), there will be an implied warranty that the paint would be fit for the ordinary purpose, and the owner could recover. If, however, the transaction is not viewed as a sale of goods but only as a sale of services, the transaction is not governed by the UCC, and no implied warranty attaches to the transaction. The Owner could not recover for the blistering paint job unless the garage expressly warranted that the paint would not blister.

While this example illustrates the impact of the UCC on contracts law, the UCC is not the only body of specialized state law that affects contracts. Another illustration involves identifiable groups of contracting parties who may be unable to protect themselves. At times a state legislature may enact special rules to protect consumers, infants, and the mentally incapacitated. The legislature may change other court made rules of contracts law as well.

Once scope issues have been resolved, the next and one of the most important questions in the analysis must be raised—"Has a contract been created?"

STEP TWO: CONTRACT FORMATION

The second step in the contracts analysis focuses on the two elements of contract formation: the offer and the acceptance.

THE OFFER

What constitutes an offer and when an offer has been made are basic inquiries at this stage. The party making the offer is the offeror. The party receiving the offer is the offeree. Because the offeror makes a promise to the offeree, the offeror is the promisor, and the offeree receiving this promise is the promisee.

What constitutes an offer deals with the components of the offer. If the offer is for a bilateral contract (a promise for a promise), the offer's components are as follows:

1. The promisor's promise
2. The consideration for the promisor's promise (e.g., the promisee's promise)
3. The fact that the promisor made a promise to induce the promisee to make a promise.

If the offer is for a unilateral contract (a promise for a performance), the offer is composed of the following components:

1. The promisor's promise
2. The consideration for the promisor's promise (e.g., the promisee's performance)
3. The fact that the promisor made a promise to induce the promisee to perform.

Consideration is what the promisor wants in exchange for his or her promise. If the promisor makes a promise without demanding something in return, the promisor's promise is "not supported by consideration" and there is "no offer." The promisor has only made a promise to make a future gift.

We have chosen to include the concept of consideration as a crucial element of both offer and acceptance. It is common to find the concept of consideration treated as a third element of contract formation: offer, acceptance, and consideration. If consideration were treated as a separate element and not a part of the offer, the conclusion might very well be "offer, but no consideration." Although this difference may appear to be semantic, it goes to the heart of what an offer is: a promise for consideration.

Even if the promisor has made a promise and has stated a consideration for his or her promise, these two elements must be connected. The promisor must make his or her promise to induce the promisee to give what the promisor says he or she is seeking. Thus the sequence of events is important.

EXAMPLE

John promises to pay Henrietta $50 if Henrietta finds and returns John's lost dog, Toby. If Henrietta had already found and returned Toby to John when John made his promise to pay Henrietta, John's promise was not intended to induce her to act. Thus there was no consideration for John's promise. John's promise was only a gift promise. If John refuses to pay Henrietta, she has no contract upon which to sue John.

THE ACCEPTANCE

If an offer has been made, attention then focuses on acceptance. The basic questions are: What constitutes acceptance and when does an attempt to accept become an effective acceptance? The components of acceptance parallel those of an offer. If the offer was for a bilateral contract (a promise for a promise) the following constitute the acceptance:

1. The promisee's promise
2. The consideration for the promisee's promise (e.g., the promisor's promise)
3. The fact that the promisee's promise was intended to secure the promisor's promise.

If the offer was for a unilateral contract (a promise for a performance), the acceptance is comprised of the following:

1. The promisee's performance
2. The consideration for the promisee's performance (e.g., the promisor's promise)
3. The fact that the promisee's performance was intended to secure the promisor's promise.

The consideration for the promisee's promise or performance is the promisor's promise.

Bilateral Contract

	Offer	
Promisor's Promise		*Promisee's Promise*
I promise to sell you my car	for	Your promise to pay me $5,000
	Acceptance	
Promisee's Promise		*Promisor's Promise*
I promise to pay you $5,000	for	Your promise to sell me your car

Unilateral Contract

Offer

Promisor's Promise		*Promisee's Performance*
I promise to sell you my car	for	Your paying me $5,000

Acceptance

Promisee's Performance		*Promisor's Promise*
My paying you $5,000	for	Your promise to sell me your car

If consideration for the promisee's promise or performance is lacking, the conclusion is "no acceptance" and not "acceptance but no consideration."

The fact that an attempt to accept an offer has taken place does not always lead to the conclusion that a contract has been formed. The attempt may be ineffective. An event may have occurred before the attempted acceptance that would have made the attempt ineffective. The offeror may have revoked the offer; the offeree may have rejected the offer before attempting to accept it; the offeror or offeree may have died; or the offer may have lapsed. If none of these events has occurred, the attempted acceptance of the offer is effective, and a contract is formed.

STEP THREE: CONTRACTS THAT ARE UNENFORCEABLE

Once a contract is formed, determining whether the contract is enforceable is the next step. The focus shifts from "freedom of contract" (that is, the parties' power to create their own contract terms and to structure their relationship as they choose) to the governmental regulation of contract. A number of policy considerations, resulting from legislative enactment or judicial decision, may preclude enforcement of the contract. These policy grounds may be grouped into three categories. The legislature or the judiciary may seek the following goals:

1. To protect a selected class of people unable to protect themselves (e.g., minors and those who are mentally incapacitated)
2. To protect a contracting party from the overreaching of the other contracting party (e.g., unconscionability, fraud, duress, mistake in a basic assumption of fact, and potential perjury due to a lack of writing [Statute of Frauds])
3. To protect the integrity of the judicial process (e.g., illegality and inappropriate forum selection).

If the contract is unenforceable, the contract may be rescinded or, depending on the nature of the problem, the contract may be reformed, thereby eliminating the obstacle precluding its enforcement.

STEP FOUR: PERFORMANCE AND BREACH OF THE CONTRACT

When the conclusion at Step Three is that the contract is enforceable, the analysis focuses on the performance and breach of the contract. Who is complaining and what is the complaint?

In a bilateral contract, the promises are reciprocal: the offeror promises the offeree and the offeree promises the offeror. The offeror, by promising the offeree, has a duty to the offeree to perform; the offeree, by being the recipient of the offeror's promise, has a right to receive the offeror's promised performance. The offeror, by having the duty, is the promisor; the offeree, by having the right, is the promisee. Therefore, when the offeror says "I promise to sell you my car," the offeror (promisor) has the duty to sell the offeree his car, and the offeree (promisee) has the right to receive the car from the offeror.

The offeree, by promising the offeror, also has a duty to the offeror to perform; the offeror, by being on the receiving end of the offeree's promise, has a right to receive the offeree's promised performance. The offeree, by having the duty, is the promisor; the offeror, by having the right, is the promisee. Therefore, when the offeree says "I promise to pay you $5,000," the offeree (promisor) has the duty to pay the offeror $5,000, and the offeror (promisee) has the right to receive $5,000 from the offeree.

Because in a bilateral contract, the offeror is both promisor and promisee and the offeree is both promisor and promisee the label promisee refers to the party who claims the unperformed right, and the label promisor refers to the party who has the duty associated with that right. Therefore, the complainant is the promisee.

If the promisee alleges that the promisor has breached a contractual duty (either by notifying the promisee that the promise will not be performed in the future or by actually not performing when the performance is due), the promisor has five responses to the promisee's allegation of breach.

1. No breach, compliance—"I am complying with the terms of the contract."

EXAMPLE

A homeowner's insurance policy provides that the insurance company will pay the Insured for all losses due to fire. When Insured's valuable art collection is stolen, she files a claim, and the insurance company rejects the claim on the ground that the loss was not due to fire. If Insured sues the insurance company for breach of contract alleging that her claim was not paid, the insurance company will respond, "No breach, compliance." The insurance company is in compliance with the terms of the contract because it does not become obligated to pay until Insured has a loss by fire. Because no fire loss has occurred, the contract has not been breached, and Insured has no cause of action for breach of contract.

2. No breach, excuse—"Although I am not complying with the terms of the contract, my nonperformance was excused, and therefore I have not breached the contract."

This response combines the promisor's admission of nonperformance under the contract with the promisor's claim that this nonperformance was excused and therefore was not a breach. "It is true that I didn't do what the promisee said I didn't do, but I was excused from doing it."

EXAMPLE

A popular singer contracts to perform for a week at a resort hotel. After the first performance, the singer becomes seriously ill and cannot perform for the remainder of the engagement. If the hotel sues the singer for breach of contract, alleging that the singer breached by not performing, the singer could respond, "No breach, excuse. Although I am not complying with the terms of the contract, I am excused from performing due to my serious illness." Unlike the first response ("No breach, compliance"), the condition (serious illness) was not an express term in the contract. Even though this condition (an act of God) was not an express term, it may excuse the singer's nonperformance. If the singer is excused, she is not in breach, and the hotel cannot maintain a cause of action for breach of contract.

3. No breach, justification—"Although I am not complying with the terms of the contract, my nonperformance was justified by your breach of this contract, and therefore I have not breached the contract."

This response to the plaintiff's allegation of breach joins the promisor's admission of nonperformance with the promisor's claim that his or her nonperformance was justified because the party alleging breach had breached the contract.

EXAMPLE

Builder contracts to build a house for Owner. Owner promises to pay every thirty days as the work progresses. Builder begins to build but Owner does not pay. After two months, Builder stops work. If Owner sues Builder for breach of contract alleging that Builder breached by stopping work, Builder would respond, "No breach, justification. My stopping work was justified because you did not pay me." Builder's nonperformance is not a breach; it is a justified nonperformance. Because Owner rather than Builder is the breaching party, Owner's action for breach of contract against Builder cannot be maintained.

This "justification" response in the civil law of contracts parallels self-defense in criminal law. For example, a storekeeper shoots a robber during an armed robbery. The death of the robber may be homicide (the killing of one human being by another human being), but the death may not be murder (the unlawful killing of a human being by another human being with malice aforethought).

4. No breach, terminated duty—"Although I am not complying with the terms of the contract, my duty to perform the contract has been terminated, and therefore I have not breached the contract."

This response contains both the promisor's admission of nonperformance and a claim that the promisor's contractual duty has ended either by agreement or by law, and therefore the promisor has not breached the contract.

EXAMPLE

Employer and Employee have a contract whereby Employer is to pay Employee "a reasonable wage." After Employee works for a month, a dispute arises between the parties about the meaning of "a reasonable wage." Employer gives Employee a check that carries the notation "Payment in Full." Employee cashes the check and then demands still more money from Employer. The Employer refuses. If Employee sues Employer for breach of contract alleging that Employer breached by not paying him a reasonable wage, Employer would respond, "No breach, my duty has been terminated." Employer's duty to pay "a reasonable wage" is terminated by the subsequent contract in the form of Employer's check with the notation "Payment in Full" and Employee's cashing the check. Because Employer is not a breaching party, Employee cannot maintain a breach of contract action. (This is an "accord and satisfaction" in contracts law and will be discussed in Chapter 7.) Although the terminating event was consensual in this case, nonconsensual terminating events are also possible. The terminating events may be consensual (substitute contract, accord and satisfaction, or novation), unilateral (release or waiver), based on reliance (estoppel), or by operation of law (statute of limitations).

5. Breach—"I admit I have breached the contract."

The fifth and final response to the plaintiff's allegation of defendant's breach is an admission by the defendant. Whether the defendant's breach is intentional or unintentional is irrelevant. The law of contracts does not evaluate the mental state accompanying nonperformance. The only question is whether defendant has not performed his or her contractual duty.

STEP FIVE: PLAINTIFF'S REMEDIES FOR THE DEFENDANT'S BREACH OF CONTRACT

If the conclusion at Step Four is that the contract has been breached, the nonbreaching party may maintain an action for breach of contract and is entitled to a remedy. The remedies for breach of contract are designed to protect not only the nonbreaching party's expectation interest, but that party's reliance and restitution interests as well.

When parties enter into a contract, both have expectations as to what the net economic gain will be once the contract has been fully performed. Protecting the injured party's expectation interest places the nonbreaching party in as good a position as if both parties had fully performed the contract according to its terms. The injured party may receive damages to compensate for the other's lack of performance. In the unusual case when money damages would be inadequate to compensate the injured party and the subject of the contract is unique, the breaching party may be ordered to deliver the subject of the contract to the injured party. This is called "specific performance." In some cases an appropriate remedy may be an order enjoining certain conduct of the promisor canceling the contract.

When parties contract, each may perform relying on the other's promise to perform. Protecting the injured party's "reliance interest" places the injured party in the position that party was in before he or she relied on the other's promise. The injured party is compensated, not on the basis of expectation, but rather for the injury suffered by relying on the other's promise. The measure of damages would be the reasonable value to the injured party of the injury suffered by relying on the other's promise.

When parties contract, one party, while performing under the contract, may confer a benefit on the other party. Protecting the injured party's "restitution interest" will place the injured party in the position that he or she was in before conferring the benefit on the other. The injured party is compensated, not on the basis of either expectation or reliance on the other's promise, but rather for the value of the benefit conferred. The measure of damages is the reasonable value of the benefit to the party receiving the benefit.

THIRD PARTY INTERESTS

Although they are not involved as a step in the contracts analysis, three other groups of parties who were not parties to the original contract (third parties) may have or may acquire an interest in the contract. The first type of third parties is the third party beneficiary to the contract. This party, if an intended beneficiary, is technically a party to the contract although he or she was not personally involved in the formation of the contract. Incidental beneficiaries, on the other hand, do not have a court protected interest. The third party beneficiary acquires rights as a result of the contract, but never acquires duties.

EXAMPLE

> Mary, wishing to leave her estate to her niece Sarah, contracts with an attorney for the drafting of her will. Sarah is the intended beneficiary of the attorney/client contract.

EXAMPLE

> The City, in preparing for the Fourth of July, hires the Stars and Stripes Fireworks Company to supply the fireworks for the celebration. John Q. Public is only an incidental beneficiary of the City/Stars and Stripes contract.

The second group of third parties consists of assignees and delegatees. Neither an assignee nor a delegatee was a party to the original contract. By an assignment, a third party acquires rights in the original contract. By a delegation, a third party agrees to perform a duty of one of the original contracting parties.

EXAMPLE

> Sally borrowed $1,000 from Friendly Finance. Friendly transferred its right to receive Sally's repayment to Easy Credit Company. Friendly's transfer of its right to receive Sally's money is an assignment of that right.

EXAMPLE

The Six Flags Coal Company contracted to sell 300,000 carloads of coal to the Ever Ready Power Company. The contract provided that the coal was to be mined at Six Flags mine # 6. Six Flags sold its mine # 6 and its contract to deliver coal to Ever Ready to A–1 Coal Company. A–1 is the delegatee of the Six Flags/Ever Ready contract.

The third group of third parties neither had a right under the original contract nor subsequently acquired a right or duty relating back to the original contract. Rather, this third party is committing a wrong by interfering with existing contract rights.

EXAMPLE

Rinaldo, a tenor, has a one year contract to sing at the Gotham Opera Company. The Metropolis Opera Company offers Rinaldo more money and thus entices him to breach his contract with the Gotham Opera Company. The Metropolis Opera Company has committed a wrong by interfering with the Rinaldo/Gotham contract.

See chart on page 15.

Section 2. A ROAD MAP FOR THE LAW OF RESTITUTION

From this functional analysis of contracts, it can be seen that not all transactions progress through the second, third, and fourth steps of the road map so that a dissatisfied party can obtain a remedy for breach of contract. A number of obstacles may block the party's path to a remedy for breach of contract. A contract may not have been formed. If a contract is formed, the contract may be unenforceable. If the contract is enforceable, the injured party may not be able to prove that the other party has breached the contract.

If the injured party cannot reach the fifth step, he or she cannot obtain a remedy for breach of contract. If, however, the injured party has conferred a benefit on the other party, another cause of action, known as a cause of action for restitution, may be available. This cause of action for restitution should not be confused with the restitution remedy for a breach of contract action. The distinction is necessary because the requirements for each are quite different. Restitution as a cause of action is not based on breach of a contractual duty but rather on a breach of a "quasi-contractual" duty. The courts impose this quasi-contractual duty to avoid an unjust result (an unjust enrichment). The law of contracts and the law of restitution are interrelated, and the contracts analysis may be expanded to explain this interrelationship.

A contracts/restitution analysis must begin with the same steps as the contracts analysis. Historically, courts have approved a restitution cause of action only when the law of contracts did not provide a cause of action for breach of contract. The underlying theory is that it would be unjust to permit the party receiving a benefit

CONTRACTS ANALYSIS

STEP 1
SCOPE—DETERMINING THE APPLICABLE LAW

STEP 2
CONTRACT FORMATION

→ no contract (no cause of action for breach of contract)

contract

STEP 3
CONTRACTS THAT ARE UNENFORCEABLE

→ unenforceable contract (no cause of action for breach of contract)

enforceable contract

STEP 4
PERFORMANCE AND BREACH OF THE CONTRACT

→ no breach, compliance (no cause of action for breach of contract)

→ no breach, excuse (no cause of action for breach of contract)

→ no breach, justification (no cause of action for breach of contract)

→ no breach, duty terminated (no cause of action for breach of contract)

breach (cause of action for breach of contract)

STEP 5
PLAINTIFF'S REMEDIES FOR THE DEFENDANT'S BREACH OF CONTRACT

expectation interest | reliance interest | restitution interest

---

conferred by the other party to retain this benefit without compensating the party conferring the benefit.

Restitution as a remedy, however, may be a remedy for breach of either a contractual or a quasi-contractual duty. A contractual duty is consensual and created by the parties themselves. The contracting parties have created reciprocal rights and duties; the defendant has breached a contractual duty; and the plaintiff, in the performance of his or her contractual duty, has conferred a benefit on the defendant and is entitled to be restored to the position he or she was in before the benefit was conferred. The courts infer a quasi-contractual duty, which they impose because one party is being unjustly enriched at the expense of the other.

Although the common thread of restitution as a cause of action is unjust enrichment, the thread runs through not one but many causes of action, all labeled restitution. While the law of contracts follows the same rules for all problems and is therefore a unified system, the law of restitution is in reality many islands of law related only by the common thread of unjust enrichment. Because restitution actions are exceptions to general rules otherwise known collectively as the law of contracts and thus related to the law of contracts, a functional analysis for breach of contract provides reference points to the general restitution action rules. Additionally, restitution as a cause of action can be distinguished from restitution as a remedy for breach of contract by following the analysis for breach of contract.

Although maintaining the law of restitution as a body of law separate from the law of contracts is essential to preserving the law of contracts as we know it, understanding the relationship of the law of contracts and the law of restitution is necessary.

The following approach to their interrelationship is based on the premise that the law of contracts is primary and therefore dominant. The law of restitution is secondary and should be employed only when the law of contracts fails to yield relief to the party who has conferred a benefit on another. Focusing attention initially on the analysis for breach of contract eliminates unnecessary duplication between contracts and restitution. The plaintiff does not need, and will not be given, the choice of proceeding in restitution or in contract.

The contracts/restitution analysis begins with step one, "scope," and then proceeds to step two, "Contract Formation." If the conclusion from step two is that an offer has not been made, a cause of action for restitution may be available only if one party has conferred a benefit on the other.

If an offer has been extended, restitution as a cause of action is unavailable even if a benefit has been conferred on one of the parties. This is true whether or not the offer has been accepted. The offeror who makes an offer that is not accepted has chosen to assume a risk by conferring a benefit on the offeree prior to binding the offeree by way of contract.

EXAMPLE

Township and Landowner are involved in negotiations concerning the lease of land for drilling a water well. Township makes Landowner an offer and in the process reveals information concerning the water table that Landowner did not previously know. Landowner rejects the offer, drills the well himself, and markets the water.

Township cannot successfully sue Landowner for breach of contract because Landowner rejected Township's offer and no contract was created.

Because Township cannot maintain a breach of contract action, Township will search for another cause of action. If Township investigates a restitution cause of action, it will find that this cause of action also could not be maintained. Although the information conveyed by Township to Landowner was a benefit to Landowner, courts hold that when an offeror makes an offer and in the process reveals information to the offeree, the offeror should know that the offeree may use this information without accepting the offer. Thus Township-offeror must bear the risk that the offeree will use the information concerning the water table.

The offeror who makes an offer that is accepted must proceed to Step Three of the contracts analysis to avoid duplication of causes of action because the restitution cause of action was intended to provide relief only when a breach of contract action was unavailable. The existence of a contract precludes the offeror from seeking restitution as a cause of action unless restitution as a cause of action is available at a later stage in the contracts analysis. The restitution cause of action may be available when the contract is unenforceable (Step Three) or the promisor has not breached the contract (Step Four).

Once a contract has been created, the analysis moves to Step Three, "Contracts that Are Unenforceable." If the conclusion from Step Three is that the contract is unenforceable, a restitution action may be available only if one party has conferred a benefit on the other.

If the contract is enforceable, the analysis focuses on Step Four, "Performance and Breach of the Contract." If the conclusion at Step Four is that the defendant has not breached the contract and the plaintiff is thereby precluded from maintaining a breach of contract action, then for each response to the allegation of breach, the party who has conferred a benefit should consider restitution as a cause of action.

Under the defendant's first response to breach ("No breach, compliance"), the situation may be such that the promisor will never be required to perform (the condition precedent to the promisor's performance has not and will never occur), and the promisee has conferred a benefit on the promisor.

EXAMPLE

Buyer contracted with Seller to purchase Seller's farm. The contract required a substantial down payment and gave Buyer sixty days to find a lender who would lend at 6.5 percent interest. Although the contract did state that Buyer did not have to complete the purchase if Buyer could not find appropriate financing, the contract failed to state whether Seller would retain the down payment if financing was unavailable. Buyer paid Seller the down payment, but could not find financing at 6.5 percent. Buyer canceled the contract, but Seller refused to return Buyer's down payment.

Buyer could not successfully maintain a breach of contract cause of action against Seller. Although the contract was enforceable, Seller did not breach any terms of the contract because the contract did not call for the return of the down payment.

Buyer, however, may have an action for restitution against Seller for the return of the down payment.

Under the defendant's second response to breach ("No breach, excuse"), the promisee may have conferred a benefit on the promisor even though the promisor's performance may be excused.

EXAMPLE

Under a contract for sale, Buyer purchases goods from Seller, and Seller agrees to deliver them to Buyer. At the time of the sale, the goods are stored in Seller's warehouse. The contract calls for Buyer to pay Seller before the goods are delivered. Buyer prepays Seller, but before Seller has an opportunity to deliver the goods, a fire destroys the warehouse and its contents. A shortage of raw materials makes it impossible for Seller to manufacture more goods, and substitute goods are not available in the marketplace. The contract does not discuss what happens to the prepayment in this situation. Naturally, Seller refuses to return the prepayment.

Buyer has an enforceable contract, but may not successfully maintain a cause of action for breach of contract (not shipping the goods) because seller was excused. Buyer may have a cause of action for restitution (for return of the prepayment) because he conferred a benefit on Seller.

Under the defendant's third response to breach ("No breach, I was justified in not performing due to your breach"), the breaching party (the promisee) may have conferred a benefit on the nonbreaching party even though the nonbreaching party was justified in not performing due to the other's breach.

EXAMPLE

Contractor began construction of a building according to the contract, which provided for full payment at the completion of the job. Prior to reaching the point of substantial performance, Contractor, without justification, ceased work. The building's Owner refused to pay Contractor for the work done before Contractor's breach.

Contractor cannot successfully maintain a breach of contract action against Owner because Contractor and not Owner has breached the contract.

The breaching Contractor may maintain a cause of action for restitution because the completed work was a benefit to Owner.

Under the defendant's fourth response to breach ("No breach, my duty has been terminated"), if the promisor is not the breaching party and the promisee has conferred a benefit on the promisor without being compensated, it would seem, at least in theory, that the promisee could have a cause of action for restitution. Our research has not yielded any case law dealing with this situation.

The point must be reemphasized that in all the situations discussed so far, a cause of action for restitution has not been an alternative to a cause of action for breach of contract. The promisee may not elect a restitution action over a breach of contract action. A restitution action is unavailable if a breach of contract action is available. When a cause of action for restitution exists, it is not an alternative but is the sole cause of action. Therefore, if the defendant chooses the fifth response to the plaintiff's allegation of breach ("I breached the contract"), the nonbreaching party may not maintain a restitution action because a breach of contract action is available.

CONTRACTS/RESTITUTION ANALYSIS

STEP 1
SCOPE—DETERMINING THE APPLICABLE LAW

|

STEP 2
CONTRACT FORMATION

→ no contract (no cause of action for breach of contract) → benefit conferred (possible restitution cause of action)

contract

|

STEP 3
CONTRACTS THAT ARE UNENFORCEABLE

→ unenforceable contract (no cause of action for breach of contract) → benefit conferred (possible restitution cause of action)

enforceable contract

|

STEP 4
PERFORMANCE AND BREACH OF THE CONTRACT

→ no breach, compliance (no cause of action for breach of contract) → benefit conferred (possible restitution cause of action)

→ no breach, excuse (no cause of action for breach of contract) → benefit conferred (possible restitution cause of action)

→ no breach, justification (no cause of action for breach of contract) → benefit conferred (possible restitution cause of action)

→ no breach, duty terminated (no cause of action for breach of contract) → benefit conferred (possible restitution cause of action)

breach (cause of action for breach of contract)

|

STEP 5
PLAINTIFF'S REMEDIES FOR THE DEFENDANT'S BREACH OF CONTRACT

- expectation interest
- reliance interest
- restitution interest

Section 3. EVALUATING A BREACH OF CONTRACT CASE

The five step analysis used throughout this book can be used to create a decision tree, which begins with the "road map" and adds the probabilities as to how each step in the analysis will be resolved. This decision tree is useful in identifying the relevant events and decisions and putting them in their proper sequence. Someone familiar with the field of contracts law must evaluate each event and decision and assign estimated probabilities. The evaluation then gives the party creating the decision tree a better understanding of both the options available and the risks associated with each option. With this information, the party is better equipped to negotiate a settlement and prepare litigation budgets.

To begin a decision tree, all of the issues involved in the transaction must be identified and organized in a logical progression. The following discussion uses the five steps in the road map to illustrate the organization of a very general decision tree. This decision tree has thirty answers based on twenty-seven issues:

1. *Scope.* Whether law A or law B applies.
2. *Contract formation.* Whether a contract has been formed.
3. *Enforcement.* Whether the contract is enforceable.
4. *Breach.* Whether the defendant has breached the contract.
5. *Remedies for breach of contract.* Whether the aggrieved party is seeking a remedy to protect an expectation, reliance or restitution interest.
6. *Expectation as a remedy for breach of contract.* Whether an expectation remedy is available for this breach of contract.
7. *Reliance as a remedy for breach of contract.* Whether a reliance remedy is available for this breach of contract.
8. *Restitution as remedy for breach of contract.* Whether a restitution remedy is available for this breach of contract.
9. *Restitution as a cause of action.* Whether a restitution action is available if a contract has not been formed.
10. *Remedy for the restitution action.* Whether a restitution remedy is available for this restitution action.
11. *Restitution as a cause of action.* Whether a restitution action is available if a contract has been formed but is unenforceable.
12. *Remedy for the restitution action.* Whether a restitution remedy is available for this restitution action.
13. *Restitution as a cause of action.* Whether a restitution action is available if the enforceable contract has not been breached by the defendant.
14. *Remedy for the restitution action.* Whether a restitution remedy is available for this restitution action.
15. *Issues 15–27.* The same as Issues 2–14 except using law B rather than law A.

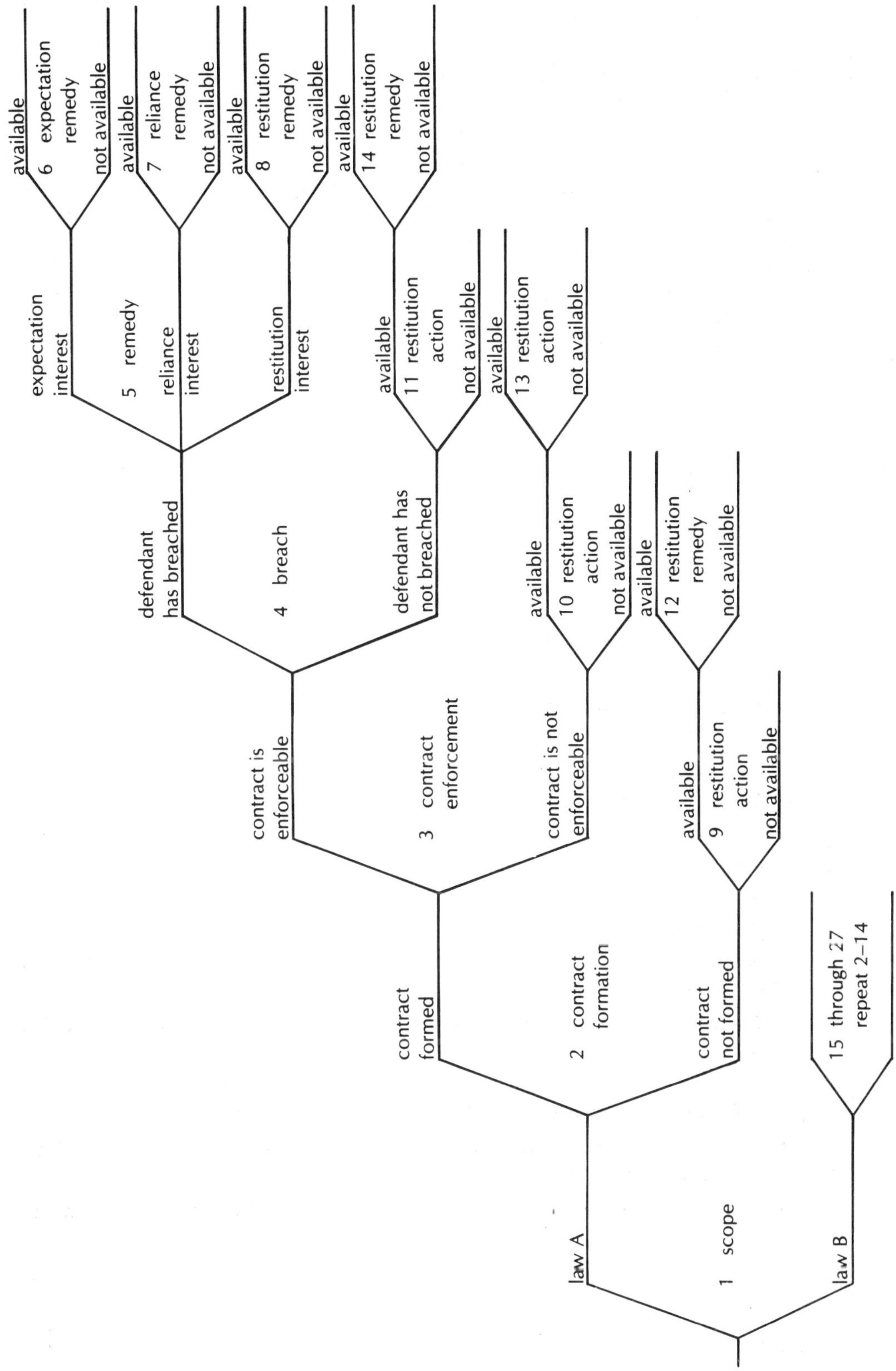
1 scope
law A
law B
2 contract formation
contract formed
contract not formed
3 contract enforcement
contract is enforceable
contract is not enforceable
4 breach
defendant has breached
defendant has not breached
5 remedy
expectation interest
reliance interest
restitution interest
6 expectation remedy
7 reliance remedy
8 restitution remedy
9 restitution action
10 restitution action
11 restitution action
12 restitution remedy
13 restitution action
14 restitution remedy
available
not available
15 through 27 repeat 2–14

As an illustration of a decision tree, consider a situation involving the sale of goods. Do not concern yourself with the applicable law at this point in the book. This example is only intended to give you an idea of how a decision tree works.

EXAMPLE

Southwest Meat Packers processes buffalo. Among its by-products are buffalo hides. BB Industries manufactures western wear. Southwest and BB entered into an oral arrangement whereby Southwest would sell BB all of its buffalo hides over an eighteen-month period. The arrangement was contingent on BB finding appropriate financing. Although Southwest did not sign the "contract," BB sent Southwest a memorandum of the agreement and did not receive a response from Southwest. When BB notified Southwest that it was ready for the first shipment, Southwest responded that it would not ship unless BB prepaid. BB refused. Southwest did not ship, and BB is interested in recovering lost profits because it was unable to find buffalo hides on the open market.

This problem involves seven related issues.

1. Did the contingency concerning financing prevent the contract from being formed, that is, was BB's promise illusory?
2. If BB's promise was illusory so that no contract was formed, would BB be entitled to a restitution action for any benefit BB conferred on Southwest?
3. If BB's promise was not illusory so that a contract was formed, was the contract enforceable against Southwest even though it did not sign the writing?
4. If the contract was not enforceable against Southwest because it did not sign the writing, would BB be entitled to a restitution action for any benefits it conferred on Southwest?
5. If the contract was enforceable against Southwest under the confirmation exception to the Statute of Frauds (UCC § 2–201(2)), did Southwest breach the contract by not shipping hides, or was Southwest's nonperformance justified by BB's refusal to prepay?
6. If BB's refusal to prepay justified Southwest in withholding shipment so that Southwest was not in breach, would BB be entitled to a restitution action (as a breaching plaintiff) for any benefits it conferred on Southwest?
7. If BB's refusal to prepay did not justify Southwest's withholding shipment so that Southwest was in breach, could BB recover for lost profits or were lost profits too uncertain?

Let us assume hypothetically the following probabilities as to the outcome of each issue. These probability estimates should be made by an attorney who has expertise in this field and is familiar with these issues. The estimates will be subjective.

Several attorneys could be consulted, and an average or mean of their estimates could be used. A computer program could be written and various probability combinations could be tested. Record keeping after the fact is useful in verifying and refining the subjective estimates.

- 70 percent probability that BB's promise is not illusory and therefore the contract has been formed.
- 55 percent probability that under UCC § 2–201(2) the contract is enforceable.
- 40 percent probability that Southwest was not justified in withholding shipment and therefore has breached.
- 80 percent probability that BB will be awarded damages for lost profits.
- 10 percent probability that BB would be entitled to a restitution action if the contract was not formed.
- 60 percent probability that BB would be entitled to a restitution action if the contract was formed but was unenforceable.
- 40 percent probability that BB would be entitled to a restitution action if Southwest was not in breach.

The decision tree would take the following form:

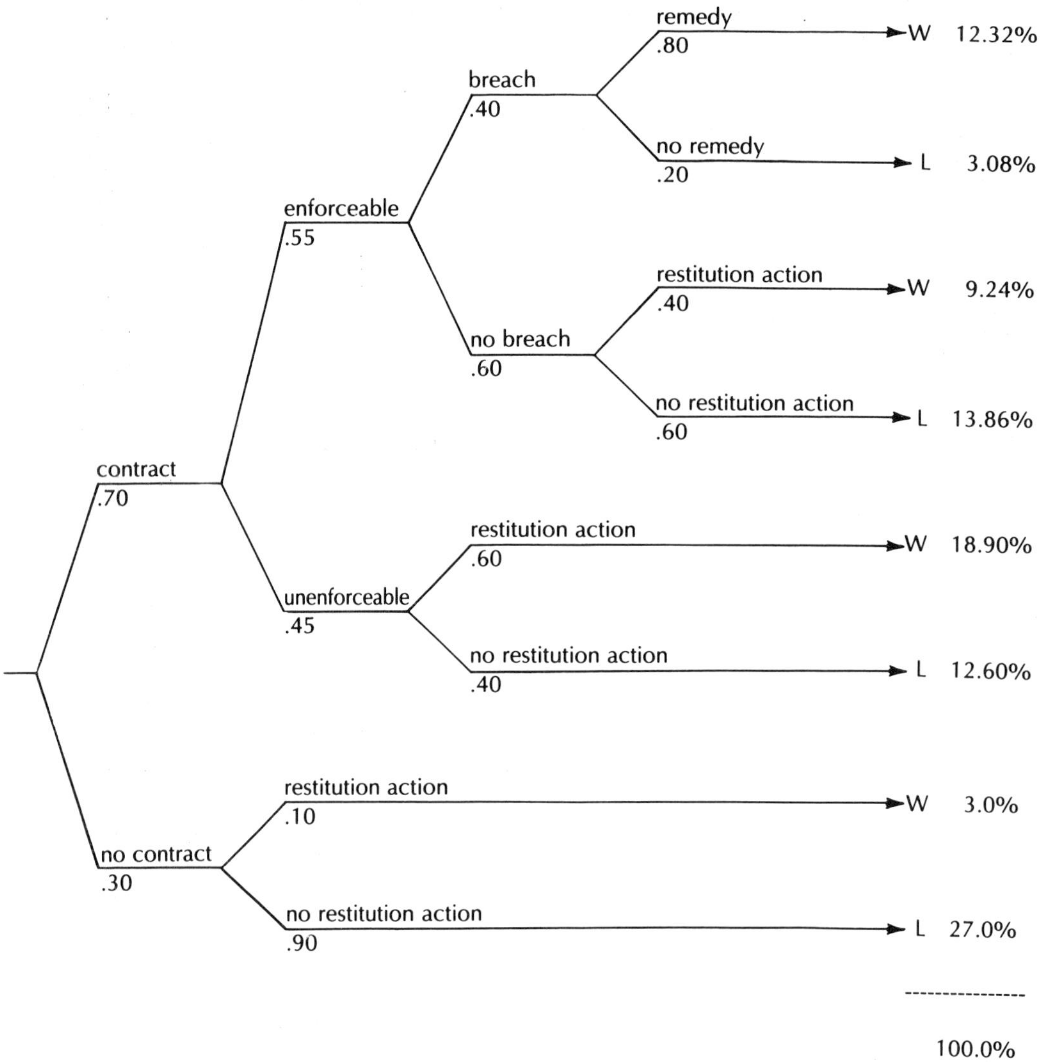

The decision tree establishes a logical relationship among the various issues in a case. The computation of each conclusion involves multiplying the probability for each issue along that route. For example, the uppermost route has a 12.32 percent probability (.7 × .55 × .4 × .8). The total probabilities of all the routes should equal 100 percent.

Our hypothetical decision tree can now be interpreted in light of the probabilities of each outcome. First, BB has a 15 percent chance of maintaining a breach of contract action, but only a 12 percent chance of recovering lost profits. BB has a 3 percent chance of maintaining a cause of action for breach of contract but with only nominal damages. Second, BB has a 31 percent chance of maintaining a restitution action for the benefit it has conferred on Southwest. In this scenario, BB's recovery would be measured by the reasonable value of the benefits conferred on Southwest and not lost profits. Third, BB has a 53 percent chance of being unable to maintain a successful cause of action, either breach of contract or restitution. On the basis of this information, BB can better evaluate its future course of action.

While the BB/Southwest decision tree presents an overview of the steps of the breach of contracts/restitution analysis, decision trees can be developed for each step of the analysis. We will periodically return to the decision tree as we progress through the contracts/restitution road map.

PART I

Step One: Scope—Determining the Applicable Law

Chapter 2
Selecting the Rules of the Game

2

SELECTING THE RULES OF THE GAME

The threshold step in a contracts problem involves determining the rules for playing the game. This is commonly referred to as "scope." Scope questions come in a variety of forms. Part One of this book introduces you to three: (1) selecting the rules when federal and state laws conflict; (2) selecting the rules when more than one state has an interest in the transaction (and the dispute would be resolved differently under the rules of the various states); and (3) selecting the rules from among the various sets of rules within a state.

The following decision tree relates these issues to one another.

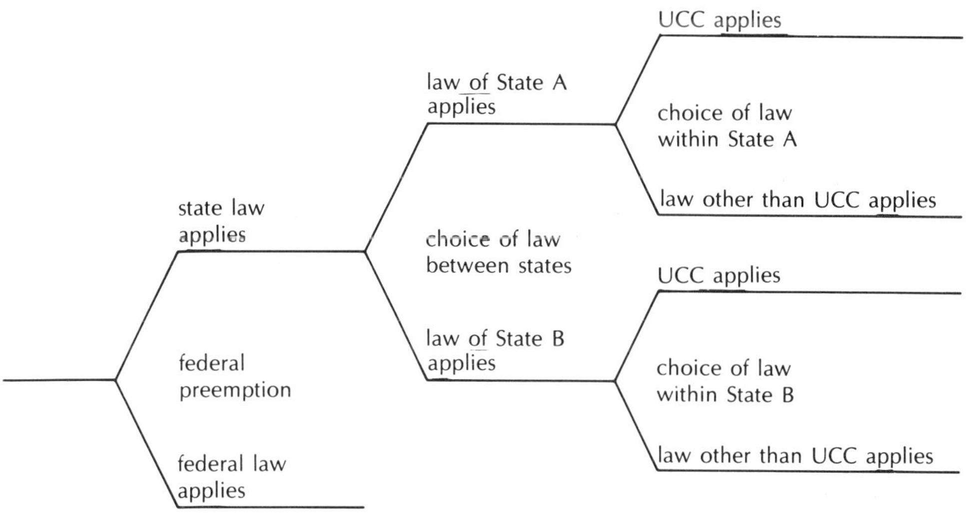

The subject of Part One of this book is complex and goes well beyond an introductory course in contracts law. We believe, however, that students preparing to become paralegals or legal assistants should have a passing acquaintance with all of the issues that arise during the analysis of a contract. Students should at least be aware that a problem exists, even though the solution is beyond the boundaries of this course. The valuable time of a paralegal or legal assistant is not well spent researching the law of Oregon when federal law applies, investigating the law of Ohio when the law of Wisconsin applies, or relying on Massachusetts case law when the Massachusetts version of the Uniform Commercial Code applies. In light of our limited goal, we plan to confine ourselves to a rudimentary coverage of scope.

Section one introduces the issues that arise when federal law and state law conflict. Section two investigates selection of the rules of the game where more than one state has an interest in the transaction. Section three explores the selection of the rules when the state has several sets of rules.

Section 1. SELECTING THE RULES WHEN FEDERAL AND STATE LAWS CONFLICT

In some instances federal preemption may cause state law, whether case law or statute, to be inoperative. Under the federal preemption doctrine, state law must give way to federal law when federal law either expressly regulates the matter or when a particular subject is regarded as being beyond the bounds of state action.

The area of warranties illustrates the federal preemption doctrine. Both Article Two of the Uniform Commercial Code (UCC) and the Magnuson-Moss Warranty–Federal Trade Commission Improvement Act include an extensive number of sections dealing with warranties. When these sections conflict, the federal Magnuson-Moss Warranty Act will apply rather than the state's UCC. Article Two of the UCC applies to all sales of goods. Magnuson-Moss is consumer protection legislation and therefore has a more limited scope. It only applies to consumer products, that is, those items of tangible personal property which are distributed in commerce and which are normally used for personal, family, or household purposes.

EXAMPLE

David decided to spray paint the interior of his house. Knowing little about paint sprayers, David went to Quality Hardware and asked their advice as to which sprayer he should buy. David, relying on Quality's advice that the "Quality High-Tech Sprayer" was the best for his needs, purchased the "Quality High-Tech Sprayer" for $125.99. The sprayer's package stated in large print the following warranty and disclaimer:

> This warranty is for a period of twelve months and covers defects in materials or workmanship caused in the manufacture or assembly of any part of the sprayer. Quality Dealers will correct such defects by repairing or replacing the defective part. This shall be the only warranty and all implied warranties of merchantability and fitness for a particular purpose are disclaimed.

When David began to spray paint his house, he encountered a number of difficulties and ultimately discovered that the Quality High-Tech Sprayer could not be used for indoor spraying. He attempted to return the sprayer, but Quality refused to refund his money. David sued Quality for breach of contract claiming a breach of an implied warranty of fitness for a particular purpose under section 2–315 of the UCC. Section 2–315 provides:

> Where the seller at the time of contracting has reason to know any particular purpose for which the goods are required and that the buyer is relying on the seller's skill or judgment to select or furnish suitable goods, there is unless excluded or modified under the next section an implied warranty that the goods shall be fit for such purpose.

Quality responded that the implied warranty of fitness for a particular purpose was disclaimed on the sprayer's package; that this disclaimer was in writing and was conspicuous; and that it therefore conformed to the requirements for an effective disclaimer under section 2–316(2) of the UCC.

> (2) Subject to subsection (3), to exclude or modify the implied warranty of merchantability or any part of it the language must mention merchantability and in case of a writing must be conspicuous, and **to exclude or modify any implied warranty of fitness the exclusion must be by a writing and conspicuous. Language to exclude all implied warranties of fitness is sufficient if it states, for example, that "There are no warranties which extend beyond the description on the face thereof."** (Emphasis added.)

David admitted that the disclaimer of the implied warranty would be effective under section 2–316 of the UCC but argued that section 2–316 of the UCC was preempted by section 108 of the Magnuson-Moss Warranty—Federal Trade Commission Improvement Act (U.S.C.A. tit. 15, § 2308 (1984)). Section 108 provides:

> (a) **No supplier may disclaim** or modify (except as provided in subsection (b)) **any implied warranty to a consumer with respect to such consumer product if (1) such supplier makes any written warranty to the consumer with respect to such consumer product,** or (2) at the time of sale, or within 90 days thereafter, such supplier enters into a service contract with the consumer which applies to such consumer product.
>
> (b) For purposes of this title (other than section 104(a)(2)), implied warranties may be limited in duration to the duration of a written warranty of reasonable duration, if such limitation is conscionable and is set forth in clear and unmistakable language and prominently displayed on the face of the warranty.
>
> (c) **A disclaimer,** modification, or limitation **made in violation of this section shall be ineffective for purposes of this title and State law.** (Emphasis added.)

Because section 108(a) of the Magnuson-Moss Warranty Act, restrictions on disclaimers, is federal law, it would apply to this transaction rather than the disclaimer provision of the UCC, which is state law. David would prevail in a breach of contract action. At the time of contracting, Quality had reason to know that David would use the sprayer for interior painting, and David relied on Quality's skill or judgment in selecting a suitable sprayer. Quality, therefore, impliedly warranted that the sprayer would be fit for the purposes for which David would be using it. This implied warranty was disclaimed under UCC section 2–316(2) because it was in writing and was conspicuous. This implied warranty was not disclaimed under federal law because Quality had made a written warranty as to the sprayer. Quality could, under section 108(b), limit this implied warranty to the duration of the written warranty (twelve months), but Quality could not disclaim the implied warranty in its entirety. Quality's attempt to disclaim the implied warranty was ineffective under section 108(c). Even if Magnuson-Moss had not had a section such as 108(c), the attempted disclaimer would still have been ineffective because federal law would control under the preemption doctrine.

Another illustration of federal preemption involves door-to-door sales.

EXAMPLE

On Monday evening, Sarah Wilson was at home when the door bell rang. When she went to the door, she found Mary Jones, a sales representative for the Carefree Vacuum Cleaner Company. Sarah was impressed with Mary's demonstration of her product and contracted to purchase the vacuum cleaner with payments over a three-month period. On Wednesday, Sarah telephoned the Carefree Vacuum Cleaner Company informing them that she had changed her mind and that she was cancelling the contract.

Carefree disregarded Sarah's attempt to cancel and shipped the vacuum. When Sarah refused to accept the delivery, Carefree sued Sarah for breach of contract.

The subject of the sale, the vacuum cleaner, qualifies under the UCC Article Two definition of goods; therefore Article Two of the Uniform Commercial Code governs the transaction. Article Two of the UCC is silent on the cooling-off period for door-to-door sales and consequently treats door-to-door sales transactions the same as other types of sales transactions. Under the UCC Sarah would be in breach of contract for rejecting the shipment.

Some states have enacted the Uniform Consumer Credit Code (UCCC). Assume Sarah lives in a state that has enacted the UCCC. Also assume that Carefree did not give Sarah written notice of her right to cancel. When the UCC and UCCC are in conflict, the UCCC takes precedence over UCC provisions. Section 1.103 of the UCCC states:

> Unless displaced by the particular provisions of this Act, the Uniform Commercial Code and the principles of law and equity, including the law relative to capacity to contract, principal and agent, estoppel, fraud, misrepresentation, duress, coercion, mistake, bankruptcy, or other validating or invalidating cause supplement its provisions. In the event of inconsistency between the Uniform Commercial Code and this Act the provisions of this Act control.

The UCCC regulates home solicitation sales. Section 3.502 of the UCCC provides the buyer with a right to cancel:

> (1) Except as provided in subsection (5), in addition to any right otherwise to revoke an offer, the buyer may cancel a home solicitation sale until midnight of the third business day after the day on which the

buyer signs an agreement or offer to purchase which complies with this Part.

(2) Cancellation occurs when the buyer gives written notice of cancellation to the seller at the address stated in the agreement or offer to purchase.

(3) Notice of cancellation, if given by mail, is given when it is properly addressed with postage prepaid and deposited in a mailbox.

(4) Notice of cancellation given by the buyer need not take a particular form and is sufficient if it indicates by any form of written expression the intention of the buyer not to be bound by the home solicitation sale.

(5) The buyer may not cancel a home solicitation sale if, by a separate dated and signed statement that is not as to its material provisions a printed form and describes an emergency requiring immediate remedy, the buyer requests the seller to provide goods or services without delay in order to safeguard the health, safety, or welfare of natural persons or to prevent damage to property the buyer owns or for which he is responsible, and

(a) the seller in good faith makes a substantial beginning of performance of the contract before the buyer gives notice of cancellation, and

(b) in the case of goods, they cannot be returned to the seller in substantially as good condition as when received by the buyer.

Section 3.503 of the UCCC establishes requirements for the home solicitation form of agreement and the statement of the buyer's rights.

(1) In a home solicitation sale, unless the buyer requests the seller to provide goods or services without delay in an emergency (subsection (5) of Section 3.502), the seller shall present to the buyer and obtain his signature to a written agreement or offer to purchase that designates as the date of the transaction the date on which the buyer actually signs and contains a statement of the buyer's rights that complies with subsection (2). A copy of any writing required by this subsection to be signed by the buyer, completed at least as to the date of the transaction and the name and mailing address of the seller, shall be given to the buyer at the time he signs the writing.

(2) The statement shall either:

(a) comply with any notice of cancellation or similar requirement of any trade regulation rule of the Federal Trade Commission which by its terms applies to the home solicitation sale; or

(b) appear under the conspicuous caption: "BUYER'S RIGHT TO CANCEL," and read as follows: "If you decide you do not want the goods or services, you may cancel this agreement by mailing a notice to the seller. The notice must say that you do not want the goods or services and must be mailed before midnight of the third business day after you sign this agreement. The notice must be mailed to:

____

(insert name & mailing address of seller)

(3) Until the seller has complied with this section the buyer may cancel the home solicitation sale by notifying the seller in any manner and by any means of his intention to cancel.

Because Carefree did not give Sarah the appropriate notice of her right to cancel, Sarah's telephone call was an appropriate notice of cancellation under subsection (3), and the contract was terminated. Sarah was not in breach for rejecting the shipment.

The Federal Trade Commission (FTC) has also dealt with home solicitation sales. The FTC promulgated the Federal Trade Commission Regulations for Door-to-Door Sales, which deal with the cooling off period for such sales. These regulations are found in 16 C.F.R. § 429.1.

Assume that when the sale was concluded on Monday evening, Mary gave Sarah a copy of the sales agreement along with a preprinted statement in 5 point type that told Sarah that she had a right to cancel the contract within three days and that written notice of cancellation was required. Under the UCCC, Carefree's notice of cancellation complied with section 3.503(2)(b) so that Sarah's cancellation by telephone was ineffective as a notice of cancellation. By rejecting the shipment, Sarah has breached the contract.

This transaction, however, is also governed by federal law. The FTC requirements are more specific than those specified by the UCCC. Section 429.1 provides:

> In connection with any door-to-door sale, it constitutes an unfair and deceptive act or practice for any seller to:
>
> (a) Fail to furnish the buyer with a fully completed receipt or copy of any contract pertaining to such sale at the time of its execution, which is in the same language, e.g., Spanish, as that principally used in the oral sales presentation and which shows the date of the transaction and contains the name and address of the seller, and in immediate proximity to the space reserved in the contract for the signature of the buyer or on the front page of the receipt if a contract is not used and in boldface type of a minimum size of 10 points, a statement in substantially the following form:
>
> "YOU, THE BUYER, MAY CANCEL THIS TRANSACTION AT ANY TIME PRIOR TO MIDNIGHT OF THE THIRD BUSINESS DAY AFTER THE DATE OF THIS TRANSACTION. SEE THE ATTACHED NOTICE OF CANCELLATION FORM FOR AN EXPLANATION OF THIS RIGHT."
>
> (b) Fail to furnish each buyer, at the time he signs the door-to-door sales contract or otherwise agrees to buy consumer goods or services from the seller, a completed form in duplicate, captioned "NOTICE OF CANCELLATION", which shall be attached to the contract or receipt and easily detachable, and which shall contain in ten point bold face type the following information and statements in the same language, e.g., Spanish, as that used in the contract:
>
> NOTICE OF CANCELLATION
>
> *(enter date of transaction)*
>
> ____________________
>
> *(Date)*
>
> YOU MAY CANCEL THIS TRANSACTION, WITHOUT ANY PENALTY OR OBLIGATION, WITHIN THREE BUSINESS DAYS FROM THE ABOVE DATE.

IF YOU CANCEL, ANY PROPERTY TRADED IN, ANY PAYMENTS MADE BY YOU UNDER THE CONTRACT OR SALE, AND ANY NEGOTIABLE INSTRUMENT EXECUTED BY YOU WILL BE RETURNED WITHIN 10 BUSINESS DAYS FOLLOWING RECEIPT BY THE SELLER OF YOUR CANCELLATION NOTICE, AND ANY SECURITY INTEREST ARISING OUT OF THE TRANSACTION WILL BE CANCELED.

IF YOU CANCEL, YOU MUST MAKE AVAILABLE TO THE SELLER AT YOUR RESIDENCE, IN SUBSTANTIALLY AS GOOD CONDITION AS WHEN RECEIVED, ANY GOODS DELIVERED TO YOU UNDER THIS CONTRACT OR SALE; OR YOU MAY IF YOU WISH, COMPLY WITH THE INSTRUCTIONS OF THE SELLER REGARDING THE RETURN SHIPMENT OF THE GOODS AT THE SELLER'S EXPENSE AND RISK.

IF YOU DO MAKE THE GOODS AVAILABLE TO THE SELLER AND THE SELLER DOES NOT PICK THEM UP WITHIN 20 DAYS OF THE DATE OF YOUR NOTICE OF CANCELLATION, YOU MAY RETAIN OR DISPOSE OF THE GOODS WITHOUT ANY FURTHER OBLIGATION. IF YOU FAIL TO MAKE THE GOODS AVAILABLE TO THE SELLER, OF IF YOU AGREE TO RETURN THE GOODS TO THE SELLER AND FAIL TO DO SO, THEN YOU REMAIN LIABLE FOR PERFORMANCE OF ALL OBLIGATIONS UNDER THE CONTRACT.

TO CANCEL THIS TRANSACTION, MAIL OR DELIVER A SIGNED AND DATED COPY OF THIS CANCELLATION NOTICE OR ANY OTHER WRITTEN NOTICE, OR SEND A TELEGRAM, TO ______________________________,
[Name of seller]

AT ____
[Address of seller's place of business]

NOT LATER THAN MIDNIGHT OF ________
[Date]

I HEREBY CANCEL THIS TRANSACTION.

__________ ______________________________
(date) *(Buyer's Signature)*

The Federal Trade Commission Regulations preempts either the silence of the UCC or the provision in the UCCC if a conflict arises. Comment 5 to section 3.501 of the UCCC addresses the issue of conflict between the UCCC and the FTC Regulations:

> 5. A seller subject to [the Home Solicitation Sales part of the UCCC] may also be subject to the FTC Regulation on Cooling Off Period for Door-to-Door Sales. In the event of direct inconsistency between that Regulation and this Act, that Regulation prevails.

Because Carefree's notice of cancellation was printed in 5 point type, rather than 10 point (5 point type is substantially smaller than 10 point type), Carefree's notice did not satisfy the necessary notice of the FTC Regulations. Carefree's failure to give the appropriate notice was an unfair and deceptive practice under the FTC Regulations. Sarah could use this unfair and deceptive practice to claim that her contract with Carefree was unconscionable and therefore unenforceable under the Uniform Commercial Code.

Section 2. SELECTING THE RULES WHEN MORE THAN ONE STATE HAS AN INTEREST IN THE TRANSACTION

The law of contracts is generally a creation of state law. The individual states and the District of Columbia determine for themselves what the law of contracts will be for their respective jurisdictions. Consequently, there are fifty-one separate bodies of contracts law, one for each state and the District of Columbia. Fortunately, many rules of contracts law are the same from jurisdiction to jurisdiction. Nevertheless, differences do exist. Furthermore, transactions frequently span several states. When the laws of these states differ, the outcome of a dispute may vary according to which state's law applies.

Which state's law applies when the laws of different states conflict? The answer may be provided by the contracting parties. When the contract was formed, the parties may have chosen the state whose laws would apply to the transaction. If the parties did not select the state or made an ineffective selection, then the answer is found in the choice of law rules of the forum state (the state where the lawsuit is filed). Unfortunately, several choice of law rules exist, producing different results.

A. Selection of the Law by the Parties

Contracting parties can choose the law of a particular state to govern their contractual rights and duties and include their choice as a provision in the contract.

EXAMPLE

A choice of law provision could take the following form: "This Agreement shall be governed and interpreted in accordance with the laws of the State of Indiana."

Because parties contract to create predictability in their relationship, courts will give effect to the parties' own choice of applicable law. This deference has become known as the "party autonomy" rule. The autonomy rule, however, is not a rule without limitations. If the contracting parties select a state and incorporate it as a provision in their contract, then the court in the forum state will enforce this choice of law provision unless (1) the chosen state has no substantial relationship to the parties or the transaction or (2) the result obtained from the applicability of the law of the chosen state would be contrary to the forum state's public policy.

PROBLEM 1: *S. Leo Harmonay, Inc. v. Binks Manufacturing Co.* involves an action by Harmonay, a New York corporation, and Binks, a Delaware corporation with its principal place of business in Illinois, for breach of a construction contract. The action was filed in the United States District Court for the Southern District of New York.

The construction site was a General Motors automobile assembly plant in Tarrytown, New York. GM, seeking to expand its assembly plant, contracted with Binks, as one of its general contractors. Binks subcontracted out the mechanical piping work to Harmonay at a cost of approximately two million dollars.

Harmonay claimed that Binks breached the contract by causing certain project delays that resulted in an increased cost of materials, labor inefficiencies, and excess supervision during an acceleration period; that Harmonay was entitled to a markup for overhead and profit for overtime work performed; and that Harmonay should be compensated for its field office costs incurred after the original job completion date.

The subcontract, a standard printed form, provided that the "contract resulting from the acceptance of this order is to be construed according to the law of the state from which this order issues, which is printed on the opposite side hereof." Binks's corporate headquarters' address in Franklin Park, Illinois, was clearly the state printed on the form. Binks argued that Illinois law should govern the dispute, and that the law of Illinois incorporates by reference the exculpatory "no damages for delay" clause for extra work contained in the GM specifications of the Binks/GM prime contract. Therefore, Binks contends that all claims for compensation for extra work are barred by the incorporation of that clause. Harmonay counters that the choice of law provision in the subcontract is unenforceable because Illinois lacks a substantial relationship to the transaction and therefore New York law, rather than Illinois law, should govern. Under New York law, a "no damages for delay" clause would not be incorporated into the subcontract, and Harmonay could recover.

Review the following excerpt from *S. Leo Harmonay, Inc. v. Binks Manufacturing Co.*, 597 F.Supp. 1014, 1024–25 (S.D.N.Y.1984), and determine whether the court applied Illinois or New York law and why:

I. Choice of Law

Jurisdiction in this case rests on diversity of citizenship, 28 U.S.C. § 1332, and therefore the Court must apply the substantive law of the forum state, including the conflict of law rules. *See Klaxon v. Stentor Elec. Mfg. Co.*, 313 U.S. 487, 61 S.Ct. 1020, 85 L.Ed. 1477 (1941). Thus, New York law applies to the conflicts question raised herein. *See La Beach v. Beatrice Foods Co.*, 461 F.Supp. 152 (S.D.N.Y.1978); *Business Incentives Co., Inc. v. Sony Corp. of America*, 397 F.Supp. 63 (S.D.N.Y.1975).

While it is true that some jurisdictions give determinative effect to a choice-of-law clause and thereby follow the so-called "autonomy rule," *see* Note, *Effectiveness of Choice-of-Law Clauses in Contract Conflicts of Law: Party Autonomy or Objective Determination?*, 82 Colum.L.Rev. 1659, 1660 (1982), New York is not one of them. *See La Beach, supra; Southern Intern. Sales Co. v. Potter & Brumfield*, 410 F.Supp. 1339 (S.D. N.Y.1976); *Business Incentives Co., supra; Fricke v. Isbrandtsen Co.*, 151 F.Supp. 465 (S.D.N.Y.1957).

A better rule, suggested by Judge Learned Hand, is that such clauses are prima facie valid and will be upheld absent a showing that they result from fraud or overreaching, that they are unreasonable or unfair, or that enforcement would contravene a strong public policy of the forum. *See Krenger v. Pennsylvania R. Co.,* 174 F.2d 556, 560–61 (2d Cir.) (L. Hand, Ch. J., concurring), *cert. denied,* 338 U.S. 866, 70 S.Ct. 140, 94 L.Ed. 531 (1949); *Bense v. Interstate Battery System of America, Inc.,* 683 F.2d 718, 721–22 (2d Cir.1982); *Richardson Greenshields Securities, Inc. v. Metz,* 566 F.Supp. 131, 133 (S.D.N.Y.1983).

The "substantial relationship" approach followed in New York, which parallels Judge Hand's rule, is stated succinctly in Restatement (Second) of Conflicts of Law § 187. *See Nakhleh v. Chemical Construction Corp.,* 359 F.Supp. 357 (S.D.N.Y.1973). In relevant part, that section states:

> "(2) The law of the state chosen by the parties to govern their contractual rights and duties will be applied, even if the particular issue is one which the parties could not have resolved by an explicit provision in their agreement directed to that issue (i.e., questions of validity, formalities and capacity) unless either
>
> (a) the chosen state has no substantial relationship to the parties . . . or
>
> (b) application of the law of the chosen state would be contrary to a fundamental policy of a state which has a materially greater interest than the chosen state . . ."

Thus, although New York does recognize the choice-of-law principle that parties to a contract have a right to choose the law to be applied to their contract, *see Compania de Inversiones Internacionales v. Industrial Mortgage Bank of Finland,* 269 N.Y. 22, 198 N.E. 617 (1935), this freedom of choice on the part of the parties is not absolute. *See Nakhleh, supra.*

With respect to the substantial relationship test, the New York Court of Appeals has held that while the parties' choice of law is to be given considerable weight, the law of the jurisdiction with the "most significant contacts" is to be applied. *Haag v. Barnes,* 9 N.Y.2d 554, 559–60, 175 N.E.2d 441, 216 N.Y.S.2d 65 (1961); *see La Beach, supra,* at 155–56; *Southern Intern., supra,* at 1341.

Under this analysis, the parties' "choice" of Illinois law in the Binks standard printed form diminishes when viewed against the facts of the case. The only Illinois contact is that it is the principal place of defendant's business. The contract itself was executed in Michigan. On the other hand and most impressive are these factors: the place of performance of the work was in New York, all negotiations for the extra work and other claims occurred in New York, the prime contract is governed by the law of New York, and plaintiff, a New York corporation, has its principal place of business in New York. Illinois has no substantial relationship to the parties and New York would seem to have a materially greater interest in the application of its law. In light of the foregoing, the rights and duties of the parties to the contract are to be governed by the law of New York, despite the "agreement" of the parties to the contrary.

PROBLEM 2: *Ryder Truck Lines, Inc. v. Goren Equipment Co.* involved a contract for the sale of seventy-five used diesel engines. Ryder, a Florida corporation with its headquarters in Florida, sold the engines to Goren, a Georgia corporation with its principal place of business in Georgia. Goren buys used truck engines and engine parts from companies like Ryder for resale to other trucking industry companies in the United States and internationally.

Upon receiving the seventy-five engines, Goren became dissatisfied and fell behind in its payments. Ryder sued Goren in the United States District Court for the Northern District of Georgia alleging a breach of contract. Goren responded with allegations of duress, fraud, and the unenforceability of the liquidated damages provision. The contract stated that Florida law would apply to any dispute between the parties.

Review the following excerpt from *Ryder Truck Lines, Inc. v. Goren Equipment Co.,* 576 F. Supp. 1348, 1354 (N.D. Ga.1983), and determine whether the court applied Georgia or Florida law and why:

A. *Choice of Law*

In resolving the various claims presented in this diversity action, the federal court must follow the Georgia conflict of laws rules. *Klaxon Co. v. Stentor Electric Manufacturing Co.,* 313 U.S. 487, 61 S.Ct. 1020, 85 L.Ed. 1477 (1941). Georgia's conflicts rule states that the law of the state where the contract is made and performed will govern the validity and interpretation of the contract, unless the parties have chosen the law of a particular state to govern their contractual rights and responsibilities. In that event, the choice of law provision in the contract will be applied, except where the chosen state has no substantial relationship to the parties or the transaction, or the result obtained from the applicability of the law of the chosen state would be contrary to Georgia's public policy. *See, 5 Encyclopedia of Georgia Law, Conflict of Laws,* §§ 27, 11; *Restatement (Second) of Conflict of Laws,* § 187 (1971). Cf. *Nasco v. Gimbert,* 239 Ga. 675, 238 S.E.2d 368 (1977).

In the case at bar, paragraph 9 of the January contract provides that the agreement shall be governed by the laws of Florida. The issues of fraud and duress, however, relate to the validity of the contract as a result of alleged pre-contract misrepresentations, and are matters outside the contract. Furthermore, contracts procured by fraud and/or duress are contrary to the fundamental policy of the state of Georgia, as is a damages provision in a contract which purports to be liquidated damages, but instead is a penalty to deter a person from breaching the contract. As these issues involve matters of public policy in Georgia, the court will apply Georgia law in resolving the issues of fraud, duress, and the enforceability of the liquidated damages provision, notwithstanding the parties' choice of Florida law provision in the Contract. On the other hand, the court does not find the questions of interest and attorney's fees to be matters of important public policy where such items are provided for in the contract. These issues are governed by the agreement, and therefore Florida law will be applied in deciding these issues.

B. The Law Governing in the Absence of an Effective Choice by the Parties

The following is a general discussion of several conflict of law rules used in the field of contracts when the parties have not included a choice of law provision in their contract. The choice of law rule specified by the forum state determines which state's law will govern.

EXAMPLE

A Texas Buyer, in preparation for a Fourth of July program, contracted to purchase one thousand cases of fireworks from an Oklahoma Manufacturer-Seller. Seller shipped the cases to Buyer in Texas. As Buyer was unloading and storing the fireworks, they exploded severely injuring Buyer. Four years and two months after the explosion, Buyer filed a breach of contract action in a Texas court seeking damages for breach of an implied warranty of merchantability under Oklahoma's version of the Uniform Commercial Code. The contract did not include a choice of law provision.

Seller contended that the Texas court should apply Texas rather than Oklahoma law. Under the Texas version of the UCC (§ 2–725), "An action for breach of any contract for sale must be commenced within **four** years after the cause of action has accrued." (Emphasis added.) "A cause of action accrues when the breach occurs, regardless of the aggrieved party's lack of knowledge of the breach. A breach of warranty occurs when tender of delivery is made. . . ." Under the Oklahoma version of the UCC, the statute of limitations has been extended to **five** years. Therefore, if Oklahoma law applies, the suit is timely. If Texas law applies, the suit is barred by the statute of limitations.

Because the lawsuit was filed in a Texas court, Texas is the forum state. The Texas court will use the Texas choice of law rules to resolve whether the Texas court should use Texas or Oklahoma law.

Which choice of law rule applies is often a complex question. Jurisdictions do not share a uniform solution. One choice of law rule applies the law of the place of the making of the contract. Generally, the place of the making of the contract is the place where the last act necessary to form the contract occurs. The place of the last act may be the place of acceptance, the place of delivery of a document, or the regular place of business of the party who accepts the offer.

Another choice of law rule applies the law of the place of performance of the contract. This would be the place where the contract specifies that the performance is to occur.

A third choice of law rule (proposed by the Restatement (Second) of Conflicts) applies the law of the state with the most significant contacts or relationship with the transaction. This rule is called the "center of gravity," "grouping of contacts," or "most significant relationship theory." This Restatement rule gives effect to the stated intent of the parties. If the contract fails to express the intent of the parties, the Restatement looks at the following list of contacts:

1. Place of contracting
2. Place of negotiation of the contract
3. Place of performance
4. Location of the subject matter of the contract

   and

5. Domicile, residence, nationality, place of incorporation, and place of business of the parties.

If the place of the making of the contract and the place of negotiating are the same, courts will tend to use the law of that place.

The following example illustrates application of these basic conflict of law rules.

EXAMPLE

Gary, a resident of State A and a captain in the U.S. Army, was stationed in West Germany. During his tour of duty, he purchased a BMW and planned to have it shipped back to the United States through a port at State C. Gary, while home in State A, mailed an offer to Barbara in State B to sell her his BMW. Gary's offer stated that the car would be delivered to Barbara at the port in State C. On the following Tuesday, Gary, having second thoughts about his offer to Barbara, mailed a letter to her revoking his previous offer. On Wednesday, not knowing that Gary had sent a letter of revocation, Barbara mailed a letter to Gary accepting his offer. On Thursday, Barbara received Gary's letter of revocation. On Friday, Gary received Barbara's letter of acceptance. When Barbara telephoned Gary demanding the car, Gary refused.

Under the laws of States A, B, and C, acceptance of an offer sent by mail is effective when the letter of acceptance is sent. Therefore Barbara's letter of acceptance would be effective on Wednesday, the date it was mailed.

State B and State A, however, have different rules governing revocation of the offer. Under State B's law, revocation is effective when sent. Therefore Gary's letter of revocation would be effective on Tuesday, the day it was sent. Gary's offer no longer existed for Barbara to accept, and a contract was not formed because under State B's law the revocation was effective before the attempted acceptance was effective. Because a contract was never formed in the first place, Gary's failure to deliver the BMW could not constitute a breach under State B's law.

Under State A's law, revocation is effective when received. Because the attempted revocation was effective on Thursday and the acceptance was effective on the previous Wednesday, Gary's offer was accepted, and his attempted revocation arrived too late to be effective. Gary's failure to deliver the BMW constituted a breach of contract. Does the law of State B or State A apply? Could the law of State C, whatever it is, apply because the car was to be delivered in State C?

Under the law of the place of the making of the contract, the law of State B would probably apply because Barbara mailed her acceptance in State B.

Under the place of performance rule, the law of State C will probably govern because delivery was to be made there.

Under the Restatement's most significant relationship theory, the place of contracting is State B, where Barbara accepted. The place of negotiating could be both State B and State A, especially if negotiations were made by mail. The place of performance would be State C where delivery was to be made; the location of the subject matter is West Germany; and the domiciles and residences of the parties are State B and State A. Under the Restatement rule, it is difficult to predict which law will be applied since it depends on how the forum jurisdiction will view the contacts.

At times, depending on the circumstances, some jurisdictions use a combination of rules. In the following case, *Zlotnick v. MacArthur,* determine the following:

1. The forum state.
2. Whether the parties included a choice of law provision in their contract.
3. The states that had some relationship to the formation and performance of the contract.
4. Which state's choice of law rule this court uses.
5. The steps in the choice of law rule used by the court.
6. The application of the facts to the choice of law rule.

Before you begin to read *Zlotnick v. MacArthur,* a few words concerning how you should brief your cases may be helpful. Preparing your own written briefs is critical to understanding the dynamics of the law of contracts. As you read the cases included in this book, find the following in each case:

1. Pre-litigation facts.
2. Action—who is suing whom and for what (include the cause of action and the relief sought).
3. Decision—for whom the trial court decided; who appealed; for whom the appellate court decided.
4. Issue—the specific question presented to the court for its decision.
5. Rule—the legal statement that governs the resolution of the issue (the principle to be followed in other cases as well).
6. Application—the court's application of the rule to the facts.
7. Conclusion—how the issue was resolved based on the application of the rule to the facts.
8. The issue in context of the analysis—where the issue in the case is in the contracts analysis (for example, scope, contracts formation, enforcement, breach, or remedy).

Briefing a case will help you organize the opinion and weed out extraneous material. Briefing will give you organized information that aids in determining why a particular case is important. As you develop briefing skills, you will be able to start making distinctions that will allow you to predict whether cases with slightly different facts should be decided similarly and why.

Zlotnick v. MacArthur

United States District Court, N.D. Illinois, 1982.
550 F. Supp. 371.

Memorandum and Order

MORAN, District Judge.

Plaintiff Albert Zlotnick ("Zlotnick") brought this action pursuant to this court's diversity jurisdiction against J. Roderick MacArthur ("MacArthur") and the Bradford Exchange, Ltd. ("Bradford"), claiming that he is entitled to a finder's fee in connection with defendant's acquisition of a New

York company known as Hammacher-Schlemmer, Inc. ("Hammacher-Schlemmer"). In Count I of the complaint plaintiff seeks recovery of the fee based on an alleged oral agreement with MacArthur, the president of Bradford, to pay Zlotnick if Bradford actually acquired Hammacher-Schlemmer. Alternatively, Count II is based on the theory of *quantum meruit.*

Defendants have moved for summary judgment on the grounds that under the applicable principles of conflict of laws New York law governs this action, and that the New York Statute of Frauds (N.Y.Gen.Oblig.Law § 5–701(a)(10) (McKinney)) bars plaintiff's claim. For the reasons discussed below, the motion for summary judgment is granted.

Factual Background

Zlotnick, a New York resident, is a business-finder and an investor, operating out of both New York and Florida. In late April 1978 Zlotnick learned that Hammacher-Schlemmer was being offered for sale by Gulf and Western Industries ("G & W"). Hammacher-Schlemmer is a New York corporation located in New York, G & W is a Delaware corporation with its principal place of business and corporate headquarters in New York. Soon thereafter plaintiff, from his office in New York City, telephoned MacArthur, an Illinois resident, in Morton Grove, Illinois, and informed MacArthur that he knew of a business in New York which might match the business objectives of Bradford. According to plaintiff MacArthur expressed interest in the deal and agreed to pay one-half of Zlotnick's finder's fee if his company purchased the business. (Dep. of A. Zlotnick, p. 22.) Zlotnick then told MacArthur the name of the company and MacArthur asked Zlotnick to send more information regarding Hammacher-Schlemmer to a Bradford executive in Illinois.

On May 4, 1978 Zlotnick sent to Bradford headquarters a written confirmation of the finder's fee agreement, along with the financial information which MacArthur had requested. During the next several weeks plaintiff and defendants engaged in numerous phone conversations and Zlotnick arranged a meeting for May 18, 1978 in New York City between the seller and defendants, so that the parties could discuss the proposed sale, and to enable the potential purchasers to inspect the business.

Shortly thereafter Zlotnick met with MacArthur in New York, at which time MacArthur told Zlotnick that he did not intend to pay plaintiff any fee and, moreover, that his company had no interest in acquiring Hammacher-Schlemmer.

Nevertheless, defendants continued negotiating directly with the sellers, and on April 28, 1980 G & W and Bradford executed a purchase agreement at G & W's headquarters in New York. The closing for the sale of Hammacher-Schlemmer also took place in New York.

Based on these facts, defendants have moved for summary judgment on both counts of the complaint. Plaintiff does not dispute that under New York law an agreement to pay a finder's fee is not enforceable unless it is in writing. *See Cohn v. Geon Intercontinental Corp.,* 62 A.D.2d 1161, 404 N.Y.S.2d 206 (1978). Nor does plaintiff deny that the purported agreement to pay a fee was oral. Instead, Zlotnick contends that Illinois law governs this action and permits the recovery of a finder's fee—whether oral or written—once it is shown that the finder was the "procuring cause" of the acquisition, and that the acquisition actually took place through his efforts. *Ehrman v. Cook Electric Co.,* 630 F.2d 529 (7th Cir.1980). Thus, the sole issue for resolution is whether this court should apply New York or Illinois law.

The Choice of Law Principles

In a diversity action a federal court must follow the conflict-of-law rules prevailing in the state in which it sits. *Klaxon Co. v. Stentor Electric Manufacturing Co.,* 313 U.S. 487, 61 S.Ct. 1020, 85 L.Ed. 1477 (1941).

Under traditional Illinois conflict of law principles,[2] the validity, construction and obligation of a contract are determined by the law of the place where it is made and performed. *Walker v. Lovitt,* 250 Ill. 543, 95 N.E. 631 (1911). Where the place of performance differs from the place of making the contract, and the agreement is to be performed wholly in one jurisdiction, then the law of the place of performance governs. *Ehrman v. Cook Electric Co.,* 468 F.Supp. 98, 99 (N.D.Ill.1979), *aff'd* 630 F.2d 529 (7th Cir.1980). If more than one place of performance is involved, the place of contracting determines the construction of the document. *Charles O. Finley & Co., Inc. v. Kuhn,* 569 F.2d 527, 542 (7th Cir.), *cert. denied* 439 U.S. 876, 99 S.Ct. 214, 58 L.Ed. 2d 190 (1978). Finally, in a "multifaceted situation where the place of making is arguable and performance takes place in several states, the Seventh Circuit Court of Appeals has ruled that Illinois applies the law of the state with the most significant contacts to the transaction." *Ehrman v. Cook Electric, supra,* 468 F.Supp. at 99–100. *See P.S. & E. Inc. v. Selastomer Detroit, Inc.,* 470 F.2d 125, 127 (7th Cir.1972).

In this case it appears not only that the place of execution and performance differ, but additionally that both took place in more than one jurisdiction. *See Adams Laboratories, Inc. v. Jacobs Engineering Co.,* 486 F.Supp. 383, 389 (N.D.Ill.1980). "Negotiations" between Zlotnick and MacArthur took place via a telephone conversation between New York and Illinois, and the contract could arguably be said to have been executed in either state.[3] Much of the performance under the contract took place in New York, where Zlotnick acquired information concerning Hammacher-Schlemmer, and part of the performance conceivably took place in Illinois, since Zlotnick communicated the information he discovered to Bradford headquarters in Morton Grove. Accordingly, this case fits precisely within what Judge Robson described in *Ehrman* as

2. Illinois courts seem to be moving away from their traditional "mechanistic" approach and towards the "most significant contacts" test. In a recent decision the Seventh Circuit noted this development in a footnote:

> There is some indication that the Illinois rule may be changing. In *Champagne v. W.E. O'Neil Construction Co.,* 77 Ill.App.3d 136, 32 Ill.Dec. 609, 395 N.E.2d 990 (1st Dist.1979), the Second Restatement's "most significant contacts" test was extended from tort to contract claims.

Overseas Development Disc Corp. and Universal Development Corp. v. Sangamo Construction Co., Inc., 686 F.2d 498 at 510 n. 43 (7th Cir.1982). *But see D.P. Service, Inc. v. A.M. International,* 508 F.Supp. 162, 164 (N.D.Ill.1981) ("Illinois has not yet adopted the most significant contacts" approach for contract choice-of-law questions and there is not sufficiently strong indication that the Illinois Supreme Court is moving in this direction to justify the court following this new approach), *NII Metals Service, Inc. v. ICM Steel Corp.,* 514 F.Supp. 164, 166 (N.D.Ill.1981).

The most significant relations test particularly makes sense in circumstances like the case at bar, where the contract is "made" during a telephone conversation between persons in two states. This court suspects, moreover, that cases which rely on the traditional approach do so without question only because it would make little difference in result, whichever test was employed.

Since the "most significant relations" test is appropriate here under the established choice-of-law principles, it need not be determined whether the Illinois Supreme Court, faced with the facts in this case, would abandon the "old" approach and turn to an examination of which forum has the most contact with the transaction.

3. It is, as defendant notes, difficult to justify the conclusion that the contract was executed in Illinois simply because a phone call happened to be placed into that state. The reasoning behind the choice-of-laws principles logically bear little real relationship to the fortuitous circumstance of who happened to place a phone call. Further, there appears to be no rational explanation for finding that the "offer moves along the phone lines to the jurisdiction of its receipt (Illinois), while the acceptance does not, and remains exclusively in the jurisdiction of its origin." (Defendant's Reply Memorandum in support of its Motion for Summary Judgment.)

a multifaceted situation.

In *Ehrman,* the plaintiff, a New York finder, contacted Cook Electric in Illinois by telephone and suggested that he could interest Northern, a Canadian company, in merging with Cook. Ehrman then contacted Northern in Canada and later sent Northern information about Cook. The district court held that the making of the finder's fee agreement, and its performance, arguably take place in several states. In these circumstances conflict-of-law rules of Illinois dictate that the district court apply the law of the state with the most significant contact to the transaction. Contrary to plaintiff's suggestion, the fact that the instant case involves only two states rather than the three jurisdictions implicated in *Ehrman,* makes no difference; the crucial question is not how many, but whether there is more than one jurisdiction involved. Accordingly, this case, like *Ehrman,* is governed by the "significant contacts" test.

Several courts have had occasion to identify the significant contacts to be considered in a finder's fee transaction. As defendants note, such factors include (1) the location of the acquired company; (2) the state where the closing of the acquisition took place; (3) the state where the benefits accrue; and (4) the state where the offer to perform the finder's services was sent. *See Ehrman, supra,* 468 F.Supp. at 100; *Havenfield Corp. v. H & R Block, Inc.,* 509 F.2d 1263, 1268 (8th Cir.), *cert. denied* 421 U.S. 999, 95 S.Ct. 2395, 44 L.Ed.2d 665 (1975). *Cf. Denny v. American Tobacco Co.,* 308 F.Supp. 219 (N.D.Cal.1970).

Consideration of the first two criteria clearly point to New York. Hammacher-Schlemmer is a New York corporation, and the closing took place in New York. As for the third factor, both New York and Illinois would likely receive the benefits of the acquisition. Finally, while Illinois was the state into which the offer was sent, this factor should be given the least weight. Just as valid would be to add into the equation that the *acceptance* was "sent" into New York, cancelling out the inference that one party came into the other's state and thereby accepted the protection and assumed the burdens of that state's laws.

Based on these facts, and the additional consideration that the vast majority of the acts constituting performance under the contract occurred in New York, this court finds that New York has the most significant relation to the cause of action.

And because New York precludes an action for *quantum meruit* or for enforcement of a contractual arrangement based on an oral contract, defendants' motion for summary judgment is granted.

PROBLEM 3: Charles Ball, a citizen and resident of Great Britain, and Pleasant Valley Farm, a Kentucky corporation, entered into an agreement whereby Ball agreed to sell Pleasant Valley a horse named "William the Conqueror" for $40,000. The agreement provided that (1) the purchase price was to be made within one month after Pleasant Valley resold the horse, or within nine months of the date of this agreement, whichever was earlier; (2) delivery of the horse by Ball was to be made in two weeks to a carrier in Great Britain designated by Pleasant Valley; and (3) the agreement would not become enforceable until the horse's sound physical health was confirmed by an examination by the Royal Breeders Clinic, performed at Ball's expense. The examination at the clinic revealed no illnesses or problems other than a previously existing ligament disease in the horse's forelegs, which apparently had not worsened since a prior examination two years before.

Ball delivered William the Conqueror to the commercial shipper designated by Pleasant Valley. The horse was transported to the United States, and then delivered to Pleasant Valley. A short time later, Pleasant Valley notified Ball that it was rescinding "the sales contract on the ground that William the Conqueror was lame." Ball refused to rescind the agreement or to accept the return of the horse. Instead Ball demanded full payment of the purchase price.

Should the law of Great Britain or the law of Kentucky govern this dispute?

PROBLEM 4: Jane and Dan Ramsey, State A residents, purchased automobile insurance from a First Rate Insurance Company agent located in State A. The policy insured not only Jane and Dan Ramsey but also their son, Randy. Randy's car was listed in the policy along with two other automobiles garaged at the State A residence of his parents. When the insurance policy was issued, the First Rate agent knew that Randy's car would not be garaged in State A, but would be garaged at his State B residence.

For each of the three vehicles listed, the policy provided uninsured motorist coverage in the amount of $10,000.

After the policy was issued, Randy was fatally injured in a head-on collision between his car and another car in State B. The driver of the second vehicle, a State B resident, carried no public liability insurance. At the time of the accident, Randy was a resident of State B. He was employed in State B and had a State B driver's license. The car he was driving was originally purchased in State B by his mother, who still held title, although Randy was in the process of purchasing it from her when he died.

The Ramseys brought suit against First Rate in State B because State B law provides for "stacking" of uninsured motorist coverage. Stacking permits the total amount of uninsured motorist coverage provided for all vehicles listed in an insurance policy to be applied to the damages resulting from an accident involving only one of the vehicles. Under stacking, the Ramseys would receive $30,000, the total amount of coverage provided for the three vehicles listed in their policy. State A law does not provide stacking so the Ramseys would receive only $10,000, the amount of coverage provided for one vehicle. Should the State B court use State B or State A law?

Section 3. SELECTING THE RULES WHEN A STATE HAS SEVERAL SETS OF RULES

The previous section explored the various choice of law rules used in determining the rules of the game when more than one state has an interest in the transaction. Once the appropriate state has been determined, attention focuses on the laws within that state. The law of contracts within a state comes from two primary sources: the legislature and agencies (statutes, codes, and regulations) and the courts (case law).

PROBLEM 5: In the cases reported for your jurisdiction, find and describe a recent case dealing with the law of contracts.

PROBLEM 6: In the statutes for your jurisdiction, find and describe the patchwork of statutes dealing with the law of contracts.

PROBLEM 7: In the statutes for your jurisdiction, find and describe the codes dealing with the law of contracts. Compare and contrast the miscellaneous statutes with the codes.

When the legislature enacts a statute addressing a specific issue, the law has been codified. Courts are not free to ignore the legislative mandate and create their own law.

EXAMPLE

A general rule under case law (court made law) is that a person who enters into a contract while a minor may disaffirm the contract while still a minor or within a reasonable time after reaching majority. Suppose that Mary Smith purchases a VCR when she is seventeen years old. Six months after turning eighteen, Mary decides that she no longer wants the VCR and wants her money back. She therefore seeks to disaffirm the contract. Under the court made law, Mary has a reasonable time after reaching majority (age eighteen) to disaffirm. If the merchant resists Mary's attempt to disaffirm, the court will be asked to determine whether six months after reaching eighteen was a reasonable time under the facts of this case. If, however, the legislature has enacted a statute that states that one year after reaching majority is a reasonable time to disaffirm, the statutory rule applies, rather than the case law. The courts cannot ignore a statute. The courts, however, have the duty to interpret the statute in light of the facts of the case before them.

When dealing with a code, such as the UCC, the lawyer's approach should differ from the approach involving an isolated statute and case law. First, the lawyer should review the relevant documents made by the parties. Next, the lawyer should consult relevant code law, not case law. The code is the primary, principal, and often preemptive source of law. Do not disregard the code. The code is an integrated document with interrelated sections. It includes definitions as well as rules.

PROBLEM 8: In the statutes for your jurisdiction, find the Uniform Commercial Code and list the titles to its eleven articles.

PROBLEM 9: In the Uniform Commercial Code for your jurisdiction, find and list the titles to ten sections in Article Two that define one or more terms.

Article Two of the UCC, dealing with the sale of goods, provides 104 interrelated sections on the law of contracts as it pertains to the sale of goods. Therefore, as a threshold question, one must determine whether the transaction is controlled by Article Two of the UCC or by the case law of the jurisdiction. If the UCC applies, the rules in the case law are irrelevant, unless the case law interprets the UCC or the UCC is silent on the issue. UCC section 1–103 provides:

> Unless displaced by the particular provisions of this Act, the principles of law and equity, including the law merchant and the law relative to capacity to contract, principal and agent, estoppel, fraud, misrepresentation, duress, coercion, mistake, bankruptcy, or other validating or invalidating cause shall supplement its provisions.

The name "Uniform Commercial Code" is a misnomer. The code is not limited to commercial transactions. For example, the Uniform Commercial Code controls the contract between two neighbors for the sale of a used lawn mower as well as the contract between two large corporations for the sale of steel beams.

Article Two of the UCC is limited, however, to "transactions in goods." The term "transactions," although not defined in the code, has generally been limited to sales. Therefore, Article Two, as its short title indicates, is the law of sale of goods. Because Article Two is generally limited to sales, it does not govern transactions that are pure leases.

Article Two applies to transactions in "goods," a term that is defined to mean all things that are movable at the time of identification to the contract for sale, other than the money in which the price is to be paid, investment securities, and things in action. Whether a particular sales transaction is governed by Article Two instead of other statutory or case law rules may, therefore, depend on whether the subject of the sale was within the UCC's definition of "goods."

PROBLEM 10: Which of the following transactions are controlled by Article Two of the UCC?

1. An employment contract
2. A contract to sell natural gas (after it has been extracted from a well)
3. A contract to sell electricity
4. A contract to sell advertising time on the radio
5. A contract to sell an airplane ticket
6. A contract to sell a cow with her calf
7. A contract to sell the Empire State Building
8. A contract to sell an automobile
9. A contract to sell timber standing in a forest
10. A contract to sell a business

Because Article Two governs transactions for the sale of goods but not for the sale of services, a difficult question is posed when the sale is a mixed or hybrid transaction. Hybrid transactions are contracts for both parts or materials and labor. Examples include the sale and installation of an air conditioning system; the repair of an automobile; the construction of a bridge; the charge for a blood transfusion; and the charge for a beauty treatment.

PROBLEM 11: List five contracts that involve sale of goods only; five that do not involve sale of goods; and five that are hybrid (some sale of goods and some sale of a service).

When faced with a hybrid transaction, courts most frequently use the rule that Article Two is applicable if the sales aspect predominates and is inapplicable if the service aspect predominates. This is known as the predominant factor test. In addition to the predominant factor test, some courts find that Article Two applies to the transaction only if the services were a necessary adjunct to the sale of goods or in a case based on breach of warranty, only if the cause of action is based on the defective goods rather than on the defective service.

In *Colorado Carpet Installation, Inc. v. Palermo,* the Palermos entered into an oral contract for the purchase and installation of carpeting, other flooring materials, and bathroom tile for their home in Colorado. The Palermos claimed that the contract, because it was not in writing, was unenforceable under section 2–201 of the UCC. If this transaction is a sale of goods, then Article Two of the UCC applies, and the contract is unenforceable because it was not in writing. If this transaction is not a sale of goods, then Article Two is inapplicable, and the contract is enforceable regardless of whether it was oral or written. Was this a hybrid or mixed transaction? What test did the court use to determine whether the transaction was a sale of goods? What factors did the court consider when working with the test? What facts did the court apply to each factor?

Colorado Carpet Installation, Inc. v. Palermo

Supreme Court of Colorado, 1983.
668 P.2d 1385.

EN BANC.

QUINN, Justice.

We granted certiorari to review the decision of the court of appeals in *Colorado Carpet Installation, Inc. v. Palermo,* 647 P.2d 686 (Colo.App.1982). The court of appeals, in reversing the trial court, held that an oral agreement involving the purchase and installation of carpeting and other flooring materials was a contract for the sale of goods within the meaning of section 4–2–201(1), C.R.S.1973, of the Uniform Commercial Code, rather than a service contract, and that the contract was unenforceable because the goods did not qualify under section 4–2–201(3)(a), C.R.S.1973, for the "specially manufactured goods" exception to the "writing" requirement of section 4–2–201(1), C.R.S.1973. We affirm the judgment of the court of appeals.

I.

In July 1980 Colorado Carpet Installation, Inc., doing business as Sierra Range Carpets, Inc. (Colorado Carpet), commenced an action in the District Court of Adams County against Fred and Zuma Palermo for breach of contract. The claim was based on an alleged oral agreement in which the Palermos agreed to pay $4,775.75 to Colorado Carpet for the purchase and installation of carpeting, other flooring materials, and bathroom tile for the Palermo home in Thornton, Colorado. The Palermos in their answer denied the existence of a contract and affirmatively asserted that the statute of frauds, section 4–2–201(1), C.R.S.1973, rendered any such agreement unenforceable.

The controversy was tried to the court and arose as follows. Colorado Carpet is a

Colorado corporation engaged in the business of selling and installing carpeting, tile and other flooring materials. In April 1980, Jack Duran, the president of Colorado Carpet, began negotiations with the Palermos for the sale and installation of carpeting, carpet padding, tile and vinyl floor covering in the downstairs and upstairs areas of their home. Colorado Carpet did not maintain an actual retail store or warehouse for these materials, but arranged to purchase them from other distributors. In the course of his negotiations with the Palermos, Duran delivered carpet samples to the Palermo home, measured the home, and assisted Mrs. Palermo in locating at local retail outlets the type and brand of flooring materials that she wanted. Further negotiations ensued, including a written proposal from Duran.

This written proposal, which referred to Colorado Carpet as "the seller" and to the Palermos as "the customer," stated that Colorado Carpet offered for the Palermos' acceptance the following items: a total of 195 square yards of Seduction and Amaretto carpeting, along with padding, at $15.95 per square yard, for a total price of $3110.45; 48 square yards of kitchen carpeting at $8.50 per square yard, for a total price of $399.50; 55 square yards of deck carpeting at $7.50 per square yard, for a total price of $412.50; approximately 220 square feet of ceramic tile at $3.50 per square foot, for a total price of $770; and 9 square yards of vinyl floor covering at $9.50 per square yard, for a total price of $85.50. The proposal expressly included all labor. According to Duran, the source of Colorado Carpet's profit from such a transaction would be the markup on the sale of the materials and not their installation, the latter being provided at cost. He estimated the labor cost at $2.00 per square yard for installing the upstairs, downstairs and kitchen carpeting, and $1.50 per square foot for installing the tile.

Although the Palermos never made a written acceptance of Colorado Carpet's proposal, Duran testified that Mrs. Palermo orally accepted the proposal on or about April 25, 1980, shortly after he submitted it to her. Mrs. Palermo, in contrast, denied accepting the written proposal. It was her testimony that neither she nor her husband ever agreed to purchase any carpeting from Colorado Carpet and that she had contacted Duran only about a tiling job for the upstairs and downstairs bathrooms.

On April 30 and May 1, 1980, Colorado Carpet placed orders with Georgia and California manufacturers for the Seduction (downstairs) and the Amaretto (upstairs) carpeting. These orders called for both carpets to be cut into segments measuring 12 feet by 73 feet in order to permit effective installation in the upstairs and downstairs sections of the Palermo home. The orders were filled in due course, and the carpets were eventually delivered to a Denver warehouse. Colorado Carpet deferred ordering the carpet padding and kitchen carpet at this time because these were stock items and could be purchased immediately before the installation was to commence.

Colorado Carpet purchased and delivered the ceramic tile to the Palermo home for eventual installation in the upstairs and downstairs bathrooms. Mrs. Palermo, however, had a disagreement with Colorado Carpet's tile man over some repair work in connection with the tile installation and arranged with some other contractor to supply and install other tile. Duran, on behalf of Colorado Carpet, attempted unsuccessfully to renegotiate with the Palermos but to no avail. Colorado Carpet removed its tile from the home, returned half of it to the supplier for a refund and sold the other half. It also shipped the Seduction carpeting back to the California manufacturer in exchange for some credit and was able to sell the Amaretto carpeting to a local purchaser.

The trial court found that Colorado Carpet's proposal for the sale and installation of the carpeting and other materials had been orally accepted by the Palermos, thereby resulting in a contract, and determined that the contract was enforceable for two reasons: first, the agreement constituted a service contract for the performance of labor, rather than a contract for the sale of goods, and thus was not subject to the "writing" requirement of the statute of frauds section of the Uniform Commercial Code, section 4–2–201(1), C.R.S.1973; and second, even if the entire agreement was construed as a contract for the sale of goods, that part of the agreement relating to the purchase and installation of carpeting fell within the "specially manufactured goods" exception to the statute of frauds, section 4–2–201(3)(a), C.R.S.1973, and thus was enforceable on that basis. The court awarded damages to Colorado Carpet in the amount of $1,356.50, based upon lost profits, labor, and storage and shipping costs in connection with all the carpeting and padding ordered under the contract, not just the upstairs and downstairs carpeting. The court of appeals reversed the judgment, reasoning that although the agreement was a contract for the sale of goods, it did not satisfy the "specially manufactured goods" exception to the statute of frauds. We granted certiorari to consider whether the oral agreement in question constituted a contract for the sale of goods within the meaning of section 4–2–201(1) of the Uniform Commercial Code, and, if so, whether it qualified for the "specially manufactured goods" exception of section 4–2–201(3)(a).

II.

We first address the court of appeals' determination that the contract was one for the sale of goods, rather than for the performance of labor or services. We conclude that the agreement in question involved a contract for the sale of goods as contemplated by section 4–2–201(1), C.R.S.1973.

This section prohibits the enforcement of contracts "for the sale of goods for the price of $500 or more ... unless there is some writing sufficient to indicate that a contract for sale has been made between the parties and signed by the party against whom enforcement is sought...." By its terms, the statute applies only to contracts for the sale of goods, and not to contracts for labor or services. *E.g., Robertson v. Ceola,* 225 Ark. 703, 501 S.W.2d 764 (1973); *George F. Mueller & Sons, Inc. v. Northern Illinois Gas Co.,* 12 Ill.App.3d 362, 299 N.E.2d 601 (1973); 3 R. Duesenberg & L. King, *Bender's Uniform Commercial Code Service* § 2.02[4] at 2–24 (1982); *cf. Samuelson v. Chutich,* 187 Colo. 155, 529 P.2d 631 (1974) (statutory warranties imposed by Uniform Sales Act not applicable to *service* contracts). The Uniform Commercial Code defines "goods" to mean "all things (including specially manufactured goods) which are movable at the time of identification to the contract for sale other than the money in which the price is to be paid, investment securities ... and things in action." Section 4–2–105(1), C.R.S.1973. A "sale," by statutory definition, "consists in the passing of title from the seller to the buyer for a price," and a "contract for sale" includes a present sale of goods as well as a contract to sell goods at a future time. *Id.* 4–2–106(1).

In this case the subject of the contract involved "goods" because the carpeting and other materials were movable at the time that Colorado Carpet procured them for installation pursuant to the agreement. Since the agreement contemplated that title to the carpeting and other materials would pass to the Palermos, it constituted a "contract for sale." The scope of the contract, however, included not only the sale of goods but also the performance of labor or service. Thus, we must determine whether such a mixed contract qualified as a contract for the sale of goods or, instead, constituted a contract for labor or service outside the scope of section 4–2–201(1), C.R.S.1973.

The performance of some labor or service frequently plays a role in sales transactions. "Goods," however, are not the less "goods" merely because labor or service may be essential to their ultimate use by the purchaser. The mere furnishing of some labor or service, in our view, should not determine the ultimate character of a contract for purposes of section 4–2–201(1) of the Uniform

Commercial Code. Rather, the controlling criterion should be the primary purpose of the contract—that is, whether the circumstances underlying the formation of the agreement and the performance reasonably expected of the parties demonstrates the primary purpose of the contract as the sale of goods or, in contrast, the sale of labor or service. We agree in this respect with the following statement in *Bonebrake v. Cox,* 499 F.2d 951, 960 (8th Cir.1974):

> "The test for inclusion or exclusion is not whether [goods and services] are mixed, but, granting that they are mixed, whether their predominant factor, their thrust, their purpose, reasonably stated, is the rendition of service, with goods incidentally involved (*e.g.,* contract with artist for painting) or is a transaction of sale, with labor incidentally involved (*e.g.,* insulation of a water heater in a bathroom)."

Accord, e.g., Care Display, Inc. v. Didde-Glaser, Inc., 225 Kan. 232, 589 P.2d 599 (1979); *Burton v. Artery Co., Inc.,* 279 Md. 94, 367 A.2d 935 (1977); *Meyers v. Henderson Construction Co.,* 147 N.J.Super. 77, 370 A.2d 547 (1977). *See generally* Annot., *Applicability of U.C.C. Article 2 to Mixed Contracts for Sale of Goods and Services,* 5 A.L.R. 4th 501 (1981).

This "primary purpose" test, we believe, is designed to promote one of the expressed statutory policies of the Uniform Commercial Code—"[t]o simplify, clarify, and modernize the law governing commercial transactions." Section 4–1–102(2)(a), C.R.S. 1973. Useful factors to consider in determining whether "goods" or "service" predominates include the following: the contractual language used by the parties, *see, e.g., Triangle Underwriters, Inc. v. Honeywell, Inc.,* 604 F.2d 737 (2d Cir.1979); *Bonebrake v. Cox, supra; Fifteenth Street Investment Co. v. People,* 102 Colo. 571, 81 P.2d 764 (1938); whether the agreement involves one overall price that includes both goods and labor or, instead, calls for separate and discrete billings for goods on the one hand and labor on the other, *see, e.g., Triangle Underwriters, Inc. v. Honeywell, Inc., supra; Aluminum Company of America v. Electro Flo Corp.,* 451 F.2d 1115 (10th Cir.1971); the ratio that the cost of goods bears to the overall contract price, *see, e.g., Lincoln Pulp & Paper Co., Inc. v. Dravo Corp.,* 436 F.Supp. 262 (D.Me.1977); *Van Sistine v. Tollard,* 95 Wis. 2d 678, 291 N.W.2d 636 (Wis.Ct.App. 1980); and the nature and reasonableness of the purchaser's contractual expectations of acquiring a property interest in goods (goods being defined as things that are movable at the time of identification to the contract, section 4–2–105(1), C.R.S.1973), *see generally* Marshall, *The Applicability of the Uniform Commercial Code to Construction Contracts,* 28 Emory L.J. 335, 365–76 (1979).

Considering the contract under these guidelines, we are satisfied that, as a matter of law, its primary purpose was the sale of goods and not the sale of labor or service. The language in Colorado Carpet's proposal referred to the parties as "seller" and "customer." In addition, the agreement called for an overall contract price that included both the cost of goods and labor, and, as the trial evidence established, the charge for labor was slight in relation to the total contractual price. Finally, the carpeting and other materials were movable when Colorado Carpet procured them for the purpose of selling them to the Palermos. The fact that these materials might later be installed in the Palermo home and assume the character of fixtures does not undermine the primary purpose of the contract as one for a sale of goods. *See Saliba v. Reed Electric Co.,* 90 Colo. 287, 8 P.2d 1095 (1932). We therefore agree with the court of appeals that the agreement between Colorado Carpet and the Palermos constituted a contract for the sale of goods, with labor or service only incidentally involved, and thus within the statute of frauds provisions of the Uniform Commercial Code.

PROBLEM 12: Apply the factors used by the court in *Colorado Carpet* to the following transactions. Is the transaction a sale of goods?

1. A hospital gives a patient a blood transfusion and charges the patient $35 a pint.
2. A doctor X-rays a patient and presents her with an itemized statement.
3. A doctor operates on a patient and implants a pacemaker.

Responding to the vast increase of blood transfusions and other medically related cases, many state legislatures have amended their codes to limit the scope of Article Two. The Alabama Code § 7–2–314(4) (1984) illustrates one such amendment:

> (4) Procuring, furnishing, donating, processing, distributing, or using human whole blood, plasma, blood products, blood derivatives, and other human tissues such as corneas, bones or organs for the purpose of injecting, transfusing, or transplanting any of them in the human body is declared for all purposes to be the rendition of a service by every person participating therein and whether any remuneration is paid therefor is declared not to be a sale of such whole blood, plasma, blood products, blood derivatives, or other human tissues.

PROBLEM 13: What were the competing interests that the legislature had to consider before enacting this piece of legislation? In your opinion, did the legislature appropriately balance these interests?

The following case of *Coffee v. Cutter Biological,* raises an AIDS issue. Mr. Coffee, a hemophiliac, contracted AIDS through an infusion of Cutter's product "antihemophilia factor Koate." Coffee and his wife sued Cutter for damages based on products liability and negligence claims. As a defense to the products liability claim, Cutter raised the Connecticut blood shield statute. The blood shield statute is not located in title 42a of the Connecticut General Statutes, the title dealing with the Connecticut version of the Uniform Commercial Code. Rather this statute is located in title 19a, a title dealing with anatomical donations.

1. What did the legislature gain by not locating the blood shield statute in the Uniform Commercial Code?
2. Compare this statute with the Alabama blood statute set forth above. What are the differences and are they significant?
3. What words and phrases in the blood shield statute did the *Coffee* court find necessary to discuss to resolve this dispute?
4. Do you agree with the court's reasoning in barring the Coffees' products liability claim?
5. Although the Coffees brought their action on products liability, a strict liability tort action, would the court have reached the same result had the action been brought under an implied warranty of merchantability under the Uniform Commercial Code?

Coffee v. Cutter Biological

United States Court of Appeals, Second Circuit, 1987.
809 F.2d 191.

Before MESKILL,* MINER and ALTIMARI, Circuit Judges.

MINER, Circuit Judge:

John T. Coffee and Meg Coffee appeal from a partial summary judgment of the United States District Court for the District of Connecticut (Burns, J.), entered in favor of Cutter Biological and Miles Laboratories, Inc., commercial producers of blood component products. Mr. Coffee, a hemophiliac who contracted acquired immune deficiency syndrome ("AIDS"), brought suit together with his wife under the provisions of Connecticut's product liability statute, Conn. Gen.Stat. § 52–572m *et seq.*, alleging that he was exposed to the AIDS virus (or retrovirus) when he received an infusion of appellees' product, "antihemophilia factor (Human) Koate" ("Koate"). The district court held that Connecticut's "blood shield" statute, Conn.Gen.Stat. § 19a–280, barred appellants' product liability claim. We affirm.

I. Background

Appellants instituted this diversity suit in the district court on April 4, 1985, basing their claims on Connecticut's product liability statute, Conn.Gen.Stat. § 52–572m *et seq.* They alleged that appellant John Coffee, while he was a patient at Norwalk Hospital, received an infusion containing Koate, a product manufactured by appellees. Appellants further asserted that the unaltered Koate was in a defective and dangerous condition when administered—contaminated with the AIDS virus—and caused Mr. Coffee to contract AIDS. In the original complaint, appellants sought recovery of damages resulting from Mr. Coffee's illness and for Mrs. Coffee's loss of consortium and expenses incurred in caring for her husband.

Appellees moved, pursuant to Fed.R.Civ. P. 12(b)(6), to dismiss the complaint, contending that the claims were barred by Connecticut's blood shield statute, Conn.Gen. Stat. § 19a–280. By order dated November 5, 1985, Judge Burns converted the motion to dismiss to one for summary judgment, and invited the parties to submit additional materials and arguments for her consideration. In opposition to the motion for summary judgment, appellants argued that there was a genuine issue of material fact as to whether Koate was a "component, fraction or derivative" of blood or blood plasma, as described in the blood shield statute. They also asserted that Connecticut's blood shield statute did not bar product liability claims and that, in any event, the statute was not intended to apply to commercial producers of blood products.

In a decision dated May 2, 1985, the district court held that Conn.Gen.Stat. § 19a–280 barred appellants' product liability claims. Judge Burns concluded that the statute was intended to apply to commercial producers of blood products and that there was no disputed issue of material fact regarding the composition of Koate. However, because Connecticut's Product Liability Act prevents a plaintiff from asserting common law theories of liability when a claim is brought under the Act, Conn.Gen.Stat. § 52–572n(a), *see Daily v. New Britain Machine Co.,* 200 Conn. 562, 512 A.2d 893 (1986), Judge Burns permitted appellants to amend their complaint prior to rendering a

* Although Judge Meskill was present at oral argument, he took no part in the decision of this case. *See* 2d Cir.R. 0.14(b).

final decision on the summary judgment motion.[1]

On June 2, 1986, a "substitute complaint" was submitted containing the product liability claims and adding negligence claims. The district court then granted appellees' motion for summary judgment on the product liability claims and directed the entry of a partial summary judgment, *see* Fed.R.Civ.P. 54(b), for appellees. This appeal followed.

II. Discussion

Appellants challenge the district court's determination that the Connecticut blood shield statute bars product liability claims and that the statute applies to commercial manufacturers and distributors of blood products. The statute provides that

> [t]he implied warranties of merchantability and fitness shall not be applicable to a contract for the sale of human blood, blood plasma, or other human tissue or organs from a blood bank or reservoir of such other tissues or organs. Such blood, blood plasma, and the components, derivatives or fractions thereof, or tissue or organs shall not be considered commodities subject to sale or barter, but shall be considered as medical services.

Conn.Gen.Stat. § 19a–280.

Under Connecticut rules of statutory construction, the reviewing court is to be guided by the language, purpose and legislative history of the statute in question. *See Anderson v. Ludgin,* 175 Conn. 545, 400 A.2d 712 (1978). The intent of the legislature generally must be found in the words of the statute itself, if the language is plain and unambiguous. *Connecticut Theater Foundation, Inc. v. Brown,* 179 Conn. 672, 427 A.2d 863 (1980); *McIlwain v. Moser Farms Dairy, Inc.,* 40 Conn.Supp. 230, 488 A.2d 102 (Super.Ct. 1985). The words employed normally should be accorded their natural and usual meaning. *Jones v. Civil Service Commission,* 175 Conn. 504, 509, 400 A.2d 721, 724 (1978). Although the parties agree that Connecticut's blood shield statute is clear, their respective interpretations of that statute differ dramatically.

We agree with the district court that Connecticut's blood shield statute was intended to preclude the assertion of product liability claims arising out of a contract for the sale of blood components. The plain and unambiguous words of the statute itself clearly state that supplying blood or blood derivatives is to be considered a medical service. Senate Bill 885, which ultimately was codified as the blood shield statute, contained a "statement of purpose" to the same effect. Because transactions involving blood and blood components are to be considered services, as opposed to sales, they are outside the purview of Connecticut's product liability statute, Conn.Gen.Stat. § 52–572m *et seq.; cf. Acme Cotton Products Co. v. Lockwood Green Engineers,* 10 Conn.L.Trib. No. 34, at 10, 11 (Super.Ct. Aug. 20, 1984) (architectural services not a "product" within purview of Connecticut Product Liability Act).

As the district court noted, blood shield statutes in other states uniformly have been interpreted as barring strict liability claims, whether or not the statute contains an express bar to such claims. *See, e.g., Iannucci v. Yonkers General Hospital,* 59 A.D.2d 887, 399 N.Y.S.2d 39 (App.Div.1977) (construing New York statute similar to Connecticut's), *appeal dismissed,* 44 N.Y.2d 837, 406 N.Y.S.2d 757, 378 N.E.2d 120 (1978); *Hyland Therapeutics v. Superior Court,* 175 Cal.App.3d 509, 220 Cal.Rptr. 590 (Ct.App. 1985) (construing similar California statute). *See generally* Annot., 24 A.L.R.4th 508, 519–24 (1983). In addition, at least one

1. On February 6, 1986, the district court was informed by appellees' counsel that Mr. Coffee had died. Because his death had not yet been reflected on the record, the district court elected to continue treating Mr. Coffee as a party.

If appellants choose to pursue their negligence claims in the district court, a motion for substitution should be made pursuant to Fed.R.Civ.P. 25(a)(1).

Connecticut court has held that Conn.Gen. Stat. § 19a–280 precludes product liability claims. *Depray v. St. Francis Hospital & Medical Center,* 12 Conn.L.Trib. No. 14, at 25 (Super.Ct. Dec. 19, 1985). Moreover, as the district court correctly noted, allowing plaintiffs to circumvent the exemption of blood and blood derivatives applicable to implied warranty claims by permitting them to pursue claims under the product liability statute would defeat the obvious legislative intent of distinguishing blood and blood derivatives from ordinary merchandise.

Through a tortured reading of the language of Conn.Gen.Stat. § 19a–280, appellants interpret the statute's second sentence as meaning only that contracts for sales of blood will not be subject to implied warranties. Appellants' proffered interpretation would render the statute's second sentence meaningless, because the second sentence would become a mere reiteration of the first. We cannot assume that the Connecticut legislature intended such surplusage. *See Berger v. Tonken,* 192 Conn. 581, 589, 473 A.2d 782, 786 (1984); *State v. Roque,* 190 Conn. 143, 150, 460 A.2d 26, 30 (1983). Appellants contend that the blood shield statute's legislative history supports their reading of the statute. The brief legislative remarks prior to enactment of Conn.Gen.Stat. § 19a–280 lend scant support for appellants' statutory construction. Senator Pac, the only senator to speak on the bill, referred to the statute as absolving hospitals from liability for implied warranties *or guarantees.* Statement of Sen. Pac, Sen. Hearings, S.B. 885 (May 17, 1971). Aside from the fact that the legislative history is so slight, the word "guarantee" in this context is quite ambiguous, and conceivably could refer to the absolute guarantee of a strict liability claim.

Appellants' claim that the Connecticut blood shield statute should not apply to commercial producers of blood products similarly is without merit. Because the statute protects only sales originating from a "blood bank," appellants argue that commercial producers and distributors of blood and blood component products such as appellees are excluded from protection by the statute. Appellants support their overly narrow definition of a blood bank by referring to legislative history and dictionary definitions. However, Senator Pac's brief reference to the benefits accruing to hospitals and volunteer donor programs as a result of the statute's enactment simply fails to address the scope of the statute's reach. In addition, appellants' dictionary references are singularly unhelpful. *See, e.g., Webster's Third New International Dictionary* 237 (1981) ("a place for storage of . . . blood or plasma").

We agree with the district court that Conn.Gen.Stat. § 19a–280 should apply to commercial producers of blood. Although the term "blood bank" is undefined in the blood shield statute, a definition is supplied in Connecticut's anatomical donations statute. As the district court noted, a "bank or storage facility" is defined in Conn.Gen. Stat. § 19a–272(a) as "a facility for storage of human bodies or parts thereof." "Parts" is further defined to include blood. *Id.* § 19a–272(e). Under the anatomical donations statute, therefore, a blood bank is a facility for the storage of human blood. This definition, of course, does not apply expressly to the blood shield statute. However, under Connecticut precedent, when the legislature has not provided a definition for an essential statutory term, the court may refer to definitions set forth in other statutes. *See Link v. City of Shelton,* 186 Conn. 623, 627, 443 A.2d 902, 903–04 (1982). Such an extrapolation is particularly appropriate in this instance because the statutes are related. Transfers of blood donated pursuant to the anatomical donations statute receive protection from liability under the blood shield statute.

Appellants also attempt to raise a disputed issue of material fact: whether Koate is a blood component, derivative or fraction within the meaning of Conn.Gen.Stat. § 19a–280. However, as the district court correctly emphasized, even appellants' expert, Dr. James O'Brien, conceded that Koate is a product derived from human blood. Dr. O'Brien merely distinguished Koate from other blood products by referring to the manner in which Koate is advertised, packaged and distributed. Appellants do not dispute the fact that Koate is a blood component product—instead, they continue to assert that significant differences in the production, marketing and distribution of Koate separate it from other blood component products. We fail to see how these considerations can alter the nature of the product itself.

III. Conclusion

For the foregoing reasons, the judgment of the district court is affirmed.

PART II

Step Two: Contract Formation

Introduction
A Transactional Guide to Contract Formation

Chapter 3
The Pre-Offer Phase

Chapter 4
The Offer Phase

Chapter 5
The Post-Offer/Pre-Acceptance Phase

Chapter 6
The Acceptance Phase

Chapter 7
The Post-Acceptance Phase

Chapter 8
Drafting a Contract

INTRODUCTION

A TRANSACTIONAL GUIDE TO CONTRACT FORMATION

After answering the threshold questions (whether federal or state law applies to the transaction, which state's law applies to the transaction, and what body of law within that state applies to the transaction), attention can focus on the contract itself. Have the parties formed a contract, and if so, what are its terms?

Part Two investigates the four phases of contract formation; the modification of an existing contract (the post-acceptance phase); and drafting a contract.

- Chapter 3. The Pre-Offer Phase
- Chapter 4. The Offer Phase
- Chapter 5. The Post-Offer/Pre-Acceptance Phase
- Chapter 6. The Acceptance Phase
- Chapter 7. The Post-Acceptance Phase
- Chapter 8. Drafting a Contract

Evaluating whether the parties have formed a contract follows the transaction's evolution from beginning to end. All of the events relating to the formation of the contract are recorded along a time line.

Consider a situation where the ABC Equipment Company is attempting to sell a tractor to Green Construction Company. The time line might be as follows:

7/1	7/2	8/1	8/5
Green asks ABC for information about a tractor.	ABC gives Green a price list and brochure.	Green sends a purchase order form for tractor #100 (list price $5,000) for delivery on 8/15.	ABC notifies Green that the price has increased by $500.

8/10	8/15	9/1	9/15
Green notifies ABC that it expects the tractor at the list price.	Delivery date passes without delivery of the tractor.	ABC delivers the tractor.	ABC bills Green $5,500 (list price plus $500).

Once all the events have been recorded, each event, beginning with the first, is evaluated for its legal significance, if any. If more than one legal conclusion can be drawn from an event, the evaluation proceeds using first one conclusion and then the second.

The legal conclusions correspond with the four phases present during the formation of a contract: (1) pre-offer; (2) offer; (3) post-offer/pre-acceptance; and (4) acceptance.

In the pre-offer phase, the parties become acquainted with each other. They begin negotiating although neither is ready to make an offer, to give the other the power to conclude the transaction, or to say "I will give you this for that and if you say 'Yes' we have a deal." The parties are still formulating and preserving their options. Neither is ready to be bound.

When one party has enough information and is ready to enter into a binding transaction, that party makes an offer requesting an exchange. "I will do this if you will do that." The offeror states what the offeror will do in exchange for what the other party, the offeree, must do. Implicit in the offer is the offeror's statement, "I will be bound by the terms that I have stated if you say 'yes.' "

The third phase, post-offer/pre-acceptance, may last no longer than a split second or may extend for hours, days, weeks, or even months. This post-offer/pre-acceptance phase is a waiting period for the offeror. The offeror waits for the offeree to either accept or reject the offer. The longer the wait, the greater the opportunity for the transaction to go awry.

A number of events can occur that will cause the offer to die before an attempted acceptance: (1) The offeror may reconsider the wisdom of the offer and revoke it, in which case the offeree no longer has an offer to accept. (2) The offeree may decide that a contract on the offeror's terms would not be in his or her own best interest and therefore reject the offer. A rejection extinguishes the offer. Because an offer no longer exists, the offeree may assume the role of offeror and propose an offer (known as a counteroffer) with more favorable terms. (3) The offer may have stated a time limit within which it must be accepted. If not accepted within this time, the offer ceases to exist and lapses. (4) If the offer does not state how long the offeree has to accept, the offer will cease to exist (lapse) after the offeree has had a reasonable time to accept. (5) Finally, the offeror or offeree could die or become incapacitated, or the subject matter of the offer could be destroyed before the offer was accepted.

If the offer continues to live, the offeree can accept the offer. To accept the offer, the offeree assents to the terms the offeror has proposed. Because the offeror has control of the offer ("the offeror is the master of his or her offer"), the offer is made on a "take it or leave it" basis. If the offeree finds the terms of the offer unacceptable, the offeree can reject the offer and propose his or her own offer. But if the offeree accepts the offeror's offer on the offeror's terms, the offeree's acceptance concludes the transaction, and a contract is formed.

Sometimes, the parties wish to change the terms of the existing contract or to correct an error in the written contract. They are now in the post-acceptance phase of contract formation, and they do not have the same flexibility that existed during prior phases. Although the relationship of the parties can be changed after a contract has been formed, they have surrendered their "freedom to contract" and now must follow the often intricate rules imposed upon them by the law.

3

THE PRE-OFFER PHASE

The seeds for a contract are sown in the pre-offer phase of contract formation. Some mature into offers. Section one investigates the transition when the pre-offer phase ends and an offer begins. Other seeds wither and die. Section two probes whether the parties are always free to just walk away if negotiations do not mature into an offer. Subsection A explores the role of reliance when negotiations fail to produce an offer. Subsection B examines the role of restitution when negotiations fail to produce an offer.

Section 1. WHEN DOES THE PRE-OFFER PHASE END AND AN OFFER BEGIN?

The pre-offer phase (also known as preliminary negotiation) begins with the first communication. The communication may be as simple as a telephone call, a letter, or a personal visit asking whether the other party can perform or promise to perform a service or supply a product. The parties may pass quickly through this phase to "offer" or dwell at the pre-offer stage for months or even years. Some parties never progress to offer and the transaction ends. Others may skip the pre-offer phase and begin their communications with an offer.

Classifying communications as "pre-offer" is not important. What is important is determining whether an offer has been made. Pre-offer (preliminary negotiation) takes place prior to offer. Terms discussed during the preliminary negotiation that do not find their way into the offer are irrelevant.

Because the threshold question is whether the communication is an offer or merely preliminary negotiation, the pre-offer phase requires some understanding of what is meant by "offer." The Restatement (Second) of Contracts section 24 provides a formal definition of offer:

> An offer is the manifestation of willingness to enter into a bargain, so made as to justify another person in understanding that his assent to that bargain is invited and will conclude it.

Professor Corbin, in his article "Offer and Acceptance, and Some of The Resulting Legal Relations," 26 Yale L.J. 169, 181–82 (1917), defines an offer as "an act whereby one person confers upon another the power to create contractual relations between them. . . . [The] act of the offeror operates to create in the offeree a power . . .; thereafter the voluntary act of the offeree alone will operate to create the new relations called a contract." In practical terms the offeror, to create this power, must state the terms of the contract so nothing remains for the offeror to negotiate once the offeree assents to these terms. The offeree, by accepting the terms, forms the contract.

The following statements illustrate the difference between pre-offer and offer:

1. "What will you take for your car?"
2. "I will give you $1,500 for your car."

The first ("What will you take for your car?") is a potential buyer's request for information. The potential buyer can evaluate the owner's response and decide whether the terms stated are acceptable. Even if the potential buyer likes the owner's terms, the buyer still must respond to the owner's offer for a contract to be formed. The buyer's request is only preliminary negotiation, not an offer.

The second statement ("I will give you $1,500 for your car") is not a request for information. It is a statement of the buyer's willingness to be bound according to the terms specified. By making the terms definite rather than seeking a subsequent opportunity to evaluate the owner's response, the buyer has made an offer. The buyer has given the owner the power to form a contract by accepting the buyer's terms. If the owner accepts the buyer's offer, a contract is formed. Nothing is left for the owner to negotiate, and the buyer is bound by the original terms.

As we continue through Chapter 3, you do not need a full understanding of the concept of offer because this chapter deals with the transaction prior to the making of the offer. Chapter 4 explores the concept of offer in greater detail, and you will be given an opportunity to analyze whether certain communications are offers or merely preliminary negotiation.

Section 2. WHEN NEGOTIATIONS END WITHOUT AN OFFER— IS THAT ALL THERE IS?

If negotiations end without one party making an offer, is that all there is? Are the parties free to walk away from each other without any obligations? Unfortunately, the answer is more complex than a simple "yes" or "no." The answer depends on the facts of each transaction and requires an evaluation of the interests that contracts law seeks to protect.

When dealing with contractual relationships, the courts recognize and protect three interests: expectation, reliance, and restitution. Because it is easier to introduce these interests once a contract has been created, let us move ahead of our road map and for purposes of discussion, assume a contract exists and one of the parties has breached. After discussing the expectation, reliance, and restitution interests in this context, we will return to determine whether the courts recognize and protect these three interests in the pre-offer phase.

EXPECTATION

Why does one party enter into a contract with another? When parties contract, each has "expectations": expectations relating to what he or she will give under the contract (duty or obligation) and expectations relating to what he or she will receive under the contract (right or benefit).

EXAMPLE

"I promise to pay you $5,000 for your promise to sell me your car." Buyer expects to give $5,000 and expects to receive the car. If Seller responds "I promise to sell you my car for your promise to pay me $5,000," Seller expects to give the car and expects to receive $5,000. If one party fails to perform his or her duty according to the expectation of the other party under the contract (that is, the party breaches the contract), the injured party is entitled to receive that which he or she expected under the contract. In other words, the injured party is placed in a position as good as he or she would have been in had each contracting party fully performed.

1. If Seller delivered the car to Buyer and Buyer refused to pay, Seller should be entitled to receive his or her expectation—payment for the car ($5,000).
2. If Buyer was to pay several days before Seller was to deliver the car, but Buyer did not pay (and Seller therefore did not deliver), Seller is still entitled to his or her expectation under the contract.

   If Seller sells the car to a third party for $4,700, a price $300 less than he or she was to receive under the original contract, Seller is entitled to $300 from breaching Buyer. Breaching Buyer will compensate Seller for the difference between what was actually received under the substitute contract (the contract between Seller and the third party) and what he or she "expected" to receive under the original contract.

Compensation for protection of an expectation interest

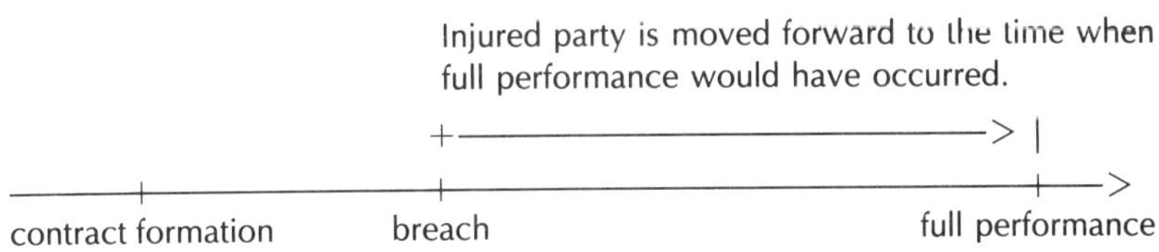

The breaching party compensates the injured party according to the injured party's expectations. The remedy is measured by the reasonable value of the expectation, as determined by the reasonable person standard.

Because the contracting parties have expectations in mind (this is one of the reasons why they contract), they have expectation interests in the contract. The courts recognize that each party may have a "reliance" and a "restitution" interest in addition to the expectation interest.

RELIANCE

What does reliance mean? Rely means "to trust, to depend." If, after forming a contract, neither party acts or refrains from acting while depending on the terms of the contract, neither party has a reliance interest. For a reliance interest to exist, one party must be influenced by the other party's promise and act or refrain from acting while under this influence. If one party relies on the contract and begins to perform, he or she has a reliance interest that the courts can protect. Without the contract, the relying party would not have performed. To compensate the injured party for an injury resulting from his or her reliance, the courts place the injured party in the position he or she was in before the act of reliance took place.

EXAMPLE

Annette, a sculptor, from San Francisco, was hired by the New York City Parks Commission to create a sculpture for Central Park. Under the contract, Annette would be paid a $10,000 commission upon completion of her work. Under the contract, she was required to provide her own transportation and room and board.

The contract gave Annette the opportunity to have her work displayed in New York City. She anticipated that this was the break she needed. She knew that she would lose money under the arrangement because she would have to move all of her equipment from her studio in San Francisco, pay her own transportation and room and board, and pay for materials.

After Annette had purchased materials for her project and had traveled to New York City with her equipment, the Parks Commission notified her that it was cancelling her contract. If Annette sued the commission for breach of contract, she could recover under her reliance interest for her expenses for moving herself and her equipment from San Francisco to New York City and for the costs of the materials that she purchased in anticipation of performing the contract (less the value of the materials).

Although compensation for injury to an expectation interest generally yields a greater dollar amount than compensation for injury based on reliance, in some situations recovery for an injury to a reliance interest will exceed that for expectation.

EXAMPLE

Retailer contracted with Manufacturer for the exclusive right to sell Manufacturer's products. The contract stated that Retailer could not sell products from competing manufacturers and required liquidation of its existing inventory of competitive products within two weeks. Retailer held a "super sale" to liquidate its inventory of competitive products and sold them at a loss. When the time came for Manufacturer to supply Retailer with its products, Manufacturer refused and thus breached the contract. To protect Retailer's expectation interest, a court would have to speculate to determine Retailer's profits for products that it never received and never sold. Therefore Retailer may not recover any damages for injury to its expectation interest. If, on the other hand, a court were to protect Retailer's reliance interest, Retailer could recover for its loss in selling its existing inventory because this loss would not have occurred if Retailer had not relied on Manufacturer's promise under the contract. Compensating Retailer for its loss places it in the position it was in prior to its reliance (prior to liquidation).

Compensation for protection of a reliance interest

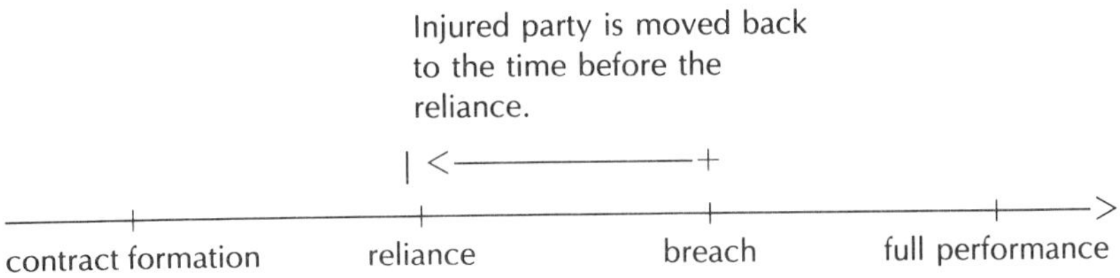

The breaching party compensates the injured party for the injury caused by the injured party's reliance. The remedy is measured by the cost of the injured party's reliance.

RESTITUTION—UNJUST ENRICHMENT

The third interest a court may protect is the injured party's restitution interest. This restitution interest exists when the injured party has conferred a benefit (an enrichment) on the breaching party. To compensate the injured party for conferring the benefit on an undeserving party, the courts will require the breaching party to compensate the injured party for the benefit conferred. Courts determine the value of the benefit by measuring its reasonable value to the breaching party, the party who was enriched.

EXAMPLE

Owner's home had a leaky roof that needed repair. Owner contracted with Roofing Company for a new roof. Roofing Company began by removing the old roof and then proceeded to shingle the roof. When three quarters of the new roof was in place, Owner fired Roofing Company.

Roofing Company sued Owner for breach of contract. Because Roofing Company wanted to do a job in Owner's neighborhood (hoping that this would lead to additional contracts), the price quoted to Owner was at cost. Roofing Company can seek damages based on its restitution interest rather than on its expectation. Compensation under Roofing Company's restitution interest is the reasonable value to the Owner of the partially completed roof.

It should be noted that, generally, recovery for an injury to the injured party's expectation interest yields more than recovery for an injury to the injured party's restitution interest. Although an injured party will rarely receive compensation for an injury to his or her restitution interest that exceeds compensation for an injury to his or her expectation (interest), these situations do exist.

EXAMPLE

Homeowner hired Contractor to install a swimming pool for $7,000. Contractor began to install the pool, but before the pool was completed, Owner decided he did not like the pool (even though it was installed according to contract specifications) and fired Contractor without cause. Before the wrongful termination, Contractor had spent $5,000 on materials and labor. To complete the job, Contractor would have had to spend another $3,000. In other words, Contractor had made a bad deal (a losing contract) and only by a stroke of good luck (the wrongful termination) was Contractor justified in not finishing the work. Because Contractor conferred a benefit on Owner (the partially completed pool), the nonbreaching Contractor is entitled to compensation for the injury to his or her restitution interest. If the reasonable value of the partially completed pool to the breaching party is $5,000, the injured Contractor should recover $5,000. Had Contractor sought compensation for injury to his or her expectation interest, recovery would have been less than $5,000. Under the expectation formula, Contractor was entitled to the prorated contract price—$\frac{5}{8} \times$ $7,000 or $4,375.

Compensation for protection of a restitution interest

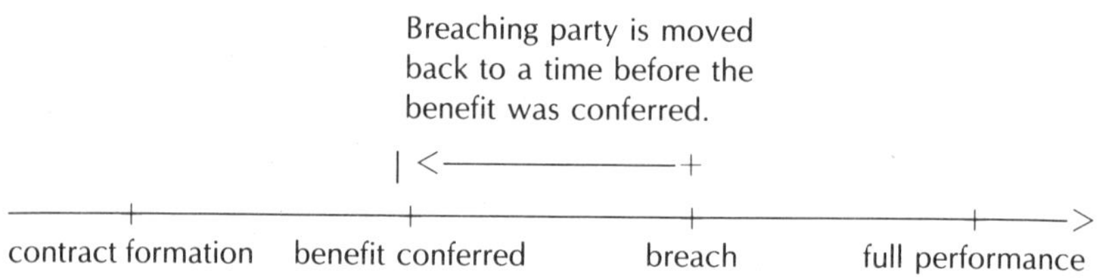

The breaching party compensates the injured party for the benefit received. Courts measure the remedy by the reasonable value of the benefit to the breaching party.

Having developed the three interests that a court may protect in a breach of contract action, we now return to our discussion of the pre-offer phase.

PRE–OFFER EXPECTATION INTEREST

Because a contract is not formed in the pre-offer phase, neither party has expectations based on a contract. Therefore, if the parties walk away without a contract being formed, neither could successfully claim injury to an expectation interest. This leaves the other two interests: reliance and restitution.

PRE–OFFER RELIANCE INTEREST

In the pre-offer phase, if one party acts or refrains from acting because he or she is relying on the other party's encouragement, a reliance interest that courts may protect comes into being even though no offer has been made.

EXAMPLE

New World Corporation and Green Construction Company are negotiating for construction of a new production plant for New World. At this time, although neither has made an offer to the other, New World says to Green, "Although I am not ready to make you an offer now, you should buy a large earthmover so you can start work as soon as we contract." If Green buys the earthmover but New World never makes an offer, Green has suffered an injury by relying on New World's encouragement. Should Green be compensated for the loss suffered by purchasing the earthmover?

PRE–OFFER RESTITUTION INTEREST

The third interest, the restitution interest, is based on unjust enrichment. A benefit has been conferred by one person on another. It would be unjust to permit the person receiving the benefit to retain it without compensating the person who conferred the benefit.

EXAMPLE

A doctor was driving to her office when she came upon an automobile-motorcycle accident. The cyclist, having been thrown from his motorcycle, was unconscious and bleeding profusely. The doctor rendered professional services and stopped the bleeding. The cyclist was taken to the hospital where he recovered from the accident. The cyclist would have died before being taken to the hospital had the doctor not rendered aid. Because the cyclist was unconscious, he was in no position to make an offer to the doctor for medical services. Should the doctor be compensated for her services?

The following material explores the roles of reliance and restitution when negotiations fail to produce an offer.

A. The Role of Reliance When Negotiations Fail to Produce an Offer

Although traditional contracts law emphasizes expectation interests, several cases in recent years have permitted recovery although the transaction never progressed beyond the pre-offer phase. Because a contract had not been formed, recovery was based on reliance rather than on the breach.

The most famous case in this area, *Hoffman v. Red Owl Stores, Inc.,* was decided by the Wisconsin Supreme Court in 1965. Joseph Hoffman operated a bakery in Wautoma, Wisconsin, where his success led him to consider expanding his operations to include a grocery store. With this in mind, he contacted a Red Owl representative to discuss establishing a Red Owl franchise store in Wautoma.

The first half of the following appellate court opinion chronicles the negotiations between Hoffman and various Red Owl representatives. Listing the various discussions between the parties sequentially will help you understand this opinion. Concentrate on what the Red Owl representatives requested and what Hoffman did in response to these requests. Consider whether there was a "cost" to Hoffman associated with each of his responses. As you sequence each episode, decide whether either Red Owl or Hoffman made an offer for the franchise. When the relationship between the parties deteriorated and they walked away from each other, had an offer for the franchise been made or were the parties still in the pre-offer phase of the transaction?

In the second half of the opinion, focus on Justice Currie's statements for the court. When Hoffman was awarded a judgment against Red Owl, did the court base recovery on a breach of contract theory or on a different theory? If the latter, does the court identify this theory? Under the theory of recovery used by the court, was recovery intended to compensate Hoffman for an injury based on his expectation or for an injury suffered as a result of his reliance? What did Hoffman need to prove to be entitled to a recovery under this theory?

Hoffman v. Red Owl Stores, Inc.

Supreme Court of Wisconsin, 1965.
26 Wis. 2d 683, 133 N.W.2d 267.

McFADDEN, Judge.

Action by Joseph Hoffman (hereinafter "Hoffman") and wife, plaintiffs, against defendants Red Owl Stores, Inc. (hereinafter "Red Owl") and Edward Lukowitz.

The complaint alleged that Lukowitz, as agent for Red Owl, represented to and agreed with plaintiffs that Red Owl would build a store building in Chilton and stock it with merchandise for Hoffman to operate in return for which plaintiffs were to put up and invest a total sum of $18,000; that in reliance upon the above mentioned agreement and representations plaintiffs sold their bakery building and business and their grocery store and business; also in reliance on the agreement and representations Hoffman purchased the building site in Chilton and rented a residence for himself and his family in Chilton; plaintiffs' actions in reliance on the representations and agreement disrupted their personal and business life; plaintiffs lost substantial amounts of income and expended large sums of money as expenses. Plaintiffs demanded recovery of damages for the breach of defendants' representations and agreements.

The action was tried to a court and jury. The facts hereafter stated are taken from the evidence adduced at the trial. Where there was a conflict in the evidence the version favorable to plaintiffs has been accepted since the verdict rendered was in favor of plaintiffs.

Hoffman assisted by his wife operated a bakery at Wautoma from 1956 until sale of the building late in 1961. The building was owned in joint tenancy by him and his wife. Red Owl is a Minnesota corporation having its home office at Hopkins, Minnesota. It owns and operates a number of grocery supermarket stores and also extends franchises to agency stores which are owned by individuals, partnerships and corporations. Lukowitz resides at Green Bay and since September, 1960, has been divisional manager for Red Owl in a territory comprising Upper Michigan and most of Wisconsin in charge of 84 stores. Prior to September,

1960, he was district manager having charge of approximately 20 stores.

In November, 1959, Hoffman was desirous of expanding his operations by establishing a grocery store and contacted a Red Owl representative by the name of Jansen, now deceased. Numerous conversations were had in 1960 with the idea of establishing a Red Owl franchise store in Wautoma. In September, 1960, Lukowitz succeeded Jansen as Red Owl's representative in the negotiations. Hoffman mentioned that $18,000 was all the capital he had available to invest and he was repeatedly assured that this would be sufficient to set him up in business as a Red Owl store. About Christmastime, 1960, Hoffman thought it would be a good idea if he bought a small grocery store in Wautoma and operated it in order that he gain experience in the grocery business prior to operating a Red Owl store in some larger community. On February 6, 1961, on the advice of Lukowitz and Sykes, who had succeeded Lukowitz as Red Owl's district manager, Hoffman bought the inventory and fixtures of a small grocery store in Wautoma and leased the building in which it was operated.

After three months of operating this Wautoma store, the Red Owl representatives came in and took inventory and checked the operations and found the store was operating at a profit. Lukowitz advised Hoffman to sell the store to his manager, and assured him that Red Owl would find a larger store for him elsewhere. Acting on this advice and assurance, Hoffman sold the fixtures and inventory to his manager on June 6, 1961. Hoffman was reluctant to sell at that time because it meant losing the summer tourist business, but he sold on the assurance that he would be operating in a new location by fall and that he must sell this store if he wanted a bigger one. Before selling, Hoffman told the Red Owl representatives that he had $18,000 for "getting set up in business" and they assured him that there would be no problems in establishing him in a bigger operation. The makeup of the $18,000 was not discussed; it was understood plaintiff's father-in-law would furnish part of it. By June, 1961, the towns for the new grocery store had been narrowed down to two, Kewaunee and Chilton. In Kewaunee, Red Owl had an option on a building site. In Chilton, Red Owl had nothing under option, but it did select a site to which plaintiff obtained an option at Red Owl's suggestion. The option stipulated a purchase price of $6,000 with $1,000 to be paid on election to purchase and the balance to be paid within 30 days. On Lukowitz's assurance that everything was all set plaintiff paid $1,000 down on the lot on September 15th.

On September 27, 1961, plaintiff met at Chilton with Lukowitz and Mr. Reymund and Mr. Carlson from the home office who prepared a projected financial statement. Part of the funds plaintiffs were to supply as their investment in the venture were to be obtained by sale of their Wautoma bakery building.

On the basis of this meeting Lukowitz assured Hoffman: "* * * [E]verything is ready to go. Get your money together and we are set." Shortly after this meeting Lukowitz told plaintiffs that they would have to sell their bakery business and bakery building, and that their retaining this property was the only "hitch" in the entire plan. On November 6, 1961, plaintiffs sold their bakery building for $10,000. Hoffman was to retain the bakery equipment as he contemplated using it to operate a bakery in connection with his Red Owl store. After sale of the bakery Hoffman obtained employment on the night shift at an Appleton bakery.

The record contains different exhibits which were prepared in September and October, some of which were projections of the fiscal operation of the business and others were proposed building and floor plans. Red Owl was to procure some third party to buy the Chilton lot from Hoffman, construct the building, and then lease it to Hoffman. No final plans were ever made, nor were bids let or a construction contract entered. Some time prior to November 20, 1961, certain of the terms of the lease under which the building was to be rented by Hoffman were understood between him and Lukowitz. The lease was to be for 10 years with a rental approximating $550 a month calculated on the basis of 1 percent per month on the building cost, plus 6 percent of the land cost divided on a monthly basis. At the end of the 10–year term he was to have an option to renew the lease for an additional 10–year period or to buy the property at cost on an instalment basis. There was no discussion as to what the instalments would be or with respect to repairs and maintenance.

On November 22nd or 23rd, Lukowitz and plaintiffs met in Minneapolis with Red Owl's credit manager to confer on Hoffman's financial standing and on financing the agency. Another projected financial statement was there drawn up entitled, "Proposed Financing For An Agency Store." This showed Hoffman contributing $24,100 of cash capital of which only $4,600 was to be cash possessed by plaintiffs. Eight thousand was to be procured as a loan from a Chilton bank secured by a mortgage on the bakery fixtures, $7,500 was to be obtained on a 5 percent loan from the father-in-law, and $4,000 was to be obtained by sale of the lot to the lessor at a profit.

A week or two after the Minneapolis meeting Lukowitz showed Hoffman a telegram from the home office to the effect that if plaintiff could get another $2,000 for promotional purposes the deal could go through for $26,000. Hoffman stated he would have to find out if he could get another $2,000. He met with his father-in-law, who agreed to put $13,000 into the business provided he could come into the business as a partner. Lukowitz told Hoffman the partnership arrangement "sounds fine" and that Hoffman should not go into the partnership arrangement with the "front office." On January 16, 1962, the Red Owl credit manager teletyped Lukowitz that the father-in-law would have to sign an agreement that the $13,000 was either a gift or a loan subordinate to all general creditors and that he would prepare the agreement. On January 31, 1962, Lukowitz teletyped the home office that the father-in-law would sign one or other of the agreements. However, Hoffman testified that it was not until the final meeting some time between January 26th and February 2nd, 1962, that he was told that his father-in-law was expected to sign an agreement that the $13,000 he was advancing was to be an outright gift. No mention was then made by the Red Owl representatives of the alternative of the father-in-law signing a subordination agreement. At this meeting the Red Owl agents presented Hoffman with the following projected financial statement:

"Capital required in operation:		
"Cash	$ 5,000.00	
"Merchandise	20,000.00	
"Bakery	18,000.00	
"Fixtures	17,500.00	
"Promotional Funds	1,500.00	
"TOTAL:		$ 62,000.00
"Source of funds:		
"Red Owl 7–day terms	$ 5,000.00	
"Red Owl Fixture contract (Term 5 years)	14,000.00	
"Bank loans (Term 9 years Union State Bank		
"of Chilton	8,000.00	
"(Secured by Bakery Equipment		
"Other loans (Term No-pay) No interest		
"Father-in-law	13,000.00	

"(Secured by None)			
"(Secured by Mortgage on "Wautoma Bakery Bldg.)		2,000.00	
"Resale of land		6,000.00	
"Equity Capital: "Amount owner has "to invest:	$ 5,000.00–Cash 17,500.00–Bakery Equip.	22,500.00	
	"TOTAL:		$70,500.00"

Hoffman interpreted the above statement to require of plaintiffs a total of $34,000 cash made up of $13,000 gift from his father-in-law, $2,000 on mortgage, $8,000 on Chilton bank loan, $5,000 in cash from plaintiff, and $6,000 on the resale of the Chilton lot. Red Owl claims $18,000 is the total of the unborrowed or unencumbered cash, that is, $13,000 from the father-in-law and $5,000 cash from Hoffman himself. Hoffman informed Red Owl he could not go along with this proposal, and particularly objected to the requirement that his father-in-law sign an agreement that his $13,000 advancement was an absolute gift. This terminated the negotiations between the parties.

The case was submitted to the jury on a special verdict with the first two questions answered by the court. This verdict, as returned by the jury, was as follows:

"Question No. 1: Did the Red Owl Stores, Inc. and Joseph Hoffman on or about mid-May of 1961 initiate negotiations looking to the establishment of Joseph Hoffman as a franchise operator of a Red Owl Store in Chilton? Answer: Yes. (Answered by the Court.)

"Question No. 2: Did the parties mutually agree on all of the details of the proposal so as to reach a final agreement thereon? Answer: No. (Answered by the Court.)

"Question No. 3: Did the Red Owl Stores, Inc., in the course of said negotiations, make representations to Joseph Hoffman that if he fulfilled certain conditions that they would establish him as a franchise operator of a Red Owl Store in Chilton? Answer: Yes.

"Question No. 4: If you have answered Question No. 3 'Yes,' then answer this question: Did Joseph Hoffman rely on said representations and was he induced to act thereon? Answer: Yes.

"Question No. 5: If you have answered Question No. 4 'Yes,' then answer this question: Ought Joseph Hoffman, in the exercise of ordinary care, to have relied on said representations? Answer: Yes.

"Question No. 6: If you have answered Question No. 3 'Yes' then answer this question: Did Joseph Hoffman fulfill all the conditions he was required to fulfill by the terms of the negotiations between the parties up to January 26, 1962? Answer: Yes.

"Question No. 7: What sum of money will reasonably compensate the plaintiffs for such damages as they sustained by reason of:

"(a) The sale of the Wautoma store fixtures and inventory?
"Answer: $16,735.00.
"(b) The sale of the bakery building?
"Answer: $2,000.00.
"(c) Taking up the option on the Chilton lot?
"Answer: $1,000.00.
"(d) Expenses of moving his family to Neenah?
"Answer: $140.00.
"(e) House rental in Chilton?
"Answer: $125.00."

Plaintiffs moved for judgment on the verdict while defendants moved to change the answers to Questions 3, 4, 5, and 6 from "Yes" to "No", and in the alternative for relief from the answers to the subdivisions of Question 7 or a new trial. On March 31, 1964, the circuit court entered the following order:

"IT IS ORDERED in accordance with said decision on motions after verdict hereby incorporated herein by reference:

"1. That the answer of the jury to Question No. 7(a) be and the same is hereby vacated and set aside and that a new trial be had on the sole issue of the damages for loss, if any, on the sale of the Wautoma store, fixtures and inventory.

"2. That all other portions of the verdict of the jury be and hereby are approved and confirmed and all after-verdict motions of the parties inconsistent with this order are hereby denied."

Defendants have appealed from this order and plaintiffs have cross-appealed from paragraph 1. thereof.

Benton, Bosser, Fulton, Menn & Nehs, Appleton, for appellants.

Van Hoof, Van Hoof & Wylie, Little Chute, for respondents.

CURRIE, Chief Justice.

The instant appeal and cross-appeal present these questions:

(1) Whether this court should recognize causes of action grounded on promissory estoppel as exemplified by sec. 90 of Restatement, 1 Contracts?

(2) Do the facts in this case make out a cause of action for promissory estoppel?

(3) Are the jury's findings with respect to damages sustained by the evidence?

Recognition of a Cause of Action Grounded on Promissory Estoppel

Sec. 90 of Restatement, 1 Contracts, provides (at p. 110):

"A promise which the promisor should reasonably expect to induce action or forbearance of a definite and substantial character on the part of the promisee and which does induce such action or forbearance is binding if injustice can be avoided only by enforcement of the promise."

The Wisconsin Annotations to Restatement, Contracts, prepared under the direction of the late Professor William H. Page and issued in 1933, stated (at p. 53, sec. 90):

"The Wisconsin cases do not seem to be in accord with this section of the Restatement. It is certain that no such proposition has ever been announced by the Wisconsin court and it is at least doubtful if it would be approved by the court."

Since 1933, the closest approach this court has made to adopting the rule of the Restatement occurred in the recent case of Lazarus v. American Motors Corp. (1963), 21 Wis.2d 76, 85, 123 N.W.2d 548, 553, wherein the court stated:

"We recognize that upon different facts it would be possible for a seller of steel to have altered his position so as to effectuate the equitable considerations inherent in sec. 90 of the Restatement."

While it was not necessary to the disposition of the Lazarus Case to adopt the promissory estoppel rule of the Restatement, we are squarely faced in the instant case with that issue. Not only did the trial court frame the special verdict on the theory of sec. 90 of Restatement, 1 Contracts, but no other possible theory has been presented to or discovered by this court which would permit plaintiffs to recover. Of other remedies considered that of an action for fraud and deceit seemed to be the most comparable. An action at law for fraud, however, cannot be predicated on unfulfilled promises unless the promisor possessed the present intent not to perform. Suskey v. Davidoff (1958), 2 Wis. 2d 503, 507, 87 N.W.2d 306, and cases cited. Here, there is no evidence that would support a finding that Lukowitz made any of the promises, upon which plaintiffs' complaint is predicated, in bad faith with any present intent that they would not be fulfilled by Red Owl.

Many courts of other jurisdictions have seen fit over the years to adopt the principle of promissory estoppel, and the tendency in that direction continues. As Mr. Justice McFADDIN, speaking in behalf of the Arkansas court, well stated, that the development of the law of promissory estoppel "is an attempt by the courts to keep remedies abreast of increased moral consciousness of honesty and fair representations in all business dealings." Peoples National Bank of Little Rock v. Linebarger Construction Company (1951), 219 Ark. 11, 17, 240 S.W.2d 12, 16. For a further discussion of the doctrine of promissory estoppel, see 1A Corbin, Contracts, pp. 187, et seq., secs. 193–209; 3 Pomeroy's Equity Jurisprudence (5th ed.), pp. 211, et seq., sec. 808b; 1 Williston, Contracts (Jaeger's 3d ed.), pp. 607, et seq., sec.

140; Boyer, Promissory Estoppel: Requirements and Limitations of the Doctrine 98 University of Pennsylvania Law Review (1950), 459; Seavey Reliance Upon Gratuitous Promises or Other Conduct, 64 Harvard Law Review (1951), 913; Annos. 115 A.L.R. 152, and 48 A.L.R.2d 1069.

The Restatement avoids use of the term "promissory estoppel," and there has been criticism of it as an inaccurate term. See 1A Corbin, Contracts, p. 232, et seq., sec. 204. On the other hand, Williston advocated the use of this term or something equivalent. 1 Williston, Contracts (1st ed.), p. 308, sec. 139. Use of the word "estoppel" to describe a doctrine upon which a party to a lawsuit may obtain affirmative relief offends the traditional concept that estoppel merely serves as a shield and cannot serve as a sword to create a cause of action. See Utschig v. McClone (1962), 16 Wis.2d 506, 509, 114 N.W.2d 854. "Attractive nuisance" is also a much criticized term. See concurring opinion, Flamingo v. City of Waukesha (1952), 262 Wis. 219, 227, 55 N.W.2d 24. However, the latter term is still in almost universal use by the courts because of the lack of a better substitute. The same is also true of the wide use of the term "promissory estoppel." We have employed its use in this opinion not only because of its extensive use by other courts but also since a more accurate equivalent has not been devised.

Because we deem the doctrine of promissory estoppel, as stated in sec. 90 of Restatement, 1 Contracts, is one which supplies a needed tool which courts may employ in a proper case to prevent injustice, we endorse and adopt it.

Applicability of Doctrine to Facts of This Case

The record here discloses a number of promises and assurances given to Hoffman by Lukowitz in behalf of Red Owl upon which plaintiffs relied and acted upon to their detriment.

Foremost were the promises that for the sum of $18,000 Red Owl would establish Hoffman in a store. After Hoffman had sold his grocery store and paid the $1,000 on the Chilton lot, the $18,000 figure was changed to $24,100. Then in November, 1961, Hoffman was assured that if the $24,100 figure were increased by $2,000 the deal would go through. Hoffman was induced to sell his grocery store fixtures and inventory in June, 1961, on the promise that he would be in his new store by fall. In November, plaintiffs sold their bakery building on the urging of defendants and on the assurance that this was the last step necessary to have the deal with Red Owl go through.

We determine that there was ample evidence to sustain the answers of the jury to the questions of the verdict with respect to the promissory representations made by Red Owl, Hoffman's reliance thereon in the exercise of ordinary care, and his fulfillment of the conditions required of him by the terms of the negotiations had with Red Owl.

There remains for consideration the question of law raised by defendants that agreement was never reached on essential factors necessary to establish a contract between Hoffman and Red Owl. Among these were the size, cost, design, and layout of the store building; and the terms of the lease with respect to rent, maintenance, renewal, and purchase options. This poses the question of whether the promise necessary to sustain a cause of action for promissory estoppel must embrace all essential details of a proposed transaction between promisor and promisee so as to be the equivalent of an offer that would result in a binding contract between the parties if the promisee were to accept the same.

Originally the doctrine of promissory estoppel was invoked as a substitute for consideration rendering a gratuitous promise enforceable as a contract. See Williston, Contracts (1st ed.), p. 307, sec. 139. In other words, the acts of reliance by the promisee to his detriment provided a substitute for consideration. If promissory estoppel were to be limited to only those situations where the promise giving rise to the cause of action must be so definite with respect to all details that a contract would result were the promise supported by consideration, then the defendants' instant promises to Hoffman would not meet this test. However, sec. 90 of Restatement, 1 Contracts, does not impose the requirement that the promise giving rise to the cause of action must be so comprehensive in scope as to meet the requirements of an offer that would ripen into a contract if accepted by the promisee. Rather the conditions imposed are:

(1) Was the promise one which the promisor should reasonably expect to induce action or forbearance of a definite and substantial character on the part of the promisee?

(2) Did the promise induce such action or forbearance?

(3) Can injustice be avoided only by enforcement of the promise?

We deem it would be a mistake to regard an action grounded on promissory estoppel as the equivalent of a breach of contract action. As Dean Boyer points out, it is desirable that fluidity in the application of the concept be maintained. 98 University of Pennsylvania Law Review (1950), 459, at page 497. While the first two of the above listed three requirements of promissory estoppel present issues of fact which ordinarily will be resolved by a jury, the third requirement, that the remedy can only be invoked where necessary to avoid injustice, is one that involves a policy decision by the court. Such a policy decision necessarily embraces an element of discretion.

We conclude that injustice would result here if plaintiffs were not granted some relief because of the failure of defendants to keep their promises which induced plaintiffs to act to their detriment.

Damages

Defendants attack all the items of damages awarded by the jury.

The bakery building at Wautoma was sold at defendants' instigation in order that Hoffman might have the net proceeds available as part of the cash capital he was to invest in the Chilton store venture. The evidence clearly establishes that it was sold at a loss of $2,000. Defendants contend that half of this loss was sustained by Mrs. Hoffman because title stood in joint tenancy. They point out that no dealings took place between her and defendants as all negotiations were had with her husband. Ordinarily only the promisee and not third persons are entitled to enforce the remedy of promissory estoppel against the promisor. However, if the promisor actually foresees, or has reason to foresee, action by a third person in reliance on the promise, it may be quite unjust to refuse to perform the promise. 1A Corbin, Contracts, p. 220, sec. 200. Here not only did defendants foresee that it would be necessary for Mrs. Hoffman to sell her joint interest in the bakery building, but defendants actually requested that this be done. We approve the jury's award of $2,000 damages for the loss incurred by both plaintiffs in this sale.

Defendants attack on two grounds the $1,000 awarded because of Hoffman's payment of that amount on the purchase price of the Chilton lot. The first is that this $1,000 had already been lost at the time the final negotiations with Red Owl fell through in January, 1962, because the remaining $5,000 of purchase price had been due on October 15, 1961. The record does not disclose that the lot owner had foreclosed Hoffman's interest in the lot for failure to pay this $5,000. The $1,000 was not paid for the option, but had been paid as part of the purchase price at the time Hoffman elected to exercise the option. This gave him an equity in the lot which could not be legally foreclosed without affording Hoffman an opportunity to pay the balance. The second ground of attack is that the lot may have had a fair market value of $6,000, and Hoffman should have paid the remaining $5,000 of purchase price. We determine that it would be unreasonable to require Hoffman to have invested an additional $5,000 in order to protect the $1,000 he had paid.

Therefore, we find no merit to defendants' attack upon this item of damages.

We also determine it was reasonable for Hoffman to have paid $125 for one month's rent of a home in Chilton after defendants assured him everything would be set when plaintiff sold the bakery building. This was a proper item of damage.

Plaintiffs never moved to Chilton because defendants suggested that Hoffman get some experience by working in a Red Owl store in the Fox River Valley. Plaintiffs, therefore, moved to Neenah instead of Chilton. After moving, Hoffman worked at night in an Appleton bakery but held himself available for work in a Red Owl store. The $140 moving expense would not have been incurred if plaintiffs had not sold their bakery building in Wautoma in reliance upon defendants' promises. We consider the $140 moving expense to be a proper item of damage.

We turn now to the damage item with respect to which the trial court granted a new trial, i.e., that arising from the sale of the Wautoma grocery store fixtures and inventory for which the jury awarded $16,735. The trial court ruled that Hoffman could not recover for any loss of future profits for the summer months following the sale on June 6, 1961, but that damages would be limited to the difference between the sales price received and the fair market value of the assets sold, giving consideration to any goodwill attaching thereto by reason of the transfer of a going business. There was no direct evidence presented as to what this fair market value was on June 6, 1961. The evidence did disclose that Hoffman paid $9,000 for the inventory, added $1,500 to it and sold it for $10,000 or a loss of $500. His 1961 federal income tax return showed that the grocery equipment had been purchased for $7,000 and sold for $7,955.96. Plaintiffs introduced evidence of the buyer that during the first eleven weeks of operation of the grocery store his gross sales were $44,000 and his profit was $6,000 or roughly 15 percent. On cross-examination he admitted that this was gross and not net profit. Plaintiffs contend that in a breach of contract action damages may include loss of profits. However, this is not a breach of contract action.

The only relevancy of evidence relating to profits would be with respect to proving the element of goodwill in establishing the fair market value of the grocery inventory and fixtures sold. Therefore, evidence of profits would be admissible to afford a foundation for expert opinion as to fair market value.

Where damages are awarded in promissory estoppel instead of specifically enforcing the promisor's promise, they should be only such as in the opinion of the court are necessary to prevent injustice. Mechanical or rule of thumb approaches to the damage problem should be avoided. In discussing remedies to be applied by courts in promissory estoppel we quote the following views of writers on the subject:

"Enforcement of a promise does not necessarily mean Specific Performance. It does not necessarily mean Damages for breach. Moreover the amount allowed as Damages may be determined by the plaintiff's expenditures or change of position in reliance as well as by the value to him of the promised performance. Restitution is also an 'enforcing' remedy, although it is often said to be based upon some kind of a rescission. In determining what justice requires, the court must remember all of its powers, derived from equity, law merchant, and other sources, as well as the common law. Its decree should be molded accordingly." 1A Corbin, Contracts, p. 221, sec. 200.

"The wrong is not primarily in depriving the plaintiff of the promised reward but in causing the plaintiff to change position to his detriment. It would follow that the damages should not exceed the loss caused by the change of position, which would never be more in amount, but might be less, than the promised reward." Seavey, Reliance on Gratuitous Promises or Other Conduct, 64 Harvard Law Review (1951), 913, 926.

"There likewise seems to be no positive legal requirement, and certainly no legal policy, which dictates the allowance of contract damages in every case where the defendant's duty is consensual." Shattuck, Gratuitous Promises—A New

Writ?, 35 Michigan Law Review (1936), 908, 912.

At the time Hoffman bought the equipment and inventory of the small grocery store at Wautoma he did so in order to gain experience in the grocery store business. At that time discussion had already been had with Red Owl representatives that Wautoma might be too small for a Red Owl operation and that a larger city might be more desirable. Thus Hoffman made this purchase more or less as a temporary experiment. Justice does not require that the damages awarded him, because of selling these assets at the behest of defendants, should exceed any actual loss sustained measured by the difference between the sales price and the fair market value.

Since the evidence does not sustain the large award of damages arising from the sale of the Wautoma grocery business, the trial court properly ordered a new trial on this issue.

Order affirmed. Because of the cross-appeal, plaintiffs shall be limited to taxing but two-thirds of their costs.

In *Hoffman v. Red Owl Stores, Inc.,* the Wisconsin Supreme Court established three requirements that justify application of promissory estoppel:

1. Was the promise one that the promisor should reasonably expect to induce action or forbearance of a definite and substantial character on the part of the promisee?
2. Did the promise induce such action or forbearance?
3. Can injustice be avoided only by enforcement of the promise?

The first two present questions of fact; the third presents a policy question for the court to decide, and necessarily includes an element of discretion. To satisfy the third requirement, the plaintiff must prove to the court's satisfaction that he or she actually suffered as a result of his or her reliance.

The court derived these requirements (elements) from section 90 of the Restatement (First) of Contracts (1933):

> A promise which the promisor should reasonably expect to induce action or forbearance of a definite and substantial character on the part of the promisee and which does induce such action or forbearance is binding if injustice can be avoided only by enforcement of the promise.

After *Hoffman v. Red Owl* was decided, the American Law Institute, which drafts the Restatements, revised the Restatement of Contracts. Restatement (Second) of Contracts includes section 90 in a slightly revised form:

> (1) A promise which the promisor should reasonably expect to induce action or forbearance on the part of the promisee or a third person and which does induce such action or forbearance is binding if injustice can be avoided only by enforcement of the promise. The remedy granted for breach may be limited as justice requires.

- How does the revision of section 90 change the three requirements (elements) for promissory estoppel?

PROBLEM 1: Pursuant to its decision to begin distributing its beer in Missouri, Adolph Coors Company, a Colorado corporation, created a distribution plan which divided Missouri into thirteen separate geographical areas. In August of 1977 Coors released news reports requesting any person interested in becoming a Coors distributor to write the company requesting an application. Coors mailed formal applications and copies of Coors' "Basic Distributor Selection Guidelines" to the plaintiffs, represented principally by Leonard H. Burst, and approximately 1600 other prospective applicants. Three hundred seventy-nine applications were completed and returned to Coors of which thirty-five, including Burst's, were for the Area No. 10 distributorship. Burst was one of four applicants selected for a field interview for Area No. 10 and the only one asked to Coors' headquarters for an in-house interview. However, on February 7, 1978, Burst received a letter notifying him that his application to become a Coors distributor had been rejected. Coors found none of the original applicants for Area No. 10 satisfactory and did not award the distributorship to any of them. Instead, Coors had Coors Distributing Company, a subsidiary, handle the distribution of its products until a suitable applicant could be found. Finally, in early 1979 Coors awarded United City Distributors, which had not been one of the original thirty-five applicants, the distributorship for a part of original Area No. 10. Coors Distributing Company retained the remainder.

Based on the three requirements for promissory estoppel (update the requirements so they relate to the Restatement (Second) of Contracts), should Burst prevail in this case? *Burst v. Adolph Coors Co.,* 650 F.2d 930 (8th Cir. 1981).

B. The Role of Restitution When Negotiations Fail to Produce an Offer

Even though classical contracts law emphasized the expectation interest, it also recognized a restitution interest. The courts have protected the restitution interest by granting an injured party a restitution remedy in a breach of contract action. The courts also have created a cause of action for restitution, separate from an action for breach of contract. A restitution cause of action may arise when negotiation fails to produce an offer. This restitution cause of action will be discussed in later sections of this book.

Restitution, whether a cause of action (separate from breach of contract) or a remedy in a breach of contract action, is based on the policy of preventing "unjust enrichment." Restitution requires both of the following:

1. An enrichment (a benefit conferred by one party on another)
2. An unjust result (the retention of the benefit without compensating the party conferring the benefit would be unjust)

Finding the enrichment is often relatively easy. The difficult question is determining whether it would be unjust to allow the benefit to be retained without compensating the party conferring the benefit.

As a general rule a person who volunteers services that are neither asked for nor needed is not entitled to recover for these services. The Restatement of Restitution section 112 states the rule as follows:

> A person who without mistake, coercion or request has unconditionally conferred a benefit upon another is not entitled to restitution, except where the benefit was conferred under circumstances making such action necessary for the protection of the interests of the other or of third persons.

Thus a person who meddles in the affairs of another cannot successfully seek compensation for his or her meddling.

In the following problems, focus first on the benefit (the enrichment). Identify the benefit conferred, the party who conferred it, and upon whom it was conferred. Then consider whether it would be unjust to permit the party receiving the benefit to retain it without compensating the other party.

> *PROBLEM 2:* Last Christmas Aunt Jane gave her niece Sylvia $1,000 as a gift. Aunt Jane had hoped that Sylvia would use this money to further her education. Shortly after Christmas, Sylvia squandered $600 on fun and frolic. Should Aunt Jane be entitled to restitution of the $600 Sylvia spent? Should Aunt Jane be entitled to restitution of the remaining $400?
>
> *PROBLEM 3:* When business was slow for the Quality Paving Company, employees would cruise neighborhoods in search of vacant houses with "For Sale" signs. If the driveway was in a state of disrepair, Quality would repave the drive and send a bill to the owner. Should Quality be entitled to restitution for the new driveway?
>
> *PROBLEM 4:* Develop two fact situations in which the person conferring a benefit, not required by contract, should *not* be entitled to restitution.

The Restatement of Restitution § 112 provides an exception to the general rule of no recovery: "except where the benefit was conferred under circumstances making such action necessary for the protection of the interests of the other or of third persons." This exception removes conferring the benefit from the realm of unjustified meddling and permits restitution.

The Restatement of Restitution provides five illustrative exceptions:

1. Performance of another's noncontractual duty to supply necessaries to a third person (Restatement of Restitution § 113)
2. Performance of another's duty to a third person in an emergency (Restatement of Restitution § 114)
3. Performance of another's duty to the public (Restatement of Restitution § 115)
4. Preservation of another's life or health (Restatement of Restitution § 116)
5. Preservation of another's things or credit (Restatement of Restitution § 117)

A common thread running through each of the five exceptions to the general rule is the fact that the person who conferred the benefit must have "acted unofficiously and with intent to charge therefor."

Rather than discuss all five exceptions to the general rule, two of the more common will be discussed. The first may arise when a third party provides a family member with food, shelter, or clothing and then seeks payment from another member of that family. The second may arise when a stranger gives unrequested medical assistance and then seeks payment for those services from that patient.

1. The Performance of Another's Noncontractual Duty to Supply Necessaries to a Third Person

Restatement of Restitution § 113 provides:

> A person who has performed the noncontractual duty of another by supplying a third person with necessaries which in violation of such duty the other had failed to supply, although acting without the other's knowledge or consent, is entitled to restitution therefor from the other if he acted unofficiously and with intent to charge therefor.

The principle underlying the general rule stated in section 112 is that a person who intervenes without being requested to perform the duty of another is not entitled to compensation. Under section 113, the protection of persons entitled by law to have necessaries (things or services) supplied to them by another, ordinarily prevents the intervention, even by a stranger, from being officious. Necessaries generally include food, shelter, clothing, and medical care.

The rule does not include a right to restitution for the performance of another person's contractual duties to supply necessaries to a third person. It is limited to situations where a common law or statutory duty requires an individual to provide a third person with necessaries. The rule operates regardless of whether an emergency exists. The rule does not require the person whose duty is performed to consent to have it performed; frequently, the duty is performed over that party's protest. The rule permits restitution only from a person who has not provided necessaries as required (a breach of duty). A person seeking restitution reasonably believing that there was a breach of duty is not always entitled to restitution.

PROBLEM 5: Under state statute, a father is required to provide support for his minor children. When Mr. Stephens failed to provide his minor son, Tommy, with adequate food and clothing, a neighbor fed and clothed the child. Is this neighbor entitled to restitution?

PROBLEM 6: Would your answer to this problem be the same if a store instead of a neighbor had supplied the food and clothing?

PROBLEM 7: Would your answer be the same if Mr. Stephens had been out of town and did not know that his son was improperly fed and clothed?

PROBLEM 8: Would your answer be the same if the state had neither a common law nor a statutory rule requiring a father to support his minor children?

PROBLEM 9: Develop a fact situation in which the person conferring a benefit, not required by contract, should be entitled to restitution under the Restatement of Restitution § 113.

Care should be taken in identifying the noncontractual duty. In some states the noncontractual duties between husband and wife are not identical. The duty the husband owes to his wife may be different from that the wife owes to her husband.

PROBLEM 10: In the following statute, Oklahoma Statutes tit. 32, § 3 (1981), identify the husband's duty to support his wife and the wife's duty to support her husband. Compare these duties.

> The husband must support himself and his wife out of the community property or out of his separate property or by his labor. The wife must support the husband when he has not deserted her out of the commu-

nity property or out of her separate property when he has no community or separate property and he is unable from infirmity to support himself.

2. Preservation of Another's Life or Health

Restatement of Restitution § 116 provides:

A person who has supplied things or services to another, although acting without the other's knowledge or consent, is entitled to restitution therefor from the other if

(a) he acted unofficiously and with intent to charge therefore, and
(b) the things or services were necessary to prevent the other from suffering serious bodily harm or pain, and
(c) the person supplying them had no reason to know that the other would not consent to receiving them, if mentally competent; and
(d) it was impossible for the other to give consent or, because of extreme youth or mental impairment, the other's consent would have been immaterial.

PROBLEM 11: How should the following case be resolved?

The street car in which Harrison was riding was involved in an accident. Harrison was thrown from the street car with such force that he hit his head on the sidewalk and was rendered unconscious. A spectator summoned Dr. Wisdom, who had an office down the street. In an effort to save Harrison's life, Dr. Wisdom performed a difficult operation but Harrison died without regaining consciousness.

Was there an offer concerning the services, or was this transaction still in the pre-offer phase?

Based on the requirements (elements) in section 116 of the Restatement of Restitution, should Dr. Wisdom be entitled to recover in a restitution action against Harrison's estate?

If Dr. Wisdom should be compensated for the injury to his restitution interest, what factors are relevant in determining how much he should recover?

PROBLEM 12: Develop a fact situation in which the person conferring a benefit, not required by contract, should be entitled to restitution under the Restatement of Restitution § 116.

4

THE OFFER PHASE

Section one investigates when an offer has been made (creating the power to contract). In addition to a general study of when an offer is created, section one analyzes several special applications: the advertisement, the auction, and the joke. Section two changes the focus from when to what. Section two considers the ingredients of an offer—a promise and consideration for that promise. When is a "promise" really a promise? Puffing, illusory promises and indefinite promises do not meet the test. What is "consideration" and why is it an essential element of an offer? Motives, moral obligations, and shams do not qualify as consideration. Section three addresses the alternatives to classical consideration. In an attempt to keep the classical consideration doctrine alive, some courts and legislatures tinker with the doctrine. The more direct approach recognizes reliance as an alternative to classical consideration.

Section 1. WHEN AN OFFER HAS BEEN MADE (CREATING THE POWER TO CONTRACT)

The Restatement (Second) of Contracts § 24 defines an "offer" as

> the manifestation of willingness to enter into a bargain, so made as to justify another person in understanding that his assent to that bargain is invited and will conclude it.

A synonym for "manifestation" is "demonstration." A "manifestation of willingness" or a "demonstration of willingness" refers to the outward actions of the negotiating parties as understood by a third person watching the parties. This nonparticipant, who is evaluating whether the manifestation of willingness has occurred, is referred to as "the reasonable person" (formerly "the reasonable man"); the standard used by this nonparticipant is known as the reasonable person's standard.

The reasonable person's standard is an objective standard. What is meant by an "objective standard"? Objectivity focuses on taking the transaction at face value. If a stranger observed the negotiations, his or her conclusions would be objective. The stranger would possess only those facts appearing on the face of the negotiation. The manifestation of willingness is evaluated by this objective standard—the reasonable person's standard.

Both the Restatement (First) and the Restatement (Second) of Contracts use an objective standard for the law of contracts. Early contracts cases, however, used a subjective standard, which evaluated communications not in light of how a reasonable person would interpret them but rather on how the person making the communications would interpret them. The "meeting of the minds" concept depends on subjective evaluations by both parties to the contract. The subjective "meeting of the minds" has been replaced by the objective "manifestation of assent." Unfortunately, old phraseology dies hard. Although the standard in the Restatement's definition of contract is clearly objective, many current cases parrot subjective language. Care must be taken when reading cases that use "meeting of the minds" language.

Read the following excerpt from *Estate of Younge v. Huysmans,* 506 A.2d 282, 284–85 (N.H. 1985) and evaluate whether the court used a subjective or objective standard to reach its solution.

I. *Meeting of the Minds*

The first issue before this court is whether the writings between the parties evidenced a meeting of the minds sufficient to constitute a contract. The master found that a contract existed between the parties. We agree.

"We will uphold a master's findings 'unless they are unsupported by the evidence or are erroneous as a matter of law.' " *Campo v. Maloney,* 122 N.H. 162, 168, 442 A.2d 997, 1001 (1982) (quoting *Summit Electric, Inc. v. Pepin Brothers Const., Inc.,* 121 N.H. 203, 206, 427 A.2d 505, 507 (1981)). A meeting of the minds must occur before a contract is formed. *Turcotte v. Griffin,* 120 N.H. 292, 294, 415 A.2d 668, 669 (1980). The intent of the parties is determined by an objective standard, and not by actual mental assent. *Kilroe v. Troast,* 117 N.H. 598, 600–01, 376 A.2d 131, 133 (1977). The writing is given the meaning which a reasonable person would attach to it. *Id.* In view of the evidence taken as a whole, the writings between the Bank and the Huysmanses constitute sufficient evidence to support the master's finding that a contract existed between the parties.

In order for a memorandum to constitute sufficient evidence of a contract for the sale of land, it must be in writing, signed by the party to be charged, and must identify the parties, state the price, and describe the land. *Cunningham v. Singer,* 111 N.H. 159, 160, 277 A.2d 318, 319 (1971). In *Cunningham,* this court held that a written memorandum signed by both the plaintiff and the defendant was sufficient evidence of a contract for the purchase of land; reasonable certainty that a meeting of the minds occurred is all that is necessary to evidence a contract. *Id.* In the case before us, the Bank's August 31, 1981 letter explicitly accepts the Huysmanses' offer to buy the real estate, and the Bank accepted a check for $10,000 as a deposit from the Huysmanses. We may reasonably assume that the forthcoming purchase and sale agreement mentioned in the Bank's August 31 letter would supplement terms otherwise specified by the exchange of letters.

Although the master did not acknowledge that the second sentence of the Bank's letter, which stated that a purchase and sale agreement would be forthcoming, created an ambiguity as to whether the letter created a valid contract, the record provides a basis on which any ambiguity could be resolved to find a contract between the parties. The purchase and sale agreement and $10,000 check originally sent by the Huysmanses, the Bank's letter of August 31, 1981, and the fact that the Bank took the property off the market, all combine to provide adequate evidence to support the master's finding that the minds of the parties had met.

The manifestation by the offeror must be sufficient to justify an understanding by the offeree that his or her assent to that bargain is invited and will conclude it. A contract will be formed, and the offeror will be bound by the contract when the offeree assents. After the offeree accepts the offer, it will be too late for the offeror to unilaterally add, delete, or modify the terms of the contract. Professor Corbin defines offer in terms of one party's (the offeror's) creation of power in another (the offeree) to form a contract:

> An offer is ... an act whereby one person confers upon another the power to create contractual relations between them.... [T]he act of the offeror operates to create in the offeree a power ...; thereafter the voluntary act of the offeree alone will operate to create the new relations called a contract.

Corbin, Offer and Acceptance, and Some of The Resulting Legal Relations, 26 Yale L.J. 169, 181–82 (1917).

Fairmount Glass Works v. Grunden-Martin Woodenware Co., although an old case, provides an excellent set of facts upon which to evaluate whether a communication is an offer or merely preliminary negotiation (pre-offer). The opinion begins by describing the various communications between Grunden-Martin, the potential buyer, and Fairmount Glass, the potential seller. As you read through the opinion, place each communication in chronological sequence on a time line. Next, begin with the first communication and determine whether it was an offer or merely preliminary negotiation. Consider the following questions:

1. Did Grunden-Martin intend to be bound by its letter if Fairmount Glass responded "yes" without stating any additional or different terms, or
2. Did Grunden-Martin want Fairmount Glass to make the offer so Fairmount Glass could evaluate the terms and would be the party that responded by saying "yes"?
3. If the first Grunden-Martin letter was not the offer, was Fairmount's letter in reply the offer or was it still only preliminary negotiation?

Ask the same questions as you evaluate the Fairmount letter:

1. Did Fairmount Glass intend to be bound by this letter if Grunden-Martin responded "yes" without stating any additional or different terms?
2. If the Fairmount letter was not the offer but still only preliminary negotiations, then evaluate the remaining communications, in order, until you have either found an offer or have exhausted all the communications.

As you read *Fairmount Glass,* determine whether the judge's evaluation of each communication is based on a subjective or objective standard. Was the judge concerned with what each party thought it was saying (subjective) or how the communication would be understood by a reasonable person (objective)?

Fairmount Glass Works v. Grunden–Martin Woodenware Co.

Court of Appeals of Kentucky, 1899.
106 Ky. 659, 51 S.W. 196.

HOBSON, J. On April 20, 1895, appellee wrote appellant the following letter:

"St. Louis, Mo., April 20, 1895. Gentlemen: Please advise us the lowest price you can make us on our order for ten car loads of Mason green jars, complete, with caps, packed one dozen in a case, either delivered here, or f.o.b. cars your place, as you prefer. State terms and cash discount. Very truly, Grunden-Martin W.W. Co."

To this letter appellant answered as follows:

"Fairmount, Ind., April 23, 1895. Grunden-Martin Wooden Ware Co., St. Louis, Mo.—Gentlemen: Replying to your favor of April 20, we quote you Mason fruit jars, complete, in one-dozen boxes, delivered in East St. Louis, Ill.: Pints $4.50, quarts $5.00, half gallons $6.50, per gross, for immediate acceptance, and shipment not later than May 15, 1895; sixty days' acceptance, or 2 off, cash in ten days. Yours, truly, Fairmount Glass Works.

"Please note that we make all quotations and contracts subject to the contingencies of agencies or transportation, delays or accidents beyond our control."

For reply thereto, appellee sent the following telegram on April 24, 1895:

"Fairmount Glass Works. Fairmount, Ind.: Your letter twenty-third received. Enter order ten car loads as per your quotation. Specifications mailed. Grunden-Martin W.W. Co."

In response to this telegram, appellant sent the following:

"Fairmount, Ind., April 24, 1895. Grunden-Martin W.W. Co., St. Louis, Mo.: Impossible to book your order. Output all sold. See letter. Fairmount Glass Works."

Appellee insists that, by its telegram sent in answer to the letter of April 23d, the contract was closed for the purchase of 10 car loads of Mason fruit jars. Appellant insists that the contract was not closed by this telegram, and that it had the right to decline to fill the order at the time it sent its telegram of April 24. This is the chief question in the case. The court below gave judgment in favor of appellee, and appellant has appealed, earnestly insisting that the judgment is erroneous.

We are referred to a number of authorities holding that a quotation of prices is not an offer to sell, in the sense that a completed contract will arise out of the giving of an order for merchandise in accordance with the proposed terms. There are a number of cases holding that the transaction is not completed until the order so made is accepted. 7 Am. & Eng. Enc. Law (2d Ed.) p. 138; Smith v. Gowdy, 8 Allen, 566; Beaupre v. Telegraph Co., 21 Minn. 155. But each case must turn largely upon the language there used. In this case we think there was more than a quotation of prices, although appellant's letter uses the word "quote" in stating the prices given. The true meaning of the correspondence must be determined by reading it as a whole. Appellee's letter of April 20th, which began the transaction, did not ask for a quotation of prices. It reads: "Please advise us the lowest price you can make us on our order for ten car loads of Mason green jars. * * * State terms and cash discount." From this appellant could not fail to understand that appellee wanted to know at what price it would sell it ten car loads of these jars; so when, in answer, it wrote: "We quote you Mason fruit jars * * * pints $4.50, quarts $5.00, half gallons $6.50, per gross, for immediate acceptance; * * * 2 off, cash in ten days,"—it must be deemed as intending to give appellee the information it had asked for. We can hardly understand what was meant by the words "for immediate acceptance," unless the latter was intended as a proposition to sell at these prices if accepted immediately. In construing every contract, the aim of the court is to arrive at the intention of the parties. In none of the cases to which we have been referred on behalf of appellant was there on the face of the correspondence any such expression of intention to make an offer to sell on the terms indicated. In Fitzhugh v. Jones, 6 Munf. 83, the use of the expression that the buyer should reply as soon as possible, in case he was disposed to accede to the terms offered, was held sufficient to show that there was a definite proposition, which was closed by the buyer's acceptance. The expression in appellant's letter, "for immediate acceptance," taken in connection with appellee's letter, in effect, at what price it would sell it the goods, is, it seems to us, much stronger evidence of a present offer, which, when accepted immediately, closed the contract. Appellee's letter was plainly an inquiry for the price and terms on which appellant would sell it the goods, and appellant's answer to it was not a quotation of prices, but a definite offer to sell on the terms indicated, and could not be withdrawn after the terms had been accepted. It will be observed that the telegram of acceptance refers to the specifications mailed. These specifications were contained in the following letter: "St. Louis, Mo., April 24, 1895. Fairmount Glass-Works Co., Fairmount, Ind.—Gentlemen: We received your letter of 23rd this morning, and telegraphed you in reply as follows: 'Your letter 23rd received. Enter order ten car loads as per your quotation. Specifications mailed,'—which we now confirm. We have accordingly entered this contract on our books for the ten cars Mason green jars, complete, with caps and rubbers, one dozen in case, delivered to us in East St. Louis at $4.50 per gross for pint, $5.00 for quart, $6.50 for one-half gallon. Terms, 60 days' acceptance, or 2 per cent. for cash in ten days, to be shipped not later than May 15, 1895. The jars and caps to be strictly first-quality goods. You may ship the first car to us here assorted: Five gross pint, fifty-five gross quart, forty gross one-half gallon. Specifications for the remaining 9 cars we will send later. Grunden-Martin W.W. Co." It is insisted for appellant that this was not an acceptance of the offer as made; that the stipulation, "The jars and caps to be strictly first-quality goods," was not in their offer; and that, it not having been accepted as made, appellant is not bound. But it will be observed that appellant declined to furnish the goods before it got this letter, and in the correspondence with appellee it nowhere complained of these words as an addition to the contract. Quite a number of other letters passed, in which the refusal to deliver the goods was placed on other grounds, none of which have been sustained by the evidence. Appellee offers proof tending to show that these words, in the trade in which parties were engaged, conveyed the same meaning as the words used in appellant's letter, and were only a different form of expressing the same idea. Appellant's conduct would seem to confirm this evidence.

Appellant also insists that the contract was indefinite, because the quantity of each size of the jars was not fixed, that 10 car loads is too indefinite a specification of the quantity sold, and that appellee had no right to accept the goods to be delivered on different days. The proof shows that "10 car loads" is an expression used in the trade as equivalent to 1,000 gross, 100 gross being regarded a car load. The offer to sell the different sizes at different prices gave the purchaser the right to name the quantity of each size, and, the offer being to ship not later than May 15th, the buyer had the right to fix the time of delivery at any time before that. Sousely v. Burns' Adm'r, 10 Bush, 87; Williamson's Heirs v. Johnston's Heirs, 4 T.B. Mon. 253; Wheeler v. Railroad Co., 115 U.S. 34, 5 Sup.Ct. 1061, 1160. The petition, if defective, was cured by the judgment, which is fully sustained by the evidence. Judgment affirmed.

The question of *when* an offer has been made also arises in disputes involving advertisements, auctions, and jokes. These three variations on the theme of creation of the offer are discussed in the following sections.

A. The Advertisement

All offers discussed thus far have been directed to a specific party. Advertisements, by contrast, are made to the general public. Simply because an advertisement is directed to the general public, however, does not preclude it from being an offer. Offers need not be made to a specific party. The offer of a reward, for example, is an offer made to the general public.

No special test exists for evaluating whether an advertisement is an offer. Authorities that categorically state that an advertisement cannot be an offer miss the mark and overgeneralize. Do not rely on them. The better approach is to follow the same method used for evaluating any other potential offer.

PROBLEM 1: Compare the following two advertisements:

Saturday 9 A.M. Sharp
3 Brand New Fur Coats
Worth up to $100.00
First Come
First Served
$1 Each

with

Saturday 9 A.M.
1 Black Lapin Stole
Beautiful,
Worth $139.50 . . . $1.00
First Come
First Served

Are both advertisements offers, or are they simply invitations to negotiate? What factors did the Supreme Court of Minnesota use to determine whether these advertisements were offers or only invitations to negotiate (preliminary negotiations)?

Lefkowitz v. Great Minneapolis Surplus Store, Inc.

Supreme Court of Minnesota, 1957.
86 N.W.2d 689.

MURPHY, Justice.

This is an appeal from an order of the Municipal Court of Minneapolis denying the motion of the defendant for amended findings of fact, or, in the alternative, for a new trial. The order for judgment awarded the plaintiff the sum of $138.50 as damages for breach of contract.

This case grows out of the alleged refusal of the defendant to sell to the plaintiff a certain fur piece which it had offered for sale in a newspaper advertisement. It appears from the record that on April 6, 1956, the defendant published the following advertisement in a Minneapolis newspaper:

"Saturday 9 A.M. Sharp
3 Brand New
Fur
Coats
Worth to $100.00
First Come
First Served
$1
Each"

On April 13, the defendant again published an advertisement in the same newspaper as follows:

"Saturday 9 A.M.
2 Brand New Pastel
Mink 3–Skin Scarfs
Selling for $89.50
Out they go
Saturday. Each.... $1.00
1 Black Lapin Stole
Beautiful,
worth $139.50.... $1.00
First Come
First Served"

The record supports the findings of the court that on each of the Saturdays following the publication of the above-described ads the plaintiff was the first to present himself at the appropriate counter in the defendant's store and on each occasion demanded the coat and the stole so advertised and indicated his readiness to pay the sale price of $1. On both occasions, the defendant refused to sell the merchandise to the plaintiff, stating on the first occasion that by a "house rule" the offer was intended for women only and sales would not be made to men, and on the second visit that plaintiff knew defendant's house rules.

The trial court properly disallowed plaintiff's claim for the value of the fur coats since the value of these articles was speculative and uncertain. The only evidence of value was the advertisement itself to the effect that the coats were "Worth to $100.00," how much less being speculative especially in view of the price for which they were offered for sale. With reference to the offer of the defendant on April 13, 1956, to sell the "1 Black Lapin Stole * * * worth $139.50 * * *" the trial court held that the value of this article was established and granted judgment in favor of the plaintiff for that amount less the $1 quoted purchase price.

1. The defendant contends that a newspaper advertisement offering items of merchandise for sale at a named price is a "unilateral offer" which may be withdrawn without notice. He relies upon authorities which hold that, where an advertiser publishes in a newspaper that he has a certain quantity or quality of goods which he wants to dispose of at certain prices and on certain terms, such advertisements are not offers which become contracts as soon as any person to whose notice they may come signifies his acceptance by notifying the other that he will take a certain quantity of them. Such advertisements have been construed as an invitation for an offer of sale on the terms stated, which offer, when received, may be accepted or rejected and which therefore does not become a contract of sale until accepted by the seller; and until a contract has been so made, the seller may modify or revoke such prices or terms. Montgomery Ward & Co. v. Johnson, 209 Mass. 89, 95 N.E. 290; Nickel v. Theresa Farmers Co-op. Ass'n, 247 Wis. 412, 20 N.W.2d 117; Lovett v. Frederick Loeser & Co. Inc., 124 Misc. 81, 207 N.Y.S. 753; Schenectady Stove Co. v. Holbrook, 101 N.Y. 45, 4 N.E. 4; Georgian Co. v. Bloom, 27 Ga.App. 468, 108 S.E. 813; Craft v. Elder & Johnston Co., 38 N.E.2d 416, 34 Ohio L.A. 603; Annotation, 157 A.L.R. 746.

The defendant relies principally on Craft v. Elder & Johnston Co. supra. In that case, the court discussed the legal effect of an advertisement offering for sale, as a one-day special, an electric sewing machine at a named price. The view was expressed that the advertisement was (38 N.E.2d 417, 34 Ohio L.A. 605) "not an offer made to any specific person but was made to the public generally. Thereby it would be properly designated as a unilateral offer and not being supported by any consideration could be withdrawn at will and without notice." It is true that such an offer may be withdrawn before acceptance. Since all offers are by their nature unilateral because they are necessarily made by one party or on one side in the negotiation of a contract, the distinction made in that decision between a unilateral offer and a unilateral contract is not clear. On the facts before us we are concerned with whether the advertisement constituted an offer, and, if so, whether the plaintiff's conduct constituted an acceptance.

There are numerous authorities which hold that a particular advertisement in a newspaper or circular letter relating to a sale of articles may be construed by the court as constituting an offer, acceptance of which would complete a contract. J.E. Pinkham Lumber Co. v. C.W. Griffin & Co., 212 Ala. 341, 102 So. 689; Seymour v. Armstrong & Kassebaum, 62 Kan. 720, 64 P. 612; Payne v. Lautz Bros. & Co., City Ct., 166 N.Y.S. 844, affirmed, 168 N.Y.S. 369, affirmed, 185 App.Div. 904, 171 N.Y.S. 1094; Arnold v. Phillips, 1 Ohio Dec. Reprint 195, 3 West. Law J. 448; Oliver v. Henley, Tex.Civ.App., 21 S.W.2d 576; Annotation, 157 A.L.R. 744, 746.

The test of whether a binding obligation may originate in advertisements addressed to the general public is "whether the facts show that some performance was promised in positive terms in return for something requested." 1 Williston, Contracts (Rev. ed.) § 27.

The authorities above cited emphasize that, where the offer is clear, definite, and explicit, and leaves nothing open for negotiation, it constitutes an offer, acceptance of which will complete the contract. The most recent case on the subject is Johnson v. Capital City Ford Co., La.App., 85 So.2d 75, in which the court pointed out that a newspaper advertisement relating to the purchase and sale of automobiles may constitute an offer, acceptance of which will consummate a contract and create an obligation in the offeror to perform according to the terms of the published offer.

Whether in any individual instance a newspaper advertisement is an offer rather than an invitation to make an offer depends on the legal intention of the parties and the surrounding circumstances. Annotation, 157 A.L.R. 744, 751; 77 C.J.S., Sales, § 25b; 17 C.J.S., Contracts, § 389. We are of the view on the facts before us that the offer by the defendant of the sale of the Lapin fur was clear, definite, and explicit, and left nothing open for negotiation. The plaintiff having successfully managed to be the first one to appear at the seller's place of business to be served, as requested by the advertisement, and having offered the stated purchase price of the article, he was entitled to performance on the part of the defendant. We think the trial court was correct in holding that there was in the conduct of the parties a sufficient mutuality of obligation to constitute a contract of sale.

2. The defendant contends that the offer was modified by a "house rule" to the effect that only women were qualified to receive the bargains advertised. The advertisement contained no such restriction. This objection may be disposed of briefly by stating that, while an advertiser has the right at any time before acceptance to modify his offer, he does not have the right, after acceptance, to impose new or arbitrary conditions not contained in the

published offer. Payne v. Lautz Bros. & Co., City Ct., 166 N.Y.S. 844, 848; Mooney v. Daily News Co., 116 Minn. 212, 133 N.W. 573, 37 L.R.A., N.S., 183. Affirmed.

PROBLEM 2: Find three different types of advertisements in your local newspaper, and determine whether each is an offer or only an invitation to negotiate (preliminary negotiation).

B. The Auction

An auction may be either "with reserve" or "without reserve." Whether the auction is with or without reserve is the key to whether the auctioneer or the person making the bid is the offeror.

In an auction with reserve, the auctioneer may withdraw the goods at any time until he or she announces the completion of the sale. Therefore, the auctioneer, rather than being the offeror, is asking potential bidders to make an offer. The auctioneer evaluates the bidder's offer and either accepts it (thus concluding the sale) or rejects it by withdrawing the goods from the auction.

In an auction without reserve, the auctioneer is the offeror and the bidders are the offerees. After the auctioneer calls for bids on an article, he or she cannot withdraw that article if a bid is made within a reasonable time.

In both auctions with reserve and without reserve, a bidder may retract his or her bid up to the time the auctioneer announces the completion of the sale. The bidder's retraction of his or her bid does not revive a previous bid.

An auction "with reserve" is the most common type of auction.

C. The Joke

What a person says and what he or she actually means may be entirely different. The outward expression of the person (objective) rather than his or her secret or unexpressed intent (subjective) determines whether a statement is intended as an offer. Thus the objective intent rather than the subjective intent determines whether an offer has been extended.

A graphic illustration of this principle is the joke. In *Lucy v. Zehmer,* the Zehmers, owners of the Ferguson Farm, operated a local restaurant. One evening their old friend W.O. Lucy met them at the restaurant, and after a few drinks and a lot of talk, the Zehmers signed a writing that said that they promised to sell W.O. Lucy the Ferguson Farm for $50,000 cash. Consider the following questions as you read the case:

1. Did A.H. Zehmer believe that this was an offer or a joke?
2. Did Ida Zehmer believe that this was an offer or a joke?
3. Did W.O. Lucy believe that what the Zehmers had signed was an offer or a joke?
4. Would a reasonable person, viewing the events at the restaurant, believe that the writing was an offer or a joke?
5. What facts did you find useful in reaching your conclusions?

Lucy v. Zehmer

Supreme Court of Appeals of Virginia, 1954.
196 Va. 493, 84 S.E.2d 516.

Before EGGLESTON, BUCHANAN, MILLER, SMITH and WHITTLE, JJ.

BUCHANAN, Justice.

This suit was instituted by W.O. Lucy and J.C. Lucy, complainants, against A.H. Zehmer and Ida S. Zehmer, his wife, defendants, to have specific performance of a contract by which it was alleged the Zehmers had sold to W.O. Lucy a tract of land owned by A.H. Zehmer in Dinwiddie county containing 471.6 acres, more or less, known as the Ferguson farm, for $50,000. J.C. Lucy, the other complainant, is a brother of W.O. Lucy, to whom W.O. Lucy transferred a half interest in his alleged purchase.

The instrument sought to be enforced was written by A.H. Zehmer on December 20, 1952, in these words: "We hereby agree to sell to W.O. Lucy the Ferguson Farm complete for $50,000.00, title satisfactory to buyer," and signed by the defendants, A.H. Zehmer and Ida S. Zehmer.

The answer of A.H. Zehmer admitted that at the time mentioned W.O. Lucy offered him $50,000 cash for the farm, but that he, Zehmer, considered that the offer was made in jest; that so thinking, and both he and Lucy having had several drinks, he wrote out "the memorandum" quoted above and induced his wife to sign it; that he did not deliver the memorandum to Lucy, but that Lucy picked it up, read it, put it in his pocket, attempted to offer Zehmer $5 to bind the bargain, which Zehmer refused to accept, and realizing for the first time that Lucy was serious, Zehmer assured him that he had no intention of selling the farm and that the whole matter was a joke. Lucy left the premises insisting that he had purchased the farm.

Depositions were taken and the decree appealed from was entered holding that the complainants had failed to establish their right to specific performance, and dismissing their bill. The assignment of error is to this action of the court.

W.O. Lucy, a lumberman and farmer, thus testified in substance: He had known Zehmer for fifteen or twenty years and had been familiar with the Ferguson farm for ten years. Seven or eight years ago he had offered Zehmer $20,000 for the farm which Zehmer had accepted, but the agreement was verbal and Zehmer backed out. On the night of December 20, 1952, around eight o'clock, he took an employee to McKenney, where Zehmer lived and operated a restaurant, filling station and motor court. While there he decided to see Zehmer and again try to buy the Ferguson farm. He entered the restaurant and talked to Mrs. Zehmer until Zehmer came in. He asked Zehmer if he had sold the Ferguson farm. Zehmer replied that he had not. Lucy said, "I bet you wouldn't take $50,000.00 for that place." Zehmer replied, "Yes, I would too; you wouldn't give fifty." Lucy said he would and told Zehmer to write up an agreement to that effect. Zehmer took a restaurant check and wrote on the back of it, "I do hereby agree to sell to W.O. Lucy the Ferguson Farm for $50,000 complete." Lucy told him he had better change it to "We" because Mrs. Zehmer would have to sign it too. Zehmer then tore up what he had written, wrote the agreement quoted above and asked Mrs. Zehmer, who was at the other end of the counter ten or twelve feet away, to sign it. Mrs. Zehmer said she would for $50,000 and signed it. Zehmer brought it back and gave it to Lucy, who offered him $5 which Zehmer refused, saying, "You don't need to give me any money, you got the agreement there signed by both of us."

The discussion leading to the signing of the agreement, said Lucy, lasted thirty or forty minutes, during which Zehmer seemed to doubt that Lucy could raise $50,000. Lucy suggested the provision for having the title examined and Zehmer made the suggestion that he would sell it "complete, everything there," and stated that all he had on the farm was three heifers.

Lucy took a partly filled bottle of whiskey into the restaurant with him for the purpose of giving Zehmer a drink if he wanted it. Zehmer did, and he and Lucy had one or two drinks together. Lucy said that while he felt the drinks he took he was not intoxicated, and from the way Zehmer handled the transaction he did not think he was either.

December 20 was on Saturday. Next day Lucy telephoned to J.C. Lucy and arranged with the latter to take a half interest in the purchase and pay half of the consideration. On Monday he engaged an attorney to examine the title. The attorney reported favorably on December 31 and on January 2 Lucy wrote Zehmer stating that the title was satisfactory, that he was ready to pay the purchase price in cash and asking when Zehmer would be ready to close the deal. Zehmer replied by letter, mailed on January 13, asserting that he had never agreed or intended to sell.

Mr. and Mrs. Zehmer were called by the complainants as adverse witnesses. Zehmer testified in substance as follows:

He bought this farm more than ten years ago for $11,000. He had had twenty-five offers, more or less, to buy it, including several from Lucy, who had never offered any specific sum of money. He had given them all the same answer, that he was not interested in selling it. On this Saturday night before Christmas it looked like everybody and his brother came by there to have a drink. He took a good many drinks during the afternoon and had a pint of his own. When he entered the restaurant around eight-thirty Lucy was there and he could see that he was "pretty high." He said to Lucy, "Boy, you got some good liquor, drinking, ain't you?" Lucy then offered him a drink. "I was already high as a Georgia pine, and didn't have any more better sense than to pour another great big slug out and gulp it down, and he took one too."

After they had talked a while Lucy asked whether he still had the Ferguson farm. He replied that he had not sold it and Lucy said, "I bet you wouldn't take $50,000.00 for it." Zehmer asked him if he would give $50,000 and Lucy said yes. Zehmer replied, "You haven't got $50,000.00 in cash." Lucy said he did and Zehmer replied that he did not believe it. They argued "pro and con for a long time," mainly about "whether he had $50,000 in cash that he could put up right then and buy that farm."

Finally, said Zehmer, Lucy told him if he didn't believe he had $50,000, "you sign that piece of paper here and say you will take $50,000.00 for the farm." He, Zehmer, "just grabbed the back off of a guest check there" and wrote on the back of it. At that point in his testimony Zehmer asked to see what he had written to "see if I recognize my own handwriting." He examined the paper and exclaimed, "Great balls of fire, I got 'Firgerson' for Ferguson. I have got satisfactory spelled wrong. I don't recognize that writing if I would see it, wouldn't know it was mine."

After Zehmer had, as he described it, "scribbled this thing off," Lucy said, "Get your wife to sign it." Zehmer walked over to where she was and she at first refused to sign but did so after he told her that he "was just needling him [Lucy], and didn't mean a thing in the world, that I was not selling the farm." Zehmer then "took it back over there * * * and I was still looking at the dern thing. I had the drink right there by my hand, and I reached over to get a drink, and he said, 'Let me see it.' He reached and picked it up, and when I looked back again he had it in his pocket and he dropped a five dollar bill over there, and he said, 'Here is five dollars payment on it.' * * * I said, 'Hell no, that is beer and liquor talking. I am not going to sell you the farm. I have told you that too many times before.' "

Mrs. Zehmer testified that when Lucy came into the restaurant he looked as if he had had a drink. When Zehmer came in he took a drink out of a bottle that Lucy handed him. She went back to help the waitress who was getting things ready for next day. Lucy and Zehmer were talking but she did not pay too much attention to what they were saying. She heard Lucy ask Zehmer if he had sold the Ferguson farm, and Zehmer replied that he had not and did not want to sell it. Lucy said, "I bet you wouldn't take $50,000.00 cash for that farm," and Zehmer replied, "You haven't got $50,000 cash." Lucy said, "I can get it." Zehmer said he might form a company and get it, "but you haven't got $50,000.00 cash to pay me tonight." Lucy asked him if he would put it in writing that he would sell him this farm. Zehmer then wrote on the back of a pad, "I agree to sell the Ferguson Place to W.O. Lucy for $50,000.00 cash." Lucy said, "All right, get your wife to sign it." Zehmer came back to where she was standing and said, "You want to put your name to this?" She said "No," but he said in an undertone, "It is nothing but a joke," and she signed it.

She said that only one paper was written and it said: "I hereby agree to sell," but the "I" had been changed to "We". However, she said she read what she signed and was then asked, "When you read 'We hereby agree to sell to W.O. Lucy,' what did you interpret that to mean, that particular phrase?" She said she thought that was a cash sale that night; but she also said that when she read that part about "title satisfactory to buyer" she understood that if the title was good Lucy would pay $50,000 but if the title was bad he would have a right to reject it, and that that was her understanding at the time she signed her name.

On examination by her own counsel she said that her husband laid this piece of paper down after it was signed; that Lucy said to let him see it, took it, folded it and put it in his wallet, then said to Zehmer, "Let me give you $5.00," but Zehmer said, "No, this is liquor talking. I don't want to sell the farm, I have told you that I want my son to have it. This is all a joke." Lucy then said at least twice, "Zehmer, you have sold your farm," wheeled around and started for the door. He paused at the door and said, "I will bring you $50,000.00 tomorrow. * * * No, tomorrow is Sunday. I will bring it to you Monday." She said you could tell definitely that he was drinking and she said to her husband, "You should have taken him home," but he said, "Well, I am just about as bad off as he is."

The waitress referred to by Mrs. Zehmer testified that when Lucy first came in "he was mouthy." When Zehmer came in they were laughing and joking and she thought they took a drink or two. She was sweeping and cleaning up for next day. She said she heard Lucy tell Zehmer, "I will give you so much for the farm," and Zehmer said, "You haven't got that much." Lucy answered, "Oh, yes, I will give you that much." Then "they jotted down something on paper * * * and Mr. Lucy reached over and took it, said let me see it." He looked at it, put it in his pocket and in about a minute he left. She was asked whether she saw Lucy offer Zehmer any money and replied, "He had five dollars laying up there, they didn't take it." She said Zehmer told Lucy he didn't want his money "because he didn't have enough money to pay for his property, and wasn't going to sell his farm." Both of them appeared to be drinking right much, she said.

She repeated on cross-examination that she was busy and paying no attention to what was going on. She was some distance away and did not see either of them sign the paper. She was asked whether she saw Zehmer put the agreement down on the table in front of Lucy, and her answer was this: "Time he got through writing whatever it was on the paper, Mr. Lucy reached over and said, 'Let's see it.' He took it and put it in his pocket," before showing it to Mrs. Zehmer. Her version was that Lucy kept raising his offer until it got to $50,000.

The defendants insist that the evidence was ample to support their contention that the writing sought to be enforced was prepared as a bluff or dare to force Lucy to admit that he did not have $50,000; that the whole matter was a joke; that the writing was not delivered to Lucy and no binding contract was ever made between the parties.

It is an unusual, if not bizarre, defense. When made to the writing admittedly prepared by one of the defendants and signed by both, clear evidence is required to sustain it.

In his testimony Zehmer claimed that he "was high as a Georgia pine," and that the transaction "was just a bunch of two doggoned drunks bluffing to see who could talk the biggest and say the most." That claim is inconsistent with his attempt to testify in great detail as to what was said and what was done. It is contradicted by other evidence as to the condition of both parties, and rendered of no weight by the testimony of his wife that when Lucy left the restaurant she suggested that Zehmer drive him home. The record is convincing that Zehmer was not intoxicated to the extent of being unable to comprehend the nature and consequences of the instrument he executed, and hence that instrument is not to be invalidated on that ground. 17 C.J.S., Contracts, § 133, b., p. 483; Taliaferro v. Emery, 124 Va. 674, 98 S.E. 627. It was in fact conceded by defendants' counsel in oral argument that under the evidence Zehmer was not too drunk to make a valid contract.

The evidence is convincing also that Zehmer wrote two agreements, the first one beginning "I hereby agree to sell." Zehmer first said he could not remember about that, then that "I don't think I wrote but one out." Mrs. Zehmer said that what he wrote was "I hereby agree," but that the "I" was changed to "We" after that night. The agreement that was written and signed is in the record and indicates no such change. Neither are the mistakes in spelling that Zehmer sought to point out readily apparent.

The appearance of the contract, the fact that it was under discussion for forty minutes or more before it was signed; Lucy's objection to the first draft because it was written in the singular, and he wanted Mrs. Zehmer to sign it also; the rewriting to meet that objection and the signing by Mrs. Zehmer; the discussion of what was to be included in the sale, the provision for the examination of the title, the completeness of the instrument that was executed, the taking possession of it by Lucy with no request or suggestion by either of the defendants that he give it back, are facts which furnish persuasive evidence that the execution of the contract was a serious business transaction rather than a casual, jesting matter as defendants now contend.

On Sunday, the day after the instrument was signed on Saturday night, there was a social gathering in a home in the town of McKenney at which there were general comments that the sale had been made. Mrs. Zehmer testified that on that occasion as she passed by a group of people, including Lucy, who were talking about the transaction, $50,000 was mentioned, whereupon she stepped up and said, "Well, with the high-price whiskey you were drinking last night you should have paid more. That was cheap." Lucy testified that at that time Zehmer told him that he did not want to "stick" him or hold him to the agreement because he, Lucy, was too tight and didn't know what he was doing, to which Lucy replied that he was not too tight; that he had been stuck before and was going through with it. Zehmer's version was that he said to Lucy: "I am not trying to claim it wasn't a deal on account of the fact the price was too low. If I had wanted to sell $50,000.00 would be a good price, in fact I think you would get stuck at $50,000.00." A disinterested witness testified that what Zehmer said to Lucy was that "he was going to let him up off the deal, because he thought he was too tight, didn't know what he was doing. Lucy said something to the effect that 'I have been stuck before and I will go through with it.' "

If it be assumed, contrary to what we think the evidence shows, that Zehmer was jesting about selling his farm to Lucy and that the transaction was intended by him to be a joke, nevertheless the evidence shows that Lucy did not so understand it but considered it to be a serious business transaction and the contract to be binding on the Zehmers as well as on himself. The very next day he arranged with his brother to put up half the money and take a half interest in the land. The day after that he employed an attorney to examine the title. The next night, Tuesday, he was back at Zehmer's place and there Zehmer told him for the first time, Lucy said, that he wasn't going to sell and he told Zehmer, "You know you sold that place fair and square." After receiving the report from his attorney that the title was good he wrote to Zehmer that he was ready to close the deal.

Not only did Lucy actually believe, but the evidence shows he was warranted in believing, that the contract represented a serious business transaction and a good faith sale and purchase of the farm.

In the field of contracts, as generally elsewhere, "We must look to the outward expression of a person as manifesting his intention rather than to his secret and unexpressed intention. 'The law imputes to a person an intention corresponding to the reasonable meaning of his words and acts.' " First Nat. Exchange Bank of Roanoke v. Roanoke Oil Co., 169 Va. 99, 114, 192 S.E. 764, 770.

At no time prior to the execution of the contract had Zehmer indicated to Lucy by word or act that he was not in earnest about selling the farm. They had argued about it and discussed its terms, as Zehmer admitted, for a long time. Lucy testified that if there was any jesting it was about paying $50,000 that night. The contract and the evidence show that he was not expected to pay the money that night. Zehmer said that after the writing was signed he laid it down on the counter in front of Lucy. Lucy said Zehmer handed it to him. In any event there had been what appeared to be a good faith offer and a good faith acceptance, followed by the execution and apparent delivery of a written contract. Both said that Lucy put the writing in his pocket and then offered Zehmer $5 to seal the bargain. Not until then, even under the defendants' evidence, was anything said or done to indicate that the matter was a joke. Both of the Zehmers testified that when Zehmer asked his wife to sign he whispered that it was a joke so Lucy wouldn't hear and that it was not intended that he should hear.

The mental assent of the parties is not requisite for the formation of a contract. If the words or other acts of one of the parties have but one reasonable meaning, his undisclosed intention is immaterial except when an unreasonable meaning which he attaches to his manifestations is known to the other party. Restatement of the Law of Contracts, Vol. I, § 71, p. 74.

" * * * The law, therefore, judges of an agreement between two persons exclusively from those expressions of their intentions which are communicated between them. * * *." Clark on Contracts, 4 ed., § 3, p. 4.

An agreement or mutual assent is of course essential to a valid contract but the law imputes to a person an intention corresponding to the reasonable meaning of his words and acts. If his words and acts, judged by a reasonable standard, manifest an intention to agree, it is immaterial what may be the real but unexpressed state of his mind. 17 C.J.S., Contracts, § 32, p. 361; 12 Am.Jur., Contracts, § 19, p. 515.

So a person cannot set up that he was merely jesting when his conduct and words would warrant a reasonable person in believing that he intended a real agreement. 17 C.J.S., Contracts, § 47, p. 390; Clark on Contracts, 4 ed., § 27, at p. 54.

Whether the writing signed by the defendants and now sought to be enforced by the complainants was the result of a serious offer by Lucy and a serious acceptance by the defendants, or was a serious offer by Lucy and an acceptance in secret jest by the defendants, in either event it constituted a binding contract of sale between the parties.

Defendants contend further, however, that even though a contract was made, equity should decline to enforce it under the circumstances. These circumstances have been set forth in detail above. They disclose some drinking by the two parties but not to an extent that they were unable to understand fully what they were doing. There was no fraud, no misrepresentation, no sharp practice and no dealing between unequal parties. The farm had been bought for $11,000 and was assessed for taxation at $6,300. The purchase price was $50,000. Zehmer admitted that it was a good price. There is in fact present in this case none of the grounds usually urged against specific performance.

Specific performance, it is true, is not a matter of absolute or arbitrary right, but is addressed to the reasonable and sound discretion of the court. First Nat. Exchange Bank of Roanoke v. Roanoke Oil Co., supra, 169 Va. at page 116, 192 S.E. at page 771. But it is likewise true that the discretion which may be exercised is not an arbitrary or capricious one, but one which is controlled by the established doctrines and settled principles of equity; and, generally, where a contract is in its nature and circumstances unobjectionable, it is as much a matter of course for courts of equity to decree a specific performance of it as it is for a court of law to give damages for a breach of it. Bond v. Crawford, 193 Va. 437, 444, 69 S.E.2d 470, 475.

The complainants are entitled to have specific performance of the contract sued on. The decree appealed from is therefore reversed and the cause is remanded for the entry of a proper decree requiring the defendants to perform the contract in accordance with the prayer of the bill.

Reversed and remanded.

Section 2. THE INGREDIENTS OF AN OFFER—A PROMISE AND CONSIDERATION FOR THAT PROMISE

The previous section dealt with the question of determining when an offer has been made. An offer is made when the offeror creates the power in the offeree to form a contract. This power is created when the offeror manifests his or her willingness to enter into a contract by inviting the offeree to agree to the offeror's demands. The offeree concludes the bargain by agreeing. In other words, there is nothing remaining for the offeror to negotiate. Assent by the offeree forms the contract.

Although it may be concluded that the transaction has moved from the preliminary negotiation to the offer phase, this conclusion may be premature. In the sequence of communications, a communication may appear to be an offer, but it is still necessary to evaluate whether that communication has the necessary ingredients of an offer.

Simply stated, an offer has three ingredients:

1. The offeror must make a promise (the offeror's promise is also referred to as the promisor's promise)
2. There must be consideration for the offeror's promise (also referred to as the consideration for the promisor's promise or the "price" for the offeror's or promisor's promise)
3. The offeror's promise must be made to induce the consideration.

Although the offeror's promise must be a promise, the consideration for the offeror's promise (the "price" for the offeror's promise) may be either the offeree's promise or a performance. If the consideration is the offeree's promise, the offeror is making his or her promise to induce the offeree to make a promise. The shorthand phrase for this offer is "a promise for a promise." If the offeror is making his or her promise to induce the offeree to perform rather than promise to perform, the offer is "a promise for a performance."

Judicial opinions and treatises often refer to the promise for a promise exchange as "a bilateral contract." At this phase of the analysis, the "promise for a promise" is only an offer. The offer is still waiting to be accepted. Contract formation will not occur until acceptance of the offer occurs. Once the offer has been accepted by the offeree's promise, the contract is a bilateral contract. "Bi" is the Latin prefix meaning two. Here we have two promises between two parties. The offeror makes a promise to receive the offeree's promise; the offeree makes a promise to receive the offeror's promise.

The following sentence illustrates an offer for a bilateral contract:

I promise to sell you my car for your promise to pay me $5,000.

+————————promise to sell————————>

Offeror Offeree

<————————promise to pay $5,000————————+

Most people do not speak or write in the formal "I promise for your promise." Usually, the offer takes the form "I'll sell you my car for $5,000." "I'll sell" in formal terms means "I promise to sell," and the "$5,000" is the common form of the formal "for your promise to pay me $5,000." Because the formal designation provides clarity, common usage will be upgraded to the formal "I promise."

The second form of offer, the promise in exchange for a performance, is an offer for a unilateral contract. This offer does not affect both sides equally and therefore lacks symmetry. The offeror makes a promise to receive the offeree's performance.

The following example illustrates an offer for a unilateral contract:

I promise to sell you my car for your paying me $5,000.

+————————promise to sell————————>

Offeror Offeree

<————————paying $5,000————————+

The consideration for the offeror's promise to sell is the offeree's "paying $5,000." The offeror is not asking the offeree to promise to pay. The offeror wants the actual payment in return for his or her promise to sell.

The distinction between offers for unilateral and bilateral contracts has practical significance. If the offer proposes a unilateral contract, the offeree must perform to accept the offer. The offeree's performance is the acceptance, and upon full performance a contract is formed. If the offeree attempts to accept the offer by promising to perform, the offeree has not accepted because the offeror's terms required the offeree's performance and not his or her promise. Once the offeree has fully performed, there is nothing left for the offeree to do; he or she has no remaining duty to perform. The only party who has a duty to perform is the offeror.

If the offer proposes a bilateral contract, the offeree must promise to accept the offer. The offeree's promise may be either express (stated) or implied from the offeree's performance. A promise implied from the offeree's performance does not require full performance. Therefore, the implied promise could be quite different from the performance required to accept an offer for a unilateral contract. Once the offeree promises, a contract is formed. Each party has a duty to perform his or her promise, and each has a right to receive the other party's performance.

An offer for a unilateral contract does not become a contract until after the offeree has fully performed. Once the offeree has fully performed and a contract is formed, only the offeror has a duty to perform. The offeree has nothing else to do. Therefore, only the offeror could be the breaching party. In a bilateral contract, both parties have a duty to perform; therefore, after the contract is formed, either (or both) could be the breaching party.

Generally, once an offer for a unilateral contract has been made, the performance required for acceptance will take some time. Preparations may be necessary prior to the offeree's actual performance, and the performance itself may require days or months to complete. Only complete performance is consideration for the offeror's promise. In contrast, when an offer for a bilateral contract has been made, the acceptance in the form of a promise can be made easier and quicker than the performance. Contract formation occurs when the offeree promises and not when the offeree performs.

Most contracts are bilateral and not unilateral. "I promise to work for you for one year for your promise to pay me $800 a week." "I promise to paint your house for your promise to pay me $1,500." "I promise to build you a house for your promise to pay $125,000." "I promise to sell you this yacht for your promise to pay $17,000." Only unusual transactions are unilateral. "I promise to pay you $100 if you win the race tomorrow." "I promise to give you a half interest in Blackacre if you discover gold."

The following material explores the three ingredients (elements) of an offer: the offeror's promise, the consideration for the offeror's offer, and the inducement connecting the offeror's promise to the consideration for the offeror's offer.

A. When a "Promise" Is Really a Promise

A promise is an unequivocal assurance that something will or will not be done. "I may sell my car to you" is not unequivocal, and therefore is less than a promise. On the other hand, "I will sell you my car" is an unequivocal assurance and is a promise. The unequivocal assurance could be to refrain from doing something as well as to do something. Thus "I will not sell my car to Marylou" is as much a promise as "I will sell my car to Marylou."

Three situations in which it is difficult to determine whether a "promise" exists are puffing, the illusory promise, and the indefinite promise (indefiniteness).

1. Puffing

Puffing is an expression of opinion by a seller that is not intended as a representation of fact. If a seller's statement is puffing, it is not a representation of fact; that is, it is not an express warranty, which is a promise by the seller relating to the goods or the services to be performed. The line between puffing and warranty is often unclear and difficult to draw. Consider the following two cases: *Wat Henry Pontiac Co. v. Bradley* and *Frederickson v. Hackney.* In each case identify the seller's statement and describe the context in which it was made. Describe the buyer and the buyer's expertise in this transaction. Describe how the buyer relied on the seller's statement. Should the buyer have relied? What injury did the buyer suffer? Did the buyer suffer the injury because of the seller's statement? Did the court's opinion state the reasons for the decision or were unstated factors the real basis for the decision? Based on these facts could you have predicted the court's conclusion as to puffing or warranty?

Wat Henry Pontiac Co. v. Bradley

Supreme Court of Oklahoma, 1949.
202 Okl. 82, 210 P.2d 348.

JOHNSON, Justice.

This is an action to recover the sum of $324.56 damages for breach of an express oral warranty of a used car purchased by plaintiff, defendant in error, from the defendant, plaintiff in error, hereafter referred to as plaintiff and defendant. A trial on the merits resulted in a judgment against the defendant in the sum of $279.56. From this verdict and order overruling motion for a new trial, defendant appeals.

The plaintiff alleged that on the 22d day of October, 1944, she purchased a used Buick automobile from the defendant, paying $890 cash for same; that the same was purchased by oral contract and that the vehicle was warranted as being in first-class condition, usable and serviceable in every respect; that plaintiff relied on said representation, but that said car was not in first-class usable condition; that it was necessary to have said vehicle repaired and parts replaced, and that she expended on said car the sum of $249.56; that she suffered damages as expenses and inconvenience in the sum of $75.

A demurrer was filed and overruled, after which defendant filed an answer, denying that plaintiff had sued the proper party; denied that the contract was oral; that any recommendations were made; that plaintiff suffered any damages. Thereafter defendant filed an amendment to his answer claiming certain Federal statutes, 50 U.S.C.A. Appendix, § 906, otherwise known as O.P.A., which fixed the ceiling price on used cars, and alleged that the maximum price regulation on a car as the one involved here, without warranty was $888. To this a reply was filed denying that maximum ceiling prices of O.P.A. affected in any way the oral contract of purchase, and the cause was tried to a jury on the 6th day of May, 1947, and judgment was rendered as heretofore stated.

The defendant (plaintiff in error) in his petition in error made thirteen specifications of error. In the brief, eleven are set out, but only four specifications are urged and argued. We shall consider only those argued. We now consider defendant's proposition one: "Generally, no implied warranty of quality or fitness is present in sale of a secondhand automobile, but doctrine of caveat emptor applies."

This is the general rule as to implied warranties as stated in 42 C.J. 780, sec. 322; 60 C.J.S., Motor Vehicles, §§ 40, 41; however, the plaintiff in this case does not rely on an implied warranty, but upon an express verbal warranty, and the rule of caveat emptor does not apply where there is an express warranty of condition, and does not apply to hidden defects which are not open to discovery by the buyer. 42 C.J. 781, sec. 324; 60 C.J.S., Motor Vehicles, §§ 40, 41; International Harvester Co. v. Lawyer, 56 Okl. 207, 155 P. 617; Pierce v. Crowl, Okl.Sup., 190 P.2d 1003.

The plaintiff testified that on October 22, 1944, she went to the Wat Henry Pontiac Company, the defendant; that she contacted the manager or salesman in charge of the used cars; that she made a deal for the car; that she was with her brother; and that the brother was present during her negotiations for the purchase of the car; that she asked many questions about the car; that the seller assured her that the car was in good condition; that he had driven the car; that "this is a car we know; this is a car I can recommend"; that "it is in A–1 shape." She informed him that her husband was in Camp Shelby, Mississippi, and that her child was only seven months old; and that she wanted to be sure she was going to get there. The defendant further assured her that he knew the car, he knew the man who had brought it in, that it was "mechanically perfect" and that it would get her any place she wanted to go. That she asked to drive the car and try it out, but was told that gas rations were very short and they were not allowed to send cars out for trial, but that she had no cause to fear this car, that it was all right; that she could not see the connecting rod or crankshaft or rings; that she was not a mechanic, but was a trained nurse; that after she bought the car they gave her a certificate to send to the O.P.A. ration board to enable her to obtain a gas ration.

That after purchasing the car she drove to Chelsea, which was about fifty miles from Tulsa; that she remained there four or five days; that on the 1st of November, 1944, she started on her trip to Camp Shelby, Mississippi; that she had not driven the car more than a few blocks in Chelsea before starting on this trip; that when she got near Fort Smith, Arkansas, the car began knocking; that she took it to the Robbins Motor Co., the Buick Sales and Service, where it was repaired; that the amount which was paid by plaintiff was $249.56; that after the repairs were made the car ran "good."

The plaintiff was corroborated by her brother whose testimony was substantially the same as plaintiff's. As to the repairs, there was ample evidence of the need and reasonableness of the charges for the repairs on the car.

The salesman who sold the car testified in substance that he had been an auto mechanic for about twelve years before becoming a salesman; that he was engaged in demonstrating and selling cars; that he did not warrant the car, but explained to the buyer that the sale was without a warranty, but did state that after the deal was closed that he told plaintiff, "I would not be afraid to start, and I wouldn't have been afraid to start any place in the car, because it run as nice as you would expect a car that age to run. There wasn't anything to indicate to me that there was anything wrong with the car, if there was anything wrong with it."

The evidence adduced as to the issues involved was in conflict, each side having witnesses to substantiate their theory. Now, did these facts as stated by plaintiff, if true, constitute an oral warranty?

The rule is that to constitute an express warranty no particular form of words is necessary, and any affirmation of the quality or condition of the vehicle, not uttered as a matter of opinion or belief, made by a seller at the time of sale for the purpose of assuring the buyer of the truth of the fact and inducing the buyer to make the purchase, if so received and relied on by the buyer, is an express warranty. 42 C.J. 781, sec. 324; 60 C.J.S., Motor Vehicles, §§ 40, 41; 46 Am. Jur. 494, sec. 313.

This court in International Harvester Co. v. Lawyer, supra, said:

" 'Warranty' is a matter of intention. A decisive test is whether the vendor assumes to assert a fact of which the buyer is ignorant, or merely states an opinion, or his judgment, upon a matter of which the vendor has no special knowledge, and on which the buyer may also be expected to have an opinion and to exercise his judgment. In the former case there is a warranty; in the latter case there is not. * * *

"The buyer knew nothing about the capacity of the automobile purchased. The seller was an expert in the handling of automobiles, and was engaged in the business of demonstrating and selling the same. Held, a statement made by the seller that the automobile could be driven over the roads in a certain vicinity satisfactorily constituted a warranty and was not the expression of a mere opinion."

The facts in this case bring it squarely within the above well-settled principles of law, and the jury was justified in finding that there was an oral warranty.

However, the defendant contends that plaintiff and defendant each signed an O.P.A. "Certification of Purchaser and Seller":

"The undersigned hereby certify that they have complied with the requirements of Maximum Price Regulation No. 540, Maximum Prices for Used Passenger Automobiles, and that the actual sale price of the vehicle is not more than the maximum selling price as established by Maximum Price Regulation No. 540, and further certify that no payment directly or indirectly was or will be made in addition to the actual sale price of the vehicle as shown on this certificate.

"Sign here (Signed)

Mrs. Joe E. Bradley
"Signature of
Purchaser
"Date __________

"Sign here (Signed)

Wat Henry Pontiac
Co.
"Loise Francis
"Signature of Seller
"Date __________"

and that by reason thereof the plaintiff cannot contradict said O.P.A. statement by oral testimony as this was a written contract, and that under the provisions of 15 O.S.A. § 137, the execution of a contract in writing, whether the law requires it to be in writing or not, supersedes all the oral negotiations or stipulations concerning its matter which preceded or accompanied the execution of the instrument. Obviously, there was no contract in the O.P.A. instrument. It was merely a "certification" that the parties had complied with the requirements of the maximum price regulation for used automobiles, and was necessary for the buyer to obtain gasoline rations, but if it could be said that it constituted a part of the contract of sale, then it would not be complete and would be governed by the incomplete writing rule, see Sales, 46 Am.Jur. 499, sec. 316, and this contention is untenable under the rule announced in 46 Am.Jur. 502, sec. 321, wherein it is stated: "If the facts or affirmations relied on to prove an express warranty rest wholly or partly in parol it has been held that it is ordinarily the province of the jury to determine whether they amount to an express warranty. * * *"

Defendant's second proposition is: "Statements by a salesman as to the condition of an automobile sold at a price lower than it would sell if warranted, or such statements that he would not mind starting any where in the car were merely expressions of opinion."

Defendant argues that the facts in this case are governed by the rule that a seller is permitted to promote his wares so long as he does so in the bounds of reason, and cites Smith v. Bolster, 70 Wash. 1, 125 P. 1022, as his authority. The first paragraph of the syllabus reads: "Statements by a seller of an automobile, which had been used as a demonstrating car, and had been run about 1,500 miles, made to a buyer who knew the facts, that the car, sold for less than 20 per cent. less than the price of a new car, * * * and would go 11 miles to a gallon of gasoline on an average, were mere expressions of opinion, and did not constitute a warranty of the car."

Thus, it is obvious that in this case cited the buyer knew as much about the facts as the seller, and, of course, the buyer, knowing the facts, what the seller said was merely the expression of an opinion. The buyer here was ignorant of the facts, and the defects were hidden and not open to discovery by the buyer. The seller was an expert in handling automobiles, having served for a long period of time as an automobile mechanic before becoming a salesman; and his statements as to the condition of the car and where it could be driven constituted a warranty and not mere opinion. International Harvester Co. v. Lawyer, supra; Pierce v. Crowl, supra.

Defendant's third proposition is: "Defendant was deprived of a fair and impartial trial and his rights were prejudiced by reason of misconduct and irregularities of plaintiff's counsel."

We have carefully examined the record and observe that probably attorneys in the case have been somewhat overzealous in the presentation of the case, but we find no such conduct as would prevent a fair and impartial trial, or conduct of the plaintiff's attorney that would prejudice the rights of the defendant.

The fourth and last proposition argued by defendant is that the verdict was contrary to the evidence, was not sustained by the evidence, was contrary to law and that the trial court should have granted a new trial.

It is the well-established rule of this court in law actions where disputed questions of fact are submitted to a jury, the jury's verdict will not be disturbed on appeal where there is any evidence reasonably tending to support it. J.B. Colt Co. v. Koehn, 128 Okl. 39, 260 P. 1060.

This case being properly submitted to the jury on controverted questions of fact, and there being evidence reasonably tending to support their verdict, the judgment is affirmed, and judgment is hereby entered on the supersedeas bond.

DAVISON, C.J., ARNOLD, V.C.J., and CORN, GIBSON, LUTTRELL, HALLEY and O'NEAL, JJ., concur.

Frederickson v. Hackney

Supreme Court of Minnesota, 1924.
159 Minn. 234, 198 N.W. 806.

Action by Ivan L. Frederickson against J.M. Hackney. From an order denying a motion for new trial, plaintiff appeals. Affirmed.

STONE, J. Action by the purchaser for the breach of an alleged warranty of a Holstein Friesian bull calf. There was no express warranty and a verdict was directed for defendant on the ground that no implied warranty existed. Plaintiff appeals from the order denying his motion for a new trial.

Both plaintiff and defendant are breeders of thoroughbred Holstein Friesian cattle. Plaintiff purchased two cows from defendant. Both were with calf when delivered to him. Defendant had reserved the calves to himself, but a few days after birth of the male in question, plaintiff purchased him of defendant for $500. The ancestry of the calf was such as to justify this price, the assumption of both parties being of course that he would be a sure calf-getter when he attained his maturity. The fact proved otherwise, and, instead of having a sire of high priced cattle, plaintiff found himself with a sterile bull of no value save for beef and of little value even for that.

There is a claim of an express warranty, but none of the language used by defendant and upon which plaintiff claims to have relied was used with intent to warrant anything. Plaintiff was advised by defendant to "buy this bull and keep him" for breeding purposes; that he would be a wonderful asset and would put him "on the map." "He told me further of his blood lines and what a great record his relatives had made; * * * that his father was the greatest living dairy bull; that if I would keep him, of course, he would be a help to build up my herd."

There is nothing in that language indicating the intent of defendant to warrant the future reproductive capacity of the calf. Defendant had no right to rely upon it as such. It was trade talk of the conventional and permissible type and cannot be expanded into a warranty simply because the unusual happened and the expectations of both parties were disappointed.

There can be no more appropriate occasion for the adoption of the rule of "caveat emptor" than the sale of an immature animal, the principal value of which depends upon its later becoming a breeder. Sterility is the exception. Still there are many contingencies attending the adolescence even of brutes that would make it an anomalous thing to impose upon a vendor, who parts with the possession and responsibility for the rearing of the animal, the liability of having the sale rescinded in the event that, at maturity, the animal proves to be sterile.

The general rule, even as to mature animals, is that—

"There is no implied warranty of competency or fitness for breeding purposes in the sale of an animal although a full price is paid and the sellers know that it is bought for breeding purposes, where there is no fraud or misrepresentation and both parties are alike destitute of knowledge or the means of forming an intelligent judgment as to the fitness or capacity of the animal for that purpose. In such a sale it seems that custom, policy, and law unite in applying the maxim of caveat emptor, and that the purchaser takes the animal upon his own judgment, risking both the quality and the value of it." 1 R.C.L. 1085.

See, also, Scott v. Renick, 1 B.Mon.(Ky.) 63, 35 Am.Dec. 177; Griffin v. Runnion, 74 W.Va. 641, 82 S.E. 686; and White v. Stelloh, 74 Wis. 435, 43 N.W. 99.

Implied warranties ordinarily speak concerning the present and give assurance only as to qualities existing at the time being. They do not ordinarily speak of the future, nor of qualities later to be developed. That is the conventional field for express rather than implied warranty.

"The doctrine of implied warranty appears to be founded on an actual or presumed knowledge by the vendor, as manufacturer, grower, or producer, of the qualities and fitness of the thing sold for the purpose for which it was intended or is desired, so far as such knowledge is reasonably attainable. The rule must be held to have a rational foundation, and to be not of a purely arbitrary character. It does not impute to the seller knowledge as to qualities or fitness which no human foresight or skill can attain, and raise an implied warranty in respect to them when the vendor and purchaser are in equal condition as to means of knowledge, or the latter must have understood from the nature of the case that the information, experience, and knowledge of the vendor are not superior to his own." McQuaid v. Ross, 85 Wis. 492, 55 N.W. 705, 22 L.R.A. 187, 39 Am.St.Rep. 864.

While that statement may not sufficiently emphasize the seller's knowledge that the article will be valueless to the purchaser unless fit for a particular purpose, it shows the utter impossibility, in reason, of creating an implied warranty in a case of this kind, where neither party can know anything about what the future will prove concerning the particular qualifications expected and desired in the subject-matter of the sale.

Authorities urged to the contrary are the

"Jack Cases"—from Missouri. In a recent one (Neal v. Crowson [Mo.App.] 231 S.W. 1033), the decision was put upon the proposition that it is a matter of common knowledge among breeders that a jack has no value except for breeding purposes and therefore that the law implies a warranty that jacks are reasonably fit for that purpose.

There is much reason in that view as applied to the sale of a mature male, or possibly to one so near maturity that the intention is soon to use him as a sire. But it cannot apply to the sale of one only a few days, or a few weeks old, and from 15 to 18 months removed from the first possibility of even limited use for breeding purposes.

The Uniform Sales Act does not change the rule. Section 15 (section 6015, Gen.St. Supp.1917) does create an implied warranty that the goods shall be reasonably fit for specific purposes, "where the buyer, expressly or by implication, makes known to the seller the particular purpose for which the goods are required, and it appears that the buyer relies on the seller's skill or judgment." That does not apply here for two reasons: (1) This animal was not purchased for immediate breeding purposes. Plaintiff bought him to raise and ultimately to use as a sire. In such a case, the statute does not import a warranty against the contingencies of nature, one of which is the possibility that an animal may be impotent. (2) There is no claim here that plaintiff relied on the seller's skill or judgment. Both parties are experienced cattlemen, and neither of them knew, although both supposed, that this particular individual would be, at maturity, effective as a sire.

Order affirmed.

2. The Illusory Promise

The phrase "illusory promise" is a misnomer because an illusory promise is not a promise. It is less than a promise and does not contribute to the creation of a power in the offeree to accept an offer. An illusory promise is not an unequivocal assurance that something will or will not be done. For example, "I may sell you my car" is an illusory promise. It is not an unequivocal statement that I will sell you my car. The same is true for the statement "I will work for you next Monday if I feel like it." There is no commitment to do or refrain from doing something.

PROBLEM 3: Is the term in the writing in *Sterling Computer Systems v. Texas Pipe* a promise or an illusory promise?

Sterling Computer Systems, Inc. v. Texas Pipe Bending Co.

Court of Civil Appeals of Texas, 1974.
507 S.W.2d 282.

TUNKS, Chief Justice.

The issue in this case is the propriety of a summary judgment for the defendant in a breach of contract suit, which was granted on the theory that the contract lacked mutuality.

The appellant, Sterling Computer Systems of Texas, Inc., brought suit for breach of contract against the appellee, Texas Pipe Bending Company. In essence, the contract in question provided that Texas Pipe Bending was to provide Sterling with digitized cards and computer programs each month, with which Sterling was to perform data processing services for Texas Pipe Bending. Certain prices were quoted in the agreement, which were "based on a minimum of 20,000 digitized cards per month." The term of the agreement was to have been for one year, but after providing cards and paying in full for eight months, Texas Pipe Bending refused to further provide Sterling with digitized cards. The trial court granted Texas Pipe Bending's motion for summary judgment. Although the judgment does not so recite, it was apparently based on the argument proposed by Texas Pipe Bending that the contract was unenforcible because of the lack of mutuality. Sterling has appealed.

The relevant portion of the contract is found in a clause denominated as "LIMITATION OF LIABILITY." This clause provides in part as follows:

> SCS [Sterling] shall not be liable for its failure to profide [sic] the services herein and shall not be liable for any losses resulting to the client [Texas Pipe Bending] or anyone else by reason of such failure.

The general rule as stated in Texas Farm Bureau Cotton Ass'n v. Stovall, 113 Tex. 273, 253 S.W. 1101, 1105 (1923), is:

> [A] contract must be based upon a valid consideration, and ... a contract in which there is no consideration moving from one party, or no obligation upon him, lacks mutuality, is unilateral, and unenforcible.

Under the express terms of the contract in question Sterling would not be liable for an outright refusal to perform the data processing services. This fact renders its obligation a nullity.

Sterling cites various cases which purportedly support its position that the trial court erred in granting summary judgment for Texas Pipe Bending. The gist of these cases is that although a contract may not expressly obligate a party to perform, such an obligation may be implied by its terms. In Texas Gas Utilities Company v. Barrett, 460 S.W.2d 409 (Tex.Sup.1970), the Texas Supreme Court held, under a similar contention, that there was a mutuality of obligation. In that case the contract provided that the Gas Company would not be liable for failure to deliver when such failure was "caused by conditions beyond its reasonable control," and then enumerated certain situations which exemplified the above phrase (over none of which would the Gas Company have control). The Court noted, "It [Gas Company] was bound, however, to supply *available* natural gas to respondents. . . ." Texas Gas Utilities Company v. Barrett, *supra* 460 S.W.2d at 413. In the present case there existed no requirement that Sterling make a reasonable effort to perform. The exculpatory clause allowed Sterling to refuse to perform with impunity.

Clement v. Producers' Refining Co., 277 S.W. 634 (Tex.Comm'n App. 1925, jdgmt adopted), was another case in which mutuality was found. That case involved a contract for an agent's commission. By the terms of the agreement the principal was to pay the agent a commission on goods which "may be supplied" by the principal. Notwithstanding this provision the Commission of Appeals held that the contract impliedly obligated the principal to supply goods to the agent. However, the Court stated:

> [A]s there is no language used which would clearly indicate that the company was not obligated to furnish goods and products, the courts are not warranted in holding that no such obligation was imposed ... by its terms. Clement v. Producers' Refining Co., *supra* at 635.

The case at bar is distinguishable because the contract contained an express provision that Sterling would not be liable if it did not perform. Various other cases cited by appellant are similarly distinguishable because in those cases contracts were involved which did not expressly provide that one of the contracting parties could fail to perform without incurring liability.

As a matter of law the contract in question fails for want of mutuality. The trial court correctly granted summary judgment for the defendant, Texas Pipe Bending Company.

Affirmed.

3. The Indefinite Promise

An indefinite promise omits terms essential in enabling the courts to determine an appropriate remedy in the event the promise is breached. Take, for example, the statement "I promise to sell you a cow for your promise to pay $750." When Seller owns a Holstein herd and does not designate a specific animal, this is an indefinite promise. The animals vary in value, some are worth substantially more than $750 and some substantially less. If Seller does not deliver a cow, how will the court determine the appropriate remedy for Seller's refusal to deliver? Even if Seller does deliver a cow but Buyer complains that this was not the cow she wanted, how will the court determine whether the promise to deliver has been breached and, if breached, the appropriate remedy?

PROBLEM 4: Does the following promise suffer for indefiniteness?

I promise to pay you a reasonable sum
if you promise to work for me.

In a sale of goods transaction, the Uniform Commercial Code addresses the indefiniteness problem in two ways. First, the UCC provides a general statement in section 2–204(3):

> (3) Even though one or more terms are left open a contract for sale does not fail for indefiniteness if the parties have intended to make a contract and there is a reasonably certain basis for giving an appropriate remedy.

Second, the UCC may supply terms omitted in the contract. These terms are known as gap fillers. The gap fillers include provisions as to price (§ 2–305), place of delivery (§ 2–308), time for shipment or delivery (§ 2–309), payment or running of credit (§ 2–310), warranty of title (§ 2–312), warranty against infringement (§ 2–312), implied warranty of merchantability (§§ 2–314(1), (2)), implied warranty of usage of trade (§ 2–314(3)), and implied warranty of fitness for a particular purpose (§ 2–315).

EXAMPLE

Uniform Commercial Code § 2–305. Open Price Term.

> (1) The parties if they so intend can conclude a contract for sale even though the price is not settled. In such a case the price is a reasonable price at the time for delivery if
>
> (a) nothing is said as to price; or
>
> (b) the price is left to be agreed by the parties and they fail to agree; or

(c) the price is to be fixed in terms of some agreed market or other standard as set or recorded by a third person or agency and it is not so set or recorded.

B. Consideration for the Offeror's Promise

The second ingredient (element) of an offer is consideration for the offeror's (also referred to as the promisor's) promise. In the offer "I promise to sell you my car for your promise to pay $5,000," the phrase "for your promise to pay $5,000" is the consideration for the offeror's promise ("I promise to sell you my car").

Consideration is the "price" that the offeror expects to receive for his or her promise. "Price" has been placed in quotation marks to emphasize that the term "price" is not limited to dollars and cents. It can be anything that the law recognizes as consideration. It could be a promise to barter. "I promise to sell you my car for your promise to roof my house." The consideration for the offeror's promise can easily be found by asking "what is the price for the offeror's promise"? In this example, the "price" for the offeror's promise to sell the car is the return promise to roof the offeror's house.

Every contract has two considerations: one for the offeror's promise and the other for the offeree's promise or performance. For clarity these two considerations will be distinguished by referring to "consideration for the offeror's promise" and "consideration for the offeree's promise or performance." The term "consideration," standing alone, will be used only when a general reference to consideration is made.

The following materials discuss six consideration-related problems: the promise to make a future gift, adequacy of consideration, motive as consideration, moral obligation as consideration, sham consideration, and mutuality of obligation.

1. The Promise to Make a Future Gift

Early in the history of contracts law, the judges decided that some promises should be enforced while others should not be enforced. The promise of a future gift fell in the latter category. The only promise to make a gift that would be enforced would be that where the gift had already been made. That is, if a donor changed his or her mind and wanted the gift returned, the court would not require the gift already conveyed to be returned. On the other hand, a person who promised to make a gift in the future but who had not yet conveyed the gift, would not be forced by the court to follow through with his or her promise.

A promise to make a future gift is a one-sided promise. The promise to make a future gift requests nothing in return for the promisor's promise. A contract, on the other hand, is more than a one-sided promise. An offer for a contract requires "something" in return for the promisor's promise. This "something" is the consideration or the "price" for the offeror's promise.

In a commercial setting, most promisors seek something in exchange for their promises. If the transaction involves the sale of goods, construction, or employment, there is always an exchange. Neither party to the transaction promises to give something for nothing. The promisor's motivation in making a promise may be quite different in the commercial world than it is in a family or interpersonal setting. In the family or interpersonal setting, the promisor may make a promise and not seek something in return. When a mother promises her daughter a weekly allowance of $4.00 (with no strings attached) or a new dress for the spring dance, the mother is making nothing more than a promise of a future gift.

2. Adequacy of Consideration (the Peppercorn Theory of Contracts)

The law of contracts does not concern itself with the size or value of the consideration. The court will not investigate whether the consideration sought by the offeror is "adequate." Adequacy of consideration is irrelevant. What is relevant is that there be some consideration, no matter how small. Consideration may be as small as a peppercorn, if that is what the offeror is bargaining to receive in exchange for his or her promise.

As we all know, promises are not made to get peppercorns. Most contracts are performed, and the parties are satisfied with the results (or are not so dissatisfied that they will do anything more than grumble). In some cases, one party may feel that he or she has paid too much or received too little. At the time of contracting, the parties were free to design the contract to their own specifications. If, after the fact, one party feels dissatisfied with the terms to which he or she agreed, this is not the concern of the court. A judge will not evaluate whether one party received more under the contract than the other and will not evaluate the adequacy of the consideration.

Although the law recognizes something the size of a peppercorn as consideration, it does not recognize everything as potential consideration. "Love and affection" cannot serve as consideration. If "love and affection" were to be consideration, the entire concept of consideration would crumble because the distinction between a promise to make a future gift and a contract promise would no longer exist. All promises would have legal significance and could be enforceable regardless of whether they were intended as gifts.

3. Motive as Consideration

Motive cannot be consideration for a promise. The offeror's motive must be separated from the consideration for his or her promise.

Consider the following statement: "I promise to sell you my car for your promise to pay $5,000." The offeror's motive for promising to sell her car might be to buy a newer car, to take a trip to Europe, to bury $5,000 in a tin can in the backyard, to pay a hospital bill, or to bet on a horse. Whatever her motive or motives, and no matter how interesting or unique, motives are irrelevant. What is relevant is that there be consideration for the offeror's promise—what will be received by the offeror in return for his or her "promise to sell the car."

> *PROBLEM 5:* A budding sculptor, seeking public exposure for his work, promises to lend a large sculpture to the First Bank if First Bank will promise to exhibit it in its foyer for one year.
>
> 1. What is the sculptor's motive or motives for promising to lend the sculpture to the Bank?
> 2. What is the consideration for the sculptor's promise to lend the sculpture to the Bank?

PROBLEM 6: A grandmother promises to pay her granddaughter's tuition if the granddaughter will go to college.

1. What is the grandmother's motive for her promise to pay her granddaughter's tuition?
2. What is the consideration for the grandmother's promise to pay the tuition?

PROBLEM 7: Mary lost her wedding ring and placed an advertisement in the personal column of the local newspaper: "I promise to pay a $400 reward to the person who finds and returns my diamond ring."

1. What is Mary's motive for making the promise to pay $400?
2. What is the consideration for Mary's promise to pay $400?

4. Moral Obligation as Consideration

The fact that someone feels morally obligated to make a promise cannot be consideration for the promisor's promise. Moral obligation is not consideration. It is synonymous with motive and, as discussed in the preceding section, motive is not consideration.

PROBLEM 8: Mills nurses Wyman's emancipated son who is seriously ill. After Wyman's son dies, Wyman promises to reimburse Mills for any expenses incurred by Mills for this care. Because Wyman's son was emancipated, Wyman is under no legal obligation to reimburse Mills. If Wyman has a change of heart and subsequently refuses to pay Mills, can Mills claim that Wyman made an offer?

1. What was Wyman's motive in making his promise to reimburse Mills?
2. What was the consideration that Wyman requested in exchange for his promise to pay Mills?

5. Sham Consideration

Sham consideration is feigned or pretended consideration. Sham consideration is not consideration. The stated consideration for the promisor's promise may be a sham when the promisor is attempting to place his or her promise, which is intended as a future gift, in the form of a contract offer.

EXAMPLE

A father, intending to give his son a car as a gift, says to his son "I promise to sell you my car for your promise to pay $5,000." Because the father had no intention of receiving the $5,000 payment but had clothed his promise of a future gift in offer apparel, the stated consideration for the promisor's promise ("your promise to pay $5,000") is a sham and does not count as consideration.

Sham consideration relates to both adequacy of consideration and motive. Although a court will not investigate whether the consideration for the promisor's promise is adequate, the court might investigate whether the stated consideration is a sham. While motive will not be consideration, motive may play a role in determining whether the consideration stated is a sham.

6. Mutuality of Obligation

It is common to find the phrase "mutuality of obligation" in judicial opinions. Unfortunately, this phrase is misleading. These opinions lead the reader to believe that mutuality of obligation is an element required for contract formation. If, however, there is consideration for the promisor's promise and the promise was made to induce the promisee to promise or perform the promisor's request, then mutuality of obligation exists, and there is no additional requirement. The same is true from the promisee's point of view; that is, the promisee's promise must be made to induce the promisor's promise.

The Restatement of Contracts (Second) § 79 concisely states:

> If the requirement of consideration is met, there is no additional requirement of
>
> . . .
>
> (c) "mutuality of obligation."

Therefore, do not be concerned with "mutuality of obligation"; check to ensure that the requirement of consideration has been met.

C. The Offeror's Promise Must Be Made to Induce the Consideration

The third element of an offer is the glue that sticks the offeror's promise to the consideration for the offeror's promise. The offer anticipates a "bargained for exchange." The phrase "bargained for exchange" does not require hard bargaining with protracted negotiation. The requirement is that the offeror, by his or her promise, must be seeking the offeree's promise or performance (the consideration). The offeror's promise must be made to induce the consideration.

The following material explores three inducement problems: past consideration, preexisting duty, and conditions.

1. Past Consideration

The past consideration issue is a timing issue. The offeror must make his or her promise to induce the offeree to perform. Therefore, the offeree's performance must occur after the offeror has made his or her promise. If the offeree has already performed, the offeror would not be making his or her promise to induce the offeree to perform.

The issue of past consideration often occurs with the offeree's performance rather than the offeree's promise. Thus, a past consideration issue could occur in the situation labeled an offer for a unilateral contract.

> *PROBLEM 9:* Several months after Stan Hall was injured in an automobile accident, Stan learned that Mary Little had rendered first aid and that Mary's quick action probably saved Stan's life.

Acting upon this information, Stan promised to pay Mary $2,000 for saving his life.

1. What is the consideration for Stan's promise to pay Mary $2,000?
2. Did Stan make his promise to induce Mary to render the consideration for his promise?

PROBLEM 10: At his granddaughter's graduation, Granddad promises to pay her $5,000 for graduating with honors.

1. What is the consideration for Granddad's promise to pay $5,000?
2. Did Granddad make his promise to induce his granddaughter to render the consideration for his promise?

2. Preexisting Duty

Consideration for the offeror's promise must be free from obligation already owed to the offeror. If the offeree is operating under a duty to perform that which the offeror is currently seeking to induce, that consideration (the duty previously owed) cannot be used as consideration for the offeror's new promise. It has already been committed.

EXAMPLE

Ron Armstrong has a three-year contract to play football for the Chicago Bears at $1,000,000 a year. Ron's performance during the first year under the contract was outstanding, and the Bears decided to increase his salary for the remaining two years of the contract. The Bears promised to pay Ron $1,200,000 a year for his promise to play for them for the next two years. The consideration for the Bears' promise to pay Ron $1,200,000 a year is his promise to play for them for the next two years. This promise to play for the Bears for the next two years is a promise to which Ron is already committed in his original contract. Therefore, his promise to play for the Bears for the next two years cannot be consideration for the Bears' promise to pay him $1,200,000 a year.

The preexisting duty problem was raised in Schwartzreich v. Bauman-Basch, a case coming from the Court of Appeals of New York, the highest court in that state. Schwartzreich, a clothing designer, contracted to work for Bauman-Basch for one year at $90 a week, a handsome salary in 1917. A short time later, Schwartzreich was offered $110 a week to work for another company. Upon hearing that they might be losing Schwartzreich's services, Bauman-Basch offered to increase Schwartzreich's salary to $100 a week for the remainder of the contract term. Answer the following questions as you read the case:

1. What was the original offer by Bauman-Basch?
2. What was the consideration for Bauman-Basch's promise in that offer?
3. What was the new offer by Bauman-Basch?
4. What was the consideration for Bauman-Basch's promise in this new offer?

5. Was the consideration for Bauman-Basch's new promise the same as the consideration for Bauman-Basch's original promise?
6. Was the court able to work around the preexisting duty problem and if so, how?

Schwartzreich v. Bauman–Basch

Court of Appeals of New York, 1921.
231 N.Y. 196, 131 N.E. 887.

CRANE, J. On the 31st day of August, 1917, the plaintiff entered into the following employment agreement with the defendant:

"Bauman-Basch, Inc.
"Coats & Wraps
"31–33 East 32d Street
"New York

"Agreement entered into this 31st day of August, 1917, by and between Bauman-Basch, Inc., a domestic corporation, party of the first part, and Louis Schwartzreich, of the borough of Bronx, city of New York, party of the second part, witnesseth:

"The party of the first part does hereby employ the party of the second part, and the party of the second part agrees to enter the services of the party of the first part as a designer of coats and wraps.

"The employment herein shall commence on the 22d day of November, 1917, and shall continue for twelve months thereafter. The party of the second part shall receive a salary of ninety ($90.00) per week, payable weekly.

"The party of the second part shall devote his entire time and attention to the business of the party of the first part, and shall use his best energies and endeavors in the furtherance of its business.

"In witness whereof, the party of the first part has caused its seal to be affixed hereto and these presents to be signed, and the party of the second part has hereunto set his hand and seal the day and year first above written.

"Bauman-Basch, Inc.,
"S. Bauman.
"Louis Schwartzreich.

"In the presence of."

In October the plaintiff was offered more money by another concern. Mr. Bauman, an officer of the Bauman-Basch, Inc., says that in that month he heard that the plaintiff was going to leave and thereupon had with him the following conversation:

"A. I called him in the office, and I asked him, 'Is that true that you want to leave us?' and he said 'Yes,' and I said, 'Mr. Schwartzreich, how can you do that; you are under contract with us?' He said, 'Somebody offered me more money.' * * * I said, 'How much do they offer you?' He said, 'They offered him $115 a week.' * * * I said, 'I cannot get a designer now, and, in view of the fact that I have to send my sample line out on the road, I will give you a hundred dollars a week rather than to let you go.' He said, 'If you will give me $100, I will stay.' "

Thereupon Mr. Bauman dictated to his stenographer a new contract, dated October 17, 1917, in the exact words of the first contract and running for the same period, the salary being $100 a week, which contract was duly executed by the parties and witnessed. Duplicate originals were kept by the plaintiff and defendant.

Simultaneously with the signing of this new contract the plaintiff's copy of the old contract was either given to or left with Mr. Bauman. He testifies that the plaintiff gave him the paper but that he did not take it from him. The signatures to the old contract plaintiff tore off at the time according to

Mr. Bauman.

The plaintiff's version as to the execution of the new contract is as follows:

"A. I told Mr. Bauman that I have an offer from Scheer & Mayer of $110 a week, and I said to him: 'Do you advise me as a friendly matter—will you advise me as a friendly matter what to do; you see I have a contract with you, and I should not accept the offer of $110 a week, and I ask you, as a matter of friendship, do you advise me to take it or not.' At the minute he did not say anything, but the day afterwards he came to me in and he said, 'I will give you $100 a week, and I want you to stay with me.' I said: 'All right, I will accept it; it is very nice of you that you do that, and I appreciate it very much.' "

The plaintiff says that on the 17th of October, when the new contract was signed, he gave his copy of the old contract back to Mr. Bauman, who said: "You do not want this contract any more because the new one takes its place."

The plaintiff remained in the defendant's employ until the following December, when he was discharged. He brought this action under the contract of October 17th for his damages.

The defense, insisted upon through all the courts, is that there was no consideration for the new contract as the plaintiff was already bound under his agreement of August 31, 1917, to do the same work for the same period at $90 a week.

The trial justice submitted to the jury the question whether there was a cancellation of the old contract and charged as follows:

"If you find that the $90 contract was prior to or at the time of the execution of the $100 contract canceled and revoked by the parties by their mutual consent, then it is your duty to find that there was a consideration for the making of the contract in suit, viz., the $100 contract, and, in that event, the plaintiff would be entitled to your verdict for such damages as you may find resulted proximately, naturally, and necessarily in consequence of the plaintiff's discharge prior to the termination of the contract period of which I shall speak later on."

Defendant's counsel thereupon excepted to that portion of the charge in which the court permitted the jury to find that the prior contract may have been canceled simultaneously with the execution of the other agreement. Again the court said:

"The test question is whether by word or by act, either prior to or at the time of the signing of the $100 contract, these parties mutually agreed that the old contract from that instant should be null and void."

The jury having rendered a verdict for the plaintiff, the trial justice set it aside and dismissed the complaint on the ground that there was not sufficient evidence that the first contract was canceled to warrant the jury's findings.

The above quotations from the record show that a question of fact was presented and that the evidence most favorable for the plaintiff would sustain a finding that the first contract was destroyed, canceled, or abrogated by the consent of both parties.

The Appellate Term was right in reversing this ruling. Instead of granting a new trial, however, it reinstated the verdict of the jury and the judgment for the plaintiff. The question remains, therefore, whether the charge of the court, as above given, was a correct statement of the law or whether on all the evidence in the plaintiff's favor a cause of action was made out.

Can a contract of employment be set aside or terminated by the parties to it and a new one made or substituted in its place? If so, is it competent to end the one and make the other at the same time?

It has been repeatedly held that a promise made to induce a party to do that which he is already bound by contract to perform is without consideration. But the cases in this state, while enforcing this rule, also recognize that a contract may be canceled by mutual consent and a new one made. Thus Vanderbilt v. Schreyer, 91 N.Y. 392, 402, held that it was no consideration for a guaranty that a party promise to do only that which he was before legally bound to perform. This court stated, however:

"It would doubtless be competent for parties to cancel an existing contract and make a new one to complete the same work at a different rate of compensation, but it seems that it would be essential to its validity that there should be a valid cancellation of the original contract. Such was the case of Lattimore v. Harsen, 14 Johns. 330."

In Cosgray v. New England Piano Co., 10 App.Div. 351, 353, 41 N.Y.Supp. 886, 888, it was decided that where the plaintiff had bound himself to work for a year at $30 a week, there was no consideration for a promise thereafter made by the defendant that he should, notwithstanding, receive $1,800 a year. Here it will be noticed there was no termination of the first agreement which gave occasion for Bartlett, J., to say in the opinion:

"The case might be different if the parties had, by word of mouth, agreed wholly to abrogate and do away with a pre-existing written contract in regard to service and compensation, and had substituted for it another agreement."

Any change in an existing contract, such as a modification of the rate of compensation, or a supplemental agreement, must have a new consideration to support it. In such a case the contract is continued, not ended. Where, however, an existing contract is terminated by consent of both parties and a new one executed in its place and stead, we have a different situation and the mutual promises are again a consideration. Very little difference may appear in a mere change of compensation in an existing and continuing contract and a termination of one contract and the making of a new one for the same time and work, but at an increased compensation. There is, however, a marked difference in principle. Where the new contract gives any new privilege or advantage to the promisee, a consideration has been recognized, though in the main it is the same contract. Triangle Waist Co., Inc., v. Todd, 223 N.Y. 27, 119 N.E. 85.

If this which we are now holding were not the rule, parties having once made a contract would be prevented from changing it no matter how willing and desirous they might be to do so, unless the terms conferred an additional benefit to the promisee.

All concede that an agreement may be rescinded by mutual consent and a new agreement made thereafter on any terms to which the parties may assent. Prof. Williston, in his work on Contracts, says (volume 1, § 130a):

"A rescission followed shortly afterwards by a new agreement in regard to the same subject-matter would create the legal obligations provided in the subsequent agreement."

The same effect follows in our judgment from a new contract entered into at the same time the old one is destroyed and rescinded by mutual consent. The determining factor is the rescission by consent. Provided this is the expressed and acted upon intention, the time of the rescission, whether a moment before or at the same time as the making of the new contract, is unimportant.

The decisions are numerous and divergent where one of the parties to a contract refuses to perform unless paid an additional amount. Some states hold the new promise to pay the demand binding though there be no rescission. It is said that the new promise is given to secure performance in place of an action for damages for not performing (Parrot v. Mexican Central Railway, 207 Mass. 184, 93 N.E. 590, 334 L.R.A.[N.S.] 261), or that the new contract is evidence of the rescission of the old one and it is the same as if no previous contract had been made (Coyner v. Lynde, 10 Ind. 282; Connelly v. Devoe, 37 Conn. 570; Goebel v. Linn, 47 Mich. 489, 11 N.W. 284, 41 Am.Rep. 723); or that unforeseen difficulties and hardships modify the rule (King v. Duluth, etc., Ry. Co., 61 Minn. 482, 63 N.W. 1105), or that the new contract is an attempt to mitigate the damages which may flow from the breach of the first (Endriss v. Belle Isle Ice

Co., 49 Mich. 279, 13 N.W. 590). See Anson's Law of Contract (Huffcut's Amer. Ed.) p. 114, § 138. To like effect are Blodgett v. Foster, 120 Mich. 392, 79 N.W. 625; Scanlon v. Northwood, 147 Mich. 139, 110 N.W. 493; Evans v. Oregon & Washington R. Co., 58 Wash. 429, 108 Pac. 1095, 28 L.R.A.(N.S.) 455; Main Street, etc., Co. v. Los Angeles Traction Co., 129 Cal. 301, 61 Pac. 937.

The contrary has been held in such cases as Carpenter v. Taylor, 164 N.Y. 171, 58 N.E. 53; Price v. Press Publishing Co., 117 App.Div. 854, 103 N.Y.Supp. 296; Davis & Co. v. Morgan, 117 Ga. 504, 43 S.E. 732, 61 L.R.A. 148, 97 Am.St.Rep. 171; Alaska Packers' Association v. Domenico, 117 Fed. 99, 54 C.C.A. 485; Conover v. Stillwell, 34 N.J.Law, 54, 57; Erny v. Sauer, 234 Pa. 330, 83 Atl. 205, Ann.Cas.1913C, 1241. In none of these cases, however, was there a full and complete rescission of the old contract and it is this with which we are dealing in this case. Rescission is not presumed; it is expressed; the old contract is not continued with modifications; it is ended and a new one made.

The efforts of the courts to give a legal reason for holding good a promise to pay an additional compensation for the fulfillment of a pre-existing contract is commented upon in note upon Abbott v. Doane (163 Mass. 433, 40 N.E. 197, 47 Am.St.Rep. 465) in 34 L.R.A. 33, 39, and the result reached is stated as follows:

"The almost universal rule is that without any express rescission of the old contract the promise is made simply for additional compensation, making the new promise a mere nudum pactum."

As before stated, in this case we have an express rescission and a new contract.

There is no reason that we can see why the parties to a contract may not come together and agree to cancel and rescind an existing contract, making a new one in its place. We are also of the opinion that reason and authority support the conclusion that both transactions can take place at the same time.

For the reasons here stated, the charge of the trial court was correct, and the judgments of the Appellate Division and the Appellate Term should be affirmed, with costs.

HISCOCK, C.J., and HOGAN, CARDOZO, McLAUGHLIN, and ANDREWS, JJ., concur.

CHASE, J., dissents.

Judgments affirmed.

3. Conditions versus Consideration

While past consideration and pre-existing duty are timing problems, the condition/consideration problem does not involve timing. Like the past consideration problem, the condition/consideration problem relates to the offer for a unilateral contract (the promise for a performance). The condition/consideration problem is a question of pure inducement: Did the offeror make a promise to induce the offeree's performance, or did the offeree perform in order to be in a position to receive the offeror's promise of a future gift? Was the offeree's performance the consideration for the offeror's promise or merely a condition that must be fulfilled by the offeree so the offeree will be in position to receive the offeror's promise of a future gift?

PROBLEM 11: Professor Williston, in his treatise on Contracts (1 Williston on Contracts 445 (Jaeger 3d ed. 1957), used the following illustration to demonstrate the difference between consideration and a condition: "[A] benevolent man says to a tramp,—'If you go around the corner to the clothing store there, you may purchase an overcoat on my credit.' "

1. What is the benevolent man's promise?
2. What was required of the tramp for him to receive the bounty of the benevolent man's promise?
3. What would a reasonable person believe was the benevolent man's motivation in asking the tramp to "go around the corner to the clothing store"?
4. Was the benevolent man asking for an exchange (a promise to purchase a coat in exchange for the tramp's walk) or did the benevolent man not seek an exchange but only that the tramp be in a position to receive the gift?

PROBLEM 12: A father told his son that if the son would move back to town, the father would start him in business.

1. What was the father's promise?
2. What was either the consideration for the father's promise or a condition for receiving the father's promise?
3. What would a reasonable person believe was motivating the father—an exchange or a gift promise if the son is in a position to receive the father's promise of a future gift?

Section 3. ALTERNATIVES TO CLASSICAL CONSIDERATION

Under classical contracts law, consideration for the promisor's promise is an essential element of an offer. Without consideration, the promisor's promise is merely a promise to make a future gift and is unenforceable in court. Rigid adherence to this consideration doctrine in the past often led to unnecessarily harsh results. Modern contracts law employs two constructive methods to rectify this imbalance. The first involves legislative and judicial tinkering with the classical doctrine. The second introduces reliance as an alternative to consideration.

A. Tinkering With the Classical Doctrine

Both legislative bodies and courts tinker with the classical consideration doctrine. A legislature, by statute, may substitute a writing or a writing with a statement of intent to be bound for consideration. A statute could take one of the following forms:

> A written promise signed by the person promising is not unenforceable for lack of consideration.
>
> A written promise signed by the person promising is not unenforceable for lack of consideration if the writing contains an express statement, in any form of language, that the signer intends to be legally bound.

Rather than substitute a writing or a writing with an additional express statement, the legislature may alter the rule about which party has the burden of proving consideration. Traditional contracts law required the party introducing the contract to prove offer and acceptance, including the element of consideration for the promisor's promise. The following pair of statutes, Oklahoma Statutes Annotated title 15, §§ 114 & 115 (1981), shifts the burden of proof from the party introducing the contract to the party challenging the contract. A number of states have this statutory pattern.

> A written instrument is presumptive evidence of a consideration.
>
> The burden of showing a want of consideration sufficient to support an instrument lies with the party seeking to invalidate or avoid it.

These illustrative statutes apply to all transactions. A legislature may, however, write with a finer pen. It may eliminate the need for consideration in a specific type of transaction rather than in all transactions. Article Two of the Uniform Commercial Code, which has been enacted by the legislatures of all states except Louisiana, provides a good example. Article Two deals with transactions involving a sale of goods. UCC § 2–209(1) provides:

> (1) An agreement modifying a contract within this Article needs no consideration to be binding.

PROBLEM 13: Describe how the legislature is tinkering with the classical consideration doctrine in the following statute. Does the statute apply to all types of contracts or only to a specific type of transaction? Does the statute dispense with the need for consideration, or does it merely substitute something in its place?

> Every contract in writing hereafter made shall import a consideration in the same manner and as fully as sealed instruments have heretofore done.

PROBLEM 14: Describe how the legislature is tinkering with the classical consideration doctrine in the following statute. Does the statute apply to all types of contracts or only to a specific type of transaction? Does the statute dispense with the need for consideration, or does it merely substitute something in its place?

> An offer by a merchant to buy or sell goods in a signed writing which by its terms gives assurance that it will be held open is not revocable, for lack of consideration, during the time stated or if no time is stated for a reasonable time, but in no event may such period of irrevocability exceed three months; but any such term of assurance on a form supplied by the offeree must be separately signed by the offeror.

The legislatures have not been the only tinkerers with the classical consideration doctrine. The courts, at times, also have been active. The following case, ***Webb v. McGowin,*** presents an excellent illustration. On August 3, 1925, Joe Webb, an employee of the W.T. Smith Lumber Company was clearing the upper floor of a company mill by dropping the wood on that floor to the ground below. While Webb was in the act of dropping a 75–pound pine block from the upper floor to the ground below, he saw J. Greeley McGowin standing on the ground below. Webb knew that he could remain safely on the upper floor of the mill and allow the block to drop, but the block would fall on McGowin and cause him serious injury or death. Webb chose to hold on to the block as it fell to the ground, thus diverting it from McGowin's direction. McGowin was saved, but Webb suffered serious bodily injuries that left him crippled for life. On September 1, 1925, McGowin promised to pay Webb $15 every two weeks for the remainder of Webb's life in consideration for Webb's having prevented McGowin from sustaining death or serious bodily harm and in consideration of the injuries Webb received. The payments, made for almost nine years, were discontinued when McGowin died.

Webb sued McGowin's estate for breach of contract, and the estate responded by claiming a lack of consideration for McGowin's promise to pay. Webb's injury and saving of McGowin's life occurred before McGowin made his promise to pay Webb $15 every two weeks. McGowin's promise to pay did not induce Webb to act.

The Court of Appeals of Alabama found in favor of Webb. How does the court tinker with the classical consideration doctrine to resolve the timing problem? The consideration was performed before the promisor promised; therefore, the promisor's promise was not made to induce the promisee to perform. Is the court's attempted analogy between a physician and a patient sound? Was there a contract in the physician/patient situation or was relief based on restitution as a cause of action? (See the discussion of Restatement of Restitution § 116, Chapter 3). Is the court's reliance on the wayward bull case, *Boothe v. Fitzpatrick,* also misplaced because that too was a restitution cause of action?

We have discussed the inability of a moral obligation to serve as consideration. (See page 110.) In *Webb v. McGowin,* the court linked moral obligation with a material benefit received by the promisor. The court stated that the moral obligation was the consideration for the promisor's promise (see paragraph number 2 in the court's opinion). Do you agree with this rationale?

The court referred to an alternative solution involving a prior legal or equitable obligation, which has become unenforceable, followed by subsequent promise to pay (see paragraph number 3). Is this rationale applicable to this case? Did McGowin have either a legal or equitable obligation to pay Webb before he made his promise to Webb?

Do you agree with the outcome? Do you agree with either rationale? If you agree with the outcome but disagree with the rationale, suggest a better rationale. Could the promise to pay have occurred by implication when McGowin looked up and saw the block with his name on it, teetering on the edge of the upper floor of the mill?

Webb v. McGowin

Court of Appeals of Alabama, 1935.
27 Ala. App. 82, 168 So. 196, certiorari denied, 232 Ala. 374, 168 So. 199 (1936).

1. The averments of the complaint show that appellant saved McGowin from death or grievous bodily harm. This was a material benefit to him of infinitely more value than any financial aid he could have received. Receiving this benefit, McGowin became morally bound to compensate appellant for the services rendered. Recognizing his moral obligation, he expressly agreed to pay appellant as alleged in the complaint and complied with this agreement up to the time of his death; a period of more than 8 years.

Had McGowin been accidentally poisoned and a physician, without his knowledge or request, had administered an antidote, thus saving his life, a subsequent promise by McGowin to pay the physician would have been valid. Likewise, McGowin's agreement as disclosed by the complaint to compensate appellant for saving him from death or grievous bodily injury is valid and enforceable.

Where the promisee cares for, improves, and preserves the property of the promisor, though done without his request, it is sufficient consideration for the promisor's subsequent agreement to pay for the service, because of the material benefit received. Pittsburg Vitrified Paving & Building Brick Co. v. Cerebus Oil Co., 79 Kan. 603, 100 P. 631; Edson v. Poppe, 24 S.D. 466, 124 N.W. 441, 26 L.R.A.(N.S.) 534; Drake v. Bell, 26 Misc. 237, 55 N.Y.S. 945.

In Boothe v. Fitzpatrick, 36 Vt. 681, the court held that a promise by defendant to pay for the past keeping of a bull which had escaped from defendant's premises and been cared for by plaintiff was valid, although there was no previous request, because the subsequent promise obviated that objection; it being equivalent to a previous request. On the same principle, had the promisee saved the promisor's life or his body from grievous harm, his subsequent promise to pay for the services rendered would have been valid. Such service would have been far more material than caring for his bull. Any holding that saving a man from death or grievous bodily harm is not a material benefit sufficient to uphold a subsequent promise to pay for the service, necessarily rests on the assumption that saving life and preservation of the body from harm have only a sentimental value. The converse of this is true. Life and preservation of the body have material, pecuniary values, measurable in dollars and cents. Because of this, physicians practice their profession charging for services rendered in saving life and curing the body of its ills, and surgeons perform operations. The same is true as to the law of negligence, authorizing the assessment of damages in personal injury cases based upon the extent of the injuries, earnings, and life expectancies of those injured.

In the business of life insurance, the value of a man's life is measured in dollars and cents according to his expectancy, the soundness of his body, and his ability to pay premiums. The same is true as to health and accident insurance.

It follows that if, as alleged in the complaint, appellant saved J. Greeley McGowin from death or grievous bodily harm, and McGowin subsequently agreed to pay him for the service rendered, it became a valid and enforceable contract.

2. It is well settled that a moral obligation is a sufficient consideration to support a subsequent promise to pay where the promisor has received a material benefit, although there was no original duty or liability resting on the promisor. Lycoming County v. Union County, 15 Pa. 166, 53 Am.Dec. 575, 579, 580; Ferguson v. Harris, 39 S.C. 323, 17 S.E. 782, 39 Am.St.Rep. 731, 734; Muir v. Kane, 55 Wash. 131, 104 P. 153, 26 L.R.A.(N.S.) 519, 19 Ann.Cas. 1180; State ex rel. Bayer v. Funk, 105 Or. 134, 199 P. 592, 209 P. 113, 25 A.L.R. 625, 634; Hawkes v. Saunders, 1 Cowp. 290; In re Sutch's Estate, 201 Pa. 305, 50 A. 943; Edson v. Poppe, 24 S.D. 466, 124 N.W. 441, 26 L.R.A.(N.S.) 534; Park Falls State Bank v. Fordyce, 206 Wis. 628, 238 N.W. 516, 79 A.L.R. 1339; Baker v. Gregory, 28 Ala. 544, 65 Am.Dec. 366. In the case of State ex rel. Bayer v. Funk, supra, the court held that a moral obligation is a sufficient consideration to support an executory promise where the promisor has received an actual pecuniary or material benefit for which he subsequently expressly promised to pay.

The case at bar is clearly distinguishable from that class of cases where the consideration is a mere moral obligation or conscientious duty unconnected with receipt by promisor of benefits of a material or pecuniary nature. Park Falls State Bank v. Fordyce, supra. Here the promisor received a material benefit constituting a valid consideration for his promise.

3. Some authorities hold that, for a moral obligation to support a subsequent promise to pay, there must have existed a prior

legal or equitable obligation, which for some reason had become unenforceable, but for which the promisor was still morally bound. This rule, however, is subject to qualification in those cases where the promisor, having received a material benefit from the promisee, is morally bound to compensate him for the services rendered and in consideration of this obligation promises to pay. In such cases the subsequent promise to pay is an affirmance or ratification of the services rendered carrying with it the presumption that a previous request for the service was made. McMorris v. Herndon, 2 Bailey (S.C.) 56, 21 Am.Dec. 515; Chadwick v. Knox, 31 N.H. 226, 64 Am.Dec. 329; Kenan v. Holloway, 16 Ala. 53, 50 Am.Dec. 162; Ross v. Pearson, 21 Ala. 473.

Under the decisions above cited, McGowin's express promise to pay appellant for the services rendered was an affirmance or ratification of what appellant had done raising the presumption that the services had been rendered at McGowin's request.

4. The averments of the complaint show that in saving McGowin from death or grievous bodily harm, appellant was crippled for life. This was part of the consideration of the contract declared on. McGowin was benefited. Appellant was injured. Benefit to the promisor or injury to the promisee is a sufficient legal consideration for the promisor's agreement to pay. Fisher v. Bartlett, 8 Greenl. (Me.) 122, 22 Am.Dec. 225; State ex rel. Bayer v. Funk, supra.

5. Under the averments of the complaint the services rendered by appellant were not gratuitous. The agreement of McGowin to pay and the acceptance of payment by appellant conclusively shows the contrary.

From what has been said, we are of the opinion that the court below erred in the ruling complained of; that is to say, in sustaining the demurrer, and for this error the case is reversed and remanded.

Reversed and remanded.

SAMFORD, Judge (concurring).

The questions involved in this case are not free from doubt, and perhaps the strict letter of the rule, as stated by judges, though not always in accord, would bar a recovery by plaintiff, but following the principle announced by Chief Justice Marshall in Hoffman v. Porter, Fed.Cas. No. 6,577, 2 Brock. 156, 159, where he says, "I do not think that law ought to be separated from justice, where it is at most doubtful," I concur in the conclusions reached by the court.

Webb v. McGowin involved a promise to pay for a benefit already received by McGowin, the promisor, and for a detriment already suffered by Webb, the promisee. The following case, *Watkins & Son, Inc. v. Carrig,* presents a different type of transaction—one involving a promise to pay additional sums for performance already due under a pre-existing contract.

Watkins & Son, a contractor, entered into a written contract with Carrig to excavate a cellar for Carrig at a stated price. Soon after the excavating began, Watkins discovered solid rock and became disenchanted with the payment terms under the contract. Watkins and Carrig discussed the matter, and Carrig orally agreed to pay nine times the unit price for any rock excavated. Watkins completed the excavation, which proved to be two-thirds rock. When Carrig refused to pay the higher price, Watkins sued for breach of contract. Carrig defended on the ground that his promise to pay the higher price was without consideration because Watkins was under a pre-existing duty resulting from the prior contract to excavate at the lower price.

Should Watkins & Son receive the higher price? Where does Justice Allen of the New Hampshire Supreme Court find the consideration for Carrig's promise to pay the higher amount? Do you agree with the result? Do you agree with the rationale? If you agree with the result but not with the rationale, what better rationale do you suggest?

Watkins & Son, Inc. v. Carrig

Supreme Court of New Hampshire, 1941.
91 N.H. 459, 21 A.2d 591.

ALLEN, Chief Justice. . . .

The issue whether the grant of relief constituted a valid contract is one of difficulty. The basic rule that a promise without consideration for it is invalid leads to its logical application that a promise to pay for what the promisor already has a right to receive from the promisee is invalid. The promisee's performance of an existing duty is no detriment to him, and hence nothing is given by him beyond what is already due the promisor. But the claim is here made that the original contract was rescinded, either in full or in respect to some of its terms, by mutual consent, and since any rescission mutually agreed upon is in itself a contract, the claim of a promise to pay for performance of a subsisting duty is unfounded. The terms of the contract of rescission are of course valid if the rescission is valid. The defendant's answer to this claim is well stated in this quotation from Williston, Contr., 2d Ed., § 130a: "But calling an agreement an agreement for rescission does not do away with the necessity of consideration, and when the agreement for rescission is coupled with a further agreement that the work provided for in the earlier agreement shall be completed and that the other party shall give more than he originally promised, the total effect of the second agreement is that one party promises to do exactly what he had previously bound himself to do, and the other party promises to give an additional compensation therefor."

With due respect for this eminent authority, the argument appears to clothe consideration with insistence of control beyond its proper demands. With full recognition of the legal worthlessness of a bare promise and of performance of a subsisting duty as a void consideration, a result accomplished by proper means is not necessarily bad because it would be bad if the means were improper or were not employed.

It is not perceived that the requirement of consideration is necessarily disregarded in spite of the net result of a promise to pay more for less, without additional obligation of the promisee. If the process in reaching such a result is inoffensive to the doctrine of consideration, the result does not become a naked promise. If in analysis of the transaction compliance with the elements of a valid contract may be found, it is hardly a perversion of principle to give the steps taken recognition. The result being reasonable, the means taken to reach it may be examined to determine their propriety.

In common understanding there is, importantly, a wide divergence between a bare promise and a promise in adjustment of a contractual promise already outstanding. A promise with no supporting consideration would upset well and long-established human interrelations if the law did not treat it as a vain thing. But parties to a valid contract generally understand that it is subject to any mutual action they may take in its performance. Changes to meet changes in circumstances and conditions should be valid if the law is to carry out its function and service by rules conformable with reasonable practices and understandings in matters of business and commerce.

Rescission in full or in modification being intended, it should be effective although the result benefits only one party and places a burden only on the other. It is the fact of rescission rather than the effect of it that determines its legal quality. The difference between a rescission unrelated to a new contract and one interdependent with a new contract, with the result the same in each case, signifies no failure of consideration in the latter case. The result, whatever it may be, is indecisive of the contractual character of the transaction. The steps taken being pointed out by the law, the result should not be held an idle one. Merger of the rescission and promise into one transaction does not destroy them as elements composing the transaction.

In another analysis of the transaction, more than a naked promise to pay more than the promisor owed appears. The promise was accompanied by the mutual understanding that the terms of the contract were to be modified. The conclusion follows that if the promisor had the right under the contract to have rock excavated at the same price as was to be paid for other material, he surrendered it. Conceding that the plaintiff did no more than the contract called for, yet if it was presented with a discharge from its duty, as an element of the transaction, by application of the law of gifts a completed discharge of a liability was validly effected. The form of statement by which one surrenders a right, if the law does not have special requirements for it, may be in any words showing the act to be one of making a present. The gift here was not of the promise to pay more, but of release of the plaintiff's duty to work for less. Whether it was, in its character and form, a gift to which the law attaches validity, is to be considered.

The foregoing views are considered to meet the reasonable needs of standard and ethical practices of men in their business dealings with each other. Conceding that the plaintiff threatened to break its contract because it found the contract to be improvident, yet the defendant yielded to the threat without protest, excusing the plaintiff, and making a new arrangement. Not insisting on his rights but relinquishing them, fairly he should be held to the new arrangement. The law is a means to the end. It is not the law because it is the law, but because it is adapted and adaptable to establish and maintain reasonable order. If the phrase justice according to law were transposed into law according to justice, it would perhaps be more accurately expressive. In a case like this, of conflicting rules and authority, a result which is considered better to establish "fundamental justice and reasonableness" (Cavanaugh v. Boston & M. Railroad, 76 N.H. 68, 72, 79 A. 694, 696), should be attained. It is not practical that the law should adopt all precepts of moral conduct, but it is desirable that its rules and principles should not run counter to them in the important conduct and transactions of life.

Exceptions overruled.

B. Reliance as an Alternative to Consideration

Legislative and judicial tinkering have produced results in a crazy quilt fashion. Sometimes judicial tinkering has resolved only the dispute between a specific plaintiff and defendant. Legislative tinkering has been limited to certain types of transactions, such as sale of goods, or has distinguished written from nonwritten promises. This tinkering has not produced a solution applicable to all transactions.

Currently emerging in the courts is a solution that applies to all transactions. It is based on reliance as an alternative to consideration. The Restatement (Second) of

Contracts § 90, entitled "Promise Reasonably Inducing Action or Forbearance," has become the focus for this movement:

> (1) A promise which the promisor should reasonably expect to induce action or forbearance on the part of the promisee or a third person and which does induce such action or forbearance is binding if injustice can be avoided only by enforcement of the promise. The remedy granted for breach may be limited as justice requires.

This is the second time that we have discussed reliance as an alternative. The first reference to reliance was during our discussion of the pre-offer phase. At the pre-offer phase, neither party attempted to make an offer and the discussion was clearly preliminary negotiation. One party, however, relied on a statement made by the other during the preliminary negotiation. In that situation, a cause of action for reliance might be available to the party relying on the statement.

In contrast, here the transaction has moved beyond preliminary negotiation. One party has done exactly what he or she set out to do—make a promise to the other. This promise was not an offer because the promisor's promise lacked consideration. A common situation is the promisor's promise to make a future gift. There the promisor's promise lacks consideration and is therefore not an offer. If the promisee relies on the promisor's promise to make a future gift at a "cost" to the promisee, should not the promisee be compensated for his or her injury? The four elements of reliance as an alternative to consideration are

1. a promise;
2. the promisor's reasonable expectation that the promise will induce action or forbearance;
3. the promise does induce such action or forbearance; and
4. injustice can be avoided only by enforcement of the promise.

The Restatement (Second) of Contracts § 90 makes the point that "The remedy granted for breach may be limited as justice requires." Thus the remedy may not necessarily protect the expectation interest, a remedy that would place the aggrieved party in the position he or she would have been in if the contract had been fully performed. Rather, the remedy for breach of the promisor's promise may be limited to compensation for the injury induced by the promisee's reliance on the promisor's promise.

EXAMPLE

A father promised his twenty-two-year-old son $20,000 when his son became twenty-five. In anticipation of receiving $20,000 at age twenty-five, the son spent $17,000 on a new car, a purchase he would not have made if his father had not promised him the gift. When the son became twenty-five, the father refused to pay. Because the father's promise was for a future gift, there was no consideration for the father's promise and it would not constitute an offer. Had the father made an offer to the son and the son accepted, the son would be entitled to his expectation—$20,000 at age twenty-five. Because no offer and thus no contract were made, the son is not entitled to protection of his expectation interest. If reliance is a substitute for consideration, the father's promise is enforceable. The son, however, may not be entitled to $20,000, his expectation had the father fully performed. The son would be entitled to a remedy that "may be limited as justice requires." Because the action is based on reliance, the remedy should be based on reliance as well. Therefore the son's reliance interest should be protected, and he should recover for his injury suffered by relying—$17,000 or less.

The following two cases, *Ricketts v. Scothorn* and *Feinberg v. Pfeiffer Co.,* illustrate the use of reliance before and after the promulgation of Restatements of Contracts § 90. In *Ricketts,* a case involving the early evolution of the reliance doctrine, Mrs. Scothorn had been given a $2,000 note by her grandfather. When her grandfather died and his executor refused to pay, should Mrs. Scothorn be able to enforce his note?

Focus on the court's rationale. Do you agree that the grandfather's promise was without consideration? In looking for precedent, does the court agree with the rationale of the church and college cases that "the expenditure of money or assumption of liability by the donee on the faith of the promise constitutes a valuable and sufficient consideration"? What rationale did the *Ricketts* court prefer?

The court used the phrase "equitable estoppel." Compare the elements for "equitable estoppel" in *Ricketts* with those set forth previously for reliance (see Chapter 3). In this context, equitable estoppel means the party challenging the lack of consideration for his or her promise is precluded from doing so because his or her promise induced the other party to rely to his detriment. If equitable estoppel is taken to its logical conclusion, the preclusion of the lack of consideration argument leaves the promise as if it had consideration and thus an offer. The offer forms a contract, and the contract is enforced as are all other contracts. Thus the nonbreaching party would be entitled to protection of his or her expectation, reliance, or restitution interests and not just his or her reliance interest. What interest did the *Ricketts* court protect?

Ricketts v. Scothorn

Supreme Court of Nebraska, 1898.
57 Neb. 51, 77 N.W. 365.

SULLIVAN, J. In the district court of Lancaster county the plaintiff, Katie Scothorn, recovered judgment against the defendant, Andrew D. Ricketts, as executor of the last will and testament of John C. Ricketts, deceased. The action was based upon a promissory note, of which the following is a copy: "May the first, 1891. I promise to pay to Katie Scothorn on demand, $2,000, to be at 6 per cent. per annum. J.C. Ricketts."

The material facts are undisputed. They are as follows: John C. Ricketts, the maker of the note, was the grandfather of the plaintiff. Early in May—presumably on the day the note bears date—he called on her at the store where she was working. What transpired between them is thus described by Mr. Flodene, one of the plaintiff's witnesses: "A. Well, the old gentleman came in there one morning about nine o'clock, probably a little before or a little after, but early in the morning, and he unbuttoned his vest, and took out a piece of paper in the shape of a note; that is the way it looked to me; and he says to Miss Scothorn, 'I have fixed out something that you have not got to work any more.' He says, none of my grandchildren work, and you don't have to. Q. Where was she? A. She took the piece of paper and kissed him, and kissed the old gentleman, and commenced to cry." It seems Miss Scothorn immediately notified her employer of her intention to quit work, and that she did soon after abandon her occupation. The mother of the plaintiff was a witness, and testified that she had a conversation with her father, Mr. Ricketts, shortly after the note was executed, in which he informed her that he had given the note to the plaintiff to enable her to quit work; that none of his grandchildren worked, and he did not think she ought to. For something more than a year the plaintiff was without an occupation, but in September, 1892, with the consent of her grandfather, and by his assistance, she secured a position as bookkeeper with Messrs. Funke & Ogden. On June 8, 1894, Mr. Ricketts died. He had paid one year's interest on the note, and a short time before his death expressed regret that he had not been able to pay the balance. In the summer or fall of 1892 he stated to his daughter, Mrs. Scothorn, that if he could sell his farm in Ohio he would pay the note out of the proceeds. He at no time repudiated the obligation. We quite agree with counsel for the defendant that upon this evidence there was nothing to submit to the jury, and that a verdict should have been directed peremptorily for one of the parties. The testimony of Flodene and Mrs. Scothorn, taken together, conclusively establishes the fact that the note was not given in consideration of the plaintiff pursuing, or agreeing to pursue, any particular line of conduct. There was no promise on the part of the plaintiff to do, or refrain from doing, anything. Her right to the money promised in the note was not made to depend upon an abandonment of her employment with Mayer Bros., and future abstention from like service. Mr. Ricketts made no condition, requirement, or request. He exacted no quid pro quo. He gave the note as a gratuity, and looked for nothing in return. So far as the evidence discloses, it was his purpose to place the plaintiff in a position of independence, where she could work or remain idle, as she might choose. The abandonment of Miss Scothorn of her position as bookkeeper was altogether voluntary. It was not an act done in fulfillment of any contract obligation assumed when she accepted the note. The instrument in suit, being given without any valuable consideration, was nothing more than a promise to make a gift in the future of the sum of money therein named. Ordinarily, such promises are not enforceable, even when put in the form of a promissory note. Kirkpatrick v. Taylor, 43 Ill. 207; Phelps v. Phelps, 28 Barb. 121; Johnston v. Griest, 85 Ind. 503; Fink v. Cox, 18 Johns. 145. But it has often been held that an action on a note given to a church, college, or other like institution, upon the faith of which money has been expended or obligations incurred, could not be successfully defended on the ground of a want of consideration. Barnes v. Perine, 12 N.Y. 18; Philomath College v. Hartless, 6 Or. 158; Thompson v. Board, 40 Ill. 379; Irwin v. Lombard University, 56 Ohio St. 9, 46 N.E. 63. In this class of cases the note in suit is nearly always spoken of as a gift or donation, but the decision is generally put on the ground that the expenditure of money or assumption of liability by the donee on the faith of the promise constitutes a valuable and sufficient consideration. It seems to us that the true reason is the preclusion of the defendant, under the doctrine of estoppel, to deny the consideration. Such seems to be the view of the matter taken by the supreme court of Iowa in the case of Simpson Centenary College v. Tuttle, 71 Iowa, 596, 33 N.W. 74, where Rothrock, J., speaking for the court, said: "Where a note, however, is based on a promise to give for the support of the objects referred to, it may still be open to this defense [want of consideration], unless it shall appear that the donee has, prior to any revocation, entered into engagements, or made expenditures based on such promise, so that he must suffer loss or injury if the note is not paid. This is based on the equitable principle that, after allowing the donee to incur obligations on the faith that the note would be paid, the donor would be estopped from pleading want of consideration."

According to the undisputed proof, as shown by the record before us, the plaintiff was a working girl, holding a position in which she earned a salary of $10 per week, Her grandfather, desiring to put her in a position of independence, gave her the note, accompanying it with the remark that his other grandchildren did not work, and that she would not be obliged to work any longer. In effect, he suggested that she might abandon her employment, and rely in the future upon the bounty which he promised. He doubtless desired that she should give up her occupation, but, whether he did or not, it is entirely certain that he contemplated such action on her part as a reasonable and probable consequence of his gift. Having intentionally influenced the plaintiff to alter her position for the worse on the faith of the note being paid when due, it would be grossly inequitable to permit the maker, or his executor, to resist payment on the ground that the promise was given without consideration. The petition charges the elements of an equitable estoppel, and the evidence conclusively establishes them. If errors intervened at the trial, they could not have been prejudicial. A verdict for the defendant would be unwarranted. The judgment is right, and is affirmed.

In *Feinberg v. Pfeiffer Co.,* Mrs. Feinberg, a longtime employee of the Pfeiffer Company, was promised retirement income when she retired. Eighteen months later, Feinberg, relying on Pfeiffer's promise, retired. When Pfeiffer Company changed management and subsequently refused to pay, should Mrs. Feinberg be able to enforce the company's promise?

Focus on the court's rationale. Do you agree that the Pfeiffer Company's promise was without consideration?

Why does the court use the phrase "promissory estoppel" rather than "equitable estoppel"? Should the term "estoppel" even be used? Would "reliance" or "detrimental reliance" be a better term? Does the Restatement of Contracts § 90 use the term "estoppel"?

What is the rationale used by the *Feinberg* court to resolve the dispute? Does Feinberg's recovery protect her expectation or reliance interest?

Feinberg v. Pfeiffer Co.

Court of Appeals of Missouri, 1959.
322 S.W.2d 163.

DOERNER, Commissioner.

This is a suit brought in the Circuit Court of the City of St. Louis by plaintiff, a former employee of the defendant corporation, on an alleged contract whereby defendant agreed to pay plaintiff the sum of $200 per month for life upon her retirement. A jury being waived, the case was tried by the court alone. Judgment below was for plaintiff for $5,100, the amount of the pension claimed to be due as of the date of the trial, together with interest thereon, and defendant duly appealed.

The parties are in substantial agreement on the essential facts. Plaintiff began working for the defendant, a manufacturer of pharmaceuticals, in 1910, when she was but 17 years of age. By 1947 she had attained the position of bookkeeper, office manager, and assistant treasurer of the defendant, and owned 70 shares of its stock out of a total of 6,503 shares issued and outstanding. Twenty shares had been given to her by the defendant or its then president, she had purchased 20, and the remaining 30 she had acquired by a stock split or stock dividend. Over the years she received substantial dividends on the stock she owned, as did all of the other stockholders. Also, in addition to her salary, plaintiff from 1937 to 1949, inclusive, received each year a bonus varying in amount from $300 in the beginning to $2,000 in the later years.

On December 27, 1947, the annual meeting of the defendant's Board of Directors was held at the Company's offices in St. Louis, presided over by Max Lippman, its then president and largest individual stockholder. The other directors present were George L. Marcus, Sidney Harris, Sol Flammer, and Walter Weinstock, who, with Max Lippman, owned 5,007 of the 6,503 shares then issued and outstanding. At that meeting the Board of Directors adopted the following resolution, which, because it is the crux of the case, we quote in full:

"The Chairman thereupon pointed out that the Assistant Treasurer, Mrs. Anna Sacks Feinberg, has given the corporation many years of long and faithful service. Not only has she served the corporation devotedly, but with exceptional ability and skill. The President pointed out that although all of the officers and directors sincerely hoped and desired that Mrs. Feinberg would continue in her present position for as long as she felt able, nevertheless, in view of the length of service which she has contributed provision should be made to afford her retirement privileges and benefits which should become a firm obligation of the corporation to be available to her whenever she should see fit to retire from active duty, however many years in the future such retirement may become effective. It was, accordingly, proposed that Mrs. Feinberg's salary which is presently $350.00 per month, be increased to $400.00 per month, and that Mrs. Feinberg would be given the privilege of retiring from active duty at any time she may elect to see fit so to do upon a retirement pay of $200.00 per month for life, with the distinct understanding that the retirement plan is merely being adopted at the present time in order to afford Mrs. Feinberg security for the future and in the hope that her active services will continue with the corporation for many years to come. After due discussion and consideration, and upon motion duly made and seconded, it was—

"Resolved, that the salary of Anna Sacks Feinberg be increased from $350.00 to $400.00 per month and that she be afforded the privilege of retiring from active duty in the corporation at any time she may elect to see fit so to do upon retirement pay of $200.00 per month, for the remainder of her life."

At the request of Mr. Lippman his sons-in-law, Messrs. Harris and Flammer, called upon the plaintiff at her apartment on the same day to advise her of the passage of the resolution. Plaintiff testified on cross-examination that she had no prior information that such a pension plan was contemplated, that it came as a surprise to her, and that she would have continued in her employment whether or not such a resolution had been adopted. It is clear from the evidence that there was no contract, oral or written, as to plaintiff's length of employment, and that she was free to quit, and the defendant to discharge her, at any time.

Plaintiff did continue to work for the defendant through June 30, 1949, on which date she retired. In accordance with the foregoing resolution, the defendant began paying her the sum of $200 on the first of each month. Mr. Lippman died on November 18, 1949, and was succeeded as president of the company by his widow. Because of an illness, she retired from that office and was succeeded in October, 1953, by her son-in-law, Sidney M. Harris. Mr. Harris testified that while Mrs. Lippman had been president she signed the monthly pension check paid plaintiff, but fussed about doing so, and considered the payments as gifts. After his election, he stated, a new accounting firm employed by the defendant questioned the validity of the payments to plaintiff on several occasions, and in the Spring of 1956, upon its recommendation, he consulted the Company's then attorney, Mr. Ralph Kalish. Harris testified that both Ernst and Ernst, the accounting firm, and Kalish told him there was no need of giving plaintiff the money. He also stated that he had concurred in the view that the payments to plaintiff were mere gratuities rather than amounts due under a contractual obligation, and that following his discussion with the Company's attorney plaintiff was sent a check for $100 on April 1, 1956. Plaintiff declined to accept the reduced amount, and this action followed. Additional facts will be referred to later in this opinion.

Appellant's next complaint is that there was insufficient evidence to support the court's findings that plaintiff would not have quit defendant's employ had she not known and relied upon the promise of defendant to pay her $200 a month for life, and the finding that, from her voluntary retirement until April 1, 1956, plaintiff relied upon the continued receipt of the pension installments. The trial court so found, and, in our opinion, justifiably so. Plaintiff testified, and was corroborated by Harris, defendant's witness, that knowledge of the passage of the resolution was communicated to her on December 27, 1947, the very day it was adopted. She was told at that time by Harris and Flammer, she stated, that she could take the pension as of that day, if she wished. She testified further that she continued to work for another year and a half, through June 30, 1949; that at that time her health was good and she could have continued to work, but that after working for almost forty years she thought she would take a rest. Her testimony continued:

"Q. Now, what was the reason—I'm sorry. Did you then quit the employment of the company after you—after this year and a half? A. Yes.

"Q. What was the reason that you left? A. Well, I thought almost forty years, it was a long time and I thought I would take a little rest.

"Q. Yes. A. And with the pension and what earnings my husband had, we figured we could get along.

"Q. Did you rely upon this pension? A. We certainly did.

"Q. Being paid? A. Very much so. We relied upon it because I was positive that I was going to get it as long as I lived.

"Q. Would you have left the employment of the company at that time had it not been for this pension? A. No.

"Mr. Allen: Just a minute, I object to that as calling for a conclusion and conjecture on the part of this witness.

"The Court: It will be overruled.

"Q. (Mr. Agatstein continuing): Go ahead, now. The question is whether you would have quit the employment of the company at that time had you not relied upon this pension plan? A. No, I wouldn't.

"Q. You would not have. Did you ever seek employment while this pension was being paid to you—A. (interrupting): No.

"Q. Wait a minute, at any time prior—at any other place? A. No, sir.

"Q. Were you able to hold any other employment during that time? A. Yes, I think so.

"Q. Was your health good? A. My health was good."

It is obvious from the foregoing that there was ample evidence to support the findings of fact made by the court below.

We come, then, to the basic issue in the case. While otherwise defined in defendant's third and fourth assignments of error, it is thus succinctly stated in the argument in its brief: " . . . whether plaintiff has proved that she has a right to recover from defendant based upon a legally binding contractual obligation to pay her $200 per month for life."

It is defendant's contention, in essence, that the resolution adopted by its Board of Directors was a mere promise to make a gift, and that no contract resulted either thereby, or when plaintiff retired, because there was no consideration given or paid by the plaintiff. It urges that a promise to make a gift is not binding unless supported by a legal consideration; that the only apparent consideration for the adoption of the foregoing resolution was the "many years of long and faithful service" expressed therein; and that past services are not a valid consideration for a promise. Defendant argues further that there is nothing in the resolution which made its effectiveness conditional upon plaintiff's continued employment, that she was not under contract to work for any length of time but was free to quit whenever she wished, and that she had no contractual right to her position and could have been discharged at any time.

Plaintiff concedes that a promise based upon past services would be without consideration, but contends that there were two other elements which supplied the required element: First, the continuation by plaintiff in the employ of the defendant for the period from December 27, 1947, the date when the resolution was adopted, until the date of her retirement on June 30, 1949. And, second, her change of position, i.e., her retirement, and the abandonment by her of her opportunity to continue in gainful employment, made in reliance on defendant's promise to pay her $200 per month for life.

We must agree with the defendant that the evidence does not support the first of these contentions. There is no language in the resolution predicating plaintiff's right to a pension upon her continued employment. She was not required to work for the defendant for any period of time as a condition to gaining such retirement benefits. She was told that she could quit the day upon which the resolution was adopted, as she herself testified, and it is clear from her own testimony that she made no promise or agreement to continue in the employ of the defendant in return for its promise to pay her a pension. Hence there was lacking that mutuality of obligation which is essential to the validity of a contract.

. . .

But as to the second of these contentions we must agree with plaintiff. By the terms of the resolution defendant promised to pay plaintiff the sum of $200 a month upon her retirement. . . .

Section 90 of the Restatement of the Law of Contracts states that: "A promise which the promisor should reasonably expect to induce action or forbearance of a definite and substantial character on the part of the promisee and which does induce such action or forbearance is binding if injustice can be avoided only by enforcement of the promise." This doctrine has been described as that of "promissory estoppel," as distinguished from that of equitable estoppel or estoppel in pais, the reason for the differentiation being stated as follows:

> "It is generally true that one who has led another to act in reasonable reliance on his representations of fact cannot afterwards in litigation between the two deny the truth of the representations, and some courts have sought to apply this principle to the formation of contracts, where, relying on a gratuitous promise, the promisee has suffered detriment. It is to be noticed, however, that such a case does not come within the ordinary definition of estoppel. If there is any representation of an existing fact, it is only that the promisor at the time of making the promise intends to fulfill it. As to such intention there is usually no misrepresentation and if there is, it is not that which has injured the promisee. In other words, he relies on a promise and not on a misstatement of fact; and the term 'promissory' estoppel or something equivalent should be used to make the distinction." Williston on Contracts, Rev.Ed., Sec. 139, Vol. 1.

In speaking of this doctrine, Judge Learned Hand said in Porter v. Commissioner of Internal Revenue, 2 Cir., 60 F.2d 673, 675, that " . . . 'promissory estoppel' is now a recognized species of consideration." . . .

Was there such an act on the part of plaintiff, in reliance upon the promise contained in the resolution, as will estop the defendant, and therefore create an enforceable contract under the doctrine of promissory estoppel? We think there was. One of the illustrations cited under Section 90 of the Restatement is: "2. A promises B to pay him an annuity during B's life. B thereupon resigns a profitable employment, as A expected that he might. B receives the annuity for some years, in the meantime becoming disqualified from again obtaining good employment. A's promise is binding." This illustration is objected to by defendant as not being applicable to the case at hand. The reason advanced by it is that in the illustration B became "disqualified" from obtaining other employment *before* A discontinued the payments, whereas in this case the plaintiff did not discover that she had cancer and thereby became unemployable until *after* the defendant had discontinued the payments of $200 per month. We think the distinction is immaterial. The only reason for the reference in the illustration to the disqualification of A is in connection with that part of Section 90 regarding the prevention of injustice. The injustice would occur regardless of when the disability occurred. Would defendant contend that the contract would be enforceable if the plaintiff's illness had been discovered on March 31, 1956, the day before it discontinued the payment of the $200 a month, but not if it occurred on April 2nd, the day after? Furthermore, there are more ways to become disqualified for work, or unemployable, than as the result of illness. At the time she retired plaintiff was 57 years of age. At the time the payments were discontinued she was over 63 years of age. It is a matter of common knowledge that it is virtually impossible for a woman of that age to find satisfactory employment, much less a position comparable to that which plaintiff enjoyed at the time of her retirement.

The fact of the matter is that plaintiff's subsequent illness was not the "action or forbearance" which was induced by the promise contained in the resolution. As the trial court correctly decided, such action on plaintiff's part was her retirement from a lucrative position in reliance upon defendant's promise to pay her an annuity or pension. In a very similar case, Ricketts v. Scothorn, 57 Neb. 51, 77 N.W. 365, 367, 42 L.R.A. 794, the Supreme Court of Nebraska said:

> " . . . According to the undisputed proof, as shown by the record before us, the plaintiff was a working girl, holding a position in which she earned a salary of $10 per week. Her grandfather, desiring to put her in a position of independence, gave her the note accompanying it with the remark that his other grandchildren did not work, and that she would not be obliged to work any longer. In effect, he suggested that she might abandon her employment, and rely in the future upon the bounty which he promised. He doubtless desired that she should give up her occupation, but, whether he did or not, it is entirely certain that he contemplated such action on her part as a reasonable and probable consequence of his gift. Having intentionally influenced the plaintiff to alter her position for the worse on the faith of the note being paid when due, it would be grossly inequitable to permit the maker, or his executor, to resist payment on the ground that the promise was given without consideration."

The Commissioner therefore recommends, for the reasons stated, that the judgment be affirmed.

PER CURIAM.

The foregoing opinion by DOERNER, C., is adopted as the opinion of the court. The judgment is, accordingly, affirmed.

WOLFE, P.J., and ANDERSON and RUDDY, JJ., concur.

PROBLEM 15: Marylou Maxwell, an honors student in high school, was offered a full tuition scholarship by Utopia College. Marylou turned down partial scholarships from other colleges so she could attend Utopia. After the second week of classes, Marylou was informed that Utopia could not honor its commitment to give her a full scholarship.

Did Utopia College make an offer to Marylou? What were the promisor's promise and the consideration for the promisor's promise?

If Utopia College did not extend an offer to Marylou because its promise lacked consideration, is there an alternative ground upon which she could recover? Could Marylou satisfy the four elements of reliance? Would she be entitled to protection of her expectation or reliance interest?

5

THE POST-OFFER/PRE-ACCEPTANCE PHASE

Not all offers are accepted. Many things can happen prior to acceptance: the offeree may fail to act in time and the offer will lapse; the offeror may revoke the offer; the offeree may reject the offer; the offeror or offeree may die or become incapacitated before the offer is accepted.

In some situations, the offeree may need time to decide whether to accept or reject the offer. Every minute the offeree takes to think about the offer is an additional minute the offeror has to revoke the offer. The risk of revocation can be eliminated if the offeror and offeree enter into a subsidiary contract while the offer is pending. This subsidiary contract is called an option contract. Classical contracts law required the parties to agree expressly to the option contract. Modern contracts law may imply an option contract when the offeree has relied on the offeror's promise in the original offer.

Section one of this chapter discusses the death of the offer prior to acceptance. Section two considers the offer that refuses to die; that is, an offer with a subsidiary express or implied option contract.

Section 1. THE DEATH OF AN OFFER PRIOR TO ACCEPTANCE

After the offeror has made an offer thereby conferring the power of acceptance on the offeree, the offeree's power can be terminated in several ways:

1. By the offeree's inaction
2. By the offeror's revocation of the offer
3. By the offeree's rejection of the offer
4. By death or incapacity of the offeror or offeree.

A. Death of the Offer by the Offeree's Inaction

An offer may state a termination date: "This offer will end at noon on Saturday, July 16th." Unless the offeree accepts by that time, the offer ceases to exist. A provision of this type gives the parties some certainty. The offeror knows that if the offeree fails to accept the offer before the specified date, the offeror is free to make other plans without informing the offeree. The offeree, on the other hand, knows there is only a limited time in which to decide to accept the offer. Although the offeror could revoke the offer prior to expiration of the stated time, at least the offeree knows the time in which the decision to accept must be made (provided the offeror does not revoke prior to the offeree's attempted acceptance).

PROBLEM 1: Describe a situation in which the offeror would find it desirable to have an express termination date in the offer.

If the offer fails to state the time at which it will cease to exist, the offer will end after a reasonable time. What is "a reasonable time" will vary with each transaction.

EXAMPLE

An offeree should have a substantially shorter time to accept an offer to sell grapes than an offer to sell an encyclopedia.

PROBLEM 2: What factors should be considered when determining whether an offer has lapsed because it has not been accepted within a reasonable time?

PROBLEM 3: Apply your factors from Problem 2 to the following situations. Determine when the offer will lapse.

1. An offer to sell Blackacre (100 acres of undeveloped farmland near the backside of nowhere).
2. An offer by the Ringling Brothers Circus to sell Sally, a trained elephant, to the Bumbling Brothers Circus.
3. An offer to sell a truckload of vine-ripened tomatoes to Safeway Stores.
4. An offer to buy a used automobile from the automobile's current owner.

PROBLEM 4: Of the previous four situations, which offer has the shortest and which the longest reasonable time, and why?

B. Death of the Offer by Revocation of the Offer

Prior to the time an offer lapses, the offeror may revoke it. As master of the offer, the offeror may terminate the power of acceptance as well as create it.

Revocation does not require an incantation. The only requirement for revocation is that it be clear to the offeree that the offer has been revoked. Revocation may take place as a result of direct or indirect communication between the offeror and offeree.

EXAMPLE

The offeree may learn from a reliable source that the offeror has contracted with a third party for the subject matter.

In the following case, *Hoover Motor Express Co. v. Clements Paper Co.,* record each event on a time line. Is the first event an offer or preliminary negotiation? Work through your time line until you come to the offer. Now look for the acceptance. What occurred before the acceptance? Was the language used by Hoover a revocation? Change the facts to strengthen Hoover's assertion that its statement was a revocation. Then change the facts to weaken Hoover's assertion that its statement was a revocation.

Hoover Motor Express Co. v. Clements Paper Co.

Supreme Court of Tennessee, 1951.
241 S.W.2d 851.

TOMLINSON, Justice.

On November 19, 1949 Hoover Motor Express Company, Inc. made and delivered to Clements Paper Company a written offer with reference to the purchase of certain real estate. There was no consideration paid for the offer. On January 20, 1950 Clements Paper Company made a written acceptance of that offer. Hoover refused to go forward with the transaction and Clements Paper Company brought suit for specific performance or, in the alternative, for damages. Hoover defended on the ground that it had withdrawn the offer before its acceptance. The Chancellor and the Court of Appeals concurred in sustaining the bill of Clements Paper Company and ordered a reference to the master for ascertainment of damages. The controversy was then presented to this Court by Hoover's petition for certiorari wherein it is insisted (1) that there is no concurrent finding on the controlling fact question; hence, that the evidence on that question may be reviewed de novo by this Court, and (2) that, assuming a concurrent finding on that question of fact, such finding is contrary under the law applicable to all the material evidence upon the question. The writ was granted and oral argument had.

All are agreed that in order to convert into a contract an offer for which no consideration was paid there must be an acceptance of that offer before it is withdrawn. The Chancellor found that Clements had shown by a preponderance of the evidence that Hoover had breached "the written contract entered into by and between the parties". Implicit in such conclusion is the finding that Hoover had not withdrawn the offer before its acceptance. The Court of Appeals expressly found that the offer had not been withdrawn before acceptance. There was, therefore, a concurrent finding of the two Courts upon that controlling question of fact.

If there is any material evidence to sustain the above stated concurrent finding of fact then this Court is bound thereby not only as to that finding but as well to an inference or conclusion reasonably drawn from the evidence that it is a fact. Conaway v. New York Life Ins. Co., 171 Tenn. 290, 295, 102 S.W.2d 66. Therefore, since we cannot consider the case de novo, we must look to the evidence most favorable to Clements and determine from it whether there is therein any material evidence in support of this concurrent finding or any testimony that reasonably supports an inference or conclusion that the offer had not been withdrawn before its acceptance on January 20.

Clements was represented in this transaction by its Vice-President, Mr. Williams. He wrote the letter of January 20, 1950 accepting the offer. It is not contended in behalf of Clements that there was any acceptance prior to that date. Williams closes that letter with this statement: "We are ready to comply with our part of this agreement and are calling on you to do the same." The statement just quoted suggests the thought that its author, Mr. Williams, realized at the time he wrote the letter that something previously had occurred which caused him to anticipate that Hoover might not "comply" by going forward with its prior offer, Mr. Williams' letter of acceptance notwithstanding. This is important in that it throws light upon the construction placed by Williams upon a phone conversation had on January 13, 1950 by him with Hoover.

Williams had been authorized by Clements Paper Company some time in December to accept the written offer made by Hoover on November 19. It would, therefore, have been a simple matter for him then to have written the letter of acceptance which he finally wrote on January 20. The record leaves no doubt of the fact that Williams intended to accept the offer provided he could not get from Hoover a substantially better trade that he, Williams, had in mind. He, therefore, withheld acceptance and undertook on several occasions to get in touch with Hoover for the purpose of procuring, if he could, that better trade. Fortunately for Williams, in so far as the keeping alive of the offer is concerned, he never got around to conveying to Hoover the changes or additions he had in mind. But he did take a step to that end on January 13, 1950 by phoning Hoover with the idea of promoting his proposition. It is upon the legal effect that must be given that phone conversation, *as testified to by Williams,* that the outcome of this case must depend. If it can be given a construction which reasonably supports the concurrent finding mentioned that construction must be given.

Mr. Williams testified that he got Mr. Hoover on the phone on January 13 and "told him that we were ready to go through with it and I would like to discuss it with him". The matter which he testifies that he wanted to discuss with Mr. Hoover was whether Hoover would permit Clements to retain an easement for certain purposes through the property which Hoover had offered to buy.

Williams testifies that in reply to Williams' statement that he, Williams, wanted to discuss the offer with Hoover that Hoover replied "Well, I don't know if we are ready. We have not decided, we might not want to go through with it".

Williams made several other statements in his testimony as to what Hoover said in this phone conversation. The following are quotations from Williams' testimony: "He said he thought they might not go through with it."

"Q. After you had talked to him on January 13, on the telephone, that is Mr. Eph Hoover, Jr., he indicated to you that he had made other plans or in some way 'indicated' to you that the company had made other plans? A. Yes."

. . .

"Q. You had been told that they had made other plans? A. No, I had not been told. He said that he didn't think they were going through with the proposal and that he would call me on January 17."

(Hoover did not call Williams after the January 13 phone conversation.)

. . .

"A. That they had other plans in mind and he would let me know. He was not sure if he was going through with the original proposition.

"Q. Did he definitely refuse to positively commit himself on January 13 that he would go through with it? A. That is right."

. . .

"It was a very short discussion. Frankly, I was very much shocked when I heard from him that they didn't plan to go through with it. I had made my plans and had gone to the extent of having this elevation made."

The interpretation which Mr. Williams placed upon what Hoover said to him in the phone conversation of January 13 is stated in Clements' bill of complaint as follows: "This was the first information, suggestion or intimation that complainant had received that the defendant would not or might not carry out its agreement or offer."

Our problem is reduced to answering the question as to whether there can reasonably be placed upon the above quoted testimony of Williams a construction that prevents the statement of Hoover, as testified to by Williams, from amounting to a withdrawal on January 13 of the offer before it was attempted on January 20 to accept it. This is true because "the continued existence of the offer until acceptance is, however, necessary to make possible the formation of the contract." 12 American Jurisprudence, page 531.

Although there is no Tennessee case deciding the point, in so far as we can find, the general rule is that express notice, in so many words, of withdrawal before acceptance of an offer of the character we have here is not required. In 55 American Jurisprudence, page 488, under a discussion of "Termination of Offer", there appears in the text, supported by reference to decisions, this statement: "It is sufficient to constitute a withdrawal that knowledge of acts by the offerer inconsistent with the continuance of the offer is brought home to the offeree."

The same principle is declared to be the law in the text of 17 Corpus Juris Secundum, Contracts, § 50, page 398 in this language: "it being sufficient that the person making the offer does some act inconsistent with it, as, for example, selling the property, and that the person to whom the offer was made has knowledge of such act."

Re-statement of the Law of Contracts, Section 41, page 49, has this to say: "Revocation of an offer may be made by a communication from the offeror received by the offeree, which states or implies that the offeror no longer intends to enter into the proposed contract, if the communication is received by the offeree before he has exercised his power of creating a contract by acceptance of the offer."

Re-statement of the Law of Agency, Section 88 expresses it thus: "Conduct manifesting to the agent or the principal that the third person no longer consents to the transaction constitutes a withdrawal."

In Coleman v. Applegarth, 68 Md. 21, 11 A. 284, 287, quoting with approval from the English case of Dickinson v. Dodds, L.R. 2 Ch.Div. 463, it is said: "That being the state of things, it is said that the only mode in which Dodds could assert that freedom (freedom from the offer) was by actually and distinctly saying to Dickinson, 'Now I withdraw my offer.' It appears to me that there is neither principle nor authority for the proposition that there must be an express and actual withdrawal of the offer, or what is called a retraction. It must, to constitute a contract, appear that the two minds were as one, at the same moment of time; that there was an offer continuing up to the time of the acceptance. If there was not such a continuing offer, then the acceptance comes to nothing."

Applying to the undisputed testimony as furnished by Williams the rule clearly stated in all the authorities from which we have above quoted—and we find none to the contrary—we think it must be concluded that Hoover's written offer of November 19 was withdrawn on January 13 thereafter prior to its attempted acceptance on January 20, and that the concurrent finding of the Chancellor and the Court of Appeals to the contrary is not supported by any material evidence. There can be no doubt as to it being a fact that on January 13 knowledge was brought home to Williams that Hoover no longer consented to the transaction. There was, therefore, no offer continuing up to the time of the attempted acceptance on January 20.

We have been greatly concerned over the fact that the above stated conclusion which we have felt compelled to reach is contrary to the concurrent findings of two very able Courts and we have long pondered the question presented. It is our feeling that the disagreement between our Court and these Courts is due to the fact that the Chancellor and the Court of Appeals and counsel for Clements Paper Company mistakenly failed to give effect to the general rule that express notice, in so many words, of withdrawal of an offer of the character we have here is not required. Apparently, in so far as a close search reveals, our Courts of Tennessee have not heretofore been presented a case in which that rule was applicable.

The decree of the Court of Appeals and of the Chancellor will be reversed and the cause remanded for entry of a decree in keeping with this opinion. All costs in all Courts will be adjudged against Clements Paper Company.

C. Death of the Offer by Rejection of the Offer

The offer will cease to exist when an offeree rejects it. The offeree's rejection may be a pure rejection without itself being a new offer.

EXAMPLE

A–1 Used Cars does not post prices on its cars but has a big sign which reads: "Make us an offer." Tommy Thomas found a car that he liked on A–1's lot and made A–1 the following offer: "I promise to pay you $1,200 for that red convertible." A–1 responded: "You have to be kidding." A–1 has rejected Tommy's offer, and the parties no longer have an offer pending before them.

The offeree's rejection could be a new offer in addition to being a rejection. In this case, the offeree's rejection is referred to as a counteroffer, and the whole process of offer and acceptance begins again. The only difference is that the original offeree is now the offeror.

EXAMPLE

Consider the A–1/Tommy Thomas hypothetical again. This time A–1 responded: "No, but we will sell it to you for $1,500." A–1 has rejected Tommy's offer and has made its own offer, now known as a counteroffer.

Once the offeree has rejected an offer, the offeree cannot accept the offer. The original offer can only be accepted if one of the parties resubmits the original offer and the other accepts it. Even though the original and the new offer are identical, the offeree technically accepts the new, not the original offer.

Problem 5: On December 5, the B & O Railroad wrote the following letter to Baltimore Rolling Mill: "Please quote me prices for 500 to 3,000 tons 50–pound steel rails, and for 2,000 to 5,000 tons 50–pound iron rails."

On December 8, the Mill sent the following letter to B & O: "We do not make steel rails. For iron rails, we will sell 2,000 to 5,000 tons of 50–pound rails for $54 per ton.

On December 16, B & O sent a letter to the Mill: "Please enter our order for 1,200 tons 50–pound iron rails."

On December 18, the Mill telegraphed B & O: "We cannot book your order at present at that price."

On December 19, B & O telegraphed the Mill: "Please enter an order for 2,000 tons 50–pound iron rails."

The Mill did not respond to B & O's telegram nor did it ship the rails.

Did B & O and the Mill enter into a contract?

PROBLEM 6: Could B & O have discussed with the Mill the 1,200–ton shipment without rejecting the 2,000 to 5,000–ton offer?

D. Death of the Offer by the Death or Incapacity of the Offeror or Offeree

The Restatement (Second) of Contracts § 48 states the rule for death or incapacity of the offeror or offeree:

> An offeree's power of acceptance is terminated when the offeree or offeror dies or is deprived of legal capacity to enter into the proposed contract.

PROBLEM 7: Mary Randolph, an artist of some renown, told Joan Scott: "I will sell you my latest landscape for $25,000. Let me know by next Friday." On Wednesday, while vacationing in the Caribbean, Mary was involved in a boating accident. Although Mary died that evening in a local hospital, the news of her death was not reported in the United States until the following Saturday. Meanwhile Joan, not knowing that Mary had died the previous evening, mailed a letter attempting to accept Mary's offer. Joan even enclosed a $25,000 check.

Has Joan effectively accepted Mary's offer? Under the Restatement's rule, must the offeree know that the offeror is dead for the attempted acceptance to be ineffective?

Section 2. THE OFFER THAT REFUSES TO DIE

The offeree's power of acceptance need not be terminated by the offeror's attempted revocation, the offeree's attempted rejection, or the death or incapacity of the offeror or offeree. Some offers refuse to die. They are supported by a subsidiary contract—an option contract. Option contracts may be express or implied by law.

A. The Classical Option Contract

When an offeror makes an offer that creates in the offeree the power to accept, the offeror retains the power to revoke the offer. Under classical contracts law, the offeror may exercise this power at any time prior to acceptance by the offeree.

At times it is important for the offeree to have time to evaluate the offer without being concerned that the offeror will revoke.

EXAMPLE

A real estate developer may need several months to evaluate whether a certain location now for sale would be well suited for commercial development.

EXAMPLE

An apartment tenant may need an apartment for a year and possibly for longer if she decides not to buy a house.

EXAMPLE

A professional soccer team may want to play in a stadium for a season and have the ability to play there for the following season if the team is successful at the gate.

PROBLEM 8: Describe three additional situations where it would be advantageous for the offeree to have time to evaluate the offeror's offer, without having to be concerned with whether the offer will be revoked.

The solution to the offeree's dilemma is for the offeree to buy the offeror's power to revoke. The offeree can do this with an option contract. This contract is subsidiary to the main contract offer. The offer for the option contract is made by either the offeror or the offeree of the main contract. Because the option contract is a contract, the offer must have both the promisor's promise and consideration for the promisor's promise. In all option contracts where the offeror in the main contract is the same as the offeror in the option contract, the promisor's promise in the option offer is always the same: "I promise not to revoke my offer." The consideration for the promisor's promise may be either the promisee's promise or the promisee's performance: "for your promise to pay $100" or "for your paying $100." The offer for the option contract would be: "I promise not to revoke my offer for your promise to pay $100" or "I promise not to revoke my offer for your paying me $100."

In all option contracts where the offeree in the main contract is the offeror in the option contract, the promisee's promise in the option offer is always the same: "I promise not to revoke my offer." This promise by the promisee is the consideration for the promisor's promise: "I promise to pay $100." The offer for the option contract would be: "I promise to pay $100 for your promise not to revoke your offer."

Once the offer for the option contract has been accepted, the option contract is formed, and the offeror no longer has the power to revoke the original offer.

Example

Main contract offer:	I promise to sell you Blackacre for your promise to pay $250,000.
Option contract offer:	I promise not to revoke my offer to sell you Blackacre for $250,000 for thirty days for your promise to pay me $100.
Option contract acceptance:	I promise to pay you $100 for your promise not to revoke for thirty days your offer to sell me Blackacre for $250,000.

For the next thirty days, the offeror may not revoke the original offer to sell Blackacre to the offeree for $250,000. The option contract also provides that during the next thirty days, the offeree may reject the offer and then decide to accept it. Depending on the nature of the contract, death or incapacity of either the offeror or offeree may not terminate the offeree's power to accept the original offer.

PROBLEM 9: David promised to sell his "Mad Magazine" collection to Mary Jane for $200. When can David sell his "Mad Magazine" collection to Darron for $300 without being in breach of contract with Mary Jane?

PROBLEM 10: David promised to sell his "Mad Magazine" collection to Mary Jane for $200. Mary Jane paid David $10 for a three-month option contract. When can David sell his "Mad Magazine" collection to Darron for $300 without being in breach of contract with Mary Jane?

B. The Implied Option Contract

If the offeror enters into an express option contract, the offeror may not revoke the offer for the duration of the option contract. This protects the offeree from the offeror's change of heart. But what if the offeror and offeree have not entered into an express option contract? It is common for the offeree, without having accepted the offeror's original offer, to change his or her conduct in reliance on that offer. Will this reliance create an implied option contract? The analysis will differ depending on whether the original offer was for a unilateral or bilateral contract.

In an offer for a unilateral contract, the offer is "I promise for your performance." This type of offer (a promise for a performance) can only be accepted by the offeree's performance. Because the offeror has asked the offeree to accept by performing (and not by promising), a promise by the offeree is ineffective as acceptance.

The offeree is required to perform in full in order to accept the offer. Beginning the performance is not full performance any more than almost completing the performance is full performance. If the offeror has the power to revoke and may exercise this power at any time prior to acceptance, the offeree may begin the requested performance, only to have the offeror revoke the offer prior to the offeree's full performance. Therefore all offers for a unilateral contract would place the offeree at risk.

EXAMPLE

Farmer Jones promised to pay Simon $1,000 for Simon's painting Farmer Jones's barn. Simon began to paint and completed three sides of the barn when Farmer Jones walked up to Simon and said "Mighty nice job Simon but I revoke my offer." Because the offer was a promise for a performance, Simon could accept only by performing in full, that is, painting all four sides of the barn. Painting three sides was not full performance and the offeror could revoke prior to Simon's having fully performed. Simon did not have an express option contract that would prevent Farmer Jones from revoking his offer. Without an offer and an acceptance, Simon could not successfully sue Farmer Jones under classical contract theory for a breach of contract.

The Restatement of Contracts (Second) § 45, came to the aid of the Simons of the world with an implied option contract.

> (1) Where an offer invites an offeree to accept by rendering a performance and does not invite a promissory acceptance, an option contract is created when the offeree tenders or begins the invited performance or tenders a beginning of it.
>
> (2) The offeror's duty of performance under any option contract so created is conditional on completion or tender of the invited performance in accordance with the terms of the offer.

Under section 45, when the offeree begins the performance requested by the offeror under the original offer, an implied option contract is created which deprives the offeror of the power to revoke the original offer. Technically, the offeree's beginning of the performance is the consideration for the offeror's implied promise not to revoke. The implied option contract would stay in existence long enough for the offeree to have an opportunity to complete the performance requested in the offer. Upon completion, the offeree accepts the offer and a contract is formed.

If section 45 were operative in the Farmer Jones illustration, Farmer Jones's attempted revocation would be ineffective. When Simon began to paint the barn, an implied option contract came into being. During the life of the option contract, the offeror was powerless to revoke the offer. If Simon painted the last side of the barn, he would have completed the requested performance and thus accepted the offer. He could successfully maintain a breach of contract action if Farmer Jones refused to pay the contract price.

In an offer for a bilateral contract, the offer is "I promise for your promise." This type of offer can only be accepted by the offeree's promise to do or not do what the offeror requested. The offeree's promise may be express or implied from the offeree's conduct. Unlike the offer for a unilateral contract, which requires full performance by the offeree to constitute acceptance of the offer, the offeree in an offer for a bilateral contract has a rapid and easy method of acceptance—simply promise. If the offeree begins to perform without expressly promising the offeror, a promise implied from the offeree's performance constitutes acceptance of the offer. The problem generally is not with the offeree's beginning the performance requested by the offeror but preparing to begin the performance.

EXAMPLE

Consider Farmer Jones again. This time Farmer Jones promised to pay Simon $1,000 if Simon promised to paint Farmer Jones's barn. Simon did not respond to Farmer Jones but bought paint and brushes for the job. Before Simon told Farmer Jones that he promised to paint or before he started painting, Farmer Jones wrote Simon stating "I revoke my offer." Because the offer has not been accepted, and because Simon did not have an express option contract, Farmer Jones could revoke because the attempted revocation occurred prior to Simon's attempted acceptance. Without an acceptance, Simon could not successfully sue Farmer Jones in classical contract theory for breach of contract.

Section 45 of the Restatement (Second) of Contracts was not designed to give the Simons of the world any help in this situation. Section 45 only applies to an offer for a unilateral contract. This was an offer for a bilateral contract. The Restatement (Second) of Contracts § 87(2) was created to address the offer for a bilateral contract:

> (2) An offer which the offeror should reasonably expect to induce action or forbearance of a substantial character on the part of the offeree before acceptance and which does induce such action or forbearance is binding as an option contract to the extent necessary to avoid injustice.

Section 87(2) provides that once the offeree either begins preparation or begins performance as defined by the terms of the offer, an implied option contract is created.

EXAMPLE

When Simon bought the paint and brushes, an implied option contract was created with the beginning of the preparation acting as the consideration for the offeror's implied promise not to revoke. Simon would have a reasonable time to promise Farmer Jones.

The language of section 87(2) is not limited to the offer for a bilateral contract. Its language encompasses both offers for bilateral and unilateral contracts. By using preparation as the time for implying the option contract, section 87(2) creates the option contract at an earlier point than section 45.

EXAMPLE

> Under section 87(2), Simon's purchase of paint brushes acts as consideration for the offeror's implied promise not to revoke. Simon would have the opportunity to perform fully if the offer were for a unilateral contract or to promise to perform if the offer were for a bilateral contract.

PROBLEM 11: Describe a situation where an offeror has made an offer for a unilateral contract and attempts to revoke the offer while the offeree is preparing to perform the requested performance. Could the offeree successfully maintain a breach of contract action against the offeror using:

1. classical contract theory;
2. Restatement (Second) of Contracts § 45; or
3. Restatement (Second) of Contracts § 87(2)?

PROBLEM 12: Change the situation in Problem 11 so the offeror attempts to revoke the offer while the offeree is performing the requested performance. Answer the three questions raised in Problem 11.

PROBLEM 13: Change the situation in Problem 11 so the offer is for a bilateral contract. The offeror attempts to revoke the offer while the offeree is preparing to perform but has not promised the offeror. Answer the three questions raised in Problem 11.

PROBLEM 14: Change the situation in Problem 13 so the offeror attempts to revoke the offer while the offeree is in the act of performing the requested performance but has not promised the offeror. Answer the three questions raised in Problem 11.

6

THE ACCEPTANCE PHASE

The offer is made and the transaction passes through the post-offer/pre-acceptance phase with the offer intact. The offeror has not revoked the offer, the offeree has not rejected the offer, and neither party has become incapacitated. The time limit for acceptance (if stated in the offer) has not passed, nor has a reasonable time for accepting the offer expired. The scene is now set for the acceptance phase of the transaction.

This chapter explores a range of problems in the acceptance phase of the transaction. Section one considers the relationship between the acceptance and the offer. Must acceptance be in response to the offer? Must the offeree agree to all of the offeror's terms? Must the offeree notify the offeror that the offer has been accepted? Who can accept the offer? Section two investigates how an acceptance is made. Must the offeree promise or can the offeree be silent and simply perform the request of the offeror? Section three examines the time at which acceptance is effective. Will the effective time of acceptance differ depending on whether the offeror and offeree are face to face or dealing at a distance? Section four discusses whether restitution is an available cause of action when the offer either has or has not been accepted.

Section 1. THE INGREDIENTS OF AN ACCEPTANCE—A PROMISE OR PERFORMANCE AND CONSIDERATION FOR THAT PROMISE OR PERFORMANCE

An offer can propose either a unilateral or bilateral contract. The offer for a unilateral contract is a promise for a performance. "I promise to pay you $5,000 if you walk from New York to San Francisco." The offer for a bilateral contract is a promise for a promise. "I promise to pay you $5,000 for your promise to walk from New York to San Francisco." Therefore, the ingredients of an offer are the offeror's promise and consideration for the offeror's promise, that is, either the offeree's promise or performance.

The offeror (by the status of being the offeror) controls the transaction and is the master of the offer. The offeror establishes whether the offeree's acceptance must be by promise or performance. If the offer is for a unilateral contract, the offeree must accept by performing—in the example above, actually walking from New York to San

Francisco. If the offer is for a bilateral contract, the offeree must accept by promising—promising to walk from New York to San Francisco. The ingredients of the acceptance are the offeree's promise or performance (depending on which the offeror required) and consideration for the offeree's promise or performance. The consideration for the offeree's promise or performance is the offeror's promise.

A. The Acceptance Must Be in Response to the Offer

Because the offeror makes a promise to entice the offeree to do or refrain from doing something, the offeree's actions must be in response to the offeror's promise. It is not enough that the offeree's actions happen by coincidence to be what the offeror has requested.

1. Knowledge of the Offer

If the offer is for a bilateral contract, the offeree must have knowledge of the offer before responding with a promise. Otherwise the offeror's promise is not inducing the offeree to respond and the offeree's response is not an effective acceptance.

> *PROBLEM 1:* David, who lives in Texas, is the original owner of a 1966 Mustang, which is in mint condition. His cousin, Susan, who lives in Georgia, has often stated that she would like to buy it. David has always said it was not for sale.
>
> On March 1st, David wrote Susan that he was now ready to sell her his Mustang for $8,000. Susan received David's letter on March 4th. On March 2d, Susan, *not* knowing that David was ready to sell, decided to press David on the issue of the Mustang. She wrote him saying that she would pay $8,000 for the Mustang.
>
> David received Susan's letter on March 8th but has had second thoughts about selling his Mustang. From Susan's letter, he knows that she could not have received his letter before writing hers. If Susan does not write a second letter or telephone David, is he under contract to sell his Mustang to Susan?

If the offer is for a bilateral contract, the acceptance is the offeree's promise, an event that is completed during a relatively short period of time. A promise therefore is almost an instantaneous event. Except for factual issues regarding whether the offeree had knowledge of the offer prior to accepting, the law is straightforward. The offeror could not induce the offeree if the offeree has no knowledge of the offer.

If the offer is for a unilateral contract, the offeree's performance often requires a period of time to complete. "Walking from New York to San Francisco" could take months. "Refraining from drinking until twenty-one" could take years. When must the offeree learn of the offeror's performance? Must the offeree have knowledge of the offer before beginning the requested performance or would having knowledge before completion of performance be sufficient?

> *PROBLEM 2:* Bonney, a convicted murderer, escaped from the county jail. The City Council offered a $50,000 reward to any person who captured and returned Bonney to jail.

Bonney fled to another county and before the news of the reward spread to that county, Oliver, a private detective, captured Bonney. As Oliver was driving Bonney back to the county jail, he learned about the reward on his car radio.

If Oliver does not release Bonney and recapture him, is he contractually entitled to the reward?

PROBLEM 3: Compare the following sections from the Restatement (First) and Restatement (Second) of Contracts. Apply each to Problem 2. If the drafters of the Restatement decided to rewrite a Restatement section, what does this change mean? Which version of the Restatement do you prefer and why? Is there something positive that could be said for each?

Restatement (First) of Contracts § 53 (1932):

The whole consideration requested by the offer must be given after the offeree knows of the offer.

Restatement (Second) of Contracts § 51 (1979):

Unless the offeror manifests a contrary intention, an offeree who learns of an offer after he has rendered part of the performance requested by the offer may accept by completing the requested performance.

2. Preexisting Duty

While exploring the components of offer, we discussed the necessity of consideration for the promisor's promise to be "new" consideration and not something already required of the offeror. If the promisor requested the promisee to promise or perform some act that the promisee already had a duty to perform, the promisor's request violates the "preexisting duty" rule and the promisor's promise would lack consideration. The promisor's attempt to make an offer fails.

The same "preexisting duty" rule applies to acceptance. If the promisee requested the promisor to promise something that the promisor was already obligated to do, the promisee's request could not be consideration for the promisee's promise. The promisee's promise or performance lacks consideration. The promisee's attempt to accept the offer fails.

It is important to consider "preexisting duty" both when evaluating the attempted offer and the attempted acceptance. The offer may not involve a preexisting duty problem but the attempted acceptance may.

PROBLEM 4: William was the sole heir under his father's will. When William's father died, the executor said to William, "I promise to pay you your inheritance, if you promise to donate ten percent to charity." William responded "I promise to donate ten percent to charity if you promise to pay me my inheritance." Did the executor make an offer to William or does the attempted offer suffer from a lack of consideration due to the preexisting duty rule? If the executor has made an offer, did William accept the offer or does William's attempted acceptance lack consideration due to the preexisting duty rule?

Common application of the preexisting duty rule often occurs in the post-acceptance phase of the transaction. During that phase, the parties may try to alter their contractual duties. This attempt may occur before either party has fully performed.

EXAMPLE

A football player had a good year and wanted to renegotiate how much he would be paid under the remaining two years of his three year contract.

EXAMPLE

A homeowner, having a new house built, wants the builder to make changes in the structure as the house is being built.

If one of the parties has completely performed under the contract, the other party may still try to alter the unperformed duties. These situations will be discussed in Chapter 7 in the post-acceptance phase of the transaction.

B. The Offeree Must Agree to All of the Offeror's Terms

The offeror is the master of the offer, and as such, the offeror controls the terms of the contract.

1. Common Law Mirror Image Rule

The offeree cannot change the terms of the offer. The offeree must either promise or perform as the offeror has required and the offeree must do so to receive what the offeror has promised.

EXAMPLE

If a homeowner promises to pay a painter $1,500 to paint his house white, the painter must respond that she will paint the owner's house white for $1,500. If the painter responds with either $1,600 or gray rather than white, the attempted acceptance does not mirror the offer and is treated as a rejection of the offer. If the rejection meets the requirements of an offer, it would be considered a counteroffer, and it would be up to the original offeror (by counteroffer the original offeror becomes the offeree), the homeowner, to accept the counteroffer.

PROBLEM 5: PG Studios, a motion picture company, promised to pay Cynthia five million dollars if she promised to star in PG's new picture "ET Part II," with filming to begin on August 1st. Cynthia wrote PG that she accepted the offer but could not begin filming until August 10th. PG did not respond to Cynthia's letter. PG began filming on August 1st but used another leading lady. Was there a contract between PG Studios and Cynthia?

2. The Uniform Commercial Code § 2–207

The common law mirror image rule left the parties in an all or nothing situation. If the attempted acceptance mirrored the offer, a contract was formed, and the terms were those of the offer. If the attempted acceptance was not the mirror image, the offer was not accepted but was rejected, and the attempted acceptance became a counteroffer. If the original offeror took no further action, the parties were without a contract. If the original offeror accepted the counteroffer, a contract was formed with the terms being those of the counteroffer. This is known as the "last shot doctrine." The last offer became the "last shot," and it dictated all the terms.

The drafters of the Uniform Commercial Code sought to change the common law's mirror image rule, at least in those transactions involving a "sale of goods." The drafters recognized that in most commercial transactions that are based on an exchange of written forms, the preprinted terms on the forms neither agree nor are read before the seller delivers or the buyer accepts the delivery. The drafters set up the following scheme:

> Section 2–207. Additional Terms in Acceptance or Confirmation
>
> (1) A definite and seasonable expression of acceptance or a written confirmation which is sent within a reasonable time operates as an acceptance even though it states terms additional to or different from those offered or agreed upon, unless acceptance is expressly made conditional on assent to the additional or different terms.
>
> (2) The additional terms are to be construed as proposals for addition to the contract. Between merchants such terms become part of the contract unless:
>
> (a) the offer expressly limits acceptance to the terms of the offer;
>
> (b) they materially alter it; or
>
> (c) notification of objection to them has already been given or is given within a reasonable time after notice of them is received.
>
> (3) Conduct by both parties which recognizes the existence of a contract is sufficient to establish a contract for sale although the writings of the parties do not otherwise establish a contract. In such case the terms of the particular contract consist of those terms on which the writings of the parties agree, together with any supplementary terms incorporated under any other provisions of this Act.

Basically § 2–207(1) provides that even if the preprinted terms in the forms (the "boilerplate") do not agree, a contract is created if the "bargained for" terms (the terms inserted by the parties on the form such as price, quantity, subject matter, credit, and delivery terms) agree. Subsection (2) tells whether additional terms (terms in the second form which are not found in the first form) become terms of the contract. If the "bargained for" terms do not agree so subsection (1) cannot be used to create a contract, a contract may still be created if both parties act as if a contract exists. This contract is created under subsection (3) rather than subsection (1). Subsection (3) also pieces together the terms of the contract created under subsection (3).

PROBLEM 6: The ABC Company sent its purchase order to the Quality Brick Company for 6 million bricks at $10 per hundred. ABC's purchase order form was silent as to warranty.

Quality responded by sending its acknowledgment form which stated 6 million bricks at $10 per hundred. Preprinted on Quality's form was

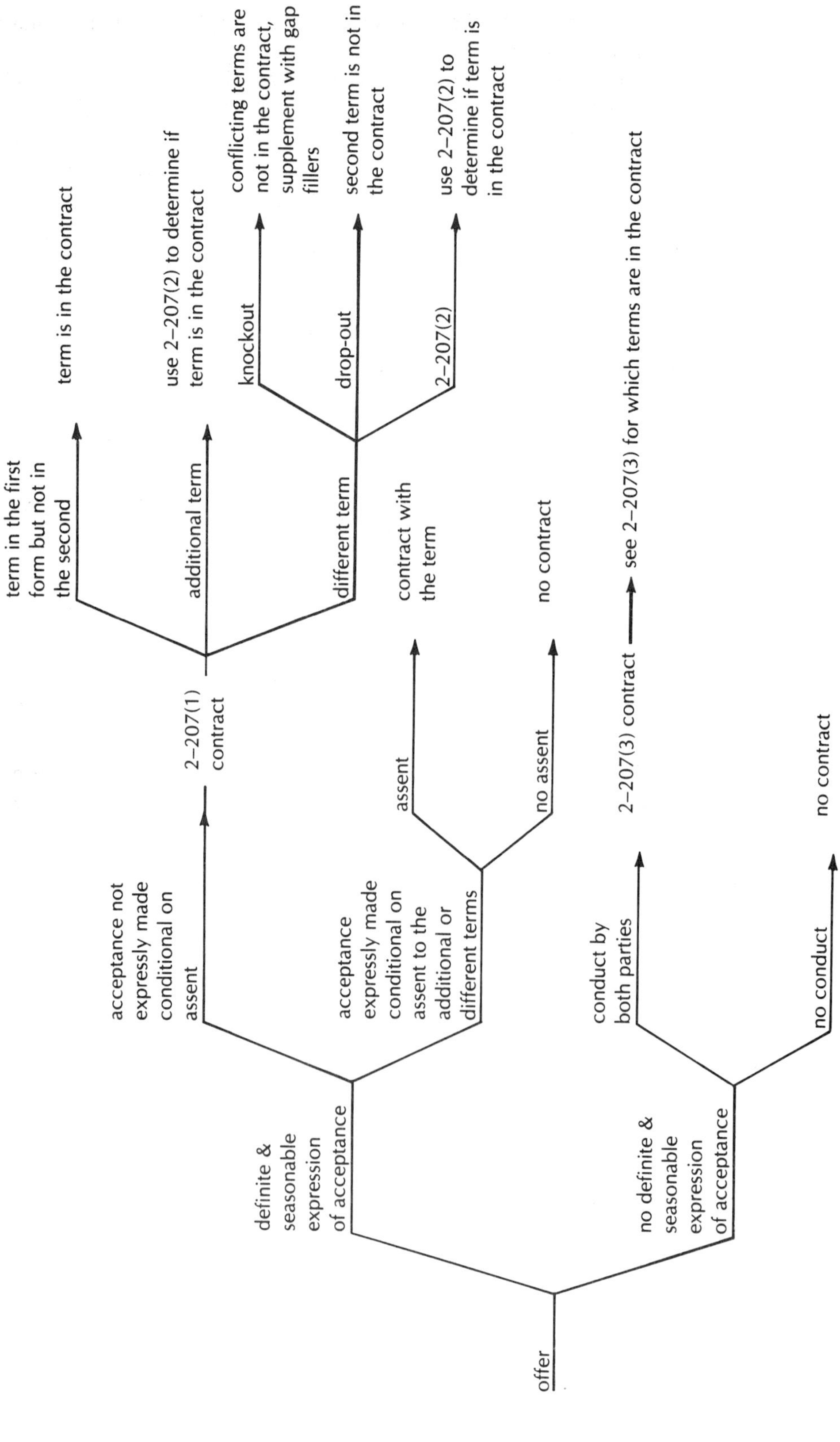
offer
definite & seasonable expression of acceptance
no definite & seasonable expression of acceptance
acceptance not expressly made conditional on assent
acceptance expressly made conditional on assent to the additional or different terms
conduct by both parties
no conduct
2–207(1) contract
assent
no assent
2–207(3) contract
no contract
term in the first form but not in the second
additional term
different term
contract with the term
no contract
see 2–207(3) for which terms are in the contract
term is in the contract
use 2–207(2) to determine if term is in the contract
knockout
drop-out
2–207(2)
conflicting terms are not in the contract, supplement with gap fillers
second term is not in the contract
use 2–207(2) to determine if term is in the contract

the statement "all bricks warranted for ninety days as to defects in materials or workmanship."

Quality sent the bricks, and ABC accepted the shipment and paid. A year later and after a winter's use, ABC noticed that some of the bricks were cracking because the bricks were improperly dried during manufacture.

Under UCC § 2–207(1) is there a contract for the sale of the bricks? If there is a contract, then under 2–207(2) is the contract with or without the limited warranty expressed in Quality's acknowledgment form?

PROBLEM 7: The ABC Company sent its purchase order to the Quality Brick Company for 6 million bricks at $10 per hundred. ABC's purchase order form was silent as to warranty.

Quality responded by sending its acknowledgment form which stated 6 million bricks at $12 per hundred. Preprinted on Quality's form was the statement "all bricks warranted for ninety days as to defects in material or workmanship."

Although the forms did not agree as to price, Quality sent the bricks and ABC accepted the shipment and paid the higher price. A year later and after a winter's use, ABC noticed that some of the bricks were cracking because the bricks were improperly dried during manufacture.

Under UCC § 2–207(1) is there a contract for the sale of the bricks? If not, is there a contract for the sale of the bricks under 2–207(3)? If there is a contract under 2–207(3), then, under 2–207(3), is the contract with or without the limited warranty expressed in Quality's acknowledgment form?

While 2–207 provides a substantial service to parties transacting business through preprinted forms, it does not resolve a number of questions. For example, subsection (2) expressly deals with "additional terms"; these are terms raised in the acceptance which were not present in the offer. Subsection (2) does not expressly address the question of different terms, that is, when the acceptance states terms contradictory to those in the offer. Subsection (2) also fails to resolve the issue of implied terms. If a term does not appear in one of the forms but is an implied term in the Code (a gap filler), and if it were to be included in the form it would be contradictory to a term in the other form, should it be implied when determining whether the term is an additional or different term or should it be implied only if the contract ultimately is silent as to that term?

For a detailed discussion of 2–207, see James J. White & Robert S. Summers, Handbook of the Law under the Uniform Commercial Code p. 24 (2d ed. West Pub. Co. 1980).

3. Mismatch: A Mistake in Understanding the Offer

An interesting problem occurs when the offeror and offeree say the same thing but mean different things.

EXAMPLE

Imagine a situation where the buyer and seller of chickens used the term "chickens" but the seller was thinking of "stewing chickens" and the buyer was thinking of "frying chickens." The seller ships the chickens to the buyer and the buyer is surprised to discover the "stewing chickens." Has a contract been formed between the parties, and if so, is the contract for stewing or frying chickens?

This mistake in understanding the terms of the offer can be resolved by considering what a reasonable person would have meant had the reasonable person been placed in this situation. If the reasonable person had meant what the offeror meant, there would be a contract and the offeror's meaning would govern. The offeree's meaning is disregarded because it does not coincide with the reasonable person's meaning, and is therefore, unreasonable.

Returning to the chickens: if the reasonable person had meant stewing chickens, and stewing chickens happened to coincide with the offeror-seller's meaning, then the contract would be for stewing chickens, and the seller would not have breached the contract. On the other hand, if the reasonable person had meant frying chickens, and frying chickens happened to coincide with the offeree-buyer's meaning, then the contract would be for frying chickens, and the seller would have breached the contract by sending stewing chickens.

> *PROBLEM 8:* In June, Mary planned a dinner party for twenty-eight people and had it catered by Le Gourmet, a French restaurant that specializes in catered dinner parties. In discussing the menu, Mary discovered that Le Gourmet had a "special" which consisted of roast duckling with all the trimmings for $60 per person. The party was a success.
>
> The next month Mary planned a second dinner party, again for twenty-eight people, and telephoned Le Gourmet and ordered "the special." Much to Mary's surprise, when dinner was served it was pheasant under glass for $100 per person.
>
> While both Mary and Le Gourmet agreed on the "the special," Mary meant the roast duckling at $60 per person while Le Gourmet meant the July special of pheasant under glass at $100 per person. Has a contract been formed between Mary and Le Gourmet and if so, was it for the duckling or the pheasant?

C. The Offeree Must Notify the Offeror That the Offer Has Been Accepted

Unless the offeror states in the offer that the offeree need not notify the offeror that the offer has been accepted, the offeree must notify the offeror. The notice will be different depending on whether the offer proposes a unilateral or a bilateral contract.

If the offer proposes a bilateral contract, the offeree must communicate his or her promise to the offeror. This communication may be oral if the parties are standing face-to-face or are communicating by telephone. If the parties are not in voice contact, then another form of communication, such as a letter, telegram, or messenger, could provide the notice.

If the offer proposes a unilateral contract, the offeree must communicate his or her performance to the offeror. If the performance, by its very nature, is known to the offeror as it occurs, then the offeree's act of performance is itself notice to the offeror. If, however, the performance occurred at a distant location so the offeror would not know about it, the offeree must, in some fashion, communicate the completion of performance to the offeror.

D. The Parties Who Can Accept the Offer

The offeror, by being master of the offer, controls who may accept the offer. An offer made to a specific party can only be accepted by that party. The offeree may not empower someone else to accept, thereby making the other person the offeree.

An offer need not, however, be limited to one party. A number of offers are made to the public in general.

EXAMPLE

A reward for information leading to the arrest and conviction of the perpetrator of a violent crime is an offer to anyone who supplies the information.

EXAMPLE

The auctioneer, who announces that the auction will be without reserve, makes an offer to all those present.

EXAMPLE

An advertisement, that contains the elements of offer, is an offer to anyone who reads the ad.

It should be noted that in all of these situations, the offer, while it may be accepted by any party, can be accepted by only one party. Only one party can supply the information, make the highest bid, or purchase each individual item advertised.

Section 2. WHAT METHOD MUST BE USED TO ACCEPT AN OFFER?

The Offeror, by being the master of the offer, not only establishes the terms of the contract (by setting the terms of the offer), but also establishes the method by which the offeree must accept the offer. The offeror may be silent as to the method of acceptance, may suggest a method, or may mandate a method. If the offeror mandates a method, then that method is the appropriate method of acceptance.

If the offeror does not mandate a method of acceptance, the general rules of contracts law apply and this takes the discussion back to offers for unilateral and bilateral contracts. If the offer is for a unilateral contract, a promise for a performance, the offer must be accepted by performance. A promise will not do; nor can a promise be used to imply the required performance. Beginning or nearly completing performance is also inadequate as the method of acceptance. Full performance is the method of acceptance unless the offeror has dictated another method.

If the offer is for a bilateral contract, a promise for a promise, rather than a promise for performance, it is accepted by a different method. The offer for this type of contract must be accepted by a promise. Full performance cannot be the method of acceptance. Full performance or even part performance, however, may imply the required promise. Implying a promise from performance is not the same as stating that the method of acceptance of an offer for a bilateral contract is performance. The method is a promise, although the promise may be implied from performance.

PROBLEM 9: The Black Forrest, a Bavarian restaurant, offered to pay Media International, an advertising agency, $40,000 for Media's planning and executing a three month advertising campaign for Black Forrest. Media telephoned Black Forrest to say that it "accepted" the offer. Has Media accepted the offer?

PROBLEM 10: Same facts as Problem 9 but instead of telephoning Black Forrest, Media began planning the campaign. Has Media accepted the offer?

PROBLEM 11: The Black Forrest offered to pay Media $40,000 for Media's promise to plan and execute a three month advertising campaign. Media telephoned Black Forrest to say that Media "accepted" the offer. Has Media accepted Black Forrest's offer?

PROBLEM 12: Same facts as Problem 11 except Media did not telephone but rather began planning the campaign. Has Media accepted Black Forrest's offer? Can you answer this question without additional facts? What would these facts be and why are they essential?

PROBLEM 13: The Black Forrest offered to pay Media $40,000 for Media's promise to plan and execute a three month advertising campaign. The offer stated that Media could accept by either notifying Black Forrest or by beginning the advertising campaign. Black Forrest first learned that Media was working on a campaign when a Black Forrest advertisement appeared in a local newspaper. Has Media accepted Black Forrest's offer?

When an offeror specifies a method of acceptance, care should be exercised to determine whether the method stated is the only method or an optional method.

EXAMPLE

Suppose that the offeror in the offer for a bilateral contract states "This offer may be accepted by beginning performance." The offeree could accept either by complying with the method stated in the offer (beginning performance) or by following the traditional method for accepting an offer for a bilateral contract (a promise).

Section 3. WHEN IS ACCEPTANCE EFFECTIVE?

An attempted acceptance is an effective acceptance when it gives notice to the offeror that the offeree has accepted. If the parties are dealing face-to-face or are in voice contact such as by telephone, the offeree has the opportunity to give the offeror instant notification.

If, however, the parties are dealing at a distance and are not in voice contact, then each party will be unaware of the other's actions. The offeror will not know that the offeree has mailed an acceptance, nor will the offeree know that the offeror has received the mailed acceptance. Each party operates in the dark for at least a part of the time.

At what point will the acceptance be effective: when the offeree posts her acceptance; when the offeror receives the offeree's acceptance; when the offeror posts his notice to the offeree that he has received her acceptance; when the offeree receives the offeror's notice that the offeror has received the offeree's acceptance; or when the offeree posts her notice to the offeror that she has received his notice that he has received her acceptance? The judges, who shaped the law, selected the least complicated approach—when the offeree posts her acceptance if posting is a medium reasonable in the circumstances. This rule has become known as the "posting" or "mailbox rule."

When the offeror sends the offeree an offer and does not specify a specific mode of acceptance, the offeror builds in the risk that before learning of this fact the offer may be accepted. The offeror had the opportunity to create an offer which would minimize these risks. If the offeror chooses not to take advantage of this opportunity, then this is the offeror's choice, and the offeror thereby assumes the risk.

> *PROBLEM 14:* The Green Thumb Landscape Company has had several serious inquiries concerning its services. Unfortunately, Green Thumb is a very small company and cannot provide its services to more than one of these prospective clients. How should Green Thumb design its offer to minimize its risks between the time the offer is extended and the acceptance is effective? Plan three approaches that focus on the time when acceptance is effective.

Section 4. IS RESTITUTION AN ALTERNATIVE TO ACCEPTANCE?

Once the offer has been made, attention focuses on acceptance. If the offeree does not accept the offer, but receives a benefit during the pre-offer and offer phases of the transaction, should the offeree be liable to the offeror in a restitution cause of action?

> *PROBLEM 15:* The City of Larkspar owned eighty acres of land at the edge of the City. On this land the City had drilled a water well from which it supplied all of its residents. Adjacent to the City's eighty acres were eighty acres owned by Beaman. The City, believing that Beaman's land also could be productive as a water supply, began negotiations with Beaman for his land. The City made Beaman an offer and subsequently received Beaman's permission to enter Beaman's property to drill a test well. The test well produced more water than either the City or Beaman thought it would. Based on this information, Beaman rejected the City's offer.

Has Beaman received a benefit from the City? Would it be unjust for Beaman to retain this benefit without compensating the City?

The situation in *Gould v. American Water Works* is slightly different from the previous problem. Gould, the landowner, offered to sell his land to the Bernards Water Company and sought to entice the Water Company by drilling a productive water well on his own land. The Water Company, now knowing that the land would produce the water required, purchased land adjacent to Gould's since that land could be purchased at a better price. Did Gould confer a benefit on the Water Company? Does this benefit constitute an enrichment? Was the Water Company unjustly enriched?

Gould v. American Water Works Service Co.

Supreme Court of New Jersey, 1958.
52 N.J. 226, 245 A.2d 14.

PER CURIAM.

The issue here is whether plaintiff, Jasper C. Gould, has a cause of action for damages against defendant The Bernards Water Company in *quasi* or implied contract based upon alleged unjust enrichment resulting from defendant's appropriation and use of information developed through plaintiff's efforts and skill in locating underground water wells. The trial court decided that the evidence created a jury question on the subject and the jury found for plaintiff Jasper Gould. The complaint against defendant American Water Works Service Co., Inc. was dismissed and has not been appealed. The Appellate Division, in an unreported opinion, reversed, holding that plaintiff was a mere volunteer and that no legal basis existed for imposing a *quasi* -contractual liability on defendant. We granted certification. 51 N.J. 182, 238 A.2d 469 (1968).

Plaintiff Jasper C. Gould is an experienced well digger. Defendant is a public utility engaged in the business of selling water to the public in Bernards Township and other localities. In 1953 plaintiff learned from a friend of many years standing, one Burd, who was in defendant's employ as a superintendent, that the company was interested in developing an additional water supply. Upon Gould's inquiry, Burd indicated the company's interest was in wells which would yield 200 to 225 gallons of water a minute. Gould asked also what the company would be willing to pay for such a well. Burd replied he was not the "boss" but he knew it would pay a fair price. Nothing further was said. The friendship between Gould and Burd was purely social. They had had no business relationships. Some time later Burd asked Gould if he would be gracious enough to talk with defendant's geologist. Gould agreed and spent two days with the geologist showing him wells Gould had dug on his own property and discussing conditions he encountered in doing so.

Thereafter, in the latter part of 1953 or early 1954, Gould spent some time drilling a well on five acres of land he owned in Bernards Township. At a depth of 365 feet the well delivered only 60 gallons a minute, so he abandoned it. He moved his equipment 80 feet farther in on his property and began to drill again. This time, after going down 670 feet, he located water and the well yielded over 200 gallons per minute. A short time later, at a social gathering, Gould told Burd he had a very good well and inquired as to whether the company would be interested in seeing a pump test on it. Burd said he would find out from his superiors, and a few days later he advised Gould his superiors would like to have such a test. In April 1954 the test was made. It revealed the well was yielding over 300 gallons a minute. In another conversation with Gould, Burd said the well was not large enough to admit defendant's pumping equipment and asked what it would cost to enlarge it from six to ten inches. It is undisputed that Gould never furnished a figure. Instead he proceeded to ream the well to a 10–inch diameter for a depth of 250 feet. He admitted that nobody connected with the water company asked him to do so.

Later in 1954, how much later does not appear, Gould met with Burd's superiors who offered $12,000 for the well. There was no discussion about whether the offer was for title to the land or an easement. The conference was a short one because Gould asked for $100,000. About a year later defendant offered $12,000 to $13,000. It was again rejected. Some time later in 1955 or in 1956 Gould reduced his asking price to $50,000, but defendant was not interested. Finally about five years later, in 1960 or 1961, defendant offered $16,000 and Gould lowered his figure to $35,000. The negotiations ended on that note and no agreement was ever reached.

Gould conceded that no representative of defendant asked or authorized him to dig a well or to prospect for water in its behalf, or ever agreed that if he dug a well which produced water at the rate of 200 gallons a minute the company would buy it from him. It appeared also that in a pretrial deposition he said:

"Q. What was the purpose in drilling this well (meaning the second well)?

A. It was speculative on my part. For the water company.

Q. You mean for the water company?

A. Yes.

Q. Did you drill it for the water company?

A. Yes.

Q. Who asked you to drill it for the water company?

A. Nobody.

Q. In other words, you drilled the well in anticipating that you would sell it to the water company?

A. Yes.

Q. That's what you were speculating on?

A. Yes."

In August 1961 defendant acquired property on the south side of Route 202 opposite Gould's acreage and began to dig 490 feet from Gould's well. In March 1962, eight years after completion of Gould's second well, defendant's digging reached 1450 feet in depth and produced sufficient water to move defendant to obtain a permanent diversionary permit from the State Division of Water Policy and Supply to divert up to 500,000 gallons of water a day from the well. About a year later plaintiff brought this action seeking damages from the water company. He alleged that defendant had been unjustly enriched as the result of plaintiff's well-digging activity and the knowledge defendant acquired thereby that water was to be found in the immediate area to an extent which defendant, as a seller of water to the public, was interested in locating and acquiring. More specifically, plaintiff claimed that defendant had encouraged him to dig wells to locate water of the volume desired. Thus when he dug such a well, and informed defendant of the location, defendant's failure to buy it coupled with the subsequent use of the information as the incentive for acquiring nearby property and digging a sufficiently productive well of its own, unjustly enriched defendant at plaintiff's expense. Therefore, plaintiff contended, in order to do justice the law ought to impose an obligation on defendant to pay plaintiff for the expenses and losses resulting from defendant's inequitable conduct.

After consideration of the entire record,

we agree with the Appellate Division that plaintiff's proof fails to establish a claim upon which relief can be granted. We concur in its declaration:

"The evidence is uncontradicted that what the plaintiff did was not done at the request of Bernards nor with any expectation at that time that he would be reimbursed by Bernards for his well digging expenses. Plaintiff * * * [Gould] dug the two wells on his property on his own initiative in the hope that if he were successful in finding an adequate water supply, he would be able to negotiate for a sale of the well or an interest in his property to the water company. The fact that the drawn-out negotiations were unsuccessful because the parties did not agree on a price affords no basis for imposing a *quasi*-contractual liability on defendant, nor is such basis to be found in the fact that defendant thereafter dug its own well approximately 500 feet away to a depth almost twice that of plaintiff's well. See Restatement, Restitution, § 2, p.15; § 112, p. 461; § 41, p. 162 (1937)."

In our judgment the plaintiff occupied the status of a volunteer who hoped that if his efforts produced a result which would interest defendant, an agreement to sell that result to defendant could be consummated. The fact that plaintiff knew defendant was interested generally in locating an additional water supply in the area would not transform his status from volunteer into an obligee when he found a source which defendant could use. Nor would the fact that defendant offered to buy the well at its price make it an obligor. And, although the act of negotiating to buy under the circumstances would not affect the legal relationship between them, it may be noted that no evidence was adduced to show that defendant did not act in good faith during the prolonged voluntary bargaining with plaintiff for the purchase of the well plaintiff had dug. Obviously plaintiff fixed an exorbitant price. Its sharply downward course from $100,000 to $35,000, roughly a drop of two-thirds of the original figure, over a period of *about seven years*, particularly in light of the water company's modest upward course of $12,000 to its final offer of $16,000, leaves no other fair inference. When the negotiations broke off, it meant that plaintiff's speculative venture had failed to achieve its ultimate purpose. If it is assumed that defendant had learned from plaintiff's unsolicited efforts that there was substantial underground water in the area, and to that extent was the recipient of a benefit, such enrichment should not be regarded as unjust enrichment creating a liability for plaintiff's expenses and losses simply because defendant, encouraged by plaintiff's experience, acquired nearby property, dug a well about 500 feet from that of plaintiff and more than twice as deep, and located an acceptable additional supply of water.

Accordingly the judgment of the Appellate Division is affirmed.

For affirmance: Chief Justice WEINTRAUB and Justices JACOBS, FRANCIS, PROCTOR, HALL, SCHETTINO and HANEMAN—7.

For reversal: None.

If the offeror makes an offer and the offeree accepts the offer, a contract is formed. The next step is to evaluate whether the contract is enforceable. Because a contract has been formed, the parties cannot consider a restitution action as an alternative. The restitution action is not an alternative to a breach of contract action. A restitution action is available only when the breach of contract action cannot be maintained. At this point in the analysis, because the offer has been accepted and a contract formed, the conclusion cannot be reached that the breach of contract action cannot be maintained.

7

THE POST-ACCEPTANCE PHASE

Once past the pre-offer, offer, post-offer/pre-acceptance, and acceptance phases, a contract exists. Chapter 7 investigates the post-acceptance phase. Section one focuses on the terms of the contract. What rules of construction should be used to interpret the language of the contract? Does the contract consist of only the written terms or does it include non-written terms as well? Does the contract include only those terms the parties have agreed upon or could it include other terms? Section two addresses errors in the written contract and when parties may correct them. Does the writing bind the parties when it differs from their prior oral agreement? Section three deals with how the parties may change a contract that they still intend to perform. Can the parties modify the terms of the contract? Section four discusses the methods by which a contract may end before it has been fully performed. Can the parties rescind the contract? Can the parties use a contract to settle a noncontractual claim? Can a contracting party pay less than the contract price as "payment in full"? The questions in sections three and four revisit a topic discussed in detail earlier, the doctrine of consideration; they are discussed here in contract formation rather than in another part of the analysis, such as "Breach" or the "Responses to Breach."

Section 1. WHAT ARE THE TERMS OF THE CONTRACT?

It is all well and good that the parties have contracted. But what have they really contracted to do? The answer clearly comes from the contract, whether oral or written. The contract should contain their rights and duties. The parties, however, may interpret the language of the contract differently or they may not agree as to which terms are included in the contract. These topics are explored next.

A. Interpreting the Language of the Contract

Words are vessels filled with ideas. Although words have standard meanings, these meanings may vary from time to time and region to region. Meanings may vary depending on whether the term is used in its general sense or as a trade term with a special meaning. Lewis Carroll, in his classic "Through the Looking-Glass", captures the full flavor in this go-around between Alice and Humpty Dumpty:

"But 'glory' doesn't mean a nice knockdown argument," Alice objected.

"When I use a word," Humpty Dumpty said, in rather a scornful tone, "it means just what I choose it to mean—neither more nor less."

"The question is," said Alice, "whether you can make words mean so many different things."

"The question is," said Humpty Dumpty, "which is to be master—that's all."

Regardless of what Humpty Dumpty believes, a contract term is interpreted according to its "plain meaning," that is, the meaning that reasonable people would give to that term. If a term has a plain meaning but one of the parties (unknown to the other party) attributes a special meaning to that term, the term will be interpreted according to its plain meaning. Because contracts are consensual, the parties may, at the time of contracting, agree to give the term a meaning other than its plain meaning.

It is common for a term to have two meanings, one meaning known by the general population and the other used in a particular trade. If both parties to the contract are members of the trade, the term is interpreted according to its trade meaning. If only one party is a member of the trade, the non-trade meaning applies. If one party is a long-standing member of the trade and the other is new to the trade, the non-trade meaning will apply unless the party new to the trade has actual knowledge of the trade meaning or the trade meaning was so generally known that actual knowledge could be inferred.

Consider the interpretation of the term "50 percent protein" in *Hurst v. W.J. Lake & Co.* Hurst, the seller of horse meat scraps, contracted to give W.J. Lake & Co., the buyer, a $5.00 discount for each ton analyzing less than 50 percent protein. When 140 tons of scraps contained protein varying from 49.53 percent to 49.96 percent, Lake claimed the discount over Hurst's objection. Could 50 percent be interpreted as 49.53 percent?

Hurst v. W.J. Lake & Co.

Supreme Court of Oregon, 1932.
141 Or. 306, 16 P.2d 627.

ROSSMAN, J.

From the portion of the pleadings which we are required to deem true, it appears that March 20, 1930, the plaintiff and the defendant entered into an agreement in writing, a copy of which follows:

"March 20, 1930.

"Messrs. Roscoe P. Hurst, Yeon Building, Portland, Oregon.

"Dear Sirs: We conform our purchase from you today as follows:

Buyer:	W.J. Lake & Co., Inc. Seattle, Washington.
Commodity:	Horse meat scraps.
Quantity:	350 tons of 2000 lbs. each.
Price:	$50.00 per ton f.o.b. cars Portland.
Terms of Payment:	Net cash in Portland on delivery with analysis certificate.
Time of Shipment:	Prior to April 20th, 1930.

Route:	As directed by buyer.
Specifications:	Minimum 50% protein, ground and sacked in 100 lb. net each. Additional specifications on supplementary page.

"Yours truly,
"W.J. Lake & Company, Inc.,
"By L.E. Branchflower.

"Accepted by:
"Roscoe P. Hurst.

"March 20, 1930.

"Mr. Roscoe P. Hurst, Yeon Building, Portland, Oregon.

"Dear Sir: In case any of the Horse Meat Scraps, covered by our purchase order No. 1352 analyzes less than 50% of protein, it is understood that W.J. Lake & Company, Inc., the buyers, are to receive a discount of $5.00 per ton.

"It is further understood that in case the buyer does not take delivery of the entire lot by April 20th, 1930, the seller agrees to carry the stock one (1) month more for 50¢ per ton additional.

"The Northwest Testing Laboratories are to instruct the warehouse in the loading and are to furnish analysis certificates, at the buyer's expense. In case of an analysis dispute findings of a refree (sic) chemist, who shall be mutually agreed upon, shall be final.

"Yours very truly,
"W.J. Lake & Co., Inc.,
"[Signed] L.E. Branchflower.
"LEB:G L.E. Branchflower.

"Accepted by:
"[Signed] Roscoe P. Hurst."

Pursuant to the contract, the plaintiff delivered to the defendant 349.25 tons of horse meat scraps which contained the following percentages of protein, and for which the defendant paid the following sums of money: 180 tons contained an excess of 50 per cent. protein, and the defendant paid for it $50 per ton; 29.25 tons contained 48.66 per cent. protein, and the defendant paid therefor $45 per ton; 140 tons contained protein varying from 49.53 per cent. to 49.96 per cent., for which the defendant paid $45 per ton. The following allegation of the complaint we are required to deem true:

"That at the time the written contract heretofore referred to for the sale of horse meat scraps was entered into on or about the 20th day of March, 1930, both plaintiff and defendant then were, and for some time prior thereto had been, engaged in the business of buying and selling horse meat scraps; that at the time said contract was entered into there was a custom and usage of trade in said business well known to both plaintiff and defendant as to the meaning of the terms 'minimum 50% protein' and 'less than 50% protein' used in the agreement between plaintiff and defendant. That by virtue of said custom so prevailing in said business of buying and selling horse meat scraps it was well known and understood among all members of the trade, including both plaintiff and defendant, that the terms 'minimum 50% protein' and 'less than 50% protein' when used in a contract for the sale of horse meat scraps with reference to a test of its protein content, meant that a protein content of not less than 49.5% was equal to and the same as a content of 50% protein. That it was further a part of said custom that where said terms 'minimum 50% protein' and 'less than 50% protein' should be used in a contract of sale it was and is the duty of the buyer to accept all horse meat scraps and pay for the same at the rate provided for a product which would test a minimum of 50% even though the chemical analysis of the product should show that the horse meat scraps actually should test as low as 49.5% protein content. That said custom in all its particulars was well known to both plaintiff and defendant and entered into and formed a part of the contract between plaintiff and defendant.

"That the said terms 'minimum 50% protein' and 'less than 50% protein' as used in said contract between plaintiff and defendant were known, understood and used in said contract by both plaintiff and defendant to have the meaning and significance given to said terms by the custom and usage heretofore alleged; that it was the intention of both the plaintiff and defendant that the said terms as used in said contract should mean that the defendant was and should be required to pay the plaintiff at the 50% protein content rate for all meat scraps delivered by plaintiff to defendant which should test as low as 49.5% protein content."

Based upon the contention that the above-quoted portion of the complaint, admitted as true by the defendant, shows that the 140 tons with a protein content of 49.53 per cent. to 49.96 per cent. should have been regarded as within the 50 per cent. protein classification, the plaintiff argues that the circuit court erred when it sustained the defendant's motion for judgment on the pleadings.

It will be observed from the foregoing (1) that there is a group of dealers who trade in the commodity known as horse meat scraps; (2) that both plaintiff and defendant are members of that group; (3) that the terms "minimum 50% protein" and "less than 50% protein" are trade terms to which the group has attached meanings different from their common ones; (4) that this usage, prevalent among this group, demanded that, whenever those terms appeared in a contract for the sale of horse meat scraps, it became the duty of the buyer to accept all scraps containing 49.5 per cent. protein or more, and to pay for them at the rate provided for scraps containing full 50 per cent. protein; and (5) that the defendant was aware of all of the foregoing when it attached its signature to the aforementioned contract.

The flexibility of or multiplicity in the meaning of words is the principal source of difficulty in the interpretation of language. Words are the conduits by which thoughts are communicated, yet scarcely any of them have such a fixed and single meaning that they are incapable of denoting more than one thought. In addition to the multiplicity in meaning of words set forth in the dictionaries, there are the meanings imparted to them by trade customs, local uses, dialects, telegraphic codes, etc. One meaning crowds a word full of significance, while another almost empties the utterance of any import. The various groups above indicated are constantly amplifying our language; in fact, they are developing what may be called languages of their own. Thus one is justified in saying that the language of the dictionaries is not the only language spoken in America. For instance, the word "thousand" as commonly used has a very specific meaning; it denotes ten hundreds or fifty scores, but the language of the various trades and localities has assigned to it meanings quite different from that just mentioned. Thus in the bricklaying trade a contract which fixes the bricklayer's compensation at "$5.25 a thousand" does not contemplate that he need lay actually 1,000 bricks in order to earn $5.25, but that he should build a wall of a certain size. Brunold v. Glasser, 25 Misc. 285, 52 N.Y.S. 1021; Walker v. Syms, 118 Mich. 183, 76 N.W. 320. In the lumber industry a contract requiring the delivery of 4,000 shingles will be fulfilled by the delivery of only 2,500 when it appears that by trade custom two packs of a certain size are regarded as 1,000 shingles, and that hence the delivery of eight packs fulfills the contract, even though they contain only 2,500 shingles by actual count. Soutier v. Kellerman, 18 Mo. 509. And, where the custom of a locality considers 100 dozen as constituting a thousand, one who has 19,200 rabbits upon a warren under an agreement for their sale at the price of 60 pounds for each thousand rabbits will be paid for only 16,000 rabbits. Smith v. Wilson, 3 Barn. & Adol. 728. Numerous other instances could readily be cited showing the manner in which the meaning of words has been contracted, expanded, or otherwise altered by local usage, trade custom, dialect influence, code agreement, etc. In fact, it is no novelty to find legislative enactments preceded by glossaries or brief dictionaries defining the meaning of the words employed in the act. Technical treatises dealing with aeronautics, the radio, engineering, etc., generally contain similar glossaries defining the meaning of many of the words employed by the craft. A glance at these glossaries readily shows that the different sciences and trades, in addition to coining words of their own, appropriate common words and assign to them new meanings. Thus it must be evident that one cannot understand accurately the language of such sciences and trades without knowing the peculiar meaning attached to the words which they use. It is said that a court in construing the language of the parties must put itself into the shoes of the parties. That alone would not suffice; it must also adopt their vernacular.

Wigmore on Evidence (2d) § 2460, points out that the interpretation of language may be thus approached: "The standard of the community, or popular standard, meaning the common and normal sense of words; the local standard including the special usages of a religious sect, a body of traders, an alien population or a local dialect; the mutual standard covering those meanings which are peculiar to both or all the parties to a transaction but shared in common by them; and the individual standard of one party to an act, as differing from that of the other party or parties, if any."

After Dean Wigmore has reviewed at length the overthrow of what he calls the traditional rule which insists that the meaning of all words is rigid and inflexible, and the development of what the terms the liberal rule which recognizes, to some extent at least, the four aforementioned standards of interpretation, he continues (section 2463): "The liberal rule, on the other hand, is today conceded practically everywhere, to permit resort in any case to the usage of a trade or locality, no matter how plain the apparent sense of the word to the ordinary reader; and some of the extreme instances are persuasive to demonstrate the fallacy of ignoring the purely relative meaning of words and the injustice of attempting to enforce a supposed rigid standard."

From Williston on Contracts, § 650, we quote: "Though Professor Thayer has said that 'In contracts it was always recognized that familiar words may have different meanings in different places, so that "every bargain as to such a thing shall have relation to the custom of the country where it is made." ' it may be doubted how far it was allowable under early law to show that a word in a written contract (or perhaps in an oral agreement) having a clear and fixed ordinary meaning bore a meaning contrary to its usual significance, if nothing in the context showed that a particular meaning was intended. But there are now numerous decisions (not all of them of recent date) where words with a clear, normal meaning have been shown by usage to bear a meaning which nothing in the context would suggest. This is not only true of technical terms, but of language which, at least on its face, has no peculiar or technical significance; though even today it is still occasionally said by courts that usage cannot control words having 'a definite legal meaning'; or cannot be used to interpret a contract unless there is an uncertainty on the face of the instrument."

From 3 Starkle on Evidence, 1033, we quote: "Where terms are used which are known and understood by a particular class of persons, in a certain special and peculiar sense, evidence to that effect is admissible for the purpose of applying the instrument to its proper subject-matter; and the case seems to fall within the same consideration as if the parties in framing their contract had made use of a foreign language which the courts are not bound to understand * * *. Conformably with these principles, the courts have long allowed mercantile instruments to be expounded according to the custom of merchants, who have a style and language peculiar to themselves, of which usage and custom are the legitimate interpreters."

From Page on Contracts, § 2028, we quote: "Usages, such as those of a trade, may be resorted to to show the special meanings of words."

From 17 C.J. Customs and Usages, p. 499, § 62, we quote: "Words technical or ambiguous on their face, or foreign or peculiar to the sciences or the arts, or to particular trades, professions, occupations or localities, are explainable where they are employed in written instruments by parol evidence of usage."

See to the same effect 27 R.C.L. Usages and Customs, p. 170, § 19, and 27 Albany Law Journal, p. 464 (reviewing many authorities), and Electric Reduction Co. v. Colonial Steel Co., 276 Pa. 181, 120 A. 116 (reviewing many authorities).

The defendant cites numerous cases in many of which the courts held that, when a contract is expressed in language which is not ambiguous upon its face the court will receive no evidence of usage, but will place upon the words of the parties their common meaning; in other words, in those decisions the courts ran the words of the parties through a judicial sieve whose meshes were incapable of retaining anything but the common meaning of the words, and which permitted the meaning which the parties had placed upon them to run away as waste material. Surely those courts did not believe that words are always used in their orthodox sense. The rulings must have been persuaded by other considerations. The rule which rejects evidence of custom has the advantage of simplicity; it protects the writing from attack by some occasional individual who will seek to employ perjured testimony in proof of alleged custom; and, if one can believe that the parol evidence rule is violated when common meaning is rejected in favor of special meaning, then the above rule serves the purpose of the parol evidence rule. Without setting forth the manner in which we came to our conclusion, we state that none of these reasons appeals to us as sufficient to exclude evidence of custom and assign to the words their common meaning only, even though the instrument is nonambiguous upon its face. The defendant argues that this court has held that custom or usage cannot be resorted to in the interpretation of the meaning of an instrument where no ambiguity appears upon its face, and cites in support of his contention Williams v. Ledbetter, 132 Or. 145, 285 P. 214; Darling-Singer Lbr. Co. v. Oriental Navigation Co., 127 Or. 655, 259 P. 420, 272 P. 275; Interior Warehouse Co. v. Dunn, 80 Or. 528, 157 P. 806; Oregon Fisheries Co. v. Elmore Packing Co., 69 Or. 340, 138 P. 862; Barnard & Bunker v. Houser, 68 Or. 240, 137 P. 227; Savage v. Salem Mills Co., 48 Or. 1, 85 P. 69, 10 Ann.Cas. 1065; Abraham v. Oregon & California R.R. Co., 37 Or. 495, 60 P. 899, 64 L.R.A. 391, 82 Am.St. Rep. 779; and Holmes v. Whitaker, 23 Or. 319, 31 P. 705. It must be admitted that language can be found in some of these decisions which lends weight to his argument. But a reading of these cases will disclose that in all of them, with the exception of Abraham v. Oregon & California R.R. Co., the party was not resorting to custom for the purpose of interpreting the language of the instrument, but for the purpose of annexing or engrafting on to the contract an additional term; in other words, he sought to prove that the written instrument did not embody the entire agreement. Such a contention invoked a principle quite different from the one with which we are now concerned. For comment see Wigmore on Evidence (2d) § 2440. In Abraham v. Oregon & California R.R. Co., the decision does not mention custom. The appellant in that case sought to prove that he and the party with whom he dealt had placed upon one of the terms of the instrument a mutual meaning distinct from its normal one.

Section 9–217, Oregon Code 1930, provides: "The terms of a writing are presumed to have been used in their primary and general acceptation, but evidence is nevertheless admissible that they have a technical, local, or otherwise peculiar signification, and were so used and understood in the particular instance, in which case the agreement shall be construed accordingly." In McCulsky v. Klosterman, 20 Or. 108, 25 P. 366, 10 L.R.A. 785, this court, after finding that the parties, both of whom belonged to the same business group, had used the term "outstanding account" in a contract as a trade term, interpreted its meaning according to the standards of the trade. In McDonald v. Supple, 96 Or. 486, 190 P. 315, Mr. Justice Bean, on behalf of this court, stated the rule governing trade terms and technical words in substantially the language of the statute. California has a statute similar to our above enactment (see Fairall's Code of Civil Procedure, § 1861, or Kerr's Cyclopedic Codes of California, § 1861), and the California courts have cited it as authority for the holding that a party may not only show that a term possesses a trade or local meaning but also that it was used in that manner. Higgins v. California Petroleum, etc., Co., 120 Cal. 629, 52 P. 1080, and County of Alameda v. Garrison, 108 Cal.App. 122, 291 P. 464. In the Higgins Case the court held that evidence was admissible to show that the term "gross ton" was a trade term to which dealers in petroleum had attached the meaning of 2,240 pounds, even though a statute of California defined a ton as "twenty hundredweight." California also has a statute (Fairall's Code of Civil Procedure, § 1870, subd. 12, and Kerr's Cyclopedic Codes of California, § 1870, subd. 12) similar to section 9–226, subd. 12, Oregon Code 1930, to which the defendant has called our attention, but that enactment did not prevent the court from the liberal holding indicated by the two above decisions. Section 9–226, subd. 12, Oregon Code 1930, reads as follows: "In conformity with the preceding provisions, evidence may be given on the trial, of the following facts: * * * Usage, to explain the true character of an act, contract, or instrument, where such true character is not otherwise plain; but usage is never admissible except as a means of interpretation. * * * "

Without setting forth herein our review of the many authorities cited in the briefs, all of which we have read with care, we state our conclusion that members of a trade or business group who have employed in their contracts trade terms are entitled to prove that fact in their litigation, and show the meaning of those terms to assist the court in the interpretation of their language.

Finally, it is suggested that the employment of the terms "minimum 50% protein" and "less than 50% of protein" indicates that the parties rejected the mercantile custom in effecting their contract. It will be recalled that under the state of the record we are compelled to regard these two terms as trade terms possessed of a special significance. We believe that it is safe to assume, in the absence of evidence to the contrary, that, when tradesmen employ trade terms, they attach to them their trade significance. If, when they write their trade terms into their contracts, they mean to strip the terms of their special significance and demote them to their common import, it would seem reasonable to believe that they would so state in their agreement. Otherwise they would refrain from using the trade term and express themselves in other language. We quote from Nicoll v. Pittsvein Coal Co. (C.C.A.) 269 F. 968, 971: "Indeed when tradesmen say or write anything, they are perhaps without present thought on the subject, writing on top of a mass of habits or usages which they take as matter of course. So (with Prof. Williston) we think that any one contracting with knowledge of a usage will naturally say nothing about the matter unless desirous of excluding its operation; if he does wish to exclude, he will say so in express terms. Williston, Contracts, § 653." Nothing in the contract repels the meaning assigned by the trade to the two above terms unless the terms themselves reject it. But, if these terms repel the meaning which usage has attached to them, then every trade term would deny its own meaning. We reject this contention as being without merit. We have considered all other contentions presented by the respondent, but have found no merit in them.

It follows that, in our opinion, the circuit court erred when it sustained the defendant's motion for judgment on the pleadings.

Reversed.

BROWN, BELT, CAMPBELL, and KELLY, JJ., concur.

RAND, J., concurs in the result.

BEAN, C.J., dissents.

B. Identifying the Terms Included in the Contract

Not all contracts need to be in writing to be enforceable. Part III (contracts that are unenforceable) explores which contracts must be in writing and what constitutes the writing (Statute of Frauds). For contract formation purposes, the need for a writing is irrelevant unless the offeror mandates that the writing will be the last act of contracting.

If, however, the parties have reduced their agreement to writing, whether the writing was or was not required for the enforcement of the contract, the question is whether the writing encompasses all the terms of the contract or only some. The answer is found in the parol evidence rule, the next topic for discussion.

1. Parol Evidence Rule

Although some contracts are created on the spur of the moment, often the contract is a product of negotiations between the parties prior to the actual time of contract formation. These negotiations may be brief or extended. Inherent in the sequence of negotiation followed by a written contract is the risk that not all terms agreed upon in the negotiation will appear in the writing. Does failure to include all of the agreed-upon terms mean those terms not incorporated into the writing are not terms of the contract? Should the answer be that the contract consists of some written and some oral terms?

Under the parol evidence rule, the contract may consist of both written and parol (including oral) terms.

> In the absence of fraud, duress, or mutual mistake, extrinsic evidence, oral or written, made prior to or contemporaneous with the final writing cannot be used to add to or contradict the final writing.

The parol evidence rule does not apply to all transactions nor does it apply to all parol evidence. First, the parol evidence rule only comes into play when the terms of the contract have been set forth in a final writing. If the parties have a writing but it is not intended as the final writing, the rule does not apply. The question that must be asked is "Has the contract been integrated?"

Second, the parol evidence rule does not apply to transactions where there has been fraud, duress, or mutual mistake. In those transactions, the parol evidence rule is inapplicable even though the contract has been integrated.

Third, the parol evidence rule only excludes extrinsic evidence of events that were prior to or contemporaneous with (at the same time as) the final writing. The rule does not exclude evidence that was created after the parties entered into the final writing.

Fourth, the parol evidence rule only excludes evidence that adds to or contradicts those terms that appear in the final writing. The rule does not exclude evidence that is intended to clarify or interpret the terms in the final writing.

PROBLEM 1: The Eldridge house needed exterior painting so Eldridge telephoned the Quality Painting Company for an estimate. Quality looked at the house and on several occasions, discussed the job with Eldridge by telephone. Finally, Eldridge agreed to pay Quality $2,000 for painting her house. When Quality finished painting the house, Eldridge refused to pay until Quality painted the garage.

Eldridge claims that during the negotiation they discussed the house and the garage and the contract was for both even though they did not specifically talk about the garage during the final telephone conversation. Quality claims that they did not discuss the garage during the final telephone conversation and therefore the contract was for the house and not the garage.

Under the parol evidence rule, does the contract include the garage?

PROBLEM 2: Same facts as Problem 1, except the final telephone conversation was followed by a final writing which spoke of the house but was silent on the garage.

Under the parol evidence rule, does the contract include the garage?

PROBLEM 3: Same facts as Problem 2 but during the negotiation, no mention was made of the garage. The parties only discussed the house for $2,000. After Quality began to paint the house, Eldridge asked Quality how much it would cost to paint the garage. Quality orally responded $500 and they orally agreed.

When Quality finished painting the house and the garage, Eldridge would only pay $2,000 because the writing only stated $2,000.

Under the parol evidence rule, has the contract been orally modified to include the garage?

PROBLEM 4: After extended negotiations, Buyer and Seller contracted for $50,000 of "chickens." Their final writing contained only the term "chickens." Upon uncrating the shipment Buyer was surprised to find "stewing chickens" instead of "fryers."

Should any prior discussion between Seller and Buyer as to the type of chicken be excluded as a violation of the parol evidence rule?

2. Supplying Omitted Terms

Irrespective of whether the contract is written, oral or a bit of both, can terms never actually discussed or agreed upon by the parties become a part of the contract? This section discusses these "omitted terms."

Regardless of whether the contract is oral or written, there are times when one contracting party would like to add a term to the contract that was never discussed. If this term is "good faith," the courts have consistently obliged the party seeking to have this term added. Therefore, both parties must exercise good faith when performing their obligations under the contract.

Care should be taken to distinguish the negotiation phase of contract formation from the performance phase. Each party must perform the contract in good faith. Neither party is required to negotiate a contract in good faith because at the pre-contract phase of the transaction, no contractual relationship exists upon which to attach the reciprocal good faith promises.

> *PROBLEM 5:* Does Pluto Computers have a duty to deal in good faith in the following situations:
>
> 1. Pluto manufactures and distributes computers worldwide. Some of its products are unique and are not yet available from any other company. Omni Unlimited, a data processing company, sought to buy several of Pluto's products, Pluto being the sole supplier of these products. Pluto refused to deal with Omni unless Omni would include in the contract its promise to buy all of its computer equipment from Pluto over the next five years.
> 2. Pluto and Omni have a contract for the purchase of sixteen computers. Omni has discussed buying an additional ten, but is hesitant to finalize the contract until it uses the sixteen computers already ordered. Pluto will not ship these computers until Omni places the second order.

If the transaction is a sale of goods, the Uniform Commercial Code will supply some omitted terms. For a discussion of the Code's "gap fillers," see page 107.

Section 2. CORRECTING ERRORS IN THE WRITTEN CONTRACT: MISTAKE IN INTEGRATION

Parties may orally contract with the understanding that one of the parties will later draft a writing to reflect the terms of the contract. Ultimately both parties may sign this written confirmation of their oral contract. The parties may even sign without thoroughly reading. Later, as the parties perform their duties, one party may be surprised to find that the writing fails to correspond to what he or she thought was agreed upon. A mistake occurred in the integration of the contract. When confronted by this alleged mistake in integration, the drafter may insist that the writing reflects the oral agreement. Can the other party have the writing reformed (altered) so it corresponds to the oral agreement?

A court has the power to reform (alter) the written evidence of a contract so it reflects the understanding of the parties. Reformation is appropriate only if clear and convincing evidence demonstrates that (1) the parties' oral agreement expresses their real intentions; (2) the writing fails to express those intentions; and (3) the failure is due to a mutual mistake or a unilateral mistake accompanied by the other party's fraudulent conduct.

A mutual mistake is a mistake that both parties shared at the time they reduced their agreement to writing. The court will reform a writing only when the parties intended their written agreement to say one thing and, by mistake, it expressed something else. The fact that one of the parties denies that a mistake occurred does not prevent the court from finding a mutual mistake.

In *Bollinger v. Central Pennsylvania Quarry Stripping & Construction Co.* the Bollingers owned property near the Pennsylvania Turnpike. Central, a contractor working on the Turnpike, orally contracted with the Bollingers for permission to deposit construction waste on the Bollingers' property. Central surprised the Bollingers by dumping the construction waste without any attempt at soil reclamation.

The Bollingers contended that the writing differed from the oral agreement. What was the mistake in the integration of the contract? Did Central agree that the writing did not correspond to the oral agreement? Would a reasonable person believe that the writing did or did not correspond to the oral agreement? What would the reasonable person consider when making this determination? If Central does not agree that a mistake in integrating the contract was made, on what basis does the court conclude that the mistake in integration was mutual?

Bollinger v. Central Pennsylvania Quarry Stripping & Construction Co.

Supreme Court of Pennsylvania, 1967.
425 Pa. 430, 229 A.2d 741.

Opinion of the Court

MUSMANNO, Justice.

Mahlon Bollinger and his wife, Vinetta C. Bollinger, filed an action in equity against the Central Pennsylvania Quarry Stripping Construction Company asking that a contract entered into between them be reformed so as to include therein a paragraph alleged to have been omitted by mutual mistake and that the agreement, as reformed, be enforced.

The agreement, as executed, provided that the defendant was to be permitted to deposit on the property of the plaintiffs, construction waste as it engaged in work on the Pennsylvania Turnpike in the immediate vicinity of the plaintiffs' property. The Bollingers claimed that there had been a mutual understanding between them and the defendant that, prior to depositing such waste on the plaintiffs' property, the defendant would remove the topsoil of the plaintiffs' property, pile on it the waste material and then restore the topsoil in a way to cover the deposited waste. The Bollingers averred that they had signed the written agreement without reading it because they assumed that the condition just stated had been incorporated into the writing.

When the defendant first began working in the vicinity of the plaintiffs' property, it did first remove the topsoil, deposited the waste on the bare land, and then replaced the topsoil. After a certain period of time, the defendant ceased doing this and the plaintiffs remonstrated. The defendant answered there was nothing in the written contract which required it to make a sandwich of its refuse between the bare earth and the topsoil. It was at this point that the plaintiffs discovered that that feature of the oral understanding had been omitted from the written contract. The plaintiff husband renewed his protest and the defendant's superintendent replied he could not remove the topsoil because his equipment for that operation had been taken away. When he was reminded of the original understanding, the superintendent said, in effect, he couldn't help that.

The plaintiffs then filed their action for reformation of the contract, the Court granted the requested relief, and the defendant firm appealed. We said in Bugen v. New York Life Insurance Co., 408 Pa. 472, 184 A.2d 499:

"A court of equity has the power to reform the written evidence of a contract and make it correspond to the understanding of the parties. * * * However, the mistake must be mutual to the parties to the contract."

The fact, however, that one of the parties denies that a mistake was made does not prevent a finding of mutual mistake. Kutsenkow v. Kutsenkow, 414 Pa. 610, 612, 202 A.2d 68.

Once a person enters into a written agreement he builds around himself a stone wall, from which he cannot escape by merely asserting he had not understood what he was signing. However, equity would completely fail in its objectives if it refused to break a hole through the wall when it finds, after proper evidence, that there was a mistake between the parties, that it was real and not feigned, actual and not hypothetical.

The Chancellor, after taking testimony, properly concluded:

"We are satisfied that plaintiffs have sustained the heavy burden placed upon them. Their understanding of the agreement is corroborated by the undisputed evidence. The defendant did remove and set aside the top soil on part of the area before depositing its waste and did replace the top soil over such waste after such depositing. It follows it would not have done so had it not so agreed. Further corroboration is found in the testimony that it acted similarly in the case of plaintiffs' neighbor Beltzner."

After the Court handed down its Decree Nisi, the defendant petitioned for a rehearing on the ground of after-discovered evidence. Even assuming, without so deciding, that the so-called after-discovered evidence qualified as such, it is not clear that it was sufficiently material or relevant to bring about a change in the result reached by the Chancellor, and he so stated in his Opinion. We are satisfied that the proffered evidence would not be inconsistent with the Chancellor's findings.

Decree affirmed, costs on the appellant.

BELL, C.J., dissents.

COHEN, J., absent.

In *Nichols v. Shelard National Bank* the homeowners asked the court to reform the $30,000 second mortgage on their home to $10,000. Was the Minnesota Supreme Court correct in refusing to reform the mortgage?

Nichols v. Shelard National Bank

Supreme Court of Minnesota, 1980.
294 N.W.2d 730.

Heard before OTIS, PETERSON, and WAHL, JJ., and considered and decided by the court en banc.

WAHL, Justice.

The plaintiffs, Richard and Janice Nichols, brought this action in Hennepin County District Court seeking to have a $30,000 second mortgage on their home held by the defendant, Shelard National Bank, declared null and void. The bank counterclaimed to foreclose the mortgage. The Nichols responded by requesting that the mortgage either be declared null and void or be reformed "to embody the actual agreement of the parties." The trial court, hearing the case without a jury, ordered that the mortgage be reformed from $30,000 to $10,000 and that the mortgage, as reformed, be foreclosed. The bank argues on appeal that the trial court's findings are manifestly contrary to the evidence and that the trial court erred in reforming the mortgage instrument from $30,000 to $10,000. We reverse.

In the fall of 1973, Richard Nichols, who had been in the restaurant business for 25 years, formed Cyrano's Restaurant, Inc. Mr. Nichols was the sole shareholder and president and Mrs. Nichols was named secretary-treasurer, but she was not active in the business. Cyrano's opened in January 1974, in Plymouth, Minnesota. Defendant Shelard National Bank provided Cyrano's with a loan for $150,000 in order to equip the restaurant. The loan was secured by the equipment, as well as by the personal guaranty of Charles Belgaard, the president of the corporation that leased the restaurant building to Cyrano's. Plaintiffs also raised funds for starting the business by borrowing on their life insurance policies and refinancing their home with the Farmers and Mechanics Savings Bank of Minneapolis.

Business at the restaurant was good until early in 1975, when the Radisson Plymouth opened for business across the street from Cyrano's. Business then declined, and Cyrano's had to take a number of short-term loans for operating expenses. When defendant Shelard was unable to provide any additional financing, Nichols borrowed $15,000 from the First National Bank of Hopkins, secured by accounts receivable and inventory. In August and December 1975, defendant made two $10,000 90–day loans to Cyrano's, each of which was secured by accounts receivable and inventory. The defendant's security interest in Cyrano's was subordinate to the security interest in the same collateral held by the First National Bank of Hopkins. In November 1975, Cyrano's borrowed $25,000 from the Citizens State Bank in St. Louis Park in order to pay a portion of federal and state taxes, pledging as collateral all outstanding shares in Cyrano's. The defendant was aware that Cyrano's had borrowed from these other banks. The two $10,000 loans with defendant were renewed in February 1976, and again in April, secured by the same collateral.

Cyrano's continued to go downhill financially. By June 1976, plaintiff owed defendant approximately $110,000 on the original $150,000 note, plus $20,000 due to the renewed $10,000 notes; owed to the state and federal government for taxes; owed $25,000 to Citizens State Bank; owed food suppliers; and owed $10,000 to First National Bank of Hopkins. Early in June, the First National Bank of Hopkins stated it would foreclose on its note, and therefore put Cyrano's out of business, unless it received a $10,000 second mortgage on plaintiffs' house. Plaintiffs refused to give the requested second mortgage. Several meetings, at which the financial condition of Cyrano's was discussed, took place in May and June 1976. The parties disagree regarding exactly what transpired at these meetings.

Gerald Wright, the president of defendant Shelard National Bank, testified that on May 3, 1976, he met with plaintiff and Sheldon Wert, the chairman of the bank's board of directors, in order to discuss ways for Cyrano's to acquire additional working capital. Plans for obtaining a partner to buy into the business had fallen through. They also discussed the possibility of turning the restaurant into a disco. The plaintiff's principal suggestion, which he saw as the last resort to save his business, was to convert part of the restaurant into a peanut bar, which he felt could be done for $10,000.

On May 23 or 26, another meeting took place in Wright's office. The plaintiff gave Wright and Wert a list of creditors, showing an indebtedness of more than $235,000. The parties discussed the threat from First Hopkins to foreclose on its $10,000 note, and plaintiff was told that if defendant were to pay off the Hopkins bank, it would combine that $10,000 with the two existing $10,000 notes and secure the entire $30,000 with a second mortgage on the plaintiffs' home. Plaintiff indicated that First Hopkins had also wanted a second mortgage on his home and he had refused. He said he did not like the idea and would in any case have to talk to his wife and his attorney before deciding. Immediately after the meeting, defendant ordered a title insurance policy binder on the plaintiffs' home in the amount of $30,000, and this binder was issued on June 7, 1976.

Another meeting was held on June 22, attended by Wert, Wright, the plaintiff and his attorney, Belgaard, and Harry Yaffee, who was the general manager of Belgaard's corporation. The meeting was called in order to discuss past due payments on the large loan and past due rent payments, but the major concern of all parties was the threat by the Hopkins bank to foreclose and take all of Cyrano's inventory. There was some discussion of plaintiff's peanut bar idea; plaintiff felt it was the only opportunity left to save his restaurant. Wert told the plaintiff that the bank would lend him $10,000 only if it could renew the $20,000 in outstanding notes, combine it with the $10,000 note, and take a second mortgage on his home for $30,000. According to Wright's testimony, plaintiff's lawyer strongly objected to this plan, but by the end of the meeting the plaintiff agreed, against his lawyer's advice, because he felt it was necessary in order to stay in business. Thus, the bank's understanding of the agreement was that it would lend plaintiff $10,000 to pay off the Hopkins bank and renew the two $10,000 notes that were now due, in return for a $30,000 second mortgage on plaintiff's home. Wright testified that the bank never promised, or ever intended to promise, to lend any money to set up a peanut bar in the restaurant.

Plaintiff's understanding of the meeting and the agreement was different, however. Plaintiff testified that, although Wert was insistent upon receiving a second mortgage to secure the outstanding $20,000 he owed to the bank, plaintiff was just as insistent that he would not do this. Plaintiff testified that he indicated to Wert, against his lawyer's advice, that if he could obtain $10,000 "fresh money" to build his peanut bar and stay in business, then he would consider getting a second mortgage on his home for $10,000. He had already been working on construction of the peanut bar for about two months. His understanding was that the bank would have to pay off the Hopkins bank anyway, in order to protect its security interest in Cyrano's accounts receivable and inventory, and that it would further lend him $10,000 to finish building the peanut bar, secured by a second mortgage for $10,000. Plaintiff said he discussed whether or not to agree to a $10,000 mortgage with his attorney and decided to do it, against his attorney's advice. Plaintiff's attorney also testified that the mortgage was to be for $10,000. Plaintiff testified he would never have signed a $30,000 note to pay off money already owed without receiving any "fresh money" to enable him to continue his business.

A note and mortgage were drawn up by the bank in the amount of $30,000. There is no question that plaintiff and his wife came into the bank approximately one week after the June 22 meeting and signed six documents which set out that the mortgage was for $30,000. Plaintiffs said they did not read the documents but relied on their understanding of the agreement reached at the June 22 meeting that the mortgage would be for $10,000.

The First Hopkins note was paid by defendant on June 28, 1976. Plaintiff apparently never received any money to construct his peanut bar. At the time of trial, the unpaid balance on the $30,000 note was $27,855.78.

The issue for our determination is whether the trial court erred in reforming the mortgage instrument. Plaintiffs argue that the reformation ordered by the trial court is justified because of a mutual mistake of fact. A written instrument can be reformed by a court if the following elements are proved: (1) there was a valid agreement between the parties expressing their real intentions; (2) the written instrument failed to express the real intentions of the parties; and (3) this failure was due to a mutual mistake of the parties, or a unilateral mistake accompanied by fraud or inequitable conduct by the other party. *Theros v. Phillips,* 256 N.W.2d 852, 857 (Minn.1977); *Fritz v. Fritz,* 94 Minn. 264, 102 N.W. 705 (1905). These facts must be established by evidence which is clear and consistent, unequivocal and convincing. *Id.*

The evidence, even when viewed in the light most favorable to the plaintiff, does not support the trial court's order for reformation, under a theory of either mutual mistake or unilateral mistake and misrepresentation. Were there fraud, misrepresentation or inequitable conduct by the defendant, reformation would be proper; but, even accepting the plaintiff's testimony as true, no fraud by the bank can be found. Plaintiff was not told by Wright when he signed the documents that they were for $10,000. Defendant testified he told plaintiff they were for $30,000, and plaintiff testified Wright said nothing about the amount of the mortgage. Moreover, in order to have a mutual mistake, it is necessary that both parties agree as to the content of the document but that somehow through a scrivener's error the document does not reflect that agreement. There is no evidence here of scrivener's error, since the documents did reflect the defendant's understanding of the agreement.

When both parties acted in good faith and neither misled the other, but nevertheless each party was mistaken and thought he was making a different contract from what the other party supposed he was making, reformation is not an appropriate remedy. *Bancharel v. Patterson,* 64 Minn. 454, 67 N.W. 356 (1896). Absent ambiguity, fraud or misrepresentation, a mistake of one of the parties alone as to the subject matter of the contract is not a ground for reformation. *Olson v. Shephard,* 165 Minn. 433, 206 N.W. 711 (1926).

Furthermore, had plaintiffs read the documents before they signed them, their mistake as to the contents would have been discovered before they suffered any harm. Were this court to allow reformation, it would not only destroy the defendant's right to rely on plaintiffs' written assent to the agreement, but would reward plaintiffs for their negligence. Unfortunate as the situation may be for the plaintiffs, this case illustrates the reason for the Statute of Frauds, requiring most contracts to be in writing: to prevent a party from being held responsible by oral, and perhaps false, testimony, for a contract he claims he never made. "[T]he purpose of the statute is to guard not only against the dishonesty of parties and the perjury of witnesses, but against the misunderstanding and mistakes of honest men." 73 Am.Jur.2d *Statute of Frauds* § 510 (1974).

Reversed.

Section 3. MODIFYING A CONTRACT

After the creation of a contract but before full performance, the needs of the contracting parties may change. Performance of the contract may no longer be in their best interest. The parties may desire to modify the terms of the contract so it keeps pace with their needs. This section explores this problem.

Once parties enter into a bilateral contract, each party's promise is consideration for the other's promise.

EXAMPLE

"I promise to sell you Blackacre for your promise to pay $500,000 cash."
"I promise to pay $500,000 cash for your promise to sell me Blackacre."
Buyer's promise to pay $500,000 in cash is consideration for Seller's

promise to sell Blackacre; Seller's promise to sell Blackacre is consideration for Buyer's promise to pay $500,000 in cash.

Assume Buyer becomes a little short on cash and would like to modify the contract so she can pay $300,000 cash and $200,000 plus interest in one year. Seller, knowing that $500,000 is a good price, is willing to modify the contract so Buyer has more time to pay. The dialogue, translated into offer format, might be something like this:

> "I promise to sell you Blackacre for your promise to pay me $300,000 cash and $200,000 plus interest in one year." The consideration for Seller's promise to sell Blackacre is Buyer's promise to pay $300,000 cash and $200,000 plus interest in one year. Under the original contract, Buyer had the duty to pay $500,000. Buyer's new promise adds the duty to pay interest on $200,000 to the promise to pay $500,000. Seller is asking for new consideration from Buyer. Seller has made a new offer.

Now check Buyer's attempted acceptance: "I promise to pay you $300,000 cash and $200,000 plus interest in one year for your promise to sell me Blackacre." The consideration for Buyer's promise to pay $300,000 cash and $200,000 plus interest in one year is Seller's promise to sell Blackacre. Under the original contract, Seller had the duty to sell Blackacre to Buyer. Buyer is not asking for new consideration from Seller. Buyer, under the original contract, is already entitled to the original consideration. Seller has a preexisting duty to sell Buyer Blackacre. Without new consideration for Buyer's promise, the attempted acceptance fails. The modification is a contract and must follow the same rules of contract formation required for the original contract. Because the offer to modify cannot be accepted (preexisting duty precludes consideration), the attempt at modification fails.

PROBLEM 6: The Bon Appetit Bakery Company contracted with Samantha Mills to host a fifteen episode TV cooking show sponsored by Bon Appetit. The contract provided that Ms. Mills would receive $200,000 per episode. Filming of all episodes would take place at the WFUN studios in Boston. Before the filming began, Ms. Mills demanded that Bon Appetit increase her salary to $250,000 an episode. Bon Appetit agreed. Bon Appetit paid Ms. Mills $250,000 for the first fourteen episodes but only $200,000 for the last.

Was the contract successfully modified thus entitling Ms. Mills to an additional $50,000 for the last episode?

PROBLEM 7: Same facts as in Problem 6 except that the attempted modification called for sixteen rather than fifteen episodes. Was the contract successfully modified so Ms. Mills was entitled to an additional $50,000 for the last episode?

PROBLEM 8: Same facts as in Problem 7 except that the attempted modification called for fourteen rather than fifteen episodes. Was the contract successfully modified so Ms. Mills was entitled to an additional $50,000 for the last episode?

PROBLEM 9: Same facts as in Problem 6 except that the attempted modification called for the filming to be in southern France rather than in Boston. Was the contract successfully modified so Ms. Mills was entitled to an additional $50,000 for the last episode?

PROBLEM 10: Same facts as in Problem 6 except that the original contract offer was for a unilateral rather than a bilateral contract. Was there a successful modification so Ms. Mills was entitled to an additional $50,000 for the last episode?

Recently, state legislatures have addressed the modification issue. The Uniform Commercial Code made the most uniform and sweeping changes for the sale of goods. Section 2–209(1) provides:

> An agreement modifying a contract within this Article needs no consideration to be binding.

PROBLEM 11: How would Problem 6 be resolved under the UCC?

PROBLEM 12: The Quality Glue Company contracted to sell to the Heirloom Furniture Company all of its glue requirements for the next year at $10 a barrel. Three months into the contract, Quality raised its price to $11 a barrel with Heirloom's consent. Has the contract price been successfully modified from $10 to $11 a barrel? Assume that this jurisdiction has enacted the UCC.

Section 4. ENDING A CONTRACT BEFORE IT HAS BEEN FULLY PERFORMED

After the creation of a contract but before it has been fully performed, the needs of the contracting parties may change. Performance of the contract may no longer be in their best interest. The parties may want to end their contractual duties without the contract being fully performed. This section investigates terminating contractual duties when neither party has fully performed, terminating contractual duties when one party has fully performed, terminating a noncontractual duty, and terminating contractual or noncontractual duties with a "payment in full" check.

A. Terminating a Contractual Duty When Neither Party Has Fully Performed

Contracting parties may agree to terminate their contractual duties when neither party has fully performed. Because neither has fully performed, both have contractual duties. To rescind the contract, the parties must follow the same rules of contracts law used when they formed the original contract. The rescission has an offer and an acceptance. The offer consists of the promisor's promise and the consideration for the promisor's promise. "I promise to release you from your contract duties to me for your promise to release me from my contract duties to you." The acceptance consists of the promisee's promise and the consideration for the promisee's promise (the mirror image of the offer). "I promise to release you from your contract duties to me for your promise to release me from my contract duties to you." When the promisee promises, the promisor's offer is accepted and the rescission contract is formed. A rescission releases both parties from their contractual obligations. The duties of both parties under the original contract are terminated.

PROBLEM 13: Tom, a standup comic, contracted with the Village Theatre of Victor, New York, to perform during the first two weeks of August. In mid-July Tom received an offer to perform at a Las Vegas hotel which would substantially benefit his career. The Village Theatre does not want to lose Tom.

Can Tom rescind the contract?

PROBLEM 14: Susan, an interior decorator, contracts to work for Design Today for one year at a salary of $1,000 a week. After working for three months, Susan is invited to join another interior decorating firm with an increase in salary. Design Today has encouraged Susan to accept the new position because business at Design Today has been rather slow.

Draft a rescission that will free both Susan and Design Today from their duties under their contract.

B. Terminating a Contractual Duty When One Party Has Fully Performed

When the decision to rescind surfaces, not all parties have outstanding duties. One party may have fully performed while the other party may have only partially performed. The party who has fully performed may still want to release the other. This type of release cannot follow contract form. Because one party has fully performed, that party no longer owes a duty to the other party. Without a duty being owed by both parties, consideration for one of the promises to release is missing. "I promise to release you from your duty for your promise to release me from my duty" becomes "I promise to release you from your duty for no consideration." Without consideration the attempted offer fails. Without an offer, the attempted rescission contract fails.

PROBLEM 15: Roberta, an artist, sold Jim a bronze sculpture for $2,500. Roberta delivered the sculpture to Jim and, he paid her $1,500. The next month Jim paid Roberta $500.

Upon reflection, Jim decided $2,500 was too high a price for the sculpture and he wanted to be released from his duty to pay the outstanding $500. Jim presented Roberta with a writing which said "I, Roberta, promise to release Jim from his duty to pay me $500 for Jim's promise to release me from my duties to him." The writing also stated "I, Jim, promise to release Roberta from her duties to me for her promise to release me from my duty to pay her $500."

If both parties sign the writing, has Roberta contracted to release Jim?

If one party has fully performed, that party can unilaterally release the other party. The transaction would not be a contract because the promise to release would lack consideration. The promisor, however, can confer a gift on the party who has contractual duties. The subject of the gift would be the promisor's right to that performance. The promisor's statement would be "I give you my right." The law of gifts would apply to the promisor's promise.

> *PROBLEM 16:* Could Roberta, in Problem 15, release Jim from his duty to pay $500? Should the failed attempt to contract be treated as a gift?

A dispute concerning either the existence or the amount of the claim must exist. Without a dispute, the claim is certain and a preexisting duty exists to pay the claim. The preexisting duty cannot be consideration for the promise to release the claim. The consideration must be new consideration and not consideration that is already owed.

> *PROBLEM 17:* Sam borrowed $100 from Ted and promised to repay it. When Sam kept delaying repayment, Ted promised to release Sam from his duty to pay $100 if Sam would promise to pay $75. Sam, naturally, was eager to promise.
>
> Have they settled the claim for $75? Was there a contract between Sam and Ted for $75? What is the consideration for Ted's promise?

> *PROBLEM 18:* Ted gave Sam $100. Ted thought it was a loan; Sam a gift. It is unclear to a reasonable person whether the transaction was a loan or a gift. Later Ted told Sam "I promise to release you from your obligation to repay me $100 if you will promise to pay me $50."
>
> If Sam promises, have they contracted?

> *PROBLEM 19:* Over several months, Mary borrowed a substantial sum of money from Liz. Their record keeping left something to be desired and neither knew the exact amount of the debt. Mary promised to pay Liz $1,200 if Liz would release Mary from all of her obligations.
>
> If Liz promises, have they contracted?

C. Terminating a Noncontractual Duty

The release parties use for settling noncontractual claims must meet the requirements of contracts law. The release consists of an offer and an acceptance. The offer has the promisor's promise and consideration for the promisor's promise.

EXAMPLE

> "I promise to pay you $1,000 for your promise to release your claim against me." The "promise to release" is the consideration for the promisor's "promise to pay $1,000."

> *PROBLEM 20:* While eating at the Pink Penguin, a local bar and grill, Erma began to choke on a piece of meat. A patron dislodged the obstruction and saved Erma's life. Erma threatened to sue the Pink Penguin although she knew that her own carelessness had caused the incident.

The Pink Penguin promises to pay Erma $1,500 if she promises not to sue. Erma promises.

Have the parties formed a contract?

PROBLEM 21: Stephanie was walking on the sidewalk in a downtown business district when a bucket suddenly struck her head. A window washer on the twentieth floor of a local office building had been using the bucket. Pedestrians were not warned that someone was washing windows. Stephanie spent four days in the hospital and missed six weeks of work.

The window washer promised to pay Stephanie $3,000 for her promise to release her claim against him.

Have they formed a contract?

D. Terminating a Contractual or Noncontractual Duty With a "Payment in Full" Check—The Accord and Satisfaction

"Accord and satisfaction" is another variation on the theme of ending a contract before it has been fully performed. In this transaction, one party writes a check to the other and states on the bottom or back of the check "this check is taken in full payment of the obligation." The "accord" is a contract to pay a stated amount to discharge a prior obligation. It begins with a traditional offer, a promise for consideration. In the offer for the accord, the drawer of the check promises to pay the payee the amount stated on the check as full payment in exchange for the payee's promise to take this stated amount as full payment for the drawer's prior obligation. While this discussion presents the accord as a bilateral contract (a promise for a promise), an accord could be a unilateral contract (a promise for a performance) if the consideration for the drawer's promise were not "the payee's promise to take the stated amount as full payment of the drawer's obligation" but rather "the payee's taking the stated amount as full payment of the drawer's obligation."

By promising to take the stated amount as full payment in exchange for the drawer's promise to pay the stated amount as full payment, the payee accepts the offer and forms the accord contract. The payee's performance of his or her promise (exercising dominion over the check by an act such as negotiating the check) is the satisfaction—satisfaction being no more than the performance of the accord contract. If the payee does not expressly promise to take the stated amount as full payment, the payee's promise may be implied from its performance (exercising dominion over the check). Thus when the payee negotiates the check, this exercise of dominion acts as both the acceptance of the offer for the accord and the satisfaction of the accord.

The accord and satisfaction promotes fairness by protecting the bona fide expectations of the drawer who tenders payment on the condition that it will be accepted as payment in full and provides a method of settling disputes without litigation.

Because the accord is merely a contract, the traditional rules of offer and acceptance, including the rules of consideration, apply. For an offer to exist under classical contracts law, there must be consideration for the drawer's promise. The consideration for "the drawer's promise to pay the stated amount as full payment" would be "the payee's new promise to take the lesser amount as full payment." The situation gives rise to an offer. For an acceptance to exist, there must be consideration for the payee's promise. The consideration for the "payee's promise to take the lesser amount as full payment" would have to be (under the mirror image rule) "the drawer's promise to pay the lesser amount as full payment."

If either the existence or the amount of the drawer's obligation is in dispute, the notation "payment in full" is significant. When either the existence or amount of the drawer's duty under the original contract is in dispute, the drawer's promise to pay a stated amount as full payment, by not reaffirming a preexisting duty, can be consideration for the payee's promise to take the stated amount as full payment. With this acceptance of the offer, an accord contract comes into being. Performance of the accord contract, the payee's exercise of dominion over the check, is the satisfaction. Upon satisfaction, the original contract duties are discharged.

EXAMPLE

The Quality Nursery contracted to landscape the Rainbow Mall to Rainbow's specifications. The contract provided that the price would be "a reasonable price."

After Quality landscaped the Mall according to Rainbow's specifications, Quality sent Rainbow a bill for $20,000. Rainbow sent Quality a check for $18,000. The check carried the notation "payment in full."

Rainbow's offer in the original contract was: "I promise to pay you a reasonable price for your promise to landscape the Mall according to my specifications." Quality's acceptance was: "I promise to landscape your Mall according to your specifications for your promise to pay me a reasonable price."

By sending the check for $18,000, Rainbow made an offer for an accord contract: "I promise to pay you $18,000 for your promise to accept this amount as full payment of my disputed obligation to you." The amount is in dispute because Quality claims the reasonable amount is $20,000 and Rainbow claims the reasonable amount is $18,000. If Rainbow cashes the check, then it accepts the offer of the accord. Rainbow's actions would amount to "I promise to accept $18,000 as full payment of your disputed obligation to me for your promise to pay me $18,000."

If neither the existence nor the amount of the drawer's obligation is in dispute, the drawer has a preexisting contractual duty to pay the undisputed higher amount. A promise to pay only a part of that undisputed amount cannot be new consideration for the payee's promise and thus is not an acceptance of the accord offer.

Without acceptance and thus without an accord contract, the drawer's notation on the check, "payment in full," is irrelevant and the payee may exercise dominion over the check without losing his or her right to enforce the drawer's original promise to pay.

EXAMPLE

The Quality Nursery contracted to landscape the Rainbow Mall to Rainbow's specifications. The contract provided that the price would be $20,000.

After Quality landscaped the Mall according to Rainbow's specifications, Quality sent Rainbow a bill for $20,000. Rainbow sent Quality a check for $18,000. The check carried the notation "payment in full."

Rainbow's offer in the original contract was: "I promise to pay you $20,000 for your promise to landscape the Mall according to my specifications." Quality's acceptance was: "I promise to landscape your Mall according to your specifications for your promise to pay me $20,000."

Although Rainbow sent a check for $18,000, it did not make an offer for an accord contract. Neither Rainbow's obligation to pay nor the amount that it was obligated to pay was in dispute. The contract clearly established the amount of the obligation as $20,000. Rainbow had a preexisting duty to pay $20,000 and therefore its promise to pay less could not be consideration for Quality's promise to take $18,000 as full payment.

If Quality cashes the $18,000 check, Rainbow is still obligated to Quality for $2,000. An accord and satisfaction has not been made.

Even if the drawer's obligation is neither unliquidated nor in dispute, new consideration for the payee's promise to do something that the drawer was not legally obligated to do already is consideration for the promisee's promise to take the lesser amount as full payment. If, for example, the payee required the drawer to promise to pay a day or even an hour before the debt is due, pay at a different place, pay a third person, or pay in personal property or anything other than money, then the drawer's promise would be consideration for the payee's promise to take the lesser amount as full payment.

EXAMPLE

Jane borrowed $2,000 from Sally and promised to repay her in one year at six percent interest. The amount due would be $2,120. A week before the loan was due, Jane sent Sally a check for $2,100 with the notation "payment in full." If Sally accepts the check, she has accepted Jane's offer for an accord contract. Although neither the existence of Jane's obligation nor the amount of it was in dispute, Jane's promise to pay before the due date would be consideration to support Sally's promise to accept the lesser amount as full payment.

PROBLEM 22: The Quality Print Company ordered 10,000 reams of paper from Excel Paper, Inc., at $2.00 a ream. After the paper was delivered, Quality sent Excel a check for $15,000 with the notation "payment in full." If Excel cashes the check, does Excel still have a claim against Quality for $5,000?

PROBLEM 23: The Evertite Pool Company contracted to seal Jones's leaking swimming pool for "a reasonable price." After sealing the pool, Evertite sent Jones a bill for $800. Jones, believing that a reasonable price was $500, sent Evertite a check for $500 with the notation "payment in full." If Evertite cashes the check, does it still have a claim against Jones for $300?

When a dispute exists, classical contracts law prevents the payee from rejecting the offer for the accord by altering the notation on the check. The payee, however, may negotiate the check without discharging the drawer if an accord cannot be proven or the payee does not see the obscure "payment in full" notation.

8

DRAFTING A CONTRACT

Chapters 3, 4, 5, 6, and 7 have taken you through the evolution of a contract: pre-offer, offer, post-offer/pre-acceptance, acceptance, and post-acceptance. We now have a contract and we know its terms. Some contracts must be in writing to be enforceable. Others are enforceable without a writing. Even those contracts that do not need to be in writing often are written. Chapter 8 briefly discusses the art of drafting a written contract.

Drafting contracts involves skills that you can develop and hone. The ability to write well is the most valuable tool a paralegal can acquire. The following material provides some suggestions for drafting a well-written contract. These suggestions also apply to drafting well-written memoranda and briefs. Reflect upon your own writing. Can some of these tips improve your writing?

Section 1. DRAFTING A BETTER CONTRACT

To paraphrase George Orwell, all contracts are equal, but some contracts are more equal than others.

A. Draft from an Outline

Before drafting develop an outline for the contract. An outline helps the drafter present the terms of the contract in a logical, orderly fashion. An outline prevents the omission or duplication of essential terms.

Begin the outlining process by defining the purpose of the contract. Next, following the organizational structure of the road map (see Chapter 1), develop a check list of items that the contract might or should address.

PROBLEM 1: The following is the beginning of a check list. What items would you add or delete from this list?

1. Scope
   The applicable state law if the parties decide to select the applicable state law (that is, choice-of-laws provision)

2. Contract formation
   a. The offeror's duties
   b. The offeree's duties
   c. The timing and dependence of the performance of the duties to one another
   d. Events or conditions necessary to create the duty
   e. Events or conditions necessary to terminate the duty
   f. Whether all the terms of this contract will be set forth in this writing and, if so, whether the writing should so state (that is, merger clause)
3. Enforcement
   a. If the contract must be in writing to be enforceable, what terms should the writing contain and who must sign
   b. If the contract could be held unenforceable, what should be the alternative course of action of the parties
4. Breach
   a. Definition of breach
   b. Significance of breach
5. Remedies for the Aggrieved Party
   a. The aggrieved party's remedies
   b. Alternative methods of dispute resolution in lieu of litigation (for example, mediation or arbitration)
   c. A statement relating to costs and attorneys' fees
   d. The forum in which litigation would take place

B. Be Brief

Omit surplus words. State your meaning clearly and concisely. More words do not make a better contract. Wordiness only creates an opportunity for ambiguity and confusion. Eliminate unnecessary paragraphs, sentences, phrases, and words. Good writing stresses conciseness.

A single word can often substitute for a verbose phrase:

afford an opportunity	allow, let
and/or	or
as to whether	whether
at that point in time	then
due to the fact that	because
during the period when	when
during the time that	during, while
file an action against	sue
force and effect	force, effect
for the reason that	because
free and clear	free, clear
full and complete	full, complete

from the point of view	from, or
good consideration	consideration
have an impact on	affect
have a tendency to	tend
insofar as . . . is concerned	(omit entirely and start with the subject)
null, void, and of no further effect	void
point in time	time
prior to	before
subsequent to	after
suffer and permit	permit
sufficient consideration	consideration
there is no doubt but that	doubtless, no doubt
the question as to whether	whether, the question whether
this is a topic that	this topic
void contract	no contract
written document	document
written instrument	instrument

Many such phrases are compound prepositions:

by means of	by
by reason of	because of
by virtue of	by, under
for the period of	for
for the purpose of	to
in accordance with	by, under
inasmuch as	since
in connection with	with, about, concerning
in favor of	for
in instances in which	when
in lieu thereof	instead
in order to	to
in regard to	about
in relation to	about, concerning
in spite of the fact that	although
in terms of	in
in the nature of	like
in view of	because
on the basis of	by, from

on the part of	by
until such time as	until
with the exception of	except
with reference to	about, concerning
with regard to	about, concerning
with respect to	on, about

PROBLEM 2: Remove the unnecessary verbiage from the following paragraph.

1. The lessor, party of the first part, agrees
2. to lease, rent and/or otherwise allow the lessee,
3. party of the second part, to use, occupy and
4. hereafter during the term of this lease, make use
5. of lessor's, said party of the first part's premises.
6. The lessee, said party of the second part, shall
7. compensate, pay and/or remit to the lessor, said
8. party of the first part, for and in consideration
9. of the said agreement of lease, rent and/or
10. otherwise use lessor's, said party of the first
11. part's premises, the dollar sum of Two Thousand
12. Dollars ($2,000.00).

C. Simplify Your Language

Use clear, concise terms. Avoid synonyms. If you mean "rooster," use "rooster." If you mean "hen," use "hen." If you mean "rooster" but use "chicken," a synonym, the reader might believe you mean "hen." Do not confuse your reader by using different words to refer to the same object or idea.

Avoid "legalese." Legalese does not make a writing "legal." Legalese only makes a writing pompous and confusing.

EXAMPLE

Said Jack and said Jill went up the said hill to fetch a said pail of said water.

When removing "said" from your writing, also remove "heretofore," "one," "whereas," and any other legalese that you might find.

Remove the following:

aforementioned
aforesaid
forthwith

hereafter
hereby
herein
hereinafter
heretofore
herewith
one
said
thence
whereas

"Minimize confusion by referring to parties by name rather than designating them "the party of the first part" and "the party of the second part."

Avoid indefinite pronouns such as "it, they, this, who, and which." An indefinite pronoun only adds confusion. When possible, substitute a noun for a pronoun.

PROBLEM 3: Rewrite the following sentences to eliminate the indefinite pronouns:

1. In this law review article it states that paralegals are real assets.
2. They say that the program for legal assistants is one which benefits students.
3. This text is written so that it can be put together one chapter after another.
4. There is a house, it stands on a hill.

Avoid "etc." "Etc." gives the reader no new information and only demonstrates that either the writer does not know or is too lazy to tell the reader.

EXAMPLE

"The bride received gifts from New York, Florida, California, etc." Rewrite to avoid "etc.", "The bride received gifts from many states including New York, Florida and California."

Simplify your drafting style. Group similar terms together.

EXAMPLE

The seller shall deliver the goods to buyer's store. The buyer shall pay the seller upon delivery. The seller will pay the cost of shipping. The buyer will inspect the goods upon delivery. The goods are sold "as is." The buyer shall insure the goods during transit.

The seller shall:

1. sell the goods "as is;"
2. deliver the goods to the buyer's store; and

3. pay the cost of shipping.

The buyer shall:
1. pay the seller upon delivery;
2. inspect the goods upon delivery; and
3. insure the goods during transit.

PROBLEM 4: Redraft the following by deleting the legalese and grouping the lessor's duties and lessee's duties.

WITNESSETH: that the party of the first part, for and in consideration of the rents, covenants and agreements hereinafter contained, does, and by these presents, demise, lease and rent, for a period of six months from the first day of June, 1987, to the party of the second part, the following described property, to-wit:

The party of the second part, for and in consideration of the use and possession of said premises for said period, does hereby agree to pay unto the party of the first part, the sum of Three Thousand Dollars ($3,000.00), said sum to be paid in the following amounts and at the time herein designated, to-wit:

On the first day of June, 1987, the sum of Five Hundred Dollars ($500.00), and on the first day of each and every month thereafter the sum of Five Hundred Dollars ($500.00), until the total sum of Three Thousand Dollars ($3,000.00) shall have been fully paid.

THE PARTY OF THE SECOND PART further agrees to keep and maintain all portions of the building let to him by the terms of this contract in as good state of repair as the same are turned over to him.

THE SECOND PARTY further agrees to be responsible and pay for the repair of any damage done to any of the buildings or grounds by any of his family or guests.

THE SECOND PARTY agrees to hold said first party free from any and all expenses for lights, heat or any other expense incident to the occupant of said property.

THE PARTY OF THE SECOND PART shall not engage, or allow any other person, pet or animal to engage in, any conduct that will disturb the quiet and peaceful enjoyment of the other tenants, the party of the first part, or the neighbors of second party, or use the premises for any purpose whatsoever which violates the laws of the United States, the State of New Hampshire, or the City of Concord.

D. Use Base Verbs and the Active Voice

Activate your writing with verbs. Replace nouns with verbs. The purest verb form is the base verb (for example, collide, decide, pay). Verbs give sentences movement and life. Nouns do not. Use the base verb rather than its derivative noun.

collide	collision
decide	decision
pay	payment

PROBLEM 5: Identify four additional base verbs and their derivative nouns.

PROBLEM 6: Write a sentence using each of the four derivative nouns from Problem 5. Then rewrite the sentence changing the noun to a verb.

Replace forms of the verb "to be" (is, are, be) with active verbs (run, skip, jump).

EXAMPLE

"The ruling was made by the trial judge" becomes "The trial judge ruled."

Active voice energizes your writing. Substitute active for passive verbs. With active voice, the subject of the sentence acts.

EXAMPLE

"Tom called the police."

With passive voice, the subject of the sentence is acted upon.

EXAMPLE

"The police were called by Tom."

Passive voice usually requires more words than active voice. In our illustration, the passive voice requires a supporting verb (were) and a preposition (by).

Passive voice creates detached abstraction within the sentence. With the active voice, the reader readily understands who is doing what to whom. With passive voice, who is doing what to whom is often unclear.

E. Avoid Sexist Language

"Every man for himself" is history. Sexist language should be deleted from your writing. Several tips are useful:

1. Avoid expressions that imply value judgments based on sex.

EXAMPLE

"Are you a man or a mouse?"
"A difficult task is a man's work."
"Don't be such a weak sister."
"He refused to do woman's work."

2. Change the wording of male-oriented expressions to include both men and women.

EXAMPLE

"reasonable man" becomes "reasonable person"
"gentlemen of the jury" becomes "members of the jury"
"Dear Sir" becomes "Dear Madam or Sir"

3. Replace sex-based descriptions and titles with non-sex-based descriptions and titles.

EXAMPLE

"workman" becomes "worker"
"newsman" becomes "journalist"
"fireman" becomes "firefighter"

4. Use parallel construction when referring to both sexes.

EXAMPLE

"man and wife" becomes "husband and wife."

5. Avoid masculine singular pronouns when not referring to a male. While "he or she" can be used in moderation, it is often best to rewrite the sentence.
   a. Omit the pronoun if it is unnecessary.

EXAMPLE

"The average citizen feels that he is doing his duty by voting" becomes "The average citizen feels a duty to vote."

EXAMPLE

"Every person has his constitutional rights" becomes "Every person has constitutional rights."

   b. Use the second person rather than the third person.

EXAMPLE

"Each voter must cast his own ballot" becomes "As a voter, you must cast your own ballot."

   c. Use the plural rather than the singular.

EXAMPLE

"Every spring the farmer plows his fields" becomes "Every spring farmers plow their fields."

EXAMPLE

"The policeman risks his life on a daily basis" becomes "Police officers risk their lives daily."

F. Check for Spelling, Punctuation, and Grammatical Errors

Common spelling errors should be eliminated from your writing. Do not expect a secretary to correct your work. Errors will reflect upon you and not your secretary. Keep a list of words you tend to misspell.

Example

The following are common spelling errors:

accommodate	not accomodate
alright	not all right
coming	not comming
defendant	not defendent
demurrer	not demurer
judgment	not judgement
occurred	not ocurred or occured

Check punctuation.

Eliminate grammatical errors from your writing. A common error is to write "it's" for "its" and "its" for "it's." "It's" is a contraction, meaning "it is." "Its" is a possessive pronoun.

EXAMPLE

"It's February 2d and the groundhog saw its shadow."

"Irregardless" is improper. Use "regardless." Check "to," "too," and "two" as well as "between" and "among."

These suggestions are but a brief introduction to better drafting. A number of helpful books are available. They include: G. Block, *Effective Legal Writing* (Foundation Press 1981); L. Glorfeld, D. Lauerman, & N. Stageberg, *A Concise Guide for Writers* (Holt, Rinehart & Winston 4th ed. 1977); D. Lambuth, *The Golden Book on Writing* (Viking Press 1964); D. Mellinkoff, *The Language of the Law* (Little, Brown & Co. 1963); C. Miller & K. Swift, *The Handbook of Nonsexist Writing* (Harper & Row 1980); W. Strunk & E.B. White, *The Elements of Style* (MacMillan 3d ed. 1979); R. Wydick, *Plain English for Lawyers* (Carolina Academic Press 1979).

Section 2. DRAFTING EXERCISE

PROBLEM 7: One of your firm's clients is in the process of hiring a tutor to teach and care for her four children. The tutor will receive room and board, a salary, and insurance benefits. Draft a contract (not to exceed two pages) that details all rights and duties of each party. Create your own facts as you need additional information. Keep in mind the material discussed in section one of this chapter.

PART III

Step Three: Contracts That are Unenforceable

INTRODUCTION

Although parties are free to create their own contracts, courts will not enforce all contracts. The legislatures and courts determine whether a party shall be free from the contract. Chapter 9 considers precluding the enforcement of the contract to protect a class, such as infants and mental incompetents. Chapter 10 explores precluding the enforcement of the contract to protect a party against the other party's overreaching through unconscionability, fraud, duress, or mistake in a basic assumption of fact. Chapter 11 investigates precluding the enforcement of the contract to protect the judicial process from becoming involved in nonjudicial type activity such as illegality, perjury, and inappropriate forum shopping.

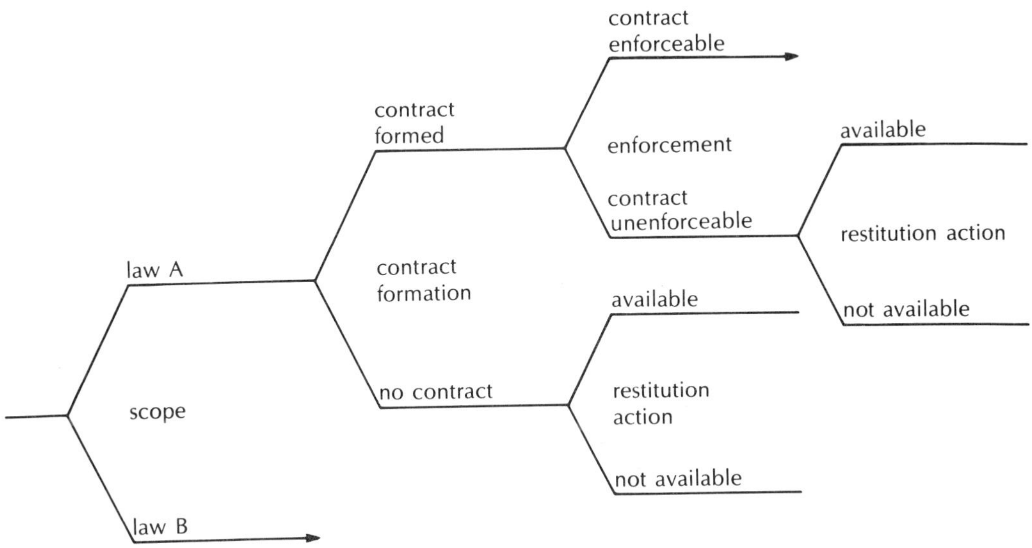

9

PROTECTING A CLASS

At times either the legislature or the court will find a class of people particularly vulnerable in the market place. Without some protection by the legislature or the court, members of these classes are at the mercy of the unscrupulous. Rather than deal with each transaction as it arises, the law protects all members of the class in all their contract transactions. Instead of precluding all members of the vulnerable class from contracting, they are permitted to contract as are individuals who are not members of these classes. The members of the protected class, however, are given the power to unilaterally rescind their contracts.

This chapter investigates two protected classes, the infant and the mental incompetent.

Section 1. INFANCY

Infants have long been a protected class. According to early criminal law, a child under seven lacked the mental capacity to form the necessary intent to commit a crime. The law presumed that children between seven and fourteen lacked the mental capacity to form the necessary intent, however, this presumption was rebuttable. Although some changes have taken place, modern criminal statutes still give children special status.

Early contracts law, which was based on the meeting of the minds, viewed infants as mindless and therefore infants could not contract. Their "contracts" were "void." Modern contracts law, which is based on the manifestation of assent, gives infants the power to contract. Unlike criminal law, contracts law does not classify children into age categories: those too young to contract; those presumed to have the ability to contract, although the presumption is rebuttable; and those who can contract. Modern contracts law permits all children to contract but gives the child the power to disaffirm the contract, even after the other party has fully performed. Also, unlike the criminal law that protects the child under seven and gives limited protection to a child between seven and fourteen, contracts law established the age of protection as minority which meant twenty-one. Most modern statutes have rolled this age back to eighteen.

A. Infancy as a Defense to a Breach of Contract Action

As a general rule, people may disaffirm contracts that they made during minority if the disaffirmance occurs during minority or within a reasonable time after reaching adulthood. Of the two contracting parties, only the minor has the power to disaffirm. The power to disaffirm is one-sided. The fact that the infant willfully misrepresents his or her age at the time of contract formation does not preclude the infant from disaffirming. The infant may be liable in a separate tort action for misrepresentation.

PROBLEM 1: Lucy, age sixteen, contracted to buy an encyclopedia from the publisher for $1,000. Lucy paid the $1,000 and received her encyclopedia. Six months later Lucy decided that she did not want the encyclopedia.

Could Lucy disaffirm the contract, return the encyclopedia, and get her money back?

PROBLEM 2: Lucy, age sixteen, contracted to buy a gold pendant heirloom from Sly's Jewelry Store for $200. Lucy paid the $200 and received the pendant. Over the next six months the price of gold increased dramatically, and the pendant increased in value to $400.

Could Sly disaffirm the contract, return Lucy's $200, and get the pendant back?

If the price of gold decreased dramatically, and the pendant decreased in value to $100, could Lucy disaffirm the contract, return the pendant, and get her $200 back?

An infant may disaffirm a contract for a reasonable time after reaching majority. A reasonable time will vary depending on the circumstances. Some factors that may shed light on "reasonable time" may include whether either side has performed, the nature of that performance, the ability of the infant to disaffirm, and the prejudice to be suffered by the infant's delay in disaffirming.

PROBLEM 3: Just before going to college, Belinda, age seventeen, entered into three contracts. Should she have the same length of time after reaching majority (age eighteen) to disaffirm each?

1. Belinda contracts to model for an agency after she graduates from college.
2. Belinda buys a VCR from Quality Electronics and takes it to college.
3. Belinda buys a registered Setter from Doctor Pets and takes her to college.

In each of these situations, would it matter whether Belinda was going to college near home or far away?

B. Restitution for the Infant and the Other Contracting Party

When infants exercise their power to disaffirm, three events take place. The first event is the disaffirmance of the contract, which terminates the performance of the contract. If the contract specifies that the infant still has duties to perform, the disaffirmance ends those outstanding duties. The infant is no longer bound to follow the contract.

The other contracting party could not successfully sue the infant for refusing to perform. Once the infant exercises the power to disaffirm, the other party may not enforce the contract.

The second event involves restoring the infant to the position the infant was in before contracting. The restoration focuses on what the infant gave the other contracting party. If, for example, the infant has paid for an item, the party receiving payment should return it to the infant. If the infant conveyed real or personal property, the party receiving the real or personal property should return it to the infant. Even if the real property has been conveyed to a subsequent purchaser who purchased in good faith and without notice of the fact that the preceding vendor was an infant, the infant may still reclaim the real property. Personal property, however, may not be reclaimed by the infant from a subsequent bona fide purchaser for value.

PROBLEM 4: Jeremy, age seventeen, purchased a used Ford from Friendly Motors for $1,500. He paid for his car with $1,000 cash and trade-in of his old Chevy. Shortly after delivering his Chevy to Friendly, paying the money, and taking delivery of the Ford, Jeremy was involved in an accident in which his Ford was totaled.

Can Jeremy disaffirm the contract and recover $1,000 from Friendly? Can he recover the Chevy from Friendly?

If Friendly has sold the Chevy to Alice who purchased it in good faith and without notice that it had been previously owned by a minor, can Jeremy recover his Chevy from her?

The third event involves *some* restoring of the other contracting party to a pre-contract position. This party is not necessarily completely restored to the position he or she was in before contracting. Rather the infant must return to this party *only* what the infant received under the contract *and* still has in his or her possession. If the infant no longer has what was given, then the infant need not return it.

PROBLEM 5: In Problem 4, what, if anything, must Jeremy return to Friendly Motors?

PROBLEM 6: In Problem 3, what, if anything, must Belinda return to her various sellers?

An infant may use disaffirmance of the contract as either an offensive or defensive weapon. The infant may disaffirm, discontinue performing under the contract, and wait until the other contracting party files a breach of contract action seeking a remedy for the infant's breach. In that case, the disaffirmance precludes the enforcement of the contract and the breach of contract action is unsuccessful. On the other hand, the infant may disaffirm, discontinue performing, and take a more aggressive posture. The infant may file a restitution action to recover the benefit conferred on the other contracting party. Regardless of whether the infant is the plaintiff or defendant, the infant may disaffirm, seek restitution of the benefits conferred, and restore what he or she has to the other contracting party. If the infant is the plaintiff rather than the defendant, many courts will charge the infant for the use and depreciation of what the infant received. This charge will be in the form of an offset.

PROBLEM 7: Should there be a difference in whether or how much the infant should receive in the following two situations:

1. Mary Alice, age sixteen, purchased a used Pinto from Friendly Ford for $1,500. She took delivery of the Pinto and financed it over twenty-four months. After driving the Pinto for a year, Mary Alice disaffirmed the contract, ceased making payments, and returned the Pinto to Friendly Ford. Friendly Ford sued Mary Alice for breach of contract claiming that she breached the contract by not continuing to pay her installments.

   What, if anything, should be restored to Mary Alice?
2. Using the same facts, assume that instead of financing the car, Mary Alice paid cash. Mary Alice sued Friendly Ford in a restitution action seeking the return of her payments.

   What, if anything, should be restored to Mary Alice?

   Should the answers to these two problems be the same or different? Why?

C. Liability of the Infant for Necessaries

An infant may disaffirm a contract for necessaries (that is, food, clothing, shelter, medical services, and education). What constitutes necessary food, clothing, shelter, medical services, and education varies depending on the infant's status.

While the infant may disaffirm a contract for necessaries, the infant is still liable for the necessaries. Liability is based on a restitution action rather than a breach of contract action. This distinction may be important to the infant. Under the contract, the infant is liable for the contract price. Under a restitution action, the infant is only liable for the reasonable value to him or her.

PROBLEM 8: Donald, age sixteen, was involved in an automobile accident and was charged with leaving the scene of an accident. Donald hired the firm of Ambrose and Pete to defend him. Through their efforts the charge was reduced and Donald pleaded guilty and paid a fine. The bill from Ambrose and Pete was $400. After discovering that most other law firms charge $200 for this service, Donald disaffirmed the contract and refused to pay Ambrose and Pete.

Does Donald have the power to disaffirm? If yes, then could the firm successfully maintain a restitution action against Donald and if so, for how much?

D. Statutory Variations

A number of states have varied these general themes.

PROBLEM 9: How do the following statutes vary the general themes discussed:

1. Oklahoma Statutes tit. 15, § 19 (1981):

   Section 19. Disaffirmance of Minor's Contract

   In all cases other than those specified herein, the contract of a minor may be disaffirmed by the minor himself, either before his majority or within one (1) year's time afterwards; or, in case of his death within that period, by his heirs or personal representatives. Provided, that any minor between the ages of sixteen (16) and eighteen (18) who has paid for any repairing, supplying or equipping on any type of a motor vehicle may disaffirm said contract in like manner only by restoring the consideration to the party from whom it was received.

2. Illinois Revised Statutes ch. 40, §§ 2203–1, 2203–2, & 2205 (1985):
Section 2203–1. Minor

"Minor" means a person 16 years of age or over, and under the age of 18, subject to this Act.

Section 2203–2. Mature Minor

"Mature minor" means a person 16 years of age or over and under the age of 18 years who has demonstrated the ability and capacity to manage his own affairs and to live wholly or partially independent of his parents or guardian.

Section 2205. Rights and Responsibilities of Emancipated Minor

(a) A mature minor ordered emancipated under this Act shall have the right to enter into valid legal contracts, and shall have such other rights and responsibilities as the court may order that are not inconsistent with the specific age requirements of the State or federal constitution or any State or federal law.

(b) A mature minor who is partially emancipated under this Act shall have only those rights and responsibilities specified in the order of the court.

3. California Civil Code §§ 35, 35a, & 36 (West 1982):
Section 35. Minors; Disaffirmance of Contracts

In all cases other than those specified in Sections 36 and 37, the contract of a minor may be disaffirmed by the minor himself, either before his majority or within a reasonable time afterwards; or, in case of his death within that period, by his heirs or personal representatives.

Section 35a. Minors; Disaffirmance of Contracts; Goods Not Recoverable From Innocent Purchaser

If before the contract of a minor has been disaffirmed the goods which he has sold have been transferred to another purchaser who bought them in good faith for value and without notice of the transferor's defect of title, the minor can not recover the goods from an innocent purchaser.

Section 36. Minors; Contracts Not Disaffirmable

(a) Contracts not disaffirmable. A contract, otherwise valid, entered into during minority, cannot be disaffirmed upon that ground either during the actual minority of the person entering into such contract, or at any time thereafter, in the following cases:

1. Necessaries. A contract to pay the reasonable value of things necessary for his support, or that of his family, entered into by him when not under the care of a parent or guardian able to provide for him or them; provided, that these things have been actually furnished to him or to his family.

2. Artistic or creative services; judicial approval. (A) A contract or agreement pursuant to which such person is employed or agrees to render artistic or creative services, or agrees to purchase, or otherwise secure, sell, lease, license, or otherwise dispose of literary, musical or dramatic properties (either tangible or intangible) or any rights therein for use in motion pictures, television, the production of phonograph records, the legitimate or living stage, or otherwise in the entertainment field, if the contract or agreement has been approved by the superior court in the county in which such minor resides or is employed or, if the minor neither resides in or is employed in this state, if any party to the contract or agreement has its principal office in this state for the transaction of business.

(B) As used in this paragraph, "artistic or creative services" shall include, but not be limited to, services as an actor, actress, dancer, musician, comedian, singer, or other performer or entertainer, or as a writer, director, producer, production executive, choreographer, composer, conductor, or designer.

3. Professional sports contracts; judicial approval. A contract or agreement pursuant to which such person is employed or agrees to render services as a participant or player in professional sports, including, but without being limited to, professional boxers, professional wrestlers, and professional jockeys, if the contract or agreement has been approved by the superior court in the county in which such minor resides or is employed or, if the minor neither resides in or is employed in this state, if any party to the contract or agreement has its principal office in this state for the transaction of business.

(b) Judicial approval; procedure; extent. The approval of the superior court referred to in paragraphs (2) and (3) of subdivision (a) may be given upon the petition of either party to the contract or agreement after such reasonable notice to the other party thereto as may be fixed by said court, with opportunity to such other party to appear and be heard; and its approval when given shall extend to the whole of the contract or agreement, and all of the terms and provisions thereof, including, but without being limited to, any optional or conditional provisions contained therein for extension, prolongation, or termination of the term thereof.

Section 2. MENTAL INCOMPETENCY

Early contracts law, under the meeting of the minds theory, denied the power to contract to the mentally incompetent. A "contract" by a party who was mentally infirm was "void." Modern contracts law (manifestation of assent) gives the mentally infirm the power to contract and the power to disaffirm the contract. Only the party who is mentally infirm has the power to disaffirm. The other party to the contract does not have this power.

Although a person suffering from mental incompetence may disaffirm the contract, the definition of mental incompetence will vary from state to state. Traditionally, the legislatures and courts measured contractual mental capacity by what is largely a "cognitive" test. Under this standard the court inquired whether the mind was so affected as to render the contracting party wholly and absolutely unable to comprehend and understand the nature of the transaction. This standard governing competency to contract evolved when psychiatric knowledge was primitive. This standard failed to account for those who by reason of mental illness were unable to control their conduct even though their cognitive ability seemed unimpaired.

Some courts and the drafters of the Restatement of Contracts have modernized the standard. The Restatement (Second) of Contracts § 15 (1979) provides the following version:

> (1) A person incurs only voidable contractual duties by entering into a transaction if by reason of mental illness or defect
>
> (a) he is unable to understand in a reasonable manner the nature and consequence of the transaction, or
>
> (b) he is unable to act in a reasonable manner in relation to the transaction and the other party has reason to know of his condition.
>
> (2) Where the contract is made on fair terms and the other party is without knowledge of the mental illness or defect, the power of avoidance under Subsection (1) terminates to the extent that the contract has been so performed in whole or in part or the circumstances have so changed that avoidance would be unjust. In such a case a court may grant relief as justice requires.

Subsection (1)(a) retains the cognitive test, the ability to understand. Subsection (1)(b) includes a volitional test, an inability to act in a reasonable manner. The tests are alternatives. A person can disaffirm if by reason of mental illness or defect, that person cannot understand or cannot act in a reasonable manner. This permits people who understand but cannot control their actions to disaffirm their contracts. It should be noted that the power to disaffirm under subsection (1)(b) is limited to those situations where the other party had reason to know of the condition.

PROBLEM 10: Thelma Simmons, a sixty-year-old Medville schoolteacher, suffered a nervous breakdown and was placed on medical leave. Her illness was diagnosed as involving involutional psychosis, melancholia type and her psychiatrist suspected that she suffered from cerebral arteriosclerosis. While on disability, she contracted with her teachers' retirement system to provide her the maximum retirement benefits during her lifetime with no benefits to her beneficiaries upon her death. She did not tell her husband, who was relying on the continuation of her retirement benefits as his sole means of support if she predeceased him.

Four months after contracting with the retirement system, Mrs. Simmons died, leaving her husband penniless.

Can Mrs. Simmons' executor disaffirm her contract with the retirement system?

10

PROTECTING A PARTY AGAINST OVERREACHING

When a legislature or court protects a class, it protects all the members of that class. All minors, for example, may disaffirm their contracts. Neither past contracting experience nor marriage lessens the benefit (protection) from being in the class. The protection extends to all contracts made while that person was a member of the protected class.

Rather than protect a class, a legislature or court may narrow its approach and protect the contracting party on a transaction by transaction basis. This chapter explores four situations where the legislatures or courts may protect a contracting party from the overreaching of the other party. Section one considers unconscionable and adhesion contracts. Section two analyzes fraud and misrepresentation. Section three investigates duress and undue influence. Section four discusses the contract with a mistake in a basic assumption of fact.

Section 1. UNCONSCIONABILITY AND ADHESION CONTRACTS

If one party's will is imposed upon an unwilling or even unwitting party during contract formation, the contract is a "contract of adhesion." What constitutes "the imposition of will" may be different from case to case. First, the negotiations may not be between equals. An automobile dealership, with its disproportionately strong economic power, will dictate the terms of a sale through the use of the standardized automobile purchase contract. Second, the imposition of will may arise when no opportunity to bargain over the terms exists. The standardized contract may be offered on a take-it-or-leave-it basis. Third, the imposition of will may arise when one party is unfamiliar with the terms. Terms may be hidden in the fine print of a standardized contract and the problem compounds itself when there is little opportunity to read and discuss the terms.

While standardized contracts illustrate adhesion contracts, nonstandardized contracts can be adhesion contracts as well. Nonstandardized contracts could involve a party with superior bargaining power who dictates the terms, terms presented on a take-it-or-leave-it basis, or terms that one party either does not understand or does not have the opportunity to understand.

Unconscionability includes a theme found in adhesion contracts—the use of superior bargaining power to force unreasonably favorable terms upon a party. The entire contract need not be unconscionable. The unconscionability challenge may be leveled at the entire contract or only one term in the contract.

A. Unconscionability as a Defense to a Breach of Contract Action

To determine whether a contract or a contract term is unconscionable evaluate from the time of contract formation. The contract or contract term must be unconscionable at the time of contract creation. If events subsequent to contract formation make the performance of the contract a severe hardship, the contract cannot be challenged as unconscionable.

Courts generally recognize unconscionability as an absence of meaningful choice on the part of one of the parties together with contract terms which are unreasonably favorable to the other party. Whether the first element of the test, "an absence of meaningful choice on the part of one of the parties," is present in a particular case can only be determined once all the circumstances surrounding the transactions are considered. Absence of meaningful choice has two components: the imbalance in bargaining power and a knowledge of the terms. A gross inequality of bargaining power will lead to the conclusion of absence of meaningful choice even if the other party had knowledge of the terms. If, however, the inequality of bargaining power is not gross, there still might be an absence of meaningful choice if the other party had little or no knowledge of the contract's terms. This lack of knowledge may occur when the terms are hidden in a maze of fine print or minimized by deceptive sales practices. Even with a term that is clearly set forth, a party must be given a reasonable opportunity to become acquainted with the term.

EXAMPLE

A contract written in English does not inform a buyer who can read only Spanish.

An absence of meaningful choice on the part of one of the parties alone does not produce an unconscionable contract. The absence of meaningful choice must be coupled with a contract term which unreasonably favors the other party. If the term is not unreasonably favorable, the term is not unconscionable even though there was a gross inequality of bargaining power, because the party with superior bargaining power has not taken advantage of that power.

Deciding whether the term is "reasonable" or "fair" cannot be done in a vacuum. The term must be considered in light of the circumstances existing when the contract was made. The general commercial background and the commercial needs of the particular trade or case shed light on reasonableness.

PROBLEM 1: Over the past several years Ms. Williams purchased a number of household items from Walker-Thomas Furniture Company for \$1,400. When the balance was reduced to \$164, Ms. Williams purchased a

> $515 stereo set from Walker-Thomas. Because the stereo was purchased on credit, Walker-Thomas knew that Ms. Williams, a single parent with seven children, was receiving a welfare check of only $218 a month.
>
> The loan was secured with collateral—the stereo set and all other merchandise purchased at the store on which credit was still extended. The loan provided that each monthly payment would be prorated as to all purchases. Therefore, no item would be free from Walker-Thomas's security interest until all items were free.
>
> Ms. Williams defaulted on her loan and Walker-Thomas brought an action to replevy all of the merchandise she bought from them. Is the cross-collateral provision unconscionable? Consider first whether the cross-collateral provision was unreasonably favorable to Walker-Thomas. If yes, then consider whether Ms. Williams suffered from an absence of meaningful choice. Consider the relative bargaining power. Consider whether Ms. Williams had little or no knowledge of the cross-collateral provision.

When a transaction involves a sale of goods, the Uniform Commercial Code simplifies the court's inquiry when the issue of unconscionability arises. Section 2–302 provides:

> (1) If the court as a matter of law finds the contract or any clause of the contract to have been unconscionable at the time it was made the court may refuse to enforce the contract, or it may enforce the remainder of the contract without the unconscionable clause, or it may so limit the application of any unconscionable clause as to avoid any unconscionable result.
>
> (2) When it is claimed or appears to the court that the contract or any clause thereof may be unconscionable the parties shall be afforded a reasonable opportunity to present evidence as to its commercial setting, purpose and effect to aid the court in making the determination.

In a case involving a sale of goods, UCC § 2–302 applies and the court *must* consider whether the contract or a contract term is unconscionable. This "reasonable opportunity to present evidence" is mandated by section 2–302(2).

In cases *not* involving the sale of goods, courts often are reluctant to consider whether a contract or term is unconscionable. Some courts, however, have used UCC § 2–302 by analogy in nonsale-of-goods transactions. *Lloyd v. Service Corporation of Alabama, Inc.* presents an interesting expansion of 2–302 unconscionability. Patricia Lloyd was raped in her apartment after her requests for repairs necessary for security went unheeded by the lessor. She sued the lessor in negligence for physical injury and emotional distress. The lessor's defense was based on the exculpatory clause in the residential lease contract that Lloyd signed when she leased the apartment. Lloyd asserted that the exculpatory clause was unconscionable by analogy to Uniform Commercial Code section 2–302. Should the court have analogized to 2–302?

Lloyd v. Service Corporation of Alabama, Inc.

Supreme Court of Alabama, 1984.
453 So. 2d 735.

EMBRY, Justice.

This is an appeal occasioned by a Jefferson County trial court's grant of summary judgment against Patricia H. Lloyd in a tort action.

I

The circumstances from which the conflict developed are as follows: On 1 April 1979, Patricia Lloyd, a young Birmingham woman, leased an apartment at Shadowood Circle, a residential apartment complex owned by John T. Strain. The printed form lease agreement which Lloyd signed contained the following clause:

> "As a part of the consideration hereof, the lessee hereby covenants and agrees to hold the Lessor, the Lessor's Rental Agents, and the Servants and Employees of either, free and harmless from any and all liability for claims for damages, or other claims for personal injury, or death, sustained by Lessee, or sustained by any other person, while on the leased premises or adjacent thereto during the terms of this lease as the result of negligence, or other conduct of the lessor, or of the Lessor's Servants, Agents or Employees."

Such is generally known as an "exculpatory clause." It operates to release the lessor from liability for future negligent conduct, so that he or she can negligently cause the lessee injury, yet avoid the otherwise fixed legal responsibility to compensate the lessee.

After moving into the apartment, Lloyd realized the sliding glass patio door in her apartment had been installed improperly so that the locking mechanism was operable from the outside. Also, because the door slid on the wrong runner, it did not open and shut properly. Due to this defective installation, there was an exposed and open area around the glass. Lloyd notified Strain of these problems on a number of occasions, but he did not repair the door.

On 8 September 1980, Strain assigned to Service Corporation of Alabama, Inc. (Service), his leasehold rights, title, and interest in Shadowood Circle Apartments. Service began immediately to convert the apartments into condominiums, but allowed Lloyd to remain in her apartment under the preexisting lease. As part of this conversion, Service removed the draperies from almost all of the units in Lloyd's building.

On 29 September 1980, Lloyd was awakened early in the morning by a burglar. When encountered, the burglar fled as he had entered, through Lloyd's bedroom window, which he had unlocked from the outside.

Lloyd immediately reported the incident to the police. The next day she complained to Service, requesting that it take the following steps to provide security for her apartment: 1) replace her sliding glass door so that the locking mechanism could not be disengaged from the outside; 2) place screens on all the windows to prevent entrance through the apartment windows; and 3) replace the draperies in the empty units. Service did not make any of the repairs at that time, but eventually began to rehang the draperies.

During the last week of November 1980, Lloyd repeatedly observed a strange man on the premises near her apartment and reported the incidents to a deputy sheriff, who investigated the man. Lloyd notified Service employees of this investigation and asked that Service make the repairs which she had previously requested. Service did not accommodate Lloyd's requests.

On 27 December 1980, Lloyd was assaulted and raped in her apartment. The rapist entered Lloyd's apartment by disengaging the locking mechanism on the sliding glass door from the outside.

Subsequently, Lloyd filed a complaint in Jefferson County Circuit Court against Service Corporation. In her complaint, she alleges that Service was negligent in failing and refusing to repair the defective sliding glass door. She alleges that Service's negligence proximately caused the physical injury and emotional distress she suffered because she was raped. A later amendment to that complaint further alleges that Service Corporation's negligence in *providing security* proximately caused her injuries.

Service filed a motion to dismiss and a subsequent motion for summary judgment based upon the presence of the exculpatory clause in Lloyd's lease. After hearing oral arguments, the trial court granted summary judgment in favor of Service based on the presence of the exculpatory clause in the lease agreement. That court entered final judgment in accordance with Rule 54(b), ARCP. Lloyd appealed to this court. She contends the trial court erred in granting summary judgment in favor of Service based on the exculpatory clause.

II

Lloyd acknowledges, as indeed she must, that this is a request for reexamination and reconsideration of our treatment, in Alabama, of exculpatory clauses in residential leases as valid and enforceable. She contends, because such clauses are typically part of adhesive contracts, that they are not truly bargained for, and that their enforcement is against the public interest.

Service argues that modification of our present law is not needed and points to this court's strong policy in favor of freedom of contract. Service contends that change, even if needed, should be initiated by our Legislature. We have supplied ample authority to support these arguments.

Exculpatory contract provisions have, in various other circumstances, been found by this court to be void on the grounds of being contrary to public policy. See *Alabama Great So. R.R. v. Sumter Plywood Corp.*, 359 So.2d 1140 (Ala.1978); *Housing Authority of Birmingham District v. Morris*, 244 Ala. 557, 14 So.2d 527 (1943); *Smith v. Kennedy*, 43 Ala.App. 554, 195 So.2d 820 (1966), cert. den., 280 Ala. 718, 195 So.2d 829 (1966). The rationale behind these holdings is that such clauses tend to encourage negligence and, in circumstances where there is a strong public interest to discourage negligence, the clauses should be unenforceable.

As Service Corporation notes, in Alabama, residential leases have consistently been characterized as *not* involving the public interest and exculpatory clauses therein as *not* violative of public policy. Lloyd begs our reconsideration of this issue and our acknowledgement that, at least when not fairly bargained for between parties having substantially equal bargaining power, exculpatory clauses in residential leases are violative of public policy in Alabama.

A single, but two-pronged, issue is presented. First, whether there is, at this time, a public policy justification for modification of the law in Alabama regarding the enforcement of exculpatory clauses in residential leases. Second, whether such a change, if needed, should originate with the judiciary.

III

The issue whether it is contrary to the public interest to allow escape from liability in a specific situation involves a complex of considerations. Among the factors we will consider and which other courts have considered in order to make such a determination regarding residential leases are: whether the service provided by the underlying contract is one necessary to the public; whether a significant number of people are compelled to seek the service; whether the transaction places one party to the contract under the control of the other and subject to his or her carelessness; the relative bargaining power of the parties and whether there is stated legislative policy against judicial enforcement of "unconscionable" contracts. See *Henrioulle v. Marin Ventures, Inc.*, 20

Cal.3d 512, 573 P.2d 465, 143 Cal.Rptr. 247 (1978), and *Weaver v. American Oil Co.,* 257 Ind. 458, 276 N.E.2d 144 (1971).

First, it is clear we no longer live in an era of the occasional rental of rooms in a home or over the corner store. The rental industry provides a basic necessity of life, shelter, to thousands of inhabitants of this state. Approximately 30% of the total occupied housing units in the state are rental units. In Birmingham, the state's largest metropolitan area, approximately 47% of the total housing units are rental units.

It requires no imagination to see that the rental industry is now a major commercial enterprise which directly touches the lives of thousands of people who depend on it for shelter. If the rental industry was small, the effect of the use of exculpatory clauses in residential leases would be minuscule. However, the existence of a large number of leases containing exculpatory clauses affects thousands of citizens who are concerned with the quality and safety of housing offered for rent in the state. See, e.g., *McCutcheon v. United Homes Corp.,* 79 Wash. 2d 443, 486 P.2d 1093, 1098 (1971).

Second, it is evident that modern residential lease transactions subject tenants to the carelessness of the landlord. That has not always been true. During the past several decades, there have been occurring important societal changes in relationships between landlords and tenants in Alabama. In the past, many Alabama tenants were farmers. In agrarian situations, land, not housing, was the important part of a rental arrangement. A tenant would rent a property "as is," but he had the right to improve the dwelling.

Since simple carpentry and construction skills were part of a farmer's basic knowledge in that area, it was easy for him to make his house "livable," according to the standards of the day. He did not need to know about plumbing, electricity, elevators, or other modern necessities. In comparison, as is illustrated by Patricia Lloyd's circumstances, the modern urban tenant is almost totally dependent upon the landlord to make repairs and is vulnerable to his or her refusal to do so.

Third, the very nature and effect of the exculpatory clause makes clear the lack of bargaining power on the part of the tenant when negotiating a lease agreement. In his special concurrence in *Taylor v. Leedy and Co.,* 412 So.2d 763, 766 (Ala.1982), Justice Faulkner spoke to this problem:

> "Clearly, landlords have greater bargaining power than tenants in residential leases. A tenant must live somewhere. The tenant has no meaningful choices. He can accept this landlord or go to another landlord who charges the same rent and asks the tenant to sign the same standard form lease. In other words, the modern standard form lease is in essence an adhesion contract. A survey of residential leases in Alabama would show that almost all leases contain these exculpatory clauses. A reasonable person with equal bargaining power would not accept a term whereby they or their children may be injured or killed, and they would have no recourse against the guilty party. . . ."

Concern with this problem has developed because of the increasing use, in Alabama, of the standardized mass contract by business enterprises. Traditionally, a contract was the result of free bargaining of parties brought together by the play of the market, parties who met each other on a footing of approximate economic equality. Today, however, an individual consumer often faces an enterprise with strong bargaining power and position. That consumer, in need of goods or services, is frequently not in a position to shop around for better terms, because all competitors use the same clauses. *Weaver v. American Oil Co.,* 257 Ind. 458, 276 N.E.2d 144, 147 (1971).

There is a nationwide trend for courts to refuse to enforce agreements proven to be unconscionable. An unconscionable contract has been defined as one "such as no man in his sense and not under delusion would make on the one hand, and as no honest and fair man would accept on the other." *West Point-Pepperell, Inc. v. Brad-*

shaw, 377 F.Supp. 154 (M.D.Ala.1974) (quoting *Hume v. United States,* 132 U.S. 406, 10 S.Ct. 134, 33 L.Ed. 393 (1889)).

Reflecting that general trend, our Legislature has expressed a clear concern for consumers in a situation analogous to that here considered. In § 7–2–302, Code 1975, the legislative body has mandated that the Alabama judiciary not enforce "unconscionable" clauses in sales agreements. We think it reasonable to surmise that, because our Legislature has expressed so strong a concern for the effect of unequal bargaining power on sales agreements, its concern with the issue relative to the provision of the basic human need of shelter is substantially stronger.

For the above reasons we find the enforcement of "unbargained for" exculpatory clauses in residential leases against the best interests of the citizens of Alabama and contrary to public policy. We now proceed to determine whether a change in the law should be effected by the judiciary.

IV

While the preferred method for modification of a rule of law is by legislative action, it is clearly within the power of the judiciary, and, at times, appropriate for the judiciary, to change an established rule of law. A number of factors lead this court to the conclusion that it is here appropriate. We will discuss three of our primary considerations below.

First, the judiciary originally created this rule of law. It has not been altered, amended, or expanded upon by our legislative body. In this circumstance, where a judicial creation has become outmoded or unjust in application, it is more often appropriate for the judicial body to act to modify the law. Further, it is not uncommon for the Legislature to defer to the court's wisdom regarding such a rule of law. See *Jackson v. City of Florence,* 294 Ala. 592, 320 So.2d 68, 73 (1975); *Haney v. City of Lexington,* 386 S.W.2d 738, 741 (Ky. 1964); and *Holytz v. City of Milwaukee,* 17 Wis.2d 26, 115 N.W.2d 618, 626 (1962). *McAndrew v. Mularchuk,* 33 N.J. 172, 193, 162 A.2d 820, 832 (1960).

Second, this is a tort law issue. An unjust tort law may *indirectly* affect every citizen of the state, but it will almost never *directly* affect enough people at any given point in time to generate a great deal of attention. It is not likely, therefore, to be placed on the Legislature's crowded agenda for consideration. For that reason, tort law issues are, when certain other factors are present, proper subjects for judicial reform.

Last, when it has determined that a judicially created law is unjust in its application, this court cannot long permit itself to be used as an instrument of inequity by refusing to act to change the law. To do so undermines our credibility in the public perception. The judicial branch of government cannot avoid action. It must continuously apply the law to resolve the conflicts between citizens of this state. To continue to apply a judicially created rule this court has recognized as obsolete and unjust is a violation of its integrity.

In *United States v. Bethlehem Steel Corp.,* 315 U.S. 289, 326, 62 S.Ct. 581, 599, 86 L.Ed. 855 (1942), Justice Frankfurter, of the United States Supreme Court, described the judiciary's responsibility regarding this problem:

> "It is said that familiar principles would be outraged if Bethlehem were denied recovery on these contracts. But is there any principle which is more familiar or more firmly embedded in the history of Anglo-American law than the basic doctrine that the courts will not permit themselves to be used as instruments of inequity and injustice? Does any principle in our law have more universal application than the doctrine that courts will not enforce transactions in which the relative positions of the parties are such that one has unconscionably taken advantage of the necessities of the other?
>
> "These principles are not foreign to the law of contracts. Fraud and physical duress are not the only grounds upon which courts refuse to enforce contracts. The law is not so primitive that it sanc-

tions every injustice except brute force and downright fraud. More specifically, the courts generally refuse to lend themselves to the enforcement of a 'bargain' in which one party has unjustly taken advantage of the economic necessities of the other. . . ."

For this court to continue to sanction the enforcement of exculpatory clauses in adhesive contracts and thereby encourage landlords to neglect the duties imposed on them by law for the protection of tenants is to allow itself to "be used as [an instrument] of inequity and injustice."

We think that, under these circumstances, the responsibility for modification of the law rests with this court. The enforcement of adhesive exculpatory clauses in modern residential leases where not explicitly bargained for by the parties cannot be rationally defended. In fact, it is almost incredible that we have so long allowed landlords to shift the consequences of their negligence to tenants in that manner. We thus proceed to consider the manner in which the law should be modified.

V

As above noted, our Legislature has expressed strong concern for the effect of the consumer's unequal bargaining power when purchasing goods, by enacting § 7–2–302, Code 1975. In light of that clear statement of legislative policy and this court's determination that exculpatory clauses in residential leases are violative of public policy where not "bargained for," we think it reasonable for this court to apply § 7–2–302 by analogy to lease agreements. At least one state has done so. See *Weaver v. American Oil Co.,* 257 Ind. 458, 276 N.E.2d 144 (1971). There is authority for such treatment.

Therefore, when a lessee can show that an exculpatory provision in a residential lease contract is in fact an unconscionable one, due to a prodigious amount of bargaining power on behalf of the lessor, which is used to the lessor's advantage, causing a great hardship and risk to the lessee, the contract provision, or the contract as a whole, if not separable, is void on the grounds that the provision is contrary to public policy. The lessor seeking to enforce such a contract has the burden of showing that the provisions were explained to the lessee and came to his knowledge and that there was in fact a real and voluntary meeting of the minds and not merely an objective meeting.

We do not hold that exculpatory clauses in residential leases are void *per se.* When clearly "bargained for," such contract provisions are enforceable and valid.

We choose not to believe that any landlord, or any of his or her agents, would commit a tort deliberately, in reliance on this court's enforcement of an adhesive exculpatory clause. Therefore, we see no particular reasons why we should not apply this modified rule of law in the instant case and permit all others who have been injured, and who are not barred by the statute of limitations, to take advantage of the rule. Our prior decisions regarding this issue are reversed only to the extent that they conflict with this holding.

The judgment of the trial court that Patricia Lloyd's cause of action is barred by the exculpatory clause in her lease agreement with Service Corporation is reversed, and this cause is remanded to that court.

If section 2–302 applies, the courts may refuse to enforce the contract, to delete the unconscionable term and enforce the remainder of the contract, or to reform the unconscionable term so it no longer produces unconscionable results. Under section 2–302(2), the court may, of its own accord, raise the issue of unconscionability. Also if the issue of unconscionability is raised, the court *must* hold a hearing to determine the issue. Unconscionability is a question for the court (the judge) to resolve. It is not a question for the jury.

Unconscionability has not been a panacea for all disappointed contracting parties. A survey of the cases would indicate that a party claiming unconscionability will generally not prevail. *Fotomat Corporation of Florida v. Chanda* explores why unconscionability should be meted out judiciously.

Fotomat Corporation of Florida v. Chanda

District Court of Appeal of Florida, 1985.
464 So. 2d 626.

ORFINGER, Judge.

The defendant appeals from a final judgment awarding damages of $9,500 to plaintiff, resulting from the loss of film which plaintiff had delivered to defendant for processing. We reverse.

Plaintiff Chanda, a medical doctor, after reading a magazine article indicating that the deterioration of movie film could be avoided by transferring the images on the film to videotape, and having read a flyer distributed by defendant which advertised the availability of such service, delivered 28 rolls of already developed Super–8 movie film to one of defendant's outlets in Melbourne, Florida in April of 1980. Defendant's clerk prepared an order form which contained information necessary to identify the customer, type of film and type of videocassette ordered, and other matters incidental to the transaction, and which also contained in a conspicuous place on the sheet and in bold type, the following language:

IMPORTANT

THE WARRANTY BELOW GIVES YOU SPECIFIC LEGAL RIGHTS AND LIMITATIONS. PLEASE READ IT CAREFULLY.

By depositing film or other material with Fotomat, customer acknowledges and agrees that Fotomat's liability for any loss, damage, or delay to film during the processing service will be limit ed to the replacement cost of a non-exposed roll of film and/or a blank cassette of similar size. Except for such replacement, Fotomat shall not be liable for any other loss or damage, direct, consequential, or incidental, arising out of customer's use of Fotomat's service.

____

Customer Signature

Dr. Chanda read this clause, asked the clerk about it, and then signed it.

The film was lost and never made its way back to the plaintiff. Despite every effort on the part of defendant to locate it, it was never found nor could anyone account for its disappearance. Dr. Chanda testified that the film was of great sentimental value to him and to his family because it contained depictions of his honeymoon, the graduation ceremony at his medical school, movies of his son's birth and early life, and many memorable vacations which he and his wife had taken. In proving his damages, he was permitted to testify, over objection, on how much time and expense would be involved in duplicating so much of the lost film as was capable of duplication. This claim included travel expenses, lodging, meals, child care for his two children at home, and the overhead expense he would incur in his medical practice while he was away.

At an in-camera hearing prior to the commencement of the jury trial, the court determined that the limitation of liability clause was unconscionable at the time it was made. *See* section 672.302, Florida Statutes (1981). At the conclusion of the evidentiary portion of the trial, the court instructed the jury to disregard the loss limitation provision of the agreement in arriving at their verdict. Defendant contends that the trial court erred in permitting evidence as to plaintiff's consequential damages, and in its ruling that the limitation of liability clause was invalid as unconscionable. Because we agree that the court erred in holding the limitation of liability provision to be invalid, we need not discuss the damage issue.

Florida has adopted the Uniform Commercial Code in dealing with commercial transactions. Section 672.2–302 of the Florida Statutes (1979) states:

> (1) If the court as a matter of law finds the contract or any clause of the contract to have been unconscionable at the time it was made the court may refuse to enforce the contract, or it may enforce the remainder of the contract without the unconscionable clause, or it may so limit the application of any unconscionable clause as to avoid any unconscionable result.
> (2) When it is claimed or appears to the court that the contract or any clause thereof may be unconscionable the parties shall be afforded a reasonable opportunity to present evidence as to its commercial setting, purpose and effect to aid the court in making the determination.

The code does not attempt to define "unconscionability." Consequently, those courts which have dealt with the problem have often looked to the common law of their respective jurisdictions because, in most, this code provision is, in reality, a codification of the common law rules. In the seminal case of *Williams v. Walker-Thomas Furniture Company,* 350 F.2d 445 (C.A.D.C.1965), the court was faced with a contract entered into before the adoption by Congress of the Uniform Commercial Code for the District of Columbia, but decided after its adoption. First determining that the code provision followed the common law of the District, the court discussed unconscionability in terms of its elements:

> Unconscionability has generally been recognized to include an absence of meaningful choice on the part of one of the parties together with contract terms which are unreasonably favorable to the other party. Whether a meaningful choice is present in a particular case can only be determined by consideration of all the circumstances surrounding the transaction. In many cases the meaningfulness of the choice is negated by a gross inequality of bargaining power. The manner in which the contract was entered is also relevant to this consideration. Did each party to the contract, considering his obvious education or lack of it, have a reasonable opportunity to understand the terms of the contract, or were the important terms hidden in a maze of fine print and minimized by deceptive sales practices? Ordinarily, one who signs an agreement without full knowledge of its terms might be held to assume the risk that he has entered a one-sided bargain. But when a party of little bargaining power, and hence little real choice, signs a commercially unreasonable contract with little or no knowledge of its terms, it is hardly likely that his consent, or even an objective manifestation of his consent, was ever given to all the terms. In such a case the usual rule that the terms of the agreement are not to be questioned should be abandoned and the court should consider whether the terms of the contract are so unfair that enforcement should be withheld. (Footnotes omitted).

Id. at 449–450.

Florida has long recognized the principle that the courts are not concerned with the wisdom or folly of contracts, *Duvall v. Walton,* 107 Fla. 60, 144 So. 318 (1932), but where it is perfectly plain to the court that one party has overreached the other and has gained an unjust and undeserved advantage which it would be inequitable to permit him to enforce, a court will grant relief even though the victimized parties owe their predicament largely to their own stupidity. *Peacock Hotel, Inc. v. Shipman,* 103 Fla. 633, 138 So. 44 (1931). Decisions in Florida since the adoption of the Uniform Commercial Code appear to follow the principles espoused in the earlier cases.

In *Kohl v. Bay Colony Club Condominium, Inc.,* 398 So.2d 865 (Fla. 4th DCA), *review denied,* 408 So.2d 1094 (Fla.1981), the court reviewed the authorities on the subject and concluded that:

> The authorities appear to be virtually unanimous in declaring (or assuming) that two elements must coalesce before a case for unconscionability is made out. The first is referred to as substantive unconscionability and the other procedural unconscionability.
>
> . . .
>
> A case is made out for substantive unconscionability by alleging and proving that the terms of the contract are unreasonable and unfair.
>
> . . .

Procedural unconscionability, on the other hand, speaks to the individualized circumstances surrounding each contracting party at the time the contract was entered into. This is thoughtfully discussed by the court in *Johnson v. Mobil Oil Corp.*, 415 F.Supp. 264, 268 (E.D.Mich.1967):

> The various factors considered by the courts in deciding questions of unconscionability have been divided by the commentators into "procedural" and "substantive" categories. See J. White & R. Summers, *supra,* at 118–30. Under the "procedural" rubric come those factors bearing upon what in the *Weaver* case was called the "real and voluntary meeting of the minds" of the contracting parties: age, education, intelligence, business acumen and experience, relative bargaining power, who drafted the contract, whether the terms were explained to the weaker party, whether alterations in the printed terms were possible, whether there were alternative sources of supply for the goods in question. The "substantive" heading embraces the contractual terms themselves, and requires a determination whether they are commercially reasonable. According to J. White & R. Summers, *supra,* at 128:
>
> Most courts take a "balancing approach" to the unconscionability question, and to tip the scales in favor of unconscionability, most courts seem to require a certain quantum of procedural plus a certain quantum of substantive unconscionability.

Id. at 867–68. *See also, Bennett v. Behring Corp.*, 466 F.Supp. 689, 696 (S.D.Fla.1979).

This court has approved the "procedural-substantive" analysis in determining the question of unconscionability, and has approved *Kohl. State v. De Anza Corporation,* 416 So.2d 1173 (Fla. 5th DCA), *review denied,* 424 So.2d 763 (Fla.1982). Although rejecting the notion that the *Kohl* analysis is a rule of law, the court in *Steinhardt v. Rudolph,* 422 So.2d 884 (Fla. 3d DCA 1982), *review denied,* 434 So.2d 889 (Fla.1983), found it "generally helpful" and applied it to the facts of that case. The *Steinhardt* court nevertheless recognized the long standing principle of law that:

> All of this does not mean, however, that a court will relieve a party of his obligations under a contract because he has made a bad bargain containing contractual terms which are unreasonable or impose an onerous hardship on him. Indeed, the entire law of contracts, as well as the commercial value of contractual arrangements, would be substantially undermined if parties could back out of their contractual undertakings on that basis. " 'People should be entitled to contract on their own terms without the indulgence of paternalism by courts in the alleviation of one side or another from the effects of a bad bargain. Also, they should be permitted to enter into contracts that actually may be unreasonable or which may lead to hardship on one side. It is only where it turns out that one side or the other is to be penalized by the enforcement of the terms *of a contract so unconscionable that no decent, fairminded person would view the ensuing result without being possessed of a profound sense of injustice,* that equity will deny the use of its good offices in the enforcement of such unconscionability.' " (Citations omitted). (Emphasis added).

Id. at 890.

Applying the substantive prong of the test here, it cannot be said, as a matter of law, that the limitation clause here was unreasonable, when viewed in its commercial setting and when considering its purpose and effect. The charge for the processing service here was $31.00. The videocassette was priced at $18.95, and there was an additional $2.00 charge for an item not identified. There was unrebutted defense testimony that the limitation of liability provision was standard in the industry because, although loss and damage of film was relatively low in view of the tremendous volume of work done, no film processor would expose itself to liability for the unknown content of film without having to so greatly increase the cost to the public as to price the service out of the market. This is clearly a commercially reasonable consideration. As one court has aptly put it,

> To put the company ... in that type of situation in which it rides every tiger that a person with a camera can imagine and carry out seems to be unconscionable. That is not to say that this limitation of liability is a perfect one, but it seems a fairly reasonable one.

Aetna Casualty & Surety Co. v. Eastman Kodak Co., District of Columbia Superior Court, 10 U.C.C.Rep.Serv. 53 (1972).

Other courts have examined similar limitation clauses in film transactions and have refused to declare these provisions unconscionable. In a commercial film transaction, the court in *Posttape Associates v. Eastman Kodak Co.,* 450 F.Supp. 407 (1978) (E.D.Pa. 1978) considered a clause similar to the one here, and commented:

> It is the "unknown or undeterminable risks" which justify the utilization of a limitation in the film industry. Not only are the risks difficult to access because of the latent nature of any film defect, but also because usually the seller is not aware of the scope of the commercial film maker's undertaking.

Id. at 412. The same principle has been applied in cases where the work was noncommercial, as where an amateur photographer leaves his vacation films with a photo supply shop for processing. *Carr v. Hoosier Photo Supplies, Inc.,* 441 N.E.2d 450 (Ind.1982).

The reasonableness of the clause is demonstrated by the huge loss claimed by Dr. Chanda, compared to the cost of the service. Without a doubt the film had peculiar value to the plaintiff. Some of it was irreplaceable and all of it was of great sentimental value, but that unknown "tiger" is the very reason for the inclusion of the limitation of liability provision in the transaction. There is no way the processor can conceive of the risk it takes in accepting film for processing absent an explicit agreement to accept such risk. When the customer is made aware of the provision for limitation of liability and nevertheless proceeds with the transaction he has assented to an agreement for which there is a commercial need, if the cost of the service is to be made reasonable.

Neither can we perceive that plaintiff satisfied the procedural prong of the test. The evidence reflects that Dr. Chanda saw and read the clause in question, asked a question about it and was apparently satisfied with the answer because he signed it. He had previously suffered the loss of film at a different place of business, and it had been replaced by new film. He was a doctor, well educated, experienced in business transactions, and well aware of what he was signing. While he was given no opportunity to negotiate the terms of this agreement, he did not attempt to determine if anyone else could provide this service. Thus the evidence falls short of showing procedural unconscionability. If, as indicated by the official comment to Section 2–302 of the Uniform Commercial Code, the principle involved in the section "is one of the prevention of oppression and unfair surprise ... and not of disturbance of allocation of risks because of superior bargaining power," no such oppression or unfair surprise is shown here.

Appellee's reliance on *Mieske v. Bartell Drug Co.,* 92 Wash.2d 40, 593 P.2d 1308 (1979) is misplaced. Although the scenerio in that case is much like the one here, there is one very salient and important distinction. In *Mieske,* the plaintiff's wife, who brought the already developed film to the drug store for splicing and placing onto larger reels, was given a receipt for the film which contained a brief limitation of liability clause. It was not called to her attention nor discussed, she was not aware of it, and she had had no prior experience with or knowledge of any custom of the trade to include such provision in film transactions. The clerk who accepted the film did not recall discussing the clause with her, nor was he even sure what it meant. The court found that:

> As to course of dealings, the record is clear that Mrs. Mieske and the Bartell manager never discussed the exclusionary clause. Mrs. Mieske had never read it, she viewed the numbered slip as merely a receipt. The manager was not "too clear on what it said." There was no showing what was the language on any other receipt given in prior dealings between the parties. In summary, defendants' proof fell short of that required by the express language of [the statute].

Id. at 1313.

It is clear from the record here that the trial court refused to consider and apply the procedural/substantive test to determine the issue of unconscionability. Neither was any other objective analysis applied, but instead, the court appeared to view the unfairness of the agreement in retrospect, because of the result. The contract should have been reviewed in the light of the circumstances that existed when it was made. The judgment for plaintiff is reversed, and the cause is remanded to the trial court with directions to enter judgment for plaintiff for the cost of 28 rolls of unexposed Super–8 movie film.

REVERSED and REMANDED.

COWART, J., and POWELL, R.W., Associate Judge, concur.

B. Unconscionability as a Cause of Action

The previous discussion portrayed unconscionability as a defense to a breach of contract action. After the filing of a breach of contract action, the defendant has an opportunity to claim that the contract or a critical contract term is unconscionable and therefore unenforceable. If the court finds the contract or term unconscionable, the plaintiff may not maintain the breach of contract action.

Unconscionability also may support an action for breach of contract. In *Jones v. Star Credit Corp.* the Joneses were visited at their home by a sales representative from Your Shop At Home Service, Inc. During the visit, the Joneses purchased a $300 home freezer for $900 plus credit life insurance, credit property insurance, and sales tax. After paying over $600, the Joneses brought an action to reform the contract. Did the Joneses and Your Shop At Home Service create a contract? Could the Joneses preclude the enforcement of the price term in the contract by claiming that the price term was unconscionable? What relief did the Joneses seek from the court?

Jones v. Star Credit Corp.

Supreme Court of New York, 1969,
59 Misc. 2d 198, 298 N.Y.S.2d 264.

SOL M. WACHTLER, Justice.

On August 31, 1965 the plaintiffs, who are welfare recipients, agreed to purchase a home freezer unit for $900 as the result of a visit from a salesman representing Your Shop At Home Service, Inc. With the addition of the time credit charges, credit life insurance, credit property insurance, and sales tax, the purchase price totalled $1,234.80. Thus far the plaintiffs have paid $619.88 toward their purchase. The defendant claims that with various added credit charges paid for an extension of time there is a balance of $819.81 still due from the plaintiffs. The uncontroverted proof at the trial established that the freezer unit, when purchased, had a maximum retail value of approximately $300. The question is whether this transaction and the resulting contract could be considered unconscionable within the meaning of Section 2–302 of the Uniform Commercial Code which provides in part:

(1) If the court as a matter of law finds the contract or any clause of the contract to have been unconscionable at the time it was made the court may refuse to enforce the contract, or it may enforce the remainder of the contract without the unconscionable clause, or it may so limit the application of any unconscionable clause as to avoid any unconscionable result.
(2) When it is claimed or appears to the court that the contract or any clause thereof may be unconscionable the parties shall be afforded a reasonable opportunity to present evidence as to its commercial setting, purpose and effect to aid the court in making the determination. L.1962, c. 553, eff. Sept. 27, 1964.

There was a time when the shield of "caveat emptor" would protect the most unscrupulous in the marketplace—a time when the law, in granting parties unbridled latitude to make their own contracts, allowed exploitive and callous practices which shocked the conscience of both legislative bodies and the courts.

The effort to eliminate these practices has continued to pose a difficult problem. On the one hand it is necessary to recognize the importance of preserving the integrity of agreements and the fundamental right of parties to deal, trade, bargain, and contract. On the other hand there is the concern for the uneducated and often illiterate individual who is the victim of gross inequality of bargaining power, usually the poorest members of the community.

Concern for the protection of these consumers against overreaching by the small but hardy breed of merchants who would prey on them is not novel. The dangers of inequality of bargaining power were vaguely recognized in the early English common law when Lord Hardwicke wrote of a fraud, which "may be apparent from the intrinsic nature and subject of the bargain itself; such as no man in his senses and not under delusion would make." The English authorities on this subject were discussed in Hume v. United States, 132 U.S. 406, 411, 10 S.Ct. 134, 136, 33 L.Ed. 393 (1889) where the United States Supreme Court characterized (p. 413, 10 S.Ct. p. 137) these as "cases in which one party took advantage of the other's ignorance of arithmetic to impose upon him, and the fraud was apparent from the face of the contracts."

The law is beginning to fight back against those who once took advantage of the poor and illiterate without risk of either exposure or interference. From the common law doctrine of intrinsic fraud we have, over the years, developed common and statutory law which tells not only the buyer but also the seller to beware. This body of laws recognizes the importance of a free enterprise system but at the same time will provide the legal armor to protect and safeguard the prospective victim from the harshness of an unconscionable contract.

Section 2–302 of the Uniform Commercial Code enacts the moral sense of the community into the law of commercial transactions. It authorizes the court to find, as a matter of law, that a contract or a clause of a contract was "unconscionable at the time it was made", and upon so finding the court may refuse to enforce the contract, excise the objectionable clause or limit the application of the clause to avoid an unconscionable result. "The principle", states the Official Comments to this section, "is one of the prevention of oppression and unfair surprise". It permits a court to accomplish directly what heretofore was often accomplished by construction of language, manipulations of fluid rules of contract law and determinations based upon a presumed public policy.

There is no reason to doubt, moreover, that this section is intended to encompass the price term of an agreement. In addition to the fact that it has already been so applied (State by Lefkowitz v. ITM, Inc., 52 Misc. 2d 39, 275 N.Y.S.2d 303; Frostifresh Corp. v. Reynoso, 52 Misc.2d 26, 274 N.Y.S.2d 757, revd. 54 Misc.2d 119, 281 N.Y.S.2d 964; American Home Improvement, Inc. v. MacIver, 105 N.H. 435, 201 A.2d 886, 14 A.L.R.3d 324), the statutory language itself makes it clear that not only a clause of the contract, but the contract in toto, may be found unconscionable as a matter of law. Indeed, no other provision of an agreement more intimately touches upon the question of unconscionability than does the term regarding price.

Fraud, in the instant case, is not present; nor is it necessary under the statute. The question which presents itself is whether or not, under the circumstances of this case, the sale of a freezer unit having a retail value of $300 for $900 ($1,439.69 including credit charges and $18 sales tax) is unconscionable as a matter of law. The court believes it is.

Concededly, deciding the issue is substantially easier than explaining it. No doubt, the mathematical disparity between $300, which presumably includes a reasonable profit margin, and $900, which is exorbitant on its face, carries the greatest weight. Credit charges alone exceed by more than $100 the retail value of the freezer. These alone, may be sufficient to sustain the decision. Yet, a caveat is warranted lest we reduce the import of Section 2–302 solely to a mathematical ratio formula. It may, at times, be that; yet it may also be much more. The very limited financial resources of the purchaser, known to the sellers at the time of the sale, is entitled to weight in the balance. Indeed, the value disparity itself leads inevitably to the felt conclusion that knowing advantage was taken of the plaintiffs. In addition, the meaningfulness of choice essential to the making of a contract, can be negated by a gross inequality of bargaining power. (Williams v. Walker-Thomas Furniture Co., 121 U.S.App.D.C. 315, 350 F.2d 445.)

There is no question about the necessity and even the desirability of instalment sales and the extension of credit. Indeed, there are many, including welfare recipients, who would be deprived of even the most basic conveniences without the use of these devices. Similarly, the retail merchant selling on instalment or extending credit is expected to establish a pricing factor which will afford a degree of protection commensurate with the risk of selling to those who might be default prone. However, neither of these accepted premises can clothe the sale of this freezer with respectability.

Support for the court's conclusion will be found in a number of other cases already decided. In American Home Improvement, Inc. v. MacIver, supra, the Supreme Court of New Hampshire held that a contract to install windows, a door and paint, for the price of $2,568.60, of which $809.60 constituted interest and carrying charges and $800 was a salesman's commission was unconscionable as a matter of law. In State by Lefkowitz v. ITM, Inc., supra, a deceptive and fraudulent scheme was involved, but standing alone, the court held that the sale of a vacuum cleaner, among other things, costing the defendant $140 and sold by it for $749 cash or $920.52 on time purchase was unconscionable as a matter of law. Finally, in Frostifresh Corp. v. Reynoso, supra, the sale of a refrigerator costing the seller $348 for $900 plus credit charges of $245.88 was unconscionable as a matter of law.

One final point remains. The defendant argues that the contract of June 15, 1966, upon which this suit is based, constitutes a financing agreement and not a sales contract. To support its position, it points to the typed words "Refinance of Freezer A/C # 6766 and Food A/C # 56788" on the agreement and to a letter signed by the plaintiffs requesting refinance of the same items. The request for "refinancing" is typed on the defendant's letterhead. The quoted refinance statement is typed on a form agreement entitled "Star Credit Corporation—Retail Instalment Contract". It is signed by the defendant as "seller" and by the purchasers as "buyer". Above the signature of the buyers, they acknowledge "receipt of an executed copy of this RETAIL INSTALMENT CONTRACT" (capitalization in original). The June 15, 1966 contract by defendant is on exactly the same form as the original contract of August 31, 1965. The original, too, is entitled "Star Credit Corporation—Retail Instalment Contract". It is signed, however, by "Your Shop At Home Service, Inc." Printed beneath the signatures is the legend "Duplicate for Star". In substance and effect, the agreement of June 25, 1966 constitutes a novation and replacement of the earlier agreement. It is, in all respects, as it reads, a Retail Instalment Contract.

Having already paid more than $600 toward the purchase of this $300 freezer unit, it is apparent that the defendant has already been amply compensated. In accordance with the statute, the application of the payment provision should be limited to amounts already paid by the plaintiffs and the contract be reformed and amended by changing the payments called for therein to equal the amount of payment actually so paid by the plaintiffs.

In *Jones* the plaintiffs asked the court to reform the price term in the contract so they could keep the freezer without having to pay more than what they had already paid. Could the Joneses have asked the court to reform the price term to an amount less than what they had paid and to award them a judgment for what they paid over that amount? Some courts have expressed reluctance to go this far. One such court was the United States Court of Appeals, Eleventh Circuit, in *Cowin Equipment Co. v. General Motors Corp.* Cowin, an equipment dealer, sued General Motors, the manufacturer, for damages on the ground that the terms of its dealer sales and service agreement were unconscionable under section 2–302 of the UCC. The district court viewed the case as a Uniform Commercial Code unconscionability action for damages, held the terms unconscionable as a matter of law, and denied GM's motion for summary judgment. The Eleventh Circuit reversed and granted GM's motion for summary judgment.

What was Cowin's cause of action? On what basis did the court deny Cowin's cause of action?

While the *Cowin* court was reluctant to open a new avenue of recovery for the plaintiff, should an injured party be able to maintain a restitution action for damages independent of section 2–302 of the UCC?

Cowin Equipment Co. v. General Motors Corp.

Eleventh Circuit, United States Court of Appeals 1984.
734 F.2d 1581.

Before GODBOLD, Chief Judge, RONEY and KRAVITCH, Circuit Judges.

RONEY, Circuit Judge:

Plaintiff Cowin Equipment Co., Inc. sued

General Motors Corporation (GMC) for damages on the ground that the terms of its dealer sales and service agreement were unconscionable under § 2–302 of the Uniform Commercial Code. The district court held the provision was unconscionable as a matter of law and denied defendant's motion for summary judgment. We granted leave to appeal on the district court's 1292(b) certificate. 28 U.S.C.A. § 1292(b). We reverse on the ground that U.C.C. § 2–302, which concerns unconscionable contracts, does not create a cause of action for damages.

This is a diversity case. The agreement indicated that Ohio law would apply. The district court applied Alabama law. The parties do not contend there is any difference between Ohio law and Alabama law. Alabama and Ohio have adopted substantially identical versions of the Uniform Commercial Code (U.C.C.) provisions which are cited in this opinion. *See* Ala. Code § 7–2–302; Ohio Rev.Code Ann. § 1302.15. Consequently, we will refer to the applicable U.C.C. provisions without additional reference to their Alabama or Ohio statutory counterparts.

Briefly, the facts are as follows: In early 1978, GMC and its dealers anticipated an increase in demand for Terex heavy equipment, which GMC manufactured and Cowin sold. GMC responded by instituting a "Planned Distribution Program" (PDP), which modified the former agreement between the parties by requiring Cowin and other dealers handling Terex equipment to place non-cancellable orders in advance for equipment to be shipped between September 1, 1978 and August 1, 1979. Formerly GMC had permitted liberal cancellation, although the terms of its agreement with its dealers provided for cancellation only upon written notice received ninety days prior to the date of scheduled assembly "unless otherwise agreed at the time an order is submitted by dealer and accepted by Terex."

Cowin ordered forty-four machines in the months following. Due to a downturn in the economy, however, Cowin later attempted to cancel some of the orders. GMC refused to permit cancellation and delivered all of the machines as ordered, leaving Cowin with excess inventory. Cowin sued in December, 1980 seeking damages on grounds that the PDP terms were unconscionable. Specifically, plaintiff sought compensation for (1) interest incurred on loans necessary in order to buy equipment which defendant would not allow cancellation on; (2) insurance on the equipment; (3) storage and maintenance fees on the equipment; (4) loss incurred from sale of certain equipment sold for less than its purchase price.

The district court viewed the case as a "Uniform Commercial Code unconscionability action for damages" based on what it found to be unconscionable terms in the sales and service agreement between the parties. Our review of the Code provisions and the relevant cases persuades us that U.C.C. § 2–302 was not intended to create a cause of action, and cannot be used as a basis for damages in the instant case.

The language of § 2–302 and the Official Comment which follows it make no mention of damages as an available remedy for an unconscionable contract. This is consistent with traditional common law unconscionability theory. When the equity courts found contracts to be unconscionable, they refused specific enforcement. *See* J. White and R. Summers, *Uniform Commercial Code,* § 4–2 at 113, and § 4–8 at 130 (1972) (citing *Earl of Chesterfield v. Janssen,* 28 Eng.Rep. 82 (Ch.1750)). The remedies available to modern courts under § 2–302 are of similar equitable nature:

> (1) If the court as a matter of law finds the contract or any clause of the contract to have been unconscionable at the time it was made the court may refuse to enforce the contract, or it may enforce the remainder of the contract without the unconscionable clause, or it may so limit the application of any unconscionable clause as to avoid any unconscionable result.

U.C.C. § 2–302 (1983).

No case has been cited in which a damage

award was based on an unconscionable contract. Although apparently not decided in either Alabama or Ohio courts, the cases which have addressed the issue have consistently rejected the theory that damages may be collected for an unconscionable contract provision, citing the language of § 2–302 and its common law precursor to demonstrate that § 2–302 was not intended to provide a basis for damage recovery. *See, e.g., Bennett v. Behring Corp.,* 466 F.Supp. 689, 700 (S.D.Fla.1979).

(the equitable theory of unconscionability has never been utilized to allow for the affirmative recovery of money damages. The Court finds that neither the common law of Florida, nor that of any other state, empowers a court addressing allegations of unconscionability to do more than refuse *enforcement* of the unconscionable section or sections of the contract so as to avoid an unconscionable result.)

(citations omitted); *Whitman v. Connecticut Bank and Trust Co.,* 400 F.Supp. 1341, 1346 (D.Conn.1975) ("The 'unconscionability' provision of the Uniform Commercial Code ... carries no provision for damages; the remedy it provides is express."); *Pearson v. National Budgeting Systems, Inc.,* 297 N.Y.S.2d 59, 31 A.D.2d 792 (N.Y.App.Div. 1969) ("Section 2–302 of the Uniform Commercial Code does not provide any damages to a party who enters into an unconscionable contract."); *Vom Lehn v. Astor Art Galleries, Ltd.,* 86 Misc.2d 1, 380 N.Y.S.2d 532, 541 (N.Y.Sup.Ct.1976) ("U.C.C. § 2–302 ... makes no provision for damages, and none may be recovered thereunder."). *See also* 2 R. Anderson, *Uniform Commercial Code* § 2–302:102 (3d ed.1982) ("[t]he unconscionability section of the Code does not authorize the recovery of any damages by the buyer, the relief obtainable being limited to that stated by the Code, namely, that the court may refuse to enforce the contract or the unconscionable provision"); 15 *Williston on Contracts* § 1763A at 215 (3d ed.1972) ("a court under [§ 2–302] may not award damages to the party who enters into an unconscionable agreement").

Cowin contends that the damages requested were granted not on grounds of unconscionability of the Planned Distribution Program, but rather under the terms of the former agreement between the parties. Under Cowin's theory, unconscionability simply provides a basis for striking the "clause" containing the Planned Distribution Program which GMC asserts as an affirmative defense, rendering the former agreement applicable. Cowin thus claims that the district court's holding did not award damages under U.C.C. § 2–302.

The language used by the district court in its opinion, however, does not support this conclusion. The opinion opens by characterizing this case as "a Uniform Commercial Code unconscionability action for damages," and closes with the observation that

[w]hile unconscionability has normally been used as a shield against oppressive and unfairly surprising terms of contracts, that shield can equitably be beaten into a sword of restitution attacking those terms. The court, therefore, finds that the terms implementing the Planned Distribution Program are unconscionable as a matter of law.

The district court cited two cases in support of the above proposition, both of which involved plaintiffs who used the doctrine of estoppel offensively. *See Janke Construction Co. v. Vulcan Materials Co.,* 527 F.2d 772 (7th Cir.1976); *Mazer v. Jackson Insurance Agency,* 340 So.2d 770 (Ala.1976). Neither of these opinions concerns the Uniform Commercial Code or the doctrine of unconscionability.

Our decision on this point forecloses Cowin's attempt to recover damages on grounds of the unconscionability of the noncancellation clause. GMC's motion for summary judgment should have been granted. We need not reach defendant's alternative contention that § 2–302 does not extend to commercial contracts between large business corporations such as the ones involved in this action. We note that we have decided this case without reflection on the district court's determination that the non-cancellability provision was unconscionable. Review of the terms at issue in light of situations in which contractual provisions have been found unconscionable at common law or under § 2–302 raises a serious question as to the correctness of that decision, however. *See, e.g., Williams v. Walker-Thomas Furniture Co.,* 350 F.2d 445, 121 U.S.App. D.C. 315 (1965); *Campbell Soup Co. v. Wentz,* 172 F.2d 80 (3d Cir.1948); *Johnson v. Mobil Oil Corp.,* 415 F.Supp. 264 (E.D. Mich.1976); *American Home Improvement, Inc. v. MacIver,* 105 N.H. 435, 201 A.2d 886 (1964); *Henningsen v. Bloomfield Motors, Inc.,* 32 N.J. 358, 161 A.2d 69 (1960); *Jacobs v. Metro Chrysler-Plymouth, Inc.,* 125 Ga.App. 462, 188 S.E.2d 250 (1972); *Jones v. Star Credit Corp.,* 59 Misc.2d 189, 298 N.Y.S.2d 264 (1969). The district court's denial of defendant's motion for summary judgment is reversed and the case is remanded for entry of an appropriate judgment in accord with this opinion.

REVERSED and REMANDED.

Section 2. FRAUD AND MISREPRESENTATION

Although courts often use the terms "fraud" and "misrepresentation" interchangeably, a distinction exists. The Restatement (Second) of Contracts provides that an assertion does not have to be fraudulent to be a misrepresentation. The Restatement (Second) of Contracts § 159 (1979) defines a misrepresentation as "an assertion that is not in accord with the facts."

A statement the speaker intends as truthful may be a misrepresentation because of ignorance or carelessness.

EXAMPLE

> Jerry's Electric Company, seeking to induce Bernard to buy a particular generator, wrote Bernard a letter with the intention of describing its output correctly as "1200 kilowatts." Due to a typist's error, unnoticed by Jerry's, the letter stated that the generator's output was "2100 kilowatts." When Bernard accepted Jerry's offer, a contract was formed. After Jerry shipped the generator and Bernard accepted delivery and paid, Bernard discovered the generator's output was only "1200 kilowatts." Jerry's statement is a misrepresentation as to the output of the generator. Bernard, the party relying on the misrepresentation, may assert that the contract is unenforceable (disaffirm), return the generator and seek restitution of his purchase price.

A misrepresentation may be fraudulent. A fraudulent misrepresentation may be either fraud in the "factum" (fraud in the "essence") or fraud in the "inducement." Fraud in the "factum" involves the very character of the proposed contract, for example when one party tricks the other into signing a promissory note that the other party believes is merely a receipt. If the deceived party neither knows nor has reason to know of the character of the proposed contract, the effect of the misrepresentation is that the parties never contracted.

The typical case of fraud in the "inducement" involves a seller's misrepresentation of the quality of the goods. We will focus our attention on this latter type of fraud, fraud in the "inducement."

Whenever a party fraudulently induces another to enter into a transaction, the deceived party may disaffirm the contract, and in those cases where the defrauded party has conferred a benefit on the defrauding party, claim restitution. This power to disaffirm protects innocent parties from deliberately dishonest statements.

EXAMPLE

Marshall induces Betty to purchase a horse by making a statement that the horse is a stallion, when in fact it is a gelding, Betty can disaffirm the contract. Betty can return the gelding and, in a restitution action, recover the purchase price. She may also recover for food, maintenance, and veterinary care as measured by their reasonable value to Marshall.

The court will find the contract unenforceable when a deceived party can establish the following elements of fraud:

1. The misrepresentation must be a statement of fact and must be false.
2. The party making the statement must know or believe the statement to be false and, by making the false statement of fact, must intend to influence the other party to act or refrain from acting.
3. The person to whom the statement is made must believe and rely on the statement.
4. The statement must be sufficiently material to induce the party relying on the statement to accept the offer.

PROBLEM 2: Sylvia, of Sylvia's A–1 Used Cars, while attempting to sell Brad a car made statements to him that a particular used car had only 40,000 miles on it. After Brad expressed concern over a lit dashboard warning light indicating faulty brakes, Sylvia further stated that the brakes had been fixed. Relying on these assurances, Brad purchased the car and later discovered that Sylvia had intentionally changed the odometer reading from its prior reading of 85,000 miles and had disconnected the warning light, making it inoperative.

Can Brad disaffirm the contract on the ground that Sylvia's fraudulent conduct precludes enforcement of the contract?

PROBLEM 3: Treeland, Inc. represented to Lynn that its grape vines were healthy, free of disease, and suitable for producing wine grapes. Lynn relied on these representations in deciding to purchase the vines. The vines, however, carried a latent disease that had gone undetected by either party prior to purchase. The disease devastated the grape vines soon after purchase, rendering the grape vines incapable of bearing fruit of adequate quality or quantity for Lynn's commercial wine production.

Can Lynn disaffirm the contract on the ground that Treeland's fraudulent conduct precludes enforcement of the contract? Would it make any difference whether Lynn acted as a novice gardener or as the experienced owner of a winery?

In *Greene v. Gibraltar Mortgage Investment Corp.* Rosa Greene challenged the enforceability of a promissory note and deed of trust on her house that she signed to receive a loan. The court discusses fraud, misrepresentation, and unconscionability. Did the facts constitute fraud, misrepresentation, or both? If fraud, was this fraud in the factum or fraud in the inducement? Do the facts constitute unconscionability?

Greene v. Gibraltar Mortgage Investment Corp.

United States District Court, District of Columbia, 1980.
488 F. Supp. 177.

Memorandum Opinion

JUNE L. GREEN, District Judge.

This matter is currently before the Court on plaintiff's motions for a preliminary injunction and partial summary judgment, and defendants' oppositions thereto. Plaintiff challenges the validity of a promissory note and deed of trust on her property based on violations of the Truth-In-Lending Act, 15 U.S.C. § 1601 et seq., and the District of Columbia Usury and Loan Shark Laws. After due notice to the parties pursuant to Fed. R.Civ.P. 65(a), this matter was consolidated for trial on the merits. Upon consideration of plaintiff's motions for preliminary injunction and partial summary judgment, defendants' oppositions, the testimony of witnesses and the oral arguments of counsel at the hearings in this matter, and the entire record herein, the Court concludes for the reasons set forth below that plaintiff's motion for preliminary injunction must be granted and that plaintiff's motion for partial summary judgment is denied.

Factual Background

Plaintiff, Rosa Greene, lives in a single family residence at 1502 Emerson St., N.W., Washington, D.C. which she purchased in 1966. The purchase was financed with a loan in the amount of $26,000 from the Carey Winston Company. In the spring of 1979 Mrs. Greene fell behind in her mortgage payments. In addition, her pipes burst during the winter and she needed money to pay for plumbing repairs. Mrs. Greene contacted several loan companies by phone and was turned down each time. She then called defendant, Gibraltar Mortgage Investment Corporation, a firm located in Arlington, Virginia. She spoke with Gibraltar's president, Mr. Willis Kemper, and met subsequently with him at Gibraltar's office on June 1, 1979.

At this meeting, Mr. Kemper informed Mrs. Greene that she could not obtain a loan unless it was for a "business purpose." He discussed converting her single family home to a rooming house and encouraged her to apply for a rooming house license so that proof of a business purpose could be substantiated. Mrs. Greene gave Kemper $40.00 to process the loan application. Mr. Kemper visited the property at 1502 Emerson St. and appraised it at $49,000 without ever going inside. He left on vacation June 15th and left his secretary, Ms. Judi Boaz in charge.

In mid-June 1979, plaintiff received a letter from an attorney representing the Carey Winston Company, the holder of the first deed of trust. This letter threatened to accelerate Mrs. Greene's obligations under the note and to foreclose unless all amounts due were received by June 21, 1979. She conveyed this information to Gibraltar on June 20, 1979. On the afternoon of June 21, 1979, plaintiff executed a promissory note to Gibraltar secured by a deed of trust on her property at 1502 Emerson St. N.W. In addition to plaintiff, Ms. Boaz and Mr. J.D. Miller, the settlement attorney and one of the trustees under the deed of trust, were present.

At settlement, Mrs. Greene discovered for the first time that the principal of the note was $5,800, even though she and Mr. Kemper had only discussed a loan in the amount of $3,000. The statement of charges indicates that of this $5,800, $2,800 was deducted as a broker's fee and $290.00 was deducted in settlement fees. Immediately, Gibraltar dispatched a messenger to pay $1,581.90 directly to the Carey Winston Company that very afternoon. Plaintiff therefore only received $1,128 in proceeds allegedly to convert her home into a rooming house. The day after it was executed, Gibraltar assigned all of its interest in the note to defendant G.R. Quittschreiber. Plaintiff was to pay him $117.62 per month for five years thus paying approximately $7,000 for the use of $2,710.

In September 1979, plaintiff became unemployed and fell behind in her payments under both the first and second deeds of trust. In December, defendant Quittschreiber contacted J.D. Miller and asked him to proceed with foreclosure. Shortly, thereafter, Quittschreiber went to Mrs. Greene's home and demanded payment in person and warned her that if she heard from Mr. Miller, she would be liable for attorney's fees. Mr. Miller then sent a letter to Mrs. Greene which informed her that all payments due under the promissory note had been accelerated and that foreclosure proceedings would be initiated if the note were not paid in full.

Mr. Miller visited plaintiff the day she received the letter and suggested that he could find an investor to enter into a contractual arrangement with her. This investor, according to Mr. Miller, would make Mrs. Greene's payments through March and give her $1,000 to pay for fuel oil. She could remain in the house for a year, during which time she could buy back the contract for $10,000.

Plaintiff then contacted an attorney who initiated this action, claiming violations of federal and District of Columbia consumer protection statutes.

Discussion

The Court need not decide this case on any statutory basis for this entire transaction was tainted with fraud and misrepresentation.

A contract is void for fraud or misrepresentation where a party makes assertions not in accord with the facts regarding essential terms of the proposed contract, reasonably inducing apparent assent by one who neither knew or had reasonable opportunity to know what those essential terms were. *See* Restatement of Contracts § 475 (1932); Restatement (Second) of Contracts § 305 (Tentative Draft No. 12, 1977); *Hill v. Marston,* 82 F.2d 856, 65 U.S.App.D.C. 250 (1936). Omission or concealment of material facts can constitute a misrepresentation, just as a positive, direct assertion can. Restatement (Second) of Contracts § 306 (Tentative Draft No. 12, 1977); *Andolsum v. Berlitz School of Languages of America,* 196 A.2d 926, 927 (D.C.1964); *Borzillo v. Thompson,* 57 A.2d 195, 197–98 (D.C.1948); *see Nader v. Allegheny Airlines, Inc.,* 445 F.Supp. 168, 174 (D.D.C.1978). Where a party's assertion not in accord with the facts induces the apparent assent of another party, there is no meeting of the minds and hence no contract. *Hill v. Marston, supra; Lyon v. Smith,* 2 App.D.C. 37, 39 (1893) (deed of trust void where true rate of interest misrepresented); *Hollywood Credit Clothing v. Gibson,* 188 A.2d 318, 319 (1963). This is so even where the misrepresentation inducing assent is not deliberate. *Battelle v. Cushing,* 21 D.C. 59, 71–72 (1892); *Hollywood Credit Clothing v. Gibson, supra,* 188 A.2d at 319.

In this case, defendant failed to disclose material facts to plaintiff in the negotiations that led to the promissory note and deed of trust. First, when plaintiff discussed the terms of a loan with Mr. Kemper, they agreed that the principal amount of the loan was to be in the vicinity of $3,000, which amount she would repay at an interest rate not out of line with prevailing market rates for second mortgages. Gibraltar did not explain or disclose that it charged a fee for brokering the loan, which, in this instance, amounted to more than the actual proceeds of the loan. Second, Gibraltar failed to disclose the significance of designating the loan as a business purpose loan, which operates as a waiver of rights plaintiff might otherwise exercise under federal and local consumer protection statutes. Moreover, that this was a sham designation is evidenced by the fact that Gibraltar paid over half of the proceeds to Carey Winston Company to eliminate plaintiff's *personal* debt. These material omissions become particularly significant once the circumstances surrounding execution of the promissory note and deed of trust are examined.

Gibraltar was aware when Mrs. Greene arrived at its office on the afternoon of June 21, 1979 that she was faced with the threat of imminent foreclosure. The papers had to be signed quickly so that Gibraltar could pay Carey Winston Company by the close of business that day. Gibraltar, in scheduling the execution of the loan documents without providing sufficient opportunity to review them, and without having disclosed the additional costs of the transaction, took advantage deliberately of the fact that plaintiff was faced with the unpleasant alternative of either signing the papers as they were offered or losing her home.

The Court concludes that Gibraltar's actions in the negotiations and execution of the loan documents contain all the elements necessary to render a contract void for fraud or misrepresentation: defendants, through affirmative statements and material omissions, made assertions not in accord with the facts regarding essential terms of the proposed contract (the true "price" of the loan; the attempted waiver of consumer protections), reasonably inducing apparent assent (her signature) by one who neither knew nor had reasonable opportunity to know what those essential terms were. *See* Restatement (Second) of Contracts §§ 301–305 (Tentative Draft No. 12, 1977); *Hill v. Marston, supra.*

In addition to the above findings, the Court concludes that this entire transaction, and especially the $2,800 broker's fee charged by Gibraltar is so exorbitant and bears so little connection to any services rendered that it shocks the conscience of the Court.

The U.S. Court of Appeals for the D.C. Circuit has held that "where the element of unconscionability is present at the time a contract is made, the contract should not be enforced." *Williams v. Walker-Thomas Furniture Co.,* 350 F.2d 445, 449 (D.C.Cir. 1965). The court there set out criteria for determining the existence of unconscionability: "an absence of meaningful choice on the part of one of the parties, together with contract terms which are unreasonably favorable to the other party," and the first party's lack of "a reasonable opportunity to understand the terms of the contract." *Id.*

The foregoing discussion of the facts establishes clearly that plaintiff lacked any meaningful alternative at the time the loan documents were executed. The terms of the loan were overwhelmingly favorable to Gibraltar and Quittschreiber, who loaned $2,710 and anticipated a return of approximately $7,000. Plaintiff had no opportunity to review the papers because they had to be signed, and Carey Winston had to be paid that day. Accordingly, this transaction is not only void and unenforceable on grounds of fraud and misrepresentation, but also on grounds of unconscionability.

The Court's finding of fraud and unconscionability applies to G.R. Quittschreiber as well, who may not claim the status of a holder in due course. Apart from specific statutory limitations on the holder-in-due-course doctrine, the courts of the District of Columbia have imposed a heavy burden of proof on parties who seek to establish the status of a holder in due course. Where a transaction appears to be outside the normal course of business or usurious, courts must view with suspicion a defense of holder in due course. *Hill v. Hawes,* 144 F.2d 511, 512, 79 U.S.App.D.C. 168, 169 (1944). In that case, the Court of Appeals stated:

> We do not consider this evidence sufficient to show that the defendant was a holder in due course of the original note which he claims to have purchased. The circumstances surrounding the transaction constitute a badge of fraud which is not rebutted. Competent businessmen do not purchase notes in substantial sums executed by parties unknown to them whose credit they have not investigated.

In the present case, defendant Quittschreiber failed to produce substantial evidence to rebut the "badge of fraud" surrounding this transaction. The evidence indicated he had a close business relationship to the other defendants and that he purchased the note at a substantial discount. In addition, he did not investigate plaintiff's credit independently, rather he relied solely on Mr. Kemper's representation as to the value of the property. Accordingly, he may not claim to be a holder in due course and is barred along with the other defendants from initiating foreclosure proceedings on plaintiff's property.

In light of the foregoing discussion, the contract and deed of trust are void and unenforceable on grounds of fraud, misrepresentation and unconscionability. Defendant Quittschreiber has not carried his burden of establishing that he is a holder in due course. Plaintiff is thus under no obligation to repay any of the money she received or make any further payments to Mr. Quittschreiber. Defendants are enjoined permanently from initiating proceedings to foreclose on plaintiff's property.

Order

This matter is before the Court on plaintiff's motion to alter or amend judgment and defendants' opposition thereto. In its memorandum opinion of February 29, 1980, the Court voided a promissory note and deed of trust executed on plaintiff's property located at 1502 Emerson Street, N.W. and enjoined the trustees and the holder of the note permanently from exercising their powers of sale and commencing foreclosure proceedings on the property.

Plaintiff now seeks statutory penalties and attorney's fees prescribed under the Truth In Lending Act, 15 U.S.C. § 1640 (1976) and punitive damages. Plaintiff, however, has already received approximately $3,000 interest free as a result of the Court's ruling and is thus not entitled, in the Court's view, to any additional award.

Accordingly, it is by the Court, this 27th day of March 1980,

ORDERED that plaintiff's motion to alter or amend judgment insofar as it seeks damages under the Truth In Lending Act is hereby denied; and it is further

ORDERED that plaintiff may apply for attorney's fees only when a final decision has been rendered by the United States Court of Appeals for the District of Columbia Circuit; and it is further

ORDERED that the order entered in this action on February 29, 1980 shall be stricken and the amended order attached hereto shall be substituted therefor nunc pro tunc Feb. 29, 1980.

Section 3. DURESS AND UNDUE INFLUENCE

Duress is the use of any wrongful act or threat as a means of influencing a party to contract. Duress takes away a contracting party's "free will." Duress has two forms: duress by actual physical force or duress by threat. In duress by actual physical force, a person using physical force compels a party to "assent" to the "contract," even though that party did not intend to contract.

EXAMPLE

George presented a document in contract form to Clint for Clint's signature. When Clint refused to sign, George, who was physically stronger, grabbed Clint by the neck and forced him to sign his name. Clint's signature is an ineffective manifestation of assent and no contract is formed. Clint literally was no more than a mere "mechanical instrument" at the hands of George.

Assent may be induced by someone who is not a party to the contract. The party subject to the duress may disaffirm the contract when the third party uses duress by physical force.

Duress encompasses more than physical force. Duress may exist when one party improperly threatens another party to assent to a contract, and the threatened party has no reasonable alternative but to assent. Duress by threat includes "economic duress." In economic duress a party is wrongfully threatened with severe economic loss if the threatened party does not enter the proposed contract.

EXAMPLE

Simmons delivered a large order of merchandise to Barnes under a contract for sale. Barnes, knowing that Simmons was in urgent need of cash and was unable to borrow money, refused to pay unless Simmons reduced the contract price by half. Simmons assented to the modification. Barnes's threat amounts to duress. Simmons may disaffirm the modification.

Duress by threat has four elements:

1. There must be a threat.
2. The threat must be improper. Improper threats include threats that are either so shocking that the court will not inquire into the fairness of the resulting exchange, such as the threat of a criminal act or criminal prosecution, or threats that in themselves necessarily involve some element of unfairness, such as a breach of the duty of good faith and fair dealing under a contract (often involved with economic duress).
3. The threat must induce the victim to assent to the contract. A threat does not induce assent if the threatened party has a reasonable alternative to assenting and fails to take advantage of that alternative. Reasonable alternatives may include legal remedies or the availability of similar goods or services in the market place.

4. The threat must be sufficiently grave to induce the victim to assent. This requires a subjective determination of the victim's perception of the seriousness of the threat.

PROBLEM 4: Reese, a general contractor, was awarded a contract by the government to extend a runway at a military air base. Reese gave Hawkins a subcontract to supply the concrete. After the foundation for the runway had been prepared, Hawkins refused to deliver the concrete unless Reese both paid more than the contract price for the concrete and awarded Hawkins a subcontract on another job that Reese had. Reese agreed to modify the price and give Hawkins the second contract.

Could Reese disaffirm the modification of the first subcontract due to duress? In evaluating whether Reese could disaffirm consider

1. whether Hawkins threatened Reese
2. whether the threat was improper
3. whether the threat induced Reese to assent to the contract (whether Reese had a reasonable alternative to assenting and whether the threat was sufficiently grave to induce Reese to assent).

PROBLEM 5: Jill, who had contracted to sell goods to Ben, threatened to refuse to deliver the goods to him unless he modified the contract to increase the price. Ben did not attempt to purchase the goods elsewhere, although he knew that they were available. Being in urgent need of the goods, he agreed to the modification. Jill shipped the goods.

Could Ben disaffirm the modification due to duress? In evaluating whether Ben could disaffirm consider

1. whether Jill threatened Ben
2. whether the threat was improper
3. whether the threat induced Ben to assent to the contract (whether Ben had a reasonable alternative to assenting and whether the threat was sufficiently grave to induce Ben to assent).

When the third party uses duress by threat, the party subject to the duress cannot disaffirm the contract if the other contracting party begins performance in good faith and without reason to know of the duress. *In re Marriage of Hitchcock* illustrates duress by threat by a third party, in this case a judge. Apply the elements for duress by threat to these facts. Do you agree with the majority or the dissenting justices?

In re Marriage of Hitchcock

Supreme Court of Iowa, 1978.
265 N.W.2d 599.

Considered en banc.

MASON, Justice.

Respondent, Necia A. Hitchcock, appeals from the economic provisions of a decree granting petitioner, W.P. Hitchcock, dissolution of his marriage to Necia and from the order overruling her motion to vacate and for new trial.

September 24, 1975, Mr. Hitchcock filed a petition in the Polk District Court for dissolution of his marriage with Necia A. Hitchcock. August 17, 1976, the action came on for trial before Judge Missildine. After hearing part of Mr. Hitchcock's testimony, the court urged the parties to attempt to settle the economic matters of the dissolution. They settled and the court entered a decree August 19 in the form submitted and approved by counsel for the parties. August 27 Mrs. Hitchcock, through attorneys she had hired after the decree was entered, filed a motion to vacate the judgment and for a new trial alleging that her consent to the purported settlement was procured by undue duress upon her as a proximate result of the trial court's conduct. After an evidentiary hearing on the motion before Judge Gibson C. Holliday, the motion was overruled.

In the part of the decree from which appeal is taken the court ordered Mr. Hitchcock to pay Mrs. Hitchcock $1500 a month alimony to continue until either party dies or Necia remarries. She was to be the owner of the equity in the couple's house and Mr. Hitchcock was to pay the mortgage payments for as long as Necia retained title to the house and as long as she continued to occupy the home at least 11 months a year. Mr. Hitchcock was ordered to pay Mrs. Hitchcock $50,000 in equal yearly installments over a five-year period. She also received the household furniture, her checking and savings accounts, and all insurance policies of which she was the owner. Mr. Hitchcock received the remainder of the property including his stocks and other interests in Davis Brokerage Company.

When the parties were married in 1947 they had no substantial property. In 1948 Mr. Hitchcock went to work as a salesman for Davis Brokerage Company, a food brokerage firm with its principal office in Des Moines. In 1951 he was transferred to Davenport and eventually became the office manager there. In 1965 he returned to Des Moines as vice president of the company. In 1970 he was made president of the company and has since continued in that office.

In 1971 the founder of the company, John Davis, sold his 40,040 shares in the company to the company at $10 a share. Pursuant to an agreement with Davis, the company has paid him a portion each year of the $400,400 it owes him so that by the time of trial the company owed him $200,000.

As of December 31, 1975, Mr. Hitchcock owned 8285 shares in the company which amounted to seventy-six percent of the outstanding shares of stock and which gave him control of the company. His salary as president was $60,000 a year plus a bonus which would be paid if the company made money. In 1975 he had been paid a bonus of $16,000.

The parties disputed the value of Mr. Hitchcock's shares in the company. Although the valuations of the shares ranged from $2,000,000 to $400,000, most of the experts the parties intended to call as witnesses placed the value between $400,000 and $600,000.

Under an agreement between Mr. Hitchcock and the company, the company agreed to buy back his shares of stock upon his death or retirement for no less than $407,000. In addition, in the event of Mr. Hitchcock's death or retirement the company agreed to pay a total of $100,000 in equal monthly installments over a period of 120 months to him or to his designated beneficiaries or to his estate. In the event he was forced to terminate his employment because of disability, he was to be paid $3400 a month until he reached age 65. The company secured its commitment under this agreement with a life insurance policy on Mr. Hitchcock.

Apparently the stock was difficult to value because the value of the company could not be easily determined. The company's only real assets were its customers who could cancel their contracts with the company on 30-day notice. If the company lost a big customer it could lose money for the year. The profits of the company were entirely dependent upon the persuasiveness of its salesmen and officers.

While Mr. Hitchcock was busy rising through the ranks of Davis Brokerage, Mrs. Hitchcock was busy at home. While he worked to earn money, she worked to maintain their home and family. The couple had one daughter who at the time of trial was 25 and lived with her mother. Mrs. Hitchcock had no specialized training to help her to obtain employment. Although her age was stated at trial to be 56, the same as her husband, she was actually 63.

Prior to trial both parties disclosed the value of their assets. These assets, excluding the stock in Davis Brokerage, were as follows: (1) a jointly owned house worth fifty to sixty thousand dollars and encumbered by a twenty thousand dollar mortgage; (2) household goods and furniture worth ten to twenty thousand dollars; (3) two automobiles which together were worth $3150; (4) Mr. Hitchcock's vested interest in the company pension plan, $45,000; (5) two savings accounts, one in Mr. Hitchcock's name and one in Mrs. Hitchcock's name, with balances of $3500 and $2400 respectively; (6) 300 shares of stock in Mr. Hitchcock's name worth $600; (7) a coin collection worth $4000; and (8) 14 life insurance policies having a face value of $111,548 and cash surrender value of $20,000, each listing Mrs. Hitchcock as primary beneficiary and some listing their daughter as contingent beneficiary.

The parties also listed their expenses. Mrs. Hitchcock's expenses for herself and her daughter totaled $25,148.45 a year. She also indicated mortgage payments, taxes and insurance on their home amounted to $3192.00 a year.

Mr. Hitchcock listed his expenses as $40,488 a year, $12,000 of which was money he hoped to invest in a trust to assure continuation of alimony payments to Mrs. Hitchcock after his retirement.

At trial the first and only witness ever called was Mr. Hitchcock who was examined until the court recessed for lunch. After lunch Mrs. Hitchcock and her attorney, Donald F. Neiman, were standing in the corridor when Judge Missildine came in. The judge asked Mr. Neiman if he and Mr. Hitchcock's attorney, J. Rudolph Hansen, could join him in chambers when Mr. Hansen returned from lunch. Upon Mr. Hansen's return, the attorneys met with the judge in his chambers.

The parties and their attorneys dispute what happened from this point on. The accounts of what occurred were brought out in the hearing before Judge Holliday on Mrs. Hitchcock's motion to vacate the judgment entered by Judge Missildine and for a new trial.

Mr. Neiman: Direct Examination

In chambers Judge Missildine said he did not wish to sit and listen to how to run a brokerage business. He felt the attorneys knew more about it than he did. From what he had observed the parties appeared to be only a couple hundred dollars apart and he thought they should get together and try to work out a settlement.

The judge offered to speak to the parties if that would help. Mr. Neiman then stated he and Mr. Hansen had been working on the case for 18 months and they would both welcome any outside help. He could not remember the judge having said anything about not wanting to know the value of the Davis Company stocks.

After the meeting he returned to his client and told her the judge would like to speak with the parties. He explained to her he had the impression the judge was not going to give her any part of her husband's business.

At the meeting with the parties and their attorneys the judge repeated what he had said to the attorneys about the possibility of settlement. Mrs. Hitchcock stated she felt that after twenty-eight and one-half years she was entitled to some part of the business. The judge explained she was not entitled to any part of the business because the business was personal to her husband. It was the business that had afforded them the life to which they had become accustomed and it was the business which would produce the money with which Mr. Hitchcock would pay the alimony. The judge intended to give her the same standard of living as that to which she had become accustomed.

Upon conclusion of this meeting, Mr. Neiman met with his client again. She appeared shocked, was trembling and was almost to the point of tears. He explained to her he did not believe the judge's comments were grounds for a mistrial. He thought they should settle the case because if they went on she could possibly get less alimony than he thought her husband was willing to pay. He based this conclusion on an earlier offer of settlement and on his impression of the attitude of the court toward giving Mrs. Hitchcock a part of the business.

Mr. Neiman then entered into negotiations with the other side. After one and one-half hours a settlement was reached. He did not know why Mrs. Hitchcock had agreed to settle the case but he surmised it was because of the attitude of the court.

Mr. Neiman: Cross-Examination

He had explained to Mrs. Hitchcock prior to trial there was little chance a judge would give her any part in the business. He felt a judge would not lend much credence to their witness who would testify the business was worth $2,000,000.

During the negotiations prior to the settlement, the judge told Mr. Neiman if they could not get it settled he was ready to continue to hear the evidence. The judge also went out and told the parties to come back in and get on with the evidence. Mr. Neiman then suggested something could be done if he had more time to speak with his client.

Mr. Neiman felt he had settled the case because he could get a better deal for his client than if he tried the case. He had explained the details of the settlement to Mrs. Hitchcock but stated she might not have understood because she was very disturbed by the whole turn of events. He felt the settlement was fair.

Mrs. Hitchcock: Direct Examination

Mr. Neiman came out of the meeting between the attorneys and the judge in a very disturbed state. He explained to Mrs. Hitchcock the judge was not going to consider the value of the business. Upon hearing this she became very agitated.

At the meeting with the parties the judge explained he thought the business was a male type achievement. He explained to her she had no right to anything except to live as she had been accustomed. She was dumbfounded and shocked to hear this. She felt he was not listening to her and had prejudged her.

The judge explained he did not care to learn how a brokerage business was run. He thought the lawyers and parties should try to work out some sort of agreement.

After the meeting Mrs. Hitchcock returned to the corridor. She was shocked and felt frustrated, trapped and under duress. Some of her agitation was caused by things her husband had told her.

Mrs. Hitchcock could not remember what happened next. During the negotiations between the attorneys, she told Mr. Neiman what she wanted but did not recall whether he had kept her informed. The judge came out about 3:00 p.m. and told the parties he did not want to be there all night. Mrs. Hitchcock then asked for another five minutes and the judge went back into the courtroom.

She had agreed to a settlement but had not approved the final figures agreed upon by the attorneys. She did not know the details of the settlement until after the court's decree was entered. She was not satisfied with the settlement.

Mrs. Hitchcock: Cross–Examination

During the negotiations she knew she would have title to the house and that her husband would make the mortgage payments. She understood her husband would pay her $50,000 over a five-year period. She was aware she would get $1500 a month alimony. She admitted the only way her husband could pay the alimony was if he kept the business.

Mrs. Hitchcock was aware the judge told her he would hear the case if the parties could not settle it. She asked him for five minutes more.

When she stated she was under duress, she meant she was being forced to make a decision she should not have made. The circumstances had forced her into this position. Mental force had been exerted upon her. Her shock was caused by her realization that things were happening differently from what she had imagined.

Judge Missildine: Direct Examination

He explained to the attorneys it appeared to him the case could be settled and suggested they take some time to attempt to do so. He felt they were better versed in the facts of the case than he would be at the close of all the evidence. He stated his attitude toward the type of case presented here:

" 'Whenever there is substantial property involved, I would much rather have a settlement than a decision of the Court, because the Court can only decide a case on the evidence that is before it, and he has to determine which witnesses he is going to believe where there is a conflict,' and so on. So it is my opinion and my philosophy, wherever there is substantial property involved, a settlement is much better than any decision the Court can give them, and I told them that."

Judge Missildine: Cross–Examination

It was his impression at the trial the brokerage business was a personal one because its success depended on the person who was the head of the business. He did not recall telling Mrs. Hitchcock she had no right to any part of the business.

Mr. Hitchcock

The judge stated he felt the people involved in the case knew more about it than he did. The judge stated the value of the business was its ability to support the parties well and as long as it served that purpose, that was how the parties should value it. It is true the judge urged the parties to settle but he did not give any impression of coercion.

Judge Holliday overruled the motion to vacate and for new trial. He found the comment of the judge urging settlement was "... without bias or prejudice toward either party. The comment was made in a desire to give counsel for the respective parties 'an expression of the conclusions of the Judge up to the moment, in order that counsel may be advised what course to chart.' " He concluded there was no error, irregularity or misconduct. He did not consider whether the economic provisions of the decree were equitable.

In his conclusions of law Judge Holliday stated:

"Efforts on the part of the trial judge to expedite the proceedings and to encourage settlements out of Court are ordinarily to be commended, such efforts should never be so directed as to compell [sic] either litigant to make a forced settlement.

"The rule is well established that, within proper bounds, a trial judge should encourage the settlement of litigated cases. The question here is whether the judge's comments were within such bounds.

"A party or his counsel may always refuse to accede to a suggestion by the court. The trial court ought not to force a settlement on a party who wants a trial, but there is nothing wrong or irregular in the Court suggesting the advisability of settlement. A settlement procured under duress cannot be binding.

"...

"The record does not reveal any evidence of coercion, bias, or prejudgment on the part of the Court. On the contrary, the Court exercised a high degree of courtesy and patience, and at all times appeared to maintain an open and unprejudicial attitude.

"This Court concludes that the record does not present a situation which calls for a holding that the trial judge was guilty of misconduct which requires the granting of a new trial."

I. The issue presented by Mrs. Hitchcock's appeal from the economic provisions of the final judgment and decree terminating the marital relationship existing between her and her husband is whether the award in those respects is justified and equitable.

Section 598.21, The Code, as in force at the time material here, provided:

"Alimony—custody of children—changes. When a dissolution of marriage is decreed, the court may make such order in relation to the children, property, parties, and the maintenance of the parties as shall be justified.

"Subsequent changes may be made by the court in these respects when circumstances render them expedient."

In *Locke v. Locke,* 246 N.W.2d 246, 251 (Iowa 1976), this court said:

"A distribution of the assets of the parties in a dissolution proceedings should be based on the guidelines set out in *Schantz v. Schantz,* 163 N.W.2d 398, 405 (Iowa 1968), excluding consideration of reward or punishment on the basis of fault. *In re Marriage of Winter,* 223 N.W.2d 165, 169 (Iowa 1974). See *In re Marriage of Cooper,* 225 N.W.2d 915, 919 (Iowa 1975).

"Division of assets of parties in dissolution of marriage proceedings based on either a one-third share to wife or an equal division is not statutorily sanctioned; that which is determinative is that which would constitute an equitable and just award under the circumstances. See *In re Marriage of Cooper,* 225 N.W.2d at 919."

As pointed out by Mrs. Hitchcock, the decree in this case is not the result of a trial on the merits or an independent decision of the court. There was no written stipulation of the parties which was incorporated in and made a part of the decree in this matter. Rather, the decree entered by the trial court was in the form submitted and approved by counsel for the parties.

Within a few days after entry of the decree Mrs. Hitchcock filed a motion to vacate the decree and for a new trial. As a basis for the relief sought in the motion Mrs. Hitchcock alleged that her manifestation of assent to the settlement referred to in the decree was procured by undue duress and emotional stress induced by the trial judge's conduct in announcing his views as to what would be a just and equitable distribution of the assets of the parties under the circumstances. She further alleged she had no reasonable alternative to succumbing to the purported settlement.

As we understand, Mrs. Hitchcock insists her manifestation of assent to the purported settlement was induced by the acts and conduct of the trial judge and consequently was not effective as an expression of mutual assent necessary for the formation of a valid contract of settlement.

As stated, Judge Holliday in ruling on Mrs. Hitchcock's motion to vacate and for new trial concluded the record before him did not present a situation which called for a holding that the trial judge was guilty of misconduct which required the granting of a new trial. He specifically stated, ". . . [T]his Court does not consider the matter of the equities of the decree before the Court."

In our opinion, the question as to whether Judge Missildine's announcements relative to distribution of the assets of the parties constitutes misconduct requiring a new trial is not the issue for determination in Mrs. Hitchcock's appeal from the economic provisions of the decree.

In view of the fact there was an actual expression of assent by Mrs. Hitchcock to the distribution of the assets of the parties as set forth in the decree, the problem before this court is whether the announcements and conduct of the trial judge were sufficient to actually induce assent on the part of Mrs. Hitchcock who claims to be the victim of duress thereby rendering it inequitable to permit enforcement of the distribution as provided in the decree.

The test is subjective. Hence, "threats that would suffice to induce assent by one person may not suffice to induce assent by another. All attendant circumstances must be considered, including such matters as the age, background and relationship of the parties. ... Timid and inexperienced persons are particularly subject to threats, ... However, ... circumstantial evidence may be useful in determining whether a threat did, in fact, induce assent." See Restatement, Second, Contracts, section 317, comment c (Tentative Draft No. 12).

In our de novo review we are limited to a record of Mr. Hitchcock's testimony, the financial statements filed by the parties prior to trial (section 598.21) and the testimony of Mrs. Hitchcock, her counsel, Judge Missildine and Mr. Hitchcock relative to the events following the noon recess up until the purported settlement. Thus limited we find the announcements and conduct of the trial judge at the noon recess relative to what he considered to be a just distribution of the assets of the parties actually induced Mrs. Hitchcock's manifestation of assent to the purported settlement.

In this connection we recognize duress may be exercised by one who is not a party to the contract as well as by one who is. See Introductory Note to Topic 2, Restatement, Second, Contracts (Tentative Draft No. 12).

In section 317, comment b, *id.,* it is stated that, "A threat, even if improper, does not amount to duress if the victim has a reasonable alternative to succumbing and fails to take advantage of it." In the brief and argument filed on behalf of Mr. Hitchcock reference is made to the fact that while negotiations were in progress Judge Missildine told Mr. Neiman if they could not get the matter settled he was ready to continue to hear the evidence; at a later time Judge Missildine also told the parties to come back in and get on with the evidence. At this point Mrs. Hitchcock asked for another five minutes which the judge granted.

Under the record a finding would be justified that during the noon recess Judge Missildine announced his views as to what would constitute a fair and just distribution of the assets of the parties. The alternative for Mrs. Hitchcock was to follow the judge's suggestion and settle the matter in accordance therewith or proceed to try her case on its merits before a tribunal which had apparently prejudged the issue to be determined by the court as mandated by section 598.21, The Code. In our opinion, this is a far cry from a *reasonable* alternative as contemplated by the Restatement. We agree with Mrs. Hitchcock she did not have a reasonable alternative to succumbing.

Insofar as we are able to determine from the record the remarks attributed to Judge Missildine were made by the judge in the presence of both parties and their counsel.

From our de novo review we conclude the purported settlement relative to the distribution of the assets of the parties as set forth in the decree is voidable by Mrs. Hitchcock. It cannot logically be maintained that she ratified the settlement agreement in any manner or to any extent, particularly in view of her promptness in filing the motion to vacate.

"... Ratification results if the party who executed the contract under duress accepts the benefits flowing from it or remains silent or acquiesces in the contract for any considerable length of time after opportunity is afforded to annul or void it. ... [citing authorities]." *Gallon v. Lloyd-Thomas Company,* 264 F.2d 821, 826 (8 Cir.1959), 77 A.L.R.2d 417, 424.

We hold the distribution of the assets of the parties as set forth in the decree cannot be sustained.

. . .

MOORE, C.J., and RAWLINGS, UHLENHOPP and REYNOLDSON, JJ., concur.

LeGRAND, REES and HARRIS, JJ., dissent.

McCORMICK, J., takes no part.

LeGRAND, Justice (dissenting).

I do not agree the record in this case supports the conclusion reached by the majority, and I therefore dissent.

Mrs. Hitchcock alleges she was induced to agree to a settlement of the dissolution case in which she was the respondent because of "gross irregularity and misconduct" by the trial court.

It is interesting to note the background from which these charges arose.

The case came on for hearing as a contested dissolution matter. No minor children were involved; and, of course, fault is no longer a consideration. This left the contestants with only one battleground—property settlement and alimony.

The trial court heard evidence for half a day. After the noon recess, at which time her husband's case had not been completed, the trial court asked to see the parties and counsel in chambers. According to the record, it was then apparent the principal asset was Mr. Hitchcock's interest in a food brokerage business. The trial court suggested the case should be settled. He stated he did not feel Mrs. Hitchcock should have any interest in the business, although it should provide her with the standard of living she had been used to. The judge also made statements to the effect that he wasn't interested in learning how to run a brokerage business and that the parties could make a better settlement than he could make for them.

The parties and counsel then retired to conduct almost two hours of negotiations, during which the court indicated the trial should resume if settlement could not be reached. On one occasion, Mrs. Hitchcock asked for "another five minutes." Eventually a settlement was reached. It provided that Mrs. Hitchcock should have the homestead and that Mr. Hitchcock should pay off the incumbrance, that she should have $1,500.00 a month alimony, and property settlement of $50,000.00 to be paid over a five-year period.

Several days later a decree was entered incorporating this settlement into its terms. Mrs. Hitchcock now repudiates it because of "duress" practiced upon her by the court.

I take it my disagreement with the majority concerns only the particular facts of this case and does not rest upon a difference of opinion concerning the general principles which govern such matters. The law looks with favor upon the settlement of disputes, particularly in family and marital cases. A trial judge may, within proper limits, urge settlement. He is frequently the only catalyst from which successful negotiations may spring. *See Schraeder Iron Work, Inc. v. Lee,* 26 Cal.App.3d 621, 103 Cal.Rptr. 106, 118 (1972); *In re Trust of Dorothy Luria Mintz,* 444 Pa. 189, 282 A.2d 295, 299 (1971); *Chertkof v. Harry C. Weiskittel Co., Inc.,* 251 Md. 544, 248 A.2d 373, 376 (1968); *Gardner v. Mobil Oil Company,* 217 Cal. App.2d 220, 31 Cal.Rptr. 731, 6 A.L.R.3d 1451 (1963). *See also* Annot. 6 A.L.R.3d at p. 1459 (1966).

I accept the proposition that a trial judge should not force parties into agreements they would not otherwise make. The majority says that is what happened here. I say it didn't. Both lawyers welcomed the suggestion that they settle. Mrs. Hitchcock's lawyer testified he and his New York expert had agreed at lunch (before the judge made any suggestion) that the case should be settled because they felt Mrs. Hitchcock couldn't do as well as she expected to. In this connection Mrs. Hitchcock's attorney testified he was willing to settle the case partially because of the fact he had no confidence in his own value expert. The notion to settle did not originate with the judge, and the claim that the settlement was made reluctantly and only in the face of the court's insistence is just not borne out by the record.

It is quite true the trial court stated he felt Mrs. Hitchcock should have no proprietary interest in her husband's business; but he also said the business should afford her the same type of living style she had become accustomed to.

This was not an arbitrary or capricious opinion but was based on the judge's philosophy as to what could best serve the interests of the litigants. The business was a personal-service operation. It had no substantial net worth. Its value could be destroyed by loss of a few key accounts. It was, for all practical purposes, a one-man company. Perhaps this is best reflected by the testimony of Donald F. Neiman, Mrs. Hitchcock's lawyer, at the hearing to vacate the decree. I set out an excerpt from it:

"Q. After you came back from lunch, will you tell the Court what happened?
A. Well, we ran into Judge Missildine, and he indicated he would like to talk to Steve Hansen and myself back in Chambers when Steve got back. During that recess I had lunch with the expert witness from New York, and we discussed the outlook of the case, and this expert witness is also an attorney although he is not familiar with the courtroom, but we both concluded that from the way the evidence was going, as far as the Judge's view of it, that he would never force a sale of Davis Brokerage Company, that there was a possibility that if we could get into it, we should think about possibly settling it. This was right before Judge Missildine—
Q. What made you feel the Judge would not force a sale of the Davis Brokerage Company?
A. It is a going concern that has fifty-five salesmen and has a large sales force. It has three executives that are very key to the business, that if it were sold, there would be no guarantee for any non-competing type of thing, and basically that was what we were looking at.
Q. That was just your private surmise between the two of you?
A. Yes.
Q. The judge hadn't said anything about that?
A. No."

This appears to have been the *real* basis for the settlement. What the judge said later was not the motivating force Mrs. Hitchcock now says it was. Nor did the fact the judge made his remarks without having heard Mrs. Hitchcock's evidence amount, as she claims, to "prejudging" her case. Her testimony could not have changed the nature or character of the business, only its value. This factor played no part in what was said.

I do not quibble about whether some of the judge's remarks might have been better left unsaid or have been couched more judiciously. But when Mrs. Hitchcock's complaints are examined one by one they are so insubstantial that I find no possibility, however remote, she was coerced or that she was the victim of judicial duress.

The court made disdainful reference to an adult daughter as a "freeloader," a remark at which Mrs. Hitchcock took umbrage. However, he did so in the context that this was making Mrs. Hitchcock's alimony requirements greater than they should be.

She also resented the judge's comparison—ill advised, perhaps—of Mrs. Hitchcock's right to an interest in her husband's business to his own wife's interest in his retirement fund should they be divorced.

Another statement with which she found fault was the court's admonition to either settle or get on with the trial because he didn't "want to be here all night." Surely this was little more than a pointed prodding that trial time was wasting, without apparent results.

During all of this, Mrs. Hitchcock had the benefit of her lawyer's counsel as well as the advice of her brother, with whom she is shown to have consulted. I simply cannot accept the majority's conclusion she was forced into an improvident settlement against her will. In fact when she was pressed for proof of such fact, the best Mrs. Hitchcock could come up with was that she felt "trapped" and "frustrated" because the judge didn't "act at all the way they do on TV."

Judge Holliday found Mrs. Hitchcock's application to vacate the decree was groundless. I think that finding should be affirmed.

REES and HARRIS, JJ., join in this dissent.

Undue influence differs from duress in two ways. First, undue influence neither requires threats nor deception, although often one or the other is present. Second, undue influence requires a special relationship between the parties. Undue influence involves unfair persuasion by a party who is either in a position of dominance or in a position of trust and confidence.

Undue influence often includes the following:

1. the susceptibility of the party influenced, such as mental or physical weakness
2. the opportunity to exercise undue influence, such as a confidential relationship (including parent-child, husband-wife, attorney-client, or trustee-beneficiary)
3. a resulting transaction that enriches the party exercising the influence at the expense of the party being influenced.

A victim of undue influence may disaffirm the contract unless a third party induces the assent and the other contracting party has begun performance in good faith and without reason to know of the undue influence.

PROBLEM 6: Johnson, an elderly and illiterate man, lived with his nephew, Barker, and was dependent on him for support. Barker told Johnson that he would no longer support him unless Johnson sold Barker a tract of land called Greenacre. Johnson signed a contract selling Greenacre to Barker.

Could Johnson disaffirm the contract due to undue influence? In evaluating whether Johnson could dissaffirm consider

1. whether Johnson was susceptible to Barker's influence
2. whether Barker had the opportunity to exercise undue influence over Johnson
3. whether Barker was enriched at the expense of Johnson.

Could Johnson disaffirm the contract due to duress?

PROBLEM 7: Tom, inexperienced in business, had for years relied on the advice of his local banker, Samantha, for business advice. Samantha constantly urged Tom to sell Jean, Samantha's business associate, a tract of land called Blackacre at a price well below its fair market value. Based on this advice, Tom contracted to sell Blackacre to Jean.

Could Tom disaffirm the contract due to undue influence? In evaluating whether Tom could disaffirm consider

1. whether Tom was susceptible to Samantha's influence
2. whether Samantha had the opportunity to exercise undue influence on Tom
3. whether Samantha was enriched at the expense of Tom.

Could Tom disaffirm the contract due to duress?

Section 4. MISTAKE IN A BASIC ASSUMPTION OF FACT

Courts allow a contracting party who has been adversely affected by a mistake in a basic assumption of fact to disaffirm the contract. This form of mistake involves a situation where the parties believed they were bargaining for something different from the thing for which they actually contracted. Typically, these mistakes involve the existence or identity of the subject matter of the contract.

EXAMPLE

In the famous case of *Sherwood v. Walker,* 66 Mich. 568, 33 N.W. 919 (1887), the mistake involved the sale of Rose 2d of Aberlone, a cow that both parties believed sterile. Walker contracted to sell Rose at a sterile cow price. But before Walker delivered Rose to Sherwood, Walker discovered that Rose was with calf and worth about ten times the contract price. The court ruled that Walker could disaffirm the contract because of a mistake in a basic assumption of fact. The mistake involved the very nature of the thing for which he bargained. The facts were quite different from those on which the parties based their bargain. A barren cow is a substantially different creature from a breeder.

The comments to the Restatement (Second) of Contracts suggest three requirements a party must meet before disaffirming a contract for a mistake in a basic assumption of fact. First, the mistake must relate to a "basic assumption on which the contract was made," such as the existence or identity of the subject matter. Second, the party seeking to disaffirm must show how the mistake had a material effect on the agreed exchange of performances. Third, the mistake must not involve a risk that the party seeking relief has agreed to bear (as provided in the contract or by implication arising from the party's greater expertise). Each party bears the risk of a bad bargain which results from failure to investigate the value of the subject matter.

PROBLEM 8: Kitty contracted to sell Northridge Lumber Company a tract of timber land. The high contract price reflected the quantity and quality of the standing timber. At the time of contracting, both parties believed the timber was standing. Unknown to the parties, the timber had recently been destroyed by fire.

Did a mistake as to a basic assumption of fact exist when the parties contracted? Could Northridge show that the mistake had a material effect on the agreed exchange of performances? Did Northridge agree to bear the risk? Could Northridge disaffirm the contract by claiming a mistake in a basic assumption of fact?

Generally, courts allow disaffirmance of only those contracts in which the mistake involves the "identity" or "existence" of the subject matter, rather than mere "quality" or "value."

EXAMPLE

Costello sold Sykes ten shares of stock for $316 a share. In fact, employees of the corporation had altered the corporation's books, and the actual value of the stock was $60 a share, rather than $316 a share. Sykes could not successfully sue Costello for breach of contract to recover the contract price based on a mistake in a basic assumption of fact. The mistake relates to "attributes, quality, or value" and not as to "existence or identity" of the stocks sold.

Attorneys who have worked in this area know that this distinction is not always clear, and the application of the law to a set of facts is often difficult.

PROBLEM 9: Wood found a pretty stone and offered to sell it to Boynton. The parties expressed their ignorance as to the nature of the stone and guessed it to be a topaz. Wood sold the stone to Boynton for one dollar. Later the stone was identified as an uncut diamond worth $1,000.

Did the mistake relate to a basic assumption on which the contract was made? Could Wood show that the mistake had a material effect on the agreed exchange of performances? What risks did Wood agree to bear in entering into the contract with Boynton? Would you be surprised to learn that the court in *Wood v. Boynton,* 64 Wis. 265, 25 N.W. 42 (1885), held that Wood could not disaffirm? Can you reconcile the result in *Wood* with the illustration given about Rose 2d?

11

PROTECTING THE JUDICIAL PROCESS

In addition to protecting a class or a party against overreaching, the legislature or court may seek to protect the judicial process. Disputants should not be permitted to use the judicial process to promote nonjudicial activity such as illegality, perjury, and inappropriate forum shopping. This chapter explores these three situations in which the judicial process is protected from misuse.

Section one considers illegality and its role in the enforcement of a contract. Should the courts enforce contracts that are illegal, contracts that are legal but were procured by illegal conduct, and contracts that are legal but were performed by illegal conduct?

Section two explores whether a contract must be in writing to be enforceable. The writing requirement may protect the judicial process from perjury. If a writing is required, what satisfies the writing requirement?

Section three investigates whether a forum selection provision is enforceable. If parties specify in their contract the location where disputes will be settled, what limitations are necessary to protect the integrity of the judicial process?

Section 1. ILLEGALITY

A. Illegality as a Defense to a Breach of Contract Action

A contract may be unenforceable due to illegality. The illegality may involve the subject matter of the contract. In other cases, the subject matter of the contract may not be illegal but illegal conduct was involved in either the procurement or performance of the contract.

1. Illegal Subject Matter

A contract which violates the law is unenforceable. The court will not aid either party to an illegal contract, regardless of whether the contract has been performed by either party. The court will not become the paymaster for an illegal contract but will leave the parties where it finds them.

PROBLEM 1: James, an employee of Vernon Calhoun Packing Company, was injured on the job. Shortly after the injury, James and the Packing Company entered into a contract whereby the Packing Company promised James lifetime employment for James's promise to waive his worker's compensation claim. Five years later, the Packing Company fired James without cause. A state statute provides "No agreement by an employee to waive his or her rights to compensation under the worker's compensation law shall be valid."

Could James successfully sue the Packing Company for breach of the lifetime employment contract?

PROBLEM 2: Hope, a livestock hauler, entered into a three year contract with Cox Feedlots which provided that Cox would act as a broker and arrange hauling contracts for Hope and Hope would haul all of Cox's livestock to and from the Cox Feedlot, haul all livestock owned by third parties to and from the Cox Feedlot, and pay Cox ten percent of the gross income for the brokerage services. When the Railroad Commission declared that the brokerage fee was in reality a rebate in violation of law, Cox stopped arranging the hauling contracts with third persons for Hope.

Could Hope successfully sue Cox for breach of contract?

Because the law of the jurisdiction in which performance of the contract occurs usually governs the contract, the issue of the illegality of a contract is ordinarily determined in accordance with the law of the place where the contract is performed.

PROBLEM 3: Alex and Carrie contracted in Michigan to sell Michigan lottery tickets in Oklahoma. The contract provided that Alex would buy tickets in Michigan and Carrie would sell them in Oklahoma at a ten percent markup. The sale of lottery tickets is legal in Michigan but is illegal in Oklahoma.

Alex buys the tickets and gives them to Carrie. Having sold them in Oklahoma, Carrie refuses to give Alex the proceeds from the sale.

Could Alex successfully sue Carrie for breach of contract? Would it matter whether the case were filed in Oklahoma or Michigan?

The covenant not to compete is a variety of illegal contract. A covenant not to compete is an impermissible restraint on trade when it sweeps too broadly. Parties often use a covenant not to compete in a contract for the sale of a business. This covenant protects the buyer's purchase of the business's good will. A covenant must be reasonable in terms of subject matter, geography, and duration or it is unenforceable. The covenant may extend only to what is reasonably necessary to protect the buyer's legitimate interest in the enjoyment of the asset bought.

PROBLEM 4: Rhodes, a minority shareholder and president of SIS, a security guard business, sold his shares to SIS and left the company. The contract for sale contained the following covenant:

> Covenant by Seller not to Solicit Buyer's Customers. Seller covenants and agrees that for a period of two years from the date of this agreement, Rhodes will not, within a radius of fifty miles of City Hall,

> Philadelphia, Pennsylvania, directly or indirectly, as a corporation or as an individual, nor will any business entity or corporation of which he is an owner, shareholder, officer, employee, representative, or otherwise, either directly or indirectly, own, manage, operate, control or participate in the ownership, management, operation of or control of or be connected in any manner with or assist others in, the security guard business.

After leaving SIS, Rhodes organized and became associated with Rhodes Investigative Services, a detective agency, and with Hahn Security Service, a security guard business. Both were located in Philadelphia.

Has Rhodes breached his contract with SIS?

An employer may also use a covenant not to compete when hiring a new employee. The covenant must be reasonable in terms of the activities it prohibits the employee from doing, the geographic area in which the employee's activity is prohibited, and the length of time which the employee is prohibited from doing the activity. In addition, the covenant must be either necessary to prevent the disclosure of the employer's trade secrets or confidential lists or the employee's services must be special, unique, or extraordinary.

PROBLEM 5: Apex Sales & Service is in the business of selling and servicing fire protection equipment. When Peters applied for a job with Apex, he executed a written application which contained the following paragraph:

> I further agree that if employed and after working for the company six months or more, I elect to quit, I will not participate in the sale or service of fire protection and/or safety equipment in the Counties of Harris and/or Galveston in the State of Texas for a period of two years.

After working for Apex for more than three years, Peters quit and went to work for Delta Safety and Supply Company, a direct competitor of Apex. While at Apex, Peters had been engaged in inspecting, maintaining, testing, and repairing fire protection equipment in various business establishments, particularly in restaurants. At Delta, Peters is the shop manager and runs Delta's shop and oversees Delta's service personnel.

By working at Delta, has Peters breached his covenant not to compete with Apex? In evaluating whether Peters is in breach, consider what interest Apex had in having Peters sign the covenant. Is the enforcement of the covenant necessary to prevent disclosure of Apex's trade secrets or confidential lists? Was Peters's service special, unique or extraordinary? Is the covenant reasonable in terms of the activities that Peters is prohibited from doing, the geographic area in which Peters is prohibited from acting, and the length of time Peters is prohibited from doing them?

2. Illegal Conduct to Procure a Legal Contract

At times the subject of the contract does not involve illegal conduct. Illegal conduct, however, may be present in the procurement of this legal contract. These cases often involve the recurring theme of bribery.

EXAMPLE

Sirkin bribed an employee of the Fourteenth Street Store to have the Store purchase merchandise from him. Sirkin delivered the merchandise but later the Fourteenth Street Store refused to pay. When Sirkin sought to use the court to collect on its contract with the Store, the court refused. The illegality—bribery—led to the formation of the legal contract for sale of goods. The court said:

> Nothing could be more corrupting, nor have a greater tendency to lead to disloyalty and dishonesty on the part of servants, agents, and employees, and to a betrayal of the confidence and trust reposed in them, than these practices which the Legislature has endeavored to stamp out; and I think nothing will be more effective in stopping the growth and spread of this corrupting, and now criminal, custom than a decision that the courts will refuse their aid to a guilty vendor or vendee, or to anyone who has obtained a contract by secretly bribing the servant, agent, or employee of another to purchase or sell property, or to place the contract with him.

Sirkin v. Fourteenth Street Store, 124 A.D. 384, 108 N.Y.S. 830, 834 (N.Y. Sup. Ct. 1908).

3. Illegal Conduct in the Performance of a Legal Contract

Although a contract may not contemplate illegal activities, one of the parties may act illegally when performing the contract. Not all illegal activity in the performance of a legal contract will preclude the enforcement of the contract. The illegality must be major rather than minor and must be directly related to the performance of the contract rather than only indirectly related.

EXAMPLE

Commonwealth Pictures wanted the distribution right to certain Universal films. McConnell promised to get Commonwealth the distribution rights if Commonwealth would promise to pay McConnell a commission on the gross receipts as the films are distributed.

McConnell bribed a representative of Universal to negotiate the Commonwealth/Universal contract. Upon discovering the bribery, Commonwealth refused to pay McConnell the commission.

The Commonwealth/McConnell contract was not illegal at its inception nor did it contemplate that McConnell would use bribery to procure the Commonwealth/Universal contract. In the performance of the contract, however, McConnell committed a major illegal act (bribery) and the illegal act was directly related to his performance of the contract. Therefore McConnell is not entitled to enforce his contract with Commonwealth for the commission.

B. Restitution as a Cause of Action

As a general rule a party who enters into an illegal contract is not only unable to enforce the bargain, he or she also is unable to obtain restitution for any benefits conferred under the contract. A number of exceptions exist. Judicial opinions are unclear in this area whether the exception entitles the aggrieved party to maintain a breach of contract action or a restitution action. For the purpose of discussion, we will treat these exceptions as permitting a restitution action.

The first exception deals with parties who are not *in pari delicto* (equal fault). The rule denies restitution of benefits conferred under illegal contracts. The rule is based on the notion that when the parties are in equal fault, the court should hold for the defendant. Another phrase for the concept could be "let sleeping dogs lie." When applied to losses by one of two equally guilty parties the concept makes sense since there is no reason to shift the loss from one to the other.

When applied to windfall gains, however, one guilty party receives a profit for the illegal activity while the other suffers a loss. Why should the profit and loss not be balanced out? Why should the courts, by inaction, enforce the windfall gain?

Where the parties are not in equal fault, the exception comes into play. A court may allow restitution to the party with less fault. In *Maner v. Mydland* isolate factors for determining whether the parties were *in pari delicto.* Also consider whether the action was for restitution or breach of contract.

Maner v. Mydland

Court of Appeal of California, 1967.
58 Cal. Rptr. 740.

FOX, Associate Justice.*

Plaintiffs [1] seek to recover their investment in a stock promotion. Judgment was rendered in favor of Maner and Tepper, but in favor of defendants and against Bennett. Defendants made a motion for a new trial which was granted as to defendant Mydland but denied as to Jones and Lindsey. Maner and Tepper have appealed from the order granting Mydland a new trial, and Mydland has cross-appealed from the judgment in favor of Maner and Tepper. Bennett has appealed from the judgment in favor of defendant in his case.

In April 1961 defendants organized the AVTA Corporation (known as AVTA Corporation) for the manufacture, sale and distribution of audio-visual teaching aids. It had an authorized capital of $300,000, divided into thirty thousand shares with a par value of $10 each. The three defendants constituted the board of directors and were elected officers of the corporation.

Pursuant to an application to the Department of Investment, Division of Corporations, a permit was issued authorizing the corporation to issue not to exceed 100 of its shares to Jones, Mydland and Ray Heinz at par per share for cash. Pursuant to this permit 80 shares were issued to Jones who was president and 10 shares each to Mydland, who was vice-president and attorney for the corporation, and to Heinz.

We shall now take up these transactions in chronological sequence.

* Retired Presiding Justice, Court of Appeal, sitting under assignment by Chairman of the Judicial Council.

1. One complaint was filed by Maner. Another was filed by Tepper and Bennett. Jones, Lindsey and Mydland were defendants in each complaint. The cases were consolidated for trial. Separate findings and conclusions of law were made, but a consolidated judgment was rendered.

The Bennett Stock Purchase

On July 7, 1961, Bennett purchased five shares of stock in AVTA Corporation for $5,000 from Jones who was to contribute said funds to the capital of AVTA, and the court found that Bennett's checks were payable to the corporation. The purchase was made under an agreement prepared by Mydland (Exhibit 3) and dated on the day Bennett purchased the stock. Bennett testified that he never had any experience in corporation affairs where a permit was obtained, nor had he purchased stock in a corporation not publicly owned.

The court found "[T]hat at the time of purchasing said shares of stock in AVTA, plaintiff Arthur C. Bennett, Jr. knew that he was purchasing stock which represented a portion of the personal stock holdings in said corporation of defendant James Jones, Jr. and said plaintiff was informed that no permit was required from the Commissioner of Corporations for the purchase of said shares of stock."

Mydland testified that at the time of the purchase of said stock by Bennett he advised Bennett that the consent of the Commissioner of Corporations was necessary where an individual sells stock and the proceeds from the sale inure to the benefit of the corporation which was the case in this transaction. Mydland had discussed this matter by telephone with a deputy in the commissioner's office and he was advised that an application was necessary and the procedure was outlined that should be followed in order to get the required consent. This "included an application and a statement of satisfaction with the transfer by the transferee." No such application was filed with the commissioner and no such statement was signed by Bennett.

On this point the court found that Bennett knowingly participated and aided in the making of the sale of the shares of stock and therefore was *in pari delicto.*

The "Jones stock" was sold to Bennett for the "benefit" of the corporation. A permit or consent for such sale from the Corporations Commissioner was therefore required under section 25152, Corporations Code. And a sale without such permit or consent violated the section. (Bellerue v. Business Files Institute, Inc., 61 Cal.2d 488, 39 Cal. Rptr. 201, 393 P.2d 401.) In *Bellerue* the court stated (p. 489, 39 Cal.Rptr. p. 202, 393 P.2d p. 402):

"Section 25152 of the Corporation Code exempts from the Corporate Securities Law '. . . the sale of securities when (a) made by or on behalf of a vendor not the issuer or underwriter thereof who, being a bona fide owner of the securities, disposes of his own property for his own account, and (b) the sale is not made, directly or indirectly, for the benefit of the issuer or an underwriter of the security . . . .' A permit for the sale of stock by a vendor who was not the issuer is therefore required when the sale is made for the benefit of the issuer."

We come now to the question: Was Bennett *in pari delicto* with defendants? We have concluded that he was not.

It must be borne in mind that the purpose of the Corporate Securities Law is to protect the investing public. And the penalties therein provided are leveled against the seller and not the buyer. (Robbins v. Pac. Eastern Corp., 8 Cal.2d 241, 278, 65 P.2d 42.) Therefore a purchaser of stock is not *in pari delicto* with the corporation and its directors unless he is equally culpable with them. If such purchaser is not *in pari delicto,* the law accords him relief against the corporation and against any person who aided the corporation in making the sale or participated in the scheme to sell the securities without the requisite permit or consent. (Randall v. Beber, 107 Cal.App.2d 692, 701, 237 P.2d 994.) Mere knowledge that no permit or consent had been issued does not place a purchaser *in pari delicto.* (Randall v. Calif. L.B. Syndicate, 217 Cal. 594, 598, 20 P.2d 331; Taormina v. Antelope Mining Corp., 110 Cal. App.2d 314, 320–321, 242 P.2d 665.) In Gormly v. Dickinson, 178 Cal.App.2d 92, 103–104, 2 Cal.Rptr. 650, 657, the court stated: "Even had the plaintiffs known that the consent of the Commissioner of Corporations would have to be secured before they could receive their stock, they could not be held to be equally culpable with the sellers." In holding in Bellerue v. Business Files Institute, Inc., supra, that plaintiff, a purchaser of stock, was not *in pari delicto* with defendants the court pointed out (61 Cal.2d pp. 490–491, 39 Cal. Rptr. p. 202, 393 P.2d p. 402): "Although plaintiff subsequently became a director of B.F.I., he was not a director at the time he and defendants made the agreement under which he was to lend B.F.I. the sum of $10,000 and pay C.M.C. $10 each for 7½ shares of stock of B.F.I. Therefore, he was not *in pari delicto* with defendants. * * * " In a footnote the court observed: "The agreement was made on April 1, 1958, and plaintiff became a director of B.F.I. on May 1, 1958." The statement of the court is particularly apposite to the case at bench. Here defendant made his stock purchase and paid for it on July 7, 1961, and then became a director on September 1, 1961, according to the minutes of that date.

In Tri-Q, Inc. v. Sta-Hi Corp., 63 Cal.2d 199, at pages 218–219, 45 Cal.Rptr. 878, at page 889, 404 P.2d 486, at page 497, the court elaborated on the applicability of the principle expressed in the phrase *in pari delicto.* The court stated:

"There is no doubt that the general rule requires the courts to withhold relief under the terms of an illegal contract or agreement which is violative of public policy. [Citations.] It is also true that whatever the state of the pleadings, 'when the evidence shows that . . . [a party] in substance seeks to enforce an illegal contract or recover compensation for an illegal act, the court has both the power and duty to ascertain the true facts in order that it may not unwittingly lend its assistance to the consummation or encouragement of what public policy forbids.' (Lewis & Queen v. N.M. Ball Sons, 48 Cal. 2d 141, 147–148, 308 P.2d 713, 717.) These rules are intended to prevent the guilty party from reaping the benefit of his wrongful conduct, or to protect the public from the future consequences of an illegal contract. They do not necessarily apply to both parties to the agreement unless *both are truly* [emphasis added] *in pari delicto.* In Norwood v. Judd, 93 Cal.App.2d 276, at pp. 288–289, 209 P.2d 24, at p. 31, it was said: 'The rule that the courts will not lend their aid to the enforcement of an illegal agreement or one against public policy is fundamentally sound. The rule was conceived for the purposes of protecting the public and the courts from imposition. It is a rule predicated upon sound public policy. But the courts should not be so enamored with the Latin phrase "*in pari delicto*" that they blindly extend the rule to every case where illegality appears somewhere in the transaction. The fundamental purpose of the rule must always be kept in mind, and the realities of the situation must be considered. . . . where the defendant is the one guilty of the greatest moral fault, and where to apply the rule will be to permit the defendant to be unjustly enriched at the expense of the plaintiff, the rule should not be applied.' "

It is quite apparent that plaintiffs and defendants were not "equally culpable" in this transaction. Bearing in mind that the Corporate Securities Law is for the protection of the public and that the penalties run against the sellers of securities, it would appear clear that it was the duty of defendants to take the steps necessary to make the sale in conformity with the law. This they did not do. It is thus apparent that the defendants are "guilty of the greatest moral fault" and that the plaintiff Bennett and defendants are not "truly" *in pari delicto.* In such circumstances the rule should not be applied. (Norwood v. Judd, supra, 93 Cal.App.2d, at p. 289, 209 P.2d 24; Tri-Q, Inc. v. Sta-Hi Corp., supra, 63 Cal.2d, at p. 219, 45 Cal. Rptr. 878, 404 P.2d 486.)

The portion of the judgment in favor of defendants and against plaintiff Bennett must be reversed.

. . .

The second exception arises when the illegality is not closely related to the plaintiff's claim. The general idea is that collateral illegality should offer no obstacle to a restitution claim. (Collateral illegality also may not be an obstacle to a breach of contract claim.)

EXAMPLE

Blackcrow, a Native American, conveyed Blackacre to Smithfield who was not a Native American. Under state law, Indians could sell tobacco on Tribal land without paying state tax. The deed provided that Smithfield could also sell tobacco on Blackacre without paying state tax.

The conveyance of Blackacre is legal although the provision permitting the sale of tobacco without paying state tax was illegal. Both Blackcrow and Smithfield can seek restitution for any benefit conferred.

The third exception arises when the claimant has "repented" before accomplishing the illegal objective. Some courts have thought it desirable to permit the plaintiff to back away from the performance of an illegal transaction and get restitution. Restitution may be available when (1) the illegal purpose has not been accomplished and can be avoided by allowing the plaintiff restitution; and (2) the illegality must not have been so serious and turpitudinous in itself that the court regards the mere making of the contract as a substantial offense.

EXAMPLE

Mary Melody contracted to sing and play the piano at the My Place Lounge for the week of July 1st (Monday through Sunday). Mary sang and played Monday through Saturday but refused to perform on Sunday because state law made it illegal for bars to be open on Sunday. My Place Lounge violates state law and is open on Sundays.

Mary can maintain an action for restitution to recover the value of her service for Monday through Saturday. (Some states also would allow her to maintain a breach of contract action rather than a restitution action.)

Section 2. STATUTE OF FRAUDS

In 1677 Parliament enacted the British Statute of Frauds. This statute required certain contracts to be in writing to be enforceable. The purpose of the statute was twofold: cautionary and evidentiary. The necessity of the writing cautioned the parties that this transaction was important and that they should pay attention to what they were doing. This was not a casual transaction without legal significance. The writing also was evidentiary. The terms in the writing were the terms the parties must follow even though their memories grew dim. Certainly the opportunity for perjury was reduced by the writing.

In the United States, each state legislature enacted its own Statute of Frauds. Although variations exist from state to state, most are similar. The New Jersey statute (N.J. Stat. Ann. section 25:1–5 (West 1968)) is a typical Statute of Frauds:

Promises or Agreements Not Binding Unless in Writing

No action shall be brought upon any of the following agreements or promises, unless the agreement or promise, upon which such action shall be brought or some memorandum or note thereof, shall be in writing, and signed by the party to be charged therewith, or by some other person thereunto by him lawfully authorized:

a. A special promise of an executor or administrator to answer damages out of his own estate;
b. A special promise to answer for the debt, default or mischarge of another person;
c. An agreement made upon consideration of marriage;
d. A contract for the sale of real estate, or any interest in or concerning the same; or
e. An agreement that is not to be performed within one year from the making thereof.

While this Statute of Frauds provides a number of categories of contracts that must be in writing to be enforceable, not all the contracts that must be in writing are included. The Statute of Frauds dealing with the sale of goods is not found in the general Statute of Frauds but is in Article Two of the Uniform Commercial Code. Other Statutes of Frauds may be scattered through a state's statutes.

In 1954, the British Parliament repealed all of its Statute of Frauds except promises to answer for the debt of another and contracts for the sale of land. American legislatures, however, have been reluctant to follow suit.

This section discusses three categories of contracts that must be in writing to be enforceable: the contract that cannot be fully performed within one year, the contract for the sale of an interest in land, and the contract for the sale of goods for the price of $500 or more.

A. Contracts Which Require a Writing and What Constitutes the Writing

Not all contracts must be in writing to be enforceable. Many contracts are written even though the writing was not required for enforcement. A writing, even though not required, solves a number of problems. The act of writing a contract requires the parties to think about the terms that are to be a part of the contract. Therefore, a written contract may be more definite and refined than an oral contract. Also the writing provides each party with documentation as to what each promised to do.

If it is required that a contract be in writing to be enforceable, then what must the writing contain? The answer is found in the particular Statute of Frauds that requires the writing. Because the Statute of Frauds that requires a writing for the contract for the sale of goods for the price of $500 or more is not the same as the Statute of Frauds that requires a writing for a contract that cannot be fully performed within a year, the writing requirements are different.

1. Contract Not to Be Performed Within One Year

A contract that could be fully performed in less than a year from the time of contract formation need not be in writing to be enforceable. The one year period runs from the time of contract formation and not from the time when performance begins.

EXAMPLE

A contract for a one day concert recital that will take place fourteen months after the date of contracting is within the Statute of Frauds and must be in writing to be enforceable. The fact that the performance will only take one day is irrelevant because the critical time period is between the date of contract formation and the date of full performance. That period is fourteen months.

The probability that the contract will be fully performed within the year is irrelevant. What is necessary to bring a contract within the Statute of Frauds (so a writing is required), is the lack of any possibility (no matter how slight) that performance will be completed within a year. Whether the contract could or could not be fully performed within a year is not made with 20/20 hindsight; that is, the determination whether the contract could or could not be fully performed within one year is not made after the parties have performed. Rather the determination is made as of the date of contract formation.

PROBLEM 6: The Airport Authority hired the All-Star Construction Company to build a new terminal at the airport. Although the normal construction time for such a project was eighteen months, All-Star finished the terminal eleven months from the date of contract.

Was this contract under the Statute of Frauds so a writing was required? Is either the normal construction time or the actual construction time relevant in this determination?

The Statute of Frauds requires full performance of the contract within one year from the date of contract formation. A duty extinguished by full performance is distinguishable from a duty terminated prior to full performance.

If a duty to perform is terminated, the duty has not been fully performed. Whether a duty to perform could be terminated within a year of contract formation is irrelevant when determining whether the contract must be in writing to be enforceable.

PROBLEM 7: Atlas contracts to play football for the Seahawks for five years. Must this contract be in writing to be enforceable?

PROBLEM 8: Atlas contracts to play football for the Seahawks for as long as he can play football. Must this contract be in writing to be enforceable?

PROBLEM 9: Atlas contracts to play football for the Seahawks for five years, but if he is injured, the contract is to be terminated. Must this contract be in writing to be enforceable?

PROBLEM 10: Williams, an account executive, entered into a three year employment contract with the High Profile Advertising Agency. After working for High Profile for six months, Williams was killed in a commercial airplane accident. The employment contract provided that the heirs of any employee would receive $100,000 upon the death of the employee.

Must this contract be in writing to be enforceable?

What must be in the writing to satisfy the Statute of Frauds? The writing must state all the essential terms with reasonable certainty and the party against whom the contract will be enforced must sign it.

PROBLEM 11: Ava, a top model, contracts to pose for a high fashion magazine for two years at $10,000 a month. The contract was reduced to writing but only Ava signed it. After six months, Ava is discharged without cause. Ava brings a breach of contract action against the magazine.

Could the magazine successfully claim that the contract was unenforceable under the Statute of Frauds?

PROBLEM 12: Anna Aldrich, a realtor, was hired by Metro Realty to sell realty for Metro for two years at $2,000 a month plus commissions. The writing was rather sketchy. While it stated the term, it did not state the salary. The writing was signed by both Aldrich and Metro. In six months Aldrich is wrongfully discharged (without cause). If Aldrich sues Metro for breach of contract, could Metro successfully assert that the contract was unenforceable under the Statute of Frauds?

2. Contract for the Sale of an Interest in Land

In addition to the contract for the sale of land, the Statute of Frauds also covers the transfer of a lesser interest in real property. Therefore, to be enforceable, a lease, easement, or mortgage would be within the statute and must be in writing.

A number of states recognize a "part performance" exception to this category of the Statute of Frauds. If the buyer pays the seller and takes possession of the realty or makes a valuable improvement on the realty with the consent of the seller, a writing is not required. The unequivocal acts of the buyer, in reliance on the seller's promise, leave little doubt that a contract for the sale of the interest in the land has been made. If other remedies are inadequate, it would be unjust to permit the seller to now claim that the contract was unenforceable because it was not in writing.

Briggs v. Sackett

Superior Court of Pennsylvania, 1980.
418 A.2d 586.

Before PRICE, HOFFMAN and DOWLING, JJ.*

HOFFMAN, Judge:

Appellant's contentions may be summarized as follows: (1) the lower court applied an improper standard in evaluating appellees' claim of partial performance of an oral contract; and (2) appellees failed to sustain their burden of proof of part performance. We disagree and, accordingly, affirm the order of the court below.

Appellant, Robert Briggs, and his wife are record owners of a home located at 167 Lower Orchard Drive, Levittown, Pennsylvania. Appellees, Winfield and Emma Sackett, have occupied the home since 1962.

* Judge JOHN C. DOWLING, of the Court of Common Pleas of Dauphin County, Pennsylvania, is sitting by designation.

Mrs. Briggs and Mrs. Sackett are sisters.

The Briggs purchased the Orchard Drive home in 1955, making a $100.00 down payment and borrowing the balance of the $11,600 purchase price on a 30 year mortgage. The monthly carrying charge on the mortgage was $82.57. In late 1961, the Briggs vacated the home and, several months thereafter, in 1962, the Sacketts moved in. At that time, the Sacketts paid three months arrearages on the Briggs' mortgage and a delinquent water bill. The Sacketts have continued to occupy the Orchard Drive home until the present, paying the monthly carrying charge on the mortgage and other expenses relating to the property.

On June 23, 1976, Robert Briggs filed an ejectment action in equity against the Sacketts. The Sacketts responded that, although the Briggs were record owners of the home, the Sacketts were the equitable owners by virtue of an oral agreement of sale entered into in 1962. They further contended that, in 1961, the Briggs were in financial difficulty and did not wish the house sold at sheriff's sale because of the absence of a resale market for Levitt homes at that time. The alleged consideration for the sale of the home was the payment of the mortgage arrearages and water bill by the Sacketts. The Sacketts therefore entered a counterclaim for specific performance of the oral contract. Robert Briggs denied the existence of an agreement and alleged that the relief sought in the counterclaim was barred by the statute of frauds.

The chancellor found that an agreement between the parties existed which was removed from the statute of frauds by the doctrine of part performance. Consequently, she ordered the Briggs to execute a deed conveying the premises to the Sacketts. Robert Briggs' exceptions to the chancellor's decree were denied by the lower court en banc. The en banc court agreed with the chancellor's finding of part performance by virtue of the reliance of the Sacketts upon the oral contract and their performance pursuant to that contract. Robert Briggs then took this appeal.

The statute of frauds provides that oral contracts for the sale of land are invalid. 33 P.S. § 1. Where, however, the party seeking to enforce the conveyance has partially performed the contract, so as to render recission inequitable and unjust, the contract may be outside the operation of the statute. *See, e.g., Hancock v. Melloy,* 187 Pa. 371, 41 A. 313 (1898). "[I]t is well settled that the statute prevents the entry of a decree of specific performance against the vendor under the oral contract, . . . unless it appears that continuous and exclusive possession was taken under the contract *and* improvements were made by the vendee not readily to be compensated in money, or other equitable considerations make it impossible to do justice save by specific performance." *Haskell v. Heathcote,* 363 Pa. 184, 69 A.2d 71 (1949) (citing *Moyer v. Moyer,* 356 Pa. 184, 51 A.2d 708 (1947); *Zlotziver v. Zlotziver,* 355 Pa. 299, 49 A.2d 779 (1946); *Axe v. Potts,* 349 Pa. 345, 37 A.2d 572 (1944); *Hartzell's Estate,* 114 Pa.Super. 190, 173 A. 842 (1934)) (emphasis in original). Although some of our cases have articulated the second requirement more narrowly, requiring a showing of permanent improvements to the property, *see, e.g., Hart v. Carroll,* 85 Pa. 508, 510 (1877), the great majority of the cases employ the broader formulation of the standard quoted above. *See, e.g., Klingensmith v. Klingensmith,* 375 Pa. 178, 100 A.2d 76 (1953); *Brotman v. Brotman,* 353 Pa. 570, 46 A.2d 175 (1946). Among the relevant "equitable considerations" which may justify a decree of specific performance is the amount of time which has passed prior to the vendor's challenge to the vendee's possession. *Rarry v. Shimek,* 360 Pa. 315, 62 A.2d 46 (1948). This time factor is considered because it would be inequitable to aid one who has induced another's detrimental reliance by his failure promptly to pursue his rights. *Id.* at 321, 62 A.2d at 49.

Robert Briggs asserts that, in order to show part performance of an oral land sales contract, the vendee must prove that he has made permanent improvements to the property which could not be compensated in damages. This interpretation of the law ignores the majority of the cases which state that improvements *or* other equitable considerations may remove a land sales contract from the statute. *See Haskell v. Heathcote, supra.* Even the case relied upon by Mr. Briggs recognized the basic requirement of the doctrine that there must be "part performance by the vendee which could not be compensated in damages, and such as would make recission inequitable and unjust." *Hart v. Carroll, supra* at 510. Thus, the rule urged upon us constitutes an unnecessarily narrow interpretation of the law, and the lower court did not err in applying the broader standard of part performance articulated by our case law.

Briggs' second contention, that the Sacketts failed to sustain their burden of proof of part performance, is likewise without merit. The opinions of the chancellor and the court en banc reveal that the Sacketts moved from their home into that of the Briggs, giving up the opportunity to acquire an equity interest in another property, with the understanding that they were buying the Briggs' home. The value of this forbearance pursuant to the oral agreement with the Briggs could not be determined. Moreover, during the 14 years in which the Sacketts inhabited the home on Orchard Drive, Robert Briggs never visited, sought rent, checked on the condition of the home, or otherwise asserted any interest in the property. Under these circumstances, we agree with the conclusion of the lower court that there was sufficient evidence of part performance of the oral contract to render it specifically enforceable. The court did not abuse its discretion in so finding. *See Payne v. Kassab,* 468 Pa. 226, 234, 361 A.2d 263, 267 (1976).

Order affirmed.

---

3. Contract for the Sale of Goods for the Price of $500 or More

Section 2–201(1) of the Uniform Commercial Code mandates:

> (1) Except as otherwise provided in this section a contract for the sale of goods for the price of $500 or more is not enforceable by way of action or defense unless there is some writing sufficient to indicate that a contract for sale has been made between the parties and signed by the party against whom enforcement is sought or by his authorized agent or broker. A writing is not insufficient because it omits or incorrectly states a term agreed upon but the contract is not enforceable under this paragraph beyond the quantity of goods shown in such writing.

To come within this Statute of Frauds, there must be a contract for the sale of goods for the price of $500 or more. A transaction for the lease of goods is not a sale of goods and is not within this statute. A transaction for the sale of services is not a sale of goods and is not within this statute. A transaction for the sale of goods for the price of $499.99 is not for the price of $500.00 and is not within this statute.

PROBLEM 13: Julius orally contracted with the Overhead Door Company for the purchase and installation of overhead doors for his garage. The contract price was $510 less five percent if paid by cash or check upon completion of the installation. Prior to commencing work, Julius telephoned the Overhead Door Company and cancelled the order. Overhead Door brought an action for breach of contract against Julius.

Could Julius claim that the contract was unenforceable under UCC § 2–201(1)?

After determining that the contract is a sale of goods for the price of $500 or more and therefore must be in writing under UCC § 2–201(1), what must the writing contain? Section 2–201(1) states only three requirements. First, the writing must evidence a contract for the sale of goods. Second, the party against whom enforcement is sought must sign it. If both parties do not sign the writing, then the contract is enforceable only against the party who did sign. Third, the writing must specify a quantity, even though the quantity is inaccurate. Recovery, however, is limited to the amount stated. Other terms, although essential to the contract, such as price, time and place of payment or delivery, and warranty need not be stated.

> *PROBLEM 14:* Mom & Pop's Hamburger Haven placed an oral order for 5,000 six ounce hamburger patties with the delivery person from Quality Meats, Inc. The delivery person completed the purchase order form and gave Mom & Pop's a copy. Mom & Pop's canceled the order before it was delivered.
>
> Could Quality Meats successfully sue Mom & Pop's for breach of contract? Consider whether Mom & Pop's could successfully claim that the contract was unenforceable due to UCC § 2–201(1). What additional facts do you need to determine whether the contract was within the statute? If the contract was within the statute, what additional facts do you need to determine whether the order form would satisfy the writing required by section 2–201(1)?

Section 2–201(1) begins with the phrase "Except as otherwise provided in this section." This means that if a contract must be in writing because it is a contract for the sale of goods for the price of $500 or more, it may still be enforceable even though it does not satisfy the memorandum requirements of subsection (1). These exceptions are found in subsections (2) and (3) of 2–201:

> (2) Between merchants if within a reasonable time a writing in confirmation of the contract and sufficient against the sender is received and the party receiving it has reason to know its contents, it satisfies the requirements of subsection (1) against such party unless written notice of objection to its contents is given within 10 days after it is received.
>
> (3) A contract which does not satisfy the requirements of subsection (1) but which is valid in other respects is enforceable
>
> (a) if the goods are to be specially manufactured for the buyer and are not suitable for sale to others in the ordinary course of the seller's business and the seller, before notice of repudiation is received and under circumstances which reasonably indicate that the goods are for the buyer, has made either a substantial beginning of their manufacture or commitments for their procurement; or
>
> (b) if the party against whom enforcement is sought admits in his pleading, testimony or otherwise in court that a contract for sale was made, but the contract is not enforceable under this provision beyond the quantity of goods admitted; or
>
> (c) with respect to goods for which payment has been made and accepted or which have been received and accepted (Sec. 2–606).

Subsection (2) addresses the lack of signature in a contract between merchants. In some instances, a written confirmation sent by the party who is not being held liable under the contract may satisfy the signature requirement of the other party.

EXAMPLE

The Gotham Zoo telephoned the Pacific Meat Packing Company and placed an order for $10,000 of meat scraps. The scraps were to be delivered in three installments, with the first due one month from the date of the telephone call. Pacific sent the Zoo a written confirmation of the order. The confirmation referenced the telephone call, the quality, the price, the delivery date, and was signed by Pacific. Pacific sent the first shipment which was rejected by the Zoo. The shipment was not defective.

Does 2–201(1) preclude Pacific from enforcing this contract against the Zoo?

Does 2–201(2) provide relief for Pacific?

Subsection (3) substitutes specially manufactured goods, admissions against interest in pleadings or court proceedings, and payment and acceptance of the goods for the writing requirement.

EXAMPLE

Billy orally contracted to sell his motorcycle to Steven for $700. When Steven tendered $700, Billy refused to deliver.

Is this contract enforceable under 2–201(1)?

If Steven sued Billy for breach of contract and Billy admitted in his pleading or in court that he did contract with Steven, is the contract enforceable under 2–201(3)?

Both subsections 2 and 3 transactions constitute an unambiguous overt admission by both parties that a contract actually exists.

B. Circumvention of the Statute of Frauds Through Reliance

Earlier in this text, we discussed reliance as it relates to preliminary negotiation (see pages 69–79), to a promise made without consideration (see 123–132), and to an implied option contract (see 141–144). Some courts have begun to use reliance as a means for circumvention of the Statute of Frauds.

To defeat a Statute of Frauds defense, the party relying on the oral agreement must show more than the nonperformance of an oral contract. The party must establish that:

1. A promise was made that the promisor should have reasonably expected to induce action or forbearance on the part of the promisee.
2. The promise does induce the promisee to rely.

3. Enforcement of the oral promise is necessary to prevent injustice notwithstanding the Statute of Frauds.

The following case of *Warder & Lee Elevator, Inc. v. Britten,* illustrates the use of reliance to circumvent the Statute of Frauds. *Warder & Lee* is particularly interesting because it has a strong dissent that illustrates judicial reluctance to use reliance for this purpose. On July 4th, Britten, a farmer, orally contracted to sell 4,000 bushels of corn and 2,000 bushels of beans to the Warder & Lee Elevator for October-November delivery. Warder & Lee, acting in its normal capacity as a broker, immediately sold the corn and beans to a third party. When grain prices increased substantially during July, Britten called Lee and said he wished to "call the deal off." Lee responded "You cannot call it off. We sold this grain, and we expect delivery this fall." When it became clear that Britten would not deliver, Warder & Lee purchased grain at a higher price to cover its contract with the third person. When Warder & Lee sued Britten for breach of contract, Britten raised the Statute of Frauds as a defense. Identify the reasons that the court and the dissent give for either using or not using reliance to circumvent the Statute of Frauds. Evaluate each reason.

Warder & Lee Elevator, Inc. v. Britten

Supreme Court of Iowa, 1979.
274 N.W.2d 339.

McCORMICK, Justice.

The question in this action for breach of an oral contract to sell grain is whether the trial court erred in holding defendant's statute of frauds defense under the Uniform Commercial Code was defeated by promissory estoppel. We affirm the trial court.

This case was tried to the court at law. The trial court's findings of fact have the effect of a special verdict and we examine the evidence in the light most favorable to the judgment. We are not bound by trial court determinations of law. *Kurtenbach v. TeKippe,* 260 N.W.2d 53, 54–55 (Iowa 1977).

Plaintiff Warder & Lee Elevator, Inc., operates a grain elevator in the town of Webster. The corporation president, Francis Lee, managed the elevator for many years until he suffered a slight stroke in November 1974. He was succeeded as manager by his son James who had been an elevator employee since 1964. The Lees were the only witnesses at trial.

We recite the evidence in the light most favorable to the judgment. Francis Lee was alone in the elevator office on July 4, 1974. Defendant John W. Britten, a farmer in the area, came to the office during the morning with a friend. The elevator had purchased Britten's grain for years, and he and Lee were well acquainted. At Britten's request Lee quoted him the price the elevator would pay for new-crop corn and soybeans for fall delivery based on market prices of the prior day.

Britten offered to sell and Lee agreed for the elevator to purchase from Britten 4000 bushels of corn at $2.60 per bushel and 2000 bushels of beans at $5.70 per bushel for October-November delivery.

The elevator did not at that time require a seller to sign a memorandum or other writing to show the agreement. Instead, the only writing consisted of notes showing the terms of sale made by Lee for internal bookkeeping purposes. All of the elevator's prior purchases from Britten had been upon oral agreement, and Britten had kept his promises on each occasion. In fact, no seller had previously refused to perform an oral agreement with the elevator.

It was the custom of the elevator not to speculate in grain but to act essentially as a broker. Thus on July 5, 1974, the elevator sold the same quantities of corn and beans as were involved in the Britten purchase for fall delivery to terminal elevators at Muscatine for a few cents more per bushel.

Grain prices increased substantially during July. On July 29, 1974, Britten called Francis Lee and said he wished to "call the deal off". Lee told him: "You cannot call it off. We sold this grain, and we expect delivery this fall." Britten said he would not deliver the grain.

In an effort to mitigate its loss and to enable it to meet its commitment to sell the grain, the elevator purchased appropriate quantities of new-crop corn and beans from other farmers on and shortly after July 29.

In August 1974, James Lee met Britten on a street in Webster. Britten initiated a conversation in which he said he would not fulfill his agreement and offered $500 in settlement. Although counsel for Britten objected to the admissibility of the evidence at trial, the objection was untimely and no motion to strike was made. Lee rejected the offer. He told Britten the elevator had sold the grain and expected him to perform under his contract.

Britten sold his 1974 crop elsewhere.

The elevator brought this action against Britten for breach of the oral agreement, seeking as damages the loss it sustained in covering its delivery obligation under the July 5 contracts by which it sold the quantity of grain purchased from Britten. See § 554.2712, The Code. That loss was $6478.34, which was the amount, plus interest, for which the trial court entered judgment.

Britten offered no evidence at trial. He relied solely on the statute of frauds in § 554.2201, The Code. The elevator urged promissory estoppel in bar of the defense.

The statute of frauds applicable to the sale of crops is § 554.2201. Under this statute an oral contract for the sale of goods for a price of $500 or more is unenforceable, with certain stated exceptions. The elevator does not contend any of those exceptions is applicable. Promissory estoppel is not among them.

Authority for use of promissory estoppel to defeat the statute of frauds, if it exists, must be found under § 554.1103. It provides:

> Unless displaced by the particular provisions of this chapter, the principles of law and equity, including the law merchant and the law relative to capacity to contract, principal and agent, estoppel, fraud, misrepresentation, duress, coercion, mistake, bankruptcy, or other validating or invalidating cause shall supplement its provisions.

We have not had occasion to decide whether the provisions of § 554.2201 displace the doctrine of estoppel which would otherwise be available in accordance with § 554.1103. However, other courts which have considered the question have held the doctrine is available. Several of those decisions involved grain sales in circumstances analogous to those in the present case. See *Decatur Cooperative Association v. Urban,* 219 Kan. 171, 547 P.2d 323 (1976); *Jamestown Terminal Elevator, Inc. v. Hieb,* 246 N.W.2d 736 (N.D.1976); *Farmers Elevator Company of Elk Point v. Lyles,* 238 N.W.2d 290 (S.D.1976).

When other courts have refused to apply the doctrine they have done so because of a different view of the doctrine of promissory estoppel rather than because of any perceived statutory bar to its use. See *Cox v. Cox,* 292 Ala. 106, 289 So.2d 609 (1974); *Del Hayes & Sons, Inc. v. Mitchell,* 304 Minn. 275, 230 N.W.2d 588 (1975); *Farmland Service Coop. v. Klein,* 196 Neb. 538, 244 N.W.2d 86 (1976).

We have long recognized promissory estoppel as a means of defeating the general statute of frauds in § 622.32, The Code. See *Miller v. Lawlor,* 245 Iowa 1144, 66 N.W.2d 267 (1954); *Shell Oil Co. v. Kelinson,* 158 N.W.2d 724 (Iowa 1968); *Johnson v. Pattison,* 185 N.W.2d 790 (Iowa 1971). We see nothing in § 554.2201 which purports to require a different rule under the Uniform Commercial Code.

The listing of exceptions to the statute of frauds in § 554.2201 is plainly definitional. The provision does not purport to eliminate equitable and legal principles traditionally applicable in contract actions. Therefore it does not affect the viability of defenses to application of the rule of evidence which it defines. See White and Summers, Handbook of the Law Under the Uniform Commercial Code § 2–6 at 59 (1972) ("There is every reason to believe these remain good law, post-Code.").

If § 554.2201 were construed as displacing principles otherwise preserved in § 554.1103, it would mean that an oral contract coming within its terms would be unenforceable despite fraud, deceit, misrepresentation, dishonesty or any other form of unconscionable conduct by the party relying upon the statute. No court has taken such an extreme position. Nor would we be justified in doing so. Despite differences relating to the availability of an estoppel defense, courts uniformly hold "that the Statute of Frauds, having been enacted for the purpose of preventing fraud, shall not be made the instrument of shielding, protecting, or aiding the party who relies upon it in the perpetration of a fraud or in the consummation of a fraudulent scheme." 3 Williston on Contracts § 553A at 796 (Third Ed. Jaeger, 1960). The estoppel defense, preserved on the same basis as the fraud defense by § 554.1103, developed from this principle. "The Statute was designed as the weapon of the written law to prevent frauds; the doctrine of estoppel is that of the unwritten law to prevent a like evil." *Id.* at 797–798.

We have found no reported decision in any jurisdiction holding that the statute of frauds in the Uniform Commercial Code, defined as it is in § 554.2203, displaces principles preserved in § 554.1103. We do not believe that our legislature intended for it to do so.

We hold that the provisions of § 554.2201 do not displace the doctrine of estoppel in relation to the sale of goods in Iowa.

We recently discussed the elements of promissory estoppel in *Merrifield v. Troutner,* 269 N.W.2d 136, 137 (Iowa 1978). Those elements are (1) a clear and definite oral agreement, (2) proof that the party urging the doctrine acted to his detriment in relying on the agreement, and (3) finding that the equities support enforcement of the agreement.

In the landmark case *Miller v. Lawlor,* supra, the court defined the doctrine in similar terms and did not limit its application to situations involving unilateral promises. 245 Iowa 1154, 66 N.W.2d 273. In fact the opposite contention was urged in that case, that the doctrine should be limited to situations where a clear and definite oral agreement is established. The court found such an agreement: "We find quite definite (practically undenied) evidence of 'a clear and definite oral agreement', relied on by plaintiff to his detriment." *Id.*

The issue is whether one has acted to his detriment in reliance upon the promise of another, and it is immaterial whether that promise was unilateral or bilateral. See, generally, Williston, supra, § 553A.

Specific circumstances which justify use of the doctrine as a means of avoiding a statute of frauds defense are now expressed in Restatement (Second) of Contracts § 217A (Tent. Draft 1–7, 1973), as follows:

> (1) A promise which the promisor should reasonably expect to induce action or forbearance on the part of the promisee or a third person and which does induce the action or forbearance is enforceable notwithstanding the Statute of Frauds if injustice can be avoided only by enforcement of the promise. The remedy granted

for breach is to be limited as justice requires.

(2) In determining whether injustice can be avoided only by enforcement of the promise, the following circumstances are significant:

(a) the availability and adequacy of other remedies particularly cancellation and restitution;

(b) the definite and substantial character of the action or forbearance in relation to the remedy sought;

(c) the extent to which the action or forbearance corroborates evidence of the making and terms of the promise, or the making and terms are otherwise established by clear and convincing evidence;

(d) the reasonableness of the action or forbearance;

(e) the extent to which the action or forbearance was foreseeable by the promisor.

This section complements Restatement (Second) of Contracts § 90, the predecessor of which we previously approved. See *Miller v. Lawlor,* supra. We now approve and adopt the standard in § 217A.

This standard moots the question whether Restatement of Contracts § 90 was intended to defeat the statute of frauds. See Annot., 56 A.L.R.3d 1037, 1050–1052. The standard is consistent with our holdings permitting the doctrine to be used to defeat the general statute of frauds. It is also consistent with the decisions allowing promissory estoppel to defeat the Uniform Commercial Code statute of frauds. See *Decatur Cooperative Association v. Urban,* 219 Kan. 171, 547 P.2d 323 (1976); *Jamestown Terminal Elevator, Inc. v. Hieb,* 246 N.W.2d 736 (N.D.1976); *Farmers Elevator Company of Elk Point v. Lyles,* 238 N.W.2d 290 (S.D.1976). It provides a basis for distinguishing contrary holdings. See *Del Hayes & Sons, Inc. v. Mitchell,* 304 Minn. 275, 230 N.W.2d 588 (1975); *Farmland Service Coop., Inc. v. Klein,* 196 Neb. 538, 244 N.W.2d 86 (1976). Of course, it also obviates any distinction based upon whether the promise is unilateral or bilateral. Restatement § 217A, comment a. ("This Section is complementary to § 90, which dispenses with the requirement of consideration if the same conditions are met, but it also applies to promises supported by consideration.").

In order to obtain the benefit of the doctrine of promissory estoppel to defeat a statute of frauds defense, the promisee must show more than the nonperformance of an oral contract. See 3 Williston on Contracts § 553A (Third Ed. Jaeger, 1960). Under § 217A the defense cannot be overcome, when it is otherwise applicable, unless the promisee proves (1) the promisor should reasonably have expected the agreement to induce action or forbearance, (2) such action or forbearance was induced, and (3) enforcement is necessary to prevent injustice.

In determining whether injustice can be avoided only by enforcement of the promise, the circumstances listed in § 217A(2) must be considered. In this manner, § 217A provides a means of deciding whether the equities support enforcement of the agreement.

We must now decide whether the trial court erred in applying the doctrine of promissory estoppel in this case.

Britten contends the elevator should not have the benefit of the doctrine because it did not plead it and did not prove he knew it would rely on the oral agreement.

We find no merit in his first contention for two reasons. The statute of frauds was asserted in Britten's answer. The elevator might have pled promissory estoppel if the court had ordered a reply, but no reply was ordered. See rule 73, Rules of Civil Procedure. Furthermore, counsel for the elevator twice invoked the doctrine on the record during the course of trial, and Britten did not challenge its failure to plead it at any time in the trial court. Under these circumstances he may not complain on appeal of the elevator's failure to plead it.

Although Britten's second contention presents a closer question, we also find it is without merit. We do so because we believe substantial evidence supports the inference he expected or reasonably should have expected the agreement to induce action by the elevator. It was not necessary for the elevator to prove he actually knew it would rely on his promise. He should have known his prior dealings with the elevator gave the elevator manager every reason to believe he would keep his word. Furthermore, it is reasonable to believe that a farmer who sells grain regularly to country elevators knows they may immediately sell the grain which they purchase. In this case, Britten expressed no surprise when the elevator refused to allow him to rescind because of its sales in reliance on the agreement. Instead he sought to buy his way out of the transaction.

We conclude that the elements of promissory estoppel were supported by substantial evidence. In keeping with the standard in Restatement § 217A, we hold that injustice could be avoided only by enforcement of Britten's promise. The trial court did not err in holding the agreement was enforceable despite the statute of frauds defense.

AFFIRMED.

All Justices concur except REYNOLDSON, C.J., and ALLBEE, J., who dissent.

REYNOLDSON, Chief Justice (dissenting).

I respectfully dissent. The contract in issue falls squarely within the language and intent of the statute of frauds, § 554.2201, The Code 1973. The majority opinion, in my view, misapprehends and misapplies our rules relating to promissory estoppel. Further, the facts in this case do not bring it within the new principles pioneered in this decision.

I. In 1965 the Iowa legislature enacted the "Uniform Commercial Code—Sales." Sixty-First General Assembly, ch. 413, § 2101. It was "a complete revision and modernization of the Uniform Sales Act." D. Stanley & C. Coulter, Iowa Code Comment, 35 I.C.A. § 554.2101 at 118 (1967). Section 554.2201, the UCC's statute of frauds, underwent a substantial liberalizing overhaul designed to eliminate undesirable and overly technical features of the former law. See D. Stanley & C. Coulter, *supra,* at 145–48; 3 R. Dusenberg & L. King, Sales & Bulk Transfers under the UCC § 2.05 (1978); R. Hudson, *Contracts In Iowa Revisited,* 15 Drake L.Rev. 61, 75–77 (1966); A. Squillante, *Sales Law In Iowa Under The UCC—Article 2,* 20 Drake L.Rev. 1, 61–65 (1970).

At the same time the statute was modified to clarify that its exceptions were limited to those contained in its provisions. Before 1919 the predecessor to § 622.32, our general statute of frauds, covered "sale[s] of personal property." See § 4625, The Code 1897. In 1919 the Uniform Sales Act and its statute of frauds were enacted and the general statute was correspondingly revised. Compare §§ 554.4 and 622.32, The Code 1962. The catch-all exception in § 622.33, "or when there is any other circumstance which, by the law heretofore in force, would have taken the case out of the statute of frauds," ceased to be applicable to sales of goods. Retained as applicable, however, were the "failure to deny" and "oral evidence of the maker" exceptions contained in § 622.34 and .35 respectively. See § 554.5, The Code 1962.

The lead sentence in § 554.2201 now provides:

> Except as otherwise provided *in this section* a contract for the sale of goods for the price of five hundred dollars or more is not enforceable by way of action or defense unless there is some writing sufficient to indicate that a contract for sale has been made between the parties and signed by the party against whom enforcement is sought or by his authorized agent or broker.

(Emphasis provided.) The § 622.34 and .35 exceptions are now incorporated in (3)(b) of the section. The specific limitation of exceptions to those contained "in this section" reflects a marked change from former § 554.4.

With exceptions to the statute of frauds now specifically limited by the terms of the statute to those enumerated in its provisions, the majority's claim that promissory estoppel may be engrafted as simply another exception by virtue of § 554.1103 loses viability. Section 554.1103 permits application of other legal principles, including estoppel, "unless displaced by the particular provisions of this chapter." Plainly, the limiting language of § 554.2201 constitutes such a displacement. Had the legislature intended the concepts of §§ 90 and 217A of the tentative draft of the Restatement (Second) of Contracts to serve as an exception to its statute of frauds, it would have incorporated them as an exception in the act.

Displacing § 554.1103 with the exceptions in § 554.2201 does not render ineffectual the common-law principles contained in the former. First, they supplement other sections of the UCC except those, like § 554.2201, which provide otherwise. Second, the victim of fraud who has no legal remedy because § 554.2201 prevents proof of the oral contract is not left out in the cold. The equitable remedy of restitution is not dependent upon proof of a contract. The basic elements of equitable estoppel and fraud are (1) intentional misrepresentation, (2) innocent, reasonable and foreseeable reliance, and (3) injury. See *Walters v. Walters,* 203 N.W.2d 376, 379 (Iowa 1973), quoted in *Merrifield v. Troutner,* 269 N.W.2d 136, 137 (Iowa 1978) (equitable estoppel); *Grefe v. Ross,* 231 N.W.2d 863, 864 (Iowa 1975) (fraud). Nor is a contract enforced in those situations. Recovery is based on the injury suffered in the course of reliance. As we stated in *Grefe,* the liability is predicated on the fraud, not on any contract. 231 N.W.2d at 868. With these remedies available, the statute of frauds gives a fraudulent party little protection.

The limiting language of § 554.2201 at least ought to displace a doctrine which would gut the legislative intent of the statute. Distilled to its essence, § 217A, as interpreted by the majority, provides that if one contracting party should know the other contracting party will rely on the contract and injustice will result if the oral contract is not enforced, the statute of frauds will be ignored. It is a rare case when either promisor in a bilateral contract does not rely on the contract. *Del Hayes & Sons, Inc. v. Mitchell,* 304 Minn. 275, 284, 230 N.W.2d 588, 594 (1975). Any party to a contract should realize such reliance occurs. Most situations in which such an oral contract is breached result in injustice.

But the § 554.2201 statute of frauds obviously is designed to suffer these injustices in isolated oral contract cases in favor of the general public policy to reduce fraud and perjury, curtail litigation and controversy, and encourage written contracts in sales of goods for a price of $500 or more. It is significant that by trial time the plaintiff corporation in the case at bar was using written sales contracts with its customers.

Adopting §§ 90 and 217A as an unwritten exception to § 554.2201 will not only encourage oral contracts, it will bring a massive infusion of litigation to our overloaded courts. Trial courts will be compelled to determine, on an *ad hoc* basis, whether there was a contract, whether the promisor could "reasonably expect" the other party to rely on it, whether reasonable action or forbearance resulted, whether "justice requires" a remedy, and otherwise engage in the delicate balancing maneuvers mandated by § 217A(2).

In the final analysis, the majority opinion means written contracts are unnecessary in initial purchases of agricultural products, probably Iowa's largest economic marketplace and involving almost three billion dollars worth of goods each year. We should proceed down that road with great caution.

It is just as clear the majority is moving against a long-time trend:

> This attitude [to extend exceptions to the statute of frauds] has given way gradually, and from quite an early period the statute of frauds has frequently been spoken of as a most beneficial statute which should be liberally construed to effect its object. The wisdom of the statute is a matter within the control of the legislature, not the judiciary, but it has been said to be justified by long experience. The tendency has long been to restrict rather than to enlarge and multiply the cases of exceptions to the statute, and the right to invoke the statute as a defense is no longer regarded with disfavor. The courts should not be

tempted to turn aside from its plain provisions merely because of the hardship of the particular case. They should not be controlled by the consequences following upon an application of the statute, or deem obnoxious a law which the legislature has placed in the statutes and allowed to remain for many years, and they cannot disregard the statute. They certainly should refuse to sanction such a construction as would permit the evils that the statute was intended to prevent.

73 Am.Jur.2d Statute of Frauds § 511 (1974).

II. Aside from the above factors, I am convinced promissory estoppel is not an appropriate device to serve as an exception to the statute of frauds.

Promissory estoppel is related to equitable estoppel and the two are frequently confused. 1 Williston on Contracts § 140 at 607–09 (3d ed. 1957). We recently defined the two in *Merrifield v. Troutner,* 269 N.W.2d 136, 137 (Iowa 1978). In promissory estoppel a unilateral promise is relied upon, while in equitable estoppel reliance is placed on a misrepresentation or concealment of material fact. In either instance the party who reasonably and detrimentally relies will be protected if the equities of the situation require it, even to the extent in promissory estoppel of enforcing an otherwise gratuitous promise. See *Miller v. Lawlor,* 245 Iowa 1144, 1153, 66 N.W.2d 267, 273 (1954).

But there is no logical basis for using either equitable doctrine to enforce a bilateral, executory contract. The exchange of promises provides the requisite consideration to make such a contract valid and enforceable if its existence can be proved. To hold plaintiff corporation's immediate resale of defendant's grain constitutes detrimental reliance and makes defendant's promise to sell enforceable is unnecessary and distorts basic precepts of contract law.

Worse yet, a rule that such detrimental reliance (which is in every bilateral, executory contract to some degree) permits the promisee to avoid the statute of frauds misconceives the nature and purpose of § 554.2201.

The § 554.2201 statute of frauds is only a rule of evidence. *Stauter v. Walnut Grove Products,* 188 N.W.2d 305, 313 (Iowa 1971). It regulates the *proof* of *contracts* or *agreements* relating to sales of goods—the type of contract or agreement which should be reduced to writing. The exceptions itemized in the statute cover situations in which the legislature determined a signed writing was unnecessary to *prove* the *contract.* Promissory estoppel is a method by which courts *enforce unilateral promises. A unilateral promise is not a contract or agreement.* It follows the § 554.2201 statute of frauds does not regulate proof in those situations in which promissory estoppel may be invoked. It should also follow that promissory estoppel, as a substantive source of enforceability, has no place in a list of exceptions to a rule of evidence covering enforceable bilateral contracts.

Many courts have declined to create an additional exception based on promissory estoppel. They continue, as I am convinced we should, to view promissory estoppel as a doctrine of equity which provides only a means of enforcing unilateral promises, not a method of proving bilateral contracts. See, e.g., *Cox v. Cox,* 292 Ala. 106, 111–12, 289 So.2d 609, 613 (1974); *Tiffany Inc. v. W.M.K. Transit Mix, Inc.,* 16 Ariz.App. 415, 420–21, 493 P.2d 1220, 1225–26 (1972); *Tanenbaum v. Biscayne Osteopathic Hospital, Inc.,* 173 So.2d 492, 495 (Fla.App. 1965); *Sacred Heart Farmers Co-op Elevator v. Johnson,* 305 Minn. 324, 326–27, 232 N.W.2d 921, 922–23 (1975) (sale of grain); *Del Hayes & Sons, Inc. v. Mitchell,* 304 Minn. at 281–85, 230 N.W.2d at 592–94 (sale of grain); *Farmland Serv. Coop, Inc. v. Klein,* 196 Neb. 538, 244 N.W.2d 86 (1976) (sale of grain).

The majority distinguishes these cases as based on a view of promissory estoppel not held in Iowa. I cannot agree. Each application of promissory estoppel by this court has occurred in a case involving a unilateral promise. We have never permitted a party to evade a clear statute of frauds *proof* problem with *bilateral* contract by the promissory estoppel device.

In *Miller v. Lawlor,* 245 Iowa at 1144, 66 N.W.2d at 267, relied on by the majority, a landowner orally assured the prospective purchaser of a neighboring residence that the landowner would not obstruct a scenic view. In *Shell Oil Co. v. Kelinson,* 158 N.W.2d 724 (Iowa 1968), the alleged promise was the plaintiff's oral notice of intent to rescind its exercise of an option to purchase. In *Johnson v. Pattison,* 185 N.W.2d 790 (Iowa 1971), the owner of a large tract of land orally assured the prospective purchaser of a portion of the property previously sold to another that the area would always be used for residential purposes. In *Merrifield v. Troutner,* 269 N.W.2d at 136, we held promissory estoppel was not established because the noncustodial parent had not relied on any "promise" by the custodial parent not to seek back support payments. The noncustodial parent had not promised to relinquish visitation rights in return for the promise.

Although the relevant element in these cases has been termed "a clear and definite oral *agreement,*" taken in the context of each case the word "agreement" was always used in the sense of a unilateral, gratuitous promise, not a contract. The majority perpetuates this inaccurate terminology.

Our cases on this point trace back to *Lawlor* where this court clearly grounded its use of the doctrine on unilateral *promises* by quoting, *inter alia,* § 90 of the Restatement of Contracts, still in effect. 245 Iowa at 1153, 66 N.W.2d at 273. Of course, § 90 and its illustrations relate solely to unilateral promises. These Iowa cases the majority relies on hold only that the statute of frauds does not forbid oral proof of the unilateral promise for the purpose of establishing promissory estoppel. They do not provide authority for using oral proof of bilateral contracts in violation of the statute of frauds.

I agree that new § 217A (aided by revised § 90 as it is interpreted under the tentative draft) moots these problems and blends unilateral and bilateral promises, but that is why I would not adopt them. The tentative draft has essentially created a concept which is indistinguishable from promissory estoppel and applies it to bilateral contract proof problems.

The effect of promissory estoppel on § 554.2201 under the majority opinion is devastating. If the statute is to be repealed the policy decision should be left with the legislature.

III. Finally, it should be noted the facts in this case would not warrant application of § 217A of the Restatement Tentative Draft.

Imposition of § 217A would require proof the defendant seller in this case "should reasonably expect" that the plaintiff corporation would promptly resell the grain. There is no evidence in the transcript in this case to show defendant either knew this was plaintiff's practice or that it was a custom in the industry.

Majority seeks to supply this crucial missing proof by asserting "it is reasonable to believe a farmer who sells grain regularly to country elevators knows they may immediately sell the grain which they purchase."

Majority seems to be judicially noting not only what defendant knew about elevator operations but also the sales practices in a private industry. I doubt these matters qualify for judicial notice as being within common knowledge or capable of certain verification. *Motor Club of Iowa v. Department of Transp.,* 251 N.W.2d 510, 517 (Iowa 1977). Plaintiff corporation's operating officer did not assume defendant had this knowledge. He felt compelled to tell defendant the grain had been resold. This, of course, was long after the event and had no bearing on whether defendant should have "reasonably expect[ed]" such action.

I would reverse and remand for a new trial, during which proof of the alleged contract would be regulated by § 554.2201 undiluted by promissory estoppel.

C. Restitution as a Cause of Action

If an oral contract is unenforceable by reason of the Statute of Frauds, a restitution action may be available to prevent unjust enrichment.

1. A Contract that Cannot Be Fully Performed Within a Year

Under the Statute of Frauds, a contract which is not to be performed within one year from the date of its making is unenforceable unless it is in writing and signed by the person to be charged with the promise. Part performance does not take the contract out of the statute. Therefore, an employee rendering services in part performance of an employment contract cannot maintain an action on the contract when the employer repudiates. Courts, however, generally recognize that the employee may recover in a restitution action for the value of services rendered when the party receiving the services repudiates the contract.

> *PROBLEM 15:* Weaver contracted in writing to work for the General Chemical Company for two years at $60,000 a year. His salary was to be paid in monthly installments of $5,000. Shortly after Weaver began work, General Chemical Company became insolvent. Weaver, General Chemical, and General Metals, entered into an oral contract whereby Weaver would work for General Metals under the same arrangements he had with General Chemical and General Chemical would be discharged. After working for General Metals for several months, Weaver quit because he was not being paid.
>
> Could Weaver successfully sue General Metals in a restitution action. If Weaver could maintain the restitution action, how should his recovery be measured?

2. A Contract for the Sale of an Interest in Land

Courts generally hold that the vendee who pays money, renders services, or transfers personal property under an oral contract to transfer an interest in real estate may recover in restitution if the vendor refuses to carry out the agreement.

EXAMPLE

> A vendee makes a $1,000 down payment to the vendor under an oral contract for the purchase of a farm. Subsequently, the vendee tenders the balance of the purchase price to the vendor but the vendor refuses to accept the tender of the price and refuses to convey the farm. The vendee may recover the $1,000 down payment in a restitution action.

If the vendor has conferred a benefit on the vendee, the vendor may recover in a restitution action the reasonable value of the benefit conferred.

EXAMPLE

If the vendee, who has been in possession of the land, repudiates the oral contract for the sale of the land, the vendor may recover in a restitution action for the use and occupation of the land.

If the vendor has not conferred a benefit on the vendee, the vendor cannot maintain a restitution action.

> *PROBLEM 16:* Sammy orally contracted to sell his hot dog stand on Coney Island to Cassandra for $50,000. Several days later, Cassandra backed out of the deal. Sammy then sold his hot dog stand to Tony for $45,000.
>
> Could Sammy successfully maintain a restitution action against Cassandra?

Section 3. FORUM SELECTION PROVISIONS

At the time of contract formation, the contracting parties may select the court that will hear any dispute that may arise as the contract is being performed. The parties will actually state their selection in the contract. "All disputes arising from this contract shall be decided by the court of New Mexico." Because a court is often referred to as a forum, this provision is known as "forum selection clause."

The fact that a contract has a forum selection clause does not guarantee that all future disputes will be heard only by the named courts. If the plaintiff files an action in a court other than the court the contract named, the defendant may request the court to enforce the forum selection clause. Enforcement would require the court to transfer the action to the forum named in the contract. A court will transfer the action only if the selection clause satisfies several criteria.

If the forum selection provision violates the public policy of the named forum, a court will not enforce it.

EXAMPLE

If a breach of contract action is filed in Utah, even though the forum selection provision named New Mexico as the proper state for filing the action, the Utah court will refuse to transfer to New Mexico if the public policy in New Mexico condemns forum selection provisions.

A court will refuse to enforce a forum selection clause that is unreasonable. A provision is unreasonable if a trial in the named forum would create a serious inconvenience to any of the participants. The problems of holding a trial in the selected forum must be so great that they would effectively deny a party his or her day in court. Generally, this degree of inconvenience is extremely difficult to prove.

In *Ronar, Inc. v. Wallace,* 649 F. Supp. 310 (S.D.N.Y. 1986), Ronar, a New York corporation, and F & C, a West German corporation, entered into a written agreement under which F & C would manufacture buttons in West Germany and Ronar would distribute them in the United States and Canada. A dispute arose and Ronar filed an action before a New York court charging F & C with various contract and business-related tort claims.

A. Forum-Selection Clause

Defendants Josef Fischer and F & C move to dismiss the counts against them on the ground that a forum-selection provision in their contract with Ronar confers venue exclusively upon a court in West Germany.

Defendants have translated the provision from the German, without challenge by plaintiff, as follows: "The courts at Tirschenreuth, Federal Republic of Germany, shall have jurisdiction and venue." Affidavit of Peter Feuerle at 4, ¶ 8.

Interpretation of this clause, like that of any other contract provision, begins in familiar territory. The court's goal is to honor the legitimate expectations of the parties to the contract. *See The Bremen v. Zapata Off-Shore Co.,* 407 U.S. 1, 12, 92 S.Ct. 1907, 1914, 32 L.Ed.2d 513 (1972). To do so the court generally must enforce the specific terms that the parties have chosen because those terms reflect the agreement they have freely reached. *See id.* To be sure, courts are not always bound by contractual language. Most notably, the terms of an agreement are not enforceable when evidence of "fraud, undue influence, or overweening bargaining power" undercuts the premise that the agreement was freely negotiated. *Id.* But absent a "strong showing" of such impinging circumstances, or some other reason why enforcement would be "unreasonable and unjust," a forum-selection clause is controlling. *Id.* at 15, 92 S.Ct. at 1916; *see Mitsubishi Motors Corp. v. Soler Chrysler-Plymouth, Inc.,* 473 U.S. 614, —, 105 S.Ct. 3346, 3356, 87 L.Ed.2d 444 (1985) (freely negotiated forum-selection clause enjoys a "strong presumption in favor of enforcement").

Ronar does not allege that fraud, undue influence, or overweening bargaining power subverted the parties' free negotiation. Instead it argues simply that enforcement of their agreement would be unfair, unjust, or unreasonable. Ronar explains that it might have difficulty getting personal jurisdiction over the British defendants in West Germany, pretrial discovery would be restricted in a West German proceeding, and many of the parties and prospective witnesses reside in the United States rather than West Germany.

These questions of convenience are hardly different from the ones the Supreme Court considered in *The Bremen,* which like this case involved a dispute between a German corporation and an American one. The Court noted that the inconvenience the plaintiff might suffer by being held to its bargain clearly could have been foreseen. *The Bremen, supra,* 407 U.S. at 17–18, 92 S.Ct. at 1917–18, and in order to escape the forum-selection provision on the ground that enforcement would be unjust and unreasonable, the American party would have to sustain the heavy burden of showing that "trial in the contractual forum will be so gravely difficult and inconvenient that he will for all practical purposes be deprived of his day in court." *Id.* at 18–19, 92 S.Ct. at 1917–18.

None of the possible sources of inconvenience mentioned by Ronar strikes the court as grave. *See, e.g., Clinton v. Janger,* 583 F.Supp. 284, 288 (N.D.Ill.1984) (plaintiff's inconvenience in suing in multiple forums because one forum does not assert jurisdiction over all defendants is not unreasonable); *Karlberg European Tanspa, Inc. v. JK–Josef Kratz Vertriebsgesellschaft mbH,* 618 F.Supp. 344, 348 (N.D.Ill.1985) (neither the restricted scope of discovery in West Germany, nor the fact that most of the witnesses reside in the United States rather than West Germany, is an unreasonable inconvenience). Each inconvenience was foreseeable when the parties agreed to the West German forum. In fact, the court assumes that

> because Ronar freely entered the agreement, it not only was aware of the potential disadvantages of the German forum but received consideration for them as part of the bargain. *See Full-Sight Contact Lens Corp. v. Soft Lenses, Inc.,* 466 F.Supp. 71, 73 (S.D.N.Y.1978) (Pierce, J.). Judge Friendly's warning applies here: "There can be nothing 'unreasonable and unjust' in enforcing such an agreement; what would be unreasonable and unjust would be to allow one of the [parties] to disregard it." *AVC Nederland B.V. v. Atrium Investment Partnership,* 740 F.2d 148, 156 (2d Cir. 1984) (footnote omitted), *quoted in Luce v. Edelstein,* 802 F.2d 49, 57 (2d Cir. 1986), *aff'g in pertinent part and rev'g in part on other grounds,* No. 85 Civ. 4064 (S.D.N.Y. Aug. 7, 1985) (Carter, J.).
>
> . . .

Unequal bargaining power at the time of contract formation is also a factor. If one party held such a powerful bargaining position that the other was unable to effectively resist the inclusion of the forum selection provision, a court, on the grounds of fairness, may refuse to enforce the clause.

A final criterion is whether the forum selection clause is exclusive. A court will transfer an action to the named forum only if the provision lists that forum as the exclusive site for litigation. Exclusive language is "the court of Arizona shall have exclusive jurisdiction to hear any and all disputes arising out of this contract." Under this clause, the parties obviously have agreed that the courts of Arizona and no other courts were to hear the action. If the clause had read, "the parties, with regard to the resolution of any dispute arising under this agreement, shall submit themselves to the jurisdiction of the court of Arizona," and if the action were brought in a court outside of Arizona, the court could refuse to transfer the action. The clause merely authorized the Arizona courts to hear the claim. The clause did not designate the Arizona court as the only court that could hear the case.

> *PROBLEM 17:* Jane and Bill Anderson, residents of Atlantic, Iowa, decided it was time to buy a new car. They found a great deal at Freeway Motors in Omaha, Nebraska, only fifty miles away. They were so excited about the car that they did not notice the clause in the sales contract that said "All disputes arising from this agreement shall be litigated in the proper court of Nebraska."
>
> Unfortunately, the car was a lemon and Freeway Motors refused to make the repairs as the warranty required. The Andersons filed a breach of contract action in Iowa.
>
> Should the Iowa court grant Freeway Motors' request to transfer the action to Nebraska? If you were the Iowa judge, what additional facts would you need before you could make your decision and why?
>
> If Freeway Motors had its main office in Kansas City, Missouri, and the contract provided that "All disputes arising from this agreement shall be litigated in the proper court of Missouri," would the Iowa judge transfer to Missouri?

But the term "shall" does not guarantee that the named forum will be the exclusive forum. Consider the following case, *Sterling Forest Associates, Ltd. v. Barnett-Range Corp.* Do you agree with the court?

Sterling Forest Associates, Ltd. v. Barnett-Range Corp.

United States District Court, Eastern District of North Carolina, 1986.
643 F. Supp. 530.

Order

TERRENCE WILLIAM BOYLE, District Judge.

This is an action for negligence, gross negligence and breach of contract arising out of a Purchase Agreement entered into by plaintiff Sterling Forest Associates, Ltd. ("Sterling") and defendant Barnett-Range Corporation ("Barnett-Range"). The Agreement provided in part that plaintiff would purchase a certain tract of land and that Barnett-Range would construct a 174–unit apartment complex on the property. With regard to forum selection, the Agreement contained the following clause:

> This Agreement shall be construed and enforced in accordance with the laws of the State of California and the parties agree that in any dispute jurisdiction and venue shall be in California.

Dissatisfied with Barnett-Range's performance of its obligations under the Agreement, Sterling filed this action in the Superior Court of Wake County, North Carolina. The action was subsequently removed to this court on diversity grounds.

Now at issue before this court is the motion of defendants Barnett-Range, Hal W. Barnett and James E. Range to transfer this action to the Eastern District of California, pursuant to 28 U.S.C. § 1404(a) and (b).

Defendants ask this court to decline to exercise jurisdiction, arguing that plaintiff waived the right to sue in North Carolina when it agreed to the forum-selection clause noted above. Defendants would claim that, instead of establishing California as one possible forum for adjudication, the Agreement creates exclusive jurisdiction over the contract in California. Plaintiff argues that, while the clause assures jurisdiction in California, it tolerates jurisdiction wherever it may otherwise be found by operation of law.

Defendants contend that, even if this court should find that it has jurisdiction, it should use its discretion to transfer the case in the interests of justice and convenience to the parties and witnesses. Plaintiff opposes this contention and asserts that North Carolina is the more convenient situs for this action. This court will first address the interpretation of the forum-selection clause and will then decide which forum offers the greater convenience.

Defendants rely on the Supreme Court decision of *The Bremen v. Zapata Off-Shore Co.,* 407 U.S. 1, 92 S.Ct. 1907, 32 L.Ed.2d 513 (1972). In that case, the Court held that a forum-selection clause which specified the court where cases would be heard would be enforced unless enforcement would be "unreasonable and unjust, or that the clause was invalid for such reasons as fraud or overreaching." 407 U.S. at 15, 92 S.Ct. at 1916. While this court appreciates the considerable impact of the *Bremen* on the validity of forum-selection clauses, it does not find that case to be controlling here.

In *Bremen,* the wording of the forum-selection clause differed in a critical respect from the clause in this case. The contract in *Bremen* stated that "[a]ny dispute arising *must* be treated before the London Court of Justice." 407 U.S. at 2, 92 S.Ct. at 1909 (emphasis added). The disputed clause in this case does not use such mandatory language. The phrase employed here is far more equivocal: "jurisdiction and venue *shall* be in California." (emphasis added) The contract contains no indication as to whether this language is meant to be exclusive or merely permissive. When confronted with a similarly ambiguous clause in *Keaty v. Freeport Indonesia, Inc.,* 503 F.2d 955

(1974), the Fifth Circuit found both interpretations to be reasonable. Faced with two opposing yet reasonable interpretations of the same contract, that court invoked the traditional rule that any ambiguities should be construed against the drafter of the clause. 503 F.2d at 957.

Because the forum-selection clause does not unambiguously give exclusive jurisdiction to California, this court cannot find that the clause is mandatory. Rather, it may fairly be interpreted as having no influence on the appropriateness of other fora where actions could otherwise be properly brought. *First National City Bank v. Nanz, Inc.,* 437 F.Supp. 184, 187 (S.D.N.Y., 1975).

This court has inherent jurisdiction over the subject matter. The action was properly removed from a state forum on diversity jurisdiction. The defendants Barnett-Range Corporation and Far West Savings & Loan Association have filed responsive pleadings without challenging the jurisdiction of the court over the person of these defendants. As such, the court has personal jurisdiction. The defendants Hal W. Barnett and James E. Range challenge the jurisdiction of the court over their person in their answer (Second Defense). However, they do not make this challenge by way of Rule 12(b)(2), Fed. R.Civ.P., as required, nor do they brief the issue as required by local rule of this court (Rule 4.04, EDNC). This attack on the jurisdiction of the court over the person of these defendants is an insufficient attack, and, further, the court deems it abandoned.

No persuasive proof has been offered either that the language of the clause is mandatory or that it is permissive. The defendants, in advancing this choice of forum clause as a bar to proceedings here, have the burden of proving this defense. The defendants have failed on this point. Because the defendants have not shown that their interpretation of the clause is any more plausible than plaintiff's, defendants have not sustained their burden of proof. The court is unable to find that the clause is mandatory and therefore declines to grant relief on this ground.

It should be noted that defendants' reliance on *Mercury Coal & Coke, Inc. v. Mannesmann Pipe and Steel Co.,* 696 F.2d 315 (4th Cir., 1982), is misplaced. In that case, a permissive clause established jurisdiction in New York, despite the fact that the contract was negotiated and signed in West Virginia. Appellee Mercury attempted to enjoin appellant Mannesmann from suing in New York. The Fourth Circuit held that the clause creating jurisdiction in New York should be enforced, and the suit was allowed to proceed. The difference between the *Mercury* case and this action is fundamental. The *Mercury* court held only that a forum-selection clause written in permissive language could create jurisdiction in the specified state. It did not hold that this grant of jurisdiction destroyed jurisdiction elsewhere, in the absence of explicit language to that effect. Indeed, in *Mercury,* the court notes that Mannesmann had earlier moved to dismiss Mercury's suit in West Virginia, basing its motion on the forum-selection clause. This motion created a situation basically identical to the one now before this court. There, as here, the motion was denied. Defendants contend in this case that a permissively worded forum-selection clause creates exclusive jurisdiction in the designated forum. This principle has never been adopted anywhere in this circuit, and this court declines to accept it today.

Defendants insist that even though the court finds the forum-selection clause is not mandatory, the action should still be transferred to the Eastern District of California. They claim that, since Barnett-Range is licensed to do business there, California is a proper venue for this action under 28 U.S.C. § 1391(c). They argue in addition that the interests of justice and the convenience of the parties and the witnesses all demand that this court exercise its discretion to transfer the case under the authority of 28 U.S.C. § 1404(a). Section 1404(a), in essence, codifies the common law doctrine of *forum non conveniens.*

The plaintiff does not dispute that California would be a proper venue, and the court finds no reason to take issue on that point. However, the defendants will only prevail on a claim of *forum non conveniens* by carrying a heavy burden of proof. Unless the balance of equities is strongly in favor of the defendants, the plaintiffs' choice of forum should rarely be disturbed. *Gulf Oil Corp. v. Gilbert,* 330 U.S. 501, 509, 67 S.Ct. 839, 843, 91 L.Ed. 1055 (1947). In this case, preponderance of equities lies not on the side of the defendants, but rather with the plaintiff.

Defendants have not met their burden of proving that California is a more convenient forum. Plaintiff has supplied affidavits from several of his important witnesses who aver that they cannot or will not voluntarily go to California to testify in this case. These witnesses would be beyond the subpoena power of the California court, and their live testimony would be lost. On the other hand, defendants have not shown that holding the trial in North Carolina will necessarily make even one witness unavailable. The sole affidavit submitted in support of their motion merely lists a handful of witnesses from California and Colorado, none of whom have stated that they will not come to North Carolina. Certainly the trying of this case in North Carolina will cause some degree of inconvenience to defendants and to some of the witnesses. However, this court is not prepared to say that the possible inconvenience to defendants substantially outweighs (or, for that matter, even equals) the inconvenience which will be suffered by plaintiff if the case is transferred.

In addition, it would not serve the interests of justice to transfer this case to California. The construction project is in North Carolina, and it will be far easier for a North Carolina court to enforce its judgment, if any, than it would be for a California tribunal the width of a continent away. Additionally, justice requires that plaintiff's choice of forum be given substantial consideration. *First National City Bank,* 437 F.Supp. at 189. The reasons offered by defendants are insufficient to justify disturbing plaintiff's choice of forum.

For the foregoing reasons, it is hereby ORDERED that defendants' motion for change of venue is DENIED.

Forum selection clauses also appear in an international context. Sometimes, when parties are from different nations, they will designate the court of either one of their nations or of a neutral, third nation to hear their disputes.

EXAMPLE

In a contract between an American seller and a West German buyer, the parties might agree that "any dispute arising under this contract must be resolved before the Court of England." If the American seller files a suit in the United States and the West German buyer requests a transfer to England, the court will examine the forum selection provision in the same manner in which the court would examine a forum selection provision between domestic parties.

PROBLEM 18: The Panhandle Oil Company, a Texas corporation, hired the Euro Ship Company, a West German corporation, to tow an oil rig from Galveston, Texas, to Venezuela. Because the contract between the companies was so complex, it took many months to negotiate. The contract contained a clause stating, "The parties will submit any claims arising from this agreement to the Courts of Switzerland."

While in tow, the oil rig sank in the Gulf of Mexico near Florida's west coast. Panhandle believes that if Euro employees had acted properly, they could have saved the rig. Panhandle filed a breach of contract action against Euro in the United States District Court for the Southern District of Florida. Euro moves to transfer the action to Switzerland.

Should the Federal District Court Judge grant Euro's motion to transfer the action to Switzerland? If you were the judge, what additional facts would you need before you could make your decision and why?

PART IV

Step Four: Performance and Breach of the Contract

Chapter Twelve
The Defendant's Response to the Plaintiff's Allegation of Breach

INTRODUCTION

A contract has been formed (step two) and the contract is enforceable (step three). Step four focuses on the performance and breach of the contract. At this step, one party becomes dissatisfied with the other's performance of the contract. The dissatisfied party, that is the party who has a right to that performance under the contract, is called the promisee. The party who owes the duty to perform is called the promisor. The promisee may allege that the promisor, by an act or a forbearance (failure to act), has breached a contractual duty. This type of breach is the commonplace breach—the time for the promisor's performance has come and gone without the promisor performing. The promisor did not perform when the performance was due.

EXAMPLE

> The House of Gems, a jewelry store, contracted with Quality Printing for the printing of its Christmas catalogs. Quality promised to deliver the catalogs on November 1st; the date passed without the catalogs being delivered. Quality has breached the contract by failing to perform when the performance was due.

When the promisee receives notice that the promisor will not perform in the future, the promisee need not wait for the due date but rather may rely on the notification, make other plans, and seek an appropriate remedy. This breach is known as a breach by anticipatory repudiation. Some refer to this erroneously as an "anticipatory breach."

EXAMPLE

> The House of Gems, a jewelry store, contracted with Quality Printing for the printing of its Christmas catalogs. Quality promised to deliver the catalogs on November 1st. On October 15th Quality notified the House of Gems that the catalogs could not be delivered on November 1st. Quality's notice that it will not perform on the future date is a breach by anticipatory repudiation.

Just because the plaintiff-promisee alleges that the defendant-promisor has breached the contract does not make it so. The defendant has an arsenal of four effective responses to the plaintiff's allegation of breach. We can reduce them to shorthand phrases:

1. No breach, compliance
2. No breach, excuse

3. No breach, justification
4. No breach, terminated duty.

In the first response ("No breach, I am complying with the terms of the contract"), the defendant denies that he or she is not complying with the terms of the contract.

> Although the plaintiff alleges that I have breached the contract, I have complied with the terms of the contract. I am not in breach.

If the defendant is in compliance with the terms of the contract, the defendant has not breached the contract and the plaintiff has no cause of action for breach.

In the second response ("No breach, although I am not complying with the terms of the contract, my nonperformance was excused"), the defendant admits not performing the contract but claims that this nonperformance was excused and therefore not a breach.

> I may not be performing the contract but there is an outside event that prevents my performance. I am excused from performing, and I am not in breach.

Unlike the first response ("No breach, compliance"), the external event or condition in the second response ("No breach, excuse") was not an express term in the contract. Even though this external event or condition (an act of God) was not an express term, it may excuse the defendant's nonperformance. If the defendant is excused, the defendant is not in breach and the plaintiff cannot maintain a cause of action for breach of contract.

In the third response to the plaintiff's allegation of breach ("No breach, although I am not complying with the terms of the contract, my nonperformance was justified by your breach of this contract"), the defendant admits nonperformance but claims that the nonperformance was justified by a breach by the plaintiff.

> My nonperformance of the contract was justified by your breach of the contract. Therefore, you are the breaching party and not I.

The defendant's nonperformance is not a breach—it is a justified nonperformance much like self-defense in criminal law. Because the plaintiff rather than the defendant is the breaching party, the plaintiff cannot maintain a cause of action for breach of contract against the defendant.

In the fourth response ("No breach, although I am not complying with the terms of the contract, my duty to perform the contract has been terminated"), the defendant admits nonperformance, but claims that his or her contractual duty has ended either by agreement or by law, and therefore he or she has not breached the contract.

> I no longer have to perform according to the contract. My obligation no longer exists due to some duty terminating occurrence. I am not in breach.

The terminating occurrence may be consensual (substitute contract, accord and satisfaction, novation or estoppel), unilateral (release or waiver), or by operation of law (statute of limitations). Because the defendant is not a breaching party, the plaintiff cannot maintain a breach of contract action.

If the defendant is unsuccessful in using any of these four responses, he or she has little alternative but to admit as true the plaintiff's allegation of breach.

> Yes, I admit I breached the contract.

Whether the defendant's breach is intentional or unintentional is irrelevant. The law of contracts does not evaluate the mental state accompanying nonperformance. All that is important is whether the defendant did not perform his or her contractual duty.

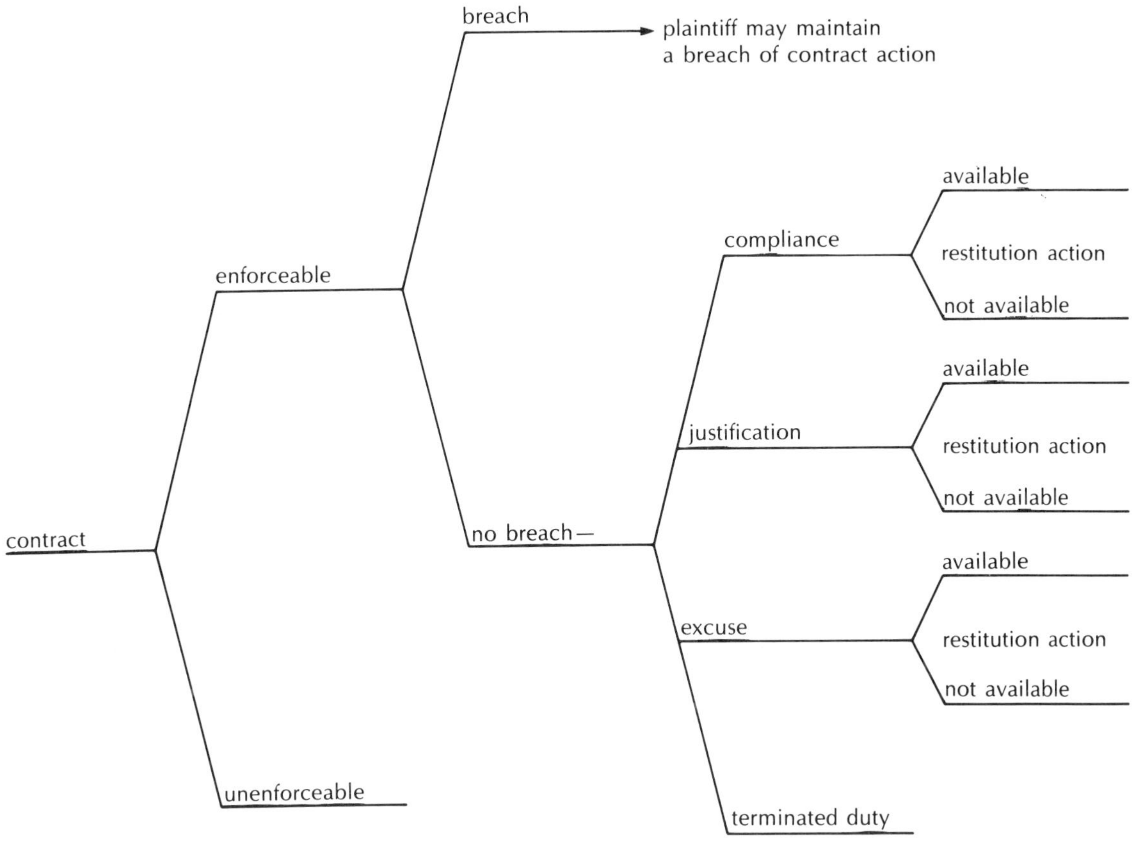

12

THE DEFENDANT'S RESPONSE TO THE PLAINTIFF'S ALLEGATION OF BREACH

This chapter focuses on the defendant's responses to the plaintiff's allegation of breach. Each of the five sections explores a different response: Section one—no breach, compliance; section two—no breach, excuse; section three—no breach, justification; section four—no breach, terminated duty; and section five—admission of breach.

Each "no breach" response, if successful, concludes the breach of contract action. The plaintiff may not maintain a breach of contract action. The no breach, compliance; no breach, excuse; and no breach, justification responses, although ending the breach of contract action, leave open the possibility of relief for unjust enrichment in a restitution action. A plaintiff, who has conferred a benefit on the defendant, may pursue a restitution action if it would be unjust to permit the defendant to retain the benefit without compensating the plaintiff. These restitution actions are explored in sections one, two, and three, along with the response that led to the conclusion that the contract was not breached.

The admission of breach sends the plaintiff into Step Five, Plaintiff's Remedies for the Defendant's Breach of Contract.

Section 1. NO BREACH, COMPLIANCE

> Although the promisee alleges that I have breached the contract, I have complied with the terms of the contract. I am not in breach.

The defendant's first response to the plaintiff's allegation of breach is "No breach, I am complying with the terms of the contract." The defendant denies that he or she has failed to comply with the terms of the contract. If the defendant is in compliance with the terms of the contract, the contract has not been breached and the defendant has no cause of action for breach of contract.

EXAMPLE

A fire insurance policy presents a classic illustration of a "no breach, compliance" response. Triplett contracted with the Lone Star Insurance Company for homeowner's insurance. Triplett promised to pay the premiums for Lone Star's promise to pay for repairs to Triplett's house for damage caused by natural disaster. Because Triplett's house was located in a flood plain, the policy excluded damage due to flooding. Several months after Triplett paid the premium, his house was damaged by a 100–year flood.

Triplett filed a claim with Lone Star but Lone Star denied the claim on the ground that the damage to the house was by flooding and the policy did not cover loss by flooding.

If Triplett filed an action against Lone Star for breach of contract, he would allege that Lone Star breached the contract by not paying the claim. Lone Star's response would be "no breach, compliance. Because the contract states that we do not have to pay for losses caused by flooding and because this loss was caused by flooding, we have no duty under the contract to pay for this loss. We are complying with the terms of the contract."

A. Finding the Terms of the Contract

If the terms of the contract are in writing, the parties will refer to the writing to determine what each party is obligated to do. It is helpful when the writing clearly states the duties of the parties and there is no dispute, but writings are seldom perfect.

In 20/20 hindsight, the terms of the writing may not have been as carefully drafted as they should have been. The parties may dispute each other's meaning. They are left with an ambiguity which needs resolution. Sometimes an ambiguity is apparent from the face of the writing (patent ambiguity). Patent ambiguities are often created by inexact pronoun reference or misleading modifiers.

EXAMPLE

The attorney told his client he needs more information.
Who needs more information, the attorney or the client?

EXAMPLE

I said when I have finished my research I will write the brief.
Does this mean: (1) I have finished my research and I will write the brief; or (2) I will write the brief when I have finished my research?

Sometimes the ambiguity is not apparent from the face of the writing but is apparent when information beyond the writing demonstrates that the term has a double meaning (latent ambiguity).

EXAMPLE

Buyer purchased from Seller 125 bales of cotton to be shipped from Bombay to Liverpool on the ship Peerless. Buyer met the ship Peerless (which sailed from Bombay) when it docked in Liverpool in October but there was no cotton. The Buyer, believing the Seller had breached the contract, purchased substitute cotton on the open market.

In December a second ship named Peerless (which also sailed from Bombay) docked in Liverpool. Although this ship carried the Buyer's cotton, the Buyer, no longer needing the cotton, rejected the shipment.

The ambiguity—two ships with the same name sailing from and to the same ports—was not apparent from the face of the contract. The ambiguity became apparent only when the Buyer discovered the existence of two ships with the same name. The ambiguity was latent.

A number of maxims and rules of construction provide some assistance, although, for every maxim or rule, a contradictory one can be found. Some common phrases are: "contract terms should be given their plain meaning"; "the terms of the contract should be strictly construed against the drafter" (*contra proferentem*); "the contract should follow the intent of the parties"; "general words which follow specific words should be limited to the same general kind or class as the specific words" (*ejusdem generis*); and "the enumeration of one thing implies the exclusion of those things not enumerated" (*expressio unius est exclusio alterius*).

If the parties had prior contractual relationships, the course of their dealings under those contracts could shed light on the current dispute. Also, if the parties have partially performed under the contract in dispute, the prior performances of the parties may provide some assistance in resolving the dispute.

Even if the writing is unambiguous, it may not reflect the agreed upon terms. The drafter who set the oral agreement into writing may have made a mistake in writing down the agreement. This is known as a mistake in the integration of the contract.

EXAMPLE

Buyer telephoned Seller to inquire the price of 2,000 crates of oranges. After negotiating, the parties settled on 2,000 crates at $10 a crate. Seller told Buyer that she would send a written confirmation of their oral contract. In typing up the confirmation, Seller erroneously typed 3,000 crates.

Seller sent the confirmation to Buyer but Buyer did not bother to read it until an extra 1,000 crates of oranges arrived. When Seller typed the confirmation with a quantity that differed from the quantity orally agreed upon, she has made a mistake in the integration of the contract.

The question then becomes whether the court should reform the writing to correct this mistake. If the parties' intent is clear and it is established that the writing was in error, the writing ought to be reformed to reflect the true intent of the parties. The problem is one of finding the true intent of the parties.

Even if the parties have a writing and the terms accurately reflect what the parties have agreed upon, a question may still arise whether the writing includes all or only some of the terms to which the parties agreed. This raises the issue of the parol evidence rule. Was this writing intended to be the final writing of the parties (that is, was the contract integrated)? Did this writing include all the terms that the parties agreed upon (that is, was this writing a total or partial integration)?

B. Condition Precedent, Concurrent Conditions, Condition Subsequent

A condition is a contingency. It is a premise upon which the fulfillment of a promise depends.

A condition may be an external event or condition.

EXAMPLE

> "I promise to come home when the sun goes down." The sun going down is a condition to the promise to come home.

A promise may be a condition to the performance of another promise. This type of promise is a "promissory condition."

EXAMPLE

> "I promise to pay you when you promise to mow the grass." The promise to mow is a condition to the promise to pay.

Conditions come in three forms; precedent, subsequent, and concurrent. A condition precedent is a duty-creating event.

EXAMPLE

> "I promise to pay for damage to your home if it is struck by lightning." Being struck by lightning is the event that creates the duty to pay. The promisor has no duty to pay until the event occurs.

A condition subsequent is a duty terminating event.

EXAMPLE

> "I promise to play tennis today unless it rains." Rain is the event that ends the duty to play tennis. The promisor has a duty to play tennis up until the time it rains.

Concurrent conditions exist when promises are conditioned on each other and both must be performed simultaneously.

EXAMPLE

"I promise to give you $200 for your promise to give me your watch." Without a statement as to who will perform first, the tender of the $200 must coincide with the tender of the watch.

C. Restitution as an Action When the Nonoccurrence of a Condition Precludes Performance of the Contract

The "no breach, compliance" response is a denial of breach. "I am not breaching, I am complying." Without a breach of the contract, the remedies for breach of contract are unavailable. Situations may exist where both the promisor and promisee are complying with the terms of the contract although the contract will require neither to perform further because a condition has terminated their duties to perform. Although neither is in breach, the promisee has at least partially performed. Situations may arise where the contract calls for the promisee to begin performance first. The promisee begins to perform his or her respective duties under the contract. Suddenly an event occurs that terminates the promisee's duty to perform further. The contract does not call upon the promisor to perform because the promisor must perform after the promisee fully performs. The performance of the contract comes to a standstill. Neither party has breached the contract. If the promisee has partially performed the contract, further complications occur. By performing, did the promisee confer a benefit on the promisor? If the promisor retains this benefit without compensating the promisee, is the promisor unjustly enriched?

PROBLEM 1: Lewis contracted to purchase Blackacre from Roberts for $85,000. The contract was subject to Lewis obtaining a twenty year mortgage for $60,000 at nine percent from a lending institution. The contract also called for an $8,500 deposit.

Lewis paid Roberts the $8,500 deposit. After exercising due diligence, Lewis was unable to find a twenty year mortgage for $60,000 at nine percent from a lending institution.

Is Lewis entitled to have his deposit returned even though the contract does not address the issue?

Section 2. NO BREACH, EXCUSE

Although the promisee alleges that I have breached the contract, I have not performed the contract because an outside event has prevented my performance. I am excused from performing, and I am not in breach.

The defendant's second response to the plaintiff's allegation of breach is "No breach, excuse." The defendant admits not complying with the terms of the contract, but asserts that this nonperformance was excused and therefore not a breach. Unlike the first response to the promisee's allegation of breach ("No breach, compliance"), the external event or condition in the second response ("No breach, excuse") was not an express term in the contract. Even though this external event or condition (an act of God) was not an express term, it may excuse the promisor's nonperformance. If the promisor is excused, the promisor is not in breach and the promisee cannot maintain a cause of action for breach of contract.

The "no breach, excuse" response has three variations: the external event made performance of the contract impossible, the external event made performance of the contract impracticable, and the external event while not making the performance of the contract impossible or impracticable did frustrate the purpose of the contract.

A. Impossibility

Cases of impossibility often involve destruction or unavailability of the subject matter of the contract. A leading case is *Taylor v. Caldwell,* 3 B. & S. 826, 122 Eng. Rep. 309 (K.B. 1863), an old English case. Taylor, an impresario, contracted to rent the Surrey Gardens and Music Hall from Caldwell for four days for the purpose of presenting four "grand concerts" and "day and night fetes" in the hall. Shortly after the parties signed a lease and before the concert dates, fire destroyed the music hall. Taylor brought a breach of contract action against Caldwell alleging that Caldwell breached the contract by failing to provide the music hall. Caldwell responded that although he did not provide the hall, his not providing the hall was excused due to the fire. The court in *Taylor v. Caldwell,* 3 B. & S. 826, 122 Eng. Rep. 309, 314–15 (K.B. 1863), held that the destruction of the music hall did excuse Caldwell from performing the contract:

> The principle seems to us to be that, in contracts in which the performance depends on the continued existence of a given person or thing, a condition is implied that the impossibility of performance arising from the perishing of the person or thing shall excuse the performance.
>
> In none of these cases is the promise in words other than positive, nor is there any express stipulation that the destruction of the person or thing shall excuse the performance; but that excuse is by law implied, because from the nature of the contract it is apparent that the parties contracted on the basis of the continued existence of the particular person or chattel. In the present case, looking at the whole contract, we find that the parties contracted on the basis of the continued existence of the Music Hall at the time when the concerts were to be given; that being essential to their performance.
>
> We think, therefore, that the Music Hall having ceased to exist, without fault of either party, both parties are excused, the plaintiffs from taking the gardens and paying the money, the defendants from performing their promise to give the use of the Hall and Gardens and other things.

The doctrine of implied conditions ultimately gave way to a more direct analysis of risk allocation. The following series of questions may be helpful in understanding the impossibility cases:

1. Did an unexpected event occur?
2. Did occurrence of the unexpected event render performance of the contract impossible?
3. Was the risk of nonperformance due to the unexpected event allocated either by contract or by custom?

4. Who should bear the risk of the defendant's nonperformance due to the unexpected event?

The first three questions sort those cases that are impossibility cases from those that are not. In *Taylor v. Caldwell* the destruction of the hall due to fire was an unexpected event. Without the music hall, the performance of the contract between Taylor and Caldwell was impossible. The contract did not allocate the risk from the destruction of the music hall due to fire.

The fourth question is simply risk allocation. Should Caldwell, the lessor, bear the risk of any loss suffered by the lessee when the unexpected fire prevents the performance of the lease?

Suppose the parties are reversed in the law suit. Caldwell, the lessor, sued Taylor, the lessee, alleging that Taylor did not finish paying on the contract. Could Taylor respond that he was excused from paying because the music hall burned down? Should Taylor, the lessee, bear the risk of any loss suffered by the lessor when the unexpected fire prevents the performance of the contract?

PROBLEM 2: In June, the Browning Agency, a creative advertising agency, contracted with Edith Edwards to send a hot air balloon over Chicago on the Fourth of July as part of an advertising campaign for Edith's Ice Cream Shoppe. High winds on the Fourth of July prevented Browning from sending up the balloon.

Edith sued Browning for breach of contract alleging that Browning breached by not sending up the balloon. Could Browning successfully maintain that her nonperformance was excused?

What was the event that led to Browning's failure to perform the contract, and was this event expected or unexpected?

PROBLEM 3: Rona contracted to create a sculpture of a moose for Andy for Christmas. Shortly before Christmas Rona completed the sculpture and arranged for it to be delivered to Andy. Before the sculpture could be delivered, a thief broke into Rona's studio and stole the sculpture. An extensive search by the police did not locate the sculpture.

Andy sued Rona for breach of contract alleging that Rona breached by not delivering the sculpture. Could Rona successfully maintain that her nonperformance was excused?

1. What was the event that led to Rona's failure to perform the contract, and was this event expected or unexpected?
2. Did the occurrence of this event render Rona's performance of the contract impossible?

If you need additional facts to resolve these questions, list the facts needed and why they are necessary.

PROBLEM 4: Gateway Industries of St. Louis contracted to lease twelve new pick-up trucks from Good Deal Motors of Detroit. Good Deal contracted with Express Railway to deliver the trucks to St. Louis. Enroute, the train derailed and the trucks were damaged.

Gateway sued Good Deal for breach of contract alleging that Good Deal breached by not delivering the trucks. Could Good Deal successfully maintain that its nonperformance was excused?

1. What was the event that led to Good Deal's failure to perform the contract, and was this event expected or unexpected?
2. Did the occurrence of this event render Good Deal's performance of the contract impossible?
3. Was the risk of nonperformance due to the unexpected event allocated either by contract or by custom?

If you need additional facts to resolve these questions, list the facts needed and why they are necessary.

PROBLEM 5: Baldwin contracted to sell Cox 2,000 tons of potatoes to be grown on Baldwin's farm in Boise, Idaho. Without any fault on Baldwin's part, a disease destroyed his entire potato crop. Cox sued Baldwin for breach of contract alleging that Baldwin breached by not delivering the potatoes. Could Baldwin successfully maintain that his nonperformance was excused?

1. What was the event that led to Baldwin's failure to perform the contract, and was this event expected or unexpected?
2. Did the occurrence of this event render Baldwin's performance of the contract impossible?
3. Was the risk of nonperformance due to the unexpected event allocated either by contract or by custom?
4. Who should bear the risk of Baldwin's nonperformance due to the unexpected event?

If you need additional facts to resolve these questions, list the facts needed and why they are necessary.

Would it make any difference if the contract had not specified that the potatoes were to be raised on Baldwin's farm?

Unexpected events making performance of the contract impossible may take the form of illness, physical incapacity, or death.

PROBLEM 6: In January, Howard contracted to perform in Roxy's motorcycle stunt show. The first show was scheduled for the end of February. In early February, Howard broke both his legs in a skiing accident. Roxy sued Howard for breach of contract alleging that Howard breached by not performing in her stunt show. Could Howard successfully maintain that his nonperformance was excused?

1. What was the event that led to Howard's failure to perform the contract, and was this event expected or unexpected?
2. Did the occurrence of this event render Howard's performance of the contract impossible?

3. Was the risk of nonperformance due to the unexpected event allocated either by contract or by custom?
4. Who should bear the risk of Howard's nonperformance due to the unexpected event?

If you need additional facts to resolve these questions, list the facts needed and why they are necessary.

Death or serious illness excuses performance when a contract specifically calls for personal performance by the party who is unable to perform. When a contracting party's death or illness does not affect the performance of the contract, the failure to perform will be a breach and not an excused nonperformance.

PROBLEM 7: Brent contracted to sell his car to Susan, who made a $500 down payment. Brent died in a boating accident before the date he was to deliver his car to Susan. When Susan tendered Brent's executor the total purchase price under the contract, the executor refused to deliver Brent's car to Susan.

Susan sued Brent's estate for breach of contract alleging that Brent breached by not delivering the car. Could Brent's executor successfully maintain that his nonperformance was excused?

1. What was the event that led to Brent's failure to perform the contract, and was this event expected or unexpected?
2. Did the occurrence of this event render Brent's performance of the contract impossible?
3. Was the risk of nonperformance due to the unexpected event allocated either by contract or by custom?
4. Who should bear the risk of Brent's nonperformance due to the unexpected event?

If you need additional facts to resolve these questions, list the facts needed and why they are necessary.

A change in law may excuse both parties to the contract. Where a previously lawful contractual duty has become illegal after contracting, both contracting parties are excused so long as the nonperforming party did not bear the risk of loss.

PROBLEM 8: On January 15, Hudson Bay Pelts Company of Toronto, Canada, contracted to sell two hundred dozen lamb pelts to American Woolen Company of Philadelphia, Pennsylvania. The contract required Hudson Bay to ship the pelts by railroad from Toronto to Philadelphia on February 20. On February 1, a United States agency outlawed the importation of lamb pelts.

American sued Hudson Bay for breach of contract alleging that Hudson Bay breached by not delivering the pelts. Could Hudson Bay successfully maintain that its nonperformance was excused?

1. What was the event that led to Hudson Bay's failure to perform the contract, and was this event expected or unexpected?

2. Did the occurrence of this event render Hudson Bay's performance of the contract impossible?
3. Was the risk of nonperformance due to the unexpected event allocated either by contract or by custom?
4. Who should bear the risk of Hudson Bay's nonperformance due to the unexpected event?

If you need additional facts to resolve these questions, list the facts needed and why they are necessary.

B. Impracticability

Impracticability cases arise when the difficulty or expense due to an unexpected event is so extreme that a court should excuse performance of the contract. What factors did the court consider in *Associated Grocers of Iowa Cooperative, Inc.?*

Associated Grocers of Iowa Cooperative, Inc. v. West

Supreme Court of Iowa, 1980.
297 N.W.2d 103.

Considered en banc.

LeGRAND, Justice.

This breach-of-contract action is the outgrowth of an unsuccessful venture by which George G. West and Lloyd G. Huffer hoped to profit from the development of real estate for industrial purposes. When their expectations were dashed, they were called upon to defend several suits arising out of that matter. This is one of them. Plaintiff obtained judgment against West and Huffer for $96,177.41. In addition, West's counterclaim against plaintiff was dismissed, and his cross-petition for indemnity against Des Moines Savings & Loan Association and Metropolitan Financial Corporation was also dismissed. This appeal followed, and we affirm.

First, it will be helpful to sort out the parties to this litigation. Lloyd G. Huffer did not resist plaintiff's claim. Judgment by default was entered against him. He is not a party to this appeal. Metropolitan Financial Corporation is a wholly owned subsidiary of Des Moines Savings & Loan Association. Their interests herein are identical. Our references throughout are to West as the sole remaining defendant and to Des Moines Savings & Loan Association for both itself and Metropolitan Financial Corporation on the third-party claim.

In September of 1971, West purchased the remaining lots in an area known as Ankeny Industrial Development Park. West intended to complete development of this area, a project which had already been started.

Part of West's plan was to secure a major purchaser for part of the area, expecting this would in turn attract other buyers and facilitate development of the property. The evidence is in dispute as to whether the commitment was conditional upon West securing a major purchaser. We do not believe this has any significance in the conclusion we reach.

In June of 1972, West entered into an option contract with Associated Grocers of

Iowa Cooperative, Inc. (AGI) which is the subject of this litigation. The option ran for ninety days and gave AGI the right to purchase Lots 10, 11, and 12 in Ankeny Industrial Development Park for a price of $5,500 per acre. The terms were later amended to provide that AGI could postpone exercising its option as to Lot 10 for five years.

The real point at issue concerns the provisions in the option which obligated West to do certain construction work. As finally agreed upon, they were as follows:

> 3. Immediately following the closing of this sale the seller hereby agrees to install roads on the north border of Lots 10, 11, and 12 and extend said road east to Delaware Avenue and seller further agrees to install a road on the east border of Lot 10 to provide access south from the property which is the subject of this proposal.
>
> 4. Seller also agrees to construct at its expense two railroad spurs from the main line of the Chicago Northwestern Railway Company to the property line of Lot 12, the location of said spurs be determined by mutual agreement between buyer and seller.

Armed with the AGI option, West secured financing from Des Moines Savings in the amount of $339,000. All of the loan proceeds were paid to him except $60,000, which was reserved for street construction. This figure was apparently arrived at by withholding 75 per cent of the estimated cost of $78,000. The city of Ankeny was to pay the remaining 25 per cent.

Approximately sixty days after West had secured financing, AGI exercised its option to purchase Lots 11 and 12 and postponed exercising its option on Lot 10. West did not install the roads nor did he construct the railroad spurs as the option specified. AGI did not begin construction for four years after exercising its option, although it paid West the full purchase price for Lots 11 and 12.

The transaction between AGI and West was completed on October 16, 1972, by delivery of a warranty deed conveying Lots 11 and 12 and reserving the option to purchase Lot 10. AGI started construction of its warehouse on Lots 11 and 12 in 1976 and completed it in 1977. The option to purchase Lot 10 was not exercised until 1977.

Eventually the city of Ankeny paved the streets described in the option and assessed AGI for its portion of the cost. AGI installed the railroad spurs at its own cost. West refused to assume any obligation for either of these expenditures for a variety of reasons which we discuss later. West was unable to sell the remaining lots in the addition. He blames this on AGI's failure to build its warehouse as an attraction to other potential buyers. In 1974 Des Moines Savings started foreclosure on the West mortgage, which was in default. A decree of foreclosure was entered, subject to AGI's option to purchase Lot 10.

Lot 10 was assessed for paving in the amount of $15,075.11. Lot 11 was assessed for $5,906.51. This was for the paving of Hulsizer Street. Lot 10 was also assessed in the amount of $8,657.26 for the paving of Iowa Street. The actual assessments were considerably less than the estimate upon which the $60,000 was withheld. The property was sold at sheriff's sale to Des Moines Savings for the amount remaining due on the indebtedness. After the expiration of the period of redemption, AGI made demand on West for reimbursement, claiming the option obligated West to pay both the paving assessment and the cost of the railroad spur lines.

The case was tried to the court and judgment went against West on all issues. He was ordered to reimburse AGI for the cost of the street paving and the railroad spurs in the total amount of $96,177.41. His counterclaim against AGI was dismissed. His third-party petition against Des Moines Savings for indemnity was dismissed. He appealed from all these adverse results.

. . .

II. Was Performance Excused Because of Impossibility or Impracticability?

West says it was impossible, or at least impracticable, for him to perform the conditions of the option. We recognized the impossibility doctrine in *Nora Springs Coop. Co. v. Brandau,* 247 N.W.2d 744, 747–48 (Iowa 1976). West now wants it extended to include impracticability as well. Without deciding this issue, we conclude the doctrine is not applicable here. *See* 17 Am.Jur.2d *Contracts,* § 402 (1964).

Nothing renders this contract impractical or impossible except West's bad judgment. West contends AGI's long delay in building, the dramatic increase in construction costs, and the mortgage foreclosure action all combined to render performance "impossible and impracticable." He cites no case authority for this proposition. We find no support for his argument. Impossibility of performance refers to extraordinary circumstances which could not have been anticipated and which arise without fault on the part of the one seeking to avoid performance. Those conditions are not present in this case. The matters about which West complains were reasonably to be anticipated and could easily have been guarded against by the parties. *Cf. Powers v. Siats,* 70 N.W.2d 344, 348–49 (Minn.1955) (fact that performance becomes economically burdensome does not excuse performance unless caused by some unforeseen contingency which alters the essential nature of the performance). . . .

In those courts that recognize impracticability as a defense, impracticability will excuse nonperformance only when the event is so unusual and unexpected as to make the performance under the new conditions entirely different from performance as contracted. The guidelines set forth in the preceding section on impossibility, with only slight modification, also serve impracticability. The modification must take into consideration that the performance in an impracticability case need not be impossible.

PROBLEM 9: Mason Company contracted with Brady to take all the gravel needed for a construction project from Brady's land. After taking 50,000 cubic yards of gravel from Brady's land, the Mason Company discovered that there was not enough gravel on Brady's land without having to dredge and dry gravel that was underwater. Because the cost of dredging and drying the gravel would have been twelve times the cost of buying dry gravel elsewhere, the Mason Company purchased 57,000 cubic yards of gravel from a third party.

Brady sued the Mason Company for breach of contract alleging that Mason breached by not taking all its gravel requirements from Brady's land. Could Mason successfully maintain that its nonperformance was excused?

1. What was the event that led to Mason's failure to perform the contract, and was this event expected or unexpected?
2. Did the occurrence of this event render Mason's performance of the contract impracticable?
3. Was the risk of nonperformance due to the unexpected event allocated either by contract or by custom?
4. Who should bear the risk of Mason's nonperformance due to the unexpected event?

If you need additional facts to resolve these questions, list the facts needed and why they are necessary.

PROBLEM 10: Weebo Manufacturing Company, a firm specializing in space-age technological equipment, contracted with the Army to develop a heat-sensitive device designed to locate nuclear-powered submarines. Midway through the project, Weebo encountered technical difficulties resulting in unexpectedly heavy production costs far in excess of any profits it would make under the contract. Weebo notified the Army that it could not develop the heat-sensitive device. The Army then contracted with The Space Age Corporation for the development of the heat-sensitive device at a contract price of five times the Weebo contract.

The Army sued the Weebo Company for breach of contract alleging that Weebo breached by not producing the heat-sensitive device. Could Weebo successfully maintain that its nonperformance was excused?

1. What was the event that led to Weebo's failure to perform the contract, and was this event expected or unexpected?
2. Did the occurrence of this event render Weebo's performance of the contract impracticable?
3. Was the risk of nonperformance due to the unexpected event allocated either by contract or by custom?
4. Who should bear the risk of Weebo's nonperformance due to the unexpected event?

If you need additional facts to resolve these questions, list the facts needed and why they are necessary.

C. Frustration of Purpose

Frustration of purpose cases involve an unexpected event that destroys the whole reason for the contract. Even though performance of the contract is still possible, courts may excuse nonperformance on the theory of failure of consideration.

EXAMPLE

An illustration is the famous English case of *Krell v. Henry,* [1903] 2 K.B. 740 (C.A.). Krell owned a suite of rooms overlooking the parade route for the coronation procession of King Edward VII. Krell contracted to lease his suite to Henry for the purpose of viewing the coronation procession. Shortly before the coronation, the King became ill and the coronation was indefinitely postponed. When Henry refused to pay Krell the balance due on the lease, Krell sued Henry. The court excused Henry's nonperformance. Though the nonhappening of the coronation did not prevent either Krell from renting the suite or Henry from paying Krell the contract price, the postponement of the coronation did destroy the value of the use of Krell's rooms to Henry during the contract period.

With a few minor variations, the guidelines used for impossibility and impracticability can be useful in understanding the frustration of purpose cases:

1. Did an unexpected event occur?
2. Did the occurrence of the unexpected event frustrate the purpose of the contract, destroying the value of performance to the defendant?
3. Was the risk of frustration due to the unexpected event allocated either by contract or by custom?
4. Who should bear the risk of the defendant's frustration of purpose due to the unexpected event?

PROBLEM 11: The summer olympic games were scheduled for the week of July 1st in Dallas, Texas. On May 1st, in anticipation of the summer olympic games, the California T–Shirt Company contracted to purchase 500,000 t-shirts bearing the Olympic logo from Channing Enterprises. On May 20th, a Soviet bloc boycott resulted in cancellation of the summer games. The California T–Shirt Company notified Channing not to ship the t-shirts.

Channing sued California for breach of contract alleging that California breached by cancelling its order. Could California successfully maintain that its nonperformance was excused?

1. What was the event that led to California's failure to perform the contract, and was this event expected or unexpected?
2. Did the occurrence of the unexpected event frustrate the purpose of the contract, destroying the value of the performance to California?
3. Was the risk of nonperformance due to the unexpected event allocated either by contract or by custom?
4. Who should bear the risk of California's nonperformance due to the unexpected event?

If you need additional facts to resolve these questions, list the facts needed and why they are necessary.

PROBLEM 12: In June, XYZ Communications contracted to lease a building from Jackson for five years for the purpose of selling satellite dishes. On December 1st, the FCC declared the use of satellite dishes by homeowners illegal. XYZ ceased operating and moved out of the building.

Jackson sued XYZ for breach of contract alleging that XYZ breached by cancelling its lease. Could XYZ successfully maintain that its nonperformance was excused?

1. What was the event that led to XYZ's failure to perform the contract, and was this event expected or unexpected?
2. Did the occurrence of the unexpected event frustrate the purpose of the contract, destroying the value of performance to XYZ?
3. Was the risk of nonperformance due to the unexpected event allocated either by contract or by custom?
4. Who should bear the risk of XYZ's nonperformance due to the unexpected event?

If you need additional facts to resolve these questions, list the facts needed and why they are necessary.

D. Restitution as a Cause of Action When Nonperformance of the Contract Is Excused

The "no breach, excuse" response is an admission of nonperformance and a denial of breach. "I am not performing but my nonperformance is excused." Without a breach of the contract, the plaintiff's remedies for the defendant's breach of contract are unavailable.

Situations may arise where the contract calls for the plaintiff to perform first. The plaintiff begins performing the contract. Suddenly an event occurs that terminates the plaintiff's duty to perform further. The defendant is not called upon to perform because the plaintiff must fully perform first. The performance of the contract comes to a standstill. Neither party has breached the contract. What about the performance that the plaintiff has already conferred on the defendant? If the defendant is able to retain this benefit without compensating the plaintiff, will the defendant be unjustly enriched?

Bell v. Carver presents the general rule that when a contractor finds it impossible to complete performance under a construction contract due to the destruction of the structure, the contractor may be entitled to an action of restitution for the value of the work which had been done prior to the destruction. Bell also raises the question of how recovery should be measured.

Bell v. Carver

Supreme Court of Arkansas, 1968.
431 S.W.2d 452.

WARD, Justice.

This is an appeal from a decree against a property owner establishing a lien to secure payment of $2,724. A brief summary of the facts out of which this litigation arises is set out below.

Facts.

R.B. Bell and his wife (appellants here) are the owners of a lot in the town of Mena on which was a building used as a cafe. On June 14, 1966 they executed a ten year lease to J.H. Cameron and his wife who were to operate the cafe. Under the terms of the lease the Camerons were to make repairs necessary for the operation of a first class restaurant. About three months later J.A. Carver, d/b/a Carver Air Conditioning Co., (appellee herein) began work on installing an air conditioner and a heating unit in the cafe building for an agreed price—whether appellants or lessees were responsible for the "agreed price" was one of the issues raised at the trial.

Before installation of said units was completed the building was practically destroyed by fire on November 1, 1966. Following the fire appellants did not choose to rebuild and the Camerons ceased trying to operate the cafe.

Pleadings. On January 26, 1967 appellee filed a complaint in chancery court, seeking (a) to recover from appellants $1291 expended for labor and $1955 expended for materials being lost as a result of the fire, and (b) to establish a lien on appellants' property to secure payment of the above items. Appellants pleaded a general denial and a cross-complaint against the Camerons alleging they were obligated, under the lease, to pay any amount due appellee. Answering the cross-complaint, the Camerons denied they were liable in any amount to appellee or appellants.

At the close of a hearing on the above issues the trial court made the following findings: appellants contracted with appellee for said installation; appellee is entitled to a judgment, on a quantum meruit basis, against appellants; said judgment is a lien on the premises (subject to a lien in favor of the Union Bank of Nena), and; when appellants satisfy said judgment they will be entitled to a judgment against the Camerons. The trial court retained jurisdiction to make any further necessary orders.

The court entered a judgment in favor of appellee in the amount of $2,727 which was less than was asked for, but appellee does not question the reduction here. Also, the Camerons have not perfected their appeal.

For a reversal appellants here rely on three separate points which we now discuss in order.

One. Appellants' first point is stated as follows:

> "The court erred in its findings of fact and conclusion of law that Appellee is entitled to judgment based upon quantum meruit."

As we understand the argument here it is contended (a) the evidence does not support the trial court's finding that appellants authorized appellee to make said installations and (b) quantum meruit was not the proper measure of damages. We find no merit in either contention.

(a) The trial court found, and it is undisputed: that the fire was not the fault of any of the parties; that appellant first contacted appellee about the installations; that Bell told appellee to start work and, that appellants and appellee agreed on the price. In addition to the above the written lease agreement does not require the Camerons to make this kind of repairs on the building. On the contrary it does give them the right (at the expiration of the lease) "to remove" any equipment installed by them. We do not think it is reasonable to presume that the lessees would have a right to remove any part of the real estate when the lease expired.

(b) Although, as appears from appellant's excellent brief, the governing rule has not always been clearly stated, we think the equitable rule, and therefore the better rule, is that appellee should be allowed to recover, in this case, on a quantum meruit basis. In the case of Coley v. Green, 232 Ark. 289, 335 S.W.2d 720, we find this statement:

> "We come then to the difficult question as to the power of this Court to apportion the insurance proceeds on the basis of the repairs made. The older cases hold that, when a special contract had been performed only in part, then there could be no recovery on a *quantum meruit* basis. Simpson v. McDonald, 2 Ark. 370; Manuel v. Campbell, 3 Ark. 324. But over the years there has been a constant tendency to find a way to prevent the working party from losing his entire outlay. In Selig v. Botts, 128 Ark. 167, 193 S.W. 534, the Court in effect, divided the contract, and allowed recovery for the part that was performed; and in Mitchell v. Caplinger, 97 Ark. 278, 133 S.W. 1032, a contractor was allowed part recovery even though the owner had to make further expenditures to complete the building."

In Williston and Thompson, Revised Edition on Contracts, Section 1975, at page 948, this statement appears:

> "One who works upon a building or other property under an indivisible contract with the owner, requiring him to complete a certain task or accomplish a certain result, cannot perform his full undertaking if the building or property in question is destroyed. He is excused from liability for his failure, because the contract required the continued existence of the building. Equally clearly he cannot sue the owner for loss of profit. If the destruction of the building was without fault on the part of the latter, he, as well as the workman, is excused from liability on the contract. But most American decisions allow recovery on a quantum meruit for the value of the work which had been done prior to the destruction."

Here, the record also reflects that part of the heater system was not destroyed and was of some benefit to appellants.

Two. It is next contended by appellants that the court erred in its findings of fact and conclusion of law that appellee is entitled to a lien on the property of appellant. Again we find no reversible error. It has been made clear by this Court that if an owner authorizes a contractor to make improvements on his land and fails to pay for same, the contractor is entitled to a lien on said land to secure payment under Ark.Stat. Ann. § 51–601 et seq. (1947).

Section 51–601, in material parts, reads:

> "Every mechanic, builder * * * or other person who shall do or perform any work upon, or furnish any material * * * for any building, erection, improvement upon land * * * under or by virtue of any contract with the owner * * * shall have * * * a lien upon such building * * * and upon the land belonging to such owner * * *."

Since, as we have already held, appellants authorized the improvements in this case, appellee is entitled to a lien on the improved property under the above quoted statute. See: Whitcomb v. Gans, 90 Ark. 469, 119 S.W. 676, and Ark. Foundry Co. v. Farrell, 238 Ark. 757, 385 S.W.2d 26.

Three. At the close of the testimony appellee moved that its pleadings be amended "to conform with the proof in view of the proof that's been submitted". The trial court granted the motion, and appellants excepted to the ruling for the reason that appellee's complaint was based on a contract and it now seeks to recover on a quantum meruit basis. Again we are unable to agree because we think, there is no showing that the trial court abused its discretion granted by statute. Ark.Stat.Ann. § 27–1160 (Repl.1962), in part, provides:

> "The Court may, at any time, in the furtherance of justice, and on such terms as may be proper, amend any pleading or proceedings by adding or striking out the name of any party, or by correcting a mistake in the name of a party, or a mistake in any other respect, or by inserting other allegations material to the case; or when the amendment does not change substantially the claim or defense, by conforming the pleadings or proceedings to the facts proved. The court may likewise, in its discretion, allow an answer or reply to be made after the time limited by this code or by an order, enlarge such time."

See also: Fuller et ux v. Fuller et ux, 240 Ark. 475, 400 S.W.2d 283, Callahan v. Farm Equipment, Inc., 225 Ark. 547, 238 S.W.2d 692, and Antrim v. McKelroy, 229 Ark. 870, 319 S.W.2d 209.

Finding no reversible error, the decree of the trial court is affirmed, and the cause is remanded for further required proceedings.

FOGLEMAN, Justice (dissenting in part).

I agree with the majority so far as the opinion goes; however, I would remand the case to the trial court for a determination by that court of the correct amount for which appellee is entitled to judgment against appellant Bell and the amount for which he is entitled to a lien on the property. As I read the briefs, appellant does challenge the correctness of the amount for which the trial court rendered judgment and granted a lien.

Appellants' first point is as stated in the majority opinion. One of the court's findings of fact was that Carver was entitled to recovery on a quantum meruit basis $2,724.00. The trial judge arrived at this amount by taking appellee's proposal for the completed job on the basis of his estimate substantially as follows:

LABOR		$1,291.00
Shop built duct	$650.00	
Prefabricated duct	421.40	
Grills & registers	163.95	
Duct insulation	125.00	
Furnaces (2); 10 ton cooling coil; 1 thermostat and 1 thermostat switch base	594.65	1,955.00
CONDENSING UNIT & CONNECTING PIPES		2,198.85
		$5,444.85

The trial judge deducted from the labor item fifty cents per man hour, leaving $1,119.00. The testimony of Carver was that he actually paid only $3.00 per hour, leaving a profit of seventy-five cents per hour on labor. The court made an allowance against this seventy-five cents per hour for supervisory expense. The trial judge also deducted $350.00 for the two furnaces removed from the building by Carver and which are useable, stating that Carver was willing to keep them. He deducted this $350.00 from the $1,955 item, leaving $1,605.00. This amount, with the balance he allowed for labor, makes up the total of $2,724.00.

I am unable to find anything in the record on which the deduction of $350.00 was based and I am also unable to find any evidence in the record of any allowance for duct work removed by Carver and retained by him which is useable.

Since these findings of fact relate to the judgment which the court based upon quantum meruit, I think that the appellant argued the question sufficiently to require our consideration. In addition to his statement on the point, he specifically states:

"For an added reason the decree is not supported by the findings of fact. Quantum meruit is measured by the value of the benefit bestowed upon the Defendant rather than the detriment incurred by the Plaintiff. Dunn v. Phoenix Village, Inc., supra. [213 F.Supp. 936 (D.C.Ark.1963)] Appellee failed to show benefit but consistently sought to prove his entitlements under the contract originally alleged, less that part remaining unperformed. The court did not make a finding of benefit to Appellant. It used the contract figures, including possible profits built into the contract prices. The court arbitrarily deducted Fifty Cents ($.50) per hour from the price of the labor as reflected on Plaintiff's exhibit # 6 as profits from the labor. It deducted Three Hundred Fifty Dollars ($350.00) from the price of materials representing the value of furnaces which Appellee now has in his possession, again, arbitrarily. No proof was offered to this effect. Some of the work alleged must have gone into the installation of the furnaces. All of the work product is gone from the building. Appellant has none of the 'benefits' remaining in his possession."

It thus appears to me that appellee failed to meet his burden of proof for recovery on quantum meruit. According to the weight of authority, the measure of recovery under the circumstances prevailing here is the reasonable value of labor performed and material furnished. See, Anno., 170 A.L.R. 980. Evidence of the contractor's estimates may be admissible as having some bearing on the recoverable values, but I do not feel that the evidence offered here is sufficient.

While there is testimony by Carver that he had approximately 18% overhead costs that had to be borne by labor, the relationship of this to the reasonable value of labor and materials does not appear. Furthermore, at different times, Carver, admitting that he took into consideration a reasonable profit on the job, testified that a reasonable profit would be 25%, but he later testified that he should have 10% profit. While profits might reasonably be considered along with evidence going to the question of reasonable value of labor and materials for the basis of recovery against Bell, still there can be no lien for profits. Withrow v. Wright, 215 Ark. 654, 222 S.W.2d 809; Cook v. Moore, 152 Ark. 590, 239 S.W. 750.

I feel that we are in somewhat the same position in which the court found itself in Withrow v. Wright, supra, where the case was remanded for a determination by the trial court of the amount for which a claimant was entitled to a lien. I would follow that precedent in this case.

In *Stein v. Shaw* an attorney contracted with a client to file a negligence action on her behalf to recover damages for personal injuries. The client agreed to pay the attorney one-third of any recovery. After the attorney instituted suit and began negotiating a settlement, he was disbarred. The disbarment action was unrelated to this client. The client found herself another attorney and her suit was ultimately settled for $4,950. Is the disbarred attorney entitled to recover in a restitution action, and if so, how much?

Stein v. Shaw

Supreme Court of New Jersey, 1951.
6 N.J. 525, 79 A.2d 310.

VANDERBILT, C.J.

The plaintiff, an attorney at law, entered into a verbal agreement with the defendant to institute a suit in her behalf for the recovery of damages for personal injuries allegedly sustained by another's negligence. Under this agreement the plaintiff was to receive one-third of any recovery. He instituted suit and opened negotiations for a settlement, both of which were pending at the time he was disbarred from the practice of law for reasons not connected in anywise with the prosecution of the defendant's suit. After the plaintiff's disbarment other attorneys were substituted for him and the defendant's suit was subsequently settled for $4,950. The defendant refused to pay the plaintiff and he then commenced this action against her, seeking in the first count to recover $1,028 as the reasonable value of his services and disbursements, and in the second count to recover on his contingent fee contract one-third of the amount of the settlement. On the defendant's motion the trial court dismissed the complaint for failure to state a cause of action. From this judgment the plaintiff appealed to the Appellate Division of the Superior Court and we have certified the appeal here on our own motion.

We are of the opinion that the plaintiff should be permitted to recover in quasi contract for the reasonable value of his services rendered and disbursements made prior to his disbarment, for otherwise the defendant will be unjustly enriched at the expense of the plaintiff. To deprive an attorney of his claim for any and all compensation for services rendered prior to his disbarment when the services are not involved in the unprofessional conduct occasioning disciplinary action, would be inequitable. There is no sound reason in law or morals for permitting the defendant to use the plaintiff's disbarment as an escape from paying him for services rendered or necessary disbursements made by him in her behalf. Article VI, Section II, paragraph 3 of the Constitution imposes on this court the duty to discipline members of the bar for the protection of society, the legal profession and the courts in preserving the due administration of justice in the State, but its exercise does not affect either civil or criminal actions by or against the attorney disciplined by the court.

If the rule were otherwise, the effect of disciplinary action would inevitably be retroactive, which is not the intent or purpose in imposing discipline. The court, moreover, would never know the extent of such retroactive punishment without an undesirable inquiry as to the extent of the attorney's pending business and the monetary value thereof. It is unthinkable that punishment should be inflicted by a court so unintelligently. These are matters, however, which should not be considered by the committees on ethics and grievances appointed by us in the several counties to aid us by investigating complaints against members of the bar and by making presentments to us where the situation requires, nor should such matters be before us in imposing discipline. Our duty of safeguarding the integrity of the bar and of keeping the fountain of justice unpolluted is sufficiently difficult and delicate as it is without further complicating it with any such extraneous matters which should in all fairness be considered in imposing discipline, if the attorney's right to bring suit for services rendered is to be impaired by us. Disbarment is not a form of outlawry. To bring economic considerations into disciplinary proceedings would not only needlessly complicate them, but would in many instances serve to defeat the essential purpose thereof.

We are aware of Davenport v. Waggoner, 49 S.D. 592, 207 N.W. 972, 45 A.L.R. 1126 (S.Dak.1926) and In re Woodworth, 85 F.2d 50 (2nd Cir.1936) which hold to the contrary, but we cannot subscribe to the theory on which they are premised, that withdrawal from a suit by reason of disbarment constitutes a voluntary abandonment of the contract without just cause. Such is actually not the fact in those cases. The contract was not voluntarily abandoned, it was automatically terminated by operation of law, when the order of the court made further performance impossible. While the plaintiff was disbarred because of his own wrongful acts, so far as this defendant is concerned he is guiltless. It is pure fiction to say that he has intentionally and without cause abandoned his contract with her. While the analogy is not complete, the effect on the client of an attorney's disbarment is the same as that in the case of Justice v. Lairy, 19 Ind.App. 272, 49 N.E. 459 (Ind.App.1898), where an attorney accepted appointment to the bench and was thereby prohibited from the further practice of law. In either situation the attorney's disability is the result of conduct wholly unrelated to his client's case. In our opinion the situation resulting here from the plaintiff's disbarment is not dissimilar to that when an attorney is incapacitated by reason of death, illness or insanity. In such cases it has been uniformly held that because of his inability to perform the contract is discharged, but that the attorney may nevertheless recover in quasi contract for the reasonable value of the services rendered, 45 A.L.R. 1135, 1158. Nor is recovery in quasi contract here barred by virtue of the express contract for a contingent fee, for as we have indicated that contract was discharged by operation of law when its performance was rendered impossible by the plaintiff's disbarment.

The fact that the defendant was compelled by virtue of the plaintiff's disbarment to retain other counsel to prosecute her claim is, of course, to be considered in determining the reasonable value of the plaintiff's services. In no event, however, should the plaintiff's recovery exceed the amount stipulated for in his express agreement less whatever reasonable sum the defendant paid other counsel to complete the case. While the express contract has been discharged and cannot serve as the measure of recovery, it does operate as a limit on the amount of the recovery in quasi contract, 6 Williston on Contracts (Rev.Ed.1938) § 1977, p. 5557; Woodward, The Law of Quasi Contracts (1913) § 125, p. 197.

In view of the conclusions we have reached, it becomes unnecessary to consider the other questions raised by the plaintiff. The judgment appealed from is reversed and the cause remanded for further proceedings in accordance with this opinion.

For reversal: Chief Justice VANDERBILT, and Justices CASE, HEHER, OLIPHANT, BURLING and ACKERSON—6.

For affirmance: Justice WACHENFELD—1.

WACHENFELD, J. (dissenting).

In In re Woodworth, D.C., 15 F.Supp. 291, 293, affirmed 85 F.2d 50 (C.C.A. 2, 1936), the court held: "On principle it cannot be doubted that when an attorney makes an agreement to prosecute a case for a fee contingent on success and is disbarred before the fee is earned, he may not collect compensation from his client for the work done. The agreed fee he cannot have, because he has not performed his engagement and the contingency on which the compensation was to rest has not happened. Reasonable compensation in lieu of the fee he cannot have, because his inability to complete his contract has been brought about by his own wrongful conduct."

I subscribe to this reasoning and conclusion and am therefore to affirm.

Adopting this rule would not complicate or bring economic considerations into disciplinary proceedings nor would it defeat their purpose. It would, in my opinion, be an added incentive to professional conduct, which is foreign to disciplinary complaints.

Admittedly, the plaintiff was disbarred because of his own wrongful act, and whether it was with reference to this particular case or not, the result, in my opinion, is the same.

The penalty falls and he can no longer represent his client because of his wrongful conduct. The result of that misconduct should be uniform, not varying with the degree of culpability or its relationship to any particular case.

"His inability to complete his contract has been brought about by his own wrongful conduct."

I would affirm the judgment.

Section 3. NO BREACH, JUSTIFICATION

My nonperformance of the contract was justified by your breach of the contract. Therefore you are the breaching party and not I.

The defendant's third response to the plaintiff's allegation of breach is "No breach, although I am not complying with the terms of the contract, my nonperformance was justified by your breach of this contract." ("Your breach justified my nonperformance.") This response couples the defendant's admission of nonperformance with the claim that the nonperformance was justified by a breach by the plaintiff. Unlike the "no breach, excuse" response, which was based on an external event (hail, locust, OPEC), the "no breach, justification" response is based on the action of the other contracting party. The defendant is *not* responding "My breach is justified by your breach." The defendant, although not admitting breach, is only admitting nonperformance. An admission of nonperformance is not the same as an admission of breach. *The defendant's nonperformance is not a breach.* Because the plaintiff rather than the defendant is the breaching party, the plaintiff cannot maintain a breach of contract action against the defendant.

A careful analysis of the justification response reveals that the defendant must prove the following:

1. The plaintiff was in breach of the contract.
2. The defendant's performance was dependent on the plaintiff's performance.
3. The plaintiff's performance was a condition precedent to the defendant's performance.
4. The magnitude of the plaintiff's breach justified the defendant's nonperformance.

This section explores these four elements of the justification response. If the defendant established these elements, he or she was justified in not performing the contract and was not in breach. Therefore, the plaintiff cannot maintain a breach of contract action. If, however, the plaintiff, the true breaching party, has conferred a benefit on the nonbreaching defendant, the breaching plaintiff could maintain a restitution action against the nonbreaching defendant. This section considers restitution as an action for the breaching plaintiff.

A. Was the Plaintiff in Breach?

The first step in the "justification response" is establishing that the plaintiff has breached the contract. If the plaintiff has not breached, the defendant cannot successfully maintain that his or her nonperformance was not a breach. The defendant's justification response will not succeed.

> *PROBLEM 13:* The Ace Painting Company contracted to paint Erica's apartment for $1,500. Erica contracted to supply the paint. When Ace arrived to paint Erica's apartment, she refused to provide them with the paint and demanded that Ace supply the paint. Ace refused and ultimately did not paint Erica's apartment. Erica then hired Russell to paint and paid Russell $2,000.
>
> Erica sued Ace for breach of contract alleging Ace breached by not painting her apartment. Ace responded, "no breach, justification."
>
> What specifically was Ace stating in its justification response? Did Erica breach the contract?

1. Entire and Divisible Performances

A contract may require one performance or a number of performances. An "entire contract" is a contract with a single performance.

EXAMPLE

> "I promise to sell you Flora, the elephant, for your promise to pay $1,500."

A "divisible contract" is a contract with separate or installment performances.

EXAMPLE

> "I promise to sell you two quarterhorses, one to be delivered this fall and the other next spring, for your promise to pay $1,500 each."

Whether a performance is entire (one performance) or divisible (multiple performances) may affect when the plaintiff breached the contract. If the performance is divisible, the plaintiff may have breached as to some of the later performances although not as to some of the earlier ones. If the plaintiff has not breached as to an early performance, the defendant may not withhold the performance that corresponds to the plaintiff's performance.

EXAMPLE

Consider the quarterhorse example. Suppose Seller delivered the first quarterhorse in the fall but refused to deliver the second in the spring. As to the fall delivery, Seller was not in breach. As to the spring delivery, Seller was in breach. If each horse was to be paid for separately, Buyer could not refuse to pay for the first horse because Seller had not breached as to the delivery of the first horse.

PROBLEM 14: The Orion Timber Company contracted to sell the Juniper Lumber Company twenty truckloads of freshly harvested trees (five truckloads of oak, five of maple, and ten of white pine). The contract provided that Juniper would pay $20,000 for each truckload of oak, $15,000 for maple, and $10,000 for pine. Orion delivered the maple and pine but did not deliver the oak. Juniper accepted the delivery of the maple and pine but subsequently refused to pay because it did not receive the oak.

Orion sued Juniper for breach of contract. What did Orion allege was Juniper's breach? If Juniper responded with a "justification response," what specifically did it say? Did Orion breach the contract? Was Orion's performance entire or divisible? What difference does this make?

2. Waiver of a Breach

Even if the plaintiff has breached the contract, the defendant might not be able to use the plaintiff's breach in its justification response if the defendant has waived the breach.

EXAMPLE

Seller contracts to sell a used car to Buyer for $2,400 with Buyer agreeing to pay in twelve monthly installments, each due on the first of the month. Buyer made the first payment on the ninth instead of on the first of the month. Seller accepted the payment but told Buyer not to let that happen again. Seller has waived Buyer's breach by ignoring the fact that the payment was late. Seller cannot later raise the late payment as a breach.

PROBLEM 15: The Horizon Construction Company received the prime contract to build a government building in Baltimore. The contract called for facing the building in Vermont marble. Horizon contracted with the Old Maine Stone Company for all of the Vermont marble that Horizon would need. Old Maine delivered New Hampshire, instead of Vermont, marble. The marbles were similar and Horizon knew when it accepted the shipment that it was New Hampshire and not Vermont marble. Horizon incorporated the marble into the structure. When the building was completed, the government refused to accept it unless the marble was changed to Vermont marble.

Could Horizon successfully sue Old Maine for breach of contract? What would Horizon allege as Old Maine's breach? Has Horizon waived Old Maine's breach?

3. Estoppel

In addition to waiver, the defendant may be estopped (precluded) from claiming that the plaintiff has breached. Unlike waiver which requires no action by the breaching party, estoppel requires that the breaching party rely on the nonbreaching party's actions.

EXAMPLE

Suppose in the sale of the car example, the first six monthly payments arrived on the ninth rather than on the first of the month. Although Buyer has been in breach by not paying on the first of each month, Seller said nothing to Buyer. Buyer relied on Seller's inaction. Seller is estopped from later raising Buyer's breach.

PROBLEM 16: In Problem 15, suppose that Old Maine had notified Horizon before shipping that it was New Hampshire rather than Vermont marble and Horizon did not object. Should Horizon be estopped from objecting after the government refuses to accept the building?

B. Was the Defendant's Performance Dependent on the Plaintiff's Performance?

For the defendant to claim a justification response, its performance must be dependent on the plaintiff's performance. If the defendant's performance is independent of the plaintiff's performance, the justification response will fail. Under modern contracts law, performances are presumed to be dependent.

PROBLEM 17: Dwayne contracted to paint Robin's portrait for Robin's promise to pay Dwayne $1,000, $200 down and the balance in $100 weekly installments. Although the painting would take about three weeks, a time was not set for its completion.

Are painting and paying independent or dependent performances?

C. Was the Plaintiff's Performance a Condition Precedent to the Defendant's Performance?

The defendant's performance must not only be dependent on the plaintiff's performance, the two performances must be scheduled in a certain order. The plaintiff's performance must occur first. The plaintiff's performance must be a condition precedent to the defendant's performance.

EXAMPLE

Tom contracted with Gary for the remodeling of Tom's kitchen. The contract required Tom to purchase the materials and Gary to do the carpentry. Tom's buying of the materials is a condition precedent to Gary's duty to remodel. If Tom does not buy materials, Gary does not have the materials with which to remodel the kitchen.

PROBLEM 18: Karen hired Stacy to tutor her in Latin. Is Karen's duty to pay a condition precedent to Stacy's tutoring or is Stacy's tutoring a condition precedent to Karen's duty to pay?

D. Did the Magnitude of the Plaintiff's Breach Justify the Defendant's Nonperformance?

The defendant may not use just any breach by the plaintiff to justify his or her nonperformance. The plaintiff's breach must be of a sufficient magnitude. If the contract is a construction contract, the plaintiff's performance must be less than "substantial performance." If the contractor has substantially performed, the owner will not be justified in nonperforming (not paying) even if the contractor did not fully perform.

PROBLEM 19: Beautiful Homes, Inc., contracted to build a house for the Culvers. Beautiful Homes promised to complete the home in ninety days and the Culvers were to pay in four installments—twenty-five percent at the time of signing the contract and twenty-five percent at the end of each month thereafter. At the end of ninety days, Beautiful Homes had the house completed except for exterior painting. Has Beautiful Homes substantially performed the contract?

If the contract is for employment rather than for construction, the language changes from "substantial performance" to "immaterial breach." An employee's immaterial breach will not justify the employer in not performing (not paying) even though the employee has not fully performed.

PROBLEM 20: The Modern Sign Company hired Alvin to solicit signs from businesses in town. The contract provided that Alvin would be paid $500 a month plus commissions. The salary was to be paid at the end of each month. After working for Modern Sign for three weeks, Alvin quit without giving the two weeks' notice required in his contract.

Was Alvin's breach material or immaterial?

If the contract is for the sale of goods, the Uniform Commercial Code governs. If the performance under evaluation relates to the goods and not to the payment and if the contract is not an installment contract, the Code (UCC § 2–601) authorizes the buyer to reject the goods that fail to conform to the contract in any respect. This is known as the perfect tender rule. UCC § 2–601 states the consequences when goods do not comply with the perfect tender rule:

Subject to the provisions of this Article on breach in installment contracts (Section 2–612) and unless otherwise agreed under the sections on contractual limitations of remedy (Sections 2–718 and 2–719), if the goods or the tender of delivery fail in any respect to conform to the contract, the buyer may

(a) reject the whole; or
(b) accept the whole; or
(c) accept any commercial unit or units and reject the rest.

EXAMPLE

John and Carol ordered a $200 wedding cake from the Elite Bakery to be delivered on April 19, at 5 P.M. Elite prepared the cake and delivered it to John and Carol's reception at 5 P.M. on April 19. As the cake was being placed on the table by Elite, the bride's mother noticed that the inscription read "John and Alice."

The cake fails to conform to the contract and can be rejected.

Although the buyer's right to reject nonconforming goods appears absolute in 2–601, the buyer's right is subject to a number of limitations. First, if the contract is an installment contract, then 2–612, rather than 2–601 applies. Perfect tender of goods in an installment is no longer required. UCC § 2–612 states:

(1) An "installment contract" is one which requires or authorizes the delivery of goods in separate lots to be separately accepted, even though the contract contains a clause "each delivery is a separate contract" or its equivalent.

(2) The buyer may reject any installment which is non-conforming if the non-conformity substantially impairs the value of that installment and cannot be cured or if the non-conformity is a defect in the required documents; but if the non-conformity does fall within subsection (3) and the seller gives adequate assurance of its cure the buyer must accept the installment.

(3) Whenever non-conformity or default with respect to one or more installments substantially impairs the value of the whole contract there is a breach of the whole. But the aggrieved party reinstates the contract if he accepts a non-conforming installment without seasonably notifying of cancellation or if he brings an action with respect only to past installments or demands performance as to future installments.

EXAMPLE

Buyer contracts to buy 300,000 tons of coal to be delivered 100,000 tons on the first day of three consecutive months. The first shipment is only 75,000 tons. Because this was an installment contract (three deliveries), Buyer cannot reject the shipment unless the shortage substantially impairs the value of that installment and the shortage cannot be cured. Furthermore, if the shortage does not substantially impair the value of the whole contract and if Seller gives adequate assurance of its cure, Buyer must accept the shipment even though it is 25,000 tons short.

Second, if the buyer exercises his or her power under 2–601 and rejects a nonconforming tender, the seller may have a right to correct the nonconformity. This is known in the Code as the seller's right to "cure." The seller does not have a right to cure in all situations but only in the following situations discussed in 2–508:

> (1) Where any tender or delivery by the seller is rejected because non-conforming and the time for performance has not yet expired, the seller may seasonably notify the buyer of his intention to cure and may then within the contract time make a conforming delivery.
>
> (2) Where the buyer rejects a non-conforming tender which the seller had reasonable grounds to believe would be acceptable with or without money allowance the seller may if he seasonably notifies the buyer have a further reasonable time to substitute a conforming tender.

EXAMPLE

Buyer contracted to purchase steel "I" beams from Seller with delivery by November 1st. Seller delivered the beams on October 7th. Buyer inspected, found the beams not to conform to the contract specifications, and rejected (UCC § 2–601). Because the time for performance has not yet expired (time for performance expires on November 1st), Seller could seasonably notify Buyer of his intention to cure (UCC § 2–508(1)). Seller then would have until November 1st to make a conforming delivery.

EXAMPLE

Consider the following case of *Wilson v. Scampoli.* Is this a 2–508(1) or 2–508(2) case? What is the difference? If the seller decided to cure, must the seller replace the goods delivered?

Wilson v. Scampoli

United States Court of Appeals, District of Columbia Circuit, 1967.
228 A.2d 848.

Before HOOD, Chief Judge, MYERS, Associate Judge, and QUINN (Associate Judge, Retired).

MYERS, Associate Judge.

This is an appeal from an order of the trial court granting rescission of a sales contract for a color television set and directing the return of the purchase price plus interest and costs.

Appellee purchased the set in question on November 4, 1965, paying the total purchase price in cash. The transaction was evidenced by a sales ticket showing the price paid and guaranteeing ninety days' free service and replacement of any defective tube and parts for a period of one year. Two days after purchase the set was delivered and uncrated, the antennae adjusted and the set plugged into an electrical outlet to "cook out." [1] When the set was turned on however, it did not function properly, the picture having a reddish tinge. Appellant's delivery man advised the buyer's daughter, Mrs. Kolley, that it was not his duty to tune in or adjust the color but that a service representative would shortly call at her house for that purpose. After the departure of the delivery men, Mrs. Kolley unplugged the set and did not use it.[2]

On November 8, 1965, a service representative arrived, and after spending an hour in an effort to eliminate the red cast from the picture advised Mrs. Kolley that he would have to remove the chassis from the cabinet and take it to the shop as he could not determine the cause of the difficulty from his examination at the house. He also made a written memorandum of his service call, noting that the television "Needs Shop Work (Red Screen)." Mrs. Kolley refused to allow the chassis to be removed, asserting she did not want a "repaired" set but another "brand new" set. Later she demanded the return of the purchase price, although retaining the set. Appellant refused to refund the purchase price, but renewed his offer to adjust, repair, or, if the set could not be made to function properly, to replace it. Ultimately, appellee instituted this suit against appellant seeking a refund of the purchase price. After a trial, the court ruled that "under the facts and circumstances the complaint is justified. Under the equity powers of the Court I will order the parties put back in their original status, let the $675 be returned, and the set returned to the defendant."

Appellant does not contest the jurisdiction of the trial court to order rescission in a proper case, but contends the trial judge erred in holding that rescission here was appropriate. He argues that he was always willing to comply with the terms of the sale either by correcting the malfunction by minor repairs or, in the event the set could not be made thereby properly operative, by replacement; that as he was denied the opportunity to try to correct the difficulty, he did not breach the contract of sale or any warranty thereunder, expressed or implied.[3]

D.C.Code § 28:2–508 (Supp. V, 1966) provides:

> (1) Where any tender or delivery by the seller is rejected because non-conforming and the time for performance has not yet expired, the seller may seasonably notify the buyer of his intention to cure and may then within the contract time make a conforming delivery.
>
> (2) Where the buyer rejects a non-conforming tender which the seller had reasonable grounds to believe would be acceptable with or without money allowance the seller may if he seasonably notifies the buyer have a further reasonable time to substitute a conforming tender.

A retail dealer would certainly expect and have reasonable grounds to believe that merchandise like color television sets, new and delivered as crated at the factory, would be acceptable as delivered and that, if defective in some way, he would have the right to substitute a conforming tender. The question then resolves itself to whether the dealer may conform his tender by adjustment or minor repair or whether he must conform

1. Such a "cook out," usually over several days, allows the set to magnetize itself and to heat up the circuit in order to indicate faulty wiring.

2. Appellee, who made his home with Mrs. Kolley, had been hospitalized shortly before delivery of the set. The remaining negotiations were carried on by Mrs. Kolley, acting on behalf of her father.

3. Appellee maintains that the delivery of a color television set with a malfunctioning color control is a breach of both an implied warranty of merchantability (D.C.Code § 28:2–314 (Supp. V, 1966)) and of an implied warranty of fitness for a particular purpose (D.C.Code § 28:2–315 (Supp. V, 1966)) and as such is a basis for the right to rescission of the sale. We find it unnecessary to determine whether a set sold under the circumstances of this case gives rise to an implied warranty of fitness for a particular purpose or whether, as appellant contends, the remedial provisions of the express warranties bind the buyer to accept these same remedial provisions as sole remedies under an implied warranty.

by substituting brand new merchandise. The problem seems to be one of first impression in other jurisdictions adopting the Uniform Commercial Code as well as in the District of Columbia.

Although the Official Code Comments do not reach this precise issue, there are cases and comments under other provisions of the Code which indicate that under certain circumstances repairs and adjustments are contemplated as remedies under implied warranties. In L & N Sales Co. v. Little Brown Jug, Inc., 12 Pa.Dist. & Co.R.2d 469 (Phila.County Ct. 1957), where the language of a disclaimer was found insufficient to defeat warranties under §§ 2–314 and 2–315, the court noted that the buyer had notified the seller of defects in the merchandise, and as the seller was unable to remedy them and later refused to accept return of the articles, it was held to be a breach of warranty. In Hall v. Everett Motors, Inc., 340 Mass. 430, 165 N.E.2d 107 (1960), decided shortly before the effective date of the Code in Massachusetts, the court reluctantly found that a disclaimer of warranties was sufficient to insulate the seller. Several references were made in the ruling to the seller's unsuccessful attempts at repairs, the court indicating the result would have been different under the Code.

While these cases provide no mandate to require the buyer to accept patchwork goods or substantially repaired articles in lieu of flawless merchandise, they do indicate that minor repairs or reasonable adjustments are frequently the means by which an imperfect tender may be cured. In discussing the analogous question of defective title, it has been stated that:

> The seller, then, should be able to cure [the defect] under subsection 2–508(2) in those cases in which he can do so without subjecting the buyer to any great inconvenience, risk or loss. Hawkland, Curing an Improper Tender of Title to Chattels: Past, Present and Commercial Code, 46 Minn.L.Rev. 697, 724 (1962). See also Willier & Hart, Forms and Procedures under the UCC, ¶ 24.07[4]; D.C.Code § 28:2–608(1)(a) (Supp. V, 1966).

Removal of a television chassis for a short period of time in order to determine the cause of color malfunction and ascertain the extent of adjustment or correction needed to effect full operational efficiency presents no great inconvenience to the buyer. In the instant case, appellant's expert witness testified that this was not infrequently necessary with new televisions. Should the set be defective in workmanship or parts, the loss would be upon the manufacturer who warranted it free from mechanical defect. Here the adamant refusal of Mrs. Kolley, acting on behalf of appellee, to allow inspection essential to the determination of the cause of the excessive red tinge to the picture defeated any effort by the seller to provide timely repair or even replacement of the set if the difficulty could not be corrected. The cause of the defect might have been minor and easily adjusted or it may have been substantial and required replacement by another new set—but the seller was never given an adequate opportunity to make a determination.

We do not hold that appellant has no liability to appellee,[4] but as he was denied access and a reasonable opportunity to repair, appellee has not shown a breach of warranty entitling him either to a brand new set or to rescission. We therefore reverse the judgment of the trial court granting rescission and directing the return of the purchase price of the set.

Reversed.

4. Appellant on appeal has renewed his willingness to remedy any defect in the tender, and thus there is no problem of expiration of his warranties. He should be afforded the right to inspect and correct any malfunction. If appellee refuses to allow appellant an opportunity to do so, then no cause of action can lie for breach of warranty, express or implied, and the loss must be borne by appellee.

Third, the buyer's right to reject nonconforming goods under 2–601 can be contracted away by the buyer. Section 2–601 expressly authorizes this consensual release of the power:

> Subject to the provisions of this Article on breach in installment contracts (Section 2–612) and *unless otherwise agreed under the sections on contractual limitations of remedy (Sections 2–718 and 2–719)*, if the goods or the tender of delivery fail in any respect to conform to the contract, the buyer may
> (a) reject the whole; or
> (b) accept the whole; or
> (c) accept any commercial unit or units and reject the rest. (Emphasis added.)

In these cases, the contracting parties will, at the time of contract, agree on what remedies will be available in the event the goods do not conform to the contract. Section 2–718(1) provides for liquidated damages:

> (1) Damages for breach by either party may be liquidated in the agreement but only at an amount which is reasonable in the light of the anticipated or actual harm caused by the breach, the difficulties of proof of loss, and the inconvenience or nonfeasibility of otherwise obtaining an adequate remedy. A term fixing unreasonably large liquidated damages is void as a penalty.

Section 2–719 discusses the contractual modification and limitation of remedies:

> (1) Subject to the provisions of subsections (2) and (3) of this section and of the preceding section on liquidation and limitation of damages,
> (a) the agreement may provide for remedies in addition to or in substitution for those provided in this Article and may limit or alter the measure of damages recoverable under this Article, as by limiting the buyer's remedies to return of the goods and repayment of the price or to repair and replacement of nonconforming goods or parts; and
> (b) resort to a remedy as provided is optional unless the remedy is expressly agreed to be exclusive, in which case it is the sole remedy.
> (2) Where circumstances cause an exclusive or limited remedy to fail of its essential purpose, remedy may be had as provided in this Act.
> (3) Consequential damages may be limited or excluded unless the limitation or exclusion is unconscionable. Limitation of consequential damages for injury to the person in the case of consumer goods is prima facie unconscionable but limitation of damages where the loss is commercial is not.

Fourth, the buyer's right to reject under 2–601 is further limited if the nonconformity deals with tender through a substitute carrier or in a substitute manner. Section 2–614(1) describes when the buyer must accept the tender made through substitute performance:

> (1) Where without fault of either party the agreed berthing, loading, or unloading facilities fail or an agreed type of carrier becomes unavailable or the agreed manner of delivery otherwise becomes commercially impracticable but a commercially reasonable substitute is available, such substitute performance must be tendered and accepted.

Fifth, the buyer's right to reject under 2–601 is still further limited in those situations where the seller is required or authorized to send the goods to the buyer and the contract does not require the seller to deliver the goods at a particular destination.

Section 2–504 defines the seller's duties and limits the buyer's right to reject to only those situations where the seller's dereliction is followed by a material delay or loss. Section 2–504 provides:

> Where the seller is required or authorized to send the goods to the buyer and the contract does not require him to deliver them at a particular destination, then unless otherwise agreed he must
>
> (a) put the goods in the possession of such a carrier and make such a contract for their transportation as may be reasonable having regard to the nature of the goods and other circumstances of the case; and
>
> (b) obtain and promptly deliver or tender in due form any document necessary to enable the buyer to obtain possession of the goods or otherwise required by the agreement or by usage of trade; and
>
> (c) promptly notify the buyer of the shipment.
>
> Failure to notify the buyer under paragraph (c) or to make a proper contract under paragraph (a) is a ground for rejection only if material delay or loss ensues.

E. Restitution as an Action for the Breaching Plaintiff

Because a breach of contract action is an action against a breaching party, and since the plaintiff, rather than the defendant, is the breaching party, the plaintiff has no cause of action against the defendant for breach of contract. The breaching plaintiff may, however, maintain a cause of action in restitution against the nonbreaching defendant if the plaintiff has conferred a benefit on the defendant.

> *PROBLEM 21:* Bradley, incarcerated for murder, hired Murphy as his legal counsel. Bradley paid Murphy $4,000 as an advance for legal services to be rendered in his defense. Before Murphy could render any legal services, Bradley committed suicide. Bradley's estate demanded that Murphy return the $4,000 and Murphy refused.
>
> If Bradley's estate sues Murphy for breach of contract, what would be the allegation of breach? What would be Murphy's response to this allegation of breach? Could the estate recover in a breach of contract action?
>
> Could Bradley's estate successfully sue Murphy in a restitution action? What benefit did Bradley confer on Murphy? Would it be unjust to permit Murphy to retain this benefit without compensating Bradley's estate?

Today, one of the more important questions dealing with the breaching plaintiff is whether the breaching purchaser of real property can recover payments made to the vendor before the purchaser's breach. Although the majority position is that restitution will not be granted, a number of jurisdictions have adopted a minority view allowing recovery and the perceptible trend is away from the rigidity of the majority rule.

Quillen v. Kelley presents the majority view. Why should the trend be away from the views expressed in this case?

Quillen v. Kelley

Court of Appeals of Maryland, 1958.
216 Md. 396, 140 A.2d 517.

PRESCOTT, Judge.

This is an appeal by the plaintiffs below from a decree of the Circuit Court for Worcester County. This decree "adjudged, ordered and decreed that the agreement of sale and purchase referred to in the proceedings is enforceable and that the petition for a declaratory decree * * * be and the same is hereby dismissed." No question is raised as to the form of the decree. It, in effect, declared that the contract entered into by the parties was not so vague and indefinite as to have been unenforceable, and the appellants were not entitled to a return of the money paid by them thereunder upon the theory that the contract was uncertain and indefinite, or upon any other theory; and we shall treat it as such.

The appellants and a certain Marie Codd Cook, as vendees, and Ethel M. Kelley and Harry P. Kelley, her husband, as vendors, entered into a written contract, dated September 1, 1952, for the purchase and sale of certain property known as "Hotel Royalton," (a hostelry whose hospitable accommodations and delectable meals are well-known throughout Maryland) together with certain chattels therein, situate in Ocean City, Maryland. The purchase price provided for in the agreement was $257,500, and the vendees obligated themselves "jointly and severally" to pay the same. Actually, however, the vendors were to receive a net amount for the property of $245,000, as $12,500 was to be paid by the vendors to Mrs. Cook, one of the vendees, who was a licensed broker, as her commission; this fact being known by all the parties.

At the time of the signing of the contract, the three vendees paid the vendors $15,000, as was provided in the agreement. The balance then remaining to be paid was $242,500. At this time, Mrs. Cook received from the vendors the sum of $5,000 on account of the commission to be paid her.

Under the terms of the agreement, a further payment of $20,000 was due on November 1, 1952. On that date, the appellants paid the vendors $12,500 in part payment of the $20,000 instalment due, and, at the request of the vendees, the vendors gave the vendees a credit of $7,500 for the balance due Mrs. Cook for her commission. Thus, the payment due on November 1, 1952, was paid in full.

The next payment due from the vendees was the sum of $40,000 which was payable on the last day of February 1953. Mrs. Cook, one of the three vendees, departed this life, intestate and hopelessly insolvent, on November 25, 1952. Shortly after her death, one of the vendees notified the vendors' attorney that the $40,000 payment due in February 1953, could not be made, and requested that the vendors agree to reduce the amount of said payment from $40,000 to $10,000, which was refused by the vendors. Thereafter, there were several conferences and meetings between the parties and their counsel, at all of which the vendees attempted to get the vendors to agree to a change in the terms of the agreement, but the vendors steadfastly adhered to the position that they expected payments in accordance with the provisions of the agreement. The vendors, being in possession of the property at the time of the vendees' default, retained possession thereof; but the record does not disclose that the vendors claimed the contract to be at an end or that they were not ready and willing to complete the contract upon compliance with its terms by the vendees, until the vendors answered the interrogatories in this suit nearly 3 years after the default.

On February 10, 1955, Ethel M. Kelley

suffered a fatal automobile accident; following her death, Harry William Kelley qualified as executor of her estate.

From the above, it will be seen that the vendees have paid unto the vendors the sum of $22,500; and the $40,000 payment due from the vendees on the last day of February, 1953, and all subsequent payments have not been made. This suit was instituted in September of 1955.

I

The appellants place their first hope of reversal on the ground of unjust enrichment. They state and earnestly urge that, even though they were in substantial default, to allow the vendors to retain their $22,500 part payments as well as the property sold by the vendors would be both inequitable and unjustifiable, and result in the unjust enrichment of the vendors at the expense of the vendees, especially as there was no provision in the subject-contract for a forfeiture. They claim the breach upon their part was neither wilful nor deliberate, and to permit the vendors to retain their money is to grant them a benefit to which they are not entitled. This presents a very interesting question, and one of growing importance throughout the country.

There can be little doubt that it was the common-law rule, which has been very generally followed and generally prevails today, that where the vendee of real property makes a part payment on the purchase price, but fails to fulfill the contract without lawful excuse, he cannot recover the payment if the vendor be ready and willing to perform his part of the contract, even though the vendor may have made a profit by reason of the default. Great United Realty Co. v. Lewis, 203 Md. 442, 446, 101 A.2d 881. And this is true whether or not the contract contains a forfeiture clause. 31 A.L.R.2d § 17, at page 96. This rule has been followed in Maryland during the course of years with a long line of decisions.

In applying this rule, there have been instances of harshness and injustice, which have caused a reconsideration of the same, in recent years, by the courts and by learned and renowned scholars and text-writers on the subject of contracts. The courts and text-writers, who do not advocate adhering to the strict common-law theory, seem to think the question of whether a plaintiff in substantial default should be given a restitutionary remedy ought to be treated in the light of the equitable rules that frown upon the enforcement of penalties and forfeitures. Both Professor Williston and Professor Corbin strongly advocate a relaxation of the harsh common-law doctrine under proper circumstances, 3 Williston, Contracts (Rev.Ed.), sec. 791; 5 Williston, op. cit., sec. 1473; 5 Corbin, Contracts, sec. 1122 etc. The common-law rule is regarded by the English Courts as unsound and intolerable. 31 A.L.R.2d at page 24. The American Law Institute recognizes the principle presented by the appellants in its famous section 357 of Restatement, Contracts, which apparently was prepared by Professor Corbin in collaboration with Justice Cardozo. 5 Corbin, Contracts, sec. 1135, n. 1. This section has been accepted in the Federal Courts, and most of the State Courts that have relaxed from the common-law rule use it as a standard. Amtorg Trading Corp. v. Miehle Printing Press, etc., 2 Cir., 206 F.2d 103; Newcomb v. Ray, 99 N.H. 463, 114 A.2d 882; Schwartz v. Syver, 264 Wis. 526, 59 N.W.2d 489, 492; Woodliff v. Al Parker Securities Co., 233 Mich. 154, 206 N.W. 499; Freedman v. Rector, etc., 37 Cal.2d 16, 230 P.2d 629, 31 A.L.R.2d 1. This Court recognized the modern trend of the law in this respect in the Lewis case, supra, 203 Md. 448, 101 A.2d 883, but decided it had no application to the facts of that case. Interesting and enlightening articles upon the subject are listed below in a foot-note.[1]

If we assume, without deciding, that the appellants' breach was not wilful or deliber-

1. 40 Yale L.J. 1013; 22 Ill.L.Rev. 315; 45 Mich.L.Rev. 935; 54 Mich.L.Rev. 871; 8 Miami Law Q. 648; 38 Minn.L.Rev. 172; 11 Wash. & Lee L.Rev. 269; 34 Tex.L.Rev. 582.

ate, and in a proper case we would accept the principles of said section 357, the appellants' position on this point still fails for, at least, two reasons. First, section 357 of Restatement, Contracts states:

"(1) Where the defendant fails or refuses to perform his contract and is justified therein by the plaintiff's own breach of duty or non-performance of a condition, but the plaintiff has rendered a part performance under the contract that is a net benefit to the defendant, the plaintiff can get judgment, except as stated in Subsection (2), for the amount of such benefit in excess of the harm that he has caused to the defendant by his own breach, in no case exceeding a ratable proportion of the agreed compensation, if

"(a) the plaintiff's breach or non-performance is not wilful and deliberate; or

"(b) the defendant, with knowledge that the plaintiff's breach of duty or non-performance of condition has occurred or will thereafter occur, assents to the rendition of the part performance, or accepts the benefit of it, or retains property received although its return in specie is still not unreasonably difficult or injurious.

"(2) The plaintiff has no right to compensation for his part performance if it is merely a payment of earnest money, or if the contract provides that it may be retained and it is not so greatly in excess of the defendant's harm that the provision is rejected as imposing a penalty.

"(3) The measure of the defendant's benefit from the plaintiff's part performance is the amount by which he has been enriched as a result of such performance unless the facts are those stated in Subsection (1b), in which case it is the price fixed by the contract for such part performance, or, if no price is so fixed, a ratable proportion of the total contract price." (Emphasis supplied.)

Thus, it is seen at the very outset that the doctrine is predicated upon the facts that the defendant refuses to fulfill his contract, is justified therein by the plaintiff's own breach, and desires to retain a benefit accruing to him as a result of the plaintiff's part performance under the contract. Comment (b) under section 357 makes this doubly clear wherein it is said: "The rules stated in the present Section are applicable *only* in those cases where the *defendant refuses* to perform as he promised and is justified in so doing by the plaintiff's breach. . . ." See also 5 Corbin, Contracts, sec. 1132, and pp. 579, 585. This is not the case of a mutual rescission of the contract. When there is no mutual rescission of the contract, there must be a showing that the vendor considers the contract at an end to entitle the vendee to restitution, for there is no right to restitution so long as the vendor is entitled to specific performance. 5 Corbin, Contracts, p. 585; Restatement, Contracts, sec. 357, comment (b). In the instant case, the evidence fails to show a refusal by the appellees to carry out their part of the contract, either before or after default by the appellants. In fact, it clearly shows that the appellees were desirous of consummating the sale: as late as May, 1953, although they had been informed as early as December, 1952, that there would be a default in the payment due in February, 1953, (and there was the actual default) we find one of the vendors calling one of the vendees over the telephone stating that the vendors were willing and anxious to carry out the contract. It is true that the vendors, in answering the interrogatories herein nearly three years after default, denied that the vendees had any further rights under the contract. In this, under the circumstances of this case, we think they were justified. But, in so far as the record is concerned, the appellees may still be ready and willing to perform the contract. As the appellants have failed to bring the case within such a factual situation as that upon which the doctrine they advance is predicated, they cannot avail themselves of the doctrine.

Second, even if the appellants had cleared the first obstacle, they still carried the burden of proof with reference to the amount they were entitled to recover. In a case of this nature (if we continue to assume, without deciding, that the principles of said section 357 correctly state the law), appellants are not entitled to recover unless it is affirmatively shown that the appellees received from the appellants' part performance more than the appellees lost, 5 Corbin, Contracts, p. 553, and to permit the appellees to retain the same would unjustly enrich them. "A person is enriched if he has received a benefit. * * * A person is unjustly enriched if the retention of the benefit would be unjust." Restatement, Restitution, sec. 1. Thus, we see that the *onus* was upon the appellants to prove the appellees received and retained from the appellants' part performance a benefit more than the appellees' loss, and, whatever that benefit was, it would be unjust to allow the appellees to retain the same. If A and B contract to purchase and sell real estate for the sum of $1,000,000, with time being of the essence of the contract, and A pays $1,000 down with the balance due in 30 days, and A defaults in the payment of the balance in 30 days, and B, thereafter, refuses to fulfill the contract because of A's default, and retains the property and the $1,000, B has received a benefit by A's part performance, but could it be seriously argued that to permit him to retain the $1,000 under a contract of these proportions would be *unjust?*

Professor Corbin ably treats this subject, 5 Corbin, Contracts, section 1132, and points out that in many of the instalment cases the amount actually paid by the plaintiff, for the restitution of which he sues, is comparatively small when considered in the light of the whole purchase-price. He considers it unlikely that in such cases the amount retained by the vendor is greater than the injury suffered from the plaintiff's breach. He points out, however, that whatever the amount, the plaintiff must show that it is greater than the injury done. The author at page 581, n. 63 feels that where the down payment is no more than 10% such proof is improbable. While not considering exactly the same principles of law as those in the instant case, in Public Industrials Corp. v. Reading Hardware Co., 3 Cir., 29 F.2d 975, a payment of $300,000 on a $3,900,000 contract was permitted to be retained; and in Mintle v. Sylvester, 202 Iowa 1128, 211 N.W. 367, retention of a payment of $35,000 on a total contract-price of $140,000 was upheld.

In said section 1132, Corbin calls attention to the fact that in some cases the down payment or the instalments paid are large in comparison to the total purchase price; and states that in such cases, if the vendee can show by proper evidence that the vendor is retaining an amount of money that, in reality, is a penalty rather than compensation for injury, he should be given judgment for restitution of that amount, and cites a substantial number of cases to support his statement. It is apparent that it would be difficult, if not impossible, to formulate a precise and comprehensive rule in those cases where the vendee proves that the vendor's benefit exceeds his loss, as to the exact percentage of the total contract-price that it would be "just" or "unjust" to permit the vendor to retain (i.e., whether or not it would amount to a penalty or a forfeiture); but each case should be considered and decided on its own facts and circumstances, and judgment rendered in accordance with justice and equity.

In the instant case, the vendors received $22,500, about 9% of the total price agreed to be paid, from the vendees. The vendees completely failed in carrying the burden of proof and showing that this amount exceeded the vendors' loss. The only evidence which they attempted to offer was the "records of the Hotel Royalton for the years 1953 and 1954," which the chancellors ruled were inadmissible. Without considering the correctness of this ruling, it is obvious, without some special proffer such as a sale at an advanced price, that the records of the operation of the Hotel for two years would not show whether the vendors had suffered a loss for the failure to consummate a sale thereof at an agreed price. The appellants, therefore, also fail upon this ground to bring themselves within the purview of unjust enrichment of the vendors, even if we assume, as above stated, that the principles of said section 357 correctly state the Maryland law with reference to unjust enrichment.

II

The appellants follow with another claim that the agreement of sale is so vague, ambiguous and indefinite that it is void, and, if so, they are entitled to a refund of the payments made thereon by them. The contract, as to be expected of one of this nature, is quite lengthy, and it would unduly enlarge this opinion to set it out in full.

It needs little, if any, citation of authority to sustain the statement that if an agreement be so vague and indefinite that it is impossible to collect from it the full intention of the parties, it is void, Strickler Engineering Corp. v. Seminar, 210 Md. 93, 101, 122 A.2d 563; Robinson v. Gardiner, 196 Md. 213, 217, 76 A.2d 354, and the vendee is entitled to a refund of any payments made upon the purchase price. Globe Home Improvement Co. v. Brothers, 204 Md. 73, 74, 102 A.2d 748. But courts are reluctant to reject an agreement, regularly and fairly made, as unintelligible or insensible. The agreement will be sustained if the meaning of the parties can be ascertained, either from the express terms of the instrument or by fair implication. The law does not favor, but leans against the destruction of contracts because of uncertainty; therefore, the courts will, if possible, so construe the contract as to carry into effect the reasonable intention of the parties if that can be ascertained. Middendorf, Williams & Co. v. Alexander Milburn Co., 134 Md. 385, 387, 388, 107 A. 7. Cf. Trotter v. Lewis, 185 Md. 528, 45 A.2d 329; Schloss v. Davis, 213 Md. 119, 131 A.2d 287.

The appellants argue on this point first that the interest charges required to be paid by the vendees are uncertain and ambiguous, and the agreement fails to provide specifically when settlement is to be made. They claim, in quite some detail, that the contract fails to state with sufficient clarity for what period or from what dates interest should be paid on different amounts. To set forth and consider each claim would require a long opinion to be much longer. We think it sufficient to say that a careful reading and re-reading of their claims and the agreement show that the contract is definite, certain and unambiguous in its requirements concerning interest charges; certainly there is no possible ambiguity therein beyond the reach of construction. Rocklin v. Eanet, 200 Md. 351, 89 A.2d 572. And, if we assume, without deciding, that an agreement of this kind must specifically provide when settlement shall take place, it is also clear and certain in this regard.

The appellants further argue that the agreement fails to state the terms and conditions of the purchase money mortgage and what amount of insurance on the property must be carried by the vendees, and these facts are fatal to its validity under the ruling of this Court in Applestein v. Royal Realty Corp., 180 Md. 274, 23 A.2d 684. That case dealt with what the Court considered an ambiguous clause in a contract relative to the payment of principal under a mortgage required to be given by a contract of sale of real estate. The Court concluded that this clause contained inconsistent requirements; but, when the case again came to this Court, 181 Md. 171, 28 A.2d 830, it was held that parol evidence and the proof of custom and usage were admissible to clear up the ambiguity. The opinion in the first case, 180 Md. at page 277, 23 A.2d at page 685, specifically pointed out that covenants to be placed in a mortgage, when they go beyond providing for the mere creation of a lien, are necessarily the subject of agreement between the parties; that matters such as whether the interest is to be paid annually, who is to be obligated to pay the taxes, or that the buildings should be insured are not essentially involved in a valid mortgage; and, if the contract between the parties be silent on such points, a provision therein for the execution of a mortgage is fully complied with by the execution of a mortgage containing no such covenants. See also Hartsock v. Mort, 76 Md. 281, 291, 25 A. 303. Compare Triebert v. Burgess, 11 Md. 452; Caplan v. Buckner, 123 Md. 590, 91 A. 481; Fifer v.

Hoover, 163 Md. 381, 163 A. 848; Rocklin v. Eanet, supra, 200 Md. 358, 89 A.2d 575.

Of course, if an attempt be made in the agreement of sale to set out a term or terms of a mortgage provided for therein such must be done by clear, definite and certain language; but additional terms, not essentially involved in creating the mortgage or lien, are not prerequisite to the agreement being clear and definite. If additional terms have been agreed upon, they, unquestionably, should be included in the contract. Kikas v. County Com'rs of Baltimore County, 200 Md. 360, 365, 89 A.2d 625; but, simply because additional terms have not been agreed upon does not, of itself, render the contract vague and uncertain. The contract in the present case provided that the unpaid instalments of the purchase price would be represented by ten "joint and several bills obligatory" payable at stated dates, which were to be secured "by the execution and delivery of a purchase money mortgage, mortgage bill of sale or such other instrument as may be necessary to properly and legally reconvey said property, real and personal, to the vendors to secure said bills obligatory * * *." Here, the intention of the parties seems perfectly clear: the balance of the purchase money was to be evidenced by "bills obligatory," and the vendees were obligated to execute a written bond or memorial, which would reconvey the property to the vendors so that the property would remain as security for the payments due from the vendees. The mere fact that the vendees were given a choice of performing this portion of the contract in any one of several ways does not render it uncertain. Restatement, Contracts, sec. 370, comment d. As was the case in Hartsock v. Mort, supra, the mortgage (or other instrument) was to create a lien upon the property in favor of the vendors; and the contract in this regard could have been completely complied with by the execution of a mortgage containing the covenants, and only the covenants, required by the contract. We find no uncertainty or ambiguity here.

Under this same heading, the alleged uncertainty and ambiguity in the contract, the appellants list no less than twelve sub-headings, with the sub-headings again divided on, at least, one occasion into three "queries." To consider and answer each of these in detail would prolong this opinion beyond reasonable bounds. Each contention has been thoroughly considered, and we are unable to discover anything therein that would warrant our determining the contract to be void as being vague, indefinite or ambiguous.

III

The appellants make as their final contention "the appellees rescinded and/or terminated the contract." As stated by them, this claim is not exactly clear, but we assume that they argue there was a mutual rescission of the contract; because, if there were no mutual rescission but merely a determination by the vendors, after the vendees' default, that the contract was at an end and that the vendors were entitled to the payments made, the right of the vendees to recover such payments would be governed by the common-law rule or the doctrine of unjust enrichment as explained in I. 5 Corbin, Contracts, sec. 1131, pp. 584–590. A contract may, of course, be rescinded by mutual assent, but a breach of contract is not an offer to rescind. The validity of an agreement to rescind a contract is governed by the same rules as in the case of other contracts; and the mutual rights of the parties are determined by the terms of the rescission agreement. 5 Corbin, Contracts, sec. 1131, p. 582. The appellants, however, are unable to obtain any succor from this source due to the fact that there is not a scintilla of evidence that the contract involved in this case was ever rescinded by mutual agreement.

Decree affirmed with costs.

If the contract were for the sale of goods, the courts would give restitutionary relief to a breaching seller. Before the enactment of the UCC, the majority of courts treated a breaching buyer of goods the same as a breaching purchaser of real property. In both cases a majority of courts refused to give the breaching buyer restitutionary relief. Under 2–718 of the UCC, the breaching buyer has gained some rights. Section 2–718 requires the seller to return to the buyer so much of the deposit or down payment as exceeds the damages which the seller in fact sustains. This reverses pre-Code authority which generally regarded a buyer's willful refusal to take proper goods as forfeiting the right to the return of the down payment.

Courts are split over whether a contractor who has not substantially performed may recover in a restitution action for benefits conferred on the nonbreaching owner. Some courts apparently reject restitution as a cause of action in these cases. Some courts permit restitution but only if the contractor's breach was not willful or "voluntary." Other courts permit restitution even where the contractor is guilty of a willful breach of the contract. If a court does permit the breaching contractor to maintain a restitution action and the contractor's costs exceed the value conferred, the contractor's recovery will be limited to the actual value to the defendant rather than the contractor's cost of construction.

Peters v. Halligan

Supreme Court of Nebraska, 1967.
182 Neb. 51, 152 N.W.2d 103.

Heard before WHITE, C.J., and CARTER, SPENCER, BOSLAUGH, SMITH, McCOWN, and NEWTON, JJ.

WHITE, Chief Justice.

The defendants Halligan appeal from a judgment of the district court foreclosing a mechanic's lien for labor and materials in the sum of $1,576.82 furnished in the construction of a basement on defendants' property.

In his petition plaintiff alleges that he was employed to construct and furnish the material for a basement on the defendants' premises and that the fair and reasonable value of the labor and material charges was in the sum of $1,576.82. Defendants, in an answer and cross-petition, allege that the plaintiff did perform work and labor on their premises under an oral contract; that the plaintiff entered into an oral contract with the defendants to construct a basement and a frame addition to the trailer home of the defendants for the agreed sum of $2,850; that thereafter the plaintiff did construct the basement; that it was defectively constructed by reason of the failure of the plaintiff to properly seal and waterproof the floor; that after construction of the basement plaintiff refused to construct the frame addition to defendants' trailer as provided under the oral contract; that the defendants were required to employ another contractor to construct the trailer house addition; and that by reason of the defective construction work in the basement and the additional cost of constructing the trailer house addition they were damaged in the sum of $1,968.20.

Outside the question of defective workmanship in the construction of the basement, the basic question involved in this case is whether the parties entered into a contract for an agreed price for the construction of a basement and the trailer house addition. In approaching this problem, we bear in mind the basic rule that a fundamental and indispensable basis of any enforceable agreement is that there be a meeting of the minds of the parties as to the essential terms and conditions of the proposed contract. Voss v. Linn, 171 Neb. 32, 105 N.W.2d 383; Griggs v. Oak, 164 Neb. 296, 82 N.W.2d 410. The evidence in this case is in irreconcilable conflict consisting of the testimony of Peters and the defendant Clinton J. Halligan. A few days prior to August 25, 1965, the Halligans contacted Peters in Ogallala, Nebraska, about the building of an addition on their trailer house which, at that time, was located on their parents' property but which they planned to move to their property south of Brule, Nebraska. Peters told them that he was building a house at that time; that he did not know whether he had time to do the job; and that he had never done anything like that before. In response to the Halligans' request, Peters went out to the trailer house to discuss the matter with them. At this time they talked about moving one wall of the trailer out to form the outside wall of the new addition and filling in the ends and the ceiling. They discussed the subfloor and the flooring, the stairwell location in the basement, the moving and possible installation of cupboards, and various other details as to the addition. At this time, the Halligans stated they wanted a basement under the trailer house that was to be constructed on their property south of Brule on which the trailer was to be moved, and there was discussion of the details of the basement construction. Peters testified that the main thing that the Halligans were interested in was to get the basement done so they could get the trailer moved to their property south of Brule. After this conversation the parties visited the Halligan place south of Brule to inspect the construction site. The basement under the trailer house was to be 20 feet by 48 feet and the basement under the new addition was to be 12 feet by 22 feet. Peters' attention was called to a spring located close to the proposed site of the basement and to a wet spot at the site of the excavation. Peters told Halligan that in order to prevent any water problem he was going to put in a polyethylene seal.

Peters testified he told the Halligans, with reference to the construction of the addition, that he did not know actually when he could do it; that he could not give them any possible date; that at all times in his conversation with them he stressed there was no way he could give an exact figure because he did not know exactly what they had in mind; that he did not know what he might run into; that he had never done anything like that before; and that the cost of an ordinary basement was at least $1,000 for the blocks and laying.

It appears from the plaintiff's evidence that he did not do any plumbing or electrical work and, in the preliminary negotiations, there was no discussion as to the electrical work or the plumbing other than hooking up a temporary toilet drain in the trailer prior to the time of the construction of the addition. The testimony is that the defendants were securing an F.H.A. loan to finance the basement and the addition. Peters testified that in giving the Halligans a figure of $1,800 on the addition and a figure of $1,000 on the basement these were only estimates and the defendants "would have to allow accordingly." The evidence shows that there were no written plans or specifications for the building of the addition or the basement and none were ever introduced into evidence in this case. Peters testified that there were some rough specifications in writing submitted to the F.H.A. for the loan but again the substance of his testimony is that this was a mere estimate and he could not give an exact figure because he did not know exactly what they wanted and because he did not know what he might run into in building the addition.

Defendant Halligan's testimony varies considerably from the plaintiff's testimony.

He testified that when Peters came out to discuss the addition they discussed "what ideas we had as far as the addition to the kitchen." He says they discussed the size of the addition, the construction and size of the basement, the floor covering, the details of the walls, the building of the walls out 12 feet from the trailer, the exterior to be aluminum covered, the interior to be of wood paneling, the ceiling, the placement of the stairway, the building of cabinets and their location, the installation of insulation and aluminum windows, the moving of the sink, and the electrical outlets around the top of the counters. They made a trip to the basement site where they discussed the details of the construction and Halligan advised Peters about the spring and asked him about a water problem in the basement. He says that the plaintiff was taking notes in a small notebook during this period of time and after these conversations Peters left and returned and told defendant Halligan that it would cost $1,850 to build the kitchen. He had previously given him a figure of $1,000 on the basement. Halligan told him that he needed these figures for the F.H.A. in order to get a loan. He does not testify that they had a specific conversation or agreement that this would be the contract price. That inference must be drawn from the following testimony on the part of Halligan: "When he told us the figures that he had, we told him that was agreeable with us, and asked him when he could start construction, ..."

We observe that no explanation appears as to why the defendant Halligan's wife did not testify in this case and corroborate his testimony. We observe further that Peters' repeated and precise testimony that the figures he furnished the Halligans were only estimates and the reasons he gave therefor stand undenied in the record by Halligan.

The basement was finished about October 25, 1965. In November or December 1965, defendants received a partial bill for $1,356 and a final one for $1,586.31. In their conversations Peters demanded payment and we observe that Halligan did not object to the amount or assert that the contract was for $1,000 but merely stated to the plaintiff that he had not finished cleaning up the material at the site of the excavation. In a conversation in the first part of November 1965, Halligan told the plaintiff that he was planning on him constructing the addition and was wondering when he could start it. Halligan not only made no objections to the bill rendered him for the cost of materials and labor but we could reasonably infer that he intended to proceed on the same basis of payment with reference to the addition when he inquired of the plaintiff and insisted that the plaintiff begin work on the addition. We are further aided in the determination of this issue by the rule that where there is irreconcilable conflict on a material issue, this court will, in determining the weight of the evidence of witnesses who appear in court to testify, consider the fact that the trial court observed them and their manner of testifying and must have accepted one version of the facts rather than the other. Uptegrove v. Elsasser, 161 Neb. 527, 74 N.W.2d 61; Brown v. Brown, 146 Neb. 908, 22 N.W.2d 148; O'Brien v. Fricke, 148 Neb. 369, 27 N.W.2d 403. The trial court must have found, in coming to the conclusion that it did, that there was no contract between the parties for the building of the basement and the addition for the agreed prices of $1,000 for the basement and $1,850 for the addition, or a total of $2,850. We come to the same conclusion.

The defendants strongly contend, nevertheless, after the basement was done, that the plaintiff Peters refused to perform the contract for the building of the trailer addition; that he gave no excuse for his action except that he would not and could not do it; that therefore he abandoned the contract; and that he is not entitled to recover on a quantum meruit basis for the reasonable cost and charge of the labor and materials furnished. There is no question, under the evidence, that in November 1965 the plaintiff informed the defendants that he could not construct the addition. Accepting defendants' own testimony in this respect, Halligan testified that the plaintiff told him that he had a man hired who he was going to send out to complete the addition on the trailer house but Halligan told him, "Well, if you are not going to complete the job, I will do my own hiring, as far as completing it." The evidence shows that the defendants did hire a contractor by the name of Hopken to construct the trailer addition on a labor and material basis at a total cost of $4,580.84 which represented the fair and reasonable cost therefor. Assuming, therefore, that the plaintiff did contract to build the trailer addition and that his failure and refusal to construct it constituted a lack of substantial performance, the question arises as to whether this action forfeits the plaintiff's right to establish a mechanic's lien for the reasonable value of his services performed and the labor and material furnished. Our mechanic's lien statute provides as follows: "Any person who shall perform any labor or furnish any material, ... for the construction, erection, improvement, repair, ... of any house, ... building, or appurtenance, ... by virtue of a contract or agreement, expressed or implied, with the owner thereof or his agents, shall have a lien to secure the payment of the same upon such house, ... building, or appurtenance and the lot of land upon which the same shall stand or the work is performed, ..." S. 52–101, R.R.S.1943.

Our mechanic's lien statutes are cumulative and remedial in nature and require a liberal construction so as to effectuate their objects and purposes, and they find their basis in the equitable principle that everyone who, by his labor and materials, contributes to the preservation or enhancement of the property of another, thereby acquires a right to compensation. Muenchau v. Swarts, 170 Neb. 209, 102 N.W.2d 129; Greenblatt v. Goldin (Fla.), 94 So.2d 355, 59 A.L.R.2d 877. We note that our statute refers to "any person" who performs labor or furnishes material "by virtue of a contract or agreement, expressed or implied" shall be entitled to a lien. The statute does not require any particular degree of performance of a contract, but simply uses the term "by virtue of a contract or agreement." It is inferable from the language of the statute itself that a person is entitled to a lien for the reasonable value of the benefit conferred upon property, irrespective of the degree of performance of the contract. The question is apparently a first impression in this state. As far as we can determine, this court has never held that even if a contractor abandons his contract, he forfeits any right to recover for material and labor actually performed of benefit and value to the defendant's property. We have held, however, in construing our mechanic's lien statutes that if the furnishing of material and labor under a contract is sufficient to create an indebtedness or liability, it is sufficient to create a lien under the provisions of the statute. Rosebud Lumber & Coal Co. v. Holms, 155 Neb. 459, 52 N.W.2d 313; Great Western Manufacturing Co. v. Hunter Bros., 15 Neb. 32, 16 N.W. 759. The general rule is that in spite of lack of substantial performance, where there has been a part performance and it has been of substantial benefit to the other party and he has accepted and retained the benefits thereof, he should not be permitted entirely to avoid the duties assumed by him under his contract, and, under such circumstances, the party partially performing is entitled to recover the reasonable or fair value of such performance, subject to the reciprocal right of the other party to recoup such damages as he has suffered from the failure of the plaintiff to perform fully or substantially his contract. 17A C.J.S. Contracts § 511, pp. 829 and 830; 17 Am.Jur.2d, Contracts, s. 379, p. 823. But the defendants claim that there can, in no case, be a recovery in case of a voluntary incompletion or abandonment of the contract, which they assert to be a fact in this case. On this question there appears to be a conflict in the authorities. It is true that in the cases cited by the defendants in some jurisdictions a party who abandons a contract or refuses to perform it cannot recover, either on the contract or on a quantum meruit, the value of the labor or materials he has expended in his partial performance. The opposite and we believe the better view is held in other jurisdictions. It is pointed out in the authorities discussing this question that a party who contracts to perform certain specified labor and to furnish materials and then breaks his contract in the first instance, without any attempt to perform it, can be made liable to pay only the damages which the other party has sustained by reason of such nonperformance, which in many instances may be trifling. A party who has entered upon a contract, even though he has not substantially performed it, may have rendered a substantial benefit to the other party, and yet be subjected to a loss of all which he has performed in the nature of damages for the nonfulfillment of the remainder of the contract, upon the technical rule that the contract must be substantially performed in order to warrant a recovery of any part of the compensation. The rule denying recovery, therefore, puts the party who partially performs his contract in a much worse position than one who wholly disregards his contract, and the other party may receive much more, by the breach of the contract than the injury he has sustained by such breach and more than he could be entitled to if he were seeking to recover damages by an action. We believe the better rule to be that a party may recover on a quantum meruit basis for partial performance for the value of benefits conferred even though he abandons the contract or refuses to perform it, subject to any counterclaim for damages that the other party has sustained by reason of the breach of the agreement. See, 17 Am.Jur.2d, Contracts, s. 380, p. 824; Pixler v. Nichols, 8 Iowa 106; Zimmerle v. Felzien, 121 Kan. 34, 245 P. 1024; Lee & Dolen v. Ashbrook, 14 Mo. 378; Parcell v. McComber, 11 Neb. 209, 7 N.W. 529, 38 Am.R. 366; McMillan v. Malloy, 10 Neb. 228, 4 N.W. 1004, 35 Am.R. 471; Britton v. Turner, 6 N.H. 481; Lynn v. Seby, 29 N.D. 420, 151 N.W. 31. We note further that the annotator in the American Jurisprudence citations above cites two Nebraska authorities in sustaining the rule we have announced herein. In McMillan v. Malloy, supra, the plaintiff entered into a contract to thresh an entire crop of wheat for the defendant. He threshed only about one-third of the crop and then sued to recover the value of his services. The court held: ". . . that the entirety of the contract having been severed by part performance, beneficial to the employer, the employee was entitled to recover the value of his labor over and above the damages sustained by a breach of the contract." More closely in point is the case of Millsap v. Ball, 30 Neb. 728, 46 N.W. 1125, wherein this court said as follows: "If we understand the position of Grove's counsel it is this: That neither a contractor nor a subcontractor can enforce a mechanic's lien where the building is not completed according to contract. We cannot accept this as a correct statement of the law. There is certainly no legislative enactment so limiting the right of the mechanic or materialman to a lien. He must establish his account; and the lien attaches for the amount found to be due thereon. If the contract for the erection of the building is not fulfilled by the contractor, it does not necessarily defeat his lien. The owner of the building is entitled to set up, as a counter-claim, any damages he has sustained by reason of the breach of the agreement, and the lien attaches for the amount actually due after deducting such damages."

We feel that the conclusion we come to follows the language and the purpose of the statute and the holding that if the furnishing of material and labor under a contract is sufficient to create an indebtedness or liability, it is sufficient to create a lien under the provisions of the statute. Rosebud Lumber & Coal Co. v. Holms, 155 Neb. 459, 52 N.W.2d 313.

We further note that there were two distinct parts to this contract, one for the construction of the basement and one for the trailer addition. The parties considered them separately, both during their negotiations and during the conversations that followed the construction of the basement. The general rule is that a party who has failed fully to perform his contract cannot recover on the contract for part performance applies only to entire indivisible, and not to severable, contracts; and there may be a recovery on the contract for a part performance of a divisible contract. 17 Am.Jur.2d, Contracts, s. 386, p. 831. We therefore hold that the plaintiff is entitled to recover on a quantum meruit basis for the reasonable cost and charge of labor and materials furnished in the construction of the defendants' basement and that the defendants' rights are fully protected because they may, and have, set up a breach of the contract as a basis for the claim of damages.

The only remaining question is whether the defendants are entitled to recover on their counterclaim for the breach of the contract. Defendants in their brief do not contend that they are entitled to any net affirmative damages but only ask that the plaintiff's petition for enforcement of the lien be dismissed. As we have noted, defendants have not proved a contract for a definite price for the building of the trailer addition. Their own evidence shows that they hired Hopken to complete the trailer addition on the basis of a reasonable cost for labor and materials. The evidence shows that the trailer addition was constructed in a substantially different manner than was contemplated in the original discussion with the plaintiff Peters. There is no evidence that there were any damages due to the delay in the construction or that the cost of the labor and materials was higher than if the plaintiff had completed the contract. On the other hand, the almost undisputed evidence is that Peters did not perform a proper and workmanlike job in waterproofing the basement. He knew there was a water problem and undertook, after discussion with the defendants, to protect the basement from water by placing polyethylene strips underneath the concrete floor. He failed to properly lap and seal the strips of polyethylene used, and drove stakes through the strips, creating holes, through which water leaked. The evidence shows that water seeped through cracks in the basement floor and that at times water collected to the extent of a 4–inch depth for which the defendants had to install a sump pump to remove the water. The defendants' evidence supplied by the contractor Hopken is that the reasonable value of the basement was reduced by the sum of $300 in this respect. The evidence shows that the reasonable cost and value of the labor and materials furnished in the basement were $1,576.82 and there appears no dispute in the evidence as to the reasonable cost and charge for these items. We therefore come to the conclusion that the plaintiff is entitled to a lien in the sum of $1,576.82 less the amount of $300 for damages due to the failure to properly perform the work of waterproofing the floor or a total net amount of $1,276.82, and the decree of the district court is modified accordingly. As modified the decree is affirmed.

Affirmed as modified.

BOSLAUGH, McCOWN, and SPENCER, Justices (concurring).

We concur in the decision of the court that the judgment of the district court as modified should be affirmed upon the ground that the contract between the parties was severable and the record will support a finding of substantial performance of the contract to construct the basement.

We do not agree that a party may recover on a quantum meruit basis for partial performance for the value of benefits conferred even though he abandons the contract or refuses to perform it, subject to any counterclaim for damages that the other party has sustained by reason of the breach of the agreement. Generally, substantial performance is a condition precedent to any recovery where there is an express contract between the parties. See, Rickertsen v. Carskadon, 172 Neb. 46, 108 N.W.2d 392; McGowan v. Gate City Malt Co., 89 Neb. 10, 130 N.W. 965.

Recovery upon a quantum meruit basis where there has been no substantial performance should be limited to the circumstances specified in Restatement, Contracts, s. 357, p. 623.

Section 4. NO BREACH, TERMINATED DUTY

I no longer have to perform according to the contract. My obligation no longer exists due to some duty terminating occurrence. I am not in breach.

The defendant's fourth response to the plaintiff's allegation of breach is "No breach, although I am not complying with the terms of the contract, my duty to perform the contract has been terminated." This "No breach, terminated duty" response couples the defendant's admission of nonperformance with a claim that the defendant's contractual duty has ended either by agreement or by law and therefore the defendant is not in breach of contract. The terminating occurrence may be consensual (substitute contract, accord and satisfaction, or novation), unilateral (release, waiver, or estoppel), or by operation of law (statute of limitations). Because the defendant is not the breaching party, the plaintiff cannot maintain a breach of contract action against the defendant.

Unlike the "no breach, compliance," "no breach, justification," and "no breach, excuse" responses, a restitution action is not available.

A. Consensual Termination of a Duty

A contractual duty may be terminated by the consent of the contracting parties. Consent will involve a contractual relationship with all the trappings of consideration. Contracts such as the substitute contract, the accord and satisfaction, and the novation illustrate termination by consent. We have or will discuss each in detail in another part of this text: substitute contract (see pages 173–175); accord and satisfaction (see pages 178–181); and novation (see pages 373–386).

B. Unilateral Termination of a Duty

A contractual duty may also be terminated by a unilateral act by the party to whom the duty is owed, the promisee. Such a termination may take the form of a release, a waiver, or estoppel. We have discussed each in detail: release (see pages 175–178); waiver (see pages 303–304); and estoppel (see page 304).

C. Termination of a Duty by Operation of Law

A contractual duty may also be terminated by operation of law. An illustration is the statute of limitations.

PROBLEM 22: Ultrasound Electronics Company contracted to purchase twenty-five TVs from Sound Warehouse, a wholesaler, for the 1983 Christmas season. Although the TVs were to be delivered by November 1, 1983, they were actually delivered on January 15, 1984, too late for Christmas.

On March 1, 1987, Ultrasound filed a breach of contract action against Sound Warehouse, alleging as breach the late delivery. If the statute of limitations for breach of contract actions is three years, could Sound Warehouse answer the allegation of breach with the "no breach, terminated duty" response?

Section 5. BREACH

Yes, I admit I breached the contract.

If the defendant is unsuccessful in using any of the four responses discussed in this chapter, he or she has little alternative but to admit as true the plaintiff's allegation that the contract has been breached.

The law of contracts does not evaluate the mental state accompanying nonperformance. Because an intentional breach will have the same significance as an unintentional breach, a contracting party may intentionally breach a contract if not performing the contract is in his or her best economic interest.

PROBLEM 23: Johnson, a fashion designer, contracted to work for Top Line Fashions for one year at $20,000 a month. After working for Top Line for two months, Johnson received an offer to work for The Ultra, another fashion designer, for $25,000 a month. Top Line replaced Johnson with Swanson at a salary of $22,000 a month.

Was Johnson's breach of contract financially beneficial to her? Did it matter whether her breach was intentional or unintentional?

If the conclusion from the Fourth Step is "breach," the plaintiff has established a cause of action against the defendant for breach of contract. The plaintiff may now consider an appropriate remedy for the defendant's breach.

If the defendant has breached the contract, the plaintiff may not seek an action in restitution even though he or she has conferred a benefit on the defendant. The plaintiff does not have the power to choose between a breach of contract action and a restitution action. The party who conferred a benefit on the other is never in a position to elect which cause of action to pursue. A restitution action is not an alternative to a breach of contract action.

This is not to say that the plaintiff may not seek restitution in a breach of contract action. The restitution sought in a breach of contract action is to protect a restitution interest, which is one of the three interests protected in a breach of contract action. This restitution remedy in a breach of contract action is not the same as a restitution remedy in a restitution action. What we have covered thus far has been the restitution action and not the restitution remedy for a breach of contract action.

PART V

Step Five: Plaintiff's Remedies for the Defendant's Breach of Contract

13

PLAINTIFF'S REMEDIES FOR THE DEFENDANT'S BREACH OF CONTRACT

Once an enforceable contract has been breached, the nonbreaching party (the injured party) may successfully maintain an action for breach of contract. The injured party is entitled to a remedy for the breaching party's breach. The remedies for breach of contract compensate the injured party not only for lost expectations under the contract (expectation interest), but also for costs incurred while relying on the contract (reliance interest) and for any benefit conferred by the injured party on the breaching party for which it would be unjust to permit the breaching party to retain without compensating the injured party (restitution interest). (See figure on the next page.) Although the injured party generally fares best with compensation based on lost expectations, compensation based on reliance or restitution may, at times, exceed compensation based on contract expectations. The following materials explore these three interests.

Section 1. PROTECTING PLAINTIFF'S EXPECTATION, RELIANCE, AND RESTITUTION INTERESTS

EXPECTATION DAMAGES

When parties contract, they have expectations about what their net economic gains will be once the contract is performed. Protecting the nonbreaching party's expectation interest places the nonbreaching party in the position he or she would have been in had both parties fully performed the contract according to its terms.

When evaluating expectation interests, courts attempt to (1) give the nonbreaching party what he or she expected to receive; and (2) have the nonbreaching party give what he or she expected to give. Thus the nonbreaching party will be placed at the point of full performance.

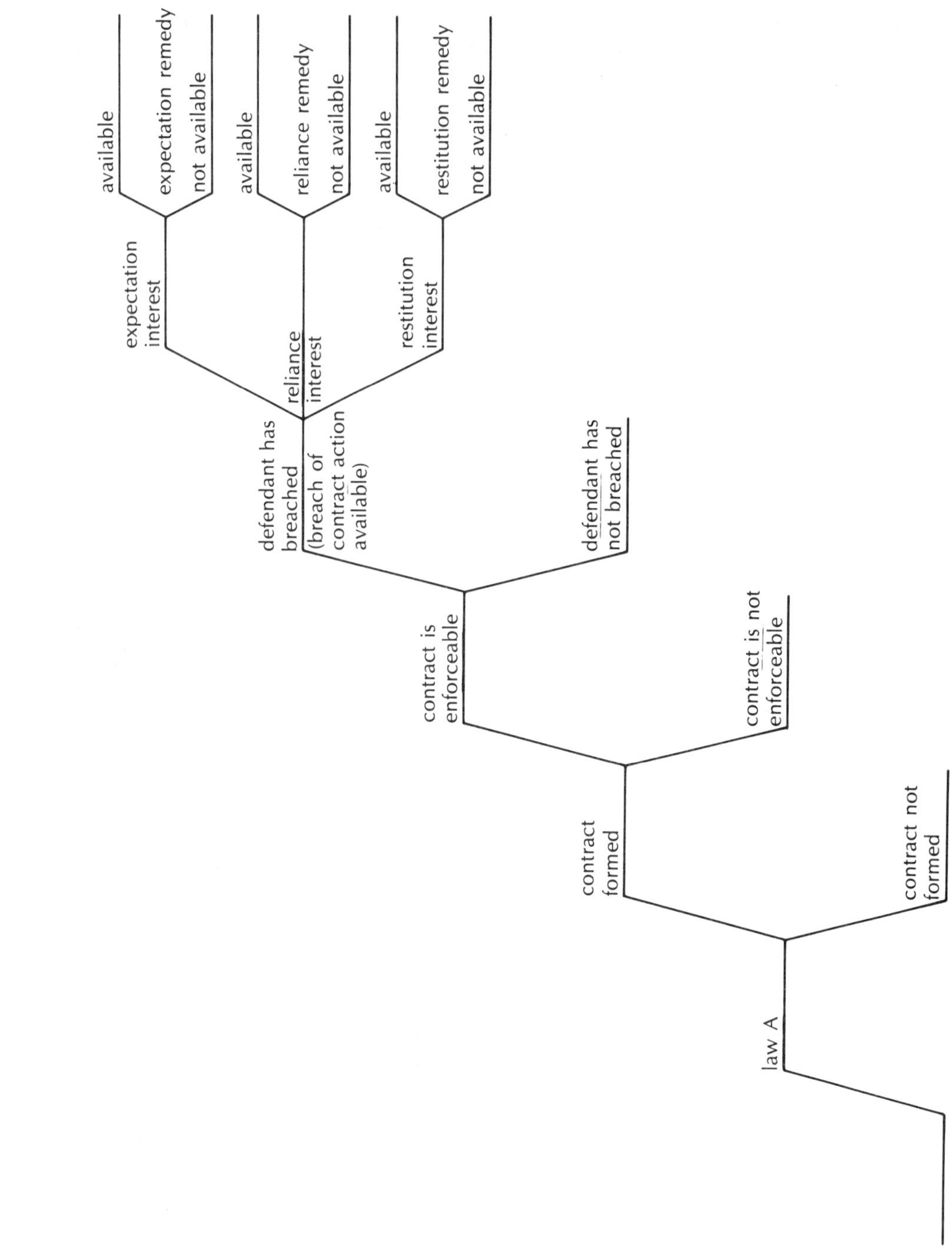

EXAMPLE

The Parkdale School District contracted with AAA Paving Company for the repaving of the District's parking lots. The contract price was $1,000,000. Shortly after entering the contract, AAA notified Parkdale that it would not pave.

Parkdale then contracted with the Quality Paving Company for the repaving at a price of $1,200,000. Parkdale sued AAA for breach of contract seeking expectation damages.

Parkdale is entitled to $200,000 in expectation damages from AAA. Parkdale, the injured party, will receive the paving (although from Quality rather than AAA) and will ultimately pay $1,000,000 to have the parking lots paved. (Parkdale will pay Quality $1,200,000 but will recoup $200,000 from AAA so Parkdale's net payment will be $1,000,000.)

The formula for expectation damages reads: *[(what the nonbreaching party expected to receive) less (what the nonbreaching party did receive)] less [(what the nonbreaching party expected to give) less (what the nonbreaching party did give)].*

The following diagram is useful in visualizing the expectation damage formula.

what the nonbreaching party expected to receive	what the nonbreaching party expected to give
what the nonbreaching party did receive	what the nonbreaching party did give

The two left quadrants are the "receiving" quadrants; the two right quadrants are the "giving" quadrants. The two left and the two right quadrants depict the two halves of the offer or the acceptance. (The diagram depicts the offer if the offeree is in breach and depicts the acceptance if the offeror is in breach.) The left quadrants deal with "for your promise to give me . . ." and the right quadrants deal with "I promise to give you. . . ." The top two quadrants are expectation and the top right subtracted from the top left represents profits. The bottom right quadrant must be subdivided between that which has been given pursuant to the contract and post-breach expenses incurred by the nonbreaching party to salvage the contract, retrieve or protect the goods or otherwise mitigate damages. These post-breach expenses are incidental damages.

what the nonbreaching party expected to receive	what the nonbreaching party expected to give
what the nonbreaching party did receive	what the nonbreaching party did give pursuant to the contract . . . . post-breach expenses (incidental damages)

In a contract for the sale of goods, the seller's incidental damages (UCC § 2–710) include:

> any commercially reasonable charges, expenses or commissions incurred in stopping delivery, in the transportation, care and custody of goods after the buyer's breach, in connection with return or resale of the goods or otherwise resulting from the breach.

The buyer's incidental damages (UCC § 2–715) include:

> expenses reasonably incurred in inspection, receipt, transportation and care and custody of goods rightfully rejected, any commercially reasonable charges, ex-

penses or commissions in connection with effecting cover and any other reasonable expense incident to the delay or other breach.

EXAMPLE

Suppose Andrew contracted to sell his watch to Bently for Bently's promise to pay Andrew $200. Andrew expected to receive $200 and to give Bently his watch. If Andrew receives $200 and gives Bently the watch, the contract is fully performed.

$200	watch
$200	watch

If Andrew receives $0 but gives Bently the watch, it would take $200 to bring Andrew up to the place where he would have been had the contract been fully performed by Bently.

$200	watch
$0	watch

If Andrew receives $50 but gives the watch, it would take $150 to bring him up to the point of full performance.

$200	watch
$50	watch

Mathematically, Andrew would need the difference between what he expected to receive and what he did receive to bring him up to what he expected to receive.

Andrew also must give what he expected to give. If he expected to give the watch and does give Bently the watch, then Andrew has given what he expected to give. But if Andrew did not give Bently the watch, Andrew must compensate Bently for the nondelivery of the watch.

Mathematically, Andrew would need to compensate Bently for the difference between what Andrew expected to give and what he did give.

$200	watch
$0	no watch

RELIANCE DAMAGES

The reliance interest does not concern itself with the nonbreaching party's expectations. Therefore, what the nonbreaching party expected to receive and what the nonbreaching party expected to give are irrelevant when computing damages based on the reliance interest. The important factors are what the nonbreaching party did give and did receive in reliance on the breaching party's promise. The formula for protecting a reliance interest reads: [*(what the nonbreaching party gave in reliance on the breaching party's promise) less (what the nonbreaching party received in reliance on the breaching party's promise)*]. Returning to the quadrant diagram, the adjustments for relevant factors are found in the lower two quadrants. Within each quadrant, only what the nonbreaching party did receive and did give in reliance on the breaching party's promise is relevant.

~~what the nonbreaching party expected to receive~~	~~what the nonbreaching party expected to give~~
what the nonbreaching party did receive based on reliance	what the nonbreaching party did give based on reliance
~~what the nonbreaching party did receive independent of reliance~~	~~what the injured party did give independent of reliance~~

EXAMPLE

If Andrew gave the watch (worth $200) and received $0, Andrew should receive $200 to place him in the position he would have been in had he not relied.

~~$200~~	~~watch~~
$0	watch (worth $200)

If the watch were worth $250 rather than $200 and he received $0, Andrew should receive $250 to place him in the position he would have been in had he not relied on the breaching party's promise.

~~$200~~	~~watch~~
$0	watch (worth $250)

On the other hand if the watch were only worth $150, Andrew should receive $150 if his reliance interest, rather than his expectation interest, were to be protected.

~~$200~~	~~watch~~
$0	watch (worth $150)

RESTITUTION DAMAGES

The restitution interest, like the reliance interest, does not concern itself with what the nonbreaching party expected to receive and what that party expected to give. The restitution interest also does not concern itself with what the nonbreaching party gave or received in reliance on the breaching party's promise. Rather the restitution interest is concerned with the benefit that the nonbreaching party conferred on the breaching party and what the nonbreaching party received for conferring that benefit. The measure of damages is the reasonable value to the party receiving the benefit, that is, the breaching party.

The diagram looks as follows:

~~what the nonbreaching party expected to receive~~	~~what the nonbreaching party expected to give~~
what the nonbreaching party did receive for conferring the benefit	what the nonbreaching party did give the breaching party
~~what the nonbreaching party did receive unrelated to conferring of the benefit~~	~~what the injured party did give but not to the breaching party~~

EXAMPLE

If Andrew gave Bently the watch worth \$200 to Andrew but worth only \$150 to Bently, and Bently did not pay Andrew the \$200 contract price, Andrew could recover, in protection of his restitution interest, only \$150, the reasonable value of the watch to Bently.

~~\$200~~	~~watch (worth \$200 to Andrew)~~
\$0	watch (worth \$150 to Bently)

If Bently had paid Andrew \$25 for the watch, Andrew could recover \$125, the reasonable value of the watch to Bently (\$150) less the amount Bently already paid Andrew for the watch (\$25).

~~\$200~~	~~watch (worth \$200 to Andrew)~~
\$25	watch (worth \$150 to Bently)

In Sullivan v. O'Connor the court discusses the injured party's three interests. Sullivan, a patient, contracted with Dr. O'Connor, a surgeon, for plastic surgery on her nose. The surgery failed to enhance her beauty and improve her appearance. The surgery in fact disfigured and deformed her nose and caused her pain and suffering beyond what she expected. Sullivan sued O'Connor for both breach of contract and negligence. The jury found Dr. O'Connor not negligent but did find that he breached his contract with Sullivan.

1. What did each party promise in the contract?
2. Was the contract enforceable?
3. Did Dr. O'Connor breach the contract?
4. As you refer to the following quadrant diagram on damages, answer the following questions.
   a. What did Sullivan expect to get?
   b. What did Sullivan get?
   c. What did Sullivan expect to give? In addition to Dr. O'Connor's fee and the clinic's or hospital's charge, what else did Sullivan expect to give? Pain and suffering for how many operations? Emotional distress for how many operations? Loss of income for how many operations?
   d. What did Sullivan give? In addition to Dr. O'Connor's fee and the clinic's or hospital's charge, what else did Sullivan give? Pain and suffering for how many operations? Emotional distress for how many operations? Loss of income for how many operations?

beautiful nose	Doctor's fee for ___ operations Clinic's fee for ___ operations Pain and suffering associated with ___ operations Emotional distress associated with ___ operations Loss of income associated with ___ operations
ugly nose	Doctor's fees for ___ operations Clinic's fees for ___ operations Pain and suffering associated with ___ operations Emotional distress associated with ___ operations Loss of income associated with ___ operations

What were Sullivan's expectation damages, reliance damages, and restitution damages? Are they the same? Did Sullivan's attorney ask for all the damages that his client was entitled to?

Sullivan v. O'Connor

Supreme Judicial Court of Massachusetts, 1973.
363 Mass. 579, 296 N.E.2d 183.

Before TAURO, C.J., and REARDON, QUIRICO, KAPLAN and WILKINS, JJ.

KAPLAN, Justice.

The plaintiff patient secured a jury verdict of $13,500 against the defendant surgeon for breach of contract in respect to an operation upon the plaintiff's nose. The substituted consolidated bill of exceptions presents questions about the correctness of the judge's instructions on the issue of damages.

The declaration was in two counts. In the first count, the plaintiff alleged that she, as patient, entered into a contract with the defendant, a surgeon, wherein the defendant promised to perform plastic surgery on her nose and thereby to enhance her beauty and improve her appearance; that he performed the surgery but failed to achieve the promised result; rather the result of the surgery was to disfigure and deform her nose, to cause her pain in body and mind, and to subject her to other damage and expense. The second count, based on the same transaction, was in the conventional form for malpractice, charging that the defendant had been guilty of negligence in performing the surgery. Answering, the defendant entered a general denial.

On the plaintiff's demand, the case was tried by jury. At the close of the evidence, the judge put to the jury, as special questions, the issues of liability under the two counts, and instructed them accordingly. The jury returned a verdict for the plaintiff on the contract count, and for the defendant on the negligence count. The judge then instructed the jury on the issue of damages.

As background to the instructions and the parties' exceptions, we mention certain facts as the jury could find them. The plaintiff was a professional entertainer, and this was known to the defendant. The agreement was as alleged in the declaration. More particularly, judging from exhibits, the plaintiff's nose had been straight, but long and prominent; the defendant undertook by two operations to reduce its prominence and somewhat to shorten it, thus making it more pleasing in relation to the plaintiff's other features. Actually the plaintiff was obliged to undergo three operations, and her appearance was worsened. Her nose now had a concave line to about the midpoint, at which it became bulbous; viewed frontally, the nose from bridge to midpoint was flattened and broadened, and the two sides of the tip had lost symmetry. This configuration evidently could not be improved by further surgery. The plaintiff did not demonstrate, however, that her change of appearance had resulted in loss of employment. Payments by the plaintiff covering the defendant's fee and hospital expenses were stipulated at $622.65.

The judge instructed the jury, first, that the plaintiff was entitled to recover her out-of-pocket expenses incident to the operations. Second, she could recover the damages flowing directly, naturally, proximately, and foreseeably from the defendant's breach of promise. These would comprehend damages for any disfigurement of the plaintiff's nose—that is, any change of appearance for the worse—including the effects of the consciousness of such disfigurement on the plaintiff's mind, and in this connection the jury should consider the nature of the plaintiff's profession. Also consequent upon the defendant's breach, and compensable, were the pain and suffering involved in the third operation, but not in the first two. As there was no proof that any loss of earnings by the plaintiff resulted from the breach, that element should not enter into the calculation of damages.

By his exceptions the defendant contends that the judge erred in allowing the jury to take into account anything but the plaintiff's out-of-pocket expenses (presumably at the stipulated amount). The defendant excepted to the judge's refusal of his request for a general charge to that effect, and, more specifically, to the judge's refusal of a charge that the plaintiff could not recover for pain and suffering connected with the third operation or for impairment of the plaintiff's appearance and associated mental distress.

The plaintiff on her part excepted to the judge's refusal of a request to charge that the plaintiff could recover the difference in value between the nose as promised and the nose as it appeared after the operations. However, the plaintiff in her brief expressly waives this exception and others made by her in case this court overrules the defendant's exceptions; thus she would be content to hold the jury's verdict in her favor.

We conclude that the defendant's exceptions should be overruled.

It has been suggested on occasion that agreements between patients and physicians by which the physician undertakes to effect a cure or to bring about a given result should be declared unenforceable on grounds of public policy. See Guilmet v. Campbell, 385 Mich. 57, 76, 188 N.W.2d 601 (dissenting opinion). But there are many decisions recognizing and enforcing such contracts, see annotation, 43 A.L.R.3d 1221, 1225, 1229–1233, and the law of Massachusetts has treated them as valid, although we have had no decision meeting head on the contention that they should be denied legal sanction. Small v. Howard, 128 Mass. 131; Gabrunas v. Miniter, 289 Mass. 20, 193 N.E. 551; Forman v. Wolfson, 327 Mass. 341, 98 N.E.2d 615. These causes of action are, however, considered a little suspect, and thus we find courts straining sometimes to read the pleadings as sounding only in tort for negligence, and not in contract for breach of promise, despite sedulous efforts by the pleaders to pursue the latter theory. See Gault v. Sideman, 42 Ill.App.2d 96, 191 N.E.2d 436; annotation, *supra,* at 1225, 1238–1244.

It is not hard to see why the courts should be unenthusiastic or skeptical about the contract theory. Considering the uncertainties of medical science and the variations in the physical and psychological conditions of individual patients, doctors can seldom in good faith promise specific results. Therefore it is unlikely that physicians of even average integrity will in fact make such promises. Statements of opinion by the physician with some optimistic coloring are a different thing, and may indeed have therapeutic value. But patients may transform such statements into firm promises in their own minds, especially when they have been disappointed in the event, and testify in that sense to sympathetic juries. If actions for breach of promise can be readily maintained, doctors, so it is said, will be frightened into practising "defensive medicine." On the other hand, if these actions were outlawed, leaving only the possibility of suits for malpractice, there is fear that the public might be exposed to the enticements of charlatans, and confidence in the profession might ultimately be shaken. See Miller, The Contractual Liability of Physicians and Surgeons, 1953 Wash.L.Q. 413, 416–423. The law has taken the middle of the road position of allowing actions based on alleged contract, but insisting on clear proof. Instructions to the jury may well stress this requirement and point to tests of truth, such as the complexity or difficulty of an operation as bearing on the probability that a given result was promised. See annotation, 43 A.L.R.3d 1225, 1225–1227.

If an action on the basis of contract is allowed, we have next the question of the measure of damages to be applied where liability is found. Some cases have taken the simple view that the promise by the physician is to be treated like an ordinary commercial promise, and accordingly that the successful plaintiff is entitled to a standard measure of recovery for breach of contract—"compensatory" ("expectancy") damages, an amount intended to put the plaintiff in the position he would be in if the contract had been performed, or, presumably, at the plaintiff's election, "restitution" damages, an amount corresponding to any benefit conferred by the plaintiff upon the defendant in the performance of the contract disrupted by the defendant's breach. See Restatement: Contracts § 329 and comment a, §§ 347, 384(1). Thus in Hawkins v. McGee, 84 N.H. 114, 146 A. 641, the defendant doctor was taken to have promised the plaintiff to convert his damaged hand by means of an operation into a good or perfect hand, but the doctor so operated as to damage the hand still further. The court, following the usual expectancy formula, would have asked the jury to estimate and award to the plaintiff the difference between the value of a good or perfect hand, as promised, and the value of the hand after the operation. (The same formula would apply, although the dollar result would be less, if the operation had neither worsened nor improved the condition of the hand.) If the plaintiff had not yet paid the doctor his fee, that amount would be deducted from the recovery. There could be no recovery for the pain and suffering of the operation, since that detriment would have been incurred even if the operation had been successful; one can say that this detriment was not "caused" by the breach. But where the plaintiff by reason of the operation was put to more pain than he would have had to endure, had the doctor performed as promised, he should be compensated for that difference as a proper part of his expectancy recovery. It may be noted that on an alternative count for malpractice the plaintiff in the *Hawkins* case had been nonsuited; but on ordinary principles this could not affect the contract claim, for it is hardly a defence to a breach of contract that the promisor acted innocently and without negligence. The New Hampshire court further refined the *Hawkins* analysis in McQuaid v. Michou, 85 N.H. 299, 157 A. 881, all in the direction of treating the patient-physician cases on the ordinary footing of expectancy. See McGee v. United States Fid. & Guar. Co., 53 F.2d 953 (1st Cir.) (later development in the *Hawkins* case); Cloutier v. Kasheta, 105 N.H. 262, 197 A.2d 627; Lakeman v. LaFrance, 102 N.H. 300, 305, 156 A.2d 123.

Other cases, including a number in New York, without distinctly repudiating the *Hawkins* type of analysis, have indicated that a different and generally more lenient measure of damages is to be applied in patient-physician actions based on breach of alleged special agreements to effect a cure, attain a stated result, or employ a given medical method. This measure is expressed in somewhat variant ways, but the substance is that the plaintiff is to recover any expenditures made by him and for other detriment (usually not specifically described in the opinions) following proximately and foreseeably upon the defendant's failure to carry out his promise. Robins v. Finestone, 308 N.Y. 543, 546, 127 N.E.2d 330; Frankel v. Wolper, 181 App.Div. 485, 488, 169 N.Y.S. 15, affd., 228 N.Y. 582, 127 N.E. 913; Frank v. Maliniak, 232 App.Div. 278, 280, 249 N.Y.S. 514; Colvin v. Smith, 276 App.Div. 9, 10, 92 N.Y.S.2d 794; Stewart v. Rudner, 349 Mich. 459, 465–473, 84 N.W.2d 816. Cf. Carpenter v. Moore, 51 Wash.2d 795, 322 P.2d 125. This, be it noted, is not a "restitution" measure, for it is not limited to restoration of the benefit conferred on the defendant (the fee paid) but includes other expenditures, for example, amounts paid for medicine and nurses; so also it would seem according to its logic to take in damages for any worsening of the plaintiff's condition due to the breach. Nor is it an "expectancy" measure, for it does not appear to contemplate recovery of the whole difference in value between the condition as promised and the condition actually resulting from the treatment. Rather the tendency of the formulation is to put the plaintiff back in the position he occupied just before the parties entered upon the agreement, to compensate him for the detriments he suffered in reliance upon the agreement. This kind of intermediate pattern of recovery for breach of contract is discussed in the suggestive article by Fuller and Perdue, The Reliance Interest in Contract Damages, 46 Yale L.J. 52, 373, where the authors show that, although not attaining the currency of the standard measures, a "reliance" measure has for special reasons been applied by the courts in a variety of settings, including noncommercial settings. See 46 Yale L.J. at 396–401.

For breach of the patient-physician agreements under consideration, a recovery limited to restitution seems plainly too meager, if the agreements are to be enforced at all. On the other hand, an expectancy recovery may well be excessive. The factors, already mentioned, which have made the cause of action somewhat suspect, also suggest moderation as to the breadth of the recovery that should be permitted. Where, as in the case at bar and in a number of the reported cases, the doctor has been absolved of negligence by the trier, an expectancy measure may be thought harsh. We should recall here that the fee paid by the patient to the doctor for the alleged promise would usually be quite disproportionate to the putative expectancy recovery. To attempt, moreover, to put a value on the condition that would or might have resulted, had the treatment succeeded as promised, may sometimes put an exceptional strain on the imagination of the fact finder. As a general consideration, Fuller and Perdue argue that the reasons for granting damages for broken promises to the extent of the expectancy are at their strongest when the promises are made in a business context, when they have to do with the production or distribution of goods or the allocation of functions in the market place; they become weaker as the context shifts from a commercial to a noncommercial field. 46 Yale L.J. at 60–63.

There is much to be said, then, for applying a reliance measure to the present facts, and we have only to add that our cases are not unreceptive to the use of that formula in special situations. We have, however, had no previous occasion to apply it to patient-physician cases.[5]

The question of recovery on a reliance basis for pain and suffering or mental distress requires further attention. We find expressions in the decisions that pain and suffering (or the like) are simply not compensable in actions for breach of contract. The defendant seemingly espouses this

5. In Mt. Pleasant Stable Co. v. Steinberg, 238 Mass. 567, 131 N.E. 295, the plaintiff company agreed to supply teams of horses at agreed rates as required from day to day by the defendant for his business. To prepare itself to fulfill the contract and in reliance on it, the plaintiff bought two "Cliest" horses at a certain price. When the defendant repudiated the contract, the plaintiff sold the horses at a loss and in its action for breach claimed the loss as an element of damages. The court properly held that the plaintiff was not entitled to this item as it was also claiming (and recovering) its lost profits (expectancy) on the contract as a whole. Cf. Noble v. Ames Mfg. Co., 112 Mass. 492. (The loss on sale of the horses is analogous to the pain and suffering for which the patient would be disallowed a recovery in Hawkins v. McGee, 84 N.H. 114, 146 A. 641, because he was claiming and recovering expectancy damages.) The court in the *Mt. Pleasant* case referred, however, to Pond v. Harris, 113 Mass. 114, as a contrasting situation where the expectancy could not be fairly determined. There the defendant had wrongfully revoked an agreement to arbitrate a dispute with the plaintiff (this was before such agreements were made specifically enforceable). In an action for the breach, the plaintiff was held entitled to recover for his preparations for the arbitration which had been rendered useless and a waste, including the plaintiff's time and trouble and his expenditures for counsel and witnesses. The context apparently was commercial but reliance elements were held compensable when there was no fair way of estimating an expectancy. See, generally, annotation, 17 A.L.R.2d 1300. A noncommercial example is Smith v. Sherman, 4 Cush. 408, 413–414, suggesting that a conventional recovery for breach of promise of marriage included a recompense for various efforts and expenditures by the plaintiff preparatory to the promised wedding. See Garfield & Proctor Coal Co. v. Pennsylvania Coal & Coke Co., 199 Mass. 22, 43, 84 N.E. 1020; Narragansett Amusement Co. v. Riverside Park Amusement Co., 260 Mass. 265, 279–281, 157 N.E. 532. Cf. Johnson v. Arnold, 2 Cush. 46, 47; Greany v. McCormick, 273 Mass. 250, 253, 173 N.E. 411. But cf. Irwin v. Worcester Paper Box Co., 246 Mass. 453, 141 N.E. 286.

proposition in the present case. True, if the buyer under a contract for the purchase of a lot of merchandise, in suing for the seller's breach, should claim damages for mental anguish caused by his disappointment in the transaction, he would not succeed; he would be told, perhaps, that the asserted psychological injury was not fairly foreseeable by the defendant as a probable consequence of the breach of such a business contract. See Restatement: Contracts, § 341, and comment a. But there is no general rule barring such items of damage in actions for breach of contract. It is all a question of the subject matter and background of the contract, and when the contract calls for an operation on the person of the plaintiff, psychological as well as physical injury may be expected to figure somewhere in the recovery, depending on the particular circumstances. The point is explained in Stewart v. Rudner, 349 Mich. 459, 469, 84 N.W.2d 816. Cf. Frewen v. Page, 238 Mass. 499, 131 N.E. 475; McClean v. University Club, 327 Mass. 68, 97 N.E.2d 174. Again, it is said in a few of the New York cases, concerned with the classification of actions for statute of limitations purposes, that the absence of allegations demanding recovery for pain and suffering is characteristic of a contract claim by a patient against a physician, that such allegations rather belong in a claim for malpractice. See Robins v. Finestone, 308 N.Y. 543, 547, 127 N.E.2d 330; Budoff v. Kessler, 2 A.D.2d 760, 153 N.Y.S.2d 654. These remarks seem unduly sweeping. Suffering or distress resulting from the breach going beyond that which was envisaged by the treatment as agreed, should be compensable on the same ground as the worsening of the patient's condition because of the breach. Indeed it can be argued that the very suffering or distress "contracted for"—that which would have been incurred if the treatment achieved the promised result—should also be compensable on the theory underlying the New York cases. For that suffering is "wasted" if the treatment fails. Otherwise stated, compensation for this waste is arguably required in order to complete the restoration of the status quo ante.[6]

In the light of the foregoing discussion, all the defendant's exceptions fail: the plaintiff was not confined to the recovery of her out-of-pocket expenditures; she was entitled to recover also for the worsening of her condition,[7] and for the pain and suffering and mental distress involved in the third operation. These items were compensable on either an expectancy or a reliance view. We might have been required to elect between the two views if the pain and suffering connected with the first two operations contemplated by the agreement, or the whole differ-

6. Recovery on a reliance basis for breach of the physician's promise tends to equate with the usual recovery for malpractice, since the latter also looks in general to restoration of the condition before the injury. But this is not paradoxical, especially when it is noted that the origins of contract lie in tort. See Farnsworth, The Past of Promise: An Historical Introduction to Contract, 69 Col.L.Rev. 576, 594–596; Breitel, J. in Stella Flour & Feed Corp. v. National City Bank, 285 App.Div. 182, 189, 136 N.Y.S.2d 139 (dissenting opinion). A few cases have considered possible recovery for breach by a physician of a promise to sterilize a patient, resulting in birth of a child to the patient and spouse. If such an action is held maintainable, the reliance and expectancy measures would, we think, tend to equate, because the promised condition was preservation of the family status quo. See Custodio v. Bauer, 251 Cal.App.2d 303, 59 Cal. Rptr. 463; Jackson v. Anderson, 230 So.2d 503 (Fla.App.). Cf. Troppi v. Scarf, 31 Mich.App. 240, 187 N.W.2d 511. But cf. Ball v. Mudge, 64 Wash.2d 247, 391 P.2d 201; Doerr v. Villate, 74 Ill.App.2d 332, 220 N.E.2d 767; Shaheen v. Knight, 11 Pa.D. & C.2d 41. See also annotation, 27 A.L.R.3d 906.

It would, however, be a mistake to think in terms of strict "formulas." For example, a jurisdiction which would apply a reliance measure to the present facts might impose a more severe damage sanction for the wilful use by the physician of a method of operation that he undertook not to employ.

7. That condition involves a mental element and appraisal of it properly called for consideration of the fact that the plaintiff was an entertainer. Cf. McQuaid v. Michou, 85 N.H. 299, 303–304, 157 A. 881 (discussion of continuing condition resulting from physician's breach).

ence in value between the present and the promised conditions, were being claimed as elements of damage. But the plaintiff waives her possible claim to the former element, and to so much of the latter as represents the difference in value between the promised condition and the condition before the operations.

Plaintiff's exceptions waived.

Defendant's exceptions overruled.

A. Expectation as a Remedy for Breach of Contract

Protection of the injured party's (the nonbreaching party's) expectation interest places the injured party in the position he or she would have been in had the contract been fully performed according to its terms. The injured party will receive what he or she expected to receive in exchange for giving what he or she expected to give.

1. Compensatory Damages

The injured party's damages are intended to compensate that party for not receiving his or her expectation under the contract. The injured party will be brought up to full performance, no more and no less. Therefore, punitive damages (that is monetary awards that punish the breaching party) are not awarded in breach of contract actions. The breaching party is not held up to the public as an example of what might happen if a party breaches.

The fact that damages for breach of contract do not include punitive damages, is consistent with the fact that the intentions of the breaching party are irrelevant. Intentional and unintentional breaches will result in the same measure of expectation damages. Therefore, a contracting party may find breaching a contract to be in his or her best economic interest. Breaching a contract and paying expectation damages may place the breaching party in a better economic position than performing the contract.

EXAMPLE

The ABC Painting Company has contracted to paint Smith's house for $3,000. Before beginning to paint, ABC breaches the Smith contract so it can paint the First Bank Building. First Bank contracts to pay ABC $12,000. Smith hires Quality Painters for $3,500. If Smith sues ABC for breach of contract, she will recover $500, the additional amount it would cost her to have her house painted. ABC may be more than willing to pay Smith $500 if it could make substantially more on the First Bank contract.

In some situations it may be difficult to decide what will place the injured party in the position he or she would have been in had the contract been fully performed. In construction contracts the issue is whether the injured party is entitled to the cost to replace (or to repair) or to only the diminished value of the subject of the contract.

EXAMPLE

Contractor builds Owner a house but mislocates an interior wall by one foot. After the house was completed, Owner discovered Contractor's error.

Even with the mislocation, the house is still quite liveable. Contractor has breached the contract by not building according to the blueprints.

Is Owner entitled to the cost to relocate the wall or only the diminished value of the house with the mislocated wall? Unless there was some overriding reason why the house was unacceptable with the mislocated wall, a relocation of the wall would have created only "economic waste." A court will generally award Owner only the diminished value in the house attributable to the mislocation.

PROBLEM 1: The Allegheny Coal Company leased ranch land from the Bar Z Ranch for the purpose of strip mining coal. The contract provided that Allegheny would reclaim the land (restore the surface) after it had completed strip mining. At the end of the lease term, Allegheny left the mining site without reclaiming the land. The value of the land would be $50 an acre if not reclaimed and $600 an acre if reclaimed. Reclaiming the land would cost $900 an acre. Should the Bar Z Ranch be entitled to the diminished value of the land or the cost to reclaim? Consider the policy arguments supporting each position.

Damages for breach of contract are limited to those that the breaching party could reasonably foresee at the time of the making of the contract as the probable result of such a breach. Foreseeable damages are either general or special damages. The classic case of *Hadley v. Baxendale,* 9 Ex. 341, 156 Eng. Rep. 145 (1854) stated the rule of foreseeability as:

> Where two parties have made a contract which one of them has broken, the damages which the other party ought to receive in respect of such breach of contract should be such as may fairly and reasonably be considered either arising naturally, i.e. according to the usual course of things, from such breach of contract itself, or such as may reasonably be supposed to have been in the contemplation of both parties, at the time they made the contract, as the probable result of the breach of it.

General damages "arise naturally, i.e., according to the usual course of things, from such breach of contract itself." In a contract for the sale of goods, what are the buyer's damages normally if the seller refuses to deliver the goods? What are the seller's damages normally if the buyer breaches by refusing to accept delivery of the goods? In a contract for employment, what are the employee's damages normally if the employer has wrongfully discharged her? What are the employer's damages normally if the employee has wrongfully quit?

Special damages do not "arise naturally, i.e., according to the usual course of things, from such breach of contract itself." Rather, special damages are those damages that "may reasonably be supposed to have been in the contemplation of both parties, at the time they made the contract, as the probable result of the breach of it." Because they may reasonably be supposed to have been in the contemplation of both parties, they are foreseeable.

PROBLEM 2: The Hunter Hotel Corporation contracted with Apex Construction Company for renovation of the hotel. The contract provided September 1st as the completion date for the renovation. Apex did not complete the renovation until October 1st and as a result, the hotel lost a convention that it scheduled during the week of September 15th. Is the Hunter Hotel entitled to recover the lost profits for the convention?

Whether a nonbreaching party can recover damages for pain and suffering and mental distress in a breach of contract action is a question of foreseeability. Generally, damages for pain and suffering or for emotional distress are not available in a breach of contract. In some instances recovery can be had for pain and suffering or emotional distress if they were the natural result of the breach so as to have been within the contemplation of the parties at the time the contract was made.

PROBLEM 3: Reconsider Sullivan v. O'Connor (page 336). The court indicated that it would permit recovery for pain and suffering and for emotional distress. Was Sullivan's pain and suffering and emotional distress foreseeable at the time of contract formation?

Damages for breach of contract must be shown with reasonable certainty. Damages that are speculative and incapable of being ascertained with reasonable certainty are not recoverable. Although damages must be certain, mathematical exactness is not required.

PROBLEM 4: Assume in Problem 2 that Apex knew at the time of contracting that the Hunter had a convention scheduled for September 15th and that if the renovation was not completed before that date, the Hunter would lose the convention and the accompanying profits. Is the Hunter entitled to recover the lost profits for the convention?

In the event of breach, the nonbreaching party has a duty to mitigate the damages. The nonbreaching party must use reasonable means to avoid or minimize damages. Mitigation may take different forms. In some situations the doctrine prevents the nonbreaching party from increasing the amount the breaching party must pay.

EXAMPLE

In a construction contract the contractor is entitled to the contract price upon completion of the structure. If the owner breaches the contract before the contractor begins to build, the contractor is entitled to her profits (contract price less the expected cost to build the structure). If the owner breaches after the contractor begins to build but before the structure is complete, the contractor is entitled to the contract price less the amount she saved by not having to complete the structure. If the contractor ignores the owner's notice not to complete the structure, the contractor cannot increase the amount due on the contract by continuing to build.

In other situations, the doctrine of mitigation requires the nonbreaching party to decrease the amount of damages the breaching party must pay.

EXAMPLE

In an employment contract, a wrongfully terminated employee must attempt to use his or her saved time productively by seeking substitute employment. If the employee does use this saved time by taking another job, the money earned from the new job will be subtracted from the money the employee expected to earn under the original contract. If the employee does not take another job but should have taken it, then the money that could have been earned from the new job will be subtracted from the money the employee expected to earn under the original contract.

PROBLEM 5: The *Daily News* hired Brenda under a one-year contract to write the local news. After three months, Brenda was wrongfully discharged. The *Chronicle,* a rival newspaper, learned of Brenda's discharge and offered her a nine month contract at ninety percent of her salary with the *Daily News.*

In determining Brenda's damages for the *Daily News*'s breach of contract, must her salary with the *Chronicle* be subtracted from her expected salary with the *Daily News* if she accepts the *Chronicle*'s offer?

Must the salary offered by the *Chronicle* be subtracted from Brenda's expected salary with the *Daily News* if she does not accept the *Chronicle*'s offer?

2. Nominal Damages

If the nonbreaching party proves a breach of contract but is unable to prove damages, the nonbreaching party is entitled to nominal damages (six cents or a dollar). A judgment for nominal damages, while not compensating the nonbreaching party in dollars and cents, does clarify the rights and duties of the parties and may include an award of court costs.

3. Injunction and Specific Performance

At times, damages may not totally compensate the nonbreaching party for his or her injury. The circumstances may be such that future injuries will occur.

EXAMPLE

A research chemist is hired by Green Farm, a farm fertilizer company, and as a part of the employment contract, the chemist promises not to work for another farm fertilizer company for two years after she ends her employment with Green Farm. After working for Green Farm for several years, the chemist quits and begins to work for another farm fertilizer company. While Green Farm is entitled to damages for the chemist's breach of her covenant not to compete, damages will not protect Green Farm from loss of its secrets that the chemist could reveal to her new employer. If the court precludes the chemist from working for her new employer for the remainder of the covenant's term, Green Farm would be better protected. This court order precluding the chemist from working for her new employer is known as an injunction.

Another remedy, specific performance, is available only when the remedy of damages would be inadequate. If in a contract for the sale of goods, the seller refuses to deliver, specific performance may be available if the goods are unique and thus are not easily replaceable on the market.

PROBLEM 6: Blue Grass Stables contracted to sell *Neal's Diamond,* an outstanding three-year-old thoroughbred and winner of the triple crown, to California Meadows, a breeding syndicate. Prior to the delivery date, Blue Grass notified California Meadows that it had decided to race *Neal's Diamond* for another year and would not deliver him to the syndicate.

1. Could California Meadows find a substitute horse on the market to replace *Neal's Diamond?*
2. Would damages (money) be an adequate remedy for California Meadows?
3. Would specific performance be an appropriate remedy?

Specific performance is not available when the breach is the failure to pay money. Money is interchangeable and not unique. Specific performance is also not available in personal service contracts. Involuntary servitude violates the Thirteenth Amendment to the United States Constitution.

PROBLEM 7: Sylvia, a female acid rock group, contracted to give a Fourth of July concert at Woodstock. Early in June, Woodstock notified Sylvia that its services were no longer needed. Should Sylvia be entitled to the remedy of specific performance for Woodstock's breach of contract?

4. Cover

Cover is a substitute. In a sale of goods, the nonbreaching buyer may need the goods and can attempt to purchase substitutes from a third party. Section 2–712(2) of the Uniform Commercial Code defines the buyer's damages:

> (2) The buyer may recover from the seller as damages the difference between the cost of cover and the contract price together with any incidental or consequential damages as hereinafter defined (Section 2–715), but less expenses saved in consequence of the seller's breach.

EXAMPLE

In early March, Farmer Jones contracted to sell his cotton crop to the ABC Cotton Gin for fifty cents a pound. Farmer Jones normally expects to harvest 100 tons of cotton. Later in March, ABC contracted to resell Farmer Jones's cotton to Quality Mills.

During the summer, when the price of cotton rose to seventy-five cents a pound, Farmer Jones notified ABC that he would not deliver his cotton to ABC. ABC then purchased cotton on the open market to meet its commitment with Quality Mills. ABC paid seventy-five cents a pound for the substitute cotton.

ABC has "covered" by buying substitute cotton. ABC is entitled to damages of twenty-five cents a pound plus its costs in finding the substitute cotton.

In an employment contract, the nonbreaching employer may need certain services and can attempt to find a substitute employee. Even though the nonbreaching party has found a substitute, he or she may still be entitled to damages. These damages include the difference in cost between what the injured party expected to pay for the services and what the injured party did pay, in addition to any expenses incurred in finding the substitute.

EXAMPLE

The Pink Panther Lounge hired Irma LaRue to sing at the Lounge on Friday and Saturday nights. The contract was for the month of December at a salary of $500 an evening. After appearing for one weekend, Irma quit so she could perform in Atlantic City. Because this was the Christmas season and most entertainers had engagements, the Lounge hired Melody Layne at a salary of $700 an evening, and she appeared through the month of December.

The Lounge is entitled to $200 for each of the remaining Friday and Saturday evenings in December. The Lounge is also entitled to any costs that it incurred in finding Ms. Layne.

---

5. Liquidated Damages

Sometimes the parties at the time of contract formation agree upon what the damages will be in the event of breach. Such a provision, if in a contract, is known as a liquidated damage clause. Not all such clauses are enforceable. When one of the parties challenges such a clause, the court will evaluate whether the clause is in fact a liquidated damage provision or merely a penalty. Clauses that are classified as penalties are unenforceable.

A clause is a liquidated damage provision and not a penalty if:

1. at the time of contract formation the damages in the event of a breach would be impossible or very difficult to estimate accurately;
2. there was a reasonable endeavor by the parties to fix a fair compensation; and
3. the amount stipulated bears a reasonable relation to probable damages and is not disproportionate to any damages reasonably anticipated.

PROBLEM 8: Reliable Property Company owned a fifty unit apartment complex. Reliable hired Felix to repaint apartments as they became vacant for $300 an apartment. The contract provided that Felix would have five days from the date of notice of vacancy to paint the apartment. The contract further provided that Felix would pay Reliable ten percent of the contract price for each day he was late. Felix finished painting the first apartment in eight days and was paid $210.

Could Felix successfully sue Reliable for breach of contract and if so, for how much? Would the following facts be relevant?

1. The apartment rents for $400 a month.
2. The apartment complex has an eighty-five percent occupancy rate.
3. The apartment was ready by the first of the month.

6. Costs and Attorney Fees

In anticipation of litigation, parties might stipulate in the contract who will pay costs. Generally, costs include filing fees, service of process, jury fees, and court officer charges, but not attorney fees. To predetermine who will pay these expenses, the contract might contain a term that states, "the party initiating litigation will pay all costs." Such a term will cause a court to levy the costs against the named party.

If the contract does not include a provision on costs, most courts will allocate costs to the losing party. Some states, however, place various limitations on this rule. For example, in Illinois, the court may apportion costs to the parties if the case is not decided on all of the issues presented. Because the rules on costs may vary from jurisdiction to jurisdiction, contracting parties must determine prior to drafting a contract which state's law will apply in the event of a breach and who will be assessed costs if the contract does not allocate costs.

Unlike costs, the nonbreaching party in a breach of contract action generally cannot recover its attorney fees from the other, even after winning the judgment. This rule has two general exceptions. First, attorney fees can be recovered if suit is brought under a statute allowing the nonbreaching party to recover attorney's fees. A statute might include the clause, "anyone bringing a cause of action under this statute may recover attorney fees, if that party has obtained a favorable judgment."

Another exception is that the parties may allocate attorney fees by contract. The agreement may state, "if litigation arises from this contract, the party obtaining a favorable judgment in such litigation may recover his or her attorney fees from the opposing party." Although most states allow the parties to allocate attorney fees, some, such as California, limit the attorney fees recoverable to "reasonable attorney fees." Because the rules on attorney fees vary from jurisdiction to jurisdiction, the parties contemplating a contract must determine prior to drafting the contract which state's law will apply in the event of a breach, whether that state will enforce an allocation of attorney fees, and whether limitation will be placed on the allocation.

B. Reliance as an Alternative Remedy for Breach of Contract

Protecting the nonbreaching party's (the injured party's) reliance interest places the nonbreaching party back in the position he or she was in prior to relying on the breaching party's promise. The reliance interest does not concern itself with the nonbreaching party's expectations. The nonbreaching party's compensation is based on what the nonbreaching party gave in reliance on the breaching party's promise, less what the nonbreaching party received in reliance on the breaching party's reliance.

While the expectation interest generally is greater than the reliance interest, instances do exist in which the reliance interest exceeds expectation.

> *PROBLEM 9:* Mary Oliver, a financial consultant in New York City, was hired by the Golden Gate Investment Company of San Francisco for $80,000 a year for three years. Mary spent a week in San Francisco finding a place to live and spent $5,000 moving her household goods to San Francisco. When she reported to work, she found that new management had taken over the investment company and her services were no longer needed. Fortunately for Mary, she was able to return to her old job in New York City at $78,000 a year.
>
> Could Mary successfully sue Golden Gate for breach of contract, and if so, for how much? Consider both Mary's expectation and reliance interests.

C. Restitution as an Alternative Remedy for Breach of Contract

Protecting the nonbreaching party's restitution interest places the breaching party back in the position he or she was in before being unjustly enriched by the nonbreaching party. The restitution interest, like the reliance interest, is unrelated to the nonbreaching party's expectations. The nonbreaching party's restitution recovery is the reasonable value of the benefit that the nonbreaching party conferred on the breaching party, less what the nonbreaching party received.

Although the expectation interest generally is greater than the restitution interest, instances do exist in which the restitution interest exceeds expectation. This will occur when the breaching party breaches a contract that was unfavorable to the nonbreaching party. The nonbreaching party is taken off the hook.

EXAMPLE

The Sunset Nursery Company contracted to landscape the Zenith Mall for $50,000. Sunset spent several weeks grading the land for trees and sod. The work took longer than Sunset had expected, due to the lack of spring rains and the hot summer that baked the soil. Zenith grew impatient and fired Sunset without cause. At the time of the termination, Sunset had spent the equivalent of $40,000 on the job and would have spent an additional $20,000 to complete it. The reasonable value of Sunset's work to Zenith was also $40,000.

Zenith breached the contract by firing Sunset without cause. Sunset is entitled to a restitution remedy for Zenith's breach of contract. Sunset's measure of damages is the reasonable value of its work to Zenith, that is, $40,000. Had Sunset sought to protect its expectation interest, it would have recovered two-thirds of the contract price ($3333.33) (two-thirds of the work was completed) or less than the value of its work.

In determining a restitution recovery, two factors come into play. Was the nonbreaching party to pay money? Did the nonbreaching party fully perform? If the nonbreaching party was to pay money and did partially perform, the nonbreaching party is entitled to restitution of the money paid.

> *PROBLEM 10:* Alexander contracted to build a barn for Herman for $30,000. Herman paid Alexander $15,000 in advance. Ultimately, Alexander did not begin to build the barn. If the barn had been built, it would have been worth only $25,000.
>
> When Herman sues Alexander for breach of contract, how much should he recover to protect his expectation interest?
>
> How much should he recover to protect his restitution interest?

If the injured party was to perform services and partially performed, then the injured party is entitled to the value of the services performed as measured by the reasonable value of the services to the breaching party. The nonbreaching party may recover the reasonable value of the services to the breaching party even though the reasonable value exceeds the prorated contract price.

EXAMPLE

A Client hired an Attorney to handle his divorce for $750. The divorce turned out to be more complicated than the Attorney originally thought and the Attorney devoted substantial time to the case. Before the Attorney could procure the divorce, the Client wrongfully discharged the Attorney. Had the Attorney computed his time in billable hours, he would have charged $1,000 as of the time of his discharge.

The Attorney is entitled to a restitution remedy for breach of contract of $1,000, the reasonable value of his services even though this exceeds the $750 contract price.

If the injured party has fully performed the services, then the contract price limits recovery.

EXAMPLE

If the Client discharged the Attorney after the Attorney procured the divorce, the Attorney would be entitled to only the contract price, $750, even though the reasonable value of his services was $1,500.

This rule contains an anomaly. The nonbreaching party may recover more than the contract price for less than full performance but no more than the contract price for full performance.

> *PROBLEM 11:* Fields, seeking a divorce from her husband, hired Bailey as her attorney. The parties agreed upon a flat legal fee of $2,500 for the completed property settlement and the divorce decree. After Bailey

had spent substantial time preparing the case, Fields reconciled with her husband and refused to pay Bailey. The case turned out to be more complicated than Bailey had originally thought and had she charged by billable hour, her fee for work performed prior to the reconciliation would easily have been $4,000.

How much should Bailey recover from Fields in an action for breach? Consider both Bailey's expectation and restitution interests.

Section 2. IS A RESTITUTION ACTION AVAILABLE FOR THE PLAINTIFF WHEN THE DEFENDANT HAS BREACHED THE CONTRACT?

A nonbreaching party does not have the luxury of selecting between a breach of contract action and a restitution action. (The restitution action should not be confused with the restitution remedies for a breach of contract action.) If a contract has been formed, it is enforceable, and if the defendant has breached, the nonbreaching party has no choice but to pursue a breach of contract action. If the nonbreaching party ignores the breach of contract action and pleads a restitution action, the breaching party can defend the restitution action by claiming the existence of an enforceable contract that has been breached.

But why would a breaching party want to defend a restitution action by stating that he or she breached the contract? The answer may be found in the baggage that accompanies each cause of action. Each cause of action has its own attributes. The difference may include: the statute of limitations, the amount of damages, the type of remedies (in a restitution action, the plaintiff may pursue an equitable lien or a constructive trust), costs and attorney fees, and the simplicity of the issues to be litigated.

PART VI

Third Party Interests

INTRODUCTION

The first five parts of this book have explored the consensual relationship between the two contracting parties. Part Six (Chapter 14) moves beyond the two parties to the contract. Section one considers the third party beneficiary contract. Section two investigates the assignment and delegation of a contract. Section three leaves the law of contracts and enters the law of torts. The topic considered is third party interference with existing contract rights.

14

THIRD PARTY INTERESTS

Section 1. THIRD PARTY BENEFICIARY CONTRACTS

A third party beneficiary contract, as its name suggests, is a contract for the benefit of a third party. Courts agree that a contract made for the benefit of a third party beneficiary may be enforced by that third party.

In a two party bilateral contract, because each party promises the other, each has a duty associated with his or her promise and a right associated with the other party's promise.

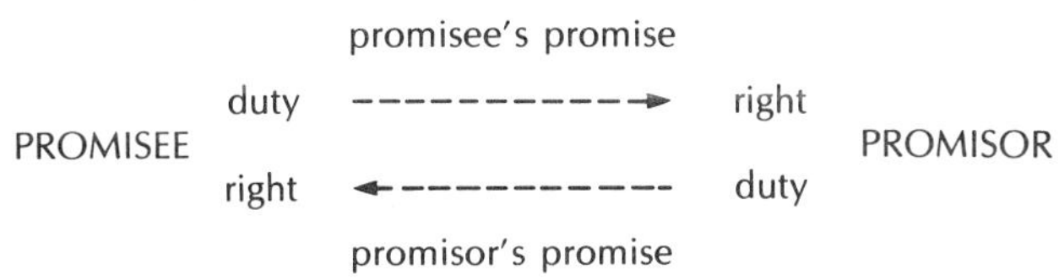

As in the two party bilateral contract, each of the two contracting parties in a third party beneficiary contract still has a duty associated with his or her promise and a right associated with the other party's promise. What is different about a third party beneficiary contract is the inclusion of the third party beneficiary. Unlike the two contracting parties who have both rights and duties, the third party beneficiary has contractual rights but no contractual duties.

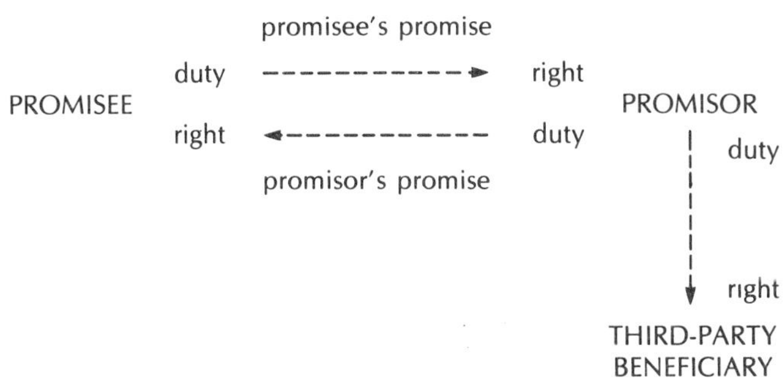

The following contract between Abigail and Pickwick Press illustrates a typical third party beneficiary contract.

EXAMPLE

Abigail, a mystery writer, promises to write a new mystery for her publisher, Fleet Street Press, if Fleet Street promises to put the royalties in trust for her godchild, Tracy. From this contract, Tracy, the third party beneficiary, owes a duty neither to Abigail nor to Fleet Street. Abigail, a contracting party, owes a duty to write for Fleet Street and Fleet Street owes both Abigail and Tracy a duty to pay Tracy. Because Fleet Street owes a duty to Tracy, Tracy has a right to have Fleet Street perform this duty.

The following diagram illustrates the parties' rights and duties:

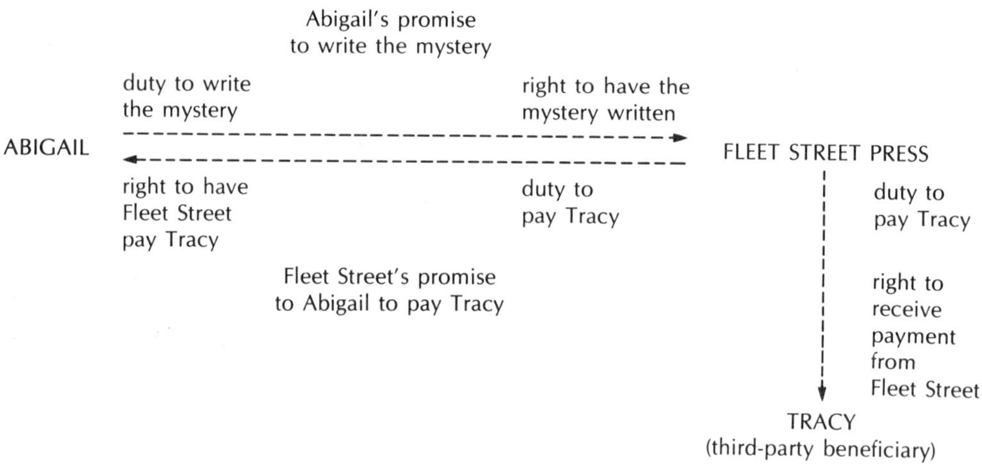

A third party beneficiary contract is subject to the same rules of contract formation as is any other contract. The consideration for Abigail's promise to write for Fleet Street is Fleet Street's promise to pay Tracy. The consideration for Fleet Street's promise to pay Tracy is Abigail's promise to write for Fleet Street.

Third party beneficiaries come in three forms: donee, creditor, and incidental. If a party contracts to give a third party a gift, the third party is a donee beneficiary. In the illustration with Abigail and Fleet Street, Tracy is a donee beneficiary.

If a party contracts to discharge a prior obligation that the promisee had with a third party, the third party is a creditor beneficiary. If, in the illustration, Tracy was not Abigail's goddaughter but rather had lent Abigail money, Tracy would have been a creditor beneficiary.

The Restatement (Second) of Contracts has moved away from the creditor-donee beneficiary distinction. In its place the Restatement uses "intended" as the label for the third party beneficiary who has an enforceable right.

A beneficiary who is neither a creditor nor a donee (intended) is an incidental beneficiary. An incidental beneficiary has no enforceable right under the contract. To determine whether a beneficiary has a right to enforce the contract, courts often use the "intent to benefit" test which examines who is to receive the performance of the contract. Courts are not in agreement in their application of the "intent to benefit" test. In some cases, the courts have held that if the *contracting parties* intended to benefit the third party, the third party is a protected beneficiary with enforceable contractual rights. If the contracting parties intended to benefit only one of themselves, any third party is an incidental beneficiary with no enforceable rights under the contract. In other cases, the courts consider only the *promisee's* intent and have said that if the *promisee* intended to benefit the third party, the third party is a protected beneficiary with enforceable contractual rights. Still other cases have emphasized the conferring of a right rather than a benefit. If the *promisee intended to confer a right on the third party,* the third party is a protected beneficiary with enforceable contractual rights.

In *Martinez v. Socoma Companies, Inc.* Socoma promised the United States Government to provide job training and at least one year of employment to a certain number of disadvantaged people in East Los Angeles. Were these residents of East Los Angeles, who were certified by the federal government as disadvantaged, donee, creditor, or incidental beneficiaries of the Socoma/Government contract?

Martinez v. Socoma Companies, Inc.

Supreme Court of California, In Bank, 1974.
11 Cal.3d 394, 521 P.2d 841, 99 Cal.Rptr. 767.

WRIGHT, Chief Justice.

Plaintiffs brought this class action on behalf of themselves and other disadvantaged unemployed persons, alleging that defendants failed to perform contracts with the United States government under which defendants agreed to provide job training and at least one year of employment to certain numbers of such persons. Plaintiffs claim that they and the other such persons are third party beneficiaries of the contracts and as such are entitled to damages for defendants' nonperformance. General demurrers to the complaint were sustained without leave to amend, apparently on the ground that plaintiffs lacked standing to sue as third party beneficiaries. Dismissals were entered as to the demurring defendants, and plaintiffs appeal.

We affirm the judgments of dismissal. As will appear, the contracts nowhere state that either the government or defendants are to be liable to persons such as plaintiffs for damages resulting from the defendants' nonperformance. The benefits to be derived from defendants' performance were clearly intended not as gifts from the government to such persons but as a means of executing the public purposes stated in the contracts and in the underlying legislation. Accordingly, plaintiffs were only incidental beneficiaries and as such have no right of recovery.

The complaint names as defendants Socoma Companies, Inc. ("Socoma"), Lady Fair Kitchens, Incorporated ("Lady Fair"), Monarch Electronics International, Inc. ("Monarch"), and eleven individuals of whom three are alleged officers or directors of Socoma, four of Lady Fair, and four of Monarch. Lady Fair and the individual defendants associated with it, a Utah corporation and Utah residents respectively, did not appear in the trial court and are not parties to this appeal.

The complaint alleges that under 1967 amendments to the Economic Opportunity Act of 1964 (81 Stat. 688–690, 42 U.S.C. §§ 2763–2768, repealed by 86 Stat. 703 (1972)) "the United States Congress instituted Special Impact Programs with the intent to benefit the residents of certain neighborhoods having especially large concentrations of low income persons and suffering from dependency, chronic unemployment and rising tensions." Funds to administer these programs were appropriated to the United States Department of Labor. The department subsequently designated the East Los Angeles neighborhood as a "Special Impact area" and made federal funds available for contracts with local private industry for the benefit of the "hard-core unemployed residents" of East Los Angeles.

On January 17, 1969, the corporate defendants allegedly entered into contracts with the Secretary of Labor, acting on behalf of the Manpower Administration, United States Department of Labor (hereinafter referred to as the "Government"). Each such defendant entered into a separate contract and all three contracts are made a part of the complaint as exhibits. Under each contract the contracting defendant agreed to lease space in the then vacant Lincoln Heights jail building owned by the City of Los Angeles, to invest at least $5,000,000 in renovating the leasehold and establishing a facility for the manufacture of certain articles, to train and employ in such facility for at least 12 months, at minimum wage rates, a specified number of East Los Angeles residents certified as disadvantaged by the Government, and to provide such employees with opportunities for promotion into available supervisorial-managerial positions and with options to purchase stock in their employer corporation. Each contract provided for the lease of different space in the building and for the manufacture of a different kind of product. As consideration, the Government agreed to pay each defendant a stated amount in installments. Socoma was to hire 650 persons and receive $950,000; Lady Fair was to hire 550 persons and receive $999,000; and Monarch was to hire 400 persons and receive $800,000. The hiring of these persons was to be completed by January 17, 1970.

Plaintiffs were allegedly members of a class of no more than 2,017 East Los Angeles residents who were certified as disadvantaged and were qualified for employment under the contracts. Although the Government paid $712,500 of the contractual consideration to Socoma, $299,700 to Lady Fair, and $240,000 to Monarch, all of these defendants failed to perform under their respective contracts, except that Socoma provided 186 jobs of which 139 were wrongfully terminated, and Lady Fair provided 90 jobs, of which all were wrongfully terminated.

The complaint contains 11 causes of action. The second, fourth, and sixth causes of action seek damages of $3,607,500 against Socoma, $3,052,500 against Lady Fair, and $2,220,000 against Monarch, calculated on the basis of 12 months' wages at minimum rates and $1,000 for loss of training for each of the jobs the defendant contracted to provide. The third and fifth causes of action seek similar damages for the 139 persons whose jobs were terminated by Socoma and the 90 persons whose jobs were terminated by Lady Fair. The first, seventh, and eighth causes of action seek to impose joint liability on Socoma, Lady Fair, and Monarch as joint venturers, alleging that they negotiated the contracts through a common representative and entered into a joint lease of the Lincoln Heights jail building. The ninth, tenth, and eleventh causes of action seek to impose the liability of the corporate defendants upon their officers and directors named as individual defendants, alleging that the latter undercapitalized their respective corporations and used the same as their *alter egos.*

Each cause of action alleges that the "express purpose of the [Government] in entering into [each] contract was to benefit [the] certified disadvantaged hard-core unemployed residents of East Los Angeles [for whom defendants promised to provide training and jobs] and none other, and those residents are thus the express third party beneficiaries of [each] contract."

. . .

Plaintiffs contend they are third party beneficiaries under Civil Code section 1559, which provides: "A contract, made expressly for the benefit of a third person, may be enforced by him at any time before the parties thereto rescind it." This section excludes enforcement of a contract by persons who are only incidentally or remotely benefited by it. (Lucas v. Hamm (1961) 56 Cal.2d 583, 590, 15 Cal.Rptr. 821, 824, 364 P.2d 685, 688.) American law generally classifies persons having enforceable rights under contracts to which they are not parties as either creditor beneficiaries or donee beneficiaries. (Rest., Contracts, §§ 133, subds. (1), (2), 135, 136, 147; 2 Williston on Contracts (3d ed. 1959) § 356; 4 Corbin on Contracts (1951) § 774; see Rest.2d Contracts (Tentative Drafts 1973) § 133, coms. b, c.) California decisions follow this classification. (Southern Cal. Gas Co. v. ABC Construction Co. (1962) 204 Cal.App.2d 747, 752, 22 Cal.Rptr. 540; 1 Witkin, Summary of Cal. Law (8th ed. 1973) Contracts, § 500.)

A person cannot be a creditor beneficiary unless the promisor's performance of the contract will discharge some form of legal duty owed to the beneficiary by the promisee. (Hartman Ranch Co. v. Associated Oil Co. (1937) 10 Cal.2d 232, 244, 73 P.2d 1163; Rest., Contracts, § 133, subd. (1)(b).) Clearly the Government (the promisee) at no time bore any legal duty toward plaintiffs to provide the benefits set forth in the contracts and plaintiffs do not claim to be creditor beneficiaries.

A person is a donee beneficiary only if the promisee's contractual intent is either to make a gift to him or to confer on him a right against the promisor. (Rest., Contracts, § 133, subd. (1)(a).) If the promisee intends to make a gift, the donee beneficiary can recover if such donative intent must have been understood by the promisor from the nature of the contract and the circumstances accompanying its execution. (Lucas v. Hamm, supra, 56 Cal.2d at pp. 590–591, 15 Cal.Rptr. 821, 364 P.2d 685.) This rule does not aid plaintiffs, however, because, as will be seen, no intention to make a gift can be imputed to the Government as promisee.

Unquestionably plaintiffs were among those whom the Government intended to benefit through defendants' performance of the contracts which recite that they are executed pursuant to a statute and a presidential directive calling for programs to furnish disadvantaged persons with training and employment opportunities. However, the fact that a Government program for social betterment confers benefits upon individuals who are not required to render contractual consideration in return does not necessarily imply that the benefits are intended as gifts. Congress' power to spend money in aid of the general welfare (U.S. Const., art. I, § 8) authorizes federal programs to alleviate national unemployment. (Helvering v. Davis (1937) 301 U.S. 619, 640–645, 57 S.Ct. 904, 81 L.Ed. 1307.) The benefits of such programs are provided not simply as gifts to the recipients but as a means of accomplishing a larger public purpose. The furtherance of the public purpose is in the nature of consideration to the Government, displacing any governmental intent to furnish the benefits as gifts. (See County of Alameda v. Janssen (1940) 16 Cal.2d 276, 281, 106 P.2d 11; Allied Architects v. Payne (1923) 192 Cal. 431, 438–439, 221 p. 209.)

Even though a person is not the intended recipient of a gift, he may nevertheless be "a donee beneficiary if it appears from the terms of the promise in view of the accompanying circumstances that the purpose of the promisee in obtaining the promise . . . is . . . to *confer upon him a right against the promisor* to some performance neither due nor supposed or asserted to be due from the promisee to the beneficiary." (Rest., Contracts, § 133, subd. (1)(a) (italics supplied); Gourmet Lane, Inc. v. Keller (1963) 222 Cal.App.2d 701, 705, 35 Cal.Rptr. 398.) The Government may, of course, deliberately implement a public purpose by including provisions in its contracts which expressly confer on a specified class of third persons a direct right to benefits, or damages in lieu of benefits, against the private contractor. But a governmental intent to confer such a direct right cannot be inferred simply from the fact that the third persons were intended to enjoy the benefits. The Restatement of Contracts makes this clear in dealing specifically with contractual promises to the Government to render services to members of the public: "A promisor bound to the United States or to a State or municipality by contract to do an act or render a service to some or all of the members of the public, *is subject to no duty* under the contract to such members to give compensation for the injurious consequences of performing or attempting to perform it, or of failing to do so, unless, . . . *an intention is manifested in the contract,* as interpreted in the light of the circumstances surrounding its formation, *that the promisor shall compensate members of the public for such injurious consequences*. . . ." (Rest., Contracts, § 145 (italics supplied); see City & County of San Francisco v. Western Air Lines, Inc. (1962) 204 Cal.App.2d 105, 121, 22 Cal.Rptr. 216.)

The present contracts manifest no intent that the defendants pay damages to compensate plaintiffs or other members of the public for their nonperformance. To the contrary, the contracts' provisions for retaining the Government's control over determination of contractual disputes and for limiting defendants' financial risks indicate a governmental purpose to exclude the direct rights against defendants claimed here.

Each contract provides that any dispute of fact arising thereunder is to be determined by written decision of the Government's contracting officer, subject to an appeal to the Secretary of Labor, whose decision shall be final unless determined by a competent court to have been fraudulent, capricious, arbitrary, in bad faith, or not supported by substantial evidence. These administrative decisions may include determinations of related questions of law although such determinations are not made final. The efficiency and uniformity of interpretation fostered by these administrative procedures would tend to be undermined if litigation such as the present action, to which the Government is a stranger, were permitted to proceed on the merits.

In addition to the provisions on resolving disputes each contract contains a "liquidated damages" provision obligating the contractor to refund all amounts received from the Government, with interest, in the event of failure to acquire and equip the specified manufacturing facility, and, for each employment opportunity it fails to provide, to refund a stated dollar amount equivalent to the total contract compensation divided by the number of jobs agreed to be provided. This liquidated damages provision limits liability for the breaches alleged by plaintiffs to the refunding of amounts received and indicates an absence of any contractual intent to impose liability directly in favor of plaintiffs, or, as claimed in the complaint, to impose liability for the value of the promised performance. To allow plaintiffs' claim would nullify the limited liability for which defendants bargained and which the Government may well have held out as an inducement in negotiating the contracts.

. . .

In providing for special impact programs, Congress declared that such programs were directed to the solution of critical problems existing in particular neighborhoods having especially large concentrations of low-income persons, and that the programs were intended to be of sufficient size and scope to have an appreciable impact in such neighborhoods in arresting tendencies toward dependency, chronic unemployment, and rising community tensions. (42 U.S.C. former § 2763.) Thus the contracts here were designed not to benefit individuals as such but to utilize the training and employment of disadvantaged persons as a means of improving the East Los Angeles neighborhood. Moreover, the means by which the contracts were intended to accomplish this community improvement were not confined to provision of the particular benefits on which plaintiffs base their claim to damages—one year's employment at minimum wages plus $1,000 worth of training to be provided to each of 650 persons by one defendant, 400 by another, and 550 by another. Rather the objective was to be achieved by establishing permanent industries in which local residents would be permanently employed and would have opportunities to become supervisors, managers and part owners. The required minimum capital investment of $5,000,000 by each defendant and the defendants' 22–year lease of the former Lincoln Heights jail building for conversion into an industrial facility also indicates the broad, long-range objective of the program. Presumably, as the planned enterprises prospered, the quantity and quality of employment and economic opportunity that they provided would increase and would benefit not only employees but also their families, other local enterprises and the government itself through reduction of law enforcement and welfare costs.

The fact that plaintiffs were in a position to benefit more directly than certain other members of the public from performance of the contract does not alter their status as incidental beneficiaries. (See Rest., Contracts, § 145, illus. 1: C, a member of the public cannot recover for injury from B's failure to perform a contract with the United States to carry mail over a certain route.) For example, in City & County of San Francisco v. Western Air Lines, Inc., supra, 204 Cal.App.2d 105, 22 Cal.Rptr. 216, the agreement between the federal government and the city for improvement of the airport could be considered to be of greater benefit to air carriers using the airport than to many other members of the public. Nevertheless, Western, as an air carrier, was but an incidental, not an express, beneficiary of the agreement and therefore had no standing to enforce the contractual prohibition against discrimination in the airport's availability for public use. The court explains the distinction as follows: "None of the documents under consideration confers on Western the rights of a third-party beneficiary. The various contracts and assurances created benefits and detriments as between only two parties—the United States and the City. Nothing in them shows any intent of the contracting parties to confer any benefit directly and expressly upon air carriers such as the defendant. It is true that air carriers, including Western, may be *incidentally* benefited by City's assurances in respect to nondiscriminatory treatment at the airport. They may also be incidentally benefited by the fact that, through federal aid, a public airport is improved with longer runways, brighter beacons, or larger loading ramps, or by the fact a new public airport is provided for a community without one. The various documents and agreements were part of a federal aid program directed to the promoting of a national transportation system. Provisions in such agreements, including the nondiscrimination clauses, were intended to advance such federal aims and not for the benefit of those who might be affected by the sponsor's failure to perform." (204 Cal. App.2d at p. 120, 22 Cal.Rptr. at p. 225.)

For the reasons above stated we hold that plaintiffs and the class they represent have no standing as third party beneficiaries to recover the damages sought in the complaint under either California law or the general contract principles which federal law applies to government contracts.

The judgments of dismissal are affirmed.

McCOMB, SULLIVAN, and CLARK, JJ., concur.

BURKE, Justice (dissenting).

I dissent. The certified hard-core unemployed of East Los Angeles were the express, not incidental, beneficiaries of the contracts in question and, therefore, have standing to enforce those contracts.

As the majority point out, we must reverse the order sustaining the demurrer in this case if we determine the written contracts incorporated into the complaint support plaintiffs' claim either on their face or under any interpretation to which the contracts are reasonably susceptible (maj. opn., p. 588). Furthermore, at this stage of the proceedings, the question of plaintiffs' ability to prove these allegations does not concern us, for plaintiffs need only plead facts showing they may be entitled to some relief. (Alcorn v. Anbro Engineering, Inc., 2 Cal. 3d 493, 496, 86 Cal.Rptr. 88, 468 P.2d 216.)

Civil Code section 1559 provides that "A contract, made expressly for the benefit of a third person, may be enforced by him at any time before the parties thereto rescind it." The general principles applicable to such contracts are set forth in Shell v. Schmidt, 126 Cal.App.2d 279, 290–291, 272 P.2d 82, 89, as follows: "[A] third party beneficiary may maintain an action directly on such a contract. [Citation.] The promise in such a situation is treated as having been made directly to the third party. [Citation.] It is no objection to an action by the third party that the contracting party (here the government) could also sue upon the contract for the same breach. [Citation.] Of course, the beneficiary must be more than incidentally benefited by the contract. An incidental beneficiary cannot successfully maintain an action. [Citation.] Whether the beneficiary is or is not an incidental one, or a beneficiary for whose express benefit the contract was entered into, is a question of construction. [Citation.] It is not required that the third party beneficiary be specifically named as a beneficiary. All that section 1559 requires is that the contract be 'made expressly for the benefit of a third person,' and 'expressly' simply means 'in an express manner; in direct or unmistakable terms; explicitly; definitely; directly.' [Citation.] [¶] *Where the contract is for the benefit of a class any members or member of the intended class may enforce it.* [Citation.] *The fact that the government is one of the contracting parties does not change the rule.*" (Italics added.)

Applying the foregoing principles to the instant case I conclude that plaintiffs are express beneficiaries of the contracts between defendants and the government and are therefore entitled to enforce the contracts.

The majority contend that the congressional purpose in enacting the Economic Opportunity Act of 1964 (including the subsequent amendments thereto creating the Special Impact Program), and the government's purpose in executing the instant contracts with defendants pursuant to the Act, was to benefit only the general public and particularly the local neighborhoods where these programs were to be implemented. Although members of plaintiffs' class "were among those whom the Government intended to benefit . . .," (maj. opn., p. 589) the benefits accruing to plaintiffs' class, according to the majority, were merely "*means* of executing the public purposes stated in the contracts and in the underlying legislation." (P. 587, italics added.)

The majority err in the above conclusion because the congressional purpose was to benefit *both* the communities in which the impact programs are established *and* the individual impoverished persons in such communities. The benefits from the instant contracts were to accrue directly to the members of plaintiffs' class, as a reading of the contracts clearly demonstrates. These direct benefits to members of plaintiffs' class were not merely the "*means* of executing the public purposes," as the majority contend (p. 589, italics added), but were the *ends* in themselves and one of the public purposes to which the legislation and subsequent contracts were addressed. Accordingly, I cannot agree with the majority that "the contracts here were designed *not* to benefit individuals as such but to utilize the training and employment of disadvantaged persons as a *means* of improving the East Los Angeles neighborhood." (Pp. 592, 593, italics added.)

The intent of the contracts themselves is expressed in their preambles: "WHEREAS, the Secretary of Labor is authorized ... to enter into contracts to provide for Special Impact Programs ... directed to the solution of the critical problems existing in particular communities and neighborhoods within urban areas of the Nation having especially large concentrations of low-income persons and [¶] WHEREAS, the President of the United States on October 2, 1967, launched a major test program to mobilize the resources of private industry and the Federal Government *to help find jobs and provide training for thousands of the Nation's hard-core unemployed, or underemployed,* by inviting private industry throughout the country to join with the agencies and departments of the Federal Government in assuming responsibility *for providing training and work opportunities for such seriously disadvantaged persons.* [¶] NOW THEREFORE, pursuant to the aforesaid statutory authority, and the directive of the President, the parties hereto, in consideration of the mutual promises herein expressed, agree as follows:. . . ." (Italics added.) By these provisions, the contracting parties clearly state as one of their purposes their intent to find jobs for the hard-core unemployed.

In accord with this expressed intent, the substantive provisions of the contracts confer a direct benefit upon the class seeking to enforce them. The contracts call for the hiring of stated numbers of hard-core unemployed from the East Los Angeles Special Impact Area for a period of at least one year at a starting minimum wage of $2.00 per hour for the first 90 days and a minimum wage of $2.25 per hour thereafter, or for the prevailing wage for the area, whichever is higher. In addition to requiring appropriate job training for such employees, the contracts also require "That the Contractor will arrange for the orderly promotion of persons so employed into available supervisory-managerial and other positions, and will arrange for all contract employees to obtain a total ownership interest not exceeding thirty (30) percent in the Contractor through an appropriate stock purchase plan. . . ." The scope of the stock purchase plans is detailed in each of the contracts.

In Lucas v. Hamm, 56 Cal.2d 583, 590, 15 Cal.Rptr. 821, 364 P.2d 685, we noted that one of the usual characteristics of a third party beneficiary contract is that performance is to be rendered directly to the beneficiary. The direct benefits to accrue to the beneficiaries as enumerated above renders inescapable the conclusion that these are third party beneficiary contracts.

Although the contracts may also benefit particular communities and neighborhoods, this fact does not preclude the maintenance of the action by plaintiffs as intended beneficiaries of the contracts. It is not necessary under Civil Code section 1559, *supra,* that a contract be exclusively for the benefit of a third party to give him a right to enforce its provisions. (Hartman Ranch Co. v. Associated Oil Co., 10 Cal.2d 232, 247, 73 P.2d 1163; Ralph C. Sutro Co. v. Paramount, 216 Cal.App.2d 433, 437, 31 Cal.Rptr. 174.) And, as will be discussed more fully, *infra,* nor does the existence of a liquidated damages clause running in favor of the government defeat plaintiffs' right to recover under the contract; the fact that the government may also bring an action for the same breach does not bar the third party beneficiary from enforcing his rights. (Shell v. Schmidt, *supra,* 126 Cal.App.2d 279, 290, 272 P.2d 82.) All that is necessary is that the third party show he is a member of a class for whose benefit the contract was made. (Shell v. Schmidt, *supra;* Ralph C. Sutro Co. v. Paramount, *supra.*) Thus, plaintiffs have standing to bring an action for the breach of defendants' contracts with the government.

. . .

The majority contend that the inclusion of liquidated damage clauses in each of the contracts limits defendants' financial risks and was intended to preclude the assertion of third party claims. (P. 590.) Yet, these clauses simply provide for various refunds of monies advanced by the government in the event of a default. These so-called "liquidated damages" clauses nowhere purport to limit damages to the specified refunds. Nothing in the contracts limits the right of the government or, more importantly, plaintiffs' class, to seek additional relief. As I noted above, the fact that the government could also sue for breach of the contracts does not affect the rights of third party beneficiaries. (Shell v. Schmidt, *supra,* 126 Cal. App.2d 279, 290, 272 P.2d 82.)

The majority also rely on the fact that, "The present contracts manifest no intent that the defendants pay damages to compensate plaintiffs or other members of the public for their nonperformance." (P. 590.) Therefore, it assertedly follows that giving plaintiffs the right to monetary benefits in lieu of performance would give to plaintiffs and the class they represent benefits never contemplated nor intended under the contracts. This argument disregards both the fact that the class was to receive a direct monetary benefit under the contracts in the form of wages, and that under well settled contract law, an aggrieved party is entitled to be compensated for all the detriment proximately caused by a breach of contract (Civ.Code, § 3300).

A contract of employment ordinarily confers upon the employee the expectation that he will obtain the work bargained for. The measure of damages for the breach of such a contract, however, is not the award of the job, but is the amount of salary the employee would have earned for the agreed upon period of service less the amount which the employer affirmatively proves the employee has earned, or with reasonable effort might have earned, from other employment. (Parker v. Twentieth Century-Fox Film Corp., 3 Cal.3d 176, 181, 89 Cal.Rptr. 737, 474 P.2d 689.) Thus, the fact that plaintiffs' class has been promised only jobs and job training does not prevent them from recovering an amount of money which will compensate them for the loss of such jobs and training, i.e., the damages proximately caused by defendants' breach. (Civ.Code, § 3300, *supra.*)

It is my conclusion, therefore, that the trial court erred in sustaining the demurrer without leave to amend. I would order the trial court to determine the propriety of plaintiffs' class action prior to proceeding upon the merits of the complaint.

TOBRINER and MOSK, JJ., concur.

PROBLEM 1: Uncle Bill promised his nephew, George, that if George would quit smoking cigarettes for one year, Uncle Bill would buy George a new Corvette. George quit smoking for a year.

1. What are the rights and duties between Uncle Bill and George?
2. Is the Chevrolet Motor Company a donee, creditor, or incidental beneficiary of this contract?
3. What are the rights and duties between Uncle Bill and the third party beneficiary?

PROBLEM 2: Alan contracted to sell Greenacre to Graham for Graham's promise to pay $250,000 according to the following plan: $10,000 to Alan's nephew Calvin as a graduation gift; $100,000 to Charge-It Credit Company as full payment of Alan's last month's charges; and $140,000 to Benton, a broker, to invest for the benefit of Alan's mother, Margaret.

1. What are the rights and duties between Alan and Graham?

2. Are Calvin, Charge-It Credit Company, and Margaret, donee, creditor, or incidental beneficiaries?
3. What are the rights and duties between Graham and the third party beneficiaries?

The distinction between intended and incidental beneficiaries is an important issue when considering breach of implied warranties in a contract for the sale of goods.

EXAMPLE

An automobile with a defective wheel was manufactured by Ford Motor Company and sold to Friendly Motors, a dealership. Friendly sold the Ford to Stanley. When Stanley was out on a Sunday drive with his girlfriend, Josephine, the wheel collapsed and the car crashed. Both Josephine and Stanley were injured.

Although Stanley could sue Friendly on his contract with Friendly, could Stanley sue Ford, the deep pocket up the distribution chain? Was Stanley a third party beneficiary of the Ford Motor Company/Friendly Motors contract? Because the three parties are in the distribution chain (as either buyers or sellers), the question is whether Stanley will be barred from suing Ford Motor on the ground that he was not in vertical privity of contract with the Ford Motor Company. The "vertical" non-privity plaintiff is a buyer in the distribution chain who did not buy directly from the defendant.

Unlike Stanley who was a buyer, Josephine was not contractually related to either Friendly or Ford. She was not in the distribution chain. The question is whether Josephine is in horizontal privity of contract with Friendly Motors. The "horizontal" non-privity plaintiff is not a buyer in the distribution chain but one who consumes, uses or is affected by the goods.

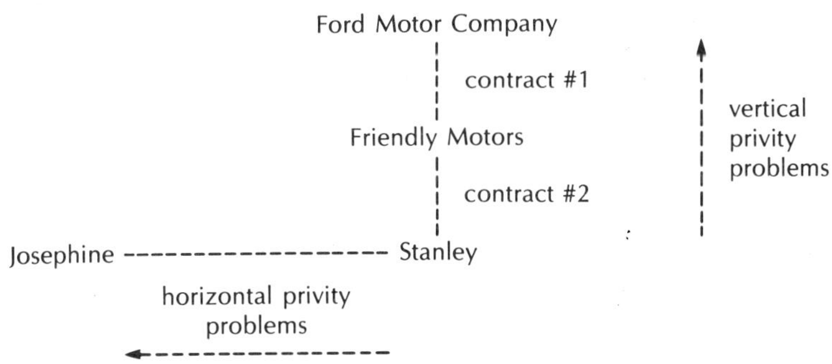

The "privity of contract" language can be translated into donee (intended) and incidental beneficiary. A third party who is in privity of contract is a donee beneficiary and has contractual rights. A third party who is not in privity of contract is an incidental beneficiary and has no contractual rights.

Because the subject matter of this illustration is a sale of goods, the Uniform Commercial Code applies. Unfortunately, the Code is silent as to the first question—whether Stanley can sue up the distribution chain. After the enactment of the Code, many courts viewed this legislative silence as indicating that such a suit is prohibited due to a lack of vertical privity of contract.

Recently, a number of courts have abrogated at least a part of the vertical privity requirement. The abrogation has been piecemeal based on the injury sustained by the aggrieved party. Products can cause three different types of injury: personal injury, property damage, and economic loss. Personal injury and property damage have traditionally been compensated under the tort action of strict liability. Breach of contract actions have traditionally compensated the aggrieved party for economic loss. Some courts, therefore, found the abrogation of vertical privity for breach of warranty cases involving economic loss a reasonable evolutionary step. Other courts found the abrogation of vertical privity for breach of warranty cases involving personal injury a reasonable evolutionary step.

The second question—whether Josephine can sue the last seller in the distribution chain—is addressed in the Code. Section 2–318 offers the states a selection among three alternatives. Alternative A extends a seller's express and implied warranty liability to family and household members and guests in the buyer's home if it is reasonable to expect that such person may use, consume or be affected by the goods.

> Alternative A
>
> A seller's warranty whether express or implied extends to any natural person who is in the family or household of his buyer or who is a guest in his home if it is reasonable to expect that such person may use, consume or be affected by the goods and who is injured in person by breach of the warranty. A seller may not exclude or limit the operation of this section.

Alternative B extends the seller's express and implied warranty liability to any person who may reasonably be expected to use the goods. Alternative B expands coverage to persons beyond the buyer's family, household, or guests.

> Alternative B
>
> A seller's warranty whether express or implied extends to any natural person who may reasonably be expected to use, consume or be affected by the goods and who is injured in person by breach of the warranty. A seller may not exclude or limit the operation of this section.

Alternative C is the broadest of the three and expands coverage to business entities.

> Alternative C
>
> A seller's warranty whether express or implied extends to any person who may reasonably be expected to use, consume or be affected by the goods and who is injured by breach of the warranty. A seller may not exclude or limit the operation of this section with respect to injury to the person of an individual to whom the warranty extends.

PROBLEM 3: Is Josephine a donee or incidental beneficiary in the Stanley/Friendly Motors contract? Is your answer the same under the three UCC alternatives of section 2–318?

In *Coombes v. Toro Co.* which alternative was enacted in Connecticut? Did the court correctly apply the facts to the law? Would the result have been the same if Connecticut had enacted either alternative B or C?

Coombes v. Toro Co.

Superior Court of Connecticut, 1979.
28 UCC Rep.Serv. 391.

DUPONT, J. Plaintiff is bringing this action to recover for personal injuries allegedly incurred when, in the course of his employment, the engine of a "three wheel utility vehicle" which he was operating stalled and the brakes failed. As a result, the vehicle rolled backwards down an incline and the plaintiff was thrown to the ground and struck by the vehicle when it overturned. The defendants are The Toro Company which manufactures this model and the Turf Products Corporation which distributes and sells it. The plaintiff-employee was a member of the maintenance crew of a golf course which purchased the vehicle for use by its workers. The action is grounded in negligence, strict tort, and breach of warranty. The defendants have moved to strike that part of the third count which sounds in breach of statutory warranty. The parties have agreed that those portions of the Motion to Strike relating to other counts need not be addressed by the court.

Defendants argue that the complaint does not state a claim upon which relief can be granted because, inter alia, count three does not allege that plaintiff is within the category of individuals protected by § 42a–2–318. Resolution of this issue in favor of the defendants is dispositive of the other claims of the Motion to Strike.

The provision governing third-party beneficiaries, CGS § 42a–2–318, was adopted in 1959 and amended in 1965. It is significant to note that although more expansive alternatives to the statute have existed since 1966,[1] the Connecticut legislature has maintained its adherence to Alternative A. The sentence pertaining to the neutrality in the statute apparently refers to developing tort law. See J. White & R. Summers, Uniform Commercial Code § 11–3 at 330–31 (1972 ed).

The Supreme Court has not yet considered whether an employee is covered by § 42a–2–318. However, in the only Superior Court case on point, Chen v. Reliable Rubber & Plastic Machinery Co., 5 CLT # 7 at 13 [25 UCC Rep 1274], September 18, 1978, the court held that an employee is not an intended beneficiary. The court relied heavily on the availability of a cause of action in strict tort. Furthermore, the majority of states which like Connecticut, have adopted Alternative A and which have considered the issue at hand have decided that the section does not extend to employees.[2]

The plaintiff urges that the spirit of various Connecticut warranty decisions should encourage the court to extend coverage to employees. The cases cited were decided under tort principles, however. It has been recognized that "an action based on strict liability is to be distinguished from liability on breach of warranty or simple negligence." De Felice v. Ford Motor Co., 28 Conn Supp 164, 168, 255 A2d 636 (1969), citing Rossignol v. Danbury School of Aeronautics, Inc., 154 Conn 549, 227 A2d 418 [4 UCC Rep 305] (1967). As a result, the import of

1. Alternative B extends warranties to "any natural person who may reasonably be expected to use, consume or be affected by the goods and who is injured in person by the breach of warranty." Alternative C extends to "any person who may reasonably be expected to use, consume or be affected by the goods and who is injured by the breach of warranty." 1A Uniform Laws Annotated 52–53 (1976).

2. The following Alternative A states have not extended the warranties to employees: Alaska, Georgia, Maryland, North Carolina, Ohio, Oklahoma, Tennessee, and West Virginia. The following Alternative A states have extended the warranties to employees: Arkansas, Florida, Maine, and Pennsylvania. 1A Uniform Laws Annotated 74–77 (1976) and 10–11 (Supp 1979).

plaintiff's cited decisions is limited.

Plaintiff also suggests that the Chen decision concerning employee coverage is not well reasoned because it is not in accord with the Connecticut decisions extending warranties and does not follow the rationale of jurisdictions which have included employees. As indicated above, however, the warranty decisions were made in accord with tort principles and the majority of Alternative A jurisdictions have denied coverage.

Motion to strike that portion of Count 3 relating to a cause of action in breach of warranty under § 42a–2–318 granted.

The third party beneficiary's rights depend on the existence and enforceability of the contract between the contracting parties. If a contract has not been formed, a third party beneficiary does not exist. If a contract exists but the contract is unenforceable, the third party beneficiary cannot enforce the contract.

EXAMPLE

Mickie contracted to sell Brent her car for Brent's promise to pay the purchase price to Mickie's debtor, Kathy. Mickie misrepresented the car's mileage as 50,000 instead of the correct mileage of 150,000. If Brent disaffirms the contract due to the misrepresentation, Brent no longer has a duty to pay Kathy.

In *Lawhead v. Booth* evaluate the following:

1. Was a contract formed between the Vests and Booth?
2. Was Keiffer an intended or incidental beneficiary?
3. Did Keiffer gain a right as a result of the Vests/Booth transaction?

Lawhead v. Booth

Supreme Court of Appeals of West Virginia, 1934.
115 W. Va. 490, 177 S.E. 283.

LITZ, Judge.

This appeal involves the validity of the alleged assumption by Rebecca A. Booth (now deceased) of a debt which defendants Zeffa Vest and E.C. Vest owed defendant Elizabeth E. Keiffer.

By deed dated April 14, 1928, Zeffa Vest and E.C. Vest, her husband, granted to Rebecca A. Booth, mother of Zeffa, lots 31 and 32 in block 48 of Center City, Cabell county, W.Va., for the recited consideration of $8,500, consisting of obligations of that amount, owing by the Vests to third persons, assumed by the grantee, including a debt of $1,250 to Elizabeth E. Keiffer secured by second deed of trust on the property conveyed. By deed of like date and as part of the same transaction, Rebecca A. Booth and husband granted the property to Zeffa Vest for a recited consideration of $1. (The evidence discloses that there was in fact no consideration of any kind.) After the execution of the latter deed, and before its recordation, Zeffa struck out her own name as grantee and inserted the name of Bettie Dwiggins. Elizabeth E. Keiffer seeks to enforce the payment of her debt against the Vests from the estate of Rebecca A. Booth because of the alleged assumption thereof by her in the Vest deed.

Proof was taken to determine (1) whether Rebecca A. Booth was mentally competent to contract at the time of the execution of the contemporaneous deeds; (2) whether the deed from the Vests was delivered; and (3) whether the two deeds were executed for the purpose of hindering, delaying, and defrauding Vests' creditors. Judgment was rendered against the estate of Rebecca A. Booth in favor of Elizabeth E. Keiffer for the full amount of her claim apparently because of affirmative findings upon these issues.

As the conveyance to Mrs. Booth and the reconveyance by herself and husband constitutes one transaction, there is no consideration for her agreement to pay the debt to Elizabeth E. Keiffer who has no higher right than the Vests, through whom she claims. "The foundation of any right the third person (to whom the promisee is obligated) may have, whether he is a sole beneficiary or a creditor of the promisee, is the promisor's contract. Unless there is a valid contract, no rights can arise in favor of anyone.... Further, if there is a contract valid at law, but subject to some equitable defense—as fraud, mistake, or failure of consideration—the defense may be set up against the third person. If the undertaking is to pay a debt or discharge a duty of the promisee, the rights of the third person can be derived only through the promisee, and whatever defense affects the latter affects the creditor." Williston on Contracts, § 394. The Vests being unable to enforce the contract because it is without consideration, Elizabeth E. Keiffer, for whom the promise was made, cannot do so.

The judgment complained of is reversed, and the answer of Elizabeth E. Keiffer in the nature of a cross-bill, against the estate of Rebecca A. Booth, deceased, dismissed.

Reversed and dismissed.

If the beneficiary consents, the contracting parties are generally free to make a subsequent agreement to discharge or modify duties to the beneficiary. If, however, the beneficiary does not consent, the beneficiary may still be able to enforce the contract despite efforts by the contracting parties to discharge or modify their duties. The trend is to allow both creditor and donee beneficiaries to enforce the contract when the beneficiary has learned of the contract and has relied on it or brought suit to enforce the contract before receiving notification of the discharge or modification. The equal treatment of creditor and donee beneficiaries in the Restatement (Second) of Contracts supports this trend.

EXAMPLE

Sneed owed Sanders $200. Sneed contracted with Johnson for Johnson to pay Sanders the $200 Sneed owed Sanders. Sneed notified Sanders that Johnson would pay his debt. Later Sneed, in exchange for Johnson's loaning Sneed his lake cabin over Labor Day weekend, released Johnson from his duty to pay Sanders. Ignorant of Sneed's attempted discharge of Johnson's duty, Sanders sued Johnson for $200. Johnson remained liable to Sanders because Sanders learned of the contract and brought suit to enforce it before receiving notice of the attempted discharge.

Section 2. THE ASSIGNMENT OF CONTRACT RIGHTS AND DELEGATION OF CONTRACT DUTIES

After a contract has been formed, it may become advantageous for one of the parties to either sell his or her contractual rights or delegate his or her contractual duties. This section introduces assignment and delegation. Rights are assigned. Duties are delegated.

A. Assignment

An assignment of a contract is the transfer to another of the contractual rights.

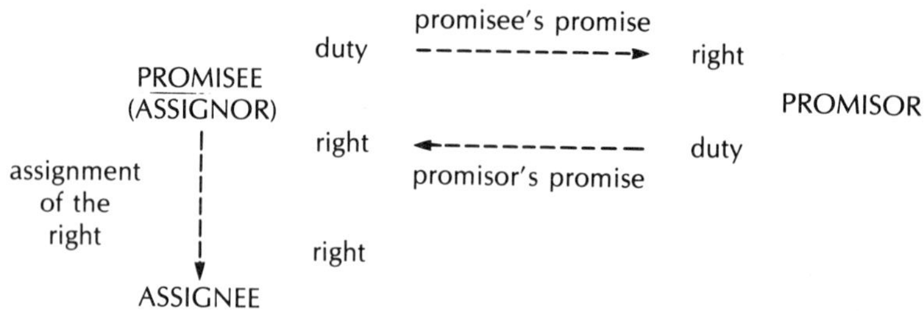

EXAMPLE

Corner Store sells a VCR to Sylvia on $300 credit. Under this contract, Corner Store has a duty to deliver the VCR to Sylvia and a right to have Sylvia pay $300. Sylvia has a duty to pay Corner Store $300 and a right to receive delivery of the VCR. Because Corner Store lacks the assets to finance its credit sales, it sells its right to payment to Friendly Finance Company. Friendly pays Corner Store in exchange for Corner Store's right to have Sylvia pay $300. Once Sylvia is notified of the assignment, she will have a duty to pay Friendly Finance. She will no longer have a duty to pay Corner Store.

In this transaction, Corner Store is the assignor, the party who transfers the right. Friendly Finance is the assignee, the party to whom the right is transferred. Sylvia is the obligor, the party who owes the duty associated with the transferred right. Because Corner Store was the original party who had the right, Corner Store is the original obligee.

Although many rights can be assigned, not all rights may be assigned. Whether a right is assignable depends on whether the transfer of the right will materially alter the duty of the obligor, the party who must perform the duty associated with that right.

PROBLEM 4: The law firm of Peabody, Anderson & Grable, hired Samantha Stevenson as their legal assistant. The contract had a one-year term. After working for the Peabody firm for several months, Samantha was notified that the firm had transferred its right to her work to O'Sullivan & Mead. Was Samantha's contract assignable?

Whether the transfer of the right will materially alter the duty of the obligor is not the only determining factor whether a contract right can be assigned. A court may place great weight on a well drafted term in the contract prohibiting the assignment of a contract right. A court may also refuse to enforce an assignment where a special relationship exists between parties. Also many states have statutes that prohibit or limit certain types of assignments.

An assignee takes the assigned rights subject to any defense which the obligor could have set up against the assignor-obligee at the time of the assignment. Common defenses include lack of consideration, misrepresentation, fraud, and duress.

> *PROBLEM 5:* A–1 Motors sold a used Volvo to Andre for $4,500. The sale was a credit sale. A–1 assigned its right to Andre's payment to Consumer Credit. Several days after Andre took possession of the Volvo, he discovered that it had a cracked block and therefore was in breach of the implied warranties of merchantability. The seriousness of this defect in the vehicle would have justified Andre in withholding his time payments.
>
> Must Andre pay Consumer Credit?

B. Delegation

A delegation of a duty is an authorization to another party to perform the duty. The party who delegates the duty is the delegator. The party who is authorized to perform the duty is the delegatee. The party who has the right to receive performance of the duty is the obligee.

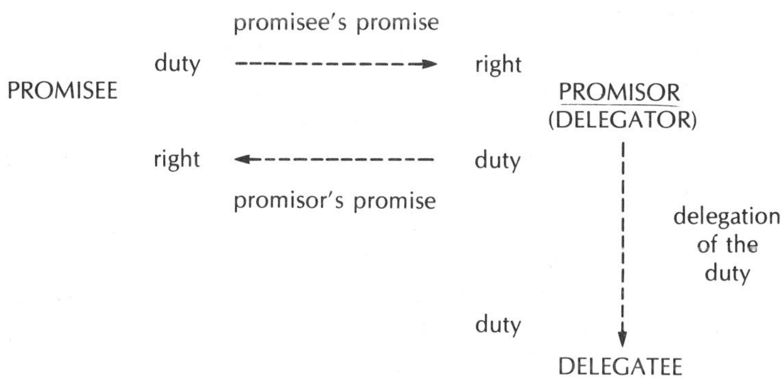

EXAMPLE

Tony had a contract with the *Evening Gazette* to deliver newspapers. Because Tony's paper route was quite lucrative, he sold it to Michael. Tony delegated his duty to deliver newspapers to Michael.

A delegation of a duty does not terminate the duty on the part of the delegator. Delegation only increases the number of parties who have the duty.

EXAMPLE

Barnes delegated his duty to clean Dell's garage to Roberts. Dell could receive performance from Barnes if Roberts fails to perform.

As was the case with the assignment, not all duties may be delegated. Whether a duty is delegable depends on whether the delegation of the duty will materially alter the right of the obligee, the party who has the right associated with that duty. The obligee may have a substantial interest in requiring the original obligor to perform, especially when the performance is "personal," involving qualities such as character, reputation, taste, or skill.

EXAMPLE

Showtime hired the Blue Notes to perform at its club. The Blue Notes could not delegate their duty to perform. Their performance is "personal" because it involves unique talent.

PROBLEM 6: Under Problem 4, could Samantha delegate her duty to work for the firm?

Even general rules have exceptions. In *Rossetti v. City of New Britain* the architectural firm of Rossetti, DiCorcia, and Mileto, a partnership, contracted with the city of New Britain to design a police station and circuit court building. DiCorcia left the partnership and assigned all of his rights and delegated all of his duties to the new partnership, Rossetti and Mileto. This included the contract to design the New Britain police station and circuit court building.

The City ultimately terminated the contract with Rossetti and Mileto and hired another architect for the project. Rossetti and Mileto sued the City for breach of contract. In *Rossetti v. City of New Britain,* 163 Conn. 283, 303 A.2d 714, 718–19 (1972), the court addressed the City's claim that the original partnership's duty was not delegable.

> As to the defendant's claim concerning the nonassignability of personal service contracts, it is indeed the general rule that contracts for personal services cannot be assigned. To be technically accurate, it is not the benefits that are nonassignable; rather, it is the duties which are nondelegable. Performance, in other words, cannot be delegated to another. 4 Corbin, Contracts, p. 439; 6 Am.Jur.2d, Assignments, § 11. Thus if a specific artist is hired to paint a picture, the artist cannot delegate his duty of performing. See La Rue v. Groezinger, 84 Cal. 281, 24 P. 42; 6 Am.Jur.2d, Assignments, § 13. Personal performance is of the essence. Agreements to render professional services as a physician or lawyer fall within this rule. Deaton v. Lawson, 40 Wash. 486, 82 P. 879; Corson v. Lewis, 77 Neb. 446, 109 N.W. 735. Whether a duty is personal such that it cannot be delegated, however, is a question of the intention of the parties to be ascertained from the contract, its nature, and the attending circumstances. Clearly, a contract to render architectural services could be one where personal performance is of the essence. Smith v. Board

of Education, 115 Kan. 155, 222 P. 101. The claims of proof, by which the charge is to be tested, do not support such a conclusion in the case at bar. The defendant's contention is that the contract was personal to the Rossetti, DiCorcia and Mileto partnership. From the claims of proof, however, it is clear that all dealings were with the plaintiff. He was the person in charge of and responsible for the contract. There was nothing offered to show an intent that the plaintiff's partners could not delegate whatever duties they had to the plaintiff. We cannot say that the court erred in its charge in this respect.

C. Substituting and Releasing a Contracting Party: The Novation

A time may come when one of the original contracting parties would like to be replaced by a party who had not been a party to the original contract. This transaction is called a "novation." A novation is a contract that discharges a party to the contract, sometimes an obligor and sometimes an obligee, and substitutes a new party in his or her place. If the new party is an obligor, the obligor may have the same or different duties as the original obligor. If the new party is an obligee, the new obligee may have the same or different rights as the original obligee. Novations come in different forms, but what is critical is that a third party, one who was not a party to the original contract, must be added and either the original obligor or obligee must be discharged.

The Restatement (Second) of Contracts § 280 (1979) defines novation as:

> a substituted contract that includes as a party one who was neither the obligor nor the obligee of the original duty.

By this definition, a novation is a contract between one or both of the original contracting parties and a third party who is added as either a new obligor or obligee. As a substituted contract, a novation replaces the original contract. The end result of a novation is the immediate discharge of one of the original contracting parties and the creation of a new duty. A novation does not exist until the discharge has been accomplished.

Because the novation is substituted for the original contract and the duties in the original contract are terminated, a party is unable to maintain a breach of contract action under the original contract.

Novations are either simple or compound. A simple novation substitutes a new obligor for the original obligor or a new obligee for the original obligee. A compound novation involves a more complex transaction where, for example, each party may be both obligor and obligee.

SIMPLE NOVATION—SUBSTITUTION OF OBLIGORS

First consider the simple novation that substitutes obligors. In the original bilateral contract, the offeror has made a promise to the offeree, and the offeree has made a promise to the offeror. The offeror owes a duty to the offeree and has a right to the offeree's promised performance. The offeree, likewise, owes a duty to the offeror and has a right to the offeror's promised performance. When the contract is executory—that is, neither party has fully performed the offeror and offeree are both obligors and obligees. Once the offeree performs, the offeror is the only remaining obligor and the offeree is the only remaining obligee. Most simple novations substitute a new obligor for the original obligor.

When a new obligor replaces the original obligor, three factual patterns are common:

(1) The obligee makes a promise to the new obligor for the new obligor's promise to the obligee.

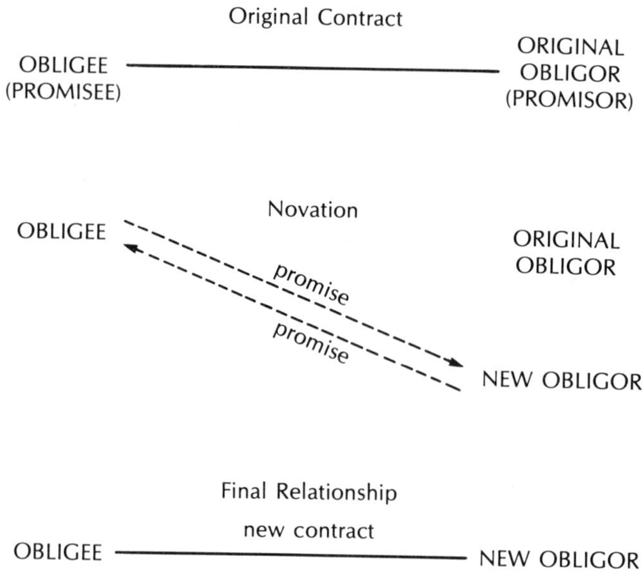

(2) The obligee makes a promise to the original obligor in exchange for the new obligor's promise to the obligee.

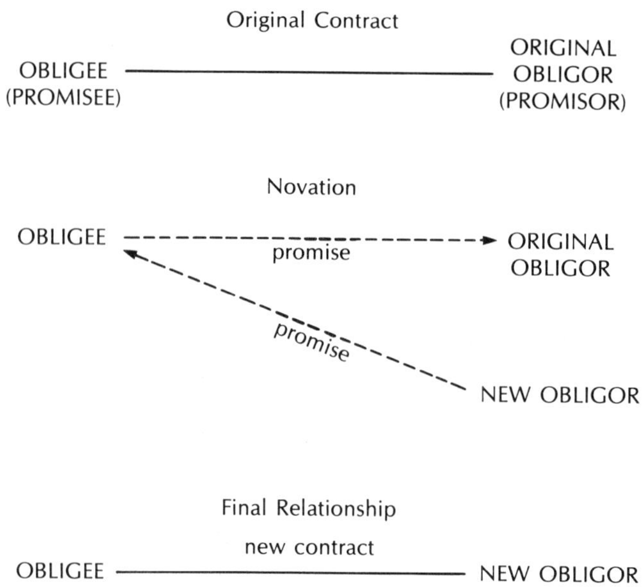

(3) The obligee makes a promise to either the original obligor or the new obligor for the new obligor's promise to the original obligor.

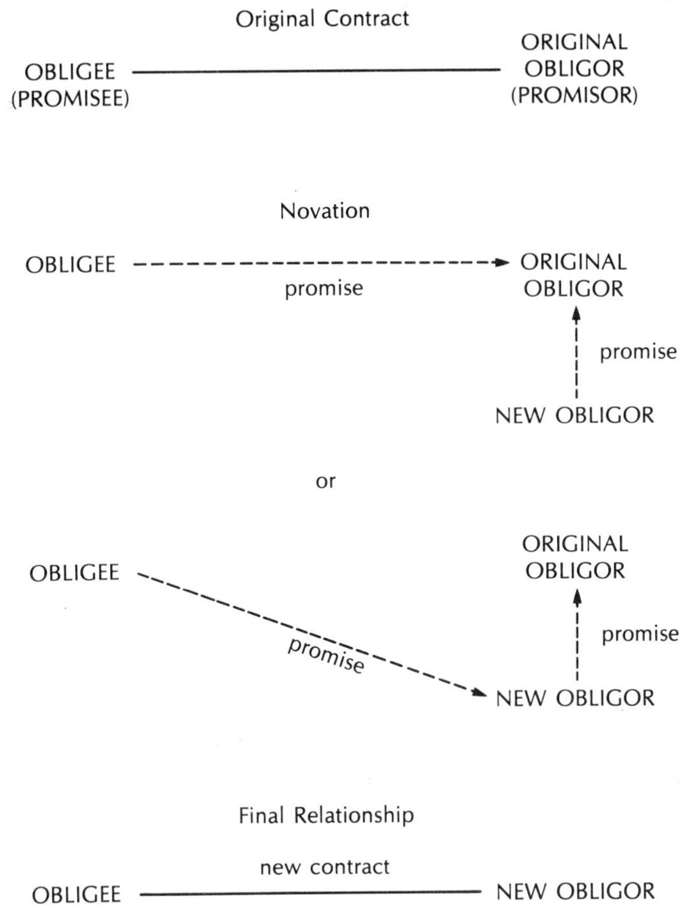

When obligors are substituted, the obligee must promise to release the original obligor. Whether the obligee promises the original obligor or the new obligor is immaterial so long as the promise to discharge is made. Without the obligee's promise to discharge, consideration does not exist for the original or the new obligor's promise. If the new contract merely adds the third party without discharging the original obligor, a novation is not created.

> *PROBLEM 7:* A Bank loaned a partnership $10,000. Subsequently, the partnership evolved into a corporation. The Bank promised the Corporation that it would discharge the partnership debt immediately if the Corporation promised to pay the Bank the amount owed by the partnership. The Corporation promised the Bank.
>
> Who was the obligee? Who was the original obligor? Who was the new obligor? When the Bank promised the Corporation and the Corporation promised the Bank, was there consideration for the Bank's promise?

Was there consideration for the Corporation's promise? Is either promise a repeat of an existing promise? Has the partnership's duty to pay the Bank been discharged? If a novation has been created, which factual pattern does this problem illustrate?

PROBLEM 8: The Bank loaned Andrew $10,000. Subsequently, the Bank promised Andrew to discharge his debt if Cynthia, a third party, promised the Bank to pay the Bank $10,000. The Bank promised Andrew to discharge him and Cynthia promised the Bank to pay it.

Who was the obligee? Who was the original obligor? Who was the new obligor? When the Bank promised Andrew, was there consideration for the Bank's promise? When Cynthia promised the Bank, was there consideration for Cynthia's promise? Is either promise a repeat of an existing promise? Once the Bank and Cynthia have promised, has Andrew's duty to the Bank been discharged? If a novation has been created, which factual pattern does this problem illustrate?

PROBLEM 9: The Bank loaned $10,000 to Andrew. The Bank promised Andrew to discharge him if Cynthia, a third party, promised Andrew that she would assume his duty to pay the Bank.

Who was the obligee? Who was the original obligor? Who was the new obligor? When the Bank promised Andrew, what was the consideration for its promise to him? When Cynthia promised Andrew, what was the consideration for her promise to him? Is either promise a repeat of an existing promise? Once the Bank and Cynthia have promised, has Andrew's duty to the Bank been discharged? If a novation has been created, which factual pattern does this problem illustrate?

PROBLEM 10: The Bank loaned $10,000 to Andrew. The Bank promised Cynthia to discharge Andrew if Cynthia, a third party, promised Andrew that she will assume his duty to pay the Bank.

Who is the obligee? Who is the original obligor? Who is the new obligor? When the Bank promised Cynthia, what was the consideration for the Bank's promise? When Cynthia promised Andrew, what was the consideration for her promise? Is either promise a repeat of an existing promise? Once the Bank and Cynthia have promised, has Andrew's duty to the Bank been discharged? If a novation has been created, which factual pattern does this problem illustrate?

Although all parties to a novation usually assent to the novation, it is unnecessary for all to assent. In the first pattern, for example, because the partnership, the original obligor, is a third party beneficiary to the novation, the lack of the partnership's assent will not preclude the formation of the novation. If, however, the partnership (the original obligor) disclaims, the disclaimer renders the novation inoperative as to the partnership.

SIMPLE NOVATION—SUBSTITUTION OF OBLIGEES

A novation may involve a change in obligee rather than a change in obligor. When a new obligee replaces the original obligee, two factual patterns are common:

(1) The original obligee promises the obligor in exchange for the obligor's promise to the new obligee.

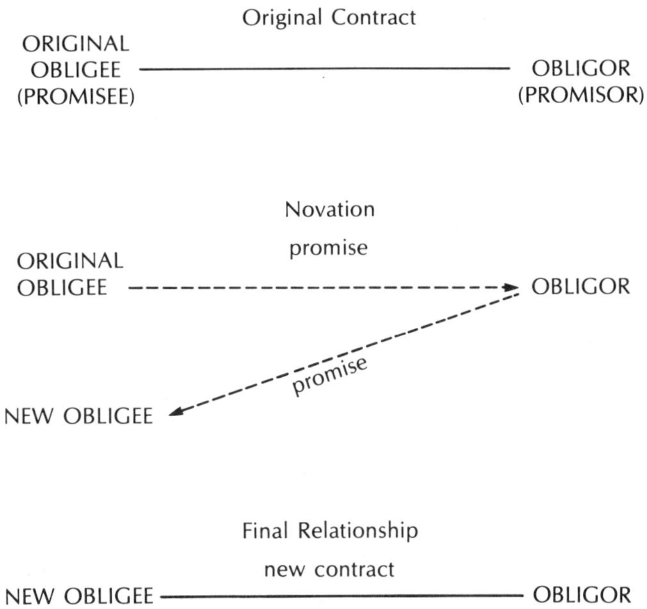

(2) The original obligee promises the obligor for the obligor's promise to the original obligee.

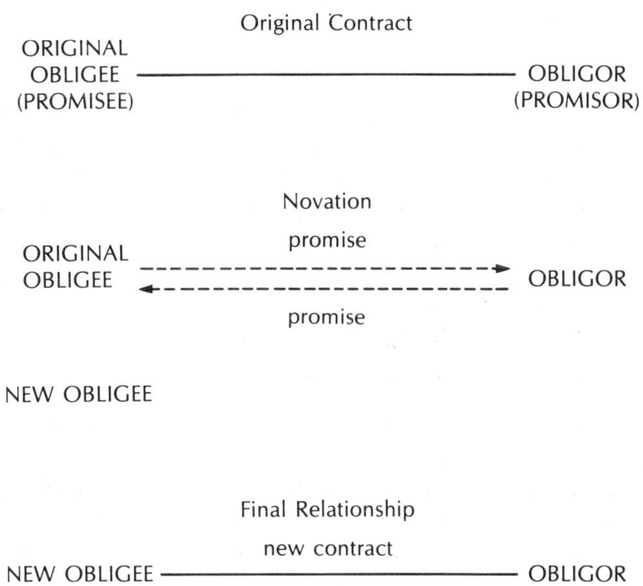

In the first pattern, the original obligee promises the obligor to discharge the obligor's duty for the obligor's promise to a third party to perform for that third party.

EXAMPLE

The Bank loaned Andrew $10,000. The Bank promised Andrew to immediately discharge his debt if Andrew promised to pay Cynthia $10,000. Andrew's promise to Cynthia was the consideration for the Bank's promise to Andrew; the Bank's promise to Andrew was the consideration for Andrew's promise to Cynthia. Neither promise was a repetition of an existing promise so neither was subject to a preexisting duty challenge. When the Bank promised Andrew and Andrew promised Cynthia, a novation resulted and Andrew's duty to pay the Bank was discharged. Cynthia became the new obligee in substitution for the original obligee, the Bank.

In the second pattern, the original obligee promises the obligor to discharge the obligor's duty if the obligor promises the original obligee to perform for a third party.

EXAMPLE

The Bank loaned Andrew $10,000. The Bank promised Andrew to immediately discharge his debt if Andrew promised the Bank to pay Cynthia, a third party, $10,000. Andrew's promise to the Bank was the consideration for the Bank's promise to Andrew; the Bank's promise to Andrew was the consideration for Andrew's promise to the Bank. Neither was a repetition of an existing promise so neither was subject to a preexisting duty challenge. When the Bank promised Andrew and Andrew promised the Bank, a novation resulted and Andrew's duty to pay the Bank was discharged. Andrew now had the duty to pay Cynthia. A new obligee, Cynthia, replaced the original obligee, the Bank. In this pattern, Cynthia, a third party beneficiary, need not consent. Cynthia, however, could disclaim and render the novation, including the discharge, inoperative from its inception.

COMPOUND NOVATION

A novation may be compound rather than simple. Two factual patterns are common. In the first a new contract replaces an executory contract where one party to the new contract was a party to the original contract. This pattern involves one original contract.

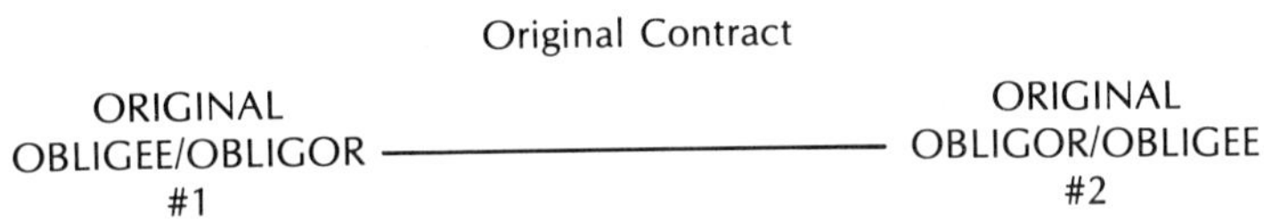

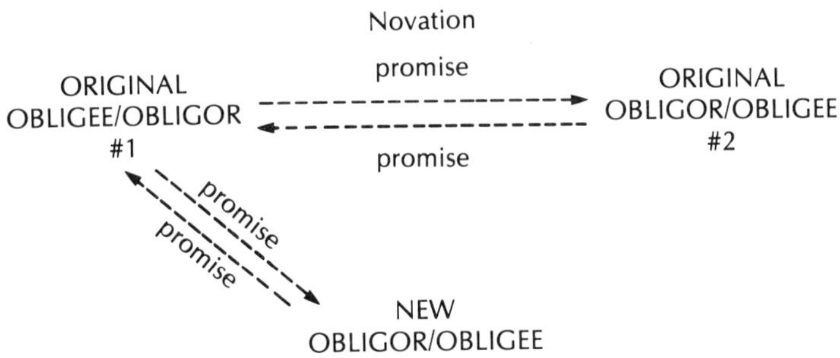

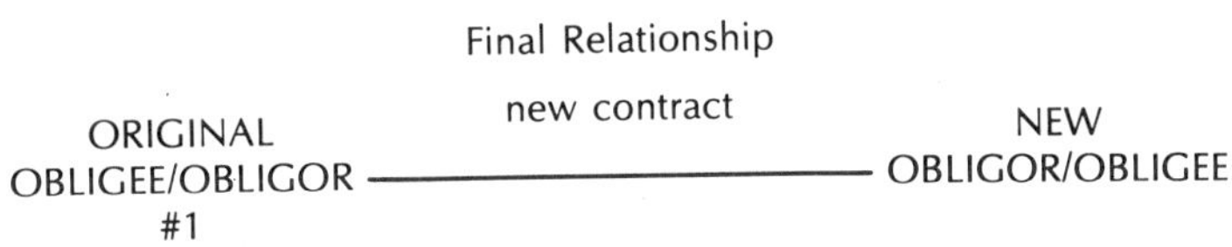

EXAMPLE

Adam promises to deliver a tractor to Ben for Ben's promise to pay Adam $1,000. Subsequently, Adam promises Ben and Carol to deliver a bulldozer to Carol and to discharge Ben's duty to pay Adam $1,000 if Ben promises to discharge Adam's duty to deliver the tractor to Ben and if Carol promises to pay $2,000 to Adam. When Adam, Ben, and Carol promise, a novation results and Adam's duty to deliver the tractor to Ben and Ben's duty to pay Adam $1,000 are discharged. Adam now has the duty to deliver the bulldozer to Carol and Carol has the duty to pay Adam $2,000.

The second pattern involves two original contracts with one party being common to both contracts. Subsequently, the three parties agree that the party common to both contracts shall drop out. The second pattern involves two original contracts with a common party.

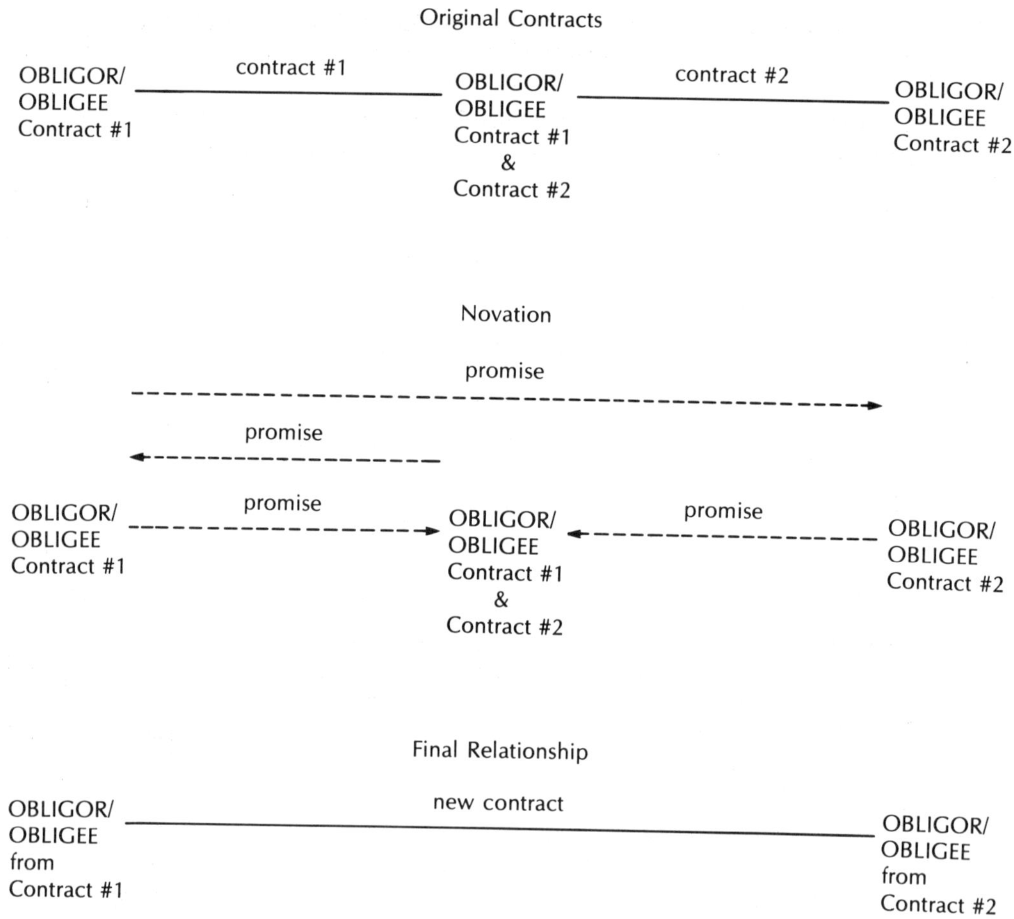

EXAMPLE

Anthony contracted with Best Construction for Best to provide materials and remodel Anthony's restaurant. Best subcontracted with the Century Lumber Company for Century to supply the materials. Century supplied the materials and Best incorporated some of these materials into Anthony's restaurant. For some reason the construction halted. Anthony promised Best and Century that Anthony would discharge Best from its duty to complete the remodeling and Anthony would pay Century what Best owed Century for the materials if Best promised to discharge Anthony from Anthony's duty to pay Best and Century promised to discharge Best from Best's duty to pay Century. When Anthony, Best, and Century promised, a novation was formed and Anthony's duty to pay Best was discharged and Best's duties to Anthony and Century were discharged. Anthony now has a duty to pay Century for the materials supplied.

Section 3. THIRD PARTY'S INTERFERENCE WITH EXISTING CONTRACT RIGHTS

In most states, one who interferes with the contractual relationship of others may be liable for harming their contractual relationship. The cause of action is known as "tortious interference with a contract."

The party claiming interference can maintain this cause of action by demonstrating that the following conditions were present:

1. an enforceable contract existed
2. the party inducing the breach knew of the contract
3. the interfering party intentionally induced the breach
4. the interfering party induced the breach unjustifiably
5. the party claiming interference was damaged by the breach of contract.

The first element, an enforceable contract, is resolved by the knowledge that you gained in Chapters 2 through 10.

The second element, knowledge of the contract, can be established by proving that the interfering party had either actual or constructive knowledge of the contract. Constructive knowledge means that the party who interfered knew facts that would cause a reasonable person to believe that a contract existed.

The third element, that the interfering party intentionally induced the breach, requires a showing that the interfering party acted to induce a breach and acted intentionally. The inducement may include threats, coercion, or economic persuasion. Some jurisdictions do not require the contract to be actually breached. These jurisdictions only require that the party somehow disrupt the contractual relationship. Generally, a party acts intentionally if he or she acts with the purpose of bringing about a particular result. Some courts reject the intent requirement and would demand only a showing that the party interfering knew his or her acts would result in a breach.

The fourth element is a showing that the party inducing the breach was unjustified in his or her actions. Generally, courts do not consider the breaching of a contract for personal gain to be "justified." Some courts go a bit further and require that the act be wrongful, malicious, or unjust, which indicates an interpretation stronger than "unjustified."

The fifth and final element is a showing that the party complaining of the interference was damaged by the interference. The most traditional aspects of harm are those damages related to the breaching of a contract.

The courts have applied various remedies in tortious interference of contract cases. One remedy is injunctive relief. The injunction forces a party to cease any activities that are designed to result in breach of a contract. If a breach has already occurred, an injunction may be of little consequence, however, courts will frequently award a traditional measure of contract damages. Also, some courts will award punitive damages.

PROBLEM 11: Carriers, Inc., delivered the *Times* newspaper to subscribers. The *Post,* a rival newspaper, liked the job that Carriers was doing so much that it hired Carriers to deliver its newspaper to its subscribers.

The Carriers/*Post* contract stated that Carriers must deliver all the newspapers that the *Post* printed.

Recently, the *Post* doubled its production, thereby placing a heavy burden on Carriers. Because of the increased burden, Carriers informed the *Times* that it might have to cancel its contract with them. Unfortunately, Carriers was the only delivery company in the town and the *Times* did not have its own delivery system.

Will the *Times* be successful in its suit against the *Post* for tortiously interfering with its contract? If so, what should be the remedy?

The following cases, *R.C. Hilton Associates, Inc. v. Stan Musial & Biggie's, Inc.* and *Ahern v. Boeing Co.,* add perspective as to how the courts deal with the tortious interference issue. Check each case for the five elements necessary for maintaining the action.

R.C. Hilton Associates, Inc. v. Stan Musial & Biggie's, Inc.

United States Court of Appeals, Eleventh Circuit, 1983.
702 F.2d 907.

Before GODBOLD, Chief Judge, RONEY, Circuit Judge, and PITTMAN *, District Judge.

GODBOLD, Chief Judge:

A real estate broker, R.C. Hilton Associates, Inc., brought this action to recover a commission on the sale of a hotel. Initially Hilton's agent visited the hotel to determine whether it was for sale. An agent of Stan Musial & Biggie's, Inc. (Musial), the owner, advised Hilton that the hotel might be for sale for $4.25 million, net to owner. Musial stated that it did not intend to pay any sales commission and that Hilton would have to make arrangements for its commission with the buyer. Hilton subsequently initiated discussions between Musial and Edward Stern. After a short period of negotiations (in which Hilton did not participate) Stern agreed to purchase the hotel for $4.12 million. No commission was paid to Hilton.

Hilton brought suit against Musial and Stern in Florida state court. The defendants removed the case to federal court based on diversity.

The complaint contains three counts: (1) a breach of contract action against Musial; (2) a claim of tortious interference with a business contract against Stern; and (3) an unjust enrichment claim against Musial for the value of services rendered. The case was referred to a United States Magistrate acting as a special master pursuant to Fed.R.Civ.P. 53. After a nonjury trial the magistrate made findings of fact and conclusions of law and recommended that judgment be entered against Hilton on all counts. The district court adopted and confirmed the magistrate's findings and conclusions. We affirm.

The district court ruled that Hilton had neither an express nor implied contract with Musial. Hilton argues that the district court's conclusion that no contract existed is inconsistent with its findings of fact. The

* Honorable Virgil Pittman, U.S. District Judge for the Southern District of Alabama, sitting by designation.

court found that Musial told Hilton that "anything over $4.25 million is yours." Hilton contends that in making this statement Musial agreed to pay a commission. To support this contention Hilton relies on the court's statement that "since the sale price was less than [$4.25 million] there is no basis for a claim predicated upon an express agreement." According to Hilton, the court concluded that an agreement would have existed had the price exceeded $4.25 million. This argument, however, is expressly refuted in both the findings of fact and conclusions of law where the district court explicitly stated that no contract existed.

Hilton next argues that, even if no formal agreement existed, a broker is entitled to recover a commission for services rendered in the sale of real estate.

> [I]n the absence of any special agreement, when a seller places property with a broker for sale, he impliedly agrees to pay a customary commission to the broker.

Kerdyk v. Hammock Oaks Estates, Inc., 342 So.2d 833, 835 (Fla.App.1977).

The authorities cited by Hilton are inapposite. In the case before us Musial did not place the property with Hilton for sale; Hilton obtained no listing. Also, Musial explicitly informed Hilton that it did not intend to pay a sales commission. "A broker cannot recover for his services unless they were rendered at the express or implied request of his employer. . . ." *City Builders' Finance Co. v. Stahl,* 90 Fla. 357, 106 So. 77, 78 (Fla.1925); *George G. Massey & Assoc. v. Borgemeister,* 297 So.2d 577 (Fla.App. 1977). The finding of no contractual liability should be affirmed.

Hilton seeks recovery from Stern for malicious interference with a "business contract." The district court concluded: "Although a claim for tortious interference may be based upon a contractual agreement which is not legally enforceable, no recovery is allowed if there is no contractual relationship at all." On appeal Hilton argues that the existence of a contract is not necessary in order to recover for tortious interference with a "business relationship." Even assuming that the court should have liberally interpreted Hilton's claim for tortious interference with contract as a claim for tortious interference with business relationship, *see Smith v. Ocean State Bank,* 335 So.2d 641 (Fla.App.1976), Hilton has failed to establish its right to recover.

To establish a claim for tortious interference with business relationship the plaintiff must prove:

> the existence of a business relationship under which the plaintiff has legal rights; an intentional and unjustified interference with that relationship by the defendant; and damage to the plaintiff as a result of the breach of the business relationship.

Fearick v. Smugglers Cove, Inc., 379 So.2d 400, 403 (Fla.App.1980).

> Initially, the broker had the burden of establishing an advantageous relationship with the seller. A broker can not recover for his services unless they were rendered at the express or implied request of his employer and a contract for services will not be implied unless the vendor knows or has reasonable grounds to believe that they were rendered with the expectation of receiving payment therefor.

Retzky v. J.A. Cantor Associates, Inc., 192 So.2d 24, 26 (Fla.App.1966). Hilton failed to prove that its services were rendered at the express or implied request of Musial. Having failed to establish an advantageous relationship with the seller, Hilton's tort claim against Stern fails.

Hilton also seeks recovery from Musial under an unjust enrichment theory. The district court denied relief, concluding:

> the Florida cases discussing broker's commissions state quite emphatically that a broker is not entitled to a commission for his services unless there is either an express contract, or one that is implied from the factual situation. The authorities thus negate the theory of unjust enrichment as a basis for the recovery of a broker's commission.

The parties did not cite, nor did our research reveal, any precedent inconsistent with the district court's decision. Even assuming that a broker could recover under an unjust enrichment theory, Hilton's claim would still fail. In *Yeats v. Moody,* 128 Fla. 658, 175 So. 719, 720 (Fla.1937), the Florida Supreme Court stated:

> It is well settled that where services are rendered by one person for another which are knowingly and voluntarily accepted, without more, the law presumes that such services are given and received in the expectation of being paid for, and will imply a promise to pay what they are reasonably worth.

In the present case Musial clearly informed Hilton that it did not intend to pay a sales commission. Thus, Hilton's services could not reasonably be "given and received in the expectation of being paid for. . . ."

AFFIRMED.

Ahern v. Boeing Co.

United States Court of Appeals, Eleventh Circuit, 1983.
701 F.2d 142.

Before HILL, KRAVITCH and HENDERSON, Circuit Judges.

KRAVITCH, Circuit Judge:

Appellants appeal from summary judgment granted to appellee by the district court. We conclude that the district court, 539 F.Supp. 1210, applied an incorrect legal standard to the facts of this case; therefore we reverse and remand for trial on the merits.

In 1976, "A & O," a partnership in which appellants were partners, entered into an agreement with Scientific Energy Engineering, Inc., ("SEE") covering the testing, production, sales, and leasing aspects of an incinerator device. A prototype of the incinerator was installed for testing on appellants' property. In May 1977, the agreement was modified to grant appellants the exclusive marketing rights to the incinerator. The agreement as modified did not contain an express durational provision, but did contain references to termination upon default of either of the parties.

SEE and A & O subsequently experienced some difficulties in their relationship, and SEE filed a state court action in September 1978, seeking declaratory relief and damages. While the state action was pending, SEE entered into negotiations with Boeing Company regarding the incinerator. On June 7, 1979, Boeing executed an option agreement with SEE and its principals, which gave Boeing an option to acquire the marketing rights to the incinerator and other products. Boeing exercised the option and on February 14, 1980, Boeing, SEE, and its principals entered into a marketing agreement. Appellants contend that this agreement directly interfered with the exclusive marketing rights that SEE had granted them.

On April 24, 1980, the state trial court entered a final declaratory judgment and declined to award SEE damages. The court found that the joint venture agreement granted certain marketing rights to the appellants, but that the contract was terminable at will by either party upon thirty days notice. Shortly after the state court judgment was entered and after the contract with Boeing had taken effect, SEE notified the appellants that it was terminating the marketing agreement with A & O. Appellants then filed this action in Florida state court seeking compensatory and punitive damages against Boeing for alleged tortious interference with the business relationship between A & O and SEE. The case was removed to federal district court pursuant to 28 U.S.C. §§ 1332 and 1441. After discovery was concluded, Boeing moved for summary judgment, and the district court granted the motion.

Under Florida law, to establish a cause of action for tortious interference, a party must demonstrate:

1. the existence of an advantageous business relationship under which that party has legal rights;
2. an intentional and unjustified interference with that relationship by the defendant; and
3. damage to the plaintiff as a result of the interference with the business relationship.

Unistar Corporation v. Child, 415 So.2d 733, 734 (Fla.3d Dist.Ct.App.1982); *Wackenhut Corporation v. Maimone,* 389 So.2d 656, 657 (Fla. 4th Dist.Ct.App.1980); *Lake Gateway Motor Inn v. Matt's Sunshine Gift Shops, Inc.,* 361 So.2d 769, 771 (Fla. 4th Dist.Ct. App.1978). The Florida courts have determined that "an action will lie where a party tortiously interferes with a contract terminable at will." *Unistar Corporation,* 415 So.2d at 734. Thus, where the plaintiff shows "an intentional and unjustified interference with an existing business relationship which causes damage to the plaintiff," a prima facie case is established, and the burden then shifts to the defendant to justify its actions. *Id.* at 734–35. "If the defendant can prove that the interference was lawful competition—a privilege which the courts recognize when the contract is terminable at will—the defendant will not be found to have committed the tort of wrongful business interference." *Id.* at 735 (citing *Insurance Field Services, Inc. v. White & White Inspection and Audit Service, Inc.,* 384 So.2d 303 (Fla. 5th Dist.Ct.App.1980); W. Prosser, *Handbook of the Law of Torts* § 129, at 932, 946 (4th ed. 1971)).

The district court focused upon this privilege of competition in granting Boeing's motion for summary judgment. The court found that Boeing was motivated by no ill will toward A & O, but only by competitive interests, a finding we do not dispute. The court, however, concluded that Florida law protects interference with at-will contracts as long as the motivation for that interference is deemed "proper." The trial court in its opinion and order granting summary judgment, stated:

> that where, as here, there is a contract terminable at will and part of defendant's motivation for interfering with that contract was to advance defendant's business interests, the interference is privileged as competition and is therefore justified as a matter of law.

We believe that the judge erred in her reading of the Florida case law. In the recent trilogy of cases cited above, the Florida courts ruled that the plaintiffs had not established the requisite unjustified interference with their business relationships. In none of the cases did the defendant actually enter into a contract that interfered with the existing at-will contract of the plaintiff. In *Lake Gateway Motor Inn,* the plaintiff was a gift shop operator who had an at-will contract with the motel. The motel notified the plaintiff that it was exercising its rights to terminate the contract upon thirty days notice. The gift shop operator then negotiated with a possible successor, but that successor also held discussions with the motel. The successor found that the motel would contract with him if he paid the motel the amount due the gift shop operator under the "buy-out" clause of the at-will contract. The court found no tortious interference because the successor and the motel had not entered into a contract interfering with the gift shop's operation. The privilege of competition, the court held, protects solicitation for future business, not interference with existing contracts. The court summarized its reasoning as follows:

> Assuming all alleged actions of the successor were as bad as the appellee paints them, (although this is disputed) said successor went to the motel and solicited a take over of the gift shop, having heard it was to be available. Such competition seems to us to be par for the course in the free enterprise system. Can not the IBM salesman solicit this court to change over from a Xerox copier? *Of course he can, unless he suggests to us that we violate a contract with Xerox in so doing.*
>
> *In the case at bar, there is no proof that the successor operator sought to persuade the motel to break a contract or strip his predecessor of some legal rights.*

Lake Gateway Motor Inn, 361 So.2d at 772 (emphasis added).

The district court concluded that the determining factor under Florida law is the motivation of the alleged tortfeasor. Motivation is *not,* however, the guiding star in the constellation of Florida's common law of tortious interference. The case law clearly demonstrates that mere self-interested and competitive solicitation will not constitute tortious interference with an at-will contract, so long as the third party does not induce the breach of or interference with that existing contract.

Viewing the facts in the light most favorable to the nonmoving party as we must in reviewing a grant of summary judgment, *Northwest Power Prods., Inc. v. Omark Indus., Inc.,* 576 F.2d 83, 85 (5th Cir.1978), *cert. denied,* 439 U.S. 1116, 99 S.Ct. 1021, 59 L.Ed.2d 75 (1979), we conclude that appellants have alleged a prima facie case showing that Boeing went much further than the mere solicitation that would be protected under Florida's privilege of competition. We hold, therefore, that appellants are entitled to present their case to a jury. The order of the district court granting summary judgment is REVERSED, and the case REMANDED for trial.

Glossary

Acceptance An acceptance is the offeree's manifestation of assent to the terms of the offer.

Accord and Satisfaction The "accord" is a contract to pay a stated amount to discharge a prior obligation. The "satisfaction" is the performance of the accord contract.

Account Stated An account stated is the debtor's and creditor's manifestation of assent to a stated sum as an accurate computation of an amount due the creditor.

Action An action is a shorthand phrase for cause of action, that is, the theory upon which relief should be granted.

Adhesion Contract An adhesion contract (contract of adhesion) is a contract formed by one party imposing his or her will upon an unwilling or even unwitting party.

Affirmance Affirmance is the manifestation, by a contracting party who has the power to avoid the contract, of a willingness to continue with the performance of the contract.

Agreement An agreement is the actual bargain of the parties as found in their language, course of dealing, usage of trade, and course of performance. Whether an agreement has legal consequences is determined by the law of contracts.

Ambiguity An ambiguity occurs when a word has two different meanings. The ambiguity may be patent (apparent on its face) or latent (apparent only in light of surrounding circumstances).

Anticipatory Repudiation Anticipatory repudiation is a shorthand phrase for "breach by anticipatory repudiation." It is a party's refusal to perform a contractual duty made prior to the time the performance is due.

Assignment An assignment is the transfer of a contractual right.

Assumpsit Assumpsit was a common law form of action that was one of the forerunners to the modern breach of contract and restitution actions. The term assumpsit meant an undertaking. Assumpsit was divided into Special Assumpsit and General (common or indebitatus) Assumpsit. An action of Special Assumpsit was brought on an express promise. An action of General Assumpsit was brought on an implied in fact or an implied by law promise.

Avoidability of damages Avoidability of damages refers to the losses that occur after a breach of contract that are preventable by the aggrieved party. A court ordinarily will not compensate an injured party for a loss that he or she could have prevented by an appropriate effort.

Bargain A bargain is an agreement between the parties.

Beneficiary A beneficiary is the recipient of a contractual promise.

Bilateral contract A bilateral contract is a contract consisting of a promise by the offeror and a reciprocal promise by the offeree.

Capacity Capacity is the legal ability a party has to contract. Some parties, such as infants and the mentally incompetent, have only limited capacity and therefore have, under some circumstances, the right to disaffirm their contracts.

Cause of Action A cause of action is the theory upon which relief should be granted. The cause of action should be distinguished from the remedy sought if the cause of action could be maintained. Breach of contract is a cause of action; damages is a remedy for breach of contract.

Certainty Certainty is the requirement that contract terms must be discernible so they provide the basis for determining breach and the appropriate remedy.

Common Law Common law has several meanings. The common law is the body of law and jurisprudential theory that originated and developed in England. Common law, as distinguished from law created by legislative enactment, is derived from custom and usage and from judicial decisions recognizing and enforcing custom and usage.

Concealment Concealment is an act intended or known to be likely to keep another party from learning a fact.

Condition A condition is an event that relates to the performance of the contract. A condition precedent is a duty creating event. The promisor does not have a duty to perform until the event occurs. A condition subsequent is a duty terminating event. The promisor no longer has a duty to perform once the event occurs. A condition is not consideration for a promise.

Conditional Promise A conditional promise is another name for promise with a condition precedent. The promisee does not have a duty to perform until the event occurs.

Consideration A contract has two "considerations"—consideration for the promisor's promise and consideration for the promisee's promise or performance. Consideration is the "price" sought by the promisor for his or her promise and the "price" sought by the promisee for his or her promise or performance.

Constructive Contract A constructive contract is not a contract because the transaction lacks the elements of a contract. A court, however, might use this terminology to impose recovery under a restitution cause of action.

Contract A contract is the total legal obligation that results from the parties' agreement. It may consist of an exchange of promises (bilateral contract) or an exchange of a promise for a performance (unilateral contract).

Counteroffer A counteroffer is an offer made by the offeree to the offeror that deals with the subject matter of the original offer made by the offeror to the offeree but with some variation in terms.

Course of Dealing A course of dealing is a sequence of previous acts and conduct between the contracting parties, which can be regarded as establishing a common basis of understanding for interpreting their expressions and other conduct.

Cover Cover is the substitute for contractual performance.

Creditor Beneficiary A creditor beneficiary is a third party beneficiary to a contract who received a right under the contract when the contract was formed to discharge a prior obligation that the promisee had with the third party beneficiary.

Cure Cure is the correction of performance so it meets the contract specifications.

Delegation A delegation is the empowering of another by the obligor to perform the obligor's contractual duty.

Detrimental Reliance Detrimental reliance is conduct by a party that was induced by another party making a promise, which would result in an injury if compensation is denied.

Divisible Contract A divisible contract is a contract with separate or installment performances.

Donee Beneficiary A donee beneficiary is a third party beneficiary to a contract who receives a gift under the contract.

Duress Duress is the use of any wrongful act or threat to influence a party to contract. Duress has two forms: duress by actual physical force and duress by threat.

Duress by Actual Physical Force This form of duress occurs when a person using physical force compels a party to "assent" to the "contract," even though that party did not intend to contract.

Duress by Threat This form of duress occurs when a person improperly threatens a party to induce assent to a contract, when the threatened party has no reasonable alternative but to assent. Duress by threat includes "economic duress."

Duty "Duty" is the correlative of "right." When one party has a duty, another will have a corresponding right. Duty means that which is owed to a party.

Economic Duress A party subjected to economic duress is wrongfully threatened with severe economic loss if he or she does not enter the proposed contract.

Entire Contract An entire contract is a contract with a single performance.

Estoppel Estoppel is the judicial preclusion of a party's assertion of a position inconsistent with his or her prior actions or promise.

Excuse Excuse is the term used to indicate that the promisor is exempted from performing under a contract by an unforeseen external event.

Express Promise An express promise is a promise stated either orally or in writing.

Expectation Interest When forming a contract, both the offeror and offeree have three interests that receive judicial protection: expectation, reliance, and restitution. The promisee's expectation interest is the promisee's interest, in the event of the promisor's breach, in acquiring the benefit of his or her bargain by being placed in as good a position as if both parties had fully performed the contract according to its terms.

Forfeiture Forfeiture is the loss of a right.

Forum State The forum state is the state in which the case is filed (the state hearing the case).

Frustration of Purpose Frustration of purpose occurs when an unexpected event destroys a party's underlying reason for contracting. Even though performance of the contract is still possible, courts may excuse nonperformance on the theory of failure of consideration.

Good Faith Good faith in the case of a merchant means honesty in fact and the observance of reasonable commercial standards of fair dealing in the trade. In the case of a nonmerchant, good faith means honesty in fact in the conduct or transaction concerned.

Gratuitous Promise (Gift Promise) If a promisor makes a gratuitous promise, the promisor does not seek consideration for his or her promise.

Guarantor A guarantor is a party whose duty is conditioned on the failure of another party's performance.

Illusory Promise An illusory promise is a statement that is less than a commitment to do or refrain from doing something. Therefore, an illusory promise is a misnomer because it is not a promise.

Implied by Law (Implied in Law) Promise The implied by law promise is neither express nor implied in fact. It is a legal fiction, not a promise, which represents the court's label attached to the set of facts so a desired result can be reached.

Implied in Fact Promise An implied in fact promise is a promise that is inferred from conduct rather than expressed orally or in writing.

Implied Promise An implied promise may be either an implied in fact or implied by law promise. The facts must be evaluated to determine whether the promise can be inferred from conduct or whether the promise is merely a legal fiction.

Impossibility Impossibility results from the occurrence of an unexpected event that renders a party incapable of performing his or her contractual duties.

Impracticability Impracticability results from the occurrence of an unexpected event that renders the performance of a contractual duty extremely difficult or expensive to perform.

Incidental Beneficiary An incidental beneficiary is a third party beneficiary to a contract who is neither a creditor nor a donee beneficiary. An incidental beneficiary receives a windfall if the contract is performed, but has no enforceable rights under the contract if it is not performed.

Indefinite Promise An indefinite promise is a statement that appears to be a promise, but omits terms essential to enable the courts to determine an appropriate remedy in the event the "promise" is breached.

Infant (Minor) An infant is a person under the legal age. In most states the legal age is eighteen.

Injunction An injunction is a writ issued by a court directing a party to refrain from a specified act.

Insolvent Insolvent may be defined differently depending on the context. A person may be insolvent when he or she has ceased to pay his or her debts in the ordinary course of business; cannot pay his or her debts as they become due; or is insolvent within the meaning of the federal bankruptcy law (the sum of the debts is greater than the fair valuation of all of the debtor's property).

Installment Contract An installment contract is one that requires or authorizes the delivery of goods or services in separate lots or increments to be separately accepted.

Integration An integration is the final written form of a contract.

Intended Beneficiary An intended beneficiary is a third party donee or creditor beneficiary. The Restatement (First) of Contracts uses the terms donee and creditor beneficiary. The Restatement (Second) of Contracts uses the term intended beneficiary.

Justification A promisor may be justified in not performing his or her contractual duties if the promisor was freed from performing due to a prior breach by the promisee.

Knowledge A person "knows" or has "knowledge" of a fact when he or she has actual knowledge of it.

Lapse Lapse is the termination of the offer through the offeree's failure to accept it within a reasonable time.

Liquidated Damages Liquidated damages are those damages agreed to by the parties at the time of contract formation that will apply to the transaction if a breach occurs.

Manifestation A manifestation is a demonstration that could be readily perceived by a third party.

Manifestation of Assent Manifestation of assent is the modern phrase that refers to the objective theory of contracts law.

Meeting of the Minds Meeting of the minds is an outdated phrase that refers to the subjective theory of contracts law.

Mirror Image The offeree must accept the offer without changing it.

Mistake Mistake may take one of five forms: (1) mistake in judgment; (2) mistake in the performance of the contract; (3) mistake in understanding the terms of the contract (mistake: misunderstanding); (4) mistake in a basic assumption of fact; and (5) mistake in the integration of the contract.

Mistake in a Basic Assumption of Fact A mistake in a basic assumption of fact occurs when a party makes an erroneous assessment of a fact basic to the contract.

Mistake in Integration A mistake in integration occurs when a party makes a clerical error in writing the terms of the contract.

Mistake in Judgment A mistake in judgment occurs when a party makes an erroneous assessment regarding how beneficial the contract will be.

Mistake in the Performance of the Contract A mistake in the performance of the contract occurs when a party makes an error by overperforming his or her contractual duty. The overperformance may include an overpayment.

Mistake: Misunderstanding A mistake in understanding the terms of a contract occurs when at the time of contract formation both contracting parties use the same manifestations, but the parties do not attach the same meaning to these manifestations.

Mistake of Fact A mistake of fact is a belief that is not in accordance with the facts.

Mistake of Law A mistake of law is a belief that is not in accordance with the law.

Mitigation Mitigation is action that the aggrieved party must take after a breach of contract to limit the damages that will arise due to the breach.

Nondisclosure A nondisclosure occurs when one party withholds information from another.

Notice A person has "notice" of a fact when he or she has actual knowledge of a fact, has received a notice or notification of a fact, or, in light of all the facts and circumstances known to him or her at the time in question, has reason to know that a fact exists.

Novation A novation is a contract that discharges a party to the contract, sometimes an obligor and sometimes an obligee, and substitutes a new party in his or her place.

Objective Standard The objective standard is the reasonable person's standard. It is based on manifestations that could be reasonably interpreted by hypothetical third persons watching the transaction.

Offer An offer is a manifestation of willingness to enter into a bargain, which justifies another person in understanding that his or her assent to that bargain is invited and will conclude it.

Offeree An offeree is the person whom the offeror invites to accept the offer.

Offeror An offeror is the person who extends the offer to the offeree.

Option Contract An option contract is a contract that limits the promisor's power to revoke the offer. An option contract has the same requirements as the main contract—promisor's promise, consideration for the promisor's promise, promisee's promise or performance, and consideration for the promisee's promise or performance.

Parol Evidence Rule The parol evidence rule is a substantive rule of contracts law that limits the terms of a contract in final written form to those in the writing. Prior or contemporaneous parol evidence cannot be used to add to or contradict terms in the final writing. Parol evidence, however, can be used to interpret terms in the final writing.

Partial Integration A partial integration is a contract that has only some of its terms in final written form.

Performance Performance must be distinguished from promise. A performance is an act or omission (doing or not doing something). A promise is the unequivocal assurance that something will or will not be done.

Preliminary Negotiation Preliminary negotiations include all discussions of the parties that occur prior to the offer.

Promise A promise is a manifestation of intention to act or refrain from acting in a specified way, which justifies a promisee's understanding that the promisor has made a commitment. A promise is an unequivocal assurance that something will or will not be done.

Promisee A promisee is the person to whom a promise is made.

Promisor A promisor is the person who makes the promise.

Promissory Estoppel Promissory estoppel is the preclusion of an assertion by the promisor that is inconsistent with a previously made promise upon which the promisee has relied.

Puffing Puffing is an expression of opinion by a seller not intended as a representation of fact.

Quantum Meruit Quantum meruit is a common count (a standard allegation) in an action of assumpsit for work and labor. It is based on an implied assumpsit or promise on the part of the defendant to pay the plaintiff as much as he reasonably deserves to have for his or her labor.

Quasi Contract A quasi contract is an implied by law or constructive contract. A quasi contract is not a contract but is a restitution cause of action based on unjust enrichment.

Reasonable Person's Standard (Reasonable Man's Standard) The reasonable person's standard is an objective rather than a subjective standard. The inquiry is how a reasonable person, having observed the transaction, perceived the transaction. The inquiry is not whether the parties mentally viewed the transaction in a common fashion. For example, if the parties dispute whether an offer was made, the legal conclusion will be that an offer was made if a reasonable person would conclude from the disputants' manifestations that an offer was made. The reasonable person's standard is used in modern contracts law.

Reformation Reformation is a judicial remedy designed to revise a writing to conform to the real agreement or intention of the parties.

Rejection Rejection is the offeree's manifestation of nonacceptance of the offer.

Release A release is the relinquishment of a right.

Reliance Interest The promisee has a reliance interest, in the event of the promisor's breach, in being returned to the position he or she was in prior to relying on the promisor's promise.

Remedy A remedy is the relief sought if a cause of action can be maintained.

Renunciation A renunciation is the abandonment of a right.

Repudiation Repudiation is the refusal to accept a right or to perform a duty.

Rescission A rescission is the abrogation of a contract. Rescission usually involves returning the parties to their pre-contract positions.

Restitution Restitution may be either a cause of action (the basis of a claim) or a remedy (the relief sought) for a breach of contract or restitution cause of action. Both forms of restitution are based on unjust enrichment.

Restitution Interest The promisee's restitution interest is his or her interest, in the event of the promisor's breach, in reacquiring any benefit that the promisee has conferred on the promisor.

Revocation Revocation is the offeror's manifestation to withdraw the offer.

Right "Right" is the correlative of "duty." When one party has a right, another will have a corresponding duty. Right means that which is due a party.

Seal An emblem or symbol affixed to a document to authenticate a signature.

Signature A signature is any symbol made by a party with a present intention to authenticate the writing as that of the signer.

Specific Performance Specific performance is a remedy whereby a court directs a party to do a specified act.

Statute of Frauds The statute of frauds is a statute forbidding enforcement of certain contracts unless they are in writing. Under the statute of frauds, for example, a contract for the sale of goods for the price of $500 or more and a contract that cannot be fully performed within one year from the time of its formation must be in writing.

Subjective Standard The subjective standard refers to a party's thinking or mental state rather than manifestations. The subjective standard is commonly referred to as the meeting of the minds.

Surety A surety is one who, by contract, is liable for the obligations of another.

Third Party Beneficiary A third party beneficiary is a party who will be benefited by the performance of a contract. A third party beneficiary may be a donee, creditor, or incidental beneficiary. An incidental beneficiary has no enforceable rights under the contract.

Third Party Beneficiary Contract A third party beneficiary contract is a contract for the benefit of a third party. This party is neither the offeror nor offeree.

Total Integration A contract is totally integrated if all of the contractual terms are in final written form.

Unconscionable A contract or contract term is unconscionable if, at the time of contract formation, one party imposed an unreasonably favorable contract or term on the other party when the other party lacked a meaningful choice in whether to accept the contract or term.

Undue Influence Undue influence involves unfair persuasion by a party who is either in a position of dominance or in a position of trust and confidence. Undue influence neither requires threats nor deception, although one or the other is often present.

Unenforceable Contract An unenforceable contract is a contract that the court will not implement.

Unilateral Contract A unilateral contract is a contract consisting of a promise by the offeror and a reciprocal performance by the offeree.

Unjust Enrichment Unjust enrichment is the underlying theory for a restitution remedy for breach of contract or a restitution cause of action. Under unjust enrichment, the plaintiff has conferred a benefit on the defendant and it would be unfair to permit the defendant to retain the benefit without compensating the plaintiff.

Usage Usage is a habitual or customary practice.

Vagueness A term suffers from vagueness if it lacks a precise meaning.

Void Contract A void contract is an agreement that has no legal effect as a contract.

Voidable Contract A voidable contract is a contract in which one or both parties have the power to avoid the legal relationship created by the contract or to ratify the contract and thus extinguish the power of avoidance.

Waiver Waiver is the intentional or voluntary relinquishment of a right.

Index